THE
SLAVEHOLDING
REPUBLIC

Don E. Fehrenbacher

The Slaveholding Republic

An Account of the United States Government's Relations to Slavery

COMPLETED AND EDITED BY

Ward M. McAfee

OXFORD

UNIVERSITY PRESS

2001

OXFORD
UNIVERSITY PRESS

Oxford   New York
Athens   Auckland   Bangkok   Bogotá   Buenos Aires   Calcutta
Cape Town   Chennai   Dar es Salaam   Delhi   Florence   Hong Kong   Istanbul
Karachi   Kuala Lumpur   Madrid   Melbourne   Mexico City   Mumbai
Nairobi   Paris   São Paulo   Shanghai   Singapore   Taipei   Tokyo   Toronto   Warsaw

and associated companies in
Berlin   Ibadan

Copyright © 2001 by Oxford University Press, Inc.

Published by Oxford University Press, Inc.
198 Madison Avenue, New York, New York 10016

Oxford is a registered trademark of Oxford University Press

Library of Congress Cataloging-in-Publication Data
Fehrenbacher, Don Edward, 1920–1997
The slaveholding republic: an account of the United States government's relations to slavery /
Don E. Fehrenbacher; completed and edited by Ward M. McAfee
p.   cm.
Includes bibliographical references and index.
ISBN 978-0-19-515805-2
1. Slavery—Political aspects—United States—History. 2. Slavery—
Government policy—United States—History. 3. United States—Politics and government—
1775–1783. 4. United States—Politics and government—1783–1865. 5. Reconstruction.
6. United States—Politics and Government—1865–1877. 7. Constitutional history—
United States. 8. Afro-Americans—Legal status, laws, etc.—History—18th century.
9. Afro-Americans—Legal status, laws, etc.—History—19th century. I. McAfee, Ward. II. Title.
E446 .F45 2001
326'.0973—dc21   00-039197

Printed in the United States of America
on acid-free paper

FOR RUTH, SUSAN, AND DAVID

CONTENTS

PREFACE

ONLY DAYS BEFORE Don Fehrenbacher died, he wrote me of his plans to finish his book, *The Slaveholding Republic*, a project he had been working on for many years: "After nearly five years of concentrating on other things, I am once again giving primary emphasis to work on my book about the federal government and slavery." This news came in the form of a handwritten Christmas note. When I heard of his death, I left the card with its message on my windowsill, in direct eyesight above my computer, the place of my work hours. It remains there as of this writing. Many months after his death, when the task of finishing the manuscript was given to me by Virginia Fehrenbacher, the card took on new meaning—a daily reminder to complete this last effort of a fondly remembered former mentor and great historian.

The thesis that he had carefully developed in the uncompleted work was straightforward: The framers of the Constitution had not intended to make slavery a national institution supported by the Union's fundamental law. Yet, over time, the antebellum federal government adopted the position that slavery was a national institution fully protected by the Constitution. Not all Americans acquiesced in this new understanding, leading to a sectionalization of politics that produced a bloody conflagration that in turn destroyed the slaveholding republic.

Don Fehrenbacher's account begins with two separate unsuccessful claims for reimbursement of injured or lost slave property made to Congress in 1828 and 1848 as a way of introducing the issue of whether or not the Constitution was universally regarded in the antebellum period as a proslavery instrument. These examples show that before the Civil

War no unanimity existed in Congress on this matter. Systematically, Professor Fehrenbacher then analyzes key constitutional provisions relating to slavery—the three-fifths clause, the slave importation clause, and the fugitive slave clause—to show that they were not intended to make the Constitution a proslavery compact. In the process, he challenges beliefs to the contrary promulgated by William Lloyd Garrison and his followers during the antebellum period and continued by many leading scholars and constitutional authorities after the Civil War, even up to our own time.

Professor Fehrenbacher argues that the Constitution was neither proslavery nor antislavery in its intent. He portrays the founders as achieving as neutral a position as they could on this subject, leaving its final resolution to later generations. In this his last manuscript, he takes the perspective of Abraham Lincoln, to whom this Pulitzer-Prize-winning historian dedicated a lifetime of study. Lincoln did not see the Constitution as a Garrisonian "agreement with hell," but rather believed that the fundamental law had been established upon a cultural assumption that slavery would remain only temporarily in a land primarily dedicated to liberty. In seeking high office, Lincoln sought to reverse a long habit that had formed after the adoption of the Constitution—the federal government's effective subservience to the slaveholding interest. This practice, Lincoln saw, had not been mandated by the Constitution itself. He and his Republican party sought to redeem for the United States the original ideals upon which it had pledged its sacred honor in the Declaration of Independence.

The part of the manuscript that Professor Fehrenbacher finished shows that relative southern political unity regarding the slavery issue helped define the national capital established in the District of Columbia as effectively proslavery in purpose and tone. Racial anxieties, northern fears of disunion, and American devotion to the principle of local self-determination contributed to this identification of slavery with the nation's symbolic center throughout the antebellum period. Indeed, the entire process of the capital's selection clearly reveals the lack of any original intent to wed the nation's destiny to the institution of slavery.

In foreign affairs, the federal government's attachment to slavery was more immediate and, in this case, intentional. In the story of Washington, D.C., federal acquiescence happened largely due to drift and inattention to the enduring importance of the matter. By contrast, in its handling of foreign relations, the federal government actively supported the institution of slavery from the very outset of the nation's existence. In ongoing negotiations with Great Britain, the United States government especially defined itself as an agent for the slaveholding interest. Challenged by England's growing commitment to the antislavery cause, American governmental officials invariably reacted as proslavery spokesmen. In domestic affairs, Americans openly disagreed regarding the desirability of slavery's expansion and perpetuation. However, in foreign affairs, American diplomats, whether from the North or the South, maintained a unanimity in favor of guarding slavery from foreign harm, even to the extent of claiming it as a constitutionally recognized national institution.

Don Fehrenbacher challenges W. E. B. Du Bois's thesis that slave importations to the United States made a mockery of the federal ban of 1808. He shows that DuBois blurred two distinctly different issues: (1) illegal slave importations, and (2) American complicity in the international maritime slave trade. In fact, the federal government was extraordinarily successful in suppressing the first of these two matters and negligent concerning the latter. Strident American nationalism and southern sensitivity over Great Britain's antislavery agenda were both instrumental in bringing about relative American inactivity in suppressing the international maritime slave trade. Racism and a domestically produced surplus of slave labor were both key in winning intersectional support for minimizing illegal slave importations. The activity of some southern extremists to reopen the importation of slaves on the eve of the Civil War was not a serious effort.

Although not authorized to do so by a strict constructionist reading of the Constitution's fugitive slave clause, Congress enacted the first Fugitive Slave Act in 1793. Northern states blocked effective enforcement of the federal law, leading to a southern outcry for more stringent legislation. The sectional crisis precipitated by California provided the opportunity for passage of a harsher Fugitive Slave Act, which became part of the Compromise of 1850. As northern civil disobedience obstructed the effectiveness of the new law, southerners became convinced that the constitutional covenant holding the Union together was broken, despite the fact that the federal government had effectively become an agent of the slaveholding interest in addressing the South's concerns.

Don Fehrenbacher wrote beginnings to both the chapters "Slavery in the Federal Territories" and "The Republican Revolution." The very clear thesis provided by him in the bulk of the manuscript that he had completed, and these direction finders to the final two chapters, enabled me to compose an ending to his work that he might have written somewhat differently had he lived, but which nonetheless is harmonious with his overall theme.

In the chapter on the territorial controversy, I emphasize the familiar theme that during the Missouri Crisis of 1819–21, constitutional interpretations were introduced by antislavery northerners challenging the republic's proslavery course. Over time, both sides in the struggle sought to constitutionalize their positions, with John C. Calhoun arguing that property rights were constitutionally protected in the western territories and Justice John McLean holding that the natural condition of the territories was free soil. Lewis Cass's theory of popular sovereignty, which was an attempt to cut a middle path between these two extremes, was also cast as a constitutional imperative. Northern antipathy to the Dred Scott decision left the issue to be decided in the political arena and eventually on the battlefield. In writing the bulk of this chapter, I was fortunately guided by a lifetime of Don Fehrenbacher's writings on this particular topic.

The Slaveholding Republic helps the modern reader see why Abraham Lincoln's election was such a shock to the South of his time. Modern Americans have come to appreciate that Lincoln and his Republicans had no immediate intent to destroy slavery in the states where it existed. From this perspective, the southern decision to secede too easily appears as either most premature or highly irrational. Indeed, it is this modern view that makes this book necessary. *The Slaveholding Republic* emphasizes the striking novelty of the Lincoln administration's restrictive attitude toward slavery. It seeks to reconstruct a sense of that novelty as it was appreciated at the time, especially in the South. With the coming of the Civil War, Lincoln's approach, which seems exceedingly cautious by modern standards, quickly evolved into what Professor Fehrenbacher termed the "Republican Revolution," which ended the anomaly of the United States as a "slaveholding republic." Appreciation of this emphasis can occur only after a careful review of the generations-long antebellum context of the federal government actively serving the slaveholding interest. This latter subject is therefore the primary focus of the book.

In the chapter "The Republican Revolution," the behaviors of southern seceders and Republicans are analyzed to explain why each side was resolute in its march toward sectional confrontation. This account challenges the currently fashionable portrait of a passive, vacillating Abraham Lincoln. After Lincoln's death, the subsequent failure of the Republican Revolution stemmed from the white majority's deep-seated racism, which kept the caste spirit of the slaveholding republic alive even after its formal demise. While the U.S. Supreme Court ultimately provided the necessary constitutional rationale for stalling the advance of the Republican Revolution, general white attitudes were more a determinant of the final result.

In closing the work, I attempt to follow the same format that Don Fehrenbacher had used in his introductory chapter. By highlighting several unrelated incidents, one in 1883 and others in 1890, I explore constitutional understandings pertinent not only for the closing of this account but also for our own time.

I thank Virginia Fehrenbacher for giving me the opportunity to complete her husband's last creative effort. I also credit both California State University, San Bernardino, colleagues Kent Schofield and Kathryn Green for their helpful comments concerning the manuscript and the CSUSB history department for temporarily releasing me from teaching duties in order to complete this work. Charles Lofgren of Claremont McKenna College, also a former student of Don Fehrenbacher, made helpful suggestions as well. Larry Gleason, Don Fehrenbacher's son-in-law, working with Quyen Nguyen, helped translate the manuscript from one computer system to another. Numerous reference librarians provided invaluable assistance. Primary among these are Chuck Eckman, Eric Heath, and Betty Lum at Stanford, and Jill Vassilakos-Long and Lisa Bartle at CSU, San Bernardino. Both Esther Eastman of Los Angeles Law Library and Arthur Buell of CSU, Stanislaus, were also of great help in insuring the accuracy of several troublesome endnotes. Bernice Lincoln and Lois McAfee provided invaluable assistance with proofreading. Virginia Fehrenbacher herself contributed most of all, reading the manuscript multiple times and overseeing all editorial changes. And, above all, I wish to thank Don Fehrenbacher for almost four decades of kind acts and assistance towards me. Carl Degler, a longtime colleague of Professor Fehrenbacher, perhaps best summarized my own recollection of the man in comments that he made in one of the many obituaries celebrating Don's life: "I knew Don as a person of strong convictions and gentle manner, a man of integrity and honest expression even in the face of disagreement. His historical achievements reflected his character."

San Bernardino, California   WARD M. McAFEE
April 2000

THE
SLAVEHOLDING
REPUBLIC

1

INTRODUCTION

DURING THE SPRING of 1828, Congress passed the "tariff of abominations," thereby adding to the excitement and confusion of the presidential contest between the incumbent John Quincy Adams and his opponent, Andrew Jackson. Partisan and sectional feeling ran high on the tariff question, but slavery did not become a prominent campaign issue. In the history of the slavery controversy, 1828 is part of an ostensibly quiet decade extending from the end of the Missouri controversy to Nat Turner's uprising and the emergence of Garrisonian abolitionism. Yet, as it happened, the House of Representatives began the year 1828 with a protracted debate that raised disturbing questions about the nature of slavery and its place in the design of the federal union.

The often heated discussion ran on through most of January and into February. At least thirty-five congressmen took part, and many of them spoke more than once. The specific matter at issue dated back thirteen years to General Jackson's famous defense of New Orleans against British assault in January 1815. A slave named Warwick, who had been impressed into military service, suffered two serious wounds from enemy fire. His owner, Marigny D'Auterive, filed a claim against the United States for $239 to cover medical expenses, loss of the slave's time while recuperating, and the depreciation of his value as property. D'Auterive also asked payment of $855 for ninety-five cords of wood and military use of a cart with horse and driver. From its Committee on Claims, the House had previously received an adverse report on the subject without taking any action. In December 1827, the committee reversed itself to the extent of reporting a

D'Auterive claim

bill for payment of the $855, but it again recommended that there be no reimbursement for the wounded Warwick. Citing earlier dispositions of similar claims, the report declared that slaves were "not put on the footing of property, and paid for, when lost to the owner in the public service."[1] That statement was what provoked the debate.

"Slaves not property! What are they then?" demanded Edward Livingston, member of a distinguished New York family who had moved to Louisiana and would in a few years become Jackson's secretary of state. "If not property," he thundered, "they are free . . . , we have no right to their service. If they are not property, the whole foundation on which the Constitution of this Union rests is shaken." Chairman Elisha Whittlesey of Ohio hastened to explain. His committee had not denied that slaves were property. Its report stated only that in circumstances such as those of the D'Auterive claim, slaves had never been treated as property by the federal government.[2] William McCoy, a member of the committee from western Virginia, joined Whittlesey in defending the report. They were dealing with a "delicate subject," he said, and it was not in the interest of the southern states to press the theoretical issue raised by Livingston. Slaves under the laws of certain states might be property "in the most complete sense of that term," but those were not the laws of the federal government, which, in dealing with slaves, "considered them as something more than property."[3]

Most southern congressmen were unhappy with such subtleties, however. Even those venturing to condemn "slavery in the abstract" nevertheless insisted that American slaves had always been recognized as property "in its full meaning, and without any qualification."[4] The laws of a southern state, said one, "secure to her citizens as completely their right to their slaves as they do to their carts and horses."[5] Another echoed him with the flat pronouncement: "If the State of Louisiana declares that slaves are property, this House must recognize them as such."[6] An Alabama member warned that rejection of the D'Auterive claim would be widely interpreted as acquiescence in the contention that slaves were not property under federal law. He called for action that would fully confirm the property rights of southern slaveholders and thus "settle the question forever."[7]

On the other hand, James Hamilton of South Carolina objected even to discussion of an issue that Congress, he said, had no power to settle.[8] Virginia's brilliant eccentric, John Randolph, emphatically agreed, declaring, "This is a question the United States Government has nothing to do with. It never had, and it never can have; for the moment it lays their unhallowed hands upon the ark of that question, it ceases to be a Government."[9] No less vehement was William Drayton, a mild-mannered but eloquent South Carolinian who would later emerge as one of the state's leading Unionists during the Nullification crisis. "I never will enter into a formal discussion, in this House, whether slaves are property," he intoned.

> I will not, in the most indirect manner, suffer an inference to be drawn from any word, or deed of mine, which, by the most strained construction, could be tortured into the semblance of an admission that the Congress of the United States has the shadow of a right to sit in judgment upon this question. If it were to assume this right, the Union would be no more. . . . Much as we love our country, we would rather see our cities in flames, our plains drenched in blood—rather endure all the calamities of civil war, than parley for an instant upon the right of any power than our own to interfere with the regulation of our slaves.[10]

Edward Everett of Massachusetts, classical scholar and conservative politician, adopted the southern point of view, maintaining that property in slaves was protected beyond any question by the just compensation clause of the Fifth Amendment.[11] Joining him was a Pennsylvanian, George Kremer, who exclaimed, "I, for one, am willing to declare, before the whole world, that I believe a slave is as much the property of his master as any thing else that he owns."[12] For the most part, however, northerners participating in the debate were disposed to contest the absolute claims of southern spokesmen. None among them espoused abolitionist principles, to be sure, and none denied that slaves were property within the jurisdiction of a slaveholding state. Instead, they sought to occupy middle ground by distinguishing state law from federal law where slavery was concerned. That strategy enabled them to reaffirm the security of slavery as a state institution, while at the same time rejecting southern efforts to define the United States unconditionally as a slaveholding republic.

The northern argument, though it varied from speaker to speaker, was fairly well summed up in one sentence by John C. Clark of New York. "I am led to the conclusion," he declared, "that slaves, for certain purposes, are persons; that their masters have in them only a qualified property; that Government, in cases of high necessity, growing out of a state of war, has a right to impress them into its military service, without the liability of being justly called on for indemnification."[13] A few northerners pressed the argument to the point of denying that the Constitution contained any recognition of slaves as property. One of them was Tristram Burges of Rhode Island, who said:

> Before we can adopt the amendment, we must first enact that persons may be property and then, that the man Warwick was the property of the claimant. In the States, such persons may be property or not, just as State laws enact: for we have no jurisdiction over the question. In this Legislature, gentlemen represent them as persons: and he, who comes here, because they are persons, cannot . . . vote that they are mere property. Our Constitution admits no representation of property; persons alone are represented. He, therefore, who votes that his constituents are property, votes to vacate his own seat on this floor.[14]

Such a reading of the Constitution could not fail to annoy and alarm the many southerners who in 1828 were already deeply concerned about the constitutional defenses of their section. One member asserted that slavery was "as much a part of the Constitution as the great right of representation." The highest judicial authority in the land, he said, had already decided that a slave was "legitimate chattel and nothing but a chattel."[15] Another speaker, responding to northern emphasis on the humanness of slaves, declared: "In the eye of the law and the Constitution, a slave is no more a 'reasonable being' than a horse or the table which stands before me. The slave is unknown to the law or the constitution, except as the property of the master."[16]

Southerners were obviously at a disadvantage in arguing their case from the text of the Constitution, which referred to slaves only as "persons" and never as "property." They occupied firmer ground when they cited the record of government practice as an authoritative guide to the established meaning of the Constitution. Among their prime exhibits were the treaties of peace with Britain in 1783 and 1815, both of which contained clauses making provision for certain slaves and "other property."[17] It was also pointed out that a direct tax on property levied by Congress in 1813 had specifically included slaves.[18] Perhaps most telling was the evidence set forth by Thomas R. Mitchell of South Carolina showing that federal courts habitually treated slaves as nothing other than "goods, wares, and merchandise" because, he said, they were required to do so by the Judiciary Act of 1789.[19] Northern congressmen could mount only weak rebuttals to this general line of argument.[20]

As the debate continued, sectional antagonism bubbled up frequently through the crust of formal courtesy. Burges, in the course of a long and florid speech, demanded to know why southerners introduced the question of slavery and then threatened disunion if it were discussed.[21] Hamilton responded with personal animosity, deriding Burges's grandiloquence and reminding him of Rhode Island's prominent part in the African slave trade.[22] William S. Archer of Virginia had earlier acknowledged a southern sensitivity "amounting, it might be, to ferocity," on the subject of slavery. "There is a belief . . . in all the slaveholding States," he said, "that a fanatical spirit exists in many of the nonslaveholding States, which would interfere, and interfere fatally, in this matter."[23] Beyond the halls of Congress, the D'Auterive controversy stirred up considerable excitement, especially in South Carolina, where Judge William Harper gloomily remarked that no other recent sectional quarrel had "done as much mischief, as . . . this trifling claim."[24]

On January 23, after nearly three weeks of oratory, the House at last began to move toward a decision. By a vote of 96 to 92, it approved an amendment authorizing payment of D'Auterive for his slave.[25] The roll call proved to be a sectional confrontation, for the amendment was supported by 92 percent of all southerners and opposed by 81 percent of all northerners. A total of 161 out of 188 congressmen voted with their respective sections. Of course the alignment also reflected partisanship in an election year when party strength was, to a considerable extent, sectionally concentrated. Supporters of Jackson tended to favor the amendment and supporters of Adams tended to oppose it. But the delegations from Pennsylvania, New York, and the three states of the Old Northwest, all of which gave electoral majorities to Jackson in 1828, nevertheless voted 55 to 12 against the amendment. Thus, in transacting some trivial legislative business that had come to be invested with symbolic importance, the House displayed a degree of sectional division usually associated with the 1850s.

Not until two weeks later did the D'Auterive bill come up for final action. Then, just as the vote was about to be taken, Charles Miner of Pennsylvania reopened the discussion. Miner, a weekly newspaper publisher and probably the most outspoken critic of slavery in Congress, had remained silent throughout the long debate but could restrain himself no longer. He held the floor for at least an hour and recapitulated most of the arguments already made against reimbursement. Declaring that the real question before the House was one of vast importance, he stated it as follows: "In what relation do slaves stand to this Government, and what obligations and duties spring from that relation?" The answer, he said, had to be drawn from the Constitution, and in that "manual and textbook" by which Congress must be guided, the African was invariably dealt with as a person rather than as property.[26]

With other speakers following Miner, the debate continued through the day until the House at last gave up the struggle. John W. Taylor of New York, who had been one of the antislavery leaders in the Missouri controversy of 1819–21, moved to recommit the bill. Again the vote was close, but the motion carried, 82 to 79, and that proved to be the end of the contest.[27] Two years later, Congress did finally pass an act paying Marigny D'Auterive $855 for the firewood and the use of his cart, horse, and driver, but he never received compensation for his wounded slave.[28]

The fundamental questions raised by the D'Auterive claim lost none of their thorniness in the decades that followed. Twenty years later, for instance, at the time of another presidential campaign, a slaveholder's claim against the United States once again set the House of Representatives to arguing whether or not slaves were property under federal law. In this instance, the petition for reimbursement was associated with a dramatic event of the second Seminole War in Florida.

Shortly before Christmas in 1835, Major Francis L. Dade started out from Fort Brooke (Tampa) with about 110 men to reinforce the garrison at Fort King, located a hundred miles to the north. Accompanying the expedition was a slave named Lewis, who had been hired from his owner, the widow of one Antonio Pacheco, to serve as guide and interpreter. By December 28, the column had reached the vicinity of Wahoo Swamp, some thirty-five miles from its destination. Then suddenly, the Seminoles launched an attack that wiped out almost the entire command. Lewis survived the "Dade massacre" and was carried off by the victors, either as a captive or as one who had been their secret ally all along. Thereafter, he apparently took part in several Indian raids on Florida settlements. In 1837, he fell into army hands and was claimed by an agent of the Pacheco estate, but the commanding officer decided instead to rid Florida of this dangerous troublemaker. He sent Lewis to join Seminoles being removed to the Indian country west of Arkansas. The Pacheco heirs, thus deprived of a slave valued at $1,000, sought recompense from the federal government.[29]

Although the Pacheco claim had already been presented unsuccessfully to three previous Congresses, its supporters did not give up, and in February 1848, the House committee on military affairs reported a bill for payment. The committee revealed itself, however, to be sharply divided along both party and sectional lines. A report accompanying the bill, endorsed only by the five southerners who composed the Democratic majority, was devoted largely to an extensive argument against the "pernicious doctrine" that slaves were not recognized as property by the Constitution. The four Whigs on the committee, all northerners, submitted a minority report in which they rejected the argument and insisted that Congress had never, "upon examination or discussion of this subject, admitted slaves to be *property*."[30]

The Pacheco debate, unlike the D'Auterive controversy, took place in the midst of a major sectional crisis over slavery—more particularly, a crisis over the status of the institution in the vast area recently conquered from Mexico. With congressional attention centered on the issue of slavery extension in its various aspects, the House did not get around to considering the Pacheco claim until the second session of the Thirtieth Congress in December 1848. Then the hall echoed with many of the arguments heard twenty years earlier. Again the more militant northerners, relying heavily on the language of the Constitution, maintained that there was no right of property in slaves under federal law. Again southerners pointed to the record of government practice as conclusive evidence to the contrary. Again debate extended over many days, and a minor piece of legislative business became emblematically significant. Thus, Joshua R. Giddings of Ohio, maintaining that the people of the free states were determined not to be involved in the guilt of slavery, warned his northern colleagues: "If we pass this bill, we shall give our most solemn sanction to that institution." Whereas Richard K. Meade of Virginia declared, "Reject it, and no slaveholder [can] longer look to Congress for protection, or to the Constitution as the broad panoply under which all may rest in safety."[31]

Debate ended on January 6, and the House proceeded to a final vote. The roll call proved to be defective, but after two days of doubt, the clerk announced that the bill had been defeated, 90 to 89.[32] At this point, the Pacheco claim may have been favorably affected by new developments in the larger sectional conflict. From the beginning of the session, antislavery forces in the chamber had been on the offensive. Already the House had emphatically reasserted the free-soil principle of the Wilmot Proviso, and on December 21, by a 98 to 88 vote, it approved an aggressively worded resolution calling for abolition of the slave trade in the District of Columbia.[33] Anger erupted throughout the slaveholding states, and a caucus of southerners in Congress entrusted to John C. Calhoun the task of drafting a southern manifesto.[34] In this atmosphere of tension, the antislavery attack lost some of its momentum. On January 10, the House voted to reconsider the slave-trade resolution and then took no further action, thus in effect rescinding it.[35] On January 19, the House also reconsidered the Pacheco bill, then passed it by a vote of 101 to 95.[36] Every southern vote was affirmative, and every negative vote was northern, but twenty-six northerners voted with the South. The sectional alignment resembled that in the D'Auterive roll call, except that southern solidarity had increased from 92 percent to 100 percent, while northern solidarity remained at about 80 percent. The bill then went to the Senate, where, with only a few weeks left in the session, it got no further than a favorable committee report.[37] Mrs. Pacheco, like Marigny D'Auterive, never obtained reimbursement for her slave.

The D'Auterive and Pacheco controversies are minor but illuminating episodes in the great American struggle over slavery. Introduction of African slavery into the British North American colonies had been essentially an unmeditated action. By the time of the Revolution there was in each colony an accumulated body of slave law that did not so much establish slavery as acknowledge its presence, sanction it, and regulate its conduct. After the achievement of independence, slavery remained what it had been before—an institution historically antecedent to the laws governing it and legally the creature of local authority. The framers of the Constitution, dealing with slavery as an incidental but troublesome circumstance, ended by extending it a kind of shamefaced recognition that included a measure of protection, but they contributed little to defining its national status.

Yet that was to be the fundamental issue in the sectional conflict—the persistent, unresolvable issue that arose in the first Congress under the Constitution and disrupted the Union seventy years later. Charles Miner stated it simply and clearly during the D'Auterive debate: "*In what relation do slaves stand to this Government?*"

The traditional answer, which has been labeled the "federal consensus," dated from the earliest years of the Republic.[38] That is, southerners were accustomed to maintaining and northerners to agreeing that, with a few exceptions specified in the Constitution, slavery was a state responsibility wholly beyond the reach of federal power. "Slavery," said William Drayton in his D'Auterive speech, "is a municipal institution, as unconnected with any control of the United States, as our corporations, our colleges, or our public charities."[39] John Randolph told his fellow congressmen that the national government had no more to do with slavery than "the Khan of Tartary."[40] Even discussion of slavery in Congress constituted intolerable intervention, some southerners argued, for discussion implied a power to act, and in any case it had a subversive effect on slaves, inspiring them with the hope of emancipation.[41] During the Pacheco debate, an angry Richard K. Meade warned northern congressmen that they must cease talking about slavery in order to preserve "the bonds of fraternity" between North and South. Otherwise, he said, the time would come "when no southern man could sleep in his bed without a guard at his door."[42]

As the D'Auterive and Pacheco controversies illustrated, however, the federal consensus did not always suit the particular desires and purposes of the slaveholding interest, which often required some kind of action by the federal government, rather than its adherence to the principle of laissez-faire. Consequently, southerners came to rely more and more upon a proslavery modification of the federal consensus first enunciated in 1800 by Henry Lee of Virginia and written into American constitutional law fifty-seven years later by Chief Justice Roger B. Taney. Congress, according to this revised version, had no authority over slavery *except the authority to protect it.*[43] In addition, the characterization of slavery as strictly a municipal institution proved troublesome for the South because it lent support to the antislavery argument that the institution existed legally only where it had been established by positive law. Thus, during the D'Auterive debate, Samuel C. Allen of Massachusetts maintained that slaves were not property outside those jurisdictions defining them as such.[44] The theoretical question became critically important with respect to the territorial expansion of the 1840s, and southerners began to develop the counterargument that abolition was municipal and slavery prescriptively universal, except where it was prohibited by the law of a sovereign state.[45] What this amounted to, as William Lowndes Yancey intimated in 1845, was a redefinition of slavery converting it into a national institution.[46] These two southern revisions of the federal consensus were combined and given classic expression by Robert Toombs of Georgia when he wrote in 1856, "Congress has no power to limit, restrain, or in any manner to impair slavery, but on the contrary, it is bound to protect and maintain it in the States where it exists, and wherever else the flag floats and its jurisdiction is paramount."[47]

Most northerners meanwhile continued to acknowledge that southern slavery was a state institution wholly immune from federal interference. Even Free Soilers and Republicans did so in emphatic terms, while at the same time asserting the constitutional authority and moral responsibility of Congress to exclude slavery from the western territories. The federal consensus thus remained operative, and in 1861 it even received the formal approval of Congress as a constitutional amendment.[48] But in the sectional struggle this acknowledgment came to be more or less beside the point. The crisis of the Union arose over conflicting sectional *revisions and extensions* of the federal consensus—all having to do with the relation of slavery to the central government.

Argument about slavery and the federal government almost always turned into argument about slavery and the intent of the Constitution. On that question the antebellum South was virtually a unit. Few southerners would have disagreed with the governor of Maryland who declared in a message to the state legislature: "The Constitution of the United States recognizes, without limitation, the institution of domestic slavery, guarantees its existence, and vindicates the right of the owner to the possession and service of the slave."[49] In the free states, on the other hand, there was much diversity of opinion. One large group, for instance, held that the Constitution was intrinsically a charter of freedom that made a few necessary concessions to slavery but pointed toward ultimate elimination of the institution. Most striking, however, was the position taken in the 1840s by William Lloyd Garrison and his wing of the abolitionist movement. The Garrisonians had come to agree completely with the southern view of the Constitution as a proslavery document.[50]

The Garrisonian interpretation, although it was too extreme for most opponents of slavery in the 1840s, retained a surprising vitality and had more adherents in the late twentieth century than ever before. During observance of the bicentennial of the Constitution in 1987, Justice Thurgood Marshall made a public attack upon the celebration in which he disparaged the achievements of the Constitutional Convention and said that he did not "find the wisdom, foresight, and sense of justice exhibited by the framers particularly profound." According to Marshall, the original Constitution was defective because it excluded women and Negroes from the right of suffrage, and, most egregiously, it perpetuated and reinforced the institution of slavery. The men of 1787 actually contributed little, he maintained, to the modern American constitutional system, with its "respect for individual freedoms and human rights."[51]

The only thing unusual about this neo-Garrisonian indictment was its source. Many of Marshall's contemporaries, white and black, shared his perception of the Constitution as a proslavery document. According to a law professor at Syracuse University, for instance, it was "permeated" with slavery, containing no less than nine clauses that "directly protected or referred to it."[52] A federal district judge in Detroit wrote to the *New York Times* that the Founding Fathers, "to our everlasting shame," expressly rejected the principle that slavery was "incompatible with the common-law principles of justice."[53]

Several scholars declared that the framers "intentionally excluded" blacks from constitutional guarantees and, indeed, placed them "outside the community of human beings."[54] A professor at Ohio State University went so far as to assert that the Constitution "directly promoted the Jim Crow codes subsequently passed by states and cities."[55] Some critics, Marshall included, even suggested that the tragedy of the Civil War must be attributed in no small part to the mistakes of the Constitutional Convention with respect to slavery.[56]

There were many dissenting responses to Marshall's speech in 1987, and similarly, there were many abolitionists in the 1840s (including Frederick Douglass) who disagreed with Garrisonian constitutional doctrine. Some went to the opposite extreme and maintained that the Constitution, if properly construed, made slavery unlawful or proscribable everywhere in the nation. The Garrisonians brushed aside such doctrine as a flight from reality and pointed to the record of the federal government as proof of the Constitution's proslavery character. "If the unanimous, concurrent, unbroken practice of every department of the Government, judicial, legislative, and executive, and the acquiescence of the whole people for fifty years do not prove which is the true construction," wrote Wendell Phillips, "then how and where can such a question be settled?"[57] A black abolitionist pointed out, however, that this line of reasoning treated implementation of the document as part of the document itself.[58] By equating the Constitution written in 1787 with the Constitution operating in the 1840s, Phillips and other Garrisonians were, in effect, holding the framers responsible not only for the original document but for all the gloss that it had acquired over more than half a century.

Thus, while federal practice in regard to slavery was guided and limited by the Constitution, conversely, the understood intent of the Constitution in regard to slavery was shaped by federal practice, which thereby had a permanent effect on the reputation of the Founding Fathers. In addition, the actual conduct of the federal government with respect to slavery from 1789 to 1860 was the standard against which southerners measured the seriousness of the threat posed by a victorious Republican party. And at the same time, the question of how the federal government *ought to act* with respect to slavery never ceased to be the essential issue in the sectional conflict. Yet the story of the federal government's involvement with slavery has been told only in bits and pieces. Most of it lies below the surface of conventional textbook history, like a submerged mountain range with just a few visible peaks rising above the waves. The story begins with one revolution that secured national independence and ends with another that heralded a "new birth of freedom."

2

SLAVERY AND THE
FOUNDING OF THE REPUBLIC

[handwritten margin notes: DoI- no ref peace treaty_ slaves are property w GB]

OF THE TWO documents that formally established the United States as a separate nation, one, the Declaration of Independence, made no direct reference to African slavery but embraced principles plainly inimical to the institution; whereas the other, the treaty of peace with Great Britain, *[handwritten: interesting]* contained a clause dealing explicitly and perfunctorily with slaves as a form of property. This inconsistency manifested at the founding was eloquently expressive of the degree to which the reach of American ideals habitually extended beyond the grasp of day-to-day practice where slavery was concerned.

Slavery at the time of the Revolution was firmly established in the five southernmost states from Maryland to Georgia, and it was more than a trivial presence in most of the others. Slaves numbered about half a million in 1780, constituting a little more than one-sixth of the national population. In the South, two persons out of every five were slaves. As a racial caste system, slavery was the most distinctive element in the southern social order. The slave production of staple crops dominated southern agriculture and eminently suited the development of a national market *[handwritten: important element in staple economy]* economy. Furthermore, slaveholders played such a vigorous part in the expansion of the American frontier that their slaves already comprised about one-sixth of the population living in Kentucky and the Southwest. Even before the great stimulus resulting from the growth of the cotton industry, slavery was by several standards a flourishing institution, integral to the prosperity of the nation. But at the same time, slavery was an institution under severe scrutiny, both as a matter of conscience and as a matter of public interest. Many Americans found it difficult to square slave-holding with the principles of Christianity, and many were troubled by the contrast between the celebration of human freedom in the Declaration of Independence and the presence of human servitude throughout so much of the Republic. For a revolutionary people, the logic of circumstance was inexorable, as a Pennsylvanian confided to his journal while traveling through Maryland in 1777. "It is astonishing," he wrote, "that men who feel the value and importance of liberty . . . should keep such numbers of the human species in a state of so absolute vassalage. Every argument which can be urged in favor of our own liberties will certainly operate with equal force in favor of that of the Negroes; nor can we with any propriety contend for the one while we withhold the other."[1]

Formation of an American government preceded the Declaration of Independence and may be said to have begun with the First Continental Congress, which met in Philadelphia from September 5 to October 26, 1774. A major achievement of the Congress was its adoption of the "Association," a program of economic sanctions aimed at suspending virtually all commercial intercourse with Great Britain. One article of the agreement called for an end to the importation of slaves after December 1 of the same year. "We will wholly discontinue the slave trade," it declared, "and will neither be concerned in it ourselves, nor will we hire our vessels, nor sell our commodities or manufactures to those who are concerned with it."[2] This emphatic wording undoubtedly reflected a certain amount of moral revulsion against the slave trade, but the article won general approval primarily as part of a strategy of vigorous resistance to British authority. The ban was reaffirmed (though in vaguer terms) by the Second Continental Congress when it resolved on April 6, 1776, "that no slaves be imported into any of the thirteen United Colonies."[3] Thus the first American governmental body organized at the national level embraced a policy disfavoring slavery to the extent of restricting its growth.

The Articles of Association were essentially hortatory, with execution depending upon local committees. It appears that the slave-trade provision was enforced about as well as other parts of the program.[4] Soon, however, when the quarrel between Britain and her colonies erupted into armed conflict, the war itself served as an effective deterrent to the importation of slaves, and enforcement ceased to be a matter of concern. Never again did the Continental Congress make any effort to curb American participation in the African slave trade. Once it came to have no direct bearing on the struggle with Britain, the problem was left entirely in the hands of the states.

It is well known that if Thomas Jefferson had had his way, the detailed indictment of George III in the Declaration of Independence would have included a paragraph blaming the British crown for the introduction of slavery into the American colonies and for the continuation of the slave trade. Jefferson's draft read in part:

> He has waged cruel war against human nature itself, violating its most sacred rights of life and liberty in the persons of a distant people who never offended him, captivating & carrying them into slavery in another hemisphere, or to incur miserable death in their transportation thither.... Determined to keep open a market where men should be bought & sold, he has prostituted his negative for suppressing every legislative attempt to prohibit or to restrain this execrable commerce.[5]

not his decision to leave it out

Congress struck out the entire passage, thus leaving a document that exalted liberty and equality but said nothing about the presence of slavery in the new nation. Jefferson later asserted that the deletion was made "in complaisance to South Carolinia and Georgia," who wanted the slave trade continued, and also to oblige certain northerners who were sensitive about their section's participation in the trade.[6] His statement seems open to question in view of the fact that just three months earlier the same Congress had voted for cessation of the slave trade. The explanation favored by some historians is that the delegates rejected the overwrought passage simply because they found it too far removed from the truth.[7] But one should also note that Jefferson's paragraph may have been especially disturbing to many southerners because, unlike the earlier resolutions of Congress on the subject, it was written in a tone of moral denunciation that could easily extend beyond the slave trade to the institution of slavery itself. In any case, despite the deletion of this one explicit reference to slavery, the general principles enunciated in the Declaration were such an obvious reproach to the institution that it could only be met by denying that the words "all men are created equal" really meant what they said.[8]

technically only referred slave trade but not slavery

With the ending of the war there came a revival of American maritime trade, including the slave trade. New England continued to provide most of the nation's slave-trading ships, while Georgia and the Carolinas continued to receive most of the imported Africans. At the same time, however, an organized antislavery movement was emerging in both Britain and the United States, concentrating its attention upon abolition of the transatlantic slave trade. The idea that Congress should lead the attack upon the trade was pressed by certain Quaker groups without success. Petitioners in 1783 did manage to inspire a favorable committee report recommending that the states be called upon to pass laws prohibiting the slave trade in accordance with the policy set forth in the old Articles of Association, but the proposal was rejected.[9] This action did not mean that Congress favored continuation of the slave trade. It reflected instead the feeling of members that they had more pressing matters to consider and ought not to spend time on a problem obviously beyond the reach of their vested legislative power.[10] It was therefore without exhortation from Congress that state after state passed prohibitory or restrictive legislation until by the late 1780s only Georgia had failed to lay any restraint upon the traffic.[11]

There can be little doubt that in the Continental Congress and elsewhere, antislavery sentiment was often muffled in the interest of national unity. During the summer of 1777, for example, two Massachusetts Revolutionary leaders, James Warren and John Adams, exchanged letters about a legislative proposal to abolish slavery in that state. Warren reported from Boston that the measure had been ordered to lie on the table lest it should have "a bad effect on the Union of the Colonies." Adams, a member of Congress, applauded the decision. "The Bill for freeing the Negroes, I hope will sleep for a Time," he declared. "We have Causes enough of Jealousy, Discord and Division, and this Bill will certainly add to the Number."[12] For the same reason, Adams had already taken a dim view of enlisting blacks in the armed forces. To Jonathan Dickinson Sergeant of New Jersey, who had drafted a plan for raising a black military unit to serve as a home guard, Adams wrote: "Your Negro Battallion will never do. S. Carolina would run out of their Wits at the least Hint of such a Measure."[13]

Nevertheless, the military struggle with Britain, while it mooted the slave-trade question, made Negro enlistment a recurring issue and one of considerable importance to the American cause. There were slaves and free blacks in the colonial forces that fought at Bunker Hill on June 17, 1775, and George Washington arrived in Cambridge two weeks later to take command of an army that had a sprinkling of color. On July 10, after a council of war, his headquarters issued an order forbidding the recruitment of British deserters, vagabonds, and Negroes.[14] In Congress, a motion calling for the discharge of all blacks serving in the Continental Army was defeated, but by mid-November, the policy of allowing no more black enlistments had congressional approval and seemed firmly established.[15] Meanwhile, however, Lord Dunmore, the royal governor of Virginia, had inaugurated a British policy of offering freedom to slaves willing to bear arms for the king. News of Dunmore's proclamation alarmed Washington. He reversed himself to the extent of authorizing the reenlistment of free black soldiers, who, he feared, might otherwise go over to the British side.[16] Congress approved, resolving on January 16, 1776, "That the free negroes who have served faithfully in the army at Cambridge, may be re-enlisted therein, but no others."[17] Still officially barred were new black recruits and all slaves, even those who had already "served faithfully."

Influenced, no doubt, by the action of Congress and the army command, several northern states took steps to exclude blacks from their militia service, but some recruiting officers went on signing them up anyhow, and eventually the pressure for more troops inspired a change of attitude throughout most of the country. By 1778, free blacks were entering service from Virginia northward, slaves and servants were sometimes being accepted as military substitutes for their masters, and Rhode Island, apparently with Washington's approval, had taken the lead in legislation encouraging and underwriting the enlistment of slaves to fill the state's continental quota.[18] In such circumstances, the question of congressional policy on the subject was bound to be reviewed.

In September of 1778, Benedict Arnold, then the commander at Philadelphia, proposed a joint expedition with French naval forces to take possession of Barbados and Bermuda. One feature of his plan was: "To engage in the marine service of the united states about 5 or 6 hundred black and Mulatto Slaves who are employed as mariners in coasting vessels, by giving to them the pay and privileges of American Seamen, and assuring them of the[ir] freedom after the war, or three years Service." Congress seems to have looked favorably on the project, but the French minister to the United States did not, and nothing further came of Arnold's proposal.[19] Another six months passed before military recruitment of slaves received formal congressional approval.

During those six months, the British launched their southern strategy by capturing Savannah and moving toward the Carolinas. The southern states lacked sufficient manpower to resist the offensive, and no sizable force could be sent to their aid from the North. The desperate circumstances lent credibility to a plan for recruiting black troops developed by John Laurens, a young South Carolinian serving on Washington's staff, and sponsored in Congress by his distinguished father, Henry Laurens. On March 29, 1779, after a favorable committee report, it was resolved that South Carolina and Georgia be urged to "take measures immediately for raising three thousand able-bodied negroes." Congress undertook to pay the owners of such enlisted slaves at a rate not exceeding $1,000 per man, and the resolution also provided: "That every negro who shall well and faithfully serve as a soldier to the end of the present war, and shall then return his arms, be emancipated and receive the sum of fifty dollars."[20]

Thus, for the first time in American history, the central government proposed military recruitment of slaves and offered to finance their manumission. More than eighty years would pass before Congress embraced any such policy again. Of course the Laurens plan required the cooperation of South Carolina and Georgia, and that was not forthcoming. Few southerners were willing to run the risk of placing guns in the hands of slaves. The Virginia government refused to do so, and it is not surprising that a similar attitude prevailed farther south.[21] "We are much disgusted here at the Congress recommending us to arm our Slaves," wrote one South Carolinian. "It was received with great resentment, as a very dangerous and impolitic Step."[22] Washington lent the proposal no open support and privately expressed a fear that arming some slaves would produce "much discontent" among those remaining in servitude.[23] On the other hand, first General Benjamin Lincoln and then General Nathaniel Greene, as American commanders in the southern theater, strongly urged that the critical need for more soldiers be met by enlisting slaves, but they were no more successful than Congress in swaying the legislatures of South Carolina and Georgia.[24]

THE SECOND CONTINENTAL Congress, after more than a year of organizing and directing American military resistance to Britain, acquired a second great responsibility in July 1776—that of establishing a permanent frame of government for the new United States of America. Richard Henry Lee's famous resolution of June 7 declaring "That these United Colonies are, and of right ought to be, free and independent States" was accompanied by another directing "That a plan of confederation be prepared and transmitted to the respective Colonies for their consideration and approbation."[25] Formation of an American union had been extensively discussed before Lee offered his resolution, and the principal organizational problem had been obvious ever since the opening session of the First Continental Congress, when Patrick Henry rose to declare that "it would be great injustice if a little Colony should have the same weight in the councils of America as a great one."[26] Virginia in 1774 had at least ten times the population of Delaware or Georgia. Yet continental unity was plainly more imperative than equitable representation, which, in any case, would have been difficult to define and administer. So this first Congress, while disclaiming any intention of setting a precedent for future congresses, decided that each colony should have one vote.[27] Despite much dissatisfaction in the more populous states, that simple solution lasted fifteen years.

Fair or unfair, state equality in congressional voting was feasible; state equality in the requisition of money and troops was not. In July of 1775, for instance, the Second Continental Congress determined that the responsibility for redeeming its bills of credit should be distributed among the states according to "the number of Inhabitants, of all ages, including negroes and mulattoes."[28] That provision, which of course displeased southerners, illustrated the fact that in any apportionment according to population, the question of whether to include slaves was bound to arise.

The actions taken in 1774 and 1775 became precedents in the summer of 1776 when a committee headed by John Dickinson set to work framing articles of confederation. In its draft submitted on July 12, the committee proposed to continue the rule of one vote per state in Congress and to apportion the expenses of the central government among the states according to their total populations.[29] The first of these provisions survived repeated attacks from representatives of the large states and was retained in the revised document finally approved by Congress on November 15, 1777. Thus the subject of slavery never entered into the decision on representation in the framing of the Articles of Confederation. But it was a different story when the delegates came to decide how the financial burden should be shared.

Americans generally agreed that taxes should be proportionate to wealth, but the task of calculating the total wealth of each state seemed so formidable that there was a strong disposition to settle for the simpler alternative of counting the producers of wealth. The proposal of the Dickinson committee reflected the judgment that population as a whole constituted the best available indicator of wealth. It was first challenged by Samuel Chase of Maryland, who on July 30 moved an amendment apportioning the government's expenses among the states according to their *white* populations only. He regarded the number of inhabitants as a "tolerably good criterion of property" but insisted that slaves were property like cattle and ought not to be counted as part of the population. John Adams responded that if the number of people was to be taken as an index of wealth, slaves must be included in the enumeration because all workers, whether freemen or slaves, were equally producers. Benjamin Harrison of Virginia denied that slave labor was as productive as free labor and suggested that "two slaves should be counted as one freeman." There, one might say, was the origin of the notorious three-fifths compromise.[30]

James Wilson of Pennsylvania also complained that Chase's amendment would stimulate the further importation of slaves, while at one point in the discussion, Thomas Lynch of South Carolina gave vent to the same menacing impatience that was expressed by some southerners during the D'Auterive and Pacheco controversies many years later. According to notes taken by Adams at the time, Lynch said: "If it is debated, whether [our] slaves are [our] property, there is an end of the confederation."[31]

The Chase amendment, which had obviously aroused strong sectional feelings about slavery, was defeated on August 1, with the seven northern states united against five southern states and only the Georgia delegation divided.[32] The issue remained unresolved until October of the following year, when the original recommendation of the Dickinson committee was discarded in favor of a somewhat less controversial but also less workable plan. First, Congress rejected a proposal that would have made almost all private property, including slaves, the basis for apportioning national expenses among the states. Then the delegates, with only the four New England states opposed, voted that such expenses should be allocated according to the estimated value of land and improvements.[33] The southern states had won their battle to exclude slaves, whether considered as persons or as property, from the calculation of how much a state must contribute to the support of the central government. Furthermore, slaves were excluded from consideration in another respect. One clause untouched by revision provided that state quotas for the land forces should be set "in proportion to the number of white inhabitants." By this rule, Massachusetts would be expected to furnish about the same number of troops as Virginia.[34] Thus the Articles of Confederation, though free of any direct reference to the institution of slavery, contained two significant concessions to the states with large slave populations.

Ratification of the Articles was largely achieved during the year 1778, but a number of state legislatures instructed their delegates in Congress to request amendments of the document before giving it formal approval. Among the proposals offered, Connecticut moved that in Article 8, the basis for allocation of common expenses be changed from lands and improvements back to total population, as the Dickinson committee's draft had provided; and three northern states sought to have troop requisitions apportioned among the states according to their total populations, rather than their white populations.[35] These and all other proposed changes were defeated because a majority in Congress feared that opening the door to even one amendment, however meritorious, would invite too much delay in the achievement of confederation.[36] Delay nevertheless ensued, as Maryland alone for more than two years refused to ratify the Articles until states claiming western lands agreed to cede them to the central government. Consequently, it was March 1, 1781, when this, the first constitution of the United States, finally went into effect.

The Confederation Congress, functioning in about the same way as its predecessor, the Second Continental Congress, presided over the achievement of American independence by virtue of military success against British forces and the treaty of peace signed in 1783. Among the many problems of the new government during the period of transition from war to peace, none was more pressing than that of revenue. Congress had no power to lay taxes or to enforce its requisitions upon the states. Furthermore, it became increasingly apparent that the apportionment of expenses according to land values, as provided for in Article 8, was never going to work. "The rule is good and plain but the question is extremely difficult," wrote the North Carolina delegates to the governor of their state.

> How shall the value be fixed? Let the appropriated Lands and their improvements be valued by the Inhabitants of the respective States and we have great reason to believe, from proofs before us, that the valuation would be unequal. . . . It is presumed that the valuation would be more uniform and just if it was made by a set of Commissioners who should view all the lands and buildings in the United States. But there is reason to believe that such process . . . would be perpetual and it would be an even chance which would come first, the fixing the Quotas or the Day of Judgment.[37]

In 1783, another attempt was made to base apportionment on population rather than land value. Northerners desiring the change recognized that they would have to make some kind of concession on slavery. A committee headed by Nathaniel Gorham of Massachusetts recommended an amendment of Article 8 whereby expenses would be apportioned among the states according to their total populations, but excluding slaves of certain ages (left unspecified).[38] There was general agreement, however, that it would be better to set a fixed ratio of slave population to free population.[39] On March 28, the committee accordingly reported a proposal that "two blacks be rated as equal to one freeman." That proportion, which had been suggested originally by Benjamin Harrison back in 1776, was satisfactory to most southerners, although a number of them still preferred the land-value basis, and some argued that 3 to 1 or 4 to 1 would be a fairer representation of the slave's productive value. On the other side, several New England delegates spoke out in favor of a four-to-three ratio. Then a move to equate three slaves with two free persons was brought to a vote and defeated, Massachusetts joining the southern states in opposition. After further discussion, James Madison, offered "proof of the sincerity of his professions of liberality" by proposing that slaves be rated at five to three. James Wilson said that he would "sacrifice his opinion to this compromise," and it passed by a vote of seven states to two, with one delegation divided. Almost immediately that decision was reversed as South Carolina deserted to the opposition, leaving only a minority of six states supporting the proposition.[40] But four days later, enough members changed their minds to produce an eight-state majority in its favor. On April 18, when the final vote was taken on the amendment to Article 8 as part of a broader revenue plan, the majority had increased to nine, with New York divided and only Rhode Island opposed.[41] "Those who voted differently from their former votes," Madison observed, "were influenced by the conviction of the necessity of the change & despair on both sides of a more favorable rate of the Slaves."[42]

The "three-fifths compromise," or "federal ratio," as it came to be called, had resulted from the determination of Congress that population instead of land ought to be the basis for allocating the expenses of the Confederation. It was the ultimate product of bargaining between northerners who wanted slaves wholly included in the calculation and southerners who wanted them wholly excluded. The proposal to split the difference evenly by counting two slaves as one free person was acceptable to the South but not to the North. In the final negotiations, accordingly, the three-fifths compromise emerged as an accommodation between the one-half compromise favored by southerners and the two-thirds compromise sought by northerners. Although racial preconceptions were always a factor in any discussion of slavery, the fraction "three-fifths" had no racial meaning. It did not represent a perception of blacks as three-fifths human. It was not intended to denote the slave's dual legal status as both person and property. Instead, it reflected a double judgment, together with a qualification insisted upon by southerners and reluctantly acquiesced in by northerners, namely: that taxation should be proportionate to wealth, that population was the best available index of wealth, and that slaves, because they were less productive than free persons, ought to be counted only fractionally as indicators of wealth. The fraction finally chosen, as Madison explained to a fellow Virginian, was simply "a compromise between the wide opinions & demands of the Southern & other States."[43]

Despite strong urging from Congress, the proposed amendment of Article 8 never went into effect because four states failed to ratify it.[44] The three-fifths compromise nevertheless remained in men's minds as an example of successful sectional accommodation on a difficult issue. Meanwhile, as the new nation struggled with various postwar problems, slavery continued to impinge now and then upon the shaping of public policy. For example, Congress in 1784 asked to be vested with certain powers over foreign trade in order to strengthen its hand in the negotiation of commercial treaties. The Georgia legislature somewhat tardily approved the exercise of such power, but with the proviso "that it do not extend to prohibit the importation of negroes."[45] Here was a plain signal that the spirit of the Revolution had not produced a consensus in favor of abolishing the African slave trade.

In addition, the Confederation Congress approved the treaty of peace with Great Britain, one clause of which provided that British forces were to withdraw from the United States without "carrying away any negroes or other property of the American inhabitants." The clause had been added belatedly to the text of the treaty at the instance of Henry Laurens, the only southern member of the American peace delegation.[46] Thus, almost casually, in the founding document that confirmed American independence, Negro slaves were recognized as property by the United States government. From 1783 onward, Congress repeatedly instructed its diplomatic emissaries abroad to seek satisfaction for the thousands of slaves carried off in disregard of the treaty.[47] When nothing came of these efforts, some southerners began to suspect that their case suffered from a lack of enthusiasm on the part of the two northerners most responsible for pressing it—John Jay, secretary of foreign affairs, and John Adams, the first American minister to Britain.[48] Jay, in a report to Congress on October 13, 1786, revealed the ambivalence and discomfort of a man whose heart was with the opponents of slavery but whose official duties required him to act virtually as a slaveholders' agent.

The report was perhaps the strongest official expression of antislavery sentiment to be heard from any person holding high executive office in the United States government down until the time of the Lincoln administration.

"Whether men can be so degraded as under any circumstances to be with propriety denominated Goods and Chattels ... is a question," Jay declared, "on which opinions are unfortunately various, even in Countries professing Christianity and respect for the rights of mankind." Nevertheless, as the treaty article confirmed, both American law and British practice recognized that man might have property in man. Jay was most concerned about those slaves who, responding to promises of freedom and protection, had fled from their masters and found refuge within British lines. The mere flight of such slaves, he maintained, did not extinguish their owners' title, and they could not be claimed by the British as booty of war because "they *were received, not taken* by the enemy." On the other hand, it would have been "cruelly perfidious," in Jay's view, if the slaves had been delivered up to their former bondage and to the severe punishments probably awaiting them. The result was a "painful dilemma." By agreeing to the treaty, "Britain bound herself to do great wrong to these Slaves; and yet by not executing it she would do great wrong to their Masters." The remedy was simple enough, however. Having kept faith with the slaves by carrying them away, the British should do justice to their masters by paying the full value for them. "In this way," Jay observed, "neither could have just cause to complain; for although no price can compensate a Man for bondage for life, yet every Master may be compensated for a runaway Slave."[49] The logic of his argument seemed impeccable, but British officials remained unresponsive, and the problem of the carried-away slaves continued to haunt Anglo-American relations for many years.

At the same time that the Confederation Congress was addressing violations of the peace treaty, it confronted the problem of slavery in the territories. The American territorial system came into existence in the 1780s as states with claims to western lands began ceding them to the United States. When the critical cession by Virginia was completed in 1784, Congress took steps to provide a frame of government for the new national domain. A committee headed by Jefferson submitted its plan for establishing at least fourteen new states in the transappalachian region. The proposed ordinance included several specific restrictions, one of which declared: "That after the year 1800 of the Christian era, there shall be neither slavery nor involuntary servitude in any of the said states, otherwise than in punishment of crimes, whereof the party shall have been duly convicted to have been personally guilty."[50]

Of course this attempt to ban slavery throughout the entire American West, as it then existed, was unacceptable to most of the southern members.

A North Carolinian moved to strike the clause, which meant that it would be retained only if seven states gave it their support. A total of fourteen delegates from the seven northern states voted unanimously for retention, but *stupid NJ* New Jersey had only one man present and so, according to the rules of Congress, its vote did not count. Nine delegates from four southern states voted 7 to 2 against retention. Jefferson's two colleagues outvoted him in the Virginia delegation, and the two North Carolina members were divided. The vote of six states to three in favor of the antislavery provision was not enough to prevent its excision, and the Ordinance of 1784, as finally enacted, therefore contained no mention of slavery.[51] In a letter written some two years later, Jefferson lamented that the voice of a single additional supporter "would have prevented this abominable crime from spreading itself across the country."[52] He was no doubt at least partly mistaken, however. Insofar as the ordinance applied to the region south of the Ohio River, where slaveholders were already well established and where no land had as yet been ceded to the United States, southern opposition probably would have prevented effective enforcement of the antislavery clause and perhaps even forced its repeal.[53]

In 1785, a congressional committee led by Rufus King of Massachusetts renewed the proposal to prohibit slavery after 1800 in all the new states created by the Ordinance of 1784, having added a provision for the recovery of fugitive slaves escaping into that region.[54] A preliminary vote indicated that northerners once again were unanimously in favor of such action and that they had the support of a few members from the upper South.[55] The King resolution never came to a final vote, however, perhaps because of a growing realization that the ordinance itself would have to be remodeled before it could be put into operation. Congress assigned the task of revision to a committee headed by Jefferson's friend James Monroe, who presented its recommendation on May 10, 1786. This document, which was in a sense the first draft of the famous Northwest Ordinance, laid out a two-stage plan of territorial government leading eventually to statehood. It said nothing about slavery. During the year that followed, the Monroe draft was debated, recommitted, redrafted, and debated again, without restoration of the antislavery clause. Congress still had the revised plan under consideration when the members of the Constitutional Convention assembled at Philadelphia in May of 1787.[56]

From 1774 until 1787, the Continental Congress and the Confederation Congress had periodically engaged in discussions and made decisions touching the institution of slavery, but never in the way of confronting it directly as a national problem. Always the concern with slavery had been incidental or auxiliary to some matter or purpose generally considered to be of greater immediate importance. Thus Congress took an interest in closing down the African slave trade only as part of the prerevolutionary struggle with Britain; it endorsed a plan for the enlistment and eventual manumission of several thousand slaves only because of a desperate need for more troops; it fashioned the three-fifths compromise only to facilitate the quest for a stable national revenue. The fundamental question of the future of slavery in a nation formally dedicated to universal freedom was simply not on the national agenda, and only a few people wanted to have it put there.[57] Of course Jefferson and several other members of Congress had sought to define the future of slavery at least with respect to its extension into new western states. But that effort had failed and, in the spring of 1787, seemed unlikely to be renewed with any hope of success.

IN 1787, WHEN Benjamin Franklin, at the age of eighty-one, served as a delegate to the Constitutional Convention, he was also elected president of the reorganized Pennsylvania Society for Promoting the Abolition of Slavery. The society requested him to deliver a memorial to the Convention urging that it devote some attention to the African slave trade, but Franklin refrained from mixing his two roles. He did not present the memorial, and, in fact, there is no record of his having said anything about slavery during the proceedings of the Convention.[58] By this time, a number of antislavery societies had been established in the United States, and their cause appeared to be prospering. Most notably, abolition had begun in the northern states and was expected to prevail eventually at least as far south as Delaware.[59] In addition, Virginia and Maryland had revised their laws to facilitate private manumission, and every state except Georgia had in some way proscribed, inhibited, or suspended the importation of slaves. All of these antislavery gains resulted from the action of state governments, dealing with what almost everyone considered to be exclusively a state problem. Neither Franklin nor any of the other delegates gathering in Philadelphia conceived of slavery as a problem waiting to be addressed by national authority. Certainly they did not think of themselves as having been empowered and charged to settle the destiny of the institution. Yet slavery, though not on the Convention's agenda, intruded frequently on its deliberations and profoundly affected several of its most important decisions. With at least half of the delegates owning slaves, the Convention, viewed as an entity, was bound to have mixed feelings on the subject. "Intent of the framers" in regard to slavery is an abstraction linking the multiplicity of individual attitudes with the unity of the Constitution. Nevertheless, a good many delegates, including some of the slaveholders, seem to have believed or hoped that somehow in the flow of time, slavery would disappear. The imprint of that expectation is visible in the document that they finally approved.

The Convention of 1787, although ostensibly called to find ways of improving the Articles of Confederation, quickly displayed a strong disposition to draft a whole new constitution for the United States. Most of the delegates were in general agreement that their primary purpose was to strengthen the national government by adding to its list of specific *powers* and by investing it with the *power* to govern effectively. But in addition, delegates from some of larger states were determined to bring about a more equitable allocation of national power by substituting proportional representation for state equality in the national legislature. Thus the "Virginia plan," which launched the work of the Convention, called for a national legislature of two houses, with representation in both apportioned among the states according to free population or contributions to the national treasury.[60] Delegates from several of the smaller states countered with the "New Jersey plan," proposing to retain the existing governmental structure of a unicameral legislature in which each state had one vote.[61] This, the most critical issue before the Convention, was resolved after much debate by the "great compromise" of July 16, which balanced state equality in one branch of Congress with representation based on population in the other.[62]

Any discussion of proportional representation necessarily raised the question of slavery and how it fitted into the emerging new design of the federal republic. In the apportionment of congressional seats among the states, were slaves to be counted as part of the population represented? This was plainly a sectional issue, but it proved to be one on which the sectional lines were never very clearly drawn in the Convention because of various complications, such as the preference of some delegates for apportionment based on wealth. If slaves were to be counted as free persons were, Virginia would have about 17 percent of the seats in the House of Representatives; if not, her share would be reduced to about 12 percent. But even 12 percent would be an improvement over the state's representation under the Articles of Confederation, which was less than 8 percent of the total. Thus, to Madison and other Virginians, as the Virginia plan itself indicated, proportional representation seemed more important than slave representation. Similarly, Pennsylvania stood to gain so much from proportional representation that its delegation (except Gouverneur Morris) tended to be conciliatory on the question of slave representation.

Since the question of counting or not counting slaves obviously had to be settled if proportional representation was to be installed, the thoughts of some delegates naturally turned to the formula approved by Congress in 1783 as a basis for distributing the expenses of the Confederation. It was James Wilson of Pennsylvania, a man of antislavery principles, who on June 11 proposed that the federal ratio be applied to the problem of representation. The Convention, sitting as a committee of the whole, promptly approved.[63] Four days later, William Paterson counterattacked by presenting the New Jersey plan, which, while clinging to the already rejected principle of complete state equality, also contained a proposal to use the federal ratio for its original purpose, that is, in the allocation of financial requisitions.[64] With these moves, the groundwork was laid for double employment of the three-fifths ratio in the Constitution.

Wilson embraced the federal ratio as strategy calculated to help secure proportional representation in both houses of Congress, which he, along with Madison, ardently supported. For Wilson at this point, the ratio was not so much a sectional compromise as it was a familiar, ready-at-hand means of clearing away a troublesome obstacle. Madison at first likewise regarded the slavery question as an impediment to the replacement of state equality with proportional representation. But at the end of June, in his desire to minimize the continuing rivalry between large states and small states, he ventured to exploit the slavery question by portraying the United States as a nation divided primarily into slaveholding and nonslaveholding sections. He suggested in place of the three-fifths compromise that legislative seats be apportioned in one house according to free inhabitants and in the other according to total population. "By this arrangement," he said, "the Southern scale would have the advantage in one House, and the Northern in the other."[65]

Hard though they tried, Madison, Wilson, and the other advocates of proportional representation were unable to hold all the ground that they had won on June 11. The opposition crystallized June 29 in a motion calling for state equality in one house of Congress. At first, the motion failed by a vote of 5 to 5, but it was incorporated in the recommendation of a committee reporting on July 5 and tentatively approved by the Convention two days later.[66] From then on, the central feature of the great compromise was substantially in place, but there followed a bitter struggle over the manner of installing proportional representation in the other house. The main issue was not the

three-fifths ratio but rather the more general question of whether the Constitution should contain *any* specific rule of apportionment. Gouverneur
Morris, who feared the potential power of new western states and thought
that representation should reflect property as well as population, wanted periodic reapportionment left to the discretion of Congress. He won a temporary
victory on July 9 when the Convention, while still considering the initial
quota of seats that it proposed to specify in the Constitution, accepted a clause
authorizing Congress in certain circumstances to revise the quota "upon the
principles of . . . wealth and number of inhabitants."[67] That would have eliminated the need for the three-fifths compromise in the Constitution, leaving
the whole question of slave representation to legislative disposal. Many delegates were unwilling to settle for such a vague arrangement, however, and
soon the Convention resumed its efforts to draft a constitutional rule of proportional representation, which meant that it must either reaffirm its
approval of the three-fifths compromise or design an acceptable alternative.

At this point, there occurred some spirited exchanges concerning slavery,
set off on July 11 by a South Carolina effort to scrap the federal ratio and base
legislative apportionment on total population. Pierce Butler, in offering the
motion, reversed earlier assertions about the low productivity of slave labor
made by southerners when the subject had been allocation of national
expenses, rather than representation. He now argued that slaves were equal
to freemen as producers of wealth and consequently ought to be represented
equally in a government "instituted primarily for the protection of property." Delegates from Massachusetts, Virginia, and North Carolina responded
adversely, indicating their continued adherence to the three-fifths compromise. Butler's proposal was defeated, 7 to 3, and when renewed the next day
by Charles Pinckney, it failed again, receiving only the votes of South Carolina and Georgia.[68]

From the opposite extreme, Gouverneur Morris declared that any representation of slaves at all would be unacceptable to the people of Pennsylvania.
He attacked the three-fifths ratio as an encouragement to the slave trade and
as having no basis in logic.[69] Morris's principal concern, however, was not
slavery but preservation of his July 9 victory. And, indeed, the argument over
slavery and the three-fifths clause, which ran intermittently for three days,
was never clear-cut, but always mixed with collateral questions: whether
wealth as well as people should be represented, whether population was the
best available index of wealth, whether apportionment should be defined in
the Constitution or left to the legislature.[70]

Morris's colleague James Wilson acknowledged that applying the three-fifths ratio to representation was hard to justify because it rested on no principle. If slaves were counted as persons, why not as whole persons? If they were counted as property, why should not other property be included in the computation? Yet these were difficulties, Wilson said, that "must be overruled by the necessity of compromise."[71] And Wilson's mood was the one that prevailed. On July 11, to be sure, the Convention voted 6 to 4 against incorporating the three-fifths ratio in a proposed national census, but the issue was somewhat confused and the division was not sectional. The negative votes came from Massachusetts, New Jersey, Pennsylvania, Delaware, Maryland, and South Carolina.[72] The Convention reversed itself the next day and endorsed the ratio by a vote of 6 to 2, with only New Jersey and Delaware opposed, while Massachusetts and South Carolina were divided.[73] In still another vote on July 13, the ratio was implicitly approved, 9 to 0, and then the Convention adopted it as part of the great compromise on July 16.[74]

By then, the three-fifths compromise had been carefully and somewhat absurdly camouflaged in the hope of making it more palatable to certain delegates. For one thing, the approved text no longer specified the three-fifths ratio but referred instead to the "ratio recommended by Congress in their Resolution of April 18, 1783." In addition, the only thing said about the apportionment of legislative seats was that "representation ought to be proportioned according to direct Taxation," after which the ratio of 1783 was applied explicitly just to direct taxation.[75] This linkage and the accompanying subterfuge, proposed by Morris and Wilson, respectively, on July 12,[76] may have had some effect on that day's voting, but the odds were always heavily in favor of the three-fifths compromise from the moment that the Convention began to move toward proportional representation in at least one branch of the national legislature. Probably the only viable alternative was Morris's proposal to leave apportionment largely in the hands of Congress, but a majority of delegates proved to be unwilling to do so. As early as June 11, the federal ratio won overwhelming approval in the committee of the whole. Opposition to it in the votes and speeches of July 11–13 sprang from mixed purposes. Feelings about slavery mingled with economic considerations, with rivalry over the geographic allocation of national power, and with a general recognition of the urgent need for compromise. South Carolina's aggressive effort to secure full representation for slaves was emphatically rejected. As for apportionment based solely on free population, no northerner at this time even ventured to propose it, and when Morris did so several weeks later, his motion failed, 10 votes to 1.[77] There was, moreover, no haggling over the fraction itself. That battle had been fought out four years earlier. One can scarcely overstate the importance of the fact that in the three-fifths ratio delegates had available a packaged compromise already ratified by eleven of the thirteen states. The ratio had become, as Rufus King later observed, "the language of all America."[78]

If the Convention's first struggle over slavery pertained to the structuring of Congress, the second such conflict grew out of the empowerment of Congress. Delegates were generally agreed that substantial control of foreign and interstate commerce must be delegated to the national government, and the first proposal along those lines was made as early as June 15 in the New Jersey plan. To no one's surprise, then, the draft constitution submitted by the Committee of Detail on August 6 contained a clause authorizing Congress to "regulate commerce with foreign nations, and among the several States." But many southerners believed that such power in the hands of the central government, if unrestricted, would be used primarily to benefit northern commerce at southern expense. Delegates from the lower South also feared that the power would be used to outlaw the African slave trade. The Committee of Detail responded sympathetically to southern apprehensions. Made up of three northerners and only two southerners, but apparently dominated in this instance by its chairman, John Rutledge of South Carolina, the committee proposed a number of glaringly sectional limitations on the commerce power and the taxing power. There was to be no tax on exports, nor any capitation tax unless apportioned in accordance with the three-fifths compromise; a two-thirds majority would be required for passage of navigation acts; and Congress was never to prohibit the importation of slaves or lay any tax upon such importation.[79]

This prosouthern package so angered Rufus King and Gouverneur Morris that on August 8 they renewed their attacks upon the three-fifths compromise, an issue supposedly settled. Morris delivered one of the Convention's strongest denunciations of slavery, calling it "a nefarious institution" and "the curse of heaven" on the states wherein it prevailed. In a concluding gust of rhetoric, he declared that he would rather be taxed to pay for all the slaves in the country than "saddle posterity with such a Constitution."[80] The prosouthern clauses did not come up for discussion until some two weeks later, by which time the commerce clause itself had been approved without opposition.[81] First to be considered was the prohibition of taxes on exports. That restriction passed, 7 to 4, with the five southern states united in its support.[82] The South was sharply divided, however, on the subject of slave importation. In the case of Maryland and Virginia, morality blended with economic interest to produce a strong desire for cessation of the trade. George Mason most eloquently condemned the "infernal traffic" and echoed the language of Morris in warning that slavery brought "the judgment of Heaven on a country." But it was Maryland's garrulous maverick Luther Martin who proposed an amendment eliminating the exemption of the slave trade from national control. Such a concession to slavery in the Constitution, he said, would be "inconsistent with the principles of the Revolution and dishonorable to the American character."[83]

The debate that followed Martin's motion began late on August 21 and extended over much of the following day. Madison, whose record is of course incomplete, noted down remarks by seventeen men, five of whom spoke more than once. Delegates from Georgia and the Carolinas insisted emphatically that their states would not ratify a Constitution in which the importation of slaves was made subject to congressional control. Charles C. Pinckney charged that Virginia, with a surplus of slaves, stood to profit from an increase in their value if importation were forbidden. A rejection of the slave-trade clause, he warned, would be the equivalent of "an exclusion of South Carolina from the Union." The most striking feature of the debate was the staunch support given the lower South by Connecticut delegates Oliver Ellsworth and Roger Sherman. In their view, the Committee of Detail's recommendations constituted a necessary compromise that ought to be accepted as written. Predicting that slavery would eventually disappear without intervention by the central government, they argued that it was better "to let the Southern States import slaves than to part with them, if they made that a sine qua non." The South Carolinians nevertheless concluded that they must yield some ground or risk total defeat. They accordingly proposed commitment of the slave-trade clause, with a view to allowing taxation of imported slaves. Some northerners wanted more than that, however, and in the end it was decided that the slave-trade clause, together with the restriction on capitation taxes and the section requiring a two-thirds vote for navigation acts, should be submitted to a committee of eleven.[84]

The committee, headed by New Jersey's vigorous and liberal-minded governor, William Livingston, reported on August 24. It proposed to retain the restriction on capitation taxes, a superfluous provision already covered in the apportionment of representation and direct taxes. Otherwise, the committee recommended that the slave trade be shielded from congressional prohibition only until the year 1800, that the trade be taxable at an average rate, and that the special requirement for navigation acts be eliminated.[85] These changes amounted to a substantial departure from the prosouthern proposals submitted by the Committee of Detail, but South Carolina sought only the minor adjustment of changing 1800 to 1808. Despite Madison's protest that a twenty-year exemption would be "dishonorable to the National character," the amendment was agreed to and the slave-trade clause approved by identical votes of 7 to 4. The three New England states combined with four southern states to form the majority. Virginia joined New Jersey, Pennsylvania, and Delaware in opposition.[86] As adopted on August 25, the slave-trade clause was in itself a compromise between the two extremes of a *total, permanent ban* and *no restriction whatever* on congressional power to prohibit the importation of slaves. The Carolinians and Georgians seem to have accepted the compromise because they believed that it was the best deal they could get. The New Englanders voted for it, declaring that they were motivated by a desire to hold the Union together, but their assertions have seldom been taken at face value. Historians have been disposed rather to view the slave-trade clause as part of a broader compromise in which the New Englanders made concessions on slavery to secure southern concessions on commerce.[87] Yet the evidence only partly bears out this interpretation.

If New England and the lower South were indeed acting in concert, it is curious that after securing approval of the slave-trade clause, they did not then seek to complete the compromise by striking out the requirement of a two-thirds vote for navigation acts. Instead, consideration of the subject was postponed until August 29, at which time four of the five southern states voted *in favor* of a two-thirds requirement for *all* federal regulation of commerce, interstate as well as foreign. Only the South Carolina delegation acted as though it were participating in an intersectional bargain on commerce and the slave trade. It joined the northern states in defeating the proposed restriction by a vote of 7 to 4. After that setback, the four other southern states gave up the struggle and assented to elimination of the section on navigation acts.[88]

The South Carolinians were all the more conciliatory at this juncture because they had decided to seek another special benefit for slavery. On August 28 and again in revised phrasing on August 29, they moved to add a clause requiring the return of slaves who had fled across state lines. Wilson and Sherman raised objections, but otherwise there was no argument, and the motion passed without an opposing vote from any state.[89] Thus, quickly and almost casually, the framers burdened the Constitution with a passage that was to have corrosive effects on national unity. No doubt they were strongly influenced by the knowledge that the Northwest Ordinance, which Congress had enacted on July 13, contained a similar provision.[90] There is, however, only meager evidence to support the thesis that the fugitive-slave clause was part of a grand compromise on slavery, secretly arranged between members of Congress and members of the Convention.[91] Moreover, in spite of the remarkable myth that later developed, there is no contemporary evidence that the sponsors of the clause labeled it a sine qua non or that the Convention regarded it as such. Ready acceptance of the clause was undoubtedly fostered by the spirit of accommodation that had begun to prevail and also by the weary desire of most delegates to finish their work and go home. Whatever the mixture of reasons may have been, it is a striking fact that the fugitive-slave clause became a part of the Constitution with virtually no discussion of its exact meaning or potential application.

As the Convention approached the end of its labors, one further concession to the slaveholding interest was extracted by South Carolina. On September 10, delegates were discussing the article providing for amendment of the Constitution when John Rutledge interposed, declaring emphatically that he could not agree "to give a power by which the articles relating to slaves might be altered by the States not interested in that property and prejudiced against it." Accordingly, a proviso was added forbidding amendment of the slave-trade clause or the capitation-tax clause before the year 1808.[92] Seven days later, most of the members present signed the final version of their historic document, which dealt with slavery in several places but never once called the institution by name.

Slavery, as a brooding presence in the land, significantly influenced the deliberations of the Constitutional Convention, but the Convention made no calculated effort to affect the institution of slavery, and its members never conceived of themselves as having any power or responsibility to do so. The intrusions of slavery into the work of the Convention were largely side effects of progress toward a new constitutional design. One such intrusion became more or less inevitable with the introduction of proportional representation at the national level; another resulted from the empowering of Congress to regulate foreign commerce. Even the fugitive-slave clause was a late-hour extension of the provision for interstate rendition of fugitives from justice. In direct confrontation, the proslavery determination of certain delegates, notably the South Carolinians, usually proved somewhat stronger than the diffuse antislavery sentiment of many others. To what extent that advantage colored the fundamental nature of the Constitution has been a matter of dispute for more than two hundred years.

EVALUATION OF THE Constitution in relation to slavery, which began as soon as the document appeared in print, corresponded in ways one would expect to the partisanship of the struggle over ratification. That is, advocates of ratification were likely to stress its proslavery features in the South and its antislavery potential in the North. Opponents of ratification tended to do the reverse. This general pattern was complicated, to be sure, by the hostility to the African slave trade in the upper South. Madison defended the twenty-year exemption of the trade from federal control as a temporary evil that was necessary to prevent "dismemberment of the Union."[93] George Mason, speaking against the Constitution, denounced the exemption as "a most disgraceful thing to America." Yet at the same time, he condemned the lack of any clause protecting the existent system of slavery from northern interference.[94] Another of Virginia's leading antifederalists, Patrick Henry, went further and argued that Congress, in its possession of power to lay taxes and provide for the common defense, would have the constitutional means of abolishing slavery completely.[95] Supporters of the Constitution in Virginia thus found themselves prodded into defending its compatibility with the institution of slavery. Madison, for instance, declared that slaveholders would have "a better security than any that now exists," and Edmund Randolph assured members of the ratification convention that even the South Carolina delegates had felt secure about their slave property under the Constitution.[96]

Proponents of ratification in South Carolina had to answer the objection that the slave-trade clause merely postponed the surrender of state control over a resource that was vital to the state's economy. Charles C. Pinckney's response was particularly revealing. He explained that whereas delegates from the middle states and Virginia had favored immediate and total prohibition of the trade, New England delegates had been more accommodating. They asked only for a time limit on the proposed exemption, and thus a compromise had been arranged. Pinckney then went on to say:

> By this settlement we have secured an unlimited importation of negroes for twenty years. Nor is it declared that the importation shall be then stopped; it may

be continued. We have a security that the general government can never emancipate them, for no such authority is granted. . . . We have obtained a right to recover our slaves in whatever part of America they may take refuge, which is a right we had not before. In short, considering all circumstances, we have made the best terms for the security of this species of property it was in our power to make. We would have made better if we could; but, on the whole, I do not think them bad.[97]

Since all the clauses directed specifically at slavery seemed to favor the institution, northern advocates of ratification encountered a good deal of criticism along antislavery lines. Part of the criticism, such as that of the Quakers, sprang from strong antislavery convictions, but another part was mainly antifederalist strategy, adopted by persons not prominently associated with the antislavery movement.[98] The slave-trade clause received the greatest amount of attention. One side denounced it as an outrageous concession to the most odious feature of the slaveholding system, while the other side praised it as a major step forward in the battle against slavery. No one in the latter group was more eloquent than James Wilson, who maintained that suppression of the slave trade would lead to total abolition. "If there was no other lovely feature in the Constitution but this one," he said, "it would diffuse a beauty over its whole countenance. Yet the lapse of a few years, and Congress will have power to exterminate slavery from within our borders."[99]

In the state ratifying conventions, slavery was a disturbing but more or less marginal issue, discussion of which was usually tailored to the primary purpose of promoting or discouraging ratification. Such discussion must be read with caution, but it did clearly reveal strong disagreement about the intent of the Constitution with respect to slavery and about the future of slavery in the new political order. The constitutional dispute was never resolved. It became especially intense in the decades preceding the Civil War, and not always as part of the controversy between North and South, for although antebellum southerners tended to see eye to eye on the subject, northerners continued to be divided. In the Illinois senatorial campaign of 1858, for instance, Stephen A. Douglas and Abraham Lincoln spent considerable time arguing whether the founders of the Republic had dealt with slavery as a permanent or an impermanent feature of American society.[100] But the most remarkable debate on the constitutional status of slavery took place within the ranks of the abolition crusade.

At one extreme of abolitionist constitutional theory were the Garrisonians, who saw in the work of the framers a document so unequivocally

proslavery that it must be renounced, they said, by all friends of libe
William Lloyd Garrison himself declared that the Constitution was an "infamous bargain" and more than that, "the most bloody and heaven-daring
arrangement ever made by men for the continuance and protection of a system of the most atrocious villany ever exhibited on earth." It was Garrison
too, of course, who coined the phrase, "a covenant with death, and an agreement with hell."[101] At the other extreme, a small group of "constitutional
utopians" not only denied that the framers had extended any protection to
slavery but went on to insist that the Constitution, if properly interpreted,
made or could make slaveholding illegal everywhere in the nation.[102] More
numerous and influential were those anti-Garrisonians who regarded the
Constitution as regrettably proslavery in certain details but antislavery in its
underlying purpose and ultimate potential. Gerrit Smith was speaking for
this group when he said that the few concessions to slavery did not "give
character to the instrument" any more than the current of a stream was
"determined by its eddies."[103]

It was the Garrisonians who, in the long run, proved to be the more persuasive theorists. Their view of the Constitution as culpably proslavery,
although endorsed at the time by relatively few Americans, was perpetuated
by abolition-minded historians after the Civil War and has gained wide acceptance in modern historical scholarship.[104] Indeed, much recent writing on the
subject is virtually an indictment of the members of the Constitutional
Convention. They are accused of passing up a golden opportunity to take
action against slavery and of drafting instead a frame of government that
legitimated and protected the institution.[105] "So firmly etched [in the Consti-
tution] was the guarantee of black bondage," says one writer, "that only a
grim and bloody war would begin to expunge it from the laws."[106]

One might think from reading many of today's neo-Garrisonians that
the members of the Constitutional Convention were free to do whatever they
liked about slavery. The Convention was severely limited, however, by its
own internal differences on the subject and by the very nature of its task,
which required the achievement of something approaching consensus on the
emerging new design of a federal republic. Along with the knowledge that
they must somehow reach substantial agreement among themselves, the delegates were limited by a constant awareness that every word they wrote
would have to pass the inspection of the state ratifying conventions. In the
circumstances, it is scarcely surprising that the framers entertained no
thought of trying to abolish slavery but left the institution unmolested as a

they did not mean to create a pro slavery document

creature of state law. Neither is it surprising that the existence of slavery should have been acknowledged in several passages or that concessions should have been made to an interest as powerful as the slaveholding class. But what was the net effect on the overall character of the Constitution? Are the neo-Garrisonians right or wrong in their insistence that the document submitted to the American people in the fall of 1787 provided "enormous protections for the peculiar institution" and was in fact "permeated" with slavery?[107]

Wendell Phillips, a leading spokesman for the Garrisonians in the 1840s, maintained that northerners in the Constitutional Convention had "bartered honesty for gain" and thus become "partners with tyrants." He named five parts of the Constitution that sacrificed liberty for the protection of slavery: (1) the apportionment of representation and direct taxes according to population, with slaves counting three-fifths; (2) the twenty-year guarantee against congressional prohibition of the foreign slave trade; (3) the provision for recovery of fugitive slaves; (4) the clause authorizing the use of the militia for suppression of insurrections; and (5) the clause promising the states federal protection against domestic violence.[108] This bill of particulars has been expanded by the neo-Garrisonians, but it remains the place to begin in any assessment of the relation between the Constitution and slavery.

According to Phillips, the three-fifths compromise was the "chief pro-slavery clause in the Constitution."[109] Down through the years, it has been denounced as a political bonus for slaveholders, as a degradation of the slave to just three-fifths of a human being, and as a constitutional legitimation of slavery. Neither of the first two complaints is well-founded, and together they are incompatible; for one implies that slaves should have counted for nothing (no-fifths) in the apportionment of representation, while the other implies that they should have been counted in full (five-fifths). The standard Garrisonian interpretation, which might be said to treat slaves as nonpersons, assumes that free population was the only appropriate basis for allocating legislative power among the states. Yet, as a matter of political theory, it made just as much sense in 1787 to base such allocation on the whole population, including slaves, women, children, and other elements of society that were not part of the body politic.[110] Thus characterization of the three-fifths clause as a *bonus* for slaveholders, resting as it does on mere assumption, is not intrinsically sounder than the view (held by Frederick Douglass, for instance) that it was a *penalty* on slaveholding.[111] One side sees a bottle three-fifths full and the other, a bottle two-fifths empty.

The five-to-three ratio, it will be remembered, had originated in earlier congressional efforts to use population as a measure of wealth when making financial requisitions on the states. More than anything else, it was an estimate of the slave's wealth-producing capacity compared with that of free men. As adopted by the Convention in 1787 and applied to the apportionment of legislative seats, the ratio was wholly arbitrary, chosen because it represented a compromise already approved by Congress and eleven of the thirteen states. The ratio did not signify that slaves were only 60 percent human or that they were partly persons and partly property. It had no substantive meaning with respect to representation.

As for the assertion of Garrisonians (in close harmony with most antebellum southerners) that the three-fifths clause gave constitutional sanction to slavery, the text of the clause lends little support to such an interpretation. "Representatives and direct Taxes," it declares, "shall be apportioned among the several States . . . according to their respective Numbers, which shall be determined by adding to the whole Number of free Persons . . . three fifths of all other Persons." Of course these words, by acknowledging the presence of persons other than free in the United States, did obliquely recognize the existence of African slavery as part of the colonial heritage, but then a clause basing apportionment solely on free population would have done the same. In any case, the phrasing carefully chosen by the framers carried no implication of national sanction or protection of the institution, and it lent no explicit reinforcement to the idea of human property. The three-fifths clause, like most compromises, can be perceived in different ways, but to label it simply proslavery or antislavery is more an act of volition than of judgment.

For many Garrisonian critics, however, the most offensive passage in the Constitution was the slave-trade clause, a single lengthy sentence weighted with circumlocution and ambiguity as follows: "The migration or importation of such persons as any of the states now existing shall think proper to admit, shall not be prohibited by the Congress prior to the year one thousand eight hundred and eight, but a tax or duty may be imposed on such importation, not exceeding ten dollars for each person."[112] This clause, moreover, was reinforced elsewhere in the Constitution by a special exemption from amendment during the twenty-year period.[113] At the time of the Constitutional Convention, the prime target of the antislavery movement in Europe and America was the foreign slave trade. To abolitionists then and later it therefore seemed particularly outrageous that the framers should have extended some measure of protection to the hated traffic.

The outrage has ever since obscured the fact that the slave-trade clause was not an independent provision of the Constitution but rather a temporary restriction on a broad power over foreign commerce—a power newly delegated to the national government and recognized at the time as having significant antislavery potential.[114] By way of elucidation, let us suppose that at the Convention a delegate proposed giving Congress the power to regulate or suppress the slave trade and that delegates from the three southernmost states responded angrily, predicting disunion as the consequence of such action. Suppose further that the Convention nevertheless adopted the proposal but appeased the rebellious southerners with a twenty-year postponement of the effective date. How would this cushioned move against the slave trade have been regarded by the American public? Surely opponents of slavery, while regretting the need for any compromise at all, would have perceived it as a partial victory for their cause. The Constitution actually approved and ratified had precisely the same effect as our imaginary antislave-trade clause. Thomas McKeon put the matter clearly when he said in the Pennsylvania ratifying convention: "Every man of candor will find more reason to rejoice that the power should be given at all, than to regret that its exercise should be postponed for twenty years."[115]

The Constitution, viewed as a whole, represented a major step forward in the crusade against further importation of slaves. This was true primarily because of the broad power created and only temporarily restricted with respect to such importation, but it was also true because of the restrictive provision itself. For, despite its proslavery purpose, the slave-trade clause is a fine example of how documental intent can stray from authorial intention. Added at the insistence of delegates from the Deep South, it turned out to be primarily antislavery in its directional force. The crucial event was the change from a permanent exemption for slave importation to one lasting just twenty years. That transformed the meaning of the slave-trade clause by setting a target date for federal prohibition of the traffic. The eminent physician Benjamin Rush was just one of many persons who immediately perceived the antislavery implications of the clause. Soon after the Philadelphia newspapers published the text of the completed Constitution, he informed an English friend that in the year 1808 there would be "an end of the African trade in America."[116] Of course, most states had already outlawed or otherwise inhibited the trade, and during the next decade it became illegal everywhere in the country. State enforcement was less than adequate, however, and any state was free to reopen the trade, as South Carolina elected to do in December

1803. Federal intervention was obviously needed for total suppression, but without the slave-trade clause, such intervention might have been hard to justify and initiate. The clause did permit the importation of some Africans—indeed, many thousands by South Carolina over a four-year period. But at the same time it *expressly confirmed* the power of Congress to prohibit the trade eventually, and more than that, it fostered a general expectation of federal legislation and federal enforcement at a designated time. When Congress passed the slave-trade act of 1807, it did so on a schedule set by the Constitution, and the vote in the House of Representatives was 113 to 5.[117]

The slave-trade clause was placed in Article I, Section 9, among the enumerated limitations on congressional authority. It temporarily suspended, and thereby plainly acknowledged, federal power to outlaw the foreign slave trade. The power was actually conferred in the clause authorizing Congress to "regulate commerce with foreign nations." But the same clause invested Congress with equivalent jurisdiction over commerce "among the several states," and if "commerce" included slave traffic in the one instance, it must have done so in the other. That inference was sustained in the act of 1807, which not only forbade the importation of slaves but also placed certain restrictions on that part of the domestic slave trade carried on in coasting vessels. Furthermore, if the power to "regulate" meant the power to prohibit in the one instance, there is no sound basis for argument that it did not mean the same thing in the other. Thus the slave-trade clause, whether or not the framers so intended, recognized congressional power to regulate or even abolish the interstate slave trade at any time after 1807.[118]

Although the clause did not mention slaves or slavery by name, the words "importation" and "duty" came closer than anything else in the Constitution to reflecting the property-holding aspect of the institution. Yet the temporary nature of the clause made it a dubious basis for any defense of slavery after 1807 and seemed to point instead toward restriction and ultimate extinction. In addition, the operation of the clause was limited from the beginning to the original states, and this, together with the Northwest Ordinance, indicated a general disposition to view slavery as the exception rather than the rule in an expanding nation. Finally, it should be noted that the slave-trade clause suspended only federal power over the importation of slaves, not federal power over all aspects of the African slave trade. As early as 1794, for example, Congress prohibited "carrying on the Slave Trade from the United States to any foreign place or country," and an act passed in 1800 outlawed all American participation in the traffic.[119] These steps, which would have been impossible under the Articles of Confederation, were taken by virtue of the commerce clause of the Constitution.

The one unambiguously proslavery provision of the Constitution was the fugitive slave clause. Here again the framers chose not to name the thing they were talking about: "No person held to service or labour in one state, under the laws thereof, escaping into another, shall, in consequence of any law or regulation therein, be discharged from such service or labour, but shall be delivered up on claim of the party to whom such service or labour may be due." The clause was not placed in Article I with the enumerated powers of Congress but appears instead in Article IV, Section 2. That whole article is about states and statehood, and the second section is about interstate comity. Of the other three sections in the article, two expressly confer power on Congress, and the other vests power more generally in the "United States"— meaning, presumably, all three branches of the federal government. There is no such conferral of power in Section 2, which lends credence to the view of the fugitive slave clause as nothing more than a declaratory limitation on state authority.[120] That view, if accurate, goes a long way toward explaining the absence of controversy in the genesis of a clause that became the basis for some of the most controversial legislation ever passed by Congress.

Without a doubt, the three-fifths clause, or some equivalent, was essential for the success of the Constitution as we know it. The slave-trade clause was probably a necessary concession to the lower South—one that proved, however, to be antislavery rather than proslavery in its ultimate effect. The fugitive-slave clause was a more gratuitous addition to the Constitution, and it alone provided slaveholders with some measure of protection, though only in vague and passive terms. Each of the three clauses dealt with a marginal feature of slavery that had some claim on national attention. None of the three recognized slavery as having any legitimacy in federal law. On the contrary, the framers were doubly careful to treat it explicitly as a state institution. Most revealing in this respect was a last-minute change in the fugitive-clause whereby the phrase "legally held to service or labour in one state" was changed to read "held to service or labour in one state, under the laws thereof." The revision made it impossible to infer from the passage that the Constitution itself legally sanctioned slavery.[121]

The two other parts of the Constitution labeled "proslavery" by Wendell Phillips were those providing for suppression of insurrections and for protection of the states against domestic violence.[122] Both clauses obviously covered various kinds of resistance to civil authority, including servile rebellion, but the 1780s were not a period of serious disturbances among the slave population. What the framers did have very much in mind was the alarming series of events in Massachusetts known as Shays's Rebellion, which had come to an end just a few months before the opening of the Convention.[123] Wendell Phillips, writing in the 1840s, conceded that the two clauses were "perfectly innocent in themselves." He nevertheless insisted that since they were potentially usable for that purpose, the clauses implicated all Americans in "the guilt of sustaining slavery."[124] Perhaps the best way to comment on such reasoning is to ask what alternatives were available to the framers. Should they have excepted slave revolts from the insurrections to be suppressed and from the domestic violence to be guarded against? Any such proposal would have been dismissed as absurd and outrageous. But then the only other option, one that likewise would have received little support in the Convention, was omission or deletion of the two clauses from the text of the Constitution. That would have deprived the federal government of needed authority—authority used as early as 1794 in the Whiskey Rebellion and invoked by Lincoln in 1861 to suppress an insurrection not of slaves, but of slaveholders.

Neo-Garrisonians of the late twentieth century have gone well beyond the Phillips indictment in stamping "proslavery" on various provisions of the Constitution. For instance, one historian maintains that the two clauses prohibiting duties on exports were partly intended to prevent both the federal government and the state governments "from taxing slavery indirectly by taxing the exported products of slave labor."[125] Only part of this interpretation is compatible with the records of the Convention, and then only if one accepts an expanded definition of "proslavery" that embraces everything conceivably beneficial to the staple-crop economy of the South. The proposed curb on *federal* power was not a strictly sectional issue; Madison spoke vigorously against the clause, while a number of northern members supported it.[126] Still, it is true that most southern delegates were, for economic reasons, opposed to allowing federal taxation of exports, and one may, if so resolved, classify such opposition as proslavery by virtue of its being prosouthern. By no stretch of definition, however, can the restriction on *state* taxation of exports be characterized as proslavery. Joined to a similar restraint on state taxation of imports, it was part of a general plan to transfer control of foreign and interstate commerce from the state governments to the federal government. The restriction was proposed by Rufus King, an outspoken critic of slavery. It was approved with the support of most northern states and despite the opposition of most southern states.[127] And there is not the slightest

evidence that any southern delegate wanted the federal Constitution to protect slaveholders from possible antislavery action by their own state
legislatures.[128]

Another neo-Garrisonian scholar identifies no fewer than fifteen provisions of the Constitution that together provided "enormous protections" for
slavery. Here are some of the items that he names in addition to those already
discussed: the creation of an electoral college (because it incorporated the
three-fifths compromise); the privileges and immunities clause (because it
applied only to citizens and therefore not to slaves); the full faith and credit
clause (because it obligated free states to recognize southern laws concerned
with slavery); the clause providing for the return of interstate fugitives from
justice (because it was a threat to persons accused of violating slave laws); and
the requirement of a three-fourths vote of the states for ratification and
amendment of the Constitution (because it gave the slaveholding states a
perpetual veto over any constitutional changes). Moreover, the very "structure of the Constitution" was proslavery, we are told, because it created a
government that "lacked the power to interfere in the domestic institutions
of the states."[129]

To this list one might well add, in the spirit of *reductio ad absurdum*: the
invention of the presidency because the executive branch so often acted in
behalf of slavery, the creation of the Supreme Court (without which there
could have been no Dred Scott decision), and the retention of state equality in
the Senate because it proved to be a bulwark of southern power. Of course the
same sort of reasoning can be used for the opposite purpose of demonstrating
that the Constitution was essentially hostile to slavery and that many of its
provisions posed threats to the institution. The commerce clause, for instance,
was generally recognized as having an antislavery potential. The territory
clause presumably invested Congress with the authority to prevent the
expansion of slavery beyond the boundaries of the original states. The power
to lay taxes, to raise armies, to make treaties, to provide for the "general
Welfare of the United States"—each could conceivably be adapted to antislavery designs. The war power of Congress represented another potential
weapon, for as slavery bred potential domestic enemies, its abolition promised
to strengthen national defenses in time of war. The time came when the military power of the president as commander in chief was actually invoked to
proclaim emancipation. The case for an antislavery Constitution is just as
strong as the case for a proslavery Constitution, but both depend upon special
pleading that ignores part of the evidence.

Unquestionably a central fact of American life in 1787, slavery must have been much on the minds of the men at Philadelphia, but its presence in the land had a stronger influence on the deliberations of the Convention than on the text of the Constitution. The few concessions to slavery in the text were, as Gerrit Smith maintained, more like eddies in a stream than part of the current.[130] Moreover, the concessions were offset by a stylistic tone of repugnance for the institution and by indications that it could be regarded as something less than permanent in American life. In short, the Constitution as it came from the hands of the framers dealt only minimally and peripherally with slavery and was essentially open-ended on the subject. Nevertheless, because it substantially increased the power of the national government, the Constitution had greater proslavery potential and greater antislavery potential than the Articles of Confederation. Its meaning with respect to slavery would depend heavily upon how it was implemented.

3

Slavery in the National Capital

On Thursday, April 13, 1848, the schooner *Pearl* sailed up the Potomac River to the Seventh Street wharf in Washington, carrying a load of wood to camouflage the real purpose for which it had come. Aboard was Daniel Drayton, a middle-aged veteran of the coasting trade, who had hired the vessel and its captain, Edward Sayres. It was a year of revolutions throughout much of Europe, and the two men found the city preparing to celebrate the recent overthrow of Louis Philippe's regime in France. A torchlight procession that evening was preceded by some extravagant oratory in one of the public squares. Speaking to an audience that probably included some members of the black population, Senator Henry S. Foote of Mississippi rejoiced that "the age of tyrants and of slavery" was drawing to a close and would soon be followed by the "universal emancipation of man from the fetters of civic oppression." Two nights later, with the wood having been sold, Drayton and Sayres were busy loading a different kind of cargo. They set sail at dawn, passed slowly down the river to Chesapeake Bay, and turned northward. But a stiff adverse wind forced them to anchor in a cove and wait for a change. By then it was Sunday night. Meanwhile, back in Washington and nearby Georgetown, about forty households had awakened that morning to find one or more of their slaves missing.[1]

This mass escape of seventy-six slaves gave rise to much excitement and a mood of vigilantism in the capital city.[2] The first hasty searches proved futile. But then a Negro drayman, vexed at not having been paid for a trip to the waterfront, revealed that all the fugitives had been carried away by the *Pearl*. Soon more than thirty armed men were embarked on a steamboat in eager pursuit. Finding the *Pearl* still at anchor near the mouth of the Potomac, they captured everyone aboard and returned triumphantly to Washington with their prisoners. A gathering mob greeted their arrival and accompanied the march from the wharf to the city jail, shouting curses and threats of summary punishment. Drayton and Sayres were nevertheless safely committed to the custody of the federal marshal, and bail was set at the excessive figure of $1,000 for each slave carried away.[3]

The cruise of the *Pearl*, although apparently arranged at the instance of a free black on behalf of his family, had all the earmarks of an abolitionist plot. The outburst of public anger in Washington was therefore directed not only against the "slave stealers" themselves but also against abolitionists in general and the local antislavery newspaper in particular. On two successive nights, unruly crowds gathered outside the offices of the *National Era*, throwing rocks at the windows and demanding that the proprietor, Gamaliel Bailey, close down his enterprise or move it to some other community. One of the leading agitators declared that the paper was "a nuisance which ought to have been reported as such by the grand jury, and expelled as such by the corporation." But Bailey, denying any complicity in the *Pearl* affair, cited his rights under the First Amendment and refused to be intimidated. President James K. Polk issued a directive forbidding government clerks to participate in the street demonstrations. The two branches of the city council met in joint session and took action to prevent further disorder. Voices of reason and authority eventually prevailed, and the mob spirit died away without having produced any serious violence.[4]

The Drayton affair had immediate repercussions on Capitol Hill, where Congress was already embroiled in a bitter dispute over the status of slavery in the newly acquired provinces of New Mexico, California, and Oregon. For three days the House of Representatives debated a resolution calling for the appointment of a committee to investigate the "lawless mob" that had been disturbing the city. Southerners were especially outraged that Joshua R. Giddings, the vehement antislavery congressman from Ohio, had visited the jail to show his sympathy for the prisoners. Accused of complicity in Drayton's venture, Giddings dissociated himself from the affair but asserted boldly that slaves had a right to free themselves by any means available to them. By such incendiary talk, said William T. Haskell of Tennessee, Giddings and other radicals in Congress were deliberately stirring up slave resistance in Washington, thereby committing felonies for which "they ought to swing as high as Haman." Abraham Venable of North Carolina, with his emotions scarcely under control, launched a sweeping attack upon Giddings and the entire anti-slavery movement. He denied that slavery was a moral or social evil but at the same time blamed Yankee slave traders for introducing the institution into the South. Professing his love for the Union, he nevertheless welcomed its dissolution with "pleasure and joy" if southerners were "continually to be taunted by fanatics and hypocrites—if their wives and little ones were to be assassinated and destroyed by intermeddling men with hearts black as hell." One speaker, Thomas H. Bayly of Virginia, undertook to demonstrate at length that American abolitionism was part of a British plot aimed at crippling the prosperity of the United States. Antislavery agitators like Giddings were therefore instruments of a foreign government, and more than that, they were advocates of servile rebellion who invited "the cutting of the throat of every white man, woman, and child" in the South. The inevitable result of their murderous designs, Bayly warned, would be bloody civil war and the total destruction of the Negro race in America.[5]

In the Senate, John P. Hale of New Hampshire set off a day of acrimonious oratory when he proposed that local governments within the District of Columbia be made liable for property damage caused by "any riotous or tumultuous assemblage of people." Hale's assertion that the bill resembled laws already operative in many states, including nearby Maryland, did not soften the fury of southern reaction. John C. Calhoun said that the measure was designed to repress "the just indignation" of the people and prevent them from "wreaking their vengeance" upon slave stealers like Drayton. He called instead for legislation "containing the highest penalties known to the law against pirates who are guilty of acts like these." At one point in a heated exchange, he exclaimed, "I would just as soon argue with a maniac from bedlam, as with the Senator from New Hampshire, on this subject." Similarly enraged, Henry Foote charged that Hale's proposal amounted to a bill for the protection of theft and that, as such, it was part of a plot to abolish slavery in the District of Columbia by making slave property unsafe there. Foote invited Hale to visit Mississippi, where, with Foote's own help if need be, he would soon "grace one of the tallest trees of the forest, with a rope around his neck." Under such fierce attack, Hale received little help or sympathy, even from his northern colleagues. In the Senate of 1848, he stood alone as an antislavery radical.[6]

Meanwhile, irate owners were claiming their runaway servants at the city jail and, in most instances, selling them promptly to dealers in the New Orleans slave market.[7] Giddings described the scene at the railroad station one day when some fifty of the Negroes were sent away "to drag out a miserable existence in the rice fields and cotton fields" of the Deep South. There were "wives bidding adieu to their husbands; mothers in an agony of despair . . . , little boys and girls weeping amid the general distress, scarcely knowing the cause of their grief." Responsibility for the shameful spectacle rested primarily with Congress, Giddings declared. "History will record the fact . . . that *we*, the members of this House, at this age of light and knowledge, and of civil liberty, maintain and keep in force a law for selling fathers and children, mothers and tender babes."[8]

Drayton and Sayres were brought to trial in July 1848. Conducting the prosecution was the federal district attorney, Philip Barton Key, whose father had written "The Star-Spangled Banner" and whose uncle, Roger B. Taney, presided over the United States Supreme Court. Acting as counsel for Drayton were the antislavery lawyer and writer, Richard Hildreth, and the noted Massachusetts educator, Horace Mann, who had recently been elected to fill the congressional seat made vacant by the death of John Quincy Adams. From the grand jury, Key had obtained 115 indictments against each man—41 on the charge of stealing slaves (one indictment for each owner) and 74 on the lesser charge of transporting runaway slaves (one indictment for each slave).[9] Tried first on one of the larceny charges, Drayton was found guilty and sentenced to twenty years in prison. But another jury refused to convict Sayres on the same charge, and Drayton's conviction was set aside by the circuit court. In the end, Key agreed to drop all the larceny charges if the two men would consent to sentencing for transportation of runaways. The punishments meted out to Drayton and Sayres were fines of $140 and $100, respectively, for each of the seventy-four slaves. With court costs added, the total for both men came to about $20,000.[10] Unable to raise that much money, Drayton and Sayres remained in the Washington jail for more than four years. They were finally pardoned in 1852 by President Millard Fillmore after consultation with his attorney general, but not until his failure to win renomination had freed him from the pressures of sectional politics.[11]

The affair of Drayton and Sayres showed once again that slavery in the national capital was an issue dangerously charged with emotion, partly because of the symbolic importance attached to it. For abolitionists, the presence of slavery in "the very household" of the Republic placed a stamp of infamy upon the entire country. "This District is the common property of the nation," Horace Mann told his fellow congressmen in 1849. "While slaves exist in it, therefore, it can be charged upon the North that they uphold slavery."[12] To southerners, on the other hand, any successful attack upon slavery in Washington would be an "entering wedge" for attacks on slavery throughout the South. It was, said Calhoun, the equivalent of "firing a train to blow up a magazine."[13]

As the Drayton affair progressed, it engaged the official attention of senators, representatives, presidents, cabinet members, the district attorney, grand and petty juries, trial and appellate judges, aldermen, councilmen, marshals, jailers, and policemen—all of whom held their positions and performed their duties by authority of the United States government. Thus it dramatized the completeness of federal involvement with slavery in the District of Columbia. It also revealed the extent to which the District had been made secure as a southern province, even though slaves and slaveholders together constituted but a small fraction of the total population.[14] Abolitionists looked upon this predominance of the slaveholding interest in Washington as one of the most egregious achievements of a conspiracy that dated back almost to the birth of the Republic. They were not totally wrong in their perception of a coherent, purposeful slave power, but the entrenchment of slavery in the national capital seems to have resulted less from deliberate planning than from chronic indifference, a few unthinking decisions, and the tacit assumption of prescriptive rights.

LOCATION OF THE national capital became a significant public issue at the close of the Revolution. The Continental Congress had met in Philadelphia throughout the war, except when the military situation prevented it. In the summer of 1783, after being threatened by a mutiny of Pennsylvania troops, Congress moved to Princeton and intensified its efforts to fix upon a permanent seat of government or "residency." The states from New York to Virginia contested vigorously for a prize expected to confer both economic advantage and political prestige. Sectional feeling was so intense that Congress adopted a proposal to have two capitals. Then, shortly before Christmas in 1784, members voted to locate the seat of government near the falls of the Delaware River on either the New Jersey or the Pennsylvania side. An effort by the Virginia delegation to substitute Georgetown on the Potomac received no support from any other state. But the decision of 1784 was rendered inoperative in 1785, primarily as a result of southern opposition. For another five years the residency question remained unresolved, while Congress, after having moved from Princeton to Annapolis and then to Trenton, made New York City its temporary home.[15]

At Philadelphia in 1787, the framers of the Constitution provided for a permanent national capital and did so virtually without controversy by avoiding the question of location. Article I authorized Congress "to exercise exclusive legislation in all cases whatsoever, over such district (not exceeding ten miles square) as may, by cession of particular states, and the acceptance of Congress, become the seat of the government of the United States." The task thus assigned did not receive official attention until late in the first session of the first Congress under the Constitution, but for many weeks earlier, the subject had inspired much discussion and intrigue.

Essentially, the contest was between a loose majority that preferred to have the seat of government in Pennsylvania and a purposeful minority of Virginians and their southern allies who still hoped to place it on the Potomac. James Madison and other Virginia leaders employed the tactic of delaying a final decision until the circumstances became more promising for their cause. Although the Pennsylvanians seemed to have the upper hand, they wasted much of their advantage in erratic political strategy and in disagreement over precisely where the capital ought to be located within their state. First they formed an alliance with the New England and New York delegations favoring some Pennsylvania location other than Philadelphia. When that arrangement fell apart, they reached an understanding with the southerners whereby the capital would be moved temporarily back to Philadelphia and then to the banks of the Potomac. The Pennsylvanians apparently counted on blocking the latter move when the time for it arrived, thus keeping the capital permanently in Philadelphia. But that was a dangerous game to play, and having second thoughts about it, they proceeded to renew their alliance with the northerners, leaving the Virginians deflated and furious.[16]

In the House of Representatives on September 3, 1789, Benjamin Goodhue of Massachusetts offered a resolution declaring that "the permanent seat of the General Government ought to be in some convenient place on the east bank of the river Susquehannah, in the State of Pennsylvania." The Susquehannah, according to one Pennsylvanian, was proposed as "the middle ground between the two extremes" of the Delaware and Potomac rivers.[17] But the Virginia leaders were not interested in such a compromise. They made speeches in praise of the Potomac and maneuvered frantically to postpone final action. Richard Bland Lee declared that any choice other than the Potomac would sacrifice southern interests and shake southern faith in the new government. An angry Madison added that if the day's proceedings could have been foreseen in 1787, Virginia might not have ratified the Constitution. In response, Theodore Sedgwick of Massachusetts exclaimed, "Will it be contended that the majority shall not govern?" And Jeremiah Wadsworth of Connecticut said he feared that if the Virginians had their way, "the whole of New England would consider the Union as destroyed."[18]

On September 4, both Lee and Madison tried in vain to substitute the Potomac for the Susquehannah in Goodhue's resolution. When Lee renewed the effort three days later, his motion was defeated, 29 to 21, with every affirmative vote coming from the South and every northerner opposing it.[19] The House then approved the Goodhue resolution and on a later day easily passed a bill incorporating its provisions.[20] Although the Pennsylvania delegation unanimously supported the measure, some of its members actually preferred a site on the Delaware and hoped that a change to that effect would be made in the Senate. The two Pennsylvania senators were bitterly at odds on the subject. William Maclay, who has been called the first Jeffersonian democrat, lived in Harrisburg on the Susquehannah and heartily favored the bill enacted by the House. Robert Morris, the Philadelphia banker renowned as the "financier of the Revolution," had promised to vote for the Susquehannah but was in fact determined that the capital should be located on the Delaware.[21]

When the bill came up for action in the Senate on September 24, there was a motion to delete the phrase "in the State of Pennsylvania." That would have opened up the possibility of locating the capital south of the Pennsylvania-Maryland line at or near the mouth of the Susquehannah. The amendment failed, however, in another interesting display of sectional consciousness. Except for a division of the Delaware senators, every southern vote was a "yea" and every northern vote a "nay."[22]

At this point, Morris offered an amendment simply striking out the Susquehannah designation without naming a substitute. He hoped thereby to unite the diverse anti-Susquehannah elements, but the Senate at first rejected his strategem. Morris promptly called for another vote on the grounds that his proposal had not been understood. Maclay protested that parliamentary procedure did not permit a motion for reconsideration by a person who had voted with the minority, but the presiding officer, Vice President John Adams, ruled against his objection. Morris also threw in a promise that the state of Pennsylvania would contribute $100,000 to the cost of locating the capital at Germantown. Maclay challenged his authority to make such a pledge. Morris replied that if necessary he would contribute the money himself. When the roll was called the Senate reversed itself and accepted the Morris amendment.

Then, after an effort in behalf of the Potomac had been defeated, Morris proposed a site near Philadelphia, including the community of Germantown. The Senate divided 9 to 9 on his motion, whereupon Vice President Adams broke the tie with a vote for Germantown.[23] Thus the Susquehannah had been discarded in favor of the Delaware, but Maclay gloomily prophesied that Morris's "perfidy" would redound to the advantage of the Potomac.[24]

The amended bill returned to the House three days before the scheduled adjournment of Congress. Southerners argued vehemently that this was virtually a new measure, requiring more time for study, but a motion to postpone it was defeated, 29 to 25. Two days later, as the members of the House prepared for their final vote, it seemed almost certain that the capital of the United States would be located permanently on the outskirts of Philadelphia. Madison had not yet given up, however. At the last moment, he proposed to add a declaration that the laws of Pennsylvania would remain in force on the chosen site until Congress provided otherwise. The obvious purpose of this innocuous but unnecessary amendment was to toss the bill back into the Senate. The House majority fell into the trap and accepted the Madison proviso before approving the Senate amendment by a vote of 31 to 24. Still, only senatorial concurrence in the minor change was needed to settle the issue in favor of Germantown. But the Senate, with its two New York members deserting the northern coalition, chose instead to postpone further action until the next session.[25] Thus, even though both houses had voted to locate the capital at Germantown, the issue remained unresolved, and that was a Fabian victory for the South.

Congress reconvened in January 1790, and it soon became clear that the situation had changed. Both houses approved a committee recommendation that they begin anew on all business left unfinished at the close of the preceding session. That wiped out the Germantown bill and made location of the capital a wide-open question once more.[26] Although Madison found little reason to be hopeful about it, the advantage was actually shifting toward the Potomac.[27] For one thing, North Carolina's ratification of the Constitution in November meant the addition of two southerners to the Senate and five to the House of Representatives.[28] Also, George Washington's strong preference for the Potomac location, generally understood though never publicly expressed, was no doubt having some effect. And Jefferson, a champion of the Potomac site since 1783, had arrived home from France to take up his post as Secretary of State.[29] Furthermore, by February, some Pennsylvania congressmen were coming to think that their best hope lay in a renewal of the bargain with the South whereby the capital would be moved temporarily to Philadelphia and then permanently to the Potomac at a later date.[30]

Again Congress waited until late in the session to take up the subject, but behind the scenes there was continual caucusing and bargaining and shifting of affiliation. Madison at one point likened the whole business to a "labyrinth for which there is no clue."[31] As an added complication, the residency question came to be linked in some degree with another major political controversy. Congress at this time was engaged in a bitter struggle over Alexander Hamilton's proposal for federal assumption of state debts, to which most southern states were strongly opposed. According to an account written later by Jefferson, he and Madison met with Hamilton and worked out an agreement whereby the assumption bill would receive the few additional southern votes needed for its passage, and the permanent seat of government would be located on the Potomac.[32] This was the famous "Compromise of 1790" that supposedly resolved the two problems threatening the safety of the Republic, but it seems to be largely a one-sided explanation. That is, enactment of the residency bill in early July probably did win some votes for assumption two weeks later, but a reverse influence is much harder to trace. From the evidence, it seems unlikely that the mere prospect of a little southern help on assumption significantly influenced the voting on the capital.[33]

What happened, essentially, in the residency struggle of 1790 was that the contest between New York and Philadelphia for temporary possession of the capital became the primary matter at issue, with both sides competing for southern support by endorsing permanent location on the Potomac. The Senate acted first, and its decision on June 28 in favor of the Potomac site was not even close, being 16 to 9. But the vote to make Philadelphia the capital for ten years was 14 to 12, and the entire bill passed by the same narrow margin on July 1. Eight days later the House gave its approval, 32 to 29.[34] And so it happened that the southern minority in Congress, by acting more consistently as a unit, won out over the North, which was divided during the first session by rivalry between the Susquehannah and the Delaware, and during the second session by the fierce competition between Philadelphia and New York for a prize that in retrospect seems insignificant. Earlier, Madison had aptly declared that the Potomac victory, if achieved, would be "the effect of a coincidence of causes as fortuitous as it [was] propitious."[35]

Of course Pennsylvanians continued to hope that the capital, once established in Philadelphia, could be kept there indefinitely, and many southerners were afraid that such might be the case. It appears that some of the opposition to creation of the Bank of the United States in 1791 reflected the fear that having such a powerful institution in Philadelphia would make it all the more difficult to move the capital to the Potomac in 1800.[36] But the energy and dispatch with which Washington carried out the provisions of the residency act gradually dispelled such apprehensions. Empowered by Congress to determine the exact site of the federal district along a seventy-mile stretch of the Potomac, he set himself speedily to the task, and, with Jefferson's help, was ready to announce his decision when Congress reassembled in January 1791. The location selected was farther downstream than most people had expected. Indeed, it extended beyond the designated limit to include Alexandria, and Washington had to ask Congress for supplementary legislation approving the change.[37] The laying out of the federal city and construction of public buildings began soon thereafter, and by the time of Washington's death in December 1799, it had become almost certain that the removal of government offices from Philadelphia to the new capital would take place on schedule the following year.[38]

Although sectional rivalry and distrust pervaded the long controversy over the national capital, the subject of slavery seems to have entered the discussion on only one occasion. A South Carolina congressman declared that Pennsylvania was the last state in which he would consent to have the seat of government located because a Quaker state was "a bad neighborhood for the South Carolinians."[39] Otherwise, no one openly supported or opposed a Pennsylvania site because slavery had been abolished in that state, and no one expressly welcomed or criticized the final outcome as a slaveholders' victory. Of course the Mason-Dixon line had not acquired its full significance in 1790. The census of that year reported about 4,000 slaves in Pennsylvania, where a program of gradual abolition was under way, and more than 30,000 in neighboring New Jersey and New York, where abolition was still unachieved. At the same time, there were grounds for hope that Virginia and Maryland would move steadily toward emancipation. Thus the distinction between slave states and free states was as yet neither clearly drawn nor permanently fixed.

To be sure, undercurrents of feeling about slavery probably had some effect on the struggle, particularly at those times when the pattern of voting became predominantly sectional. The image of the South was a slaveholding image in both northern and southern eyes. One may reasonably suspect, for instance, that there were some thoughts about slavery on the occasion when virtually every southern member of the House voted for expanding the Susquehannah bill to include Maryland, and every northerner voted against it. There, the issue seemed to be little else than whether selection of the capital site should be restricted to free territory.

No doubt every southern congressman realized that location of the capital in Pennsylvania might be of some inconvenience for slaveholding officials. Washington began to find it so soon after he made the move from New York to Philadelphia in the fall of 1790. Pennsylvania law permitted temporary residents to keep slaves with them in the state, but for no more than six months at a time. The president consequently found it advisable to shuttle his black servants back and forth between Philadelphia and Mount Vernon, in order to prevent them from claiming freedom. "I wish to have it accomplished," he wrote, "under pretext that may deceive both them and the Public."[40] Senator Pierce Butler of South Carolina, with less prudence, kept one of his slaves with him in Philadelphia for a number of years, and the man was eventually freed by the federal circuit court.[41]

A controversy precipitated in 1790 by several antislavery petitions of Quaker origin had negatively affected southern attitudes toward Philadelphia as the temporary capital. The raising of the issue, which Washington labeled "very mal-apropos,"[42] provoked more than a little southern anger at the Quakers and Pennsylvania—anger that undoubtedly spilled over into the struggle concerning the temporary capital's location. Maclay noted in his journal that the senators from South Carolina had "a most settled antipathy to Pennsylvania, owing to the doctrines patronized in that State on the subject of slavery."[43] It is not at all surprising that the states of the lower South, which were most vehement in the defense of slavery, should have aligned themselves with New York against Philadelphia in the contest for the temporary capital.[44]

Whatever the amount of southern concern about slavery in relation to the national capital, it was dispelled by the decision in favor of a site on the Potomac. Surprisingly, there were no expressions of northern uneasiness at the prospect of situating the capital between two slaveholding states. It is possible that some lawmakers from New England repressed any such uneasiness in order not to endanger passage of Hamilton's funding program, but that would not account for the indifference of later years. The Constitution endowed Congress with the power "to exercise exclusive legislation in all cases whatsoever, over such district . . . as may, by cession of particular States, . . . become the seat of the Government." Those emphatic words would certainly seem to have included the power either to establish or to prohibit slavery. Without giving the matter much thought, Congress proceeded to establish it by default.

The hundred square miles forming the District of Columbia were ceded by Maryland and Virginia with no conditions respecting slavery. Southerners later insisted that slavery in the District was protected by a tacit understanding without which the two states would not have given up their land, but the argument had no foundation in historical evidence. Congress accepted the donations in 1790 with the provision that the area should remain under state jurisdiction until the actual transfer of federal offices to the District.[45] That arrangement proved to be an entering wedge. During the next ten years, while Washington, D.C., was taking shape as a physical entity, federal officials gave little thought to the political and legal structure of the city. Then, in 1801, with the transfer at last completed, Congress provided a system of government for the District, but took the easy way out with respect to its laws by directing that those of Maryland and Virginia should continue in force. Thus, casually and silently, slavery was legitimized in the national capital. The statute doing so bore the signature of John Adams, the only nonslaveholding president in the early decades of the Republic.[46]

IN 1800, THE District of Columbia contained about 14,000 people, of whom more than 11,000 lived in the three towns of Alexandria, Georgetown, and Washington. Slaves constituted 23 percent of the District's population. That percentage would decline in each decennial census thereafter, sinking to 15 percent by 1830 and 4 percent by 1860. A majority of the slaves in the District and most of those in Washington were household servants. Washington in 1800 had a total population of 3,210 that included 623 slaves, many of whom were undoubtedly the property of public officials.[47] Thus, when Congress took over control of the District in 1801, the institution of slavery was firmly established but at the same time relatively unobtrusive and inoffensive in its urban mode. Furthermore, the fact that leading public figures like Washington and Jefferson were slave owners lent moral prestige to the institution and discouraged criticism of it.

Congress, in facing up to its duty with respect to the District of Columbia, was primarily worried, not about slavery, but about how congressional rule could be made compatible with the principle of self-government. That proved to be an impossible task. The framers of the Constitution, it soon became clear, had mandated an anomaly that simply did not fit into the design of a federal republic. Most disturbing was the fact that transfer of the District from state to national jurisdiction would deprive the inhabitants of suffrage (except for local elections) and thus install "taxation without representation" at the very center of national affairs. In addition, the transfer would presumably burden Congress with many petty details of local government. The most drastic solution to the problem was the argument of some Jeffersonians that Congress should interpret its constitutional authority as discretionary, rather   *WHAT?* than imperative, and then make the deliberate choice to leave jurisdiction permanently in the hands of the two states.[48] Such abdication of power did not receive much support in either house. Yet, even though a large majority of members favored national jurisdiction, they could not produce a satisfactory plan for carrying their purpose into effect. The proposal advanced most often without success would have mediated between the claims of federal authority and local rights by providing some kind of territorial government for the District.[49] What emerged instead from a series of acts passed in 1801 and 1802 was a jerry-built structure of troublesome complexity.

The legislation did terminate state jurisdiction in the District of Columbia, but it retained the accumulated law of two states instead of providing a single code of laws for the District. This division of the District according to its Maryland and Virginia origins continued until the retrocession of the Virginia portion in 1846. The division was further formalized by the creation of Washington and Alexandria counties on opposite sides of the Potomac. Congress alone legislated for the District as a whole, and in time both houses created standing committees to deal with District affairs. A certain amount of responsibility devolved to the president, most notably in the appointment of District officers. The early legislation established a comprehensive judicial system, with local magistrates and a circuit court for the entire District. It also provided for a United States marshal and a United States attorney as chief law enforcement officers of the District. In the two counties, the various magistrates (all appointed officials) acted collectively as boards of commissioners. After the incorporation of Washington in 1802, there were three city governments in the District, with authority extending over four-fifths of its population. Washington's bicameral city council was elective like the councils of Alexandria and Georgetown, but its mayor was until 1812 a presidental appointee who in turn appointed all other officers of the corporation. Not until 1820 did the mayoralty become an office filled by direct popular election.[50]

The law of the District of Columbia during the early decades of the nineteenth century therefore comprised the statutes and common law of Virginia and Maryland operative in 1801, as revised and supplemented by later acts of Congress, together with the ordinances of five local governing bodies. Since Congress lagged behind Virginia and Maryland in modifying old law to fit new circumstances, the District became in some ways a legal backwater. This was especially the case with the law of slavery. Still nominally in effect at the beginning of the Civil War, for instance, were certain colonial statutes imposing cruel punishments that had been generally abandoned in the southern states. Thus, according to one Maryland law of 1729, a slave convicted of murder or arson might be sentenced "to have the right hand cut off, to be hanged in the usual manner, the head severed from the body, the body divided into four quarters, the head and quarters set up in the most public places of the country where such act was committed."[51] To be sure, no such penalty was ever exacted in the District of Columbia. Obsolete but unrepealed laws of this kind served primarily as lurid illustrations in abolitionist propaganda, but they were also reminders of persistent congressional failure to provide the District with a modernized legal code purged of such barbaric penalties.

There were several major efforts at comprehensive legal reform before the Civil War, all of them unsuccessful. In 1816, Congress authorized preparation of a civil and criminal code for the District, but it failed to take any action when the work was completed.[52] In 1830, the House committee on the District of Columbia called for a complete revision of the District's laws, declaring that many penalties for crime belonged to "the barbarous ages" and that some parts of the District's black code were "revolting to humanity."[53] Congress responded to a limited degree in 1831 with legislation making imprisonment and/or a fine the punishment for most crimes. Thus whipping, mutilation, and other such penalties were abolished, but not for all offenders. In a spirited debate on the bill, it was argued that persons already unfree would have little fear of the penitentiary and that imprisonment of a slave punished the master more than the slave. Consequently, the law as finally passed applied only to free persons, leaving the physical punishments of the old slave code still formally in effect.[54] What this meant in practice was that whipping continued to be the common punishment of slaves for lesser offenses, such as damaging federal property, setting off firecrackers, shooting deer out of season, causing false alarms of fire, mistreating horses, and (in Georgetown) flying kites.[55] During the 1850s, Congress again authorized an attempt at systematic legal reform. The resulting general code included a more humane law of slavery, but when submitted to the voters of the District, as required by Congress, it was rejected by a wide margin.[56]

Of course the letter of the law may be considerably modified in the process of enforcement, and such appears to have been the case with the law of slavery in the national capital and its federal environs. The amelioration that Congress failed to provide was partly achieved in the courts, and especially in the decisions of the United States Circuit Court for the District of Columbia, over which William Cranch presided from 1805 until his death in 1855. For instance, the court interpreted the law in such a way as to limit the flow of slaves into the District; it placed restrictions on the sale of slaves for shipment to the lower South, and it tended to be indulgent toward petitioners in suits for freedom.[57] In criminal trials, punishment was generally more lenient than the letter of the law suggests. The horror stories of the abolitionists notwithstanding, only one slave was ever executed in the District.[58]

Yet, because the administration of justice is what converts the general principles of the law into concrete and personal effects, it was in the courtrooms and jails of the District that the United States government became most intimately involved with slavery. There federal authority enforced the right to own slaves, the right to buy and sell slaves, the right to bequeath and inherit slaves, and the right to recover fugitive slaves. There slaveholders were occasionally punished for mistreatment of their human property, and slaves were frequently punished for a variety of offenses. There, by the authority of the United States, a slave was sometimes set free. Only a reading of the individual cases can give one some real sense of this federal involvement with the peculiar institution.

In 1803, for example, a slave woman found guilty of stealing goods was ordered to receive twenty lashes and pay a fine of one cent.[59] In 1806, a black man was held to be legally white for the purpose of testifying in court because he had for many years acted as a person free under Maryland law by reason of having been born to a white woman.[60] In 1807, a slave was convicted of robbing a man of his watch. The circuit court for the District of Columbia sentenced him "to be burnt in the hand and whipped with one hundred stripes," an unusually severe penalty that might have been even worse if the charge had not been changed from highway robbery to plain robbery.[61] In 1823, an owner accused of beating and slashing his own slave was found not guilty by the jury, but with the added recommendation that "the court should express their strong disapprobation of similar conduct."[62] In 1834, a slave brought into the District was awarded his freedom on the technicality that his sex had not been designated on the list of imports.[63] That same year, an owner charged with beating his slave and "exposing him, so beaten, to public view" was convicted and fined a hundred dollars.[64] In 1835, Henry Frye, a slave convicted of manslaughter was sentenced only to branding and twenty-five stripes because he had acted more or less in self-defense.[65] In 1836, a white man was sentenced to one year in prison for attempting to sell a free mulatto boy into slavery.[66] Also in 1836, a slave was tried for the attempted murder of his mistress with an axe, pleading that he had been drunk at the time. Convicted and sentenced to be hanged, he was "reprieved from time to time and finally pardoned at the instance of his mistress."[67] In 1856, the Court instructed the jury that assault and battery on a slave was not indictable unless it was done "in a cruel or inhuman manner in such a place . . . as to be an annoyance or nuisance to the citizens, whose pleasure or business carry them near the scene of the infliction." The jury convicted the defendant, and the verdict was affirmed by the circuit court.[68]

The criminal law of slavery as actually enforced in the District was certainly mild in comparison with the formal law on the books to which abolitionists so often pointed with outrage. Slaves in Washington seem to have had considerable freedom. Often working on hire for persons other than their owners, they tended to be more or less indistinguishable from free blacks working for wages. Stated another way, free blacks were often treated the same as slaves. In legislating for the District of Columbia, Congress habitually treated free blacks as non-citizens, not only excluding them from suffrage and officeholding but often lumping them together with slaves. As in all slaveholding jurisdictions, the slave code merged into a black code. There were some laws that applied to all African Americans and mulattoes, whether enslaved or free, and many others that were aimed specifically at the control of free blacks. For example, Congress passed a law in 1820 empowering the city of Washington "to restrain and prohibit the nightly and other disorderly meetings of slaves, free negroes and mulattoes," and also "to prescribe the terms and conditions upon which free negroes and mulattoes may reside in the city."[69] Under this authority, a city ordinance of 1829 provided that "persons of color frequenting the Capitol square, without necessary business, and refusing to depart," should be fined as much as twenty dollars or be "confined to labor" for as many as thirty days.[70] Free blacks could not go at large after 10 P.M. without a pass; their rights of assembly were restricted; they were forbidden to engage in the sale of liquor; and they could not testify in cases involving white persons.[71] Furthermore, under a Maryland law of 1796, a "free negro or mulatto . . . found living idle, without any visible means of maintenance" could end up sold into servitude for a period not exceeding six months.[72]

For a free black in Washington, the most fearful danger was that of being claimed as a runaway slave. There, as in the slaveholding states generally, blacks were assumed to be slaves unless they could prove otherwise, such as by producing a certificate of freedom. Congress in 1801 applied the federal fugitive-slave law of 1793 to the District of Columbia, but in addition, laws inherited from Virginia and Maryland provided for the jailing of any person suspected of being a fugitive. If the prisoner, after due advertisement, went unclaimed as property and yet could not prove himself to be free, he might be sold into servitude by the federal marshal to pay for the costs of his incarceration. The abolitionist William Jay questioned whether even Turkish despotism was "disgraced by any enactment of equal atrocity."[73] Efforts to change the law were unsuccessful, southerners insisting that such a change would turn the District into a haven for runaways.[74]

At any time, the Washington jail was likely to contain a number of black persons suspected of being fugitives, but often more numerous were slaves placed there by their owners, sometimes for disciplinary reasons, sometimes as part of the process of selling them. "From the settlement . . . of Maryland to this day," declared the federal marshal in 1829, "it has been the custom and the law for masters to have the right to commit their slaves for safekeeping to the public gaols."[75] The custom was still being honored as late as the year 1862 by Lincoln's appointee, Marshal Ward H. Lamon, to the intense displeasure of many Republicans.[76] Also, the marshal sometimes had the official task of seizing and selling a slave to satisfy an adjudicated claim of the United States. The *Washington Union* of July 3, 1847, for example, carried an advertisement announcing the forthcoming sale to the highest bidder of "one negro woman, named Elizabeth, about the age of sixty years; and one negro girl, named Caroline, about the age of twenty years."[77] Upon such occasions, the federal government became, temporarily, a veritable slave owner and slave dealer.

Congress, in most of its slavery-related legislation for the District of Columbia, seems to have been concerned primarily with accommodating slaveholders. Thus, it extended the operation of the fugitive-slave law to the District; it affirmed the right of owners to hire slaves within the District; it legalized the transfer of slaves between the two counties; and it empowered the cities of the District to take various actions for the protection and control of the institution.[78] The presence of slavery in the national capital and the intimate involvement of the federal government with the slaveholding system were dramatized from time to time by incidents such as the abortive cruise of the *Pearl* and two poignant illustrations of the agony that life as a slave could entail: In 1815, a woman about to be taken away for sale in the southern market aroused much public sympathy by throwing herself from the third floor of a Washington building to the pavement below; and in 1837, another woman facing the same prospect cut the throats of two of her children and tried unsuccessfully to kill herself.[79] Tragic personal histories of this kind proved to be the best ammunition for the growing abolitionist movement. Clearly, in the nineteenth century the government of the United States became deeply enmeshed in supporting and protecting the institution of slavery. All by itself, the history of Washington, D.C., proved that.

NOT UNTIL FOUR years after the casual action by which Congress legitimized slavery in the District of Columbia did anyone try to revise or reverse it. Early in 1805, an obscure representative from New Jersey named James Sloan offered a resolution declaring that all District slaves born after July 4 of that year should be free when they reached a certain age, which he left to be specified. The times were scarcely propitious, however, for any such tampering with the institution of slavery in the Chesapeake region. Racial fears aroused by the black revolution in Haiti had been reinforced nearer at hand by the Gabriel conspiracy and a number of lesser slave disturbances in Virginia. Also, the resumption of the Napoleonic wars in Europe posed a renewed threat to the security of the United States and discouraged serious consideration of domestic issues likely to be distractive and divisive. Under the circumstances, it is perhaps less surprising that seventy-seven members of the House voted to reject Sloan's resolution than that thirty-one dared to support it. Four-fifths of the latter were Republicans, although they received no encouragement from the Jefferson administration. All but one of them were from north of the Mason and Dixon line, and they constituted more than half of all the northerners voting on the question.[80] This early sectional move against slavery in the District of Columbia, though utterly unsuccessful, nevertheless proved to be a high-water mark. Not until after the outbreak of the Civil War did another proposal for abolition in the District actually come to a vote on the floor of Congress.

The slave population of the District doubled between 1800 and 1820, remained almost stable for the next decade, and then began to decline. Slave-trade activity within the District followed a similar curve, reaching its peak in the mid-1830s, and for many residents and visitors, this was the most offensive aspect of slavery in the national capital. As early as 1802, an Alexandria grand jury lodged a formal protest against "the practice of persons coming from distant parts of the United States into this District, for the purpose of purchasing slaves, where they exhibit to our view a scene of wretchedness and human degradation, disgraceful to our characters as citizens of a free government."[81] James Madison as president was brashly needled by his young private secretary, Edward Coles, about the "gangs of Negroes, some in irons, on their way to a southern market" and the likely effect of such sights upon resident foreign diplomats.[82] Later critics returned again and again to the same theme, portraying slave coffles on Pennsylvania Avenue as shameful symbols of oppression that soiled the image of the United States before the rest of the world.

Actually, Washington was never a major slave market like Charleston or New Orleans, but it did become an important depot in the interstate slave trade. Residents of Washington County were legally free to sell their own slaves locally or in other parts of the country, but only from Maryland could they import slaves for themselves or for sale elsewhere. The law permitted importation from other states only by owners coming to take up residence, and such slaves could not be sold within three years of their arrival or they became legally free. There were no legal barriers, however, to the temporary housing of slaves in transit through the District, and what gave Washington the appearance of a thriving slave market was primarily its convenience as a station where slaves from the Chesapeake region were collected by traders for shipment to states farther south.[83]

In 1816, as part of his charge to the grand jury, Judge James S. Morsell of the District's circuit court complained about the frequency with which manacled slaves were seen on the streets of Washington. At about the same time Virginia's unpredictable congressman, John Randolph, arose to denounce the conversion of the District into "a depot for a systematic slave market—an assemblage of prisons where the unfortunate beings, reluctant, no doubt, to be torn from their connexions, and the affections of their lives, [are] incarcerated and chained down, and thence driven in fetters like beasts, to be paid for like cattle." He proposed the appointment of a committee to investigate the "inhuman and illegal traffic." The House agreed, but nothing significant resulted from the committee's labors, and before long whatever stirring there may have been about slavery in the District was swallowed up in the great struggle over slavery in Missouri.[84]

The paramount constitutional question in the Missouri controversy of 1819–20 was whether or not Congress had the power to place antislavery restrictions on a state at the time of its entry into the Union. More than once during the debate, a southerner denying that power drew a comparison with congressional authority over slavery in the national capital. For instance, Senator Richard M. Johnson of Kentucky demanded sarcastically why there was so much "heart-rending sympathy" for the slaves of Missouri and yet nothing but "cold insensibility" toward the slaves of the District of Columbia, where, he said, "emancipation rests with Congress alone."[85]

The Missouri crisis frightened American political leaders and fortified a general reluctance to touch the "delicate" subject of slavery. Furthermore, when revelation of the Denmark Vesey conspiracy shocked South Carolina in 1822, many southerners persuaded themselves that Vesey and his confederates had been inspired in no small part by the antislavery rhetoric of the Missouri debates.[86] The uprising thus seemed to confirm them in the belief that intersectional public discussion of slavery was inherently dangerous, and some South Carolinians even took to arguing that Congress, since it had no authority over the institution, had no constitutional right to discuss it. [87]

Nevertheless, despite these resistant forces, a crusade against slaveholding and slave trading in the District of Columbia got started during the 1820s. Its leading spirits at first were the Quaker journalist Benjamin Lundy and a Federalist congressman, Charles Miner of Pennsylvania. When Lundy, the most notable American abolitionist of the decade, moved from eastern Tennessee to Baltimore in 1824 with his paper, *The Genius of Universal Emancipation*, he had already begun issuing periodic demands that Congress take steps to "eradicate" slavery in the District as speedily as "the nature of things" would permit. The presence of the slave system in Washington contradicted American ideals and drew justifiable scorn from the representatives of foreign powers, he declared. Even residents not participating in the system were becoming "contaminated by its deleterious and heart-corrupting influence."[88]

In 1826, Lundy's newspaper singled out Miner and urged him to bring the subject before Congress. Miner responded with a resolution looking toward gradual abolition in the District, but the House quickly set it aside in the face of southern displeasure.[89] The next year, Maryland congressman John Barney presented a memorial drafted by Lundy and signed by various citizens of Baltimore. It called upon Congress to provide for the eventual emancipation of all children thereafter born to slave parents in the District. Three southerners spoke against Barney's motion to print the document, each giving a different reason. The grim-faced George McDuffie of South Carolina, who suffered not only from dyspepsia but from a spinal wound received in a duel, said that the attempt by residents of Maryland to interfere in the affairs of the District was impertinent, insulting, and outrageous. "If the People of the District of Columbia wish to abolish Slavery, and will present a petition to this House to that effect," he declaimed, "no man in this House will be more ready than I will to grant to the People any measure which they may deem necessary to free themselves from this deplorable evil." A member from Virginia protested that printing such a petition was not customary and that its only effect so late in the session would be "to disseminate a partial and intemperate view of the subject of slavery." Then one of Barney's Maryland colleagues concluded the discussion by warning that the ultimate purpose of the memorial went far beyond abolition in the District of Columbia. It breathed, he said, "the spirit of general emancipation." When it came to a vote, the motion to print was defeated by a large majority. In this brief but animated debate, early versions of two major southern arguments against abolition in the national capital had been set forth. One, the assertion that slavery in the District was a legitimate matter of concern only to the people of the District, embodied the principle of popular sovereignty that would later be associated with the territories. The other employed the concept of the "entering wedge" by holding that any restriction on slavery in the District would be the first step in an attack on slavery everywhere in the country.[90]

Early in 1828, as if to test McDuffie's glib promise, Lundy and other sponsors obtained more than a thousand signatures of District citizens on a petition for gradual abolition and suppression of the slave trade in the District.[91] Petitions and memorials to the same purpose were also coming to Congress from other parts of the Union. The Pennsylvania House of Representatives urged that slavery be abolished in the District, and this stimulus from home undoubtedly encouraged Charles Miner to raise the issue again.[92] On January 6, 1829, he moved a preamble and two resolutions instructing the committee for the District of Columbia to investigate the local slave trade and recommend appropriate legislation, and to "inquire into the expediency" of providing for the gradual abolition of slavery within the District. Miner expanded on his denunciatory preamble in a speech cataloguing the evils of slavery and the slave trade in Washington. The principal southern reply came from John C. Weems, a Maryland planter, who cast doubt on the accuracy of Miner's information, accused him of "improper meddling" in matters with which he had no legitimate concern, and quoted the Bible extensively to demonstrate that slavery was "justified by the Almighty." At the close of his speech, Weems introduced another argument that was to become a standard feature of southern resistance to abolition in the District. "Can anyone suppose for one moment," he demanded, "that either the State of Virginia or Maryland would have consented to have ceded to the General Government the ten miles square, if they had ever once supposed that Congress, here, in the midst of their slave population, would ever have entertained such a dangerous proposition for one moment?"[93]

By overwhelming majorities in each case, the House rejected Miner's controversial preamble, but adopted both of his resolutions. The division on the resolutions was along sectional lines, with the North showing more solidarity than the South.[94] Those southerners voting for the resolutions knew that they posed no ultimate threat. The committee for the District of Columbia was controlled by a Maryland-Virginia majority and included no outspoken critic of slavery. Six of its seven members had voted on the southern side in the D'Auterive controversy a year earlier.[95] The report of the committee, presented on January 29 by its chairman, Mark Alexander of Virginia, was essentially proslavery in spirit and yet offered significant concessions to antislavery feeling.

The report began by condemning the agitation against slavery in the District as a threat to the peace and harmony of the Union. "By keeping this subject constantly alive before the public," it declared, "false hopes of liberty are held out to the slave, exciting him to insubordination, and creating a restlessness for emancipation, rendered incompatible with the existing state of the country." The report forthrightly defended the practice of transplanting slaves southward to "a more genial and bountiful clime," and it also defended the use of public jails to accommodate the traffic. Then it went on to argue that the movement for abolition could not be justified on either constitutional or practical grounds. The power of Congress to legislate for the District, though exclusive, was not unlimited and must conform to the general principles of the Constitution. To abolish slavery in the District against the will of its people would be a despotic and therefore an unconstitutional act. Furthermore, abolition could not be constitutionally imposed without just compensation, and yet Congress lacked authority to appropriate public money for a local purpose that was not connected with the general legislation of the Union. In any case, the report added, abolition was undesirable because it would make the District a refuge for runaway negroes and manumitted slaves, the "most vicious and degraded population that could exist in any community."[96]

That particular kind of apprehension was already widespread in
trict. On January 8, the Washington County grand jury, in respon
Miner resolutions, declared that there should be no emancipation ⌐ ⌐.
"however guarded or gradual," unless it was connected with "a practicable
scheme for their removal." In the view of the jurymen, who claimed to speak
for a large majority of local citizens, the central problem was not the presence
of slavery in the District and not even the offensibly visible slave trade
(which they condemned). It was rather the growing size of the free black
population, which had increased at more than twice the rate of the white
population during the 1820s. The jury wanted public policy to be directed
toward reducing the influx of blacks and ultimately replacing the District's
black workforce with a white laboring class.[97]

The Alexander committee did respond to antislavery complaints and to
the recommendations of the grand jury by reporting a District bill of considerable range and consequence. It prohibited the importation of slaves and the
immigration of free blacks, restricted the operation of slave depots, and forbade slave sales that broke up families. But with little more than a month of
the session remaining, the measure died quietly in the committee of the
whole. A year later, the same bill met a similar fate.[98] Thus the official attitude of Congress toward slavery in the national capital remained one of
abiding indifference occasionally interrupted by flickering attention. Yet various forces at work were intensifying the struggle and making the subject a
focus of legislative turmoil and sectional conflict.

American abolitionism was entering its radical phase in which even more
aggressive attention would be given to slavery in the District of Columbia.
Benjamin Lundy had already laid down the strategy of harassment by petition that was to cause so much disturbance in Congress. Urging a flood of
petitions for abolition in the District, he elaborated: "Teaze the members with
importunities, until they are *provoked* to deeds of *justice.* They will, no doubt,
refuse compliance for a time. But as the continual falling of water will wear
the hardest rock, so a continual repetition of this demand will, in process of
time, triumph over the most obstinate resistance."[99] Such strategy was
bound to infuriate more people than it persuaded, especially in the circumstances of the early 1830s. The new antislavery militancy personified by
William Lloyd Garrison emerged at a time when the great tariff controversy
was building to its climax of nullification in South Carolina and when southerners generally were becoming more worried and defensive about slavery,
federal power, and states' rights. Then, in August 1831, the Nat Turner upris-

ing in southeastern Virginia struck fear throughout the slaveholding states and reinforced the widespread southern belief that abolitionist agitation was, in its effect, a call for servile rebellion and wholesale murder. In the District of Columbia, where racial considerations were already strengthening local resistance to abolition sentiment, the Turner uprising caused considerable anxiety and drew the populace closer to the rest of the South. Washington of the 1830s was therefore an increasingly hostile environment for critics of slavery, who nevertheless continued to view it as, in Garrison's words, "the first citadel to be taken."[100]

CHARLES MINER, TROUBLED by deafness, retired to private life in 1829 and for a time had no obvious successor as the most prominent antislavery figure in Congress. Then, in 1831, a number of possible candidates for that role arrived on the scene, including several members of the new Antimasonic party who were also strongly opposed to slavery. Notable among them were John Dickson, from Ontario County in western New York, and William Slade of Vermont, who had been dismissed from his clerkship in the State Department by the incoming Jackson administration and was now beginning the first of six consecutive terms in the House of Representatives. At the same time, sixty-four-year-old John Quincy Adams returned to Washington, as a member of the House. Still mortified by his recent expulsion from the White House, primarily at the hands of southern voters, Adams was nevertheless determined, he later said, to be a "Man of the Whole Nation."[101] His record did not give slaveholders much reason to fear him. In nearly four decades of public service, this former diplomat, senator, cabinet member, and president had never lent any open encouragement to the antislavery cause.

Adams took his seat on December 5 and a week later rose to address the House for the first time, presenting fifteen petitions from Pennsylvania Quakers for abolition of slavery and the slave trade in the District of Columbia. He mildly expressed his belief that the slave trade "might be a proper subject of legislation by Congress" and then went on to say that he did not support abolition of slavery itself in the District. As explanation, he offered only the sententious remark that "the most salutary medicines, unduly administered, were the most deadly of poisons."[102] Privately, he told one Quaker leader that he "abhorred" slavery but believed that discussion of the subject in Congress would merely lead to ill will without accomplishing anything. He also suggested that such petitions from persons outside the District amounted to "meddling with what did not concern them."[103] In this diffident manner, John Quincy Adams entered the final phase of his career and took the first step toward becoming "Old Man Eloquent."

On Adams's motion, the Pennsylvania petitions were referred to the committee for the District of Columbia, which in the Twenty-second Congress consisted of three members from Virginia, three from Maryland, and one from Pennsylvania. The committee took only seven days to prepare a report that declared: "Until the wisdom of State Governments shall have devised some practicable means of eradicating or diminishing the evil of slavery, . . . it would be unwise and impolitic, if not unjust, to the adjoining States, for Congress to interfere in a subject of such delicacy and importance."[104] Adams, busy with responsibilities as chairman of the committee on manufactures, did not even make note of the report in his diary, but it was precisely the dampening response that he had expected and desired.

Thus, at the beginning of the 1830s, the question of slavery in the District of Columbia was a political irritant but not a serious national issue. Abolition in the District had declining support from the local citizenry and no more than a handful of advocates in Congress, a body that had not taken the trouble to pass even the meliorative legislation proposed by southern committee chairmen. Petitions against slavery in the national capital were routinely sent to that "tomb of the Capulets," the committee for the District, which either silently buried them or, at most, reported adversely. This was, as Adams repeatedly pointed out, a modus operandi duly respectful of the petitioners but at the same time favorable to the South and to the preservation of sectional peace.[105] The controversy continued to smolder for several years, with both sides maneuvering for advantage. A congressman presenting a petition might move that it be printed or that it be referred to a select committee rather than to the committee for the District. At the same time, there was a growing disposition among southerners and some northerners to have the petitions laid on the table without being read, discussed, or referred. Adams and many other members believed that tabling a petition in this manner would be disrespectful to its authors and a violation of their constitutional rights. To that argument Henry Wise of Virginia replied: "It is respectful enough . . . to *receive* them." Soon even reception followed by tabling was more than Wise and many other southerners were willing to allow.

The issue became more inflammatory in 1835 against a background of unrelenting pressure from abolition societies and growing popular hostility, in the North as well as the South, to antislavery agitation. Petitioning Congress on the subject was developing into a well-organized campaign of impressive proportions, one that could no longer be dismissed as the work of a few fanatics.[106] Meanwhile, mob violence against abolitionists and free blacks, which had been increasing in the United States, reached its peak during the summer of 1835, and the city of Washington contributed dramatically to the alarming trend.[107] At the same time, a national controversy was raging over the distribution of vast quantities of abolitionist literature through the mails. In Charleston, an angry crowd had recently broken into the post office and burned the objectionable documents found there.[108] The same kind of temper pervaded Washington and proved especially deadly for a newcomer to the city, Dr. Reuben Crandall.

Crandall, whose sister Prudence had incurred imprisonment and gained national notoriety by trying to establish a school for colored girls in Connecticut, made the mistake of letting it be known that he had some antislavery pamphlets in his possession. Arrested, he was threatened with lynching by a crowd that worked off its rage in destructive forays against various tenements and churches of the free black population.[109] Rioting continued for several days, eliciting a mixture of disapproval and extenuation in the local press. The *Washington National Intelligencer*, for example, condemned the violence but attributed it to "the natural resentment inspired by the demoniacal design, on the part of a fanatical individual to stir up our negro population to insurrection and murder."[110] Crandall was indicted by the Washington grand jury for "publishing libels tending to excite sedition" among the slaves and free blacks of the District. Unable to raise bail of $5,000, he remained in jail for eight months before standing trial in April 1836. His prosecutor was Francis Scott Key, author of "The Star-Spangled Banner" and United States Attorney for the District of Columbia. Key seems to have pursued his task with a determination bordering on malevolence, but the case against Crandall was flimsy, defense attorneys were eloquent, and the jury took less than an hour to arrive at a verdict of "not guilty."[111] Thus the attempt to use the authority of the United States to punish mere possession of abolitionist literature ended in failure. Crandall's health had suffered from the long confinement, however, and he died of tuberculosis just two years later.[112]

The temper of the new Congress as it convened in December 1835 bore some resemblance to the spirit of recent antiabolitionist mobs. Most southern members were already fed up to the point of fury with the badgering of antislavery petitioners, and their attitude reflected that already forcefully expressed by a number of southern legislatures, as well as by much of the southern press. With a presidential campaign under way, it was widely recognized among northern congressmen that neither the Jacksonians nor the opposition could afford to antagonize the South. On December 16, along with about four hundred petitions on other subjects, the House received the session's first two memorials against slavery and the slave trade in the District of Columbia. Both were promptly laid on the table, one by a roll-call vote of 180 to 31, and a motion to print was also overwhelmingly defeated.[113] Such emphatic disposal did not satisfy the more militant southerners, however. When a petition from Massachusetts citizens was submitted two days later, James H. Hammond of South Carolina moved that it be rejected, saying that he could not sit there and see "the rights of the Southern People assaulted day after day, by . . . ignorant fanatics." In the Senate, where the problem had been less disturbing over the years, John C. Calhoun was ready to make the same demand for a "prompt and stern rejection" of antislavery petitions. "We must meet the enemy on the frontier, on the question of receiving," he insisted. "We must secure that important pass—it is our Thermopylae."[114]

The proposal to refuse reception of antislavery petitions lacked full southern support and failed in both houses.[115] Clearly, a majority of congressmen, including the Jacksonian leadership, wanted to steer a course between the extremes of abolitionism and Calhounism. In the Senate, after some experiment with the strategy of receiving a petition and then rejecting its content, members settled into the practice of simply tabling all motions for reception or nonreception. In the House, where the petitions continued to be more intrusive, there was a stronger desire to install some kind of rule for their control. The first attempt to do so was made by George W. Owens, a Georgia Democrat. On December 21, he offered a resolution declaring that the question of abolition in the District "ought not to be entertained by Congress," and that all petitions to that purpose "ought to be laid upon the table without reading." The Owens resolution did not come to a vote. In January, a similar resolution was offered by Leonard Jarvis of Maine, another Jacksonian Democrat, but it too got nowhere.[116] Meanwhile, the House went on wrangling over individual petitions as they were presented. At one point, members sustained a decision of the chair that the preliminary question of reception was debatable, even though the substance of a petition was not. After this action, as one congressman complained, discussion of slavery seemed likely to monopolize all the time allotted for presentation of petitions.[117]

Surprisingly, it was a South Carolinian of the Calhoun school who led the way toward something resembling compromise, damaging his own political career as he did so. Henry L. Pinckney, former editor of the *Charleston*

Mercury, proposed that all memorials and motions relating to slavery in the District of Columbia be referred to a select committee with instructions to report that Congress possessed no constitutional authority to interfere with slavery in the states and "ought not" to interfere with slavery in the District because it would be "a violation of the public faith, unwise, impolitic, and dangerous to the Union."[118] Hammond and other southern extremists were astonished and outraged. They regarded the Pinckney resolution as a virtual surrender to antislavery forces on the question of whether Congress had the constitutional power to abolish slavery in the District.[119] The House nevertheless voted overwhelmingly to follow Pinckney's lead, and he was named chairman of the special committee to which the whole problem was consigned. Speaker James K. Polk of Tennessee, a loyal Jacksonian, loaded the committee with men favorable to the resolution.[120] Shortly thereafter, Vice President Van Buren, in his role as Democratic presidential nominee, publicly embraced the Pinckney formula of compromise—that is, he opposed any interference with slavery in the District of Columbia but refused to endorse the view that such interference would be unconstitutional.[121]

More than three months passed before Pinckney submitted the committee's report, which was more general than the original instructions. It resolved that all petitions and propositions relating to slavery be laid on the table without being read or printed or acted on in any way further.[122] Some bitter debate followed, but the opposition of antislavery northerners and militant southerners was swept aside as the House on May 26, 1836, installed its first "gag rule" by a vote of 117 to 68. John Quincy Adams, when the clerk came to his name in the roll call, rose and declared: "I hold the resolution to be a direct violation of the Constitution of the United States, the rules of this House, and the rights of my constituents."[123]

THE GAG RULE of 1836 merely formalized what had already become the common practice of smothering antislavery resolutions by laying them peremptorily on the table.[124] It also may be said to have completed the transition whereby the struggle over slavery in the District of Columbia became principally a struggle over the right of petition. Of course the gag did not dampen controversy but aggravated it instead. For one thing, the abolitionists promptly accelerated the flow of petitions to Congress, as they gave primary emphasis after 1836 to opposing the annexation of Texas. Meanwhile, Adams took the lead in finding ways to evade the rule, and each session began with a battle over renewing the restriction.[125] In 1840, the House made the gag a standing rule and at the same time revised it to provide that no antislavery petition should be received by the House or "entertained in any way whatever."[126] Thus the southern extremists were at last able to rejoice at having won their fight for the principle of nonreception. Soon, however, northern support for the gag rule began to decline, and on December 3, 1844, with scarcely any commotion, the House voted to repeal it. A week later, when Adams presented a petition for abolition in the District of Columbia, it was duly referred to the committee for the District.[127]

For antislavery forces, the overthrow of the gag rule was an exciting victory but a largely symbolic one. Southern disunity and eventual defeat in the procedural struggle over reception of abolitionist petitions has tended to obscure the solidarity and success with which southerners defended slavery in the District of Columbia. Abolition in the District had the active support of few congressmen during the 1830s and never came close to realization at any time before the Civil War. Abraham Lincoln as president-elect said in December 1860 that he had "no thought" of recommending such a measure and that Congress clearly would not follow his advice if he did.[128] Perhaps most surprising is the extent to which northerners accepted southern doctrine on the subject.

In the debate that ran on for several decades, the abolitionist argument remained eloquently simple: (1) the presence of slavery and slave trading in the national capital was a national disgrace; (2) the Constitution authorized Congress to "exercise exclusive legislation in all cases whatsoever" over the federal district; and (3) that power should be used to eradicate the evil. The southern argument was more complex and eventually took on some of the qualities of fantasy.

Probably most effective in promoting southern unity on the subject was the incessantly reiterated assertion that any congressional interference with slavery in the District of Columbia would be the "entering wedge" for an attack upon slavery everywhere in the country. This was Calhoun's battle cry, and even the moderate Henry Clay asserted that the petitions for abolition in the District were steps toward the "bloody goal" of universal emancipation.[129] Most persuasive for many northerners, on the other hand, was the repeated warning that the vehement and persistent agitation of the issue threatened to disrupt the Republic. Not only southerners issued the warning. Senator Nathaniel Tallmadge of New York, even while defending the right of petition, said that such agitation must cease, lest it produce "consequences the most fatal to the peace and harmony of the Union." And

Senator Garrett D. Wall of New Jersey, in a speech opposing the outright rejection of abolition petitions, declared nevertheless that their incendiary purpose was "to dissolve our happy Union, and under a false and phrensied notion of humanity, to involve our fellow citizens in the horrors of rapine, murder and a servile war."[130]

Likewise convincing to many northerners was the argument that Congress, in its role as legislature for the District of Columbia, had no right to act against the will of the local population. Abolitionists like William Slade might respond that slavery in the nation's capital was the business of the whole nation, but the spirit of the age tended to resist anything that denied the primacy of local consent.[131] Thus, the legislatures of New Hampshire and Illinois resolved in 1837 that abolition without the consent of the District's citizens would be a breach of public faith.[132] Twelve years later, when Congressman Abraham Lincoln presented a proposal for gradual abolition in the District, he included a provision that it should go into effect only after being approved by the local electorate.[133] Throughout the following decade Lincoln continued to favor what amounted to popular sovereignty for the District, even while rejecting the same principle as applied to slavery in the territories.[134]

Southerners also had considerable northern support when they maintained, as did the Pinckney report of 1836, that abolition in the District would violate the "faith reposed in Congress" by Virginia and Maryland, without which there would have been no transfer of land.[135] It became the strategy of northern Democrats during the presidential campaign of 1836 to endorse this dubious doctrine as a setoff against their unwillingness to pronounce such abolition unconstitutional. Martin Van Buren, in his formal statement on the subject, declared that if the people of Virginia and Maryland had foreseen the agitation for abolition in the District, the cession "would not have been made except on the express condition that Congress should exercise no such power." Given the state of public opinion at the time, he added, the condition would have been "readily accepted."[136]

From retrospective conjecture of this kind there developed the myth of a compact, express or implied, between the two states and the federal government—a compact that was no less binding than a clause of the Constitution. As a matter of historical reality, it is doubtful that any concern about the future of slavery within the ceded area could have induced the leaders of Virginia and Maryland in 1790 to jeopardize location of the capital on the Potomac by demanding special protection for the institution; it is even less likely that northern congressmen, most of whom opposed the Potomac location anyhow, would have yielded to such a demand. Certainly the acts of cession contained no reservations respecting slavery in particular or property rights in general. The Maryland act of 1791, for instance, stipulated only that the cession would not affect private land titles and that the laws of Maryland would remain in operation until replaced by those of Congress. Nevertheless, the Maryland senate in 1837 resolved that abolition of slavery by Congress would be "a violation of the terms and conditions upon which the cession of the District of Columbia was made to the Federal Government," and furthermore, that "in the event of such violation, the territory included in said District, ought, and of right will, revert respectively to the States of Virginia and Maryland."[137]

As for the constitutional argument against abolition in the District of Columbia, it was essentially an expression of proslavery extremism that convinced few northerners and received substantially less than universal support among southerners. It contributed little to the successful defense of slavery in the District but had considerable influence on the growing debate over slavery in the federal territories. Constitutional attack on a proposed act of Congress may proceed by asserting a general lack of power or by pointing to a specific denial of power. The southern militants pursued both lines of argument, gaining momentum from their own frequent spasms of apprehension and anger.

It was no easy task to demonstrate that the exercise of "exclusive Legislation in all Cases whatsoever" did not include control over slavery. Some of the efforts to do so were preposterous, such as the contention of South Carolina's Francis W. Pickens that the authority of the federal government in the District of Columbia amounted to "nothing more than the right to protect its property."[138] As grounds for minimizing congressional power, Pickens and other southerners pointed to the fact that the clause authorizing "exclusive Legislation" in the District vested Congress with "like Authority" over places purchased "for the Erection of Forts, Magazines, Arsenals, dock-Yards and other needful Buildings." Jefferson Davis was just one of those who warned that if the federal government could restrict or abolish slavery in the District, it could claim the right to do likewise on all federal property in the slaveholding states.[139] But despite the carelessness of the framers in blending the two grants of authority, there was obviously a critical difference between control over federal property remaining within the jurisdiction of a state and control over an area of a hundred square miles to which the federal government had been ceded jurisdiction.

The main argument of Calhoun and the other southern militants depended heavily on the presumption, reiterated until it seemed to become an axiom, that slaveholding was a right anterior to the Constitution, which had been confirmed and guaranteed by the Constitution but at the same time remained wholly exempt from federal control.[140] This combination of protection and immunity, according to militant theory, extended to slavery wherever it existed in the Union. Therefore, congressional authority to abolish slavery in the District could not be inferred from the Constitution's general grant of legislative power over the District. "Congress," wrote a correspondent of the *Charleston Courier*, "has no more power to legislate on the subject for the District of Columbia, than it has for South Carolina."[141] And, the militants added, neither could such congressional authority be claimed as having been received from Virginia and Maryland, for the cessions of land had been made by the legislatures of the two states, which did not possess, and so could not transfer, the constitutional power to abolish slavery.[142]

The case for an absence of congressional power over slavery in the District thus amounted to little more than a tissue of flat assertions investing the institution with a special sanctity that exempted it from the plain wording of the Constitution. More plausibly, southern militants also argued that congressional authority in the District, though exclusive, was limited by various constitutional restraints on federal power, particularly those specified in the Bill of Rights. As early as 1836, Calhoun and several other southerners were contending that abolition in the District would violate the Fifth Amendment by depriving slaveholders of their property without due process of law.[143] This argument rested upon two assumptions, both open to question: (1) that slaves, though referred to only as persons in the text of the Constitution, were to be treated strictly as property under the Fifth Amendment; and (2) that abolition—even compensated, *post nati* abolition—would be legally equivalent to confiscation.[144] Calhoun himself acknowledged that his interpretation of the due process clause as a bulwark of slavery lacked broad support in the Senate.[145] He did not live to see it judicially confirmed two decades later in the Dred Scott decision.

The lack of southern unity on the subject testified to the inherent weakness of the constitutional argument against abolition in the District of Columbia. There had never been much question that state sovereignty encompassed the power to abolish slavery, and within the District, the federal government presumably had the authority and responsibilities of a state government. Thus logic as well as the language of the Constitution indicated that the power to abolish slavery had been lodged with Congress. Otherwise, said Daniel Webster, "though slavery in every other part of the world should be abolished, yet in the metropolis of this great Republic, it is established in perpetuity."[146] As a political movement, the crusade to drive slavery out of the national capital was perennially a failure, but for other than constitutional reasons. The continuing presence of the institution right up to the time of the Civil War reflected southern determination and much northern indifference, as well as racial fears, hostility to abolitionism, concern for the safety of the Union, and devotion to the principle of local self-government.

THE DISTRICT OF COLUMBIA became smaller in 1846 when Congress voted to retrocede the Virginia portion, which constituted about 30 percent of the whole and had little to do with the operation of the federal government.[147] Proposals for similar legislation returning the rest of the District to Maryland, which would have resolved the controversy over slavery, had no chance against northern opposition. Concern about slavery in Washington tended in any case to wane during the years of territorial expansion and war, but it was renewed by the dramatics of the *Pearl* affair in April 1848 and by the rising excitement over the Wilmot Proviso. In constitutional debate, some antislavery spokesmen were now taking a leaf from the southern book of strict construction. That is, besides asserting congressional power to abolish slavery in the District, they denied congressional power to establish slavery there. The logic of this strategy led to the introduction of a bill repealing that part of the District act of 1801 whereby the laws of Virginia and Maryland had been continued in force. Repeal, said the bill's sponsor, Representative John Crowell of Ohio, would remove the legal basis for slaveholding that Congress had unconstitutionally supplied. The authority to transform human beings into property and reduce them to the level of brutes, he declared, could not be sought "in doubtful construction" but must instead be given "in plain unequivocal terms." Since no such authority was expressly conferred by the Constitution, it did not exist. Therefore, all legislation of Congress that upheld slavery was "wholly unauthorized, and a palpable usurpation of power."[148] Crowell's bill neatly bypassed the southern constitutional argument and was cleverly aimed at undermining slavery in the District without formally abolishing it. Predictably, however, the measure received no consideration from the House and served only as a platform for launching one more antislavery speech.

The hopelessness of trying to get rid of slavery as a whole in the District of Columbia was demonstrated in 1848 when the Senate voted 36 to 7 against a resolution instructing the District committee to report an abolition bill.[149] To many antislavery congressmen, prohibition of the domestic slave trade in the District was a much more attainable goal. Despite a decline in the traffic, it remained the most visible and objectionable aspect of the presence of slavery in the nation's capital. Slaveholders themselves frequently acknowledged the repulsiveness of slave trading, and some southern states imposed restrictions on it. The trouble was that, in southern eyes, suppression of the District's slave trade by the federal government qualified perfectly as an "entering wedge"—one that would surely open the way to total abolition in the District and might also serve as a precedent for congressional interference with the interstate slave trade. By midcentury, it had become conventional wisdom in the South that no concession to the antislavery movement, however slight, could be anything but an invitation to further demands.

During the first session of the Thirtieth Congress, several attempts to initiate anti-slave-trade legislation proved unsuccessful.[150] But shortly after the second session began in December 1848, the House, by a vote of 98 to 88, suddenly approved the resolution of New York's Daniel Gott instructing the committee for the District of Columbia "to report a bill, as soon as practicable, prohibiting the slave trade in the said District." The action infuriated southerners already up in arms because of the continuing effort to prohibit slavery in the great expanse of territory recently conquered from Mexico. They especially resented Gott's denunciatory preamble, which by implication condemned slavery in general as "a reproach to our country throughout Christendom."[151] The immediate result was a bipartisan caucus of southern senators and representatives on December 23. Out of it emerged a committee that detailed Calhoun to draft an "address" setting forth the grievances of the South with respect to the antislavery movement. This manifesto proved satisfactory to only a minority of southern congressmen, but the furor dismayed enough northern members to produce a striking reversal. On January 10, by a vote of 119 to 81, the House reconsidered its passage of the Gott resolution.[152] Just nine days later, the same body reversed itself on another sectionally controversial issue by approving the Pacheco claim for loss of a slave during the second Seminole War.

It was during debate on January 10, 1849, that Abraham Lincoln read his bill for gradual abolition of slavery in the District of Columbia, saying that he intended to introduce it if the Gott resolution should be reconsidered. The measure, however, was not only hopeless but extraneous, containing no mention of the slave trade in the District. Nothing further came of it.[153] Caleb B.

Smith of Indiana, who would later serve in Lincoln's cabinet, was ready with a more appropriate substitute for the Gott resolution. Presented as soon as reconsideration had been voted, it instructed the committee on the District of Columbia to report a bill that would prevent the introduction of slaves into the District for sale there or elsewhere. Richard K. Meade of Virginia promptly offered an amendment calling for more effective fugitive-slave legislation.[154] Although the Speaker ruled him out of order, the idea of such a quid pro quo had thus been broached and was to prove viable in the next Congress. At the end of January, the District committee did report a bill along the lines of the Smith resolution, but it made no headway before adjournment on March 3.[155]

When the Thirty-first Congress met in December 1849, the sectional controversy over slavery in the new American Southwest had become a crisis of such intensity that it threatened to tear the nation apart. Talk of secession was common throughout the South, and even a man as seldom disposed to extremism as Alexander H. Stephens thought that the southern states should be "making the necessary preparations of men and money, arms and munitions, etc., to meet the emergency."[156] It was at this point that Henry Clay assumed the historical role for which he is probably best remembered. The legislation that became known as the Compromise of 1850 originated in a set of eight resolutions that he presented to the Senate on January 29. One of those resolutions declared that abolition of slavery in the District of Columbia would be "inexpedient" without the consent of Maryland, the consent of the people of the District, and just compensation to slave owners. Another declared that it was "expedient" to prohibit trade in slaves brought into the District "either to be sold therein as merchandise, or to be transported to other markets."[157] More than three months passed before the Clay resolutions and various other proposals were shaped by committee action into a legislative program. The compromise package reported by Clay on May 8 consisted primarily of a five-part "omnibus" bill dealing with the admission of California, territorial organization for Utah and New Mexico, the boundaries of Texas, and the public debt of Texas. In addition, the committee recommended meliorative amendments to a fugitive slave measure already under consideration by the Senate, and as the seventh and last compromise item, it reported a separate bill for suppression of the professional slave trade in the District of Columbia.[158]

Because the fugitive-slave and District bills were not included in the omnibus, they are commonly viewed as two measures that offset each other and supplemented the main body of the compromise, which was wholly concerned with problems arising from acquisition of the new American Southwest. It should be remembered, however, that the slave-trade bill was in itself a compromise balancing suppression of the slave trade with rejection of outright abolition in the District of Columbia. Furthermore, the bill merely prohibited the importation of slaves for sale within the District or in preparation for their sale elsewhere. It did not forbid local residents to import slaves for their own use, and local owners could still sell their slaves within the District or anywhere else in the country. The effect was to restore restrictions that had presumably existed under Maryland law before Congress set them aside in 1802. The bill, in short, was just a minor concession to antislavery sentiment and undoubtedly the least consequential feature of the Compromise of 1850.

Despite its mildness, a majority of southern senators were determined to oppose the District bill, which received scarcely any mention throughout most of the legislative struggle and came up for consideration very late in the session. At that time, its progress toward enactment was strongly affected by a recent slave-escape incident that inevitably revived memories of the flight of the *Pearl* two years earlier. On July 27, when debate on the omnibus bill was coming to its climax, two servants ran away from their masters, Georgia congressmen Robert Toombs and Alexander H. Stephens. There was reason to believe they had not left the city, and the police received information that led them to watch the movements of William L. Chaplin, a prominent New York abolitionist who had moved to Washington.[159] Eventually their vigilance was rewarded.

Some days later, Chaplin set out northward with the two slaves inside his carriage. At a point just beyond the District boundary, the vehicle was stopped by a body of five policemen and several civilians. One officer used a fence rail to immobilize the rear wheels, but Chaplin and the slaves were armed and defiant. When another man tried to seize the reins, he was greeted with a bullet that passed through his hat. The ensuing gun battle in the darkness lasted five or six minutes, and according to one report, at least twenty-seven shots were fired. Surprisingly, only a few minor wounds were sustained. One of the fugitives escaped in the confusion but surrendered two days later. The police arrested Chaplin and the other slave, taking them back to Washington. Chaplin was subsequently indicted in Maryland, as well as in the District of Columbia, on charges of assault with intent to kill and larceny of slaves. He spent more than four months in jail but escaped longer imprisonment by jumping bail of $6,000 in one jurisdiction and $19,000 in the other.[160]

The incident could not have been better timed for sensational effect, with the great sectional struggle in Congress approaching its climax. Again, as in 1848, there were threats of mob action in Washington, directed especially at Gamaliel Bailey and the *National Era*. Although Bailey hastened to dissociate himself from Chaplin's adventurism, the outburst of southern anger about the event itself was prolonged and aggravated by the praise that radical abolitionists heaped on Chaplin as a hero and martyr.[161] "This stealing of slaves," wrote a North Carolina congressman to his wife, "produces more irritation, more heart-burning among slaveholders, than all other causes combined."[162]

By the end of August, the Senate had passed all other parts of the compromise and was ready at last to consider the District slave-trade bill. On September 3, James A. Pearce of Maryland, with the Chaplin affair obviously in mind, offered an amendment prescribing heavier punishment for persons who encouraged or assisted runaways and requiring any such offender to reimburse the owner if an escape proved successful. The amendment, which also gave local authorities the power to exclude free blacks from the District, was readily approved, in spite of Clay's objection that it would endanger passage of the bill. Upon his motion the next day, further consideration was postponed to September 10.[163] At that time, the Senate engaged in one last burst of angry debate on the Compromise of 1850.

Robert M. T. Hunter of Virginia had led off debate on September 3 with a set speech attacking the District bill as unconstitutional and taking a step toward suppression of the interstate slave trade.[164] When discussion of the measure resumed a week later, his colleague James Mason moved to strike the first two sections, which would have eliminated Clay's bill entirely, leaving only the Pearce amendment. Prohibition of slave trading in the District, said Mason, would amount to moral condemnation of a commerce carried on in all southern states because it "was necessarily incident to the institution of slavery." For Jefferson Davis, the most egregious feature of the bill was its discriminatory interference with transit across what ought to be neutral ground. Neither Congress nor any state government, he sweepingly declared, had the right to prevent an American citizen from passing through any part of the United States with any "species of property" recognized by the Constitution. Davis nevertheless admitted that the bill had the support of an "anti-slavery majority around which sycophants, deserters, and ambitious demagogues gather." Sure enough, Mason's motion was soundly defeated, as about one-third of the southerners present voted against it.[165] But with the Pearce amendment still attached, the bill now displeased many northerners and seemed likely to fail in the House even if it should pass the Senate.

At this point, William H. Seward launched a counterattack by moving to substitute a bill for the virtually immediate abolition of slavery and emancipation of all slaves in the District. The New York senator made it plain that his provocative gesture was an expression of dissatisfaction with the Pearce amendment, which, he said, had converted the original bill "from a law meliorating slavery within the District into a law to fortify slavery and proscribe free men." Some antislavery moderates hastened to dissociate themselves from Seward, and southerners were furious that he should "throw a firebrand" into the progress toward sectional adjustment. "I consider this a proposition to dissolve the Union," declared Henry S. Foote of Mississippi, one of the architects of the compromise. Willie P. Mangum, a North Carolinian who had voted against Mason's proposal to jettison the original bill, announced that he was changing his course and would no longer support slave-trade legislation for the District. "I am satisfied," he said, "that it is impossible to satisfy certain gentlemen. To attain their objects they would wade through the blood knee-deep of the whole South....The further discussion of such subjects as this, in my judgment, only tends to operate as an entering wedge ... hazarding the existence of the Union and the safety and liberties of the South."[166]

On September 12, after discursive debate extending over three days, Seward's motion was rejected by a vote of 45 to 5, and the bill was reported from the committee of the whole to the Senate floor.[167] By that time, the House had passed all the other compromise measures, including the fugitive-slave bill. The final discussion on September 14 revealed that the Pearce amendment had lost some support from senators who feared that it would block passage of the bill. The old Missourian Thomas Hart Benton, for one, announced that he would reverse himself and vote against the amendment, however desirable it might be as a separate piece of legislation. John Bell of Tennessee disagreed, pleading in moderate tones that it was needed to make the bill less offensive to the South. Some tinkering to reduce the severity of the amendment brought an embittered Jefferson Davis to his feet with the protest that there seemed to be "a great sympathy getting up in the Senate for negro thieves." It was useless, he exclaimed, "to struggle against those who are determined to oppress us, aided as they are by those who desert us and go over to the enemy." When the decisive vote came, it proved to be fairly close, but ultimately the Pearce amendment was rejected.[168] Thus returned to its original form, the bill passed the Senate on September 16 by a vote of 33 to 19 and passed the House one day later, 124 to 59.[169] With the signature of the president on September 20, the Compromise of 1850 was completed and slave trading had been restricted in the District of Columbia.

Of the 157 votes cast for the District bill in both houses, only ten came from southerners, and six of those were from the border states of Delaware, Kentucky, and Missouri.[170] Southern hostility to the measure had been strong from the beginning and was intensified by the Chaplin incident and the defeat of the Pearce amendment. The objection was not so much to what the bill did as to what it signified. "It is the principle," said Foote, "the most unpardonable injustice towards the South—which must inflame the public mind, and must inevitably awaken apprehension that this is but the entering wedge to other and more aggressive measures which are afterwards to follow." Antislavery radicals were not at all disposed to quiet such fears. For instance, Salmon P. Chase acknowledged that the slave-trade bill was "a step towards the abolition of slavery itself." Members deceived themselves, he added, if they thought nothing more would follow.[171] Expectations of this kind proved to be mistaken, however. Slavery not only continued to exist in the District but came under no serious attack for more than a decade. Although the professional slave-trader disappeared from the scene, local slaves could still be sold within or outside the District, and a slave might still occasionally be auctioned off as part of some legal process.[172] The dismal city jail still housed slaves for the convenience of their masters, and of course the District slave code continued in force, with whipping still prescribed as the most common punishment.

THE IDEA OF a federal city had taken shape at the close of the American Revolution and may be said to have crystallized as a reaction to the humiliation that Congress suffered in the summer of 1783, when the menace of a few hundred dissatisfied soldiers caused it to flee from Philadelphia. The Constitutional Convention adopted the idea but did so without much discussion and without making any attempt to resolve the question of location. No one at the time seems to have thought through the implications of creating such a district in a country where local government was wholly under state control. Neither did anyone in the First Congress openly question the wisdom or propriety of situating the national capital within the slaveholding South. The sectional struggle in 1789–90 over location of the "residency" was largely a contest for prestige and expected commercial advantage, with slavery at most an unexpressed secondary consideration at the back of men's minds. Later Congresses almost absentmindedly legitimized slavery in the District of Columbia and put the federal government into the business of providing the kind of protection for the institution that had become standard in slaveholding states. This series of unthinking decisions had national consequences as well as concrete local effects, for it tended to characterize the United States more or less officially as a slaveholding nation. Slave-trading activities within sight and sound of the Capitol were just the most conspicuous evidence of what Congress had undeliberately wrought. Even southerners now and then expressed concern about the resulting contradiction in the image of America. John Randolph, for instance, confessed his mortification at being told by a foreigner of high rank: "You call this the land of liberty, and every day that passes things are done in it at which the despotisms of Europe would be horrorstruck and disgusted."[173]

Except for occasional protests of little significance, however, the presence of slavery in the national capital remained a matter of congressional indifference until antislavery sentiment crystallized into a reform movement of considerable force in the 1820s. Then, for about a decade, the District of Columbia became the primary focus of abolitionist attack in an increasingly bitter controversy over the federal government's relation to slavery. A major consequence of this struggle was the flowering of the concept of the "entering wedge" and the consolidation of southern resistance to any kind of restriction on slaveholding in the District. In addition, local opinion turned increasingly hostile to antislavery appeals at the very time when government, in the age of Andrew Jackson, was presumably drawing closer to the will of the people. Southern resistance to abolition in the District could thus be aligned with the democratic principle of popular consent.

Beginning in the late 1830s, the issue of slavery in the District of Columbia was first swallowed up in the battle over the right of petition and then pushed aside by the problem of the status of slavery in an expanding nation. Only the legislation of 1850 suppressing the professional slave trade in the District deviated from a general pattern of southern success that prevailed from 1789 until the outbreak of civil war. The ten-mile-square clause was itself no proslavery feature of the Constitution (not even in the jaundiced view of Garrisonians and neo-Garrisonians), but by 1861 the clause had been made proslavery by construction. Lincoln took the oath of office in a capital city that remained what it had long since become through both accident and design—a symbolic stronghold of the slave power in America.

4

Slavery in American Foreign Relations

CHATTEL SLAVERY IN a nation explicitly dedicated to human freedom was a heritage both paradoxical and dangerous for the new United States of 1776. The domestic consequences of that heritage became the central theme of nineteenth-century American history, as increasing sectional conflict led eventually to disunion, civil war, and the aftermath called reconstruction. Less familiar are the effects of the heritage upon American foreign relations and upon the image of itself that the United States presented to the rest of the world.

American victory in the Revolutionary War meant that the abstract principles of the Declaration of Independence had been successfully converted into an actual experiment in nation building. It made the new United States an international symbol, not only of revolutionary escape from external rule, but of republican self-government and personal freedom. "The example of political wisdom and felicity here to be displayed will excite emulation through the kingdoms of the earth, and meliorate the condition of the human race."[1] So spoke Joel Barlow in 1787, and the same kind of gleam was in George Bancroft's eye many years later when he declared: "Our country is bound to allure the world to freedom by the beauty of its example."[2] Freedom was the keynote. Liberty personified as a young woman soon emerged as one of the earliest symbols of American nationhood. At the beginning of the Revolution, Tom Paine had pictured freedom as "hunted round the globe" and finding her last refuge on the American shore.[3] For many a

European liberal, the struggle quickly took on similar meaning. "America" and "liberty" tended to become interchangeable terms.[4]

Proud of their own Revolution, Americans of the early national period were deeply interested in other revolutionary movements that seemed to pay them the flattery of imitation. First, of course, came the great upheaval in France, which inspired passionate renewals of the commitment to freedom in the United States. Throughout the country, local societies sprang up in support of the French revolutionary cause, issuing public appeals such as the following: "Shall we Americans, who have kindled the spark of liberty, stand aloof and see it extinguished, when burning a bright flame, in France, which hath caught it from us?"[5]

Certain conservatives like John Adams were skeptical from the beginning, and by 1793, the excesses of violence in France had alienated many more. The wars of the French Revolution divided Americans into bitterly hostile factions that soon took more definite form as the Federalist and Republican parties. Considerations of national interest and commercial welfare predominated in the shaping of public policy, but ideology was also a factor. For the better part of a decade, American foreign relations and domestic politics were strongly affected by the disposition of the emerging Jeffersonian Republicans to look upon embattled France as the old world's champion of political liberty in the tradition of the American Revolution.

That view fell out of fashion, of course, with the rise of Napoleon Bonaparte to supreme power in France, but soon there were revolutions in Latin America to celebrate, and then the revolt of the Greeks against their Turkish oppressors. Most thrilling of all, and most disappointing, were the revolutionary movements that swept across much of Europe in 1848 but eventually yielded, in one way or another, to the forces of reaction. Disturbed by the outcome, Senator Isaac P. Walker of Wisconsin questioned whether American isolationism continued to be appropriate. "What was our policy in our infancy and weakness, has ceased to be our *true* policy now that we have reached to manhood and strength," he declared. "I am for the cause of liberty and free Government, against slavery and despotism, throughout the globe." In support of that cause he was prepared to have the United States "interpose both her moral and physical power."[6] Such extravagant talk did not make much headway, however, against the traditional conception of the nation's appointed role in world history. A Tennessee congressman spoke for most Americans when he dismissed all thought of intervention in Europe. It was the American achievement, he declared, that had animated the European revolutionaries. "We will keep that light of our example burning and shining upon the pathway of nations . . . to guide them from the darkness of tyranny and despotism to the sunlight of liberty."[7]

Senator Walker's aggressive tone reflected the self-confidence of a nation that had recently expanded to the shores of the Pacific, adding more than a million square miles to its domain and reinforcing its conviction of having been born to a special destiny. Thus, when the revolutions of 1848 burst forth just a few weeks after the war between the United States and Mexico came to an end at Guadalupe Hidalgo, the New York Herald boasted that American military energy and genius had astonished all Europe. "We are," it declared, "a great, a growing, a rich, and a powerful people. We ought to take a proper position in the world, at this important crisis in European affairs."[8] Not surprisingly, some of the rhetoric of the time linked territorial expansion with the American ideal of liberty. Particularly in discussions of the annexation of Texas, expansion was often justified as a means of "extending the area of freedom." But this phrase, repeated until it became a cliché, was invested with a terrible irony, for, as an Indiana congressman bitterly complained, this "nation boasting itself to be the freest upon the earth" was being asked "to extend the area of freedom by enlarging the boundaries of slavery."[9]

The United States at midcentury was still viewed throughout much of the world as a symbol of personal liberty and self-government. Yet it had also come to be conspicuous as one of the last strongholds of slavery in Western civilization. At home, the American nation was a house divided by the slavery question, but in the conduct of foreign affairs it appeared consistently as a slaveholding republic. Meanwhile, that old enemy Britain, the very epitome of oppression in American Revolutionary rhetoric, had assumed the role of an international champion of human freedom. It was a British foreign minister who in 1843 portrayed his country as "constantly exerting herself to procure the general abolition of slavery throughout the world," and it was an American secretary of state who responded with a vehement defense of slavery, ending in the assertion that for *his* country, abolition would be a great "calamity."[10]

INVERSION OF THE standard revolutionary roles had actually begun during the Revolution itself, when slaves in large numbers sought freedom within British lines. George Washington was among those slaveholders who suffered financial losses in this manner.[11] At American insistence, the treaty of peace included a provision that the British forces must withdraw from the United

States without "carrying away any Negroes or other Property of the American Inhabitants."[12] By that wording, the treaty explicitly recognized slaves as property, something the framers of the Constitution would studiously avoid. But the clause proved ineffective. Washington himself was unable to prevent the departure of some four thousand blacks with the British evacuation of New York City, and there were similar losses elsewhere.[13] What remained to disturb Anglo-American diplomacy for many years was the question of compensation.

After the Revolution, the United States energetically pressed the claims of American slaveholders against Great Britain. The principal government spokesmen were John Adams, Gouverneur Morris, John Jay, and Thomas Jefferson—all men of antislavery convictions. But antislavery was then just a moral sentiment, while slavery was an economic interest, and in the day-to-day conduct of public business, an interest will usually have the advantage. Besides, the issue of the appropriated slaves involved other principles important to Americans, including property rights of individuals and treaty rights of the nation.

Both Great Britain and the United States failed to meet all their obligations under the treaty of peace, and reproaches on the subject were duly exchanged for more than a decade. Americans protested especially against the British refusal to evacuate certain military posts situated on American soil along the boundary between the United States and Canada. The British replied that the posts were being held in reprisal for American delinquencies with respect to treatment of Loyalists and payment of British creditors, to which Jefferson, Jay, and others responded that the British had been the first to violate the treaty by carrying off the American slaves. Jefferson even argued that the loss of their slaves was what prevented many Americans from paying their British debts.[14]

Anglo-American relations deteriorated further when Britain went to war against revolutionary France in 1793 and began to interfere with American maritime commerce. The situation soon became critical, and in 1794, President Washington sent Chief Justice John Jay to London as a special envoy seeking to resolve the differences between the two countries. Some southerners thought that Jay, a confirmed Anglophile and a friend of abolition, would not be very resolute in protecting their interests, and the results of his diplomacy seemed to bear them out. Jay, in fact, found it useless to press the slave question. British officials remained adamant, insisting, as they had before, that the provision in the peace treaty was prospective only. It did not apply, they said, to slaves that had come under British protection before the war ended. Consequently, the treaty that Jay signed contained no reference to the carried-off slaves. "We could not agree about the negroes," he wrote. "Was that a good reason for breaking up the negotiation?"[15]

The omission drew criticism even from some northern members of Congress, and it was a major reason for the bitter southern opposition that almost defeated Jay's Treaty in the Senate.[16] After senatorial approval by a bare two-thirds majority, James Madison led an attempt in the House of Representatives to withhold the appropriation necessary for carrying the treaty into effect. The slave issue was prominent in a debate that ran on for two months before the effort ended in failure. At one point in the discussion, John Heath of Virginia declared that the failure to secure payment for the slaves was the "great objection against the Treaty." When the House finally voted to support the treaty, it did so by the narrow margin of 51 to 48.[17] Thereafter, the United States government gave up its efforts to obtain satisfaction from Britain for the slaves carried off during the period of the Revolution, and the slave owners were never indemnified.[18]

There was, to be sure, a smaller group of slaveholders that did eventually win compensation for slaves taken away during and immediately after the Revolution. Beginning in 1783, the Creek Indians, who had been allies of the British, were forced to sign a series of treaties in which they agreed to return all American prisoners, including slaves, being held by them. Although only a few owners actually recovered their slaves as a consequence, others became claimants against the Creek nation. Their reimbursement was finally provided for by treaty in 1821, when the federal government, as part of the payment for a cession of land, agreed to satisfy the various claims outstanding against the Creeks.[19]

By that time, the United States had fought another war with Great Britain and was wrestling again with a postwar problem of absconded slaves. British fleets had taken away several thousand blacks from the Chesapeake region and certain other places, seemingly in direct violation of a provision in the treaty of peace. Again the British government read its own meaning into the treaty language and refused either to return the slaves or to indemnify the owners. This time, as it happened, there was to be a different outcome, but not until after many years of negotiation and labored proceedings.

As soon as diplomatic relations were reestablished in 1815, Secretary of State James Monroe raised the issue with the British chargé d'affaires in Washington and directed the new American minister in London, John Quincy

Adams, to do the same with the foreign secretary. The British officials on both sides of the Atlantic responded with a terminological argument. The first article of the Treaty of Ghent stipulated: "All territory, places, and possessions whatsoever, taken by either party from the other during the war, or which may be taken after the signing of this treaty . . . shall be be restored without delay, and without causing any destruction, or carrying away any of the artillery or other public property originally captured in the said forts or places, and which shall remain therein upon the exchange of the ratification of this treaty; or any slaves or other private property."[20] The British contended that the restrictive words "and which shall remain therein upon the exchange of the ratification of this treaty" applied to all the property mentioned, private as well as public. Since most of the slaves in question had been taken aboard British naval vessels after having run away from their masters, this interpretation would have rendered the slave clause largely meaningless. The American spokesmen insisted that the treaty, while it limited the return of public property to material still in place at the time of ratification, required the return of all private property (including slaves) held by the British on American soil or within American territorial waters when ratifications were exchanged.[21]

The grammatical structure of the disputed passage lent strong support to the American interpretation, and Adams, as one of the men who had drafted and signed the treaty, readily demonstrated that the passage in its final form was a compromise intended to establish different rules for the return of public and of private property.[22] The New Englander must have been somewhat uneasy, however, when the argument shifted toward moral ground. On one occasion, Lord Liverpool, the prime minister, took exception to his flat assertion that slaves were private property. Not exactly, said Liverpool. A table or chair, for instance, might be taken away and restored without changing its condition, but a human being was entitled to other considerations. The prime minister in his mild way was thus reasserting the British contention that men who had been promised their freedom could not in good conscience be handed back into slavery. Adams, while acknowledging the humanity of the slave, found himself duty bound to reply that the treaty recognized slaves only as property and made no distinction between them and other private property. Besides, he pointed out, the British could honor both their treaty obligations and their promises of freedom simply by reimbursing the owners of the slaves that had been taken away.[23]

Adams pursued the matter vigorously and in 1816 suggested submitting it to the arbitration of a "friendly sovereign."[24] When it came to choosing the arbiter, Britain acquiesced in the American nomination of Alexander I of Russia. Adams, who by this time had become secretary of state in the Monroe administration, found "something whimsical in the idea that the United States and Great Britain, both speaking English, should go to the Slavonian Czar of Muscovy to find out their own meaning, in a sentence written by themselves."[25]

The imperial decision, not announced until the spring of 1822, declared that the "literal and grammatical sense" of the treaty supported the American claim and that the United States was therefore entitled to "a just indemnification" for the slaves carried away.[26] The czar, as requested by the two powers, then shifted from the role of arbitrator to that of mediator in the negotiations that necessarily followed his award. The result was a convention, signed at Petersburg in July 1822, which set up a complicated procedure for ascertaining the amount to be paid. First, an Anglo-American board of two commissioners and two arbitrators were to examine the evidence and agree upon "an average value" for each slave. Then the two commissioners were to examine each claim individually, deciding upon its validity, and thus calculate the total indemnity. If the commissioners should disagree on any specific case before them or on the meaning of any stipulation in the convention, one of the arbitrators, chosen by lot, was to join in the rendering of a majority decision.[27]

On August 25, 1823, the board convened in Washington and set about the performance of its duties with the aid of a secretary, a clerk, a doorkeeper, and two messengers. The importance attached to the proceedings by the federal government is indicated in the appointment of a distinguished public figure, Langdon Cheves of South Carolina, as the American commissioner. Cheves was joined by Henry Seawell of North Carolina as the American arbitrator. In addition, the prominent Virginia lawyer George Hay, a close friend of President Monroe, attended the sessions as agent of the United States government and guardian of the claimants' interests.[28] It was approximately one year later that the four members of the board completed their first assignment by fixing the average value of the slaves at $580 for Louisiana, $390 for Alabama, Georgia, and South Carolina, and $280 for all other states.[29] In the second stage of its deliberations, however, the board ran into serious difficulties. Not unexpectedly, there was frequent disagreement between Cheves and the British commissioner, George Jackson. They differed sharply, for instance, over whether the claimants were entitled to interest on the value of their slaves. Another dispute arose over the blacks taken away from Dauphin Island in Mobile Bay, it being the British contention that the island was still under Spanish sovereignty in 1814. But what brought the board's work virtually to a standstill was Jackson's adamant refusal to submit such issues to one of the arbitrators, as provided for in the convention.[30]

Thus John Quincy Adams, who had already been officially involved in the controversy for more than ten years, found the troublesome problem still very much on his hands when he became president in 1825. With his approval, Secretary of State Henry Clay sought to bypass the cumbersome machinery of the Petersburg Convention and negotiate a new settlement fixing a definite amount of money as indemnity. The British at first responded unfavorably to Clay's overtures, and another year of seemingly fruitless diplomatic exchange ensued. It was Albert Gallatin, arriving in London as the new American minister, who managed to break the deadlock. In a convention signed November 13, 1826, Britain finally agreed to pay the American slaveholders a total of $1,204,960.[31]

Gallatin's successful diplomacy concluded the story of the carried-away slaves as a chapter in American foreign relations, but it did not mark the end of the whole affair. There remained the problem of distributing the money to more than a thousand claimants. For that task, Congress authorized the establishment of a three-man commission, limiting its term of existence to approximately one year, and directing it to use the list of claimants and the table of slave values that had been assembled by the Anglo-American board.[32] President Adams, in appointing the members of the commission, chose to enlist the further services of Langdon Cheves and Henry Seawell. His third selection was a former governor of Virginia, James Pleasants. The three commissioners, all southerners, set to work in July 1827 and soon found themselves embroiled in a bitter controversy between two groups of slaveholders.

In order to stay within the limit of $1,204,960, Congress had directed the commission to pay 75 percent of each claim when it was approved and to remit the balance, or whatever proportion of the balance remained available, after all the claims were judged. By March of 1828, awards totaling about $600,000 had been made, principally to citizens of Louisiana and Georgia.[33] Acceptable proof of a claim was easier to produce in those states than in the Chesapeake region, where British depredations had extended over a longer period. Indeed, most of the Virginia and Maryland slaves in question had probably been taken out of the country before ratification of the Treaty of Ghent and thus were not covered by the terms of the treaty.[34] The Chesapeake slaveholders nevertheless pressed their claims, believing that they had suffered more from the war than any other claimants. Some of them contrived to offer evidence of postwar removal, but it was largely hearsay or otherwise of dubious quality. Especially notable was their presentation of a good many depositions from slaves, a recourse that ran contrary to the whole legal tradition of the South. Cheves, the South Carolinian, found the anomaly deeply disturbing and warned that the introduction of such testimony would set an example sustaining the principles of abolitionism. "Ought we not to beware lest we be stirring a volcanic fire?" he asked.[35]

The Chesapeake claimants relied primarily, however, upon a broader legal strategy, pursued before the commission by no less an advocate than the attorney general of the United States, William Wirt.[36] With respect to the critical question of *when* the slaves had left the country, Wirt argued that in the absence of satisfactory evidence, postwar removal must be universally presumed and that the burden of proof rested with anyone who disputed the presumption. This bold effort to finesse the problem of inadequate verification met strong opposition from the Louisiana and Georgia claimants. They were, of course, still waiting for the 25 percent balance due them and hoped to receive payments of interest as well if the total number of awards could be restricted. Their agents consequently set about gathering evidence to prove that most of the Chesapeake slaves had been removed before the end of the war. The Chesapeake claimants, who had made no attempts to interfere with the Louisiana-Georgia awards, protested that their generous forbearance was being repaid in a most "ungracious and selfish" manner.[37]

It soon became clear that the commissioners were divided on the issue, with Seawell and Pleasants favoring the Virginia-Maryland group and Cheves on the other side. By votes of 2 to 1, the commission accepted the slave testimony, accepted Wirt's argument of presumption, and disqualified the opposing evidence on technical grounds. The Louisiana-Georgia claimants, in an effort to stave off defeat, then requested that Congress extend the life of the commission so that they might retake the suppressed testimony and seek other evidence to support their case. A bill for that purpose provoked some vehement argument in both chambers, with Virginians and Georgians doing most of the talking. In the end, Congress approved an extension only until September 1, not enough for the needs of the Louisianans and Georgians, who had wanted three months more. The commissioners managed to allocate all the money and finish their work on time, with the Chesapeake claimants remaining on the list of beneficiaries.[38]

Thus, forty-five years of controversy over British wartime removal of American slaves came to a satisfactory conclusion for the United States and for a substantial number of its slaveholders. An indemnity of $1,204,960 was for those days a sizable payment, equaling about 5 percent of the federal government's income in 1828. The result had been achieved, however, at considerable public expense and only after an inordinate expenditure of time and energy by a long line of high-ranking national officials from George Washington to Henry Clay and Albert Gallatin.[39] In the House of Representatives, the final discussion of the indemnity and its allocation took place just a few months after the memorable debate on the D'Auterive claim, in which the central issue had been whether slaves were essentially persons or property in the eyes of the federal government. Yet no congressman at that time raised the same question with respect to the slaves liberated by British forces, and no elected or appointed federal officeholder had ever raised it.[40] When it came to extracting money from Great Britain, northerners like John Quincy Adams seem to have agreed implicitly with southerners like James Monroe that those slaves were property, pure and simple, under federal law.

IT WAS ONE thing for the United States government to seek restitution for the financial losses of slaveholders resulting from enemy operations in wartime, but federal officials were no less solicitous about the peacetime problem of slaves escaping across international boundaries. For instance, slaveholders in Georgia complained repeatedly after the Revolution that Spanish Florida had become a haven for runaways. The labors of John Jay as secretary for foreign affairs under the Articles of Confederation bore fruit in 1790 when the King of Spain ordered the governor of East Florida to cooperate in closing the border to fugitives.[41] At the urging of Georgia leaders, President Washington and Secretary of State Jefferson then tried to arrange an agreement with the Spanish governor, Juan Nepomuceno de Quesada, for retroactive enforcement of the royal directive and the consequent return of all American slaves living as fugitives in Florida. Their ambitious effort failed, however, and the Georgians had to be satisfied with Quesada's promise to detain and return runaways entering Florida after the promulgation of the King's order in that province.[42]

Soon the circumstances were reversed when Jefferson received a Spanish complaint that several Georgians had crossed the border and kidnapped a number of slaves belonging to a Florida resident. At about the same time, French West Indian officials accused an American sea captain of carrying off some blacks from Martinique and selling them as slaves in Georgia. Jefferson sought the advice of Attorney General Edmund Randolph, who informed him that there was no federal law authorizing the punishment of such activities. The president did not ask Congress for appropriate legislation. Instead, Jefferson contented himself with vainly requesting the governor of Georgia to see that justice was done in the interest of international amity.[43]

With Spanish control chronically weak, Florida was the scene of much turmoil during the first two decades of the nineteenth century. When the wars in Europe and America came to an end in 1815, Spain retained possession of the colony, except that the United States had seized the area west of the Perdido River, claiming it as part of the Louisiana Purchase. Complaints again arose over the problem of slaves fleeing across the border into Florida, where they often mingled with the Seminole Indians. Slaveholders in Georgia and Alabama became especially apprehensive when they learned that several hundred blacks, together with a number of Seminoles, had occupied a fort within Spanish jurisdiction on the lower Apalachicola River. Some of these blacks were recently arrived fugitives, but many others were descendants of slaves who had sought refuge in Florida during the eighteenth century. All of them were militantly determined to retain their freedom. The fort was one built and recently evacuated by British troops, who had left a large supply of weapons and ammunition behind them. The commander of American forces in the area received emphatic instructions on the subject from his superior officer, General Andrew Jackson. "If the fort harbours the Negroes of our citizens . . . or hold[s] out inducements to the slaves of our citizens to desert from their owners' service," Jackson wrote, "this fort must be destroyed."[44]

And destroyed it was. An army regiment with two cannon and a large number of Creek allies marched southward across the border and reached the vicinity of the fort late in July of 1816. Meanwhile, two American gunboats made their way up the river and began to exchange fire with the defenders of the fort. A hot shot from one of the vessels struck the powder magazine, and in the resulting explosion, most of the fort's occupants (men, women, and children) were killed outright or mortally wounded.[45] The officer reporting the event to the secretary of the navy expressed satisfaction at this elimination of a "rendezvous for runaway slaves" that would have been "highly injurious to the neighboring states."[46] Some twenty-three years later, Congress appropriated $5,465 as prize money for the officers and men of the two gunboats. Not even Joshua R. Giddings of Ohio, then just beginning his congressional career, spoke out against this reward for what he later called "one of the darkest crimes which stains the history of any civilized nation."[47]

So began the first Seminole War, largely as a consequence of the use of federal troops in the service of Georgia and Alabama slaveholders. Indians and Florida blacks retaliated for the destruction of Negro Fort with raids on American border settlements. Late in 1817, they ambushed a supply boat on its way up the Apalachicola, killing most of the forty-man escort and all but one of the women and children on board.[48] President Monroe, in reporting these hostilities to an outraged public, described them as "unprovoked" Indian attacks.[49] He and other American officials said as little as possible about the role of escaped slaves in the border warfare. Taking personal command of a punitive campaign, General Jackson pursued the offenders into Florida and managed to crush their organized resistance after some hard fighting in which the blacks played a prominent part. This provocative conduct elicited angry protests from Spain while at the same time helping to convince the Spanish government that the province might as well be relinquished before it was taken by force. Jackson's actions sprang from mixed personal motives and national purposes, one of which, certainly, was to destroy the refuge for American fugitive slaves furnished by the black settlements of Spanish Florida.[50]

Spain's cession of Florida to the United States in 1821 simplified matters considerably but did not resolve the basic problem. Hundreds of blacks went on living in loose association with the Seminoles, often ostensibly as their slaves. White inhabitants of the region continued to charge that their runaway slaves were finding refuge among those Seminole Negroes, and the Indians in turn protested that white raiding parties made a habit of seizing blacks indiscriminately and carrying them off as fugitives. In 1823, three commissioners for the federal government, all of them southerners, arranged a treaty confining the Seminoles to a reservation in the interior of Florida. One of its provisions required the Indians to be "active and vigilant" in excluding fugitive slaves from their domain and promised a bounty for every runaway turned over to the federal Indian agent.[51] Thus the United States government entered more directly than ever before into the business of slave hunting. Throughout the territorial period in Florida, the continuing affiliation of blacks with Seminoles and the everlasting complaints about it by slaveholders had a disturbing effect on federal Indian diplomacy. In particular, the problem complicated and hindered the translocation of the southern tribes beyond the Mississippi when that melancholy project was undertaken in the 1830s. And although the second Seminole War, fought from 1835 to 1842, must be viewed primarily as a conflict over Indian removal, it too, like the earlier war, was in some respects about African Americans and slavery.[52]

American acquisition of Florida erased an international boundary that had long been attractive to fugitives, but in Louisiana, slaves could still flee across the Sabine River into Mexico. During the administration of John Quincy Adams, the federal government moved to close that line of escape. The American minister to Mexico, Joel R. Poinsett, negotiated a commercial treaty, and, under instructions from Secretary of State Henry Clay, he secured the inclusion of an article providing for the mutual return of fugitive slaves. Since Mexico had scarcely any slaves except those that Americans were beginning to bring into Texas, this would have been an arrangement beneficial only to American slaveholders on both sides of the border. Some Mexican officials raised objections to the article but acquiesced when Poinsett insisted in "very strong language" that it was indispensable.[53] In May of 1828, the United States Senate approved the treaty without a dissenting vote and without any discussion of the fugitive slave provision.[54] But in Mexico, both houses of the national legislature rejected the article. "It would be most extraordinary," ran one statement, "that in a treaty between two free republics slavery should be encouraged by obliging ours to deliver up fugitive slaves to their merciless and barbarous masters."[55] Not until several years later was a redrafted commercial treaty ratified by both nations. It contained no mention of fugitive slaves.[56]

After the annexation of Texas and its admission to the Union as a slave-holding state, followed by the American victory in the war with Mexico, the problem of international escapes from slavery shifted southwestward to the new international border at the Rio Grande. In 1855, an Austin editor asserted that about four thousand runaway slaves had found sanctuary in northern Mexico.[57] Senator Sam Houston and other Texan leaders repeatedly called the problem to the attention of federal authorities, urging a diplomatic solution before Texans took matters into their own hands. The United States government was responsive. First, Secretary of State John M. Clayton, then the American minister to Mexico, James Gadsden, and then Gadsden's successor, John Forsyth, sought an extradition treaty with Mexico that would include the return of runaway slaves, but all their negotiations failed. Forsyth reported that he could make no headway against "the British borrowed cant of philanthropy about slavery."[58]

Of course the great majority of slaves fleeing the United States headed northward to Canada. By 1860, according to the careful estimate of one historian, there were as many as thirty thousand fugitives, or children of fugitives, living in Canada West (formerly Upper Canada and later Ontario).[59] One of the first American officials to take formal notice of the problem had been John Quincy Adams. In 1819, as secretary of state, he exchanged communications on the subject with Gibbs C. Antrobus, the British chargé d'affaires in Washington. "Representations have been received at this Department," Adams wrote, "that several Negro slaves ran off last fall from their owners in the State of Tennessee and have taken refuge at Malden in Upper Canada. The owners are anxious to know if any arrangement can be made by which permission could be obtained for them to go to Canada and reobtain possession of their property."[60] Thus Adams, following precedents set by the national leaders of his father's generation, continued the practice of viewing slaves as property in international relations.

Antrobus replied: "The legislature of His Majesty's Province of Upper Canada having adopted the Law of England as the Rule of decision in all questions relative to property and civil rights, the Negroes have, by their residence in Canada, become free, whatever may have been their former condition in this country, and should any attempt be made to infringe upon this right of freedom, these Negroes would have it in their power to compel the interference of the courts of law for their protection, and the executive government could in no manner restrain or direct the judges in the exercise of their duty."[61] This pronouncement, which breathed the spirit of the famous *Somerset* decision of 1772, had been formulated by the attorney general of Upper Canada, and it proved to be virtually the British text in all subsequent discussions of the subject.[62]

After Adams became president, his secretary of state, Henry Clay, tried hard to secure an agreement with Great Britain for rendition of fugitive slaves. Clay was acting under heavy pressure from his home state; the Kentucky legislature had repeatedly invoked the aid of the federal government in the recovery of blacks fleeing to Canada. In 1826, he instructed the American minister, Albert Gallatin, to broach the subject in London. Gallatin was to suggest that a British proposal for mutual exchange of criminals be expanded to include deserters from military, naval, and merchant service, as well as "persons held to service or labour" who escaped one country into the other. What this amounted to was an offer to exchange British sailors who jumped ship in American ports for runaway slaves who managed to reach Canada. If the British government balked at incorporating such provisions in a treaty, it might be willing, Clay thought, to make informal arrangements along the same lines. If it refused to return any slaves already in Canada, it should be pressed for a promise not to receive any more.

Clay made it clear in these instructions to Gallatin that the importance of the fugitive slaves transcended their monetary value. "They are generally the most worthless of their class," he wrote, "and far, therefore, from being an acquisition which the British Government can be anxious to make, the sooner, we should think, they are gotten rid of, the better for Canada. It may be asked why, if they are so worthless, are we desirous of getting them back? The motive is to be found in the particular interest which those have who are entitled to their service, and the desire which is generally felt to prevent the example of the fugitives becoming contagious."[63]

Gallatin's efforts were wholly unsuccessful. British officials, even while administering a slaveholding empire in the West Indies, persisted in extending to Canada the principle that every person who reached British soil was free.[64] Clay, with the added stimulus of a resolution from the House of Representatives, nevertheless directed Gallatin's successor, James Barbour of Virginia, to renew negotiations on the subject.[65] In discussions with a new foreign secretary, Lord Aberdeen, Barbour carefully explained that when slaves succeeded in escaping, their example "impaired the value" of all those who remained at home. Aberdeen listened sympathetically, but said that neither English law nor English public opinion would permit the granting of any substantial remedy.[66]

Although the flight of slaves to Canada not only continued but substantially increased after 1830, the United States government made no further attempts to solve the problem by diplomatic means. As a last resort, some slaveholders began trying to recover fugitives through criminal extradition proceedings, relying on an Upper Canada law enacted in 1833. One such effort proved successful in 1842. A slave indicted in Arkansas for larceny (including theft of the horse with which he had made his escape) was returned to Arkansas by authority of the Canadian governor-general.[67] This incident provoked an outcry from abolitionists on both sides of the Atlantic. Their apprehensions increased later that same year when they learned that the Webster-Ashburton Treaty contained an article providing for mutual extradition. But in the few cases that came before them, British officials usually managed to find technical reasons for refusing to extradite runaway slaves. The most notable incident took place on the very eve of the Civil War, when a fugitive known as John Anderson reached Upper Canada after having fatally wounded a Missouri farmer who tried to capture him. Arrested and held for possible extradition as an accused murderer, Anderson was eventually released on a technicality, but not until his case had caused much public furor and inspired rival judicial proceedings in England and Canada.[68]

Thus Canada, like Mexico, successfully resisted the strenuous efforts of the United States to extend the operation of its fugitive-slave laws across international boundaries. But during the presidency of Andrew Jackson, another kind of escape from slavery began to trouble Anglo-American relations.

IN DECEMBER 1830, the brig *Comet* set sail down the Potomac from Alexandria, which was then part of the District of Columbia. Bound for New Orleans with a cargo of 164 slaves, it ran into foul weather and struck a reef in Bahamian waters off the coast of Florida. Those aboard were rescued and taken to Nassau, where British authorities freed the slaves. Two years later, the *Encomium*, carrying 46 slaves, had virtually the same experience. The American consul at Nassau protested vigorously and was told with equal force by the lieutenant governor's secretary that anyone trying to carry the Negroes away from the island would be liable to hanging.[69]

Of course the owners of the freed slaves were soon calling upon the federal government to secure either the return of their property or adequate compensation for it. Beyond such personal interest, the *Comet* and *Encomium* affairs evoked strong protest from the South in general. Coming at a time of deepening southern fear over the security of the slaveholding system, the two incidents seemed to be part of an ominous international pattern that included the Nat Turner uprising, the Garrisonian escalation of antislavery vehemence, and the triumph of abolition in the British colonies. Secretary of State Edward Livingston, in his instructions on the subject, made it plain that more was at stake than the property rights of a few slaveholders. "The doctrine that would justify the liberation of our slaves," he said, "is too dangerous to a large section of our country to be tolerated by us."[70] For the better part of a decade, beginning with Martin Van Buren in 1831, American diplomatic representatives spent an enormous amount of time arguing the slave owners' cause at the Court of St. James.

While British officials were pondering their response to these claims, a third incident further intensified the controversy. Early in 1835, the brig *Enterprise*, sailing from Alexandria to Charleston with 78 slaves, was forced by bad weather to seek shelter in Port Hamilton, Bermuda. Local customs officers seized the slaves and set them free, thereby provoking another outburst of southern complaint.[71] The next year, when Andrew Stevenson of Virginia became minister to England, he was instructed by the secretary of state, John Forsyth of Georgia, that the *Comet-Encomium-Enterprise* claims were "the most immediately pressing of the matters with which the United States Legation at London is now charged." It was the president's anxious wish, Forsyth continued, "that no time should be lost, and no exertion spared on your part to effect an early adjustment of this long pending claim."[72]

Stevenson, a former speaker of the House of Representatives, was a stalwart defender of the slaveholding interest. He set to work carrying out Forsyth's instructions soon after his arrival in London. On July 29, 1836, he dispatched a fifty-nine-page letter to Lord Palmerston, lecturing the foreign secretary on every aspect of the matter at issue. The essence of his argument was that the slaves in question were property under American law, that slavery and the domestic slave trade were not contrary to the law of nations, and that slaves on board an American ship remained within the jurisdiction of the United States even when the ship entered the waters of another nation, if it had been driven there by forces of nature. From Stevenson's emphatic language, one would never have suspected that there was any difference of opinion in the United States about the status of slavery under federal law. Slaves were recognized as property by the Constitution, he asserted in response to one of Palmerston's arguments. There was, in fact, "no distinction in principle between property in persons and property in things." Slavery as property formed "a basis of representation" in the federal government; it was "infused" into federal law and mixed itself with "all the sources" of federal authority.[73]

Nearly six months passed before Stevenson received an answer. In early January 1837, Palmerston informed him that the British government would assume financial responsibility for the slaves on the *Comet* and *Encomium*, but not for those on the *Enterprise*. The difference was that the *Enterprise* had arrived in Bermuda with its cargo of slaves after Parliament's enactment of emancipation in 1833. As a consequence, said Palmerston, the owners were "never lawfully in possession of those slaves within the British Territory." Stevenson had thus gained a partial victory, but a bitter one. Palmerston went on to declare that in the future, His Majesty's government would entertain no claim for slaves entering the British dominions, whatever the circumstances might be.[74]

After consultation with Forsyth, the American minister accepted the

British offer respecting the slaves of the *Comet* and *Encomium*, but he continued to argue vehemently the case of the *Enterprise*. His strongest language was reserved for Palmerston's statement of future British policy. That pronouncement, Stevenson said, would encourage the flight or abduction of slaves from their masters and, if adhered to, could not fail to be viewed as evidence of "a spirit hostile to the United States."[75] In this manner, he persistently identified the slaveholding interest with the American national interest. When Palmerston again ventured to differentiate slaves from other forms of property Stevenson replied at great length. "The question of property in slaves," he wrote, "is one, certainly, which the United States will never consider even open for discussion, much less the decision of a foreign government." To Forsyth, the minister wrote, "I have . . . been influenced alone by a desire to fulfil the wishes of our Government on the subject, and vindicate in a proper manner the rights of my country."[76]

Back in the United States, John C. Calhoun led the congressional attack on British conduct, calling the liberation of American slaves "one of the greatest outrages ever committed on the rights of individuals by a civilized nation."[77] After British officials had several times reaffirmed their decision respecting the *Enterprise*, Calhoun in 1840 introduced a series of resolutions in the Senate asserting the slave owners' rights under international law. He supported them in a speech that began as a strong logical argument and became an excoriation of Britain's antislavery posture, which he contrasted with that nation's repressive treatment of Ireland, India, and China. When the time came for voting on the resolutions, an obscure northern senator moved to lay them on the table, arguing that the United States should not claim the right to recover slaves from within a foreign jurisdiction. But every one of his senatorial colleagues voted against him and in support of Calhoun.[78] Six months later, as if in answer to the Senate's action, British authorities freed 38 more American slaves when another vessel, the *Hermosa*, was wrecked on one of the Bahamas.[79]

The southern element that controlled American foreign policy wanted security for the future even more than indemnity for the losses already suffered by slaveholders. Consequently, in the spring of 1838 Stevenson was instructed to cease arguing the issue on its merits and try instead to negotiate a convention providing for the disposition of all slaves that might thereafter "be carried by force, or be driven by stress of weather within the British colonies." What the United States government desired, Stevenson informed Palmerston, apparently in all seriousness, was that British authorities "refrain from forcing liberty" on such slaves. They should be either left aboard their ship or confined within a military installation until reclaimed by their owners. The foreign secretary, in his reply, did not pass up the opportunity to indulge in a little sarcasm. "It is difficult to suppose," he wrote, "that any slave who is brought into a situation in which the choice of freedom is placed within his reach can require the employment of force to induce him to avail himself of that choice." As for the proposed convention, he rejected the idea in such emphatic terms that Stevenson thought it useless to pursue the matter further.[80] The American government had thus failed again in its efforts to protect slaveholding rights beyond the limits of its jurisdiction.

Meanwhile, Palmerston and Stevenson had begun to discuss details of settling the *Comet* and *Encomium* claims, disagreeing over the number of slaves involved, the method of evaluation, and the amount of interest to be paid. The claims were referred to the Lords of the Treasury for investigation, and the settlement did not reach its final stages until 1839. On May 2 of that year, Palmerston announced that Britain would pay approximately $115,000, including interest and certain expenses, for 179 slaves liberated. The per capita value, set at close to $500, was relatively generous, considering the fact that, as Stevenson noted, "a large portion of the slaves were women and children, some of them under five years of age."[81] The American government was then left with the task of distributing the money among the claimants. About four-fifths of it actually went to insurance companies that had already reimbursed most of the slave owners.[82] The work was not finished until 1843, when Congress passed a law for the proportional distribution of $7,695 remaining in the indemnity fund. Joshua R. Giddings, who had recently been censured by the House for his antislavery vehemence, seized the opportunity to make a long speech denouncing the federal government's involvement in the protection of slavery.[83]

The subject of slavery dominated Stevenson's five years of service as American minister in London. Besides his devoted attention to the *Comet-Encomium-Enterprise* claims, he spent much time protesting the conduct of the British navy in its efforts to suppress the international slave trade. Furthermore, his own slaveholding background drew him into an unseemly public quarrel with a famous member of Parliament. At an abolitionist meeting in 1838, the Irish leader Daniel O'Connell reportedly pilloried Stevenson as "a slave-breeder, one of those beings who rear up slaves for the traffic." Stevenson took steps toward challenging O'Connell to a duel but in the end let the matter drop.[84]

Meanwhile, other events and controversies, dealt with primarily in Washington, were disturbing Anglo-American relations. For one thing, a major crisis resulted from the burning of the American steamer *Caroline* during the Canadian rebellion of 1837. It was soon followed by the renewal of a dangerous quarrel over the boundary between Maine and New Brunswick. A new British ministry headed by Sir Robert Peel decided to send a special mission to the United States to seek resolution of the accumulated differences between the two countries. The well-known British banker, Alexander Baring, now Lord Ashburton, accordingly set out for Washington early in 1842. Upon his arrival, he found himself in the midst of a new public uproar over the liberation of still another shipload of American slaves in the British West Indies.

In the autumn of 1841, the brig *Creole* was en route from Virginia to Louisiana with a cargo of tobacco and 135 slaves when a revolt broke out on board. Nineteen of the blacks, led by a man named Madison Washington, seized control of the vessel, killing one passenger during the struggle and wounding several officers and members of the crew. They then sailed to Nassau, where officials set all of the slaves free. Even the mutineers were released after being held in custody for a number of months. Orders from London forbade their return to the United States for trial, there being no Anglo-American extradition agreement in force at the time, and the local admiralty court dismissed charges against them in Nassau on grounds of insufficient evidence.[85] Thus ended the most successful slave rebellion in American history, achieved with British collaboration.[86]

Southerners were furious, and all the more so because antislavery radicals took the British side in the diplomatic controversy that followed. Release of the slaves, said Calhoun, was "the most atrocious outrage ever perpetrated on the American people,"[87] and similar expressions of anger came from the Virginian in the White House, John Tyler. Although Secretary of State Daniel Webster tried to exercise a restraining influence, Ashburton found the president "very sore and testy" about the *Creole* and "not a little disposed to be obstinate on the subject."[88] Webster condemned the British action as a violation of the law of nations and instructed the American minister in London, Edward Everett, to demand indemnification of the slave owners.[89] Tyler insisted that in addition some kind of guarantee for the future should be written into the treaty under discussion, but public opinion in England blocked any such result. "Touching on the Creole affair," Foreign Secretary Lord Aberdeen wrote to Ashburton, "I very much fear it will be impossible to give any positive security against a repetition of the same kind of proceeding." Aberdeen also refused to allow the inclusion of mutiny on the list of crimes to be made extraditable.[90]

As it finally emerged, the Webster-Ashburton Treaty settled the Northeast boundary dispute and established a policy of cooperative action against the African slave trade, but the text contained no mention of the *Creole* or of the issues associated with it. The best that Ashburton could offer was an informal promise, made without authorization from London, that British officials would avoid "officious interference" with American ships driven by necessity into West Indian ports. That meager concession nevertheless satisfied Calhoun as a temporary disposition of the problem, and it was grudgingly accepted by Tyler.[91]

Thus the claims resulting from the liberation of slaves on the *Enterprise*, *Hermosa*, and *Creole* slipped into abeyance, while the promise of British restraint in the future did nothing to resolve the important issues that had been raised. The basic question was whether the slaves, once they arrived in a West Indian port, continued to be under American jurisdiction or became subject to British municipal law. The answer depended partly upon whether slaves under international law were distinguishable or indistinguishable from ordinary property such as animals and commodities. British spokesmen maintained that their nation, having abolished slavery, was under no obligation to acknowledge within its own jurisdiction the force of any foreign law treating persons as property. American officials replied that the slave system of the British West Indies remained partly intact after 1833 because of the transitional apprenticeship system that was established, and that in any case, British domestic legislation could not unilaterally change the law of nations; that slaves aboard an American ship on the high seas were property under American law and therefore under the law of nations, and that their status remained the same if the ship was forced by distress into a foreign port. Always underlying the American argument was the assumption, still much disputed in Congress but unreservedly embraced by northerners as well as southerners in the Department of State, that according to the laws and Constitution of the United States, slaves were property and nothing else.

After a decade of further diplomatic exchanges on the subject of the freed slaves, Britain and the United States in 1853 signed a convention establishing a joint commission to deal with the extensive list of private claims outstanding against both governments. It included the customary provision that cases disagreed upon by the commission were to be submitted to an umpire. The man chosen for that post was Joshua Bates, a native

New Englander who had long been resident in London as a banking associate of the Baring family.[92] Predictably, the commissioners failed to reach agreement on the *Enterprise, Hermosa,* and *Creole* claims. Bates accordingly studied the evidence and in the winter of 1854–55 rendered decisions that turned out to be uniformly in favor of the American claimants.[93] Speaking of the *Enterprise* case, he declared: "At the time of the transaction on which this claim is founded, slavery existed by law in several countries, and was not wholly abolished in the British dominions; it could not then be contrary to the law of nations, and the *Enterprise* was as much entitled to protection as though her cargo consisted of any other description of property." And with respect to the *Creole* he said: "The municipal law of England can not authorize a magistrate to violate the law of nations by invading with an armed force the vessel of a friendly nation that has committed no offense, and forcibly dissolving the relations which by the laws of his country the captain is bound to preserve and enforce on board."[94] Bates awarded $49,000 to insurance companies for the slaves on the *Enterprise,* $16,000 to insurance companies for the slaves on the *Hermosa,* and $110,330, mostly to individuals, for the slaves on the *Creole.*[95]

The *Creole* affair had an explosive effect on American politics as well as on American diplomacy. It took place during the later stages of the long struggle over antislavery petitions sent to Congress—a struggle that had begun in 1836 and reached a dramatic climax on the floor of the House of Representatives in January 1842 with an attempt to censure John Quincy Adams. While Adams elaborately defended himself to the eventual frustration of his adversaries, American abolitionists were cheering the liberation of the *Creole* slaves and urging the British government to reject all demands for reimbursement of the slave owners. The abolitionist point of view was incorporated in a series of nine resolutions that Joshua Giddings laid provocatively before the House on March 21. Slavery, their argument ran, existed only by virtue of state law, which did not extend to the high seas. The constitutional authority of the federal government did extend to the high seas but not to the protection of slavery. Therefore, when the Negroes on board the *Creole* asserted their natural right to freedom, they "violated no law of the United States" and were "liable to no punishment."[96]

The deadly anger with which the majority received the reading of the resolutions seems to have intimidated Giddings, for he soon rose to withdraw them from consideration. But it was too late. A motion of censure, which accused him of justifying mutiny and murder, was introduced immediately, and his request for adequate time to prepare a defense was brushed aside. The motion passed the next day by a vote of 125 to 69. Giddings promptly resigned and returned home to Ohio. There, in a special election, he won the overwhelming approval of his constituents, receiving 95 percent of the votes cast. By May, he had returned to his seat in Congress.[97]

Although Giddings did not stand alone in the House of Representatives, there were at this time no such voices of antislavery radicalism in the Senate and certainly none in the executive branch of the federal government. A striking feature of the long-running controversy over slaves liberated in British West Indian ports was the consistency with which the Department of State followed proslavery theory in all diplomatic correspondence and negotiation on the subject. It made little difference whether Democrats or Whigs, southerners or northerners were in charge. Webster was just as emphatic as Forsyth, for instance, in giving American slavery the character of a national institution fully protected by the Constitution.[98]

THE UNITED STATES government, by its habitual willingness to act as an agent of slaveholders, made slavery an explicit and troublesome issue in American diplomacy, especially in relations with Great Britain. But there were also other ways in which the peculiar institution significantly influenced American foreign policy. One example deserving close attention is the attitude of the government toward Saint Domingue, the French colony that came to be known as Haiti. It was an attitude fixed during the presidency of George Washington and sustained for approximately seventy years.

The black people of Saint Domingue, most of them slaves, rose in bloody revolt during the French Revolution. Part of the dominant planter class was killed off, and the rest fled the island, many taking refuge in the United States. The blacks defeated British as well as French attempts to reestablish European control of the island and then in 1804 declared themselves to be an independent nation.[99] Americans had good reason to be grateful to the Haitians, whose successful defense of their country against Napoleonic efforts to reconquer it cleared the way for the Louisiana Purchase in 1803. Besides, the war in Europe had opened the island to American trade, and the Haitians, in breaking away from colonial rule, were paying Americans the tribute of imitation. Yet the Haitian Revolution inspired much more alarm than sympathy in the United States for it provided American slaves with a model of violent resistance and thereby embodied the worst nightmares of a slaveholding society. In southern consciousness long afterward, the very name of the place remained a synonym for their ultimate danger. "I am old enough to remember the horrors of St. Domingo," wrote Chief Justice Roger B. Taney on the eve of Lincoln's election in 1860, "and a few days will determine whether anything like it is to be visited upon any portion of our own Southern countrymen."[100]

Beginning in 1791, the Washington administration advanced over $700,000 to help the French planters of Haiti in their resistance to the revolt. Charged against the Revolutionary War debt owed to France, the money was used to buy arms and other supplies in the United States.[101] This experiment in aiding the suppression of a servile rebellion on foreign soil came to an end when the National Convention assumed power in France and decreed emancipation for the slaves of Saint Domingue. Later, as a strategic move in the undeclared naval war with France, President John Adams entered into temporary collaboration with Haitian leader Toussaint L'Ouverture, but that policy was not continued by his successor. President Jefferson favored the restoration of French control in Saint Domingue and lent some encouragement to Napoleon's plans for reconquest of the colony.[102] By 1803, the French military effort there had become a disaster, and Napoleon, giving up his dream of a new French empire in America, sold Louisiana to the United States. The Haitian declaration of independence, following soon thereafter, was not a welcome event for Jefferson. On the contrary, despite considerable opposition from commercial interests, he decided that all trade with the black revolutionaries should be suspended. Congress enacted legislation to that effect early in 1806 and renewed it the following year.[103]

The situation was complex and so were Jefferson's motives. For one thing, he feared that an independent Haiti would soon come under British domination. In addition, he probably hoped to get Napoleon's help in prying the Floridas loose from Spain. Consequently, there were elements of truth in the complaint of some Federalist critics that the embargo on trade with Saint Domingue had been dictated from Paris. But underlying such immediate strategic considerations was the visceral apprehension with which most southerners viewed this self-proclaimed nation of rebellious slaves, whose very existence cast a menacing shadow over the slaveholding states of the Union. Jefferson's own son-in-law, John Eppes, issued a warning on the floor of Congress that independence for Haiti would bring "immediate and horrible destruction on the fairest portion of America."[104]

As early as 1792, Jefferson and other Virginians had been disturbed by reports of slave plots that seemed linked to the revolt in Saint Domingue. Then, in the summer of 1800, fear became reality. A large number of armed slaves, led by a tall young black named Gabriel began to assemble near Richmond with the intention of marching on the city. But a heavy rainstorm forced them to disperse, and the conspiracy collapsed as troops called out by Governor James Monroe began arresting the ringleaders. Although no white person had been harmed, at least twenty-six slaves were hanged.[105] Many Virginians had qualms about such wholesale executions, and the General Assembly passed a resolution requesting the governor "to correspond with the President of the United States on the subject of purchasing lands without the limits of this State, whither persons obnoxious to the laws or dangerous to the peace of society may be removed."[106]

Accordingly, Monroe addressed a letter to Jefferson on the subject and in due course received a reply. The president invited the Virginians to make their request more specific, and he canvassed all the places to which "dangerous characters" like Gabriel might conceivably be exiled. For various reasons, no part of the North American continent seemed suitable. South America was a possibility. The West Indies were more promising, and Jefferson even toyed with the idea of sending rebellious blacks to Saint Domingue, where their behavior would no doubt be regarded as "meritorious" instead of "criminal." As a last resort, he concluded, there was always Africa. The Virginia legislature responded with a resolution proposing the purchase of land in Africa or South America as a place of exile for slaves guilty of conspiracy and insurrection.[107]

Jefferson, who seems to have had no doubt that this was legitimate business of the federal government, wrote to Rufus King, the American minister in London, asking him to find out if such slaves might be received in the colony of Sierra Leone. That social experiment on the west coast of Africa had been established by a private company of British abolitionists as a haven for freed slaves. Sierra Leone was already troubled by unruly elements in its population, however, and the proposal to make the colony a dumping ground for American malcontents understandably found little favor among British officials or the company's directors. King could only report that his efforts were getting nowhere. Jefferson continued to assure the Virginians that he had the matter "sincerely at heart" and would keep it under his "constant attention," but nothing further was done.[108]

The suspension of commerce with Haiti, though in effect for only two years, was continued by more general legislation affecting American foreign trade: first, the famous Jeffersonian Embargo of 1807, and then, the Non-intercourse Act of 1809. When a Massachusetts congressman proposed to exempt Haiti from the operation of the latter measure, John Randolph denounced his amendment as a threat to southern security, and it was defeated by a vote of 97 to 1.[109] In 1810, the measure known as "Macon's Bill No. 2" reopened the possibility of trade with Haiti, which at that time was divided by warfare between rival native leaders. Some of the first American vessels sent to the island ran afoul of Henri Christophe, the black ruler of northern Haiti. He seized a number of cargoes, declaring that they would serve as reimbursement for money that had been taken from him by fraud in Baltimore. The inevitable result was a list of claims that the United States government was expected to press against a nation whose existence it refused to recognize. Forty years later, those claims were still unfinished business for the Department of State.[110]

The chronic disorder in Haiti may have been sufficient reason for withholding recognition, but not after 1820. In that year, Jean Pierre Boyer reunited the country and began a long period of relatively stable rule. One immediate result was an increase in the commerce between the United States and Haiti. It amounted to more than $4 million in 1820–21, or about 4 percent of all American foreign trade that year.[111] Furthermore, in 1822, the Monroe administration, with almost unanimous support from Congress, began recognizing various Latin American republics that had secured their independence more recently than Haiti. Yet when the Boyer government requested recognition that same year, it was refused without the courtesy of a direct reply.[112] In a special message to Congress dated February 25, 1823, Monroe justified non-recognition partly on the grounds that France had not yet acknowledged the independence of her former colony.[113] This explanation coolly ignored the fact that Spain likewise had not acknowledged the independence of those Latin American nations with which the United States was in the process of establishing diplomatic relations. Significantly, when France *did* recognize Haitian independence two years later, the action had no effect on American policy.

Everyone knew that the rejection of Haiti was dictated primarily by southern sensitivities, which were painfully tender in the early 1820s. The South had been shocked by the amount of antislavery feeling manifested in the great Missouri controversy of 1819–21. Then exposure of the Denmark Vesey conspiracy in South Carolina sent a wave of alarm through all the slaveholding states during the summer of 1822—that is, just as Boyer was preparing to ask for recognition. To anxious southerners, the request seemed absurd because of Haiti's racial character and menacing because of Haiti's revolutionary tradition. An article in *Niles' Register*, a Baltimore publication, put it plainly enough. The author first praised Haiti's "enlightened government," which, he said, was more liberal than most of those functioning in Europe, but then he concluded: "The time has not yet come for a surrender of our feelings about color, nor is it fitting at any time that the public safety should be endangered."[114] Monroe, in his special message, preferred to be delicate rather than clear: "Regarding the high interest of our happy Union and looking to every circumstance which may by any possibility affect the tranquillity of any part, however remotely, and guarding against such injury by suitable precautions, it is the duty of this Government to promote by all the means in its power and by a fair and honorable policy the best interest of every other part and thereby of the whole."[115]

The official American attitude did not change when John Quincy Adams succeeded Monroe in the presidency. At one of the first Adams cabinet meetings, Secretary of State Henry Clay ventured to suggest that the independence of Haiti would probably have to be recognized before very long. Adams stated his objections to such a departure from the policy of his predecessor, and Clay apparently never raised the question again.[116] Both Monroe and Adams did send agents to look after American commercial interests in Haiti, but the Haitian government refused to take any formal notice of their presence until it had been accorded recognition.[117]

Southern concern about Haiti intruded upon one of the major proposals of the Adams administration in the realm of foreign policy—that is, upon the question of whether the United States should participate in a conference of independent American nations to be held at Panama in 1826. When Adams and Clay sought congressional approval for sending a delegation, they ran into strong opposition that was both partisan and sectional. Southerners objected especially to several items on the agenda that promised to involve the United States in international discussions of slavery. One was the possibility of cooperation for suppression of the African slave trade. Another was the question of relations with Haiti.[118]

The federal government, said Senator Robert Y. Hayne of South Carolina, had no power to interfere with the institution of slavery and must not enter into any discussion of the subject with other nations. That rule of silence extended to the problem of Haiti. "We never can acknowledge her independence," Hayne asserted. "Other States will do as they please—but let us take the high ground, that these questions belong to a class, which the peace and safety of a large portion of our Union forbids us even to discuss." His words were echoed in the House of Representatives by another South Carolinian, James Hamilton, who declared: "Haytien [sic] independence is not to be tolerated in any form. Our opinions are derived from a solemn conviction that the consequences of this recognition would be fatal to our repose. . . . The municipal laws of many of the Southern States would conflict with the provisions of a treaty containing such a recognition, and produce a concussion which must end either in the annihilation of these States, or the destruction of the power of the General Government."[119]

The emotional level of the debate was often extraordinary. John M. Berrien of Georgia, confessing that he could scarcely control his feelings on the subject, demanded: "Can the people of the South permit the intercourse which would result from establishing relations of any sort with Haiti? Is the emancipated slave, his hands yet reeking in the blood of his murdered master, to be admitted into their ports, to spread the doctrines of insurrection, and to strengthen and invigorate them, by exhibiting in his own person an example of successful revolt?" Thomas Hart Benton of Missouri spoke in the same vein. The safety of the slaveholding states, he declared, would not permit "black Consuls and Ambassadors to establish themselves in our cities, and to parade through our country, and give their fellow blacks in the United States, proof in hand of the honors which await them, for a like successful effort on their part."[120]

Both the Senate and the House did finally vote their approval of the Panama mission, but the United States, as it turned out, did not participate in the Pan-American congress of 1826 because one of its delegates died on the way and the other arrived after adjournment. The conference took no action regarding Haiti, which remained a diplomatic outcast among the independent nations of the western hemisphere.[121]

Meanwhile, the United States continued its policy of refusing recognition while promoting trade with the black republic. By 1844, the State Department was maintaining three commercial agents in Haiti, and yet recognition seemed further away than ever. In earlier decades, pressure for more formal relations with Haiti had come primarily from maritime interests, but in the late 1830s the cause was taken up by the abolitionists as a means of circumventing the gag rule against antislavery petitions. During the winter of 1838–39, Congress received more than two hundred petitions for recognition of Haiti.[122] Even a moderate southerner like Hugh Swinton

Legaré of South Carolina was provoked to violent anger. In the House of Representatives, Legaré declared that such memorials were abolitionist in purpose and amounted to declarations of war on the South. "They are treason," he declared. "Yes, sir, I pronounce the authors of such things traitors—traitors not to their country only, but to the whole human race."[123] In 1843, Congressman John Quincy Adams proposed that the House Committee on Foreign Affairs recommend establishment of a consulate in Haiti. Every other member of the committee voted against him, including three northerners whom he criticized in his diary for their "submission to the South." Adams apparently forgot that in his twelve years as secretary of state and president he had consistently opposed recognition of any kind.[124]

In 1844, after two decades of relative stability, Haiti entered another period of turmoil. The Spanish-speaking population on the eastern side of the island, which had been unwillingly annexed to Haiti in 1822, declared its independence as the Dominican Republic. The Haitian government failed in repeated efforts at reconquest but stubbornly refused to acknowledge the separation. American interest in the new republic centered on preventing Britain and France from obtaining too much influence there and on the strategic value of Samana Bay as a naval coaling station. The Dominican leadership, in seeking recognition and help from the United States, shrewdly emphasized the blackness of the Haitian population while exaggerating the number and influence of white persons in Dominican society. Actually, many if not most of the Dominicans calling themselves white were of a mixed blood that would have meant classification as Negroes in the United States. Nevertheless, even John C. Calhoun and John Tyler allowed themselves to be persuaded that the racial differences between the two parts of the island were enough to justify recognizing the Dominican government instead of treating it as a pariah like Haiti. But for a number of reasons, including the complicated international politics of the Caribbean, no such recognition was forthcoming during the antebellum years.[125] When President Millard Fillmore in 1852 ventured the suggestion that it might be time to consider establishing normal relations, not only with the Dominican Republic and Haiti, but with Liberia as well, he was tacitly pointing up the fact that the standard and much reiterated American policy of recognizing de facto governments did not extend to black nations.[126]

Of course some commercial interests went on urging recognition of Haiti as a matter of good business, and some antislavery voices went on protesting that the United States, in its treatment of Haiti, was betraying the principles of the American Revolution.[127] But the southern view prevailed as American policy continued to deny Haiti "the consideration to which her actual independence and generally acknowledged sovereignty entitled her."[128] That policy did not change until slaveholders ceased to be a major force in American politics.

MUCH MORE DIFFICULT to assess is the influence of slavery on American expansion and expansionism in the antebellum era. The presence of such influence can scarcely be doubted, but the difficulty lies in determining its weight at each juncture and whether or not it was ever predominant. No one any longer accepts at face value the abolitionist view that the acquisition of Florida, the Texan Revolution, the annexation of Texas, the war with Mexico, and the persistent efforts to acquire Cuba were components of a slaveholders' master plan for enlarging the domain of their peculiar institution.[129] Yet the "slave-power conspiracy" thesis did not miss the mark entirely. Expansionism had many sources and was as much a national as a sectional phenomenon, but in several manifestations it clearly reflected the dynamics of the slaveholding interest. Politically, moreover, expansionism was stronger in the party with the stronger southern accent—first the Jeffersonian Republicans and then the Jacksonian Democrats. The connection became more pronounced after 1840, when the Democratic party embraced expansionism with growing fervor and at the same time displayed increasing subservience to the South. Northern Democrats like James Buchanan who voted for the annexation of Texas and advocated the acquisition of Cuba were obviously doing so in part to gratify southern wishes and court southern favor. The effect of this warp in the pattern of political power was sometimes little different from what a carefully wrought conspiracy might have been expected to produce.

Concern about Florida as a haven for fugitive slaves had been one of the reasons for the aggressive American policy that led to acquisition of the province from Spain. The transfer was made by treaty, signed in 1819 but not ratified until 1821. Those, of course, were the very years of the Missouri controversy, the nation's first major crisis over slavery. Secretary of State John Quincy Adams seems to have negotiated the treaty without any qualms about enlarging the slaveholding portion of the nation. A thoroughgoing expansionist, he regarded the entire North American continent as the "proper dominion" of the United States.[130] By 1820, Adams was having some second thoughts, saying privately that the treaty perhaps ought to contain an article prohibiting slavery in the ceded territory, but he made no official proposal to that effect.[131] The scattered antislavery objections to the acquisition of Florida were offset by southern complaints about the treaty's relinquishment of American claims to Texas. President James Monroe did not regret that concession, however. Troubled by the intensity of sectional feeling displayed in the Missouri struggle, he feared that any efforts at further expansion to the southwest would cause difficulties menacing to the Union. Southerners, he concluded, should be "content with Florida for the present."[132]

No such concern inhibited the two succeeding presidents. Adams had scarcely settled into the White House in 1825 before his secretary of state, Henry Clay, was instructing the minister to Mexico, Joel R. Poinsett, to seek a boundary adjustment transferring some part of Texas to the United States. The Mexicans, Clay suggested, might find the transfer desirable because it would place their capital city nearer the center of their country.[133] For the next eleven years, the Adams and Jackson administrations, in negotiations directed and conducted almost entirely by southerners, tried repeatedly to pressure Mexico into selling all or part of Texas. Their efforts not only failed every time but made Mexican leaders increasingly suspicious and unreceptive.[134]

Then, in 1836, there came the Texan revolution. Suddenly an independent Texas appeared to be available for the taking, but Jackson proceeded with uncharacteristic restraint, waiting a full year before even extending formal recognition to the new republic. He and his handpicked successor, Martin Van Buren, knew that annexation would probably mean war with Mexico, and they also feared that it would be dangerously divisive for the Democratic party and the nation.[135] Sectional discord over slavery had already reached such an alarming level that Van Buren in his inaugural address devoted more attention to it than to any other national problem. The Texas question burst into national politics just as the House of Representatives was imposing its notorious restriction on abolitionist petitions. Throughout the North, denunciation of the gag rule merged with opposition to the annexation of Texas in a display of antislavery sentiment much broader than the abolitionist movement. It was at this time, and with Texas primarily in mind, that certain antislavery leaders began to cry out warnings against a "slave-power conspiracy" seeking to dictate national policy in its own selfish interest.[136] The atmosphere of rising tension encouraged Van Buren, a cautious man who probably had little appetite for expansion anyhow, to avoid action likely to precipitate a crisis. In the summer of 1837, his secretary of state, John Forsyth of Georgia, rejected a formal Texan request for annexation. The following year, resolutions favoring annexation failed in both houses of Congress.[137]

Clearly, antislavery feeling, together with a widespread disinclination to aggravate the slavery controversy, was impeding the extension of American sovereignty over Texas, and it continued for a time to do so. With anti-Texas sentiment heavily concentrated in the Whig party, the election of William Henry Harrison and a Whig Congress in 1840 gave annexationists no reason to hope for anything better than the four frustrating years under Van Buren. The appointment of Daniel Webster as secretary of state tended to reinforce such negative expectations. Perhaps nothing other than an extraordinary historical accident could have opened a passage through the barriers of circumstance that blocked the road to annexation. Harrison's death soon after he took office brought John Tyler, an ardent expansionist, into the White House. This crucial change did not begin to affect the government's Texas policy, however, until Tyler had broken with his party and freed himself from its restraints. The group of men who gathered about him in his political isolation included some of the leading Texas enthusiasts, such as Thomas W. Gilmer and Abel P. Upshur of Virginia, Robert J. Walker of Mississippi, and the Kentucky-born journalist, Duff Green. By the spring of 1843, when he at last eased Webster out of the cabinet, Tyler and his "Texas junto" were ready to launch a new annexation movement.[138] They faced the huge task of mobilizing American public opinion so compellingly as to extract from the Senate, with its hostile Whig majority, a two-thirds vote in favor of a treaty of annexation. This meant, more specifically, that they needed to gain the united support of southerners in both parties and the united support of Democrats in both sections. But the kind of appeal likely to promote southern solidarity would tend to aggravate sectional tensions and bring northern Democrats under increased antislavery pressure. Fortunately for the junto, national interest and southern interest in annexation could both be stimulated by exploiting certain international implications of the Texas question.

The remarkable territorial expansion of the United States in the 1840s took place against a background of intense Anglo-American rivalry and friction in various parts of the world from African waters to the Pacific Northwest. Most notably, the festering dispute over the Oregon boundary lent credence to American suspicion of British intentions in several other parts of North America. Expansionism fortified with resurgent Anglophobia became arguably a strategy of defense against the potential encroachments of a traditional enemy. Moreover, according to some influential southerners, British foreign policy posed a serious threat, not only to the national and commercial interests of the United States but also to the

institution of slavery. The historic parliamentary legislation of 1833 emancipating slaves in the British West Indies had been a shocking turn of
events for southern slaveholders, and all the more so because of the
encouragement that it gave to American abolitionists.[139] British hostility
to American slavery had been forcefully demonstrated in the series of incidents from 1831 to 1841 involving slave ships driven by circumstance into
West Indian ports. Increasingly, the British government seemed to be
acting virtually as international sponsor of the antislavery movement. The
secretary for foreign affairs, Lord Aberdeen, acknowledged in 1843 that his
country was "constantly exerting herself to procure the general abolition
of slavery throughout the world."[140]

By that time, southern apprehensions centered especially on Britain's
intentions with regard to Texas. British officials, it was said, were scheming to
bring about the abolition of slavery in that republic as a first step toward
undermining the institution in the United States. Duff Green wrote from
London, where he was serving as Tyler's executive agent, that annexation was
"the only means of preventing Texas falling into the hands of English fanatics and thus becoming a depot for smugglers and runaway slaves."[141] Andrew
Jackson became convinced of the danger and described it this way: "Great
Britain is trying to obtain the liberation of the slaves in Texas for the avowed
purpose of coercing the South and West into this measure by destroying the
value of this property and opening the way for our slaves to run away to
Texas." Abel P. Upshur, who succeeded Webster as secretary of state, confided
to Calhoun his belief that Britain was "determined to abolish slavery
throughout the American continent" and had formulated her Texas policy
with that purpose in mind.[142] Upshur and Calhoun agreed that British spon-
sorship of abolitionism masked a grand scheme to build a monopoly of world
commerce on the ruination of the American economy. The editor of the
Washington Madisonian, Tyler's political organ, hammered away at the same
theme in a number of editorials.[143] These and other southerners undoubtedly
exaggerated and perhaps even largely imagined the British threat to American slavery, but that they exaggerated their own fears is by no means so
clear.[144] Southern expansionism, like national expansionism, contained elements of defensive imperialism—that is, the disposition to forestall a
perceived threat of encroachment by making a preemptive advance. In the
southern case, this defensive mode was probably dominant, although it
blended imperceptibly with more aggressive aspirations to extend the geographic limits and political power of the slaveholding culture.

Whatever may have been the effect on southern opinion, it is unlikely that the outcry about British plans to abolitionize Texas did much good for the annexation cause in the North. There, advocates appealed to the general spirit of expansionism that would soon be epitomized in the phrase "manifest destiny." They stressed the commercial advantages of annexation and the threat that British control of Texas would pose to national security.[145] Opposition on antislavery grounds constituted a formidable obstacle, however, and had to be met more directly. One way of doing so was to attack abolitionists as subversives lending aid to the British in their plotting against the United States.[146] Another was to maintain that balancing the annexation of Texas with the acquisition of Oregon would promote sectional harmony by reaffirming and extending the tradition of the Missouri Compromise.[147] But the most unusual attempt to disarm antislavery opposition came from Robert J. Walker in a widely circulated public letter arguing that the presence of Texas in the Union would actually facilitate the extinction of slavery in the United States by gradually drawing the institution southward into Mexico, Central America, and South America.[148]

In October of 1843, as its propaganda campaign gathered momentum, the Tyler administration secretly initiated discussions of annexation with the government of Texas. Although impediments thrown up by the Texan president, Sam Houston, prolonged the negotiations for several months, the preparation of a treaty had nearly been completed when another historical accident intervened. On February 28, 1844, the explosion of a gun aboard the warship *Princeton* during a presidential excursion killed eight persons, one of whom was Secretary of State Upshur.[149] Tyler waited only a week before nominating Calhoun as Upshur's successor, and the Senate promptly voted its unanimous approval.[150] Reluctantly accepting the appointment, Calhoun arrived in Washington near the end of March and immediately set to work with the Texan representatives. The treaty of annexation was formally signed on April 12 and transmitted to the Senate ten days later. Tyler accompanied it with a message (his first official statement on the subject) in which he argued that union with Texas would benefit all parts of the United States. His only reference to slavery and the Anglo-abolitionist threat was very delicately phrased. For the southern states, he said, annexation would mean "protection and security to their peace and tranquillity, as well against all domestic and foreign efforts to disturb them."[151]

Tyler's appointment of Calhoun, the most noted defender of slavery in the country, had been announced at about the time that word of the annexation treaty was leaking out to the general public. Abolitionists were not alone in their mounting wrath at the revelations. In a lead editorial on March 16, for instance, the *Washington National Intelligencer* denounced the "unauthorized and clandestine manner" in which the administration had reversed previously established policy and "gone a-wooing" to the government of Texas. Although the treaty went before the Senate in executive session, the veil of official secrecy was soon swept aside. Benjamin Tappan of Ohio, the older brother of abolitionists Arthur and Lewis Tappan, sent his confidential copy of the treaty and accompanying papers to the *New York Evening Post*, which quickly published them. Tappan's colleagues formally reprimanded him for his "flagrant violation of the rules of the Senate and disregard of its authority," but they subsequently removed the injunction of secrecy and ordered the printing of twenty thousand copies of the documents for their own use.[152]

Exposure of the Texas documents to public view provoked a furor because they gave the impression that the primary purpose of annexation was to protect American slavery from the abolitionist plotting of Great Britain. Exposed to public view, for example, were Upshur dispatches to the American minister in London containing extravagant descriptions of the British threat, together with pronouncements on the ineradicability of slavery in the United States.[153] The most sensational item, however, was Calhoun's letter of April 18 to Richard Pakenham, the British minister in Washington. After taking perfunctory note of assurances from Lord Aberdeen that the British government had no intention of interfering with slavery in the southern states, the new secretary of state responded at length to Aberdeen's acknowledgment that Britain favored abolition everywhere in the world. He began by explaining and justifying the annexation of Texas as a response to British antislavery designs. "This step," he wrote, "has been taken as the most effectual, if not the only, means of guarding against the threatened danger." He went on to declare that every nation must determine its own racial policy and that in the United States the decision rested entirely with the individual members of the Union. The federal government had no right to interfere but only the duty to protect each state in whatever policy it might adopt with respect to the African race. After this enunciation of proslavery constitutional theory, there followed some familiar proslavery discourse on the consequences of abolition. Calhoun cited census figures to demonstrate that free blacks were the most wretched element of the American population, in contrast, he said, with southern slaves, who enjoyed a

degree of health and comfort equal to that of any laboring class in Christendom and who represented the African race's highest attainment in morals,
intelligence, and civilization. Abolition of slavery in the United States, he
concluded, would be a "calamity" for the whole country, but especially for the
slaves themselves.[154]

Historians disagree about Calhoun's motivation in sending off such an
inflammatory communication at such a critical time.[155] The letter may have
been intended to rally and unite the South on behalf of annexation. It may
have been a political maneuver against Van Buren. But most obviously it was
a move to install proslavery doctrine as official national doctrine in the conduct of foreign relations. For a man returning to appointive federal office
after an interval of nineteen years during which he had swung from nationalism to extreme sectionalism, the letter served as a kind of inaugural address
breathing defiance to the North.

Before his death, Upshur had sounded out members of the Senate and
arrived at a conviction "little short of absolute certainty" that the treaty of
annexation would be approved.[156] Whether or not this prediction was accurate at the time, Calhoun's appointment in March and publication of the
Texas documents in April dimmed the prospects of success by centering
attention more than ever on the connection between annexation and slavery.
Then in May, annexation politics were affected by a dramatic development in
presidential politics. Van Buren and Clay, by far the leading candidates in
their respective parties, had both issued anti-Texas statements. The Whigs
nominated Clay by acclamation, but at the Democratic convention, with nine
out of every ten southern delegates voting against him, Van Buren failed to
get the required two-thirds majority. Instead, after a number of ballots, the
convention nominated James K. Polk of Tennessee on an expansionist platform that called for "the reoccupation of Oregon and the re-annexation of
Texas."[157] Suddenly, Texas had become a clear-cut partisan issue in a presidential election year. Van Buren's defeat was at first detrimental to the
annexation movement, but it proved crucially beneficial in the end.

After several weeks of debate, the treaty came to a final vote on June 8
and was overwhelmingly defeated, receiving only sixteen votes when thirty-
four were needed. Eight Democrats, including some resentful friends of Van
Buren, joined twenty-seven Whigs in opposition.[158] The decision seemed
devastatingly conclusive, but a number of negative votes reflected more hostility to the president and his annexation strategy than to annexation itself,
and the Senate was in any case a dubious mirror of public sentiment on the

subject. Tyler turned immediately to the House of Representatives, control of which had been recaptured by the Democrats in the midterm elections. Together with the treaty and all documents already provided to the Senate, he sent a message proposing ratification "by some other form of proceeding."[159] He meant a joint resolution, which would require simple majorities in both houses instead of a two-thirds majority in the Senate. The first session of the Twenty-eighth Congress came to an end before any action could be attempted. When members reconvened in December 1844, Tyler's hand had been strengthened by the outcome of the presidential election.

Polk's victory over Clay, although momentous in its consequences, was by such a narrow margin that it had little meaning as a referendum on Texas or anything else. Tyler and other annexationists nevertheless hailed it as a popular mandate. "The decision of the people and the States on this great and interesting subject has been decisively manifested," the president declared in his annual message to Congress on December 3.[160] Soon a variety of annexation proposals were being introduced in each chamber. The House, with its strong Democratic majority, acted first. On January 25, it voted 120 to 98 for a joint resolution that amounted to an enabling act for the admission of Texas as a full-fledged state. The contest was much closer in the Senate, where an amended version of the resolution finally carried on February 27 by a two-vote margin. On the following afternoon, the House brushed aside last-minute antislavery efforts and concurred in the Senate's amendment with more than fifty votes to spare.[161] "The heaviest calamity that ever befell myself and my country was this day consummated," John Quincy Adams wrote in his diary.[162] Tyler promptly signed the resolution, and on March 3, 1845, his last full day in office, he sent a messenger to Texas with the offer of statehood.[163] Texas accepted and in December of that same year was formally admitted to the Union. Presidential determination had triumphed. So had the Democratic party with its expansionist agenda, and so had the southern slavocracy.

Tyler always insisted that his Texas policy was national rather than sectional in character. "I saw nothing but ... the good, the strength, the happiness, the glory of the whole country in the measure," he declared. He blamed Calhoun for the widespread impression that annexation had been undertaken primarily in the interest of slavery.[164] Surely it is true that Tyler and Polk, in embracing expansionism with so much enthusiasm, tapped into a powerful motive force that overran sectional boundaries. Annexation was supported as a matter of national pride and national purpose by a good many

Americans, including Illinois congressman John Wentworth. An antislavery Democrat who would soon be voting for the Wilmot Proviso, Wentworth told his colleagues that he hoped Oregon, Canada, Cuba, Mexico, and even Patagonia would eventually follow Texas into the Union. God had designed the original thirteen states, he said, "as the center from which civilization, religion, and liberty should radiate and radiate until the whole continent shall bask in their blessing."[165] At the same time, annexation was opposed by many Americans as a matter of national honor and prudence, the argument being that it amounted to an underhanded form of territorial conquest and that it would lead inevitably to war with Mexico.

After all such considerations are duly noted, however, slavery remains the heart of the matter. It was largely the slavery issue that made annexation so dangerously controversial for political leaders and caused the earlier rejection of Texan requests for admission to the Union. Hatred of slavery predominated in the opposition to annexation, and solicitude for slavery, particularly the fear of a British plot to make Texas an entering wedge for abolitionism, was primarily what inspired the aggressive annexation movement launched by the Tyler administration. Tyler, who as a young congressman had bitterly opposed the Missouri Compromise, was arguably the most resolute defender of slavery ever to occupy the presidency, and both of his appointees as secretary of state were proslavery zealots of the first rank.[166] Together, these men brought the slaveholding influence on American foreign policy to its apogee in their successful campaign to expand the federal Union by adding a fifteenth slave state that covered more than a quarter of a million square miles.

WRITING TO UPSHUR in August 1843 about British designs on Texas, Calhoun added: "Connected with this subject, Cuba deserves attention. Great Britain is at work there, as well as in Texas; and both are equally important to our safety."[167] During the next several years, a campaign for the annexation of Cuba got under way in various parts of the United States, overshadowed though it was by other ventures in expansionism.[168] To the South, Cuba like Texas signified both danger and opportunity. The danger was that slavery might somehow be abolished or overthrown on the island, which, said a South Carolina congressman, would then become "a second Hayti to cast the shadow of its ominous gloom over our shores."[169] As for opportunity, that presented itself in the prospect of annexation, which would not only eliminate the danger of emancipation but also strengthen southern political power within the Union and perhaps inspire further American expansion into the Caribbean and Central America. Senator Albert G. Brown of Mississippi with startling candor proclaimed in 1858: "I want Cuba, and I know that sooner or later we must have it. . . . I want Tamaulipas, Potosi, and one or two other Mexican States; and I want them all for the same reason—for the planting or spreading of slavery."[170]

In the early part of the century, however, it was the strategic importance of Cuba that most concerned American leaders, who feared British and French designs on this remnant jewel of the disintegrating Spanish empire. Presidents Jefferson and Madison both explored the possibility of acquiring the island, and Jefferson later wrote to President James Monroe: "I have ever looked on Cuba as the most interesting addition which could ever be made to our system of States. The control which, with Florida Point, this island would give us over the Gulf of Mexico, and the countries and isthmus bordering on it, . . . would fill up the measure of our political well-being."[171] At about the same time, Secretary of State John Quincy Adams was predicting that within half a century the possession of Cuba would have become "indispensable to the continuance and integrity of the Union." The laws of political gravitation, he said, made eventual annexation virtually certain, and in the meantime, the United States preferred that the island remain a Spanish colony.[172] Later pronouncements from the State Department repeatedly threatened armed intervention to keep it so. Edward Livingston (Democrat) stated in 1832, for example, that the American purpose respecting Cuba was "to preserve it in the hands of Spain, even at the expense of a war." Similarly, James Buchanan (Democrat) declared in 1848 that the United States would "resist to the last extremity" its transfer to any other European nation, and John M. Clayton (Whig) added his concurrence a year later, saying that "news of the cession of Cuba to any foreign power would, in the United States, be the instant signal for war."[173]

One other possibility was that the Cubans would declare themselves to be an independent nation. Latin American revolts against Spanish rule had already received the hearty approval of the United States, but sectional influence shaped a different national policy where Cuba was concerned. Southerners feared that a struggle for independence would disrupt Cuban society and lead to the overthrow of slavery. The result, according to Henry Clay, might be "a renewal of those shocking scenes of which a neighboring island was the afflicting theatre." With the shadow of Haiti cast over American thought on the subject, Clay sent assurances to Spain that the United

States would lend no countenance to Cuban independence movements. At the same time, he set about discouraging plans for a joint Colombian-Mexican expedition to liberate the island. During his four-year tenure as secretary of state, it became the established American policy to support maintenance of the status quo in Cuba, and that meant the continuation not only of Spanish rule, but of slavery as well.[174]

Emancipation in the British West Indies heightened American concern about Cuba, which seemed a prime target for British abolitionism allied with British imperialism. In 1843, for example, Daniel Webster directed the American consul at Havana to investigate a report of a plot to erect "a black Military Republic under British protection."[175] Such apprehensions were fed by several abortive slave uprisings on the island, including one in which a British consul was almost certainly involved. A good many Cuban Creoles favored annexation to the United States as the best way of protecting their slave system.[176] Spanish pride and British opposition made a peaceable transfer unlikely, however, and a revolutionary transfer in the Texas fashion was bound to be difficult and dangerous, as Narciso Lopez discovered when he tried it in the years 1848–51.[177] Meanwhile, the Mexican War stimulated American expansionism but at the same time impeded it by reviving the bitter controversy over the extension of slavery. The antislavery principle of the Wilmot Proviso, although aimed specifically at land conquered from Mexico, obviously applied also to Cuba and its three hundred thousand slaves. With one sectional crisis following another after 1846, and with Spain still fiercely resistant, the times were not auspicious for acquisition of the island. What seems most remarkable, in view of the overwhelming odds against success, is the dedication with which three Democratic administrations nevertheless pursued the dream of annexation.

James K. Polk, who had already presided over a vast expansion of American sovereignty, opened the bidding in 1848 by authorizing an offer of up to $100 million for Cuba. The Spanish minister of foreign affairs replied that no government official dared entertain such a proposition and that the Spanish people would rather see the island "sunk in the ocean" than have it transferred to a foreign power.[178] Negotiations for the purchase of Cuba thus seemed hopeless and were suspended for approximately five years, only to be renewed in the spring of 1854 by authority of Franklin Pierce. This was a time of crisis with Spain over the seizure of an American ship, the *Black Warrior*, in Havana harbor. It was also a time of increased alarm over the future of

Cuban slavery, for British pressure and the reform program of a new captain general seemed to be pushing matters rapidly toward emancipation. The dread prospect of an "Africanized" Cuba had induced a good many southerners to support plans for a filibustering expedition to seize control of the island. Its leader, John A. Quitman of Mississippi, expected benevolent noninterference from the Pierce administration, which at first was not entirely hostile to the venture. In the circumstances, then, a renewal of efforts to buy Cuba became the moderate alternative to more aggressive action.[179]

On April 3, Pierce's secretary of state, William L. Marcy, instructed the American minister to Spain, a hyperthyroid annexationist named Pierre Soulé, to offer as much as $130 million for Cuba. If Spain refused, Soulé was to concern himself with the problem of how to "detach that island from the Spanish dominion and from all dependence on any European power."[180] Presumably the word "detach" meant lending assistance to the achievement of Cuban independence. Marcy's militant tones were echoed and amplified six months later in the so-called Ostend Manifesto, which was actually a joint dispatch from Soulé and two other American diplomats, James Buchanan, minister to Britain, and John Y. Mason, minister to France. Written after the three men had held a conference, the document recommended seizure of Cuba if it could not be purchased and if its possession by Spain continued to threaten the security of the United States.[181] The authors justified such action "upon the very same principle that would justify an individual in tearing down the burning house of his neighbor if there were no other means of preventing the flames from destroying his own home." They went on to particularize their analogy as a reference to the danger that Cuba would "be Africanized and become a second St. Domingo, with all its attendant horrors to the white race."[182]

The ensuing public furor over the Ostend Manifesto followed soon after the political upheaval resulting from passage of the Kansas-Nebraska Act. In antislavery circles, the manifesto was received as an expression of the same malign influence that had brought about the repeal of the Missouri Compromise. "How happens it," demanded Gamaliel Bailey's *National Era*, "that the Chief Executive Officer of the People has dared to venture upon a measure of such magnitude, and involving consequences so momentous? But one answer can be given—*the Slave Power willed it, and its will is the law of this Administration*."[183] Notwithstanding Bailey's obvious bias, there was more truth than error in his pronouncement. The antebellum campaign to acquire Cuba, although it had the devoted support of northern expansionists and dough-faces, was chiefly a southern project aimed at removing a threat to southern security and extending the reach of southern power. Even more emphatically than in the case of Texas, the campaign injected antiabolitionism into American foreign policy, reflecting, as it did, southern insistence that the United States must somehow prevent emancipation on the island.

After the Ostend fiasco, the Pierce administration slackened its effort to purchase Cuba and at the same time forced abandonment of the Quitman expedition. Southern expansionists were angry at the failure of their hopes, but the return to a conservative proslavery regime in Cuba dispelled the fear of impending Africanization and thus reduced the urgency of American acquisition.[184] With the Kansas Territory embroiled in fierce political and sectional conflict over slavery, further questing after the "Pearl of the Antilles" seemed a most dubious enterprise. James Buchanan nevertheless entered the White House in 1857 with the fond hope of making annexation one of the triumphs of his presidency.[185] Prudently, he waited until the Kansas struggle had ended in a semblance of compromise. Then, in his second annual message to Congress, dated December 6, 1858, he announced his intention to resume negotiations for purchase of the island, asking first to be entrusted "with the means of making an advance to the Spanish Government," payable immediately after the signing of a treaty.[186]

Responses came from both houses, but the only significant action took place in the Senate, which had a large Democratic majority. Late in January, the Committee on Foreign Relations submitted a bill drafted by John Slidell of Louisiana appropriating $30 million for the president's use in securing the cession of Cuba. Anticipating objections to the propriety and constitutionality of such a measure, the committee, in its accompanying report, cited similar legislation passed in 1803, 1806, and 1847 to facilitate the acquisition of territory. Among the many benefits to flow from the transfer of Cuba to the United States, the committee listed effective suppression of the flourishing slave trade to the island and the "better treatment and increased happiness" that Cuban slaves would enjoy under American rule.[187]

Debate on the Slidell bill took up much of the Senate's time during February. The Republican opposition, joined by one northern Democrat and a few southern Whig-Americans, resorted to tactics of delay in the hope of preventing final action before the end of the short session. Late at night on February 25, a frustrated Albert G. Brown proposed a test vote in the form of a motion to table. The result was an emphatic 30–18 endorsement of the measure, but with the Republicans prepared to talk it to death and other legislation demanding attention, Democratic leaders decided to press no further for its passage.[188] Subsequent efforts of Slidell and Buchanan to revive the project were unsuccessful.[189]

The hope of the Buchanan administration had been that the instability of Spanish politics might produce a government momentarily willing to sign a treaty of cession, which could then be quickly sealed with a substantial down payment. Every report from Spain indicated, however, that the scheme was unrealistic and congressional debate on the subject a waste of time. Thus, in January 1859, just as Slidell was preparing to introduce his $30 million bill, the Spanish minister of foreign affairs responded to Buchanan's annual message by reiterating that "no amount of gold could ever buy Cuba," and the Spanish Senate voted its unanimous concurrence in that stand.[190] Militant annexationists tended to regard the Slidell bill as, at best, the first stage of a more aggressive program. "I am for the acquisition of Cuba," said Brown, "and I want to advertise to all the world that we mean to have it—peaceably if we can, forcibly if we must. I am willing to pay for it, or I am willing to fight for it."[191] The militants were unable to stamp their adventurous purpose on national policy, however. Although the dynamic appeal of expansionism might have overridden antislavery resistance to a treaty of purchase, it was not strong enough to mobilize public support for seizure of the island.

The failure to acquire Cuba, which is well labeled "one of the major non-events of the antebellum period,"[192] left its bitterest aftertaste in those parts of the South that were already the most disaffected. To Jefferson Davis, among others, the defeat of the Slidell bill constituted further evidence that the Union was no longer a safe place for slaveholders. Addressing a state convention of Mississippi Democrats in the summer of 1859, Davis spent more time on Cuba than on the issue of slavery in the territories. Acknowledging that "the presence of slaves in the island made it more desirable" and that he wanted to "increase the number of slaveholding constituencies in the United States," he nevertheless insisted that annexation would be as beneficial to the North as to the South and thus a truly national achievement.[193] The fact that Buchanan and Pierce had officially adopted the same line of argument must be attributed primarily to the kinetic energy of expansionism in the 1850s, but it also reveals the extent to which national interest had become identified with southern interest in the shaping of American foreign policy.

NEITHER THE GARRISONIANS nor any of their latter-day disciples have argued that the clauses of the Constitution pertaining to foreign relations were tainted with a proslavery bias. Yet in the actual conduct of diplomacy from 1789 to 1861, the federal government habitually assumed the role of a protector, and sometimes spoke even as a vindicator, of slavery. Although slave owners and their families amounted to only about 7 percent of the total population, the antebellum United States consistently presented to the rest of the world the countenance of a slaveholding republic. "The whole of their domestic policy is governed, more or less, by slavery," wrote a British reformer, the Earl of Shaftsbury. "It is the beginning and end of their movements."[194] Such an impression had become fairly common in Europe, reinforced as it was by a long train of utterances and incidents on the diplomatic scene. The Stevenson-O'Connell quarrel of 1838 and Calhoun's Pakenham letter of 1844 come to mind at once as examples, and here is one more: When the British government, after several years' occupancy of the so-called Bay Islands, agreed in 1856 to restore them to Honduras, it stipulated that slavery should never be permitted to exist therein. Endorsement of the proposed treaty between Britain and Honduras was included in a simultaneously proposed agreement between Britain and the United States (the Dallas-Clarendon Convention). A number of southerners in Congress regarded the antislavery proviso as highly offensive, however, and President Buchanan concluded that "it would be quite impossible for the Government of the United States to sanction and endorse a Treaty between Great Britain and another Power for the exclusion of Domestic Slavery from its limits." In Britain's final disposition of the Bay Islands problem, the objectionable stipulation did not appear.[195]

To abolitionists, there was no mystery about the proslavery bias in the conduct of American foreign relations. The slaveholding class, they said, had dominated the federal government from its inception and had systematically installed policies aimed at fortifying slavery. Statistics and the historical record lend considerable credence to their explanation, but the fact that the foreign policy of John Quincy Adams, both as secretary of state and as president, was more proslavery than antislavery illustrates the need to take other influences into account. The proslavery cause generally prospered in American foreign relations because it could so often be assimilated to the national interest. It coincided again and again with the dynamic force of expansionism, and it drew much strength from the traditional American hostility to Britain. It appealed to the revered principle of property rights and to racial fears that were by no means confined to the South. Furthermore, the proslavery cause benefited from the structure of American politics, which required that any northerner serving in, or aspiring to, high federal office make some kind of peace with the nation's peculiar institution. It benefited also from the inertial tendencies of government and more specifically from a good deal of incremental decision making that was perfunctory, unreflective, and more often than not in southern hands.

5

THE AFRICAN SLAVE TRADE, 1789 TO 1842

IN THE SPRING of 1800, by a vote of 67 to 5, the House of Representatives approved a Senate bill strengthening federal restrictions on American participation in the foreign slave trade. One of the five negative votes came from John Rutledge, Jr., of South Carolina, a lawyer and planter whose father had been perhaps the most influential spokesman for the slaveholding interest at the Constitutional Convention. Another dissenter was John Brown of Rhode Island, member of a leading mercantile family who had himself engaged in the slave traffic. Both men argued that the removal of slaves from Africa would continue in any case and that American citizens ought not to be excluded from a lucrative trade "which all other nations enjoyed." Brown, a huge figure of a man cut to the mold of an Elizabethan merchant adventurer, also denounced the influence of Quaker abolitionists and added as a moral argument that slaves transported from Africa to America "much bettered their condition."[1] For Rutledge, the whole issue was somewhat academic because the proposed law did not affect the *importation* of slaves, which South Carolina had suspended but could renew if she chose and which the Constitution still protected from federal proscription. To Brown, on the other hand, such legislation seemed oppressive because it interfered with an ongoing commerce of considerable importance to his state. Rhode Island, even though it had forbidden its citizens to participate in the foreign slave trade, remained the one state with a significant economic stake in the increasingly disreputable enterprise.[2]

These two principal modes of American involvement in the African slave trade—as a maritime carrier and as an import market—are sometimes inadequately differentiated. They were not only functionally distinctive and sectionally concentrated but often unconnected in practice. That is, a majority of the slaves brought to British North America and the United States during the seventeenth and eighteenth centuries were transported in European ships; and many, perhaps a majority, of the slaves carried away from Africa in American ships over that same period were taken to places other than the North American continent.[3] Only the importation mode was dealt with in the Constitution, which implicitly confirmed federal regulatory power while explicitly suspending it until 1808. But in an early resort to broad construction, the first federal House of Representatives took aim at the maritime mode with an assertion that Congress had the authority to restrain Americans from participating in the foreign slave trade.[4] The assertion was implemented by statute in 1794 and again in the supplementary act of 1800. Meanwhile, Congress had already forbidden the introduction of slaves from abroad into Mississippi Territory, and in 1804 it extended the ban to Orleans Territory and the rest of the Louisiana Purchase. So the famous act of 1807, which fulfilled the promise of the Constitution by prohibiting the importation of slaves into any part of the United States, was not a new departure but rather the climax of a sustained congressional attack on the slave trade that had begun in 1790 with what amounted to a declaration of intent.

The lopsidedness of the House vote in 1800 was surpassed in 1807 when members voted 113 to 5 for the historic prohibitory act.[5] Only three of the "nays" came from southerners and only one from the South Carolina delegation, even though that state had removed its own ban and resumed the importation of slaves in 1803. This appears to have been the closest approach to unanimity ever recorded in a congressional roll-call vote on a significant slavery issue. It expressed an aversion to the slave trade that varied in intensity but was prevalent across most of the nation. It also preceded by just ten days a similarly overwhelming vote in the British House of Commons. Almost simultaneous legislative actions in London and Washington prohibited the international slave traffic throughout the English-speaking world.[6] In another law passed thirteen years later, the United States went still further and declared slave trading to be piracy, punishable by death.

Early federal legislation concerning the African slave trade may therefore be said to have been vigorously abolitionist. Its enactment, moreover, did not cause severe sectional strain within the country but instead reflected something approaching a national consensus that seemed to promise a high level of compliance. Yet, during the next half century, violation of the slave-trade laws was common enough to raise doubts about the government's sincerity and enhance the impression of the United States as a slaveholding nation at heart. The discrepancy between law and enforcement continually incensed antislavery militants like William Jay, who called it "one of the foulest stains attached to our national administration." W. E. B. Du Bois, in his classic work on the suppression of the slave trade, described federal enforcement as apathetic and criminally lax, though not quite a total nullity. He estimated that 250,000 slaves were smuggled into the country between 1807 and 1862. Du Bois's influence is visible in much of the subsequent writing on the subject, including the statement of a British historian that down until 1861, "no serious attempt had ever been made by any American Government to enforce the laws of 1807 and 1820 declaring slave trading to be illegal." The most systematic study of the subject, published in 1963, concluded that the federal effort at enforcement expended a great deal of human energy but was nevertheless a "debacle."[7]

Thus, the history of the federal government's relation to the African slave trade begins with impressive legislation but is primarily a study of faulty enforcement. Often it is also a study of American diplomacy, since enforcement necessarily extended beyond the boundaries of the United States and became part of the international movement to suppress the traffic. The nineteenth-century American effort to enforce the slave-trade laws has obvious twentieth-century parallels that lend perspective to one's judgment of the results achieved. Commonly though somewhat inaccurately regarded as an ignoble failure, the effort may also be viewed as an early, premonitory test of the limits of criminal sanction.

ONE OF THE figures in John Trumbull's painting *Capture of the Hessians at Trenton* is Colonel Josiah Parker, a Virginian from Isle of Wight County. It was this former Revolutionary officer, described as having an "impulsive" temper, who set off the first argument about slavery in the United States House of Representatives. On May 13, 1789, just thirteen days after the inauguration of George Washington, he moved to amend a tariff bill by laying a duty of ten dollars on each imported slave. It would, he hoped, reduce "an irrational and inhuman traffic" that was contrary to the principles of the Revolution.[8]

The motion provoked a chorus of protest from northern as well as southern representatives, the chief objection being that such an issue ought not to be injected into a revenue bill. Most vehement in opposition was James Jack-

son of Georgia, a thirty-one-year-old lawyer, planter, and combative politician, who as little more than a youth had killed the lieutenant-governor of his
state in a duel. Jackson complained that Virginia, which already had enough
slaves, ought to be more considerate of the states that did not. The proposed
duty would oppress Georgia, he said. It would be discriminatory and therefore "the most odious tax Congress could impose." In the course of his
wide-ranging remarks, Jackson denounced the fashionable tendency to favor
emancipation, declaring that freed slaves would not work for a living and
usually turned into "petty larceny villains." James Madison staunchly
defended the propriety and wisdom of his colleague's proposal but concluded
after further debate that it would be better to deal with the matter in separate
legislation. Parker accordingly withdrew his amendment. When it came
before the House as an independent bill some four months later, members
voted to postpone consideration until the next session.[9] The initiative, meanwhile, was passing to certain elements outside Congress.

American Quakers, after purging their own ranks of slaveholding, had
led the formation of abolition societies from New England to Virginia. Practiced hands at lobbying state legislatures and the Continental Congress on
the subject, they were ready to press antislavery policies upon the new federal
government almost as soon as it was organized. Early in 1790, Quakers from
Pennsylvania and New York petitioned Congress to take action against the
"licentious wickedness" of the slave trade. A number of southerners in the
House reacted so hostilely that the petitions were laid on the table instead of
being referred to a committee.[10] But the very next day an even more controversial memorial arrived, sent by the Pennsylvania Abolition Society and
bearing the signature of its president, Benjamin Franklin. This document
asked not only that Congress "step to the very verge" of its power to curb the
slave trade, but also that it "countenance the restoration of liberty" to those
unhappy persons, who, in a land of freedom, were "degraded into perpetual
bondage."[11]

Such words could not fail to provoke a heated discussion. The tone was
set by representatives from South Carolina and Georgia, who issued repeated
warnings that considerate treatment of the petition would, as one man put it,
"sound an alarm and blow the trumpet of sedition in the Southern States."
On the question immediately at issue, these militant defenders of slavery
were nevertheless overwhelmed, as the House voted 43 to 14 for commitment of the Franklin petition and the Quaker petitions as well.[12]
Furthermore, the select committee appointed by the speaker, a Pennsylvan-

ian, included no one from the Deep South. The irate South Carolinians and Georgians were consequently ready for battle when the committee presented its report three weeks later. During the extensive debate that followed, they mixed proslavery argument with so much abuse of the Quakers that Madison described their conduct as "intemperate beyond all example and even all decorum."[13]

The report of the select committee was an effort to define and delimit federal power over slavery. In the revised form eventually accepted by the committee of the whole, it reaffirmed the constitutional ban on congressional prohibition of the slave trade before 1808, and it declared that Congress had no authority "to interfere in the emancipation of slaves, or in the treatment of them within any of the States." Those two disclaimers were accompanied, however, by three assertions of federal power, namely, the power to restrain American citizens from "carrying on the African trade, for the purpose of supplying foreigners with slaves"; the power to prohibit foreigners from fitting out slave-trade vessels in American ports; and the power to regulate the shipboard treatment of any slaves imported into the United States.[14]

The House itself took up the report on March 23 and, despite increased southern resistance, gave it virtual approval by voting to print it in the *Journal*.[15] Of course this action had no binding effect, especially since the Senate had refused to expend any time in serious consideration of the antislavery petitions.[16] Yet, with respect to the slave trade, the House report of 1790 obviously constituted a significant declaratory step. Quakers and other abolitionists, though disappointed at its constrictive interpretation of federal power over domestic slavery, nevertheless felt that they had been given an agenda to work with. In the years immediately following, antislavery societies concentrated much of their effort on persuading Congress to make full use of the powers claimed in the report.[17]

American slave trading had been sharply reduced during the Revolution but was well recovered by the 1790s, when American ships in some years carried perhaps as many as ten thousand slaves away from Africa.[18] Some blacks were imported legally into Georgia until 1798 and into North Carolina from 1790 to 1794. Some were introduced illegally into states where importation had been prohibited. Large numbers were also taken to Cuba and other islands in the West Indies, and this was the traffic that the federal government presumably possessed the power to regulate. Rhode Island, Connecticut, Massachusetts, and Pennsylvania had already enacted legislation forbidding their citizens to participate in the foreign slave trade.

Enforcement was something else again, however, and some traders cynically justified their noncompliance by arguing that state laws of this kind were intrusions on authority belonging to the national government under the new Constitution.[19] Adding to the pressure for curtailment of slave trading and slave importation was the black revolution in Haiti, which shocked Americans north and south into greater awareness of the perils of a slaveholding society.[20] In 1794, after having ignored the problem for several years, Congress responded to abolitionist petitions with its first slave-trade law, one that prohibited citizens and other residents of the United States from carrying on such trade to any foreign country.[21] Ready acceptance of the measure in both houses was facilitated by the prudent language of the petitions, which disclaimed any intention of asking for general abolition.[22]

The act of 1794 prescribed relatively heavy financial penalties, including forfeiture of slave ships, but it provided no specific policing mechanism and left enforcement largely to the initiative of individuals willing to bring charges against alleged offenders. Historians who dismiss the legislation as wholly ineffectual are nevertheless mistaken.[23] In Providence, for example, the town's leading African trader, Cyprian Sterry, withdrew permanently from the traffic under threat of prosecution. At about the same time, John Brown was brought to trial and ended by forfeiting the one ship that he had dispatched to the Guinea coast in defiance of the law.[24] Federal executive officers at first did nothing to promote enforcement, but by 1799, a number of prosecutions were under way with the backing of the Adams administration. Then Congress added the supplementary act of 1800, which broadened the range of prohibition, increased the penalties, and authorized United States naval vessels to seize slave ships as prizes. With several captures in West Indian waters shortly thereafter, the newly created American navy began its long and frustrating struggle to suppress the slave trade.[25]

The deterrent effect of this early legislation was only briefly visible. Following the passage of each law, Rhode Island's African trade fell off for just a year or so and then began to recover. Twenty-two cases against slavers were prosecuted in the state from 1794 to 1804, but Rhode Island ships made at least two hundred slaving voyages to Africa during that same period. Indeed, all estimates indicate that American participation in the foreign slave trade, far from declining, increased sharply after it became illegal under federal law.[26] Enforcement, it is said, was too timid, and slave traders often escaped penalties through legal stratagems and outright intimidation. Condemned vessels were sometimes repurchased at public auction for a fraction of their value, and juries proved reluctant to convict well-known local figures. Furthermore, the slave-trade interest exercised considerable political influence, persuading Thomas Jefferson in 1804, for example, to appoint one of Rhode Island's leading slave merchants as customs collector at Bristol, a major center of the trade. Not surprisingly, the number of African clearances from that port immediately shot upward.[27]

Defective enforcement is only part of the story, however. The slave-trade legislation of 1794 and 1800 ran counter to certain currents of economic change that were bound to impair its effectiveness. The wars of the French Revolution and Napoleon greatly stimulated American maritime commerce, including American participation in the Atlantic slave trade. Spain had already opened her sugar colonies to slave traders of all nations in 1789, and thereafter more than half of the Rhode Island slavers marketed their cargoes in Cuba.[28] The federal legal restraints, though they might be enough to deter some former "blackbirders," were among the lesser risks attending wartime ventures that offered tempting possibilities of extraordinary profits. The American share of slave exports from Africa consequently increased, according to one estimate, from 2 percent in the 1780s to 9 percent in the 1790s, and then to 16 percent during Jefferson's first presidential term.[29]

Meanwhile, certain influences at home were encouraging the importation of slaves into the United States, despite state embargoes that became unanimous with Georgia's action in 1798. The rapid growth of cotton production after the invention of the cotton gin, the westward advance of plantation agriculture, and the acquisition of Louisiana all tended to expand the market for slave labor. South Carolina in particular needed more field hands for its own economy at a time when it was supplying many to frontier planters. In these circumstances, slave smuggling into the Deep South seems to have flourished at the turn of the century. Captain Charles Clark of Rhode Island, after landing a black cargo at Charleston in December 1801, reported that he had seen fourteen other American ships on the African coast, most of them likewise loading slaves for Charleston.[30]

Clark's voyage was a breach of South Carolina law and Rhode Island law, but it did not violate any law of the United States. The situation changed early in 1803 when an act of Congress for the first time brought federal authority to bear on the problem of illegal slave importations. Inspired by southern fear of an influx of free blacks and troublesome slaves from the French West Indies, the new statute was drafted by southerners and passed with solid southern support. It forbade the importing of "any negro, mulatto, or other person of colour" into any state that had prohibited such entry.[31] Although the text of the law said nothing directly about slaves, its wording plainly included them. The United States collector of the customs at Charleston, a holdover Federalist appointee, promptly launched a vigorous campaign of enforcement by seizing a brig that had recently landed slaves from Africa.[32]

It seems to have been this sudden intrusion of federal power, together with the likelihood of total federal prohibition at an early date, that precipitated a change in South Carolina's slave-trade policy. Late in 1803, the legislature repealed the state's sixteen-year ban on importation. The vote of 55 to 46 in the lower house reflected the fact that South Carolinians in general, many of them sensitive to the moral vulnerability of the slave trade, were sharply divided in their feelings about reopening it. Farmers newly settled in the back country wanted more field hands at lower prices, whereas established tidewater planters feared that an influx of Africans would depress the value of their slaves and the price of cotton. Proponents of repeal justified it primarily on the grounds that the ban had proved unenforcible, but this argument, coming at a time when enforcement was actually improving as a result of federal intervention, did not carry much conviction.[33] The action of the legislature set off a slave-trading boom in Charleston. During the next four years, more than two hundred ships landed more than forty thousand Africans, many of whom were then sent on to other markets as far away as New Orleans.[34] Charles Pinckney, who became governor in 1806, declared that the trade was "mischievous" in its effect upon the local economy and "wrong" for many other reasons. He urged an immediate return to prohibition.[35]

South Carolina's decision to resume the importation of slaves was almost universally condemned throughout the rest of the country. The legislatures of North Carolina, Tennessee, and Maryland were among those passing resolutions in which they urged a constitutional amendment empowering the federal government to shut down importation immediately, instead of having to wait until 1808 to do so.[36] In Congress, the first expression of outrage came from Pennsylvanian David Bard, a former clergyman and frontier missionary. Arguing that the government should do as much to check the "horrid traffic" as the Constitution would allow, Bard renewed the proposal made fifteen years earlier by Josiah Parker—that is, he offered a resolution calling for a tax of ten dollars on every imported slave.[37]

The ensuing debate in February 1804 pointed up the complexity and eccentricity of the slave trade issue. It was asserted without contradiction that every man in the South Carolina delegation disapproved of his state's reopening the trade, and, indeed, no member of the House defended the action per se. Yet all eight South Carolinians, together with about half the other southerners and a good many northerners, opposed the ten-dollar tax. They presented a curious medley of reasons for doing so: The tax would have no effect on the volume of slave imports. It would be discriminatory against one kind of agriculture. It would amount to the censure of a sovereign state for exercising a right guaranteed by the Constitution. Its offensiveness to South Carolinians would blight expectations of their early return to a policy of prohibition. It would give federal sanction to the slave trade by drawing federal revenue from it.[38]

The strong opposition did not prevent House approval of Bard's resolution, but the implementing bill, although it apparently had majority support, was postponed and never taken up again.[39] Subsequent efforts to impose a ten-dollar tax were likewise unsuccessful. The final attempt began in December 1805 and extended over most of the session. Debate on the question had a familiar ring, as the same old arguments were met with the same old replies. Again the House passed a resolution endorsing the tax in principle, but again delay after delay ended in legislative futility. A bill was reported, debated, recommitted, rereported, postponed, and then forgotten in the final weeks of the session, when congressional attention centered on a growing maritime crisis with Britain. The last roll call vote actually favored the bill by rejecting, 69 to 42, a motion for indefinite postponement.[40]

Supporters of the ten-dollar tax consistently outnumbered the opposition, but many of them were apparently limited in their commitment. Some must have been troubled by the moral ambiguity of the tax, which in penalizing the slave trade seemed at the same time to lend it respectability; and some no doubt had misgivings about a bill that stirred up so much animosity without promising much in the way of effect. What may in fact be most surprising is not the failure of Congress to impose the tax, but rather the degree of persistence with which the matter was pressed at a time when the Constitution would soon allow total federal control. Such diligence sprang primarily from anger at South Carolina, which continued to allow the importation of slaves despite repeated assurances from its representatives that the state legislature was about to restore the policy of prohibition.[41] The volume of imports increased each year and in 1807 was triple what it had been in 1804.[42] With this perverse behavior and the widespread repugnance that it aroused, South Carolina began the long process of isolating herself psychologically from the rest of the nation. More to the immediate point, her late-hour indulgence in slave trading made it virtually certain that Congress would act decisively at the earliest possible moment.

As EARLY AS December 1805, Senator Stephen R. Bradley of Vermont proposed the enactment of a law prohibiting slave importations, to become effective on January 1, 1808. A Massachusetts congressman made the same proposal in the House some two months later. Both efforts failed because they were considered premature.[43] Then, in December 1806, Thomas Jefferson lent presidential support to the idea of prospective legislation, declaring in his annual message to Congress that it was at last possible "to withdraw the citizens of the United States from all further participation in those violations of human rights which have so long continued on the unoffending inhabitants of Africa." Timely notice, Jefferson declared, would prevent expeditions that could not be completed before January 1808. There were immediate responses in both houses, but it was the Senate bill, introduced by Bradley, that eventually became law.[44] In the broadest view, consensus prevailed throughout the proceedings, which is to say that no one in Congress dissented from the general purpose of terminating slave importations. On that subject, said Speaker Nathaniel Macon of North Carolina, there was "but one opinion."[45] When the House began to consider certain details, however, consensus dissolved in bitter disagreement, predominantly along sectional lines.

The House bill was reported on December 15 from a committee headed by Peter Early, a grim-faced young Virginian who had migrated to Georgia in the preceding decade. One section prescribed forfeiture of those slaves imported in violation of the law, which meant that they would be sold at auction by federal authority. James Sloan of New Jersey promptly moved to add a clause declaring that any slave so forfeited should be "entitled to his freedom," and the battle was on. Endorsing the object of Sloan's amendment, a Pennsylvania member demanded: "Shall we, while we are attempting to put a stop to this traffic, take upon ourselves the odium of becoming slave traders?"[46] Early and other southerners replied with considerable heat that forfeiture was absolutely necessary for effective enforcement and that no disposition of contraband slaves other than their sale would be feasible, least of all the proposal to set them free. The federal government, they argued, had no constitutional power to liberate slaves within the boundaries of a slaveholding state. Furthermore, a law ordering such liberation would pose an implied threat to all slave property. The entire southern population would rise up against it, said Early, and if any Africans should nevertheless be turned loose on the southern countryside, "not one of them would be left alive in a year."[47]

Between the extremes of freeing contraband Africans and selling them into slavery, various other dispositions were suggested.[48] Several times, for example, the idea of returning them to Africa was introduced and brushed aside as impractical. The alternative solution that ultimately proved most important came from Barnabas Bidwell, a Massachusetts Republican, who proposed to strike out the provision for forfeiture of the Africans, thereby leaving their disposal to state authority. This would mean enslavement, but not by action of the federal government. When the House emphatically rejected Bidwell's amendment on January 7, he re-allied himself with Sloan and moved to add a proviso: "That no person shall be sold as a slave by virtue of this act." The motion produced another flurry of debate, and there was a conspicuously sectional alignment in the roll call that followed, with northerners voting 54 to 13 in favor and southerners 47 to 6 against. Speaker Macon then broke the 60-to-60 tie with a negative vote, thus defeating the maximum antislavery effort of the session.[49]

Interwoven with the House debate on the disposal of contraband Africans was another about the punishment of offenders. The original bill prescribed no penalties except fines and forfeiture of property, but an amended version declared that any person transporting slaves into the United States was guilty of a felony and should suffer death. Northern congressmen were divided in their responses to this change, many of them regarding it as too severe. Southerners opposed it by a wide margin, which seemed surprising in view of the fact that the brunt of punishment would fall on northern mariners. But capital punishment for slave *trading* cut too close to the bone of slave *owning*. As James Holland of North Carolina explained, a slave trader on trial for his life might well compare himself with his southern accusers in the following manner: "It is true that I have [brought] these slaves from Africa; but I have transported them from one master to another. I am not guilty of holding human beings in bondage. But you are. You have hundreds on your plantations in this miserable condition. By your purchases you tempt traders to increase the evil." When the question came to a vote, the House rejected the death-penalty clause in favor of a compromise amendment that changed the crime to a high misdemeanor and changed the penalty to imprisonment.[50]

The day after the failure of Bidwell's anti-enslavement proviso, a dissatisfied House majority that included most northerners and some southerners voted to recommit the slave-trade bill.[51] From the newly appointed committee came a revised bill on January 20, but just one week later the Senate passed its own slave-trade bill, and the House chose thereafter to concentrate its attention on that measure.

Unfortunately, we know little about the proceedings in the Senate, where no debates or votes were recorded. Bradley's bill, amended in committee, had been approved after only brief consideration and without any reported dissent. It contained two features that seemed sure to reignite sectional controversy in the House, namely, prohibition of domestic slave trading in coastal vessels and forfeiture of contraband slaves, to be followed by their indenture for a term of years in some free state or territory.[52] Peter Early led the fight against both. Of the provision for indenture and eventual liberation of forfeited slaves he said that the southern people would resist it "with their lives." Military force, he warned, would be necessary to carry such a law into execution. He moved an amendment substituting the previously rejected Bidwell scheme of turning contraband slaves over to state authority. The House records are sketchy at this point, but it appears that antislavery sentiment wilted before southern determination that the federal government should not be involved in any program of emancipation. Early's amendment was accepted without a division. After that victory, he offered another amendment canceling the proposed ban on coastal traffic in slaves, and it too won quiet approval. The bill as a whole, having thus been well tuned to southern sensibilities, was then quickly passed with only five dissenting votes.[53]

The Senate responded favorably to most of the House's amendments, but it refused to accept the one deleting the ban on coastal slave trading. Back in the House, a South Carolinian's motion to insist on the amendment received only eleven affirmative votes, whereupon Andrew Gregg of Pennsylvania offered a motion to recede. But at this point John Randolph delivered a fiery speech. If the bill passed without the amendment, he declared, the southern people would "set the law at defiance," and he himself would lead the resistance. After Early and several others had spoken to the same effect, Gregg complaisantly withdrew his motion, and the House, reversing itself, voted to insist on the amendment.[54]

The bill accordingly went to a conference committee, which modified it so as to prohibit coastal slave trading only in vessels "of less burthen than forty tons." This compromise the Senate readily accepted, but in the House there was further resistance from Early and Randolph. The impulsive Virginian warned that the prohibition touched the right of private property and might at some future time be made "the pretext of universal emancipation."

It had the capacity, he said, "to blow up the Constitution in ruins." Nevertheless, after extensive debate, the House voted 63 to 49 to accept the recommendation of the conference committee. More than four-fifths of the northern members supported acceptance; more than three-fourths of the southerners opposed it.[55] The long struggle was over at last, and Jefferson's signature converted the bill into law on March 2, 1807. Ten months must pass, however, before it would become effective.

The prospective nature of the law encouraged a final burst of slave importations into South Carolina. At least forty Rhode Island slavers brought their cargoes into Charleston during 1807. That was a much larger number than in any previous year.[56] British arrivals were likewise numerous, and South Carolinians had steadily increased their own participation in the trade. Charleston clearances to Africa rose from nine in 1804 to a high of forty-three in 1807.[57] A bit of grim testimony to the volume of the traffic was offered by the bodies of three Africans found floating near three different docks within a two-week period in April—all presumably cast overboard in the harbor to avoid the expense of burial.[58]

One of the locally financed ships that set sail from Charleston after enactment of the prohibitory law was the *Venus*, which had one seasoned slave trader as captain and another as commercial agent. Its outbound cargo consisted primarily of rum and textiles but included a variety of other trading items, such as knives, candles, tobacco, gunpowder, bar iron, lumber, looking glasses, and snuff boxes. The *Venus* arrived off the coast of Africa in early May, but the captain's illness caused some delay, and trading at the Gambia River proved unsuccessful. Farther south in Sierra Leone, the agent took aboard eighty-two slaves for his employer, eight for himself in payment of a debt, and thirty-one to be transported for other proprietors at thirty dollars a head. These transactions consumed much time, and the *Venus* did not arrive back in Charleston until mid-December, thus completing one of the last legal slave trading ventures in American history. Two slaves had died on the voyage, and nine more died after their arrival in America. Nineteen, being rather sickly, were shipped off to be sold in Havana. Sale in Charleston of the remaining men, women, and children took several months, during which time the proprietor had to provide food, shelter, clothing, blankets, and medical attention. The average price received was about $350. Gross proceeds from the voyage were in the neighborhood of $26,000, most of which sum appears to have been offset by expenses. It is impossible to be precise about the net profit, if any was realized, because the proprietor and his agent were in sharp disagreement about the financial accounting. They ended by suing one other, each claiming that he had been cheated out of more than $4,000.[59]

Slave trading could be highly profitable, but it was a complex and hazardous enterprise, even when carried on within the law. The act of 1807 heightened the risk by making importation of slaves a federal offense everywhere in the country. As punishment for engaging in the slave trade, it prescribed forfeiture of ships, fines of up to $20,000, and imprisonment for five to ten years. In addition, persons buying or selling illegally imported slaves were subject to fines of $800 per slave.[60] Apparently, the mere enactment of the law induced more than a few men to get out of the business. The number of ships advertised for sale in Charleston as the deadline approached is one indication of its salutary effect. Also, clearances to Africa from Rhode Island ports, which had been little affected by earlier state and federal legislation, fell off sharply after 1807.[61] And with respect to execution, the law was not virtually a dead letter from the start, as some historians have maintained. On the contrary, there is considerable evidence of effective enforcement in the years immediately following its passage, and the amount of illegal importation thereafter has often been greatly exaggerated, partly because of confusion with American participation in the slave trade to other countries.[62]

The readiest American market for imported slaves continued to be the southwestern frontier, which had illicitly received many of the Africans brought into Charleston from 1804 to 1807. Louisiana planters were especially resentful of congressional insensitivity to their peculiar and pressing need for more slave labor. They protested vigorously against the legislation of 1804 excluding foreign slaves from Orleans Territory, and they were openly hostile to the general prohibitory act of 1807, insisting that it would be very harmful to the economy of their region. "I defy all the vigilance of man to prevent the introduction of slaves by some means or other," declared the mayor of New Orleans.[63] Some Negroes were smuggled across the border from West Florida, still a colony of Spain. Others were filtered into Louisiana from privateers and pirates that preyed on Spanish ships during the Latin American revolutions. One of the leading spirits was Jean Laffite, who briefly interrupted his freebooting career to lend support to Andrew Jackson at the battle of New Orleans. After the war, Laffite returned to his old piratical ways and began operating from Galveston Island. There, captured Spanish slaves could be bought for a dollar a pound. They were then taken overland into Louisiana and sold at much higher prices by dealers like Jim Bowie and his brothers, one of whom later reported that their total profit came to $65,000.[64]

Another center of privateering and smuggling was Amelia Island at the mouth of the St. Mary's River in East Florida. From there, slaves and other contraband were introduced into Georgia so openly and in such volume as to provoke eventually a military response from Washington. Late in 1817, army troops and a naval force together seized Amelia Island and held it long enough to disperse the band of adventurers that had taken control there. Four years later, an American warship forced Laffite and his followers to abandon their Galveston establishment.[65] Laffite's departure into obscurity marked the end of an era. American acquisition of Florida, together with the general decline of privateering as the Latin American nations established their independence, greatly reduced the piratical sources of slaves along the southern coast of the United States.

Smuggling of slaves into the United States did not cease entirely, of course, but the volume after 1807 and especially after 1820 was very small compared with that of earlier years.[66] Modern scholarship has greatly reduced the Du Bois estimate of 250,000 slaves brought illegally into the country between 1807 and 1862.[67] The respected authority Philip D. Curtin suggested in 1969 that an average of about 1,000 per year would be a more reasonable "shot in the dark." According to one recent time-series study, the number imported directly from Africa averaged only 1,000 per year in the second decade of the century, 200 per year in the third decade, and almost none thereafter. To this figure of only about 12,000 for the half century from 1810 to 1860, one would have to add slaves smuggled in at certain periods from Spanish Florida, Cuba, and preannexation Texas—an unknown number, but not enough to bring the total up to the Curtin estimate. Even some conspicuous southern gestures of defiance toward the slave-trade laws during the late 1850s seem to have resulted in relatively few imports.[68] It is probably safe to say that illegal importation of foreign slaves into the South after 1807 was, on average, lower in volume than the flight of fugitive slaves out of the South to the northern states and Canada. Both movements were politically inflammatory but demographically insignificant.

The exclusion of foreign slaves from the United States was made easier by the development of an interregional trade that supplied the newer agricultural areas of the Southwest with needed slave labor. In the decade of the 1850s, for instance, more than a quarter of a million slaves were transferred from the South Atlantic states, plus Kentucky and Tennessee, to the Gulf states and Arkansas.[69] But plainly, the sharp reduction in the importation of Africans after 1807 was also in no small part a consequence of federal intervention.

Compared with twentieth-century efforts to prevent the introduction of alcoholic beverages, drugs, and illegal aliens into the United States, the legislation banning importation of slaves must be regarded as relatively successful. Less effective, on the other hand, were the federal laws prohibiting American participation in the Atlantic slave trade as a whole, which continued to flourish elsewhere, even as it dwindled to insignificance with relation to American importation. During the half century from 1810 to 1860, when probably fewer than 50,000 Africans were being smuggled into the United States, about 2 million were being carried to Cuba and Brazil, more than half of them illegally.[70] In the perpetuation of that traffic certain Americans played a major role, and so did the American government.

The slave-trade act of 1807 had been in effect for only a short time when it was partially and temporarily suspended to meet a special problem that arose unexpectedly. In 1809, several thousand French refugees and their household slaves arrived in New Orleans and certain other American ports after having been expelled from Cuba. Legally, the ships and slaves were subject to forfeiture, and their owners faced other penalties, but Congress hastily passed legislation granting relief to everyone involved in the emigration. Eventually, more than seventy vessels were exempted from the operation of a statute which, it seems clear, was being diligently enforced.[71]

In his annual message of December 5, 1810, President James Madison notified Congress that the nation's slave-trade laws were being violated, but he spoke only of American involvement in the maritime traffic, not of slave importation into the United States. Six years later, however, he reported violations of both kinds and called for remedial legislation.[72] By then, the influx of contraband slaves from Florida and Texas had become flagrant enough to command attention. It was during this relatively brief period of renewed concern about importations that Congress enacted a set of three supplementary slave-trade laws.

First, in 1818, came a revision of the act of 1807, directed primarily, but not entirely, at the problem of illegal importation. The record of the proceedings is minimal and gives no indication of the rationale for changes introduced.[73] Twice the phrasing of the act of 1807 was altered in such a way as to reinforce the laws of 1796 and 1800 by making the section applicable to all slave trading and not merely to that associated with importation into the United States. Penalties for participation in the slave trade, such as fitting out a slave ship or taking aboard Africans for disposal as slaves, were substantially reduced, perhaps in the hope that they would be more readily imposed.[74] On the other hand, penalties for buying and selling illegally imported slaves were increased, and the burden was placed upon the defendant to prove that a Negro in question had not been brought into the country contrary to the law within the preceding five years.[75] In addition, the rule for equal division of fines between the government and the informer who brought charges was extended to include the proceeds of forfeitures.[76]

These revisions may have strengthened the hand of the government in policing illegal importations, but they did not satisfy dedicated enemies of the African slave trade. Antislavery agitation for a more vigorous federal program stimulated further action in the next session of Congress.[77] Leadership in the framing of the new legislation came primarily from southerners, including Henry Middleton, a South Carolina planter; Charles F. Mercer, a Virginia Federalist; and young John H. Eaton of Tennessee, who had recently completed a biography of Andrew Jackson. Furthermore, it was another Virginian, James Pindall, who proposed the death penalty for illegal importation of a slave or for the sale or purchase of such a slave. His amendment received the approval of the House but was rejected by the Senate.[78] The act of 1819, passed in the midst of the initial furor over the admission of Missouri to statehood, introduced several important changes. It authorized American war vessels to cruise on the African coast and established a system of awarding prize money and bounties to naval personnel for the capture of slave ships. It directed that federal district attorneys commence prosecution by information (rather than grand jury indictment) against persons accused of holding illegally imported slaves. And most importantly, it satisfied one of the principal antislavery demands by changing the disposition of confiscated slaves. Instead of being turned over to state authority (which in southern states meant their sale and commitment to a lifetime of servitude), they were to be placed in the hands of the local federal marshal, and the president was authorized to make arrangements for their return to Africa. With this feature particularly in mind, the drafters of the measure included a special appropriation of $100,000 to carry the law into effect.[79]

The deletion of Pindall's death-penalty amendment left many members of the House dissatisfied with the slave-trade act of 1819, and they consequently seized the first good opportunity to try again. In the spring of 1820, soon after completion of the historic Missouri Compromise, the Senate judiciary committee routinely reported a bill to continue in force for three more years an existing temporary law for the protection of American commerce against piracy, one that prescribed death as the punishment. When the

measure passed the Senate and arrived in the House, it was calculatedly referred to the committee on the slave trade. In due course, Henry Mercer as
chairman reported the bill with two additional sections that defined slave trading as piracy and imposed the death penalty. An accompanying report justified
the amendments in these terms: "Your committee cannot perceive wherein the
offence of kidnapping an unoffending inhabitant of a foreign country; of
chaining him down for a series of days, weeks, and months, amidst the dying
and the dead, to the pestilential hold of a slaveship; of consigning him, if he
chance to live out the voyage, to perpetual slavery, in a remote and unknown
land, differs in malignity from piracy, or why a milder punishment should follow the one, than the other crime." The House promptly approved the amendments and passed the bill. Back in the Senate, the revised version won
acceptance without recorded opposition. This act of 1820, made permanent
three years later, virtually completed the substantive legislation of Congress
for suppression of the African slave trade.[80]

EXECUTION OF THE slave-trade laws enacted by Congress between 1794 and
1820 depended upon customs officers, federal marshals, federal district attorneys, federal judges and juries, territorial governors, the United States Navy,
the cooperation of state authorities, and the initiative of private citizens.
Except for the ultimate responsibility of the president, there was no one person in charge and consequently little coordination of effort. The attorney
general, for example, exercised no control over the district attorneys, who
received instructions from several departments but were responsible to
none.[81] Enforcement tended to be episodic, rather than systematic, and the
engagement of federal officials in the battle against the slave trade ranged all
the way from diligence to nonfeasance, with some instances of corrupt
involvement in the traffic. Thus, the collector of customs at New Orleans who
in 1817 urgently requested a naval force to suppress the smuggling of slaves
into his district may be contrasted with the Maryland judge who in 1803
imposed penalties of one day in jail and a ten-dollar fine upon a man convicted of engaging in the foreign slave trade.[82] The most notable scandal
involved David B. Mitchell, a former governor of Georgia serving as a federal
Indian agent, who was accused of complicity in the illegal importation of
about a hundred Africans from Amelia Island in 1817. Attorney General
William Wirt, after investigating the charges, concluded that Mitchell had
"prostituted his power . . . from mercenary motives." President James Monroe removed him from office.[83]

As American importation of slaves declined while American participation in the international slave trade continued, the responsibility for initiating enforcement of the prohibitory laws rested more and more with naval commanders. By 1800, when Congress first authorized the seizure of slavers by commissioned vessels of the United States, the navy had achieved separate departmental status and something approaching parity with the army in number of personnel and money appropriated for it.[84] Several seizures were made soon after passage of the act of 1800, but otherwise naval restraint on the slave trade did not attain much more than token significance until after the War of 1812. For one thing, it appears that many American slave traders protected themselves by switching registry to one of the nations that had not yet outlawed the traffic. Then the war itself and the accompanying British blockade effectively restricted American slave trading along with other maritime commerce. But after 1815, the international traffic in slaves quickly revived, and enforcement of the laws against it became one of the main assignments of the peacetime navy.

Beginning with the seizure of Amelia Island in 1817, the Navy's efforts to suppress the slave trade in Gulf and Caribbean waters often blended with its task of protecting American commerce against piracy in those regions. The connection is illustrated in the case of the *Fenix*, an American-built Spanish vessel that was pursued and captured near Haiti in 1830 by the U.S. schooner *Grampus* after having repeatedly menaced an American merchantman. Eighty-two blacks were found aboard the *Fenix*, which apparently alternated between slave trading and piracy as opportunity presented itself.[85] The range of naval action was greatly extended in 1819, when Congress authorized cruising along the African coast. As a result of the same piece of legislation, naval operations against the slave trade came to be intimately associated with a unique American experiment in "informal colonialism."

The day after passage of the act of 1819, a committee of the American Colonization Society headed by Supreme Court Justice Bushrod Washington called upon President Monroe. Organized some thirty months earlier to promote the return of free blacks to Africa, the society hoped to enlist the federal government as a partner in its endeavors. More specifically, the committee urged that the $100,000 appropriated in the act be used to establish an African colony that would serve doubly as the return destination of captured contraband slaves and as a home for voluntary black emigrants from the United States. The society's model was the British colony of Sierra Leone on the Guinea coast. Founded by abolitionists but taken over by the Crown in 1808, it had a population made up almost entirely of liberated slaves, about half of them captured from slavers.[86]

Monroe consulted his cabinet and found it divided. Secretary of the Treasury William H. Crawford, a leading figure in the Colonization Society, strongly supported its proposal; Secretary of State John Quincy Adams was no less emphatic in his assertion that it would be unconstitutional to use government funds for such an enterprise. Attorney General William Wirt at first agreed with Adams but eventually modified his opinion under pressure from Crawford and other society members.[87] Monroe, who, like many Virginians, had been a friend of colonization ever since Gabriel's rebellion in 1800, readily put aside his strict-constructionist scruples and announced in December 1819 that he was sending a warship to Africa with two agents commissioned to make the preliminary arrangements for establishment of a station to which Africans rescued from slave ships could be sent.[88]

The resulting voyage, although officially associated only with suppression of the slave trade, was in fact "a thinly veiled colonization venture." In February 1820, the U.S. sloop-of-war *Cyane* set sail from New York harbor, along with the *Elizabeth*, a merchantman carrying tools, supplies, and eighty-six free black emigrants masquerading as hired laborers.[89] For the colonists, this first expedition proved disastrous, as did a second one the following year. Efforts to acquire a satisfactory site were unsuccessful, and disease swept away many of the blacks and all but one of the white agents accompanying them. Then, in 1821, Lieutenant Robert F. Stockton arrived on the scene in command of the U.S. schooner *Alligator*. Already a ten-year veteran of naval service at the age of twenty-six, Stockton displayed the same impetuous energy that he would bring to the conquest of California a quarter of a century later. Together with a newly appointed agent, Dr. Eli Ayres, he used threats as well as persuasion in extracting from reluctant native rulers their conveyance of title to Cape Mesurado, the region at the mouth of the St. Paul River some two hundred miles south of Sierra Leone. The price paid by the Colonization Society was approximately $300 in guns, ammunition, rum, tobacco, and other goods. Thus, in a few days of aggressive diplomacy bordering on extortion, Stockton laid the foundation for the republic of Liberia and its capital, Monrovia.[90]

Meanwhile, the navy had begun its operations against the slave trade on the African coast. In the spring of 1820, soon after her arrival with the first boatload of colonists, the *Cyane* captured seven ships, destroying three of

them and sending the other four back to New York as prizes.[91] Later in the
year, the *Cyane* was replaced by two other ships, which also made captures.[92]
By 1821, when the *Alligator* arrived, along with another schooner, the *Shark*,
commanded by Matthew G. Perry, American slave ships had largely disappeared from the coast. The flag of France now predominated in the trade.
Perry pursued and boarded two slavers but released them when they proved
to have French papers in good order. His fellow officers were especially
unhappy about the freeing of the *Caroline*, a malodorous schooner found to
have 133 slaves crammed between-deck in a space about fifteen-by-forty feet
and four feet high. The bodies of these naked creatures were so emaciated,
wrote one of the *Shark*'s midshipmen, that they resembled "Egyptian mum-
mies half-awakened into life."[93] Perry took no prizes throughout his cruise,
but the more adventurous Stockton seized four French slavers in 1821 and
dispatched them to the United States. On the way, three of them escaped
from the control of their prize crews, and the arrival of the fourth (the *Jeune
Eugenie*) in Boston harbor set off such a diplomatic disturbance that it was
released to its French owners.[94]

The flurry of congressional legislation and naval action had obviously
produced some salutary effects. By 1822, the smuggling of slaves into the
Gulf states was no longer a serious matter, according to the secretary of the
navy. A House committee announced the same year that the flag of the
United States, once so prominent in the slave trade, had "wholly disappeared
from the coasts of Africa." Lieutenant Perry confirmed that report after
returning from a second African cruise in the fall of 1822. "During my stay
upon the coast," he wrote, "I could not *even hear* of an American slaving vessel; and I am fully impressed with the belief that there is not one at present
afloat."[95] Presidents Monroe and Adams, in making similar pronouncements,
acknowledged that some Americans might be involved in the trade under the
banners of other nations, but the resolution of that problem, they indicated,
was not the responsibility of the American government.[96]

With the United States thus seeming to be no longer seriously affected
by the foreign slave trade, enforcement of the laws against the traffic not surprisingly tended to become a matter of subordinate concern among federal
officials. The navy, which had other urgent responsibilities in the 1820s, such
as establishing a Pacific station and suppressing piracy in the West Indies, did
not undertake to maintain a continuous presence on the African coast. One
visit per year of several weeks' duration was the average for two decades

after 1822, and some of those visits were little more than perfunctory calls on the naval agency in Liberia. American war vessels captured only three slavers during that twenty-year period, only one of them in African waters.[97]

The problem of suppressing the trade went unmentioned for thirteen straight years (1826–38) in the annual messages of Presidents John Quincy Adams, Andrew Jackson, and Martin Van Buren.[98] Yet the African slave trade continued to flourish as an international criminal enterprise of vast proportions. Indeed, the numerical peak of more than four centuries of transatlantic slave trading may have been reached at this time, after it had become illegal throughout most of the Western world.[99] From 1820 to 1840, importation into the Americas (principally Cuba and Brazil) averaged about 60,000 annually, and according to one leading authority, it is possible that "in 1829, more slaves crossed the Atlantic than in any other year before and after."[100] That happened to be one of the years in which no United States warship visited the coast of Africa. American involvement in this voluminous slave trade of the 1820s and 1830s was, of course, surreptitious and therefore difficult to identify. It appears to have been relatively insignificant until about 1835, but thereafter it contributed substantially to the prospering of the traffic.

The Americans most directly implicated in the contraband slave trade of the nineteenth century were, of course, those officers and crewmen who actually manned slavers and other vessels auxiliary to the traffic. Their number is unknown, but it probably never amounted to more than a few hundred at any one time, and they were scattered among the ports and ships of several nations. More significant, no doubt, was the contribution of those entrepreneurial elements in the United States that provided vessels, outfitted them, financed voyages, and furnished goods to be exchanged for slaves on the African coast. Baltimore, for example, became a major center of slave-ship construction. The light, fast brigs and schooners known as "Baltimore clippers" proved to be admirably suited for an outlawed marine commerce. To an increasing extent from the 1820s to the 1850s, slavers were American in origin.[101]

The fact of American involvement in all aspects of the foreign slave trade does not mean that it was common practice for an American captain with an American crew to sail an American ship from an American port to the African coast, load it with slaves, and carry them back across the Atlantic. The operation of what amounted to a loosely knitted international conspiracy was much more complicated than that. For one thing, after passage of the Piracy Act of 1820, citizens of the United States were reluctant to risk being caught with slaves aboard. Americans therefore generally played a much more prominent part in the outward voyage, providing ships, equipment, and trading supplies, but making real or fictitious transfers to foreign ownership somewhere along the way to Africa. A slave ship commonly carried more than one set of papers and was prepared to run up any one of several national flags in order to evade capture. The paucity of American enforcement in the 1830s, together with a tightening British-led program of international enforcement, which the United States refused to join, made the American flag an increasingly good cover for slavers. As a consequence, American involvement in the slave trade extended beyond the direct and indirect participation of certain persons to virtual complicity, however involuntary, on the part of the government and the whole nation. British vexation with this complicity seriously affected Anglo-American relations over a period of several decades.

GREAT BRITAIN, HAVING abolished the African slave trade in 1807, began the work of enforcement even while continuing its desperate struggle against Napoleonic France and fighting a second war with the United States. The return of peace in 1814–15 brought a revival of maritime commerce, including commerce in slaves, and at the same time, it terminated the wartime naval right of visit and search. Accordingly, British leaders set about promoting international action for suppression of the traffic. Declarations endorsing suppression were included, for instance, in the Treaty of Ghent and in the Final Act of the Congress of Vienna. By that time all of the principal maritime nations had either prohibited the trade or committed themselves to doing so in the near future.[102] But establishing a workable system of enforcement proved bafflingly difficult.

The central problem was that on the high seas in time of peace, international law allowed a nation only to enforce its own laws upon its own ships and citizens.[103] This meant that the dominating power of the British navy could not legally be brought to bear against the bulk of the slave trade without diplomatic arrangements sanctioning its use. British Foreign Secretary Lord Castlereagh tried several times in vain to secure the creation of an international maritime police for suppression of the trade. With more success, he also began to negotiate bilateral agreements in which the critical element was a mutual right to search suspected ships of the other nation and take them before a mixed commission for condemnation if the evidence warranted. What this mutuality would mean in practice, more often than not, was British inspection of non-British vessels. Treaties embracing some right of search were extracted from Portugal and Spain in 1817, both facilitated by subsidies of considerable size. The Netherlands signed a similar treaty in 1818 without any financial inducement. France, on the other hand, stubbornly refused to cooperate, and so did the United States.[104]

In the spring of 1818, Castlereagh broached the subject of a slave-trade agreement to Richard Rush, the newly arrived American minister. Rush sought instructions from home, and Secretary of State John Quincy Adams, with the unanimous approval of the Monroe cabinet, directed him to reply that the British treaties with Spain, Portugal, and the Netherlands were "of a character not adaptable to the institutions or to the circumstances of the United States." Castlereagh nevertheless persisted, shifting the negotiations to Washington in 1820. Again his efforts met polite but emphatic refusal.[105] Besides the already traditional American wariness of any formal connection with the European power structure, the Monroe administration had several specific objections to the British treaty design. There was considerable doubt, for instance, that the Constitution would allow participation in the proposed system of mixed commissions for trial of captured slavers.[106] Problems of this sort were obviously resolvable, however. The one real sticking point was right of search.

Having just finished fighting a war with Britain over freedom of the seas, Americans were understandably reluctant, even in a good cause, to endorse a major infringement of that freedom. "The admission of a right in the officers of foreign ships-of-war to enter and search the vessels of the United States in time of peace, under any circumstances whatever, would meet with universal repugnance in the public opinion of this country," Adams declared.[107] The British government's reiterant pleas for a mutual right of search seemed all the more presumptuous in view of its continuing refusal to make any concessions regarding impressment, the wartime practice of forcibly removing alleged British subjects from American merchant vessels. Rush expressed some of the intensity of his countrymen's feelings on the subject when he characterized impressment not only as insulting to the rights and dignity of an independent nation but as "more afflicting to humanity" than the African slave trade.[108]

In a nation still retaining much of its enmity for Britain, the administration's resolute stand on right of search was bound to be popular. Nevertheless, among members of Congress, there was a strong current of opinion running the other way. The British strategy for suppression of the slave trade rested, after all, upon compelling logic. Only an international effort could dismantle a furtive international enterprise, and as Castlereagh argued, if even one major maritime power refused to cooperate, the trade would surely continue.[109] Furthermore, it should be remembered that Castlereagh made his overtures to the United States at a time of great public concern about the influx of Africans from Florida and Texas, a concern that led to the passage of three additional laws on the subject. As early as 1817, the House committee on the slave trade recommended negotiation of agreements with other powers for suppression of the traffic. One year later, the Senate took a preliminary step in the same direction.[110] A resolution calling for such negotiations without explicitly mentioning right of search won the approval of the whole House in 1820, but it failed to get through the Senate.[111]

Each year thereafter, the issue came before Congress. A House committee report in 1821, reaffirmed in 1822, stated that a mutual right of search appeared to be "indispensable to the great object of abolition."[112] The contemporaneous dispute with France over the captured slaver *Jeune Eugenie* seemed to illustrate the wisdom of this judgment.[113] Yet the administration remained adamant. Adams, when asked by the British minister whether he could conceive of a "greater and more atrocious evil" than the slave trade, resolutely replied: "Yes, admitting the right of search by foreign officers of our vessels upon the seas in time of peace; for that would be making slaves of ourselves."[114] But this son of the Revolution, for all his nationalistic fervor, was also a New Englander made more sensitive to the slavery issue by the recent controversy over the admission of Missouri; and in addition, he was a contender for the presidential succession, needing to keep a watchful eye on the trend of public opinion. As much as any member of the executive branch he felt the impact of a House resolution passed in February 1823, requesting initiation of negotiations "for the effectual abolition of the African slave trade, and its ultimate denunciation, as piracy, under the law of nations." This time, the vote was a thunderous 131 to 9.[115]

The wording of the resolution suggested to Adams a route of graceful retreat from his and the administration's previously held position. If the maritime nations would all agree to treat the slave trade as piracy in international law, then a belligerent's right of search in wartime could be invoked, even in peacetime, against slave traders as common enemies of mankind.[116] With Monroe's approval, Adams instituted negotiations along those lines and drafted a proposed Anglo-American convention dependent upon British legislation declaring the slave trade to be piracy. He also took initial steps toward securing similar agreements with other powers. British officials were not entirely satisfied, but after extensive discussions with Rush, they accepted the convention substantially as Adams had written it. The document was signed in London on March 13, 1824, after which Parliament promptly enacted the required piracy law.[117] As its central feature, the convention authorized the naval officers of each nation "to detain, examine, capture, and deliver over for trial and adjudication ... any ship or vessel concerned in the illicit traffic of slaves, and carrying the flag of the other, or owned by any subjects or citizens of either of the two contracting parties, except when in the presence of a ship-of-war of its own nation." The primary concession to the United States was a clause that set aside the principle of joint adjudication by providing that vessels seized as slavers should be adjudged "by the tribunals of the captured party, and not by those of the captor."

It was still necessary, of course, to secure the approval of the Senate, where support for such an undertaking had never been as strong as that mobilized in the House. The task proved more difficult than anyone expected, even though Monroe pleaded eloquently that rejection of the convention would be embarrassing to the administration and injurious to its foreign policy.[118] Some senators, Adams noted in his diary, had become alarmed "lest this concert between the United States and Great Britain for suppressing the slave-trade should turn to a concert for the abolition of slavery."[119] And there was indeed growing dismay in the South about abolitionist influence on the British government, which had only recently taken some dramatic steps toward the amelioration and presumably the eventual extinction of slavery throughout the British Empire.[120]

More immediately detrimental, however, were the vagaries of domestic politics in a presidential election year. Senatorial supporters of William H. Crawford, still a candidate despite having suffered a paralyzing stroke, sought to diminish Adams's stature by defeating the treaty that he had drafted. They managed to burden it with several amendments, one of which turned out to be fatal.[121] The British ministry, although willing to accept the other modifications, refused to exclude the North American coast from the stipulated right of search. Such an exemption, its spokesmen declared, would destroy the very principle of mutuality upon which the agreement was founded. Whatever may be said for the logic and justice of this response, it closed a door that could have been more than half opened. Efforts to resolve the difference failed, and the uselessness of further negotiations became obvious a year later when the Senate overwhelmingly rejected a similar convention with Colombia that incorporated all of the Senate amendments.[122]

British leaders continued to hope that an accord so nearly concluded could somehow be revived, but the minister to the United States reported in 1831 that he had "not perceived the slightest inclination in two successive administrations to renew the negotiation." Three years later, Lord Palmerston as foreign secretary offered to yield on the one point previously at issue by exempting the American coast from a mutual search treaty. Secretary of State John Forsyth replied that it had been resolved "not to make the United States a party to any convention on the subject." His predecessor, Louis McLane, had already explained that such a policy was necessary to avoid aggravating southern excitement recently aroused by the growth of the abolitionist movement.[123] Thus domestic influences discouraged vigorous American action against the slave trade at a time when American complicity in that trade was rising to a scandalous level.

There is conflicting testimony about the extent of American involvement in the international slave trade of the 1820s, but it does not appear to have been a very substantial part of the whole. More than two-thirds of the Africans carried across the Atlantic during the decade were taken to Brazil, almost exclusively in Portuguese and Brazilian ships.[124] Only later did Americans come to play a significant role in that traffic. Similarly, Spanish and French traders dominated the transport of slaves to the Spanish and French West Indies, although there, much closer to home, some Americans were always involved. What happened in the 1830s was that Palmerston's aggressive diplomacy tightened the screws on the other maritime nations and drove slavers increasingly to the protection of the American flag.

Soon after Louis Philippe replaced the last of the Bourbon rulers on the throne of France in 1830, his government entered into a treaty with Britain accepting the principle of mutual search. French participation in the slave trade swiftly declined as a consequence.[125] By then, Britain had already prodded newly independent Brazil into signing a slave-trade convention that took effect in 1830. Brazil's legislation prohibiting the importation of slaves proved only briefly effective however, and the now illicit traffic revived dramatically in the later 1830s, for the most part under protection of the Portuguese flag. Not until 1836 did Portugal outlaw slave trading in the South Atlantic, and even then it continued to resist British pressure for a mutual-search agreement. Palmerston, at the end of his patience, accordingly secured passage in 1839 of a parliamentary act authorizing British warships to search Portuguese vessels and, if they proved to be slavers, take them before British admiralty courts for condemnation. This high-handed policy soon brought an outraged but helpless Portugal to the acceptance of a treaty. It also stimulated American entry into the Brazilian slave trade on a sizable scale.[126]

Most important of all as a stimulus to American involvement was an Anglo-Spanish treaty concluded in 1835 authorizing the seizure of vessels patently equipped for slave trading even if they had no Africans aboard. This development greatly enhanced the value of American cover in the Cuban slave trade. For example, the Baltimore owners of a 95-ton schooner, the *Ontario*, dispatched it to Havana in 1838. There, with the cooperation of the American consul, it was sold and resold, ending up nominally as the property of Eleazer Huntington, an American sea captain, but owned in fact by a Spanish slave trader named José Maria Mendez. The *Ontario* cleared for Africa under Huntington's command and flying the American flag, but with an all-Spanish crew. At the Niger River, just before 220 slaves were taken aboard, Huntington executed a sale to Mendez, who took command and ran up the Spanish flag. Until that moment, the *Ontario* had enjoyed immunity from British inspection because of its American colors and virtual immunity from American seizure because of the inadequacy of American enforcement. Fraudulent use of the flag of the United States thus served to nullify the effect of the Anglo-Spanish equipment treaty.[127] Once the *Ontario* assumed a Spanish character, it of course became subject to British capture, but only the vessel and its cargo were at risk. The Anglo-Spanish mixed commission had no power to punish the officers and crew of a condemned slave ship. They were free to find other employment in the trade.

By all accounts, the use of the American flag in the Cuban slave trade, which had not previously been very extensive, increased sharply after 1835.[128] Britain responded not only with renewed diplomatic pressure on the United States but also with more aggressive enforcement procedures. Suspected slavers flying American colors were stopped and boarded for examination of their papers. Many turned out to be actually of Spanish nationality and thus liable to search, seizure, and trial before a mixed commission, as provided by treaty. British naval commanders caught the attention of the American public when they dispatched several questionable vessels to New York for determination of their status and possible prosecution.[129] Ships proving to be bona fide American were usually allowed to continue on their way, but each instance of stoppage constituted an interference with maritime commerce and thus an "outrage" in the eyes of American officials. Andrew Stevenson, the United States minister in London, was kept busy protesting one ship seizure after another while receiving in return the Foreign Office's vigorous complaints about American complicity in the slave trade. With customary boldness, Palmerston now asserted a right to board any vessel solely for the purpose of examining its papers to determine its true nationality. Stevenson, speaking for the administration of Martin Van Buren, emphatically rejected this proposed distinction between right of search and right of visit.[130]

The confrontation over the slave trade came at a time when Anglo-American relations were strained by other difficulties, including rival claims to Oregon and the disputed Maine-New Brunswick boundary. Hostility to Britain was especially strong in the South by the late 1830s. There, the shock of West Indian emancipation had been aggravated by the *Comet, Encomium,* and *Enterprise* controversies, along with other indications of a growing abolitionist influence on British foreign policy. One specific southern fear was that Britain would pressure Spain into ceding Cuba and then use the island as a base for undermining slavery in the United States.[131] British officials in turn, whether dealing with Stevenson in London or Forsyth in Washington, saw little reason to doubt that slaveholding influence accounted in no small part for the indifference with which the State Department seemed to view all evidence of American complicity in a universally condemned but still flourishing traffic.

A case in point was the *Prova,* a Portuguese slave ship out of Havana that put into Charleston in distress and remained there three months for refitting without any interference from port authorities. It then sailed for the African coast and took on a load of slaves, only to be captured by a British warship and condemned by the joint commission at Sierra Leone in 1839. When Forsyth received full information on the incident from the British minister, he replied: "With Spanish, Portuguese, or Brazilian vessels, forced into our ports by misfortune, although engaged in the slave trade, the officers of the customs have no right to interfere." Such matters, he said, must be dealt with by the appropriate foreign consuls. (Actually, the sheltering of the *Prova* violated the first clause of the very first federal anti-slave-trade law—the one enacted in 1794.) With respect to foreign slave ships posing as American, Forsyth declared: "The United States have no authority to punish the subjects or citizens of other nations for offences committed against the laws of their own country on the high seas. . . ."[132] Yet, at the same time, Forsyth and Stevenson continued to insist that the American flag was inviolable and that British naval officers had no right to board any vessel flying it. How, then, was wrongful use of the flag to be stopped?

Especially galling to Palmerston were reports from Havana, where Spanish officials commonly connived at slave trading, that the United States consul was lending aid to the traffic. The man in question was Nicholas P. Trist, a Virginian who had married the granddaughter of Thomas Jefferson and served as Andrew Jackson's private secretary before receiving the Cuban appointment in 1833. Lukewarm in his opposition to the slave trade, which he thought beneficial to the Africans themselves, Trist seems to have believed that active intervention against the traffic was beyond the authority of his office and likely in any case to be a useless exercise. Along with that apathetic view of his responsibilities, he nursed a deep resentment of British power in general and British abolitionism in particular.[133] According to Her Majesty's slave-trade commissioners in Havana, Trist habitually signed papers for suspected slavers enabling them to sail for Africa under the protection of the American flag. In addition, for more than a year he voluntarily performed the duties of the absent Portuguese consul and in that capacity, it was said, cleared many slave ships for the African coast.[134]

When the charges against him began to appear in published British documents, Trist found himself a target of reprobation on both sides of the Atlantic. James Gordon Bennett's *New York Herald*, for example, said that there appeared to be cause for his "instant removal." John Quincy Adams expressed the common antislavery view when he concluded that the documents revealed "either the vilest treachery or the most culpable indifference to his duties."[135] Trist, who may have been the wordiest government functionary in all American history, responded vehemently and at length in official dispatches and private correspondence, as well as in a pamphlet signed: "A Calm Observer." The climax of his caustic exchange with the British commissioners was a letter of some 275 handwritten pages in which he mixed a defense of his own conduct with personal abuse of his critics and an attack on Britain's motives in her war against the slave trade.[136]

Trist had powerful friends in Washington, including the president himself, but Van Buren, facing a difficult campaign for reelection, recognized that an investigation was necessary. The special agent appointed for the task was Alexander H. Everett of Massachusetts, a Whig turned Democrat who had served as minister to Spain. Forsyth made it plain to him that the administration expected Trist to be exonerated. After spending several months in Cuba, however, Everett submitted a report severely critical of the consul's performance. Trist promptly set to work on a point-by-point reply, which he did not finish because of an "affection of the head." Even so, the completed portion

(dutifully printed by order of Congress, along with hundreds of other relevant documents) ran to 262 pages, or ten times the length of Everett's report.
With the extent of his culpability obscured by so much verbiage, Trist held on
to his post until he was removed, ostensibly for partisan reasons, by the
incoming Whig administration in 1841.[137] That did not mark the end of his
public service, however. Four years later, this American original would be
back in harness, exasperating his superiors as he negotiated the Treaty of
Guadelupe Hidalgo.

In December 1839, at the height of the furor over Trist, the president
announced that a "competent" naval force would be stationed on the African
coast. Clearly, the primary purpose of this action was to remove what Forsyth
called the "pretext" for British boarding of American merchant vessels.[138]
Actually, only two warships, the brigantine *Dolphin* and the schooner *Grampus*, were sent to Africa in 1840. The senior officer, Lieutenant John L. Paine,
carried orders that included "friendly co-operation" with the British navy. He
interpreted them broadly, to say the least, entering into an agreement with
the senior British commander that went so far as to establish a mutual right
of search. News of the agreement caused no less dismay in Washington than
delight in London. The secretary of the navy hastened to reprimand Paine and
repudiate his naive venture into diplomacy.[139]

Dolphin and *Grampus* made just one capture between them (the first in
nearly twenty years by an American warship in African waters). To be sure,
their very presence seems to have discouraged illegal use of the American
flag, thereby enabling the British fleet to take more prizes in 1840 than ever
before.[140] Palmerston was far from satisfied, however, and did not slacken his
aggressive policy. British naval commanders went on stopping American
ships to examine their papers, and American officials went on lodging stern
protests with the Foreign Office. Daniel Webster succeeded Forsyth as secretary of state, and Palmerston, his party having fallen from power, gave way to
the Earl of Aberdeen, but the controversy continued. The political change in
both governments nevertheless cleared the way for an extraordinary effort to
resolve their various differences, and in February 1842, a special British minister, Lord Ashburton, departed for the United States with full power to
negotiate a general settlement.

ASHBURTON ARRIVED IN Washington at a time of highly inflamed feelings
concerning slavery. Abolitionist petitions were still having a disruptive effect
on the deliberations of Congress, and in early February, after two weeks of

furious debate, John Quincy Adams had barely escaped formal censure by the House of Representatives. Moreover, Ashburton's mission was threatened from the start by the uproar over the recent *Creole* affair, in which the British government had displayed an apparent readiness to condone servile rebellion at sea and give asylum to its principals. For southerners, the sinister connection between British power and American abolitionism seemed well illustrated in the inflammatory Giddings resolutions of March 21, which vindicated the *Creole* uprising as a resumption of natural rights and earned the author a vote of censure such as Adams had just avoided.

It was also at the time of Ashburton's departure for the United States that Anglo-American differences over the slave trade were producing a curious turn of events in Paris. In December 1841, the five major European powers (Britain, France, Austria, Prussia, and Russia) signed a treaty embracing mutual right of search and declaring the slave trade to be piracy.[141] Now, since France and Britain were already bound by their own slave-trade convention and the other three nations had little practical concern with the problem, this new treaty seemed to serve only an emblematic purpose—except, perhaps, as the first step in a larger project. By inviting other Western countries to sign the pact, Britain might at last fulfill Castlereagh's vision of an international concert for suppression of the slave trade, with the British navy as its chief enforcing agent. That achievement would, at the very least, increase the moral pressure on laggard governments, particularly the United States. The *London Times* declared menacingly that the European states would not "brook to be thwarted" by American recalcitrance.[142] Furthermore, definition of the slave trade as piracy by a concert of nations could well mean incorporation of the principle into international law, something that courts in Europe and America had generally resisted.[143] Such a change, as John Quincy Adams had suggested back in 1824, might furnish some legal basis for peacetime visit and search without treaty authorization.

One man disturbed by these possibilities was Lewis Cass, the portly and somewhat pompous American minister to France. A Jacksonian Democrat from Michigan who had fought in the War of 1812 and retained all of his old enmity toward Britain, Cass persuaded himself that the Quintuple Treaty, taken together with the British government's persistent assertion of a right of visit, constituted a grave threat to the United States. Without any instructions from home, he launched a personal campaign to turn the French government against the treaty. In addition to lobbying among legislators, he sent an official letter of protest to Foreign Minister Francois Guizot, and he published a pamphlet setting forth emphatically the American position on right of visit and search.[144] Whatever effect Cass's intervention may have had, the Chamber of Deputies did refuse to approve the treaty, its vote coming soon after the Webster-Ashburton discussions got under way in Washington. Webster and President John Tyler, after some hesitation, endorsed his extraordinary course of action, while vexed British officials accepted the incident as one more example of American obstructionism in the war against the slave trade.[145]

Cass, an ardent nationalist more or less indifferent to the problem of slavery at home and abroad, warned that Britain's slave-trade policy, as embodied in the Quintuple Treaty, had the ulterior purpose of advancing her maritime power and securing commercial advantage. "Who can doubt," he wrote, "but that English cruisers, stationed upon that distant coast, with an unlimited right of search, and discretionary authority to take possession of all vessels frequenting those seas, will seriously interrupt the trade of other nations. . . . A trade carried on under such unfavorable circumstances cannot contend with the trade of a favored nation, who herself exercises the police of the seas, and who may be harsh or lenient, as her prejudices or interest may dictate."[146]

Besides Cass, there were other Americans, principally southerners, who responded to British criticism of the United States by impugning the motives and methods of Britain's crusade against the slave trade. Nicholas Trist, for example, maintained that British policy was inspired by selfish economic considerations and that Britain itself supplied most of the goods used in the trade. The zealous talk of his British accusers from Palmerston on down, he said, was merely the "empty cant" of men who actually wanted the traffic to continue because their political popularity or their very jobs depended on it.[147] Similarly, Charles H. Bell, commander of one of the American warships sent to Africa in 1840, reported that the cruising strategy of British naval officers seemed ill-chosen for suppression of the slave trade and was, by their own admission, aimed primarily at earning prize money. Bell also charged that at Sierra Leone, articles from condemned vessels were commonly acquired at auction by British agents, who passed them on to slave dealers. "Under these circumstances," he wrote, "I say the British Government is *not sincere in its attempts to put down the slave-trade.*"[148]

Especially effective as a voice of Anglophobia was the well-known editor, promoter, and behind-the-scenes politician, Duff Green. This self-important Kentuckian, long associated with the political fortunes of Calhoun, went to Europe in 1841 with informal credentials as Tyler's personal agent and there lent encouragement to Cass in his attack on the Quintuple Treaty. Eight years earlier, Green had developed an economic interpretation of British emancipation in the West Indies, arguing that the reform was really the work of British capitalists, particularly East Indian interests, who used abolitionist fanatics to achieve their own purposes.[149] As Ashburton was crossing the Atlantic in March 1842, Green returned to the same theme with an article on "England and America," published first by a Paris newspaper and then by an English magazine. In it, he declared that the volume of the African slave trade had been greatly exaggerated to suit British strategy. "England," he wrote, "has laboured to render the slave-trade more odious, because her purpose is to abolish slavery; not that England has any sympathy for the slave; but because England believes that, but for slave-labour in the United States, in Cuba, and Brazil she could produce cotton, rice, coffee, and sugar cheaper in India than it can be produced in the United States, Cuba, or Brazil. Her war upon the slave-trade . . . is a movement to compel the whole world to pay her tribute."[150] Green's words were important because of the weight they carried with the president and certain other American political leaders. Calhoun, for one, was soon echoing the idea that British abolitionism served primarily to facilitate the British pursuit of "dominion and commercial monopoly."[151]

In portraying British antislavery policy as driven by economic rather than humanitarian purposes, Green and others like him anticipated certain aspects of the thesis set forth a century later by the Marxist historian Eric Williams.[152] Unlike Williams, however, they mixed economic determinism with a good deal of conspiracy theory, summoning up the specter of a British grand design aimed at maritime supremacy, commercial monopoly, and universal emancipation. Southern apprehensions were heightened in the early 1840s by loose talk on both sides of the Atlantic about a possibly impending war in which Britain's most likely strategy would be to strike at American slavery, using West Indian troops to stir up black revolution throughout the South. Green was not alone in believing that such a war, if it came, would probably result from continued British harassment of American ships in the name of suppressing the African slave trade.[153]

The slave trade is commonly regarded as one of the secondary matters dealt with in the Webster-Ashburton negotiations.[154] Both men knew, however, that the issue was little less than crucial. There appears to have been some hope at first that American concessions respecting right of search might be exchanged for a British renunciation of impressment. Edward Everett, who had succeeded Stevenson as minister to England, favored just such a compromise, but neither government was willing to give any ground.[155] The Webster-Ashburton discussions accordingly turned to the only suitable alternative—a system of joint patrol. Webster sought advice from Lieutenants Paine and Bell, commanders of the two ships sent to Africa in 1840. Their reply recommended that a squadron of about fifteen ships, mainly schooners, be kept on the African coast and that arrangements be made for them to "cruise in couples" with British vessels. In a clause stricken by Webster before the letter was printed, the two officers also ventured to suggest a mutual right of visit for the sole purpose of determining a vessel's national character.[156]

The Paine-Bell report became the basis for the slave-trade agreement in the Webster-Ashburton Treaty (or Treaty of Washington), signed in its final form on August 10, 1842, and approved by the Senate ten days later. Article VIII stipulated that each nation should "maintain in service, on the coast of Africa, a sufficient and adequate squadron, or naval force of vessels, of suitable numbers and descriptions, to carry in all not less than eighty guns." The two squadrons would be "independent of each other," but were to "act in concert and cooperation."[157] Both negotiators were well satisfied with the solution, Ashburton, indeed, calling it "the very best fruit" of his mission.[158] The article nevertheless proved faulty in a number of ways. It was a mistake, for instance, to specify a minimum number of guns, without also fixing the minimum number of ships to be deployed. And, of course, the right-of-visit issue, though presumably rendered less urgent by the provision for joint cruising, remained unsettled.

When Lewis Cass learned the contents of the treaty, he protested vehemently because it did not include an explicit British renunciation of the asserted right to board American vessels. That, he told Webster, should have been a prior condition to any negotiation. Democratic senators Thomas Hart Benton and James Buchanan had argued along similar lines in their efforts to defeat the treaty. Cass resigned and returned home, but pursued his quarrel with Webster in a correspondence that became increasingly acrimonious. The treaty, he insisted, left untouched the "monstrous pretension" with which Britain sought to "introduce an entire change in the maritime police of the world."[159]

Troubled by such criticism, the president reviewed the controversy in his annual message to Congress on December 6, 1842. Again rejecting the British distinction between visit and search, he took the position that Article VIII put the whole issue to rest. "All pretense is removed," he declared, "for interference with our commerce for any purpose whatever by a foreign government."[160] That statement caused a stir in London, where Aberdeen and the prime minister, Sir Robert Peel, were under attack from the political opposition, charged with yielding too much in the treaty. They labeled Tyler's interpretation inaccurate and emphatically denied having retreated from the principle of visitation. Aberdeen wrote in January: "We still maintain, and will exercise, when necessary, our right to ascertain the genuineness of any flag which a suspected vessel may bear." England, said the *London Times*, had not abandoned "one tittle of her claim."[161] Webster labored with some success to smooth over the dispute, and Tyler helped by acknowledging in a subsequent message that neither side had made any concession of principle on the subject.[162]

The Anglo-American controversy over right of visit, though not formally resolved in 1842, was for several reasons muted in the years that followed. As expected, the presence of an American squadron on the African coast reduced the occasions for British investigation of ostensibly American ships believed to be slavers. More important, the two governments, while continuing to disagree in principle, had gradually talked their way into an accommodation. Britain claimed a right to board merchant ships suspected of illegally flying the American flag. The United States acknowledged that it had no grounds for protest when such suspicion proved to be accurate. Thus the quarrel was over instances of *mistaken* suspicion—that is, of British interference with bona fide American vessels. In December 1841, Aberdeen took the important step of virtually conceding that such mistakes constituted trespass. "If, in spite of the utmost caution," he wrote, "an error should be committed, and any American vessel should suffer loss and injury, it would be followed by prompt and ample reparation." A few months later, he made this promise more concrete when he told Everett that the government had decided to indemnify the owner of the *Tigris*, one of the ships seized in 1840.[163]

Everett was thereafter busier presenting claims for past British "outrages" than with lodging protests against new ones. He sometimes found his task embarrassing. For example, the *Douglas*, an American ship sailing under American colors, had been boarded, searched, and detained for several days before being allowed to go on its way. Everett confided to Webster that he thought the evidence strongly implicated the *Douglas* in slave trading, but he maintained in his correspondence with Aberdeen that the owner had a strong legal case for redress. Aberdeen's reply, though politely phrased, said in effect that Britain would pay damages if the United States had the indecency to ask for them. The American government, for once shamed into submission, ceased to sponsor the malodorous claim.[164]

Britain's stated willingness to make restitution for any unwarranted detention of American ships markedly reduced the tension between the two countries, but it did not put an end to controversy. There was continuing argument over which incidents called for reparation and how much should be paid in each instance. In August 1843, after more than a year of delay, Aberdeen offered an indemnity of approximately $6,000 for the *Tigris*, much less than the owner had sought. Everett replied that he had no authority to compromise the amount of a claim. The matter accordingly remained unsettled until 1854, when a mixed commission (the one that disposed of the *Creole* claims) fixed damages at about double what Aberdeen had proposed. From the same arbitrational body, the owner of the *Douglas* received a more or less nominal award of $600.[165]

Meanwhile, British naval commanders on the African coast continued to operate under virtually the same instructions that had been in effect before the Webster-Ashburton Treaty. That is, they were authorized to board any suspicious vessel flying the American flag, but solely for the purpose of determining its true nationality. If it proved to be bona fide American, the boarding officer was to leave immediately, no matter what evidence of slave trading he might see.[166] But a ship flying false colors was likely also to carry false papers, and suspicion along those lines sometimes led an officer to turn his "visit" into a search. In 1850, for example, several vessels claiming to be American were boarded and seized as prizes, their American papers having been arbitrarily labeled false. More often, British officers boarded American ships and, finding their papers in order, released them, only to learn later that they had loaded slaves and fled westward.[167]

A leading authority on the subject is therefore mistaken in his assertion that the right of visit was not exercised for fifteen years after ratification of the Webster-Ashburton Treaty.[168] In fact, British visitation of suspected ships remained an established policy, practiced infrequently but becoming somewhat more common after Palmerston returned to the Foreign Office in 1846. One vessel alone, the *Lucy Ann*, received several visits early in 1850, even though her American papers were each time found to be in order. As the boarding officer on the last visit was about to leave, he heard from below the deck "a low, indistinct murmur, wrung from the accumulated sufferings of her human cargo." The captain, when confronted, promptly announced that he was not the master. He threw the ship's papers overboard, and ordered the

American flag to be replaced with Brazilian colors. More than 500 slaves were found aboard.[169]

During those fifteen years, to be sure, complaints about British conduct were generally lodged and parried by naval commanders on station, rather than by diplomats in London and Washington. An exchange in 1850, for instance, between Levin M. Powell of the U.S.S. *John Adams* and George F. Hastings of H.M.S. *Cyclops* embraced many of the same arguments that Palmerston and Stevenson had directed at each other a decade earlier.[170] Not until the late 1850s, when the conduct of American foreign policy was in the hands of Lewis Cass, did the right-of-visit controversy escalate again to the crisis level of 1840.

6

The African Slave Trade, 1842 to 1862

THE MAN RESPONSIBLE for implementing Article VIII of the Webster-Ashburton Treaty was Tyler's secretary of the navy, Abel P. Upshur, a social conservative and proslavery radical of the Calhoun stamp who would soon replace Webster in the State Department. Like the president, Upshur at this time had his eyes fixed on Texas. There is no evidence of his giving anything beyond perfunctory attention to the problem of the slave trade. Only after months of delay did he appoint Matthew C. Perry to command the African squadron, and it was August of 1843 when Perry arrived off Cape Mesurado, where he had cruised with the *Shark* twenty-two years earlier.[1]

Upshur's instructions made it plain that the squadron's primary assignment was the protection of American commerce. "It is to be borne in mind," he wrote, "that while the U[nited] States sincerely desire the suppression of the Slave Trade, and design to exert their power, in good faith, for the accomplishment of that object, they do not regard the success of their efforts as their paramount interest nor as their paramount duty. They are not prepared to sacrifice to it any of their rights as an independent Nation, nor will the object in view justify the exposure of their own people to injurious and vexatious interruptions in the prosecution of their lawful pursuits. Great caution is to be observed, upon this point."[2]

Instead of the fifteen vessels, principally small schooners, recommended in the Paine-Bell report, Upshur put together an African squadron consisting of one frigate, two sloops-of-war, and one brigantine, only the last of which measured less than 500 tons. The squadron mounted a total of eighty-two guns and thus met the terms of the Webster-Ashburton Treaty, but scarcely in a way calculated to maximize the American effort against the slave trade. Aside from the 1,341-ton frigate *Macedonian*, these ships were not unsuited for their task, as some historians have maintained. They were simply too few for effective patrol of several thousand miles of coast.[3] Perry made matters worse by keeping the squadron together as often as not, rather than systematically dispersing it in the interest of broader surveillance. Contrary to his instructions from Upshur, he did not enter into an arrangement for joint cruising with British warships. Neither did he venture into the busy slave-trading areas south of the equator, although the instructions permitted him to do so. He spent much of his time in a variety of other activities, such as lending aid to Liberia and other colonization settlements, palavering with native rulers, and punishing earlier offenses against American citizens. During Perry's year and a half of command, the squadron took only one suspected slaver as a prize, and that primarily because the mate had been murdered.[4] Under his successor, Commodore Charles W. Skinner, six slavers were captured in about the same amount of time. The biggest catch was the *Pons*, taken off Cabinda, south of the equator, with 913 Africans aboard.[5]

Even with the flurry of activity under Skinner's command, the secretary of the navy in 1850 reported only 7 slave ships captured by the African squadron since its creation. That was an average of one a year, at an annual cost of $384,500.[6] During the same period, the British navy made over 500 captures and liberated approximately 38,000 Africans.[7] This striking contrast, though misleading in certain respects, undoubtedly reflected a differential in national commitment. British slave-trade policy, heavily influenced by British abolitionism, was designed to produce results. American policy, on the other hand, was essentially gestural, aimed primarily at screening American commerce from British interference. Successive administrations were unresponsive to advice from the squadron's commanders on how to improve its operations. They did not discontinue the assignment of frigates in favor of smaller warships, for instance, or furnish the steamers repeatedly requested, or remedy the inefficiencies of the supply system.[8] Frequently, they even allowed the strength of the squadron to fall below the treaty minimum of eighty guns. For a time during the Mexican War it consisted of three ships with a total of forty-two guns. In October 1852, Commodore Isaac Mayo reported an effective strength of seventy-one guns, fifty-one of them mounted on the frigate *Constitution*, which he labeled "entirely unfit" for slave-trade duty.[9]

Despite these and other handicaps, including the difficulty of maintaining health and morale on the African coast, the squadron's performance over the years was arguably better than the statistics would seem to indicate. Always much smaller than the British African fleet, it also had fewer opportunities for captures, being limited to the seizure of American ships. When those differences are taken into account, the American record compares less unfavorably with that of the Royal Navy.[10] Furthermore, it should be remembered that slave traders, who commonly carried more than one flag and set of papers, were readier to risk capture as non-Americans by British warships than as Americans by American warships, because they would not then face criminal prosecution and a possible death sentence. That is why slavers seldom flew the American flag *after* they had loaded their human cargoes.

As an additional explanation of the relatively small number of captures, it has been said that the American navy was authorized to seize only those ships that actually had slaves aboard. This curiously durable misinformation may have originated in 1840 with a statement by Palmerston that went uncorrected. "There is no law of the United States," he complained to the American minister, "which renders it penal for a vessel to be equipped simply for the slave trade."[11] The same mistaken notion appears to have been held by some American officials who should have known better, such as the consul at Rio de Janeiro.[12] It has certainly had a long life among historians.[13] Yet, at the very time that Palmerston made his pronouncement, Lieutenant Paine, commanding the *Grampus*, was on his way to Africa with orders to seize any American vessel equipped for slave trading even if it did not have "a single slave aboard."[14] The laws of 1800, 1818, and 1819 were repeatedly interpreted in naval instructions and in court decisions as embracing ships intended for slaving at any stage of their operations. On the federal circuit in 1823, for example, Justice Joseph Story rejected the contention that the act of 1800 applied only to the actual transportation of slaves. "Every vessel fitted out for the purpose of the slave trade," he declared, "may be truly and accurately said to be employed in that business . . . as soon as she has sailed on the voyage." Chief Justice Roger B. Taney, speaking for a unanimous Supreme Court, said virtually the same thing in a decision handed down in 1840.[15] And, in actual practice, the slave-trade prizes taken by the American navy, like those of the British navy, were more often than not ships that had no slaves aboard.

To be sure, American slave-trade law would have been stronger if, like the Anglo-Spanish treaty of 1835, it had specified what constituted slave-trading equipment. British leaders repeatedly pointed out the need for such legislation, but Congress never responded. The statutory vagueness provided loopholes for slave traders to explore in the courtroom, and it also led to circumstances that made some naval commanders overly cautious in proceeding against suspected ships. A chill of fear settled on the African squadron in 1847 when two of its officers were sued for damages by the owners of ships that had been captured as slavers and then released by federal courts. For two years thereafter, the squadron commanders deliberately shirked their duties and avoided taking any prizes.[16] The fear subsided when the suits failed, but it did not pass away entirely. A commander making a capture in 1860 wrote to the United States district attorney in New York City saying that the evidence plainly seemed to warrant condemnation of the vessel. "But should my expectations not be realized," he added, "I most earnestly hope the Court will find the cause of suspicion sufficiently strong to relieve me from all claims for damage, &c., that terror of all our naval officers who strive for conscientious discharge of their duties on this station."[17] The same year, Senator Henry Wilson of Massachusetts proposed a slave-trade bill that included a ban on suits against naval officers, but Congress took no action.[18]

To some extent, of course, the U.S. Navy's performance varied with the abilities and attitudes of the officers in charge. Among the eleven commanders of the African squadron from 1843 to 1861, some, like Skinner, launched vigorous efforts against the slave trade. Others, including Perry, followed their instructions literally and gave higher priority to the promotion of American commerce. And then there were those like Thomas J. Conover who preferred the pleasures of Madeira to cruising the Congo coast. It has been calculated that in twenty-six months of African duty, Conover's flagship, the *Cumberland* spent only twenty-six days on active patrol.[19] This laggard officer, it should be noted, was from New Jersey, whereas the man who captured the notorious *Echo* in 1858 and three other slavers in 1860 was John N. Maffit, later one of the bright lights in the Confederate navy. The record, in fact, does not lend support to the.view that southern naval officers as a class were less energetic than their northern colleagues in operations against the slave trade. An analysis of 71 ship commanders from 1843 to 1861 revealed that 15 of the 32 northerners made 24 captures, and 14 of the 39 southerners made 27 captures. In sectional terms, the honors were close to even.[20]

During the eighteen-year life of the African squadron, the international slave trade and American involvement in it went through several major changes. The half million slaves carried across the Atlantic in the 1830s had been delivered to Brazil and Cuba in a ratio of approximately 2–1, but with the Brazil trade monopolized by Portuguese and Brazilians, the American connection had been concentrated in Cuba. By the time of the Webster-Ashburton Treaty, however, Cuban imports were in sharp decline, owing to conditions on the island, as well as British enforcement procedures. The total for the 1840s amounted to less than a third of what it had been in the previous decade.[21] Meanwhile, certain developments on the international scene were stimulating a surge of American participation in the slave trade to Brazil.

The British government, by coercive legislation in 1839 and a coerced treaty in 1842, had brought Portuguese slave traders fully within the police power of the Royal Navy. Another act of Parliament in 1845 unilaterally extended British naval authority over Brazilian slave traders.[22] Yet, despite these aggressive actions, the importation of Africans into Brazil, after slackening somewhat in the early 1840s, returned to a near-record level of more than 50,000 per year during the second half of the decade.[23] The continuing influx, a response to the undiminished need for additional slave labor in an expanding plantation economy, was facilitated by Brazil's egregious failure to enforce its own slave-trade laws. But it also became increasingly obvious that American enterprise was contributing heavily to the success of the traffic and, indeed, far outweighed the American naval effort to suppress it. "The slave trade is almost entirely carried on under our flag and in American built vessels," wrote George H. Proffitt, the United States minister to Brazil in 1844.[24] The traders, he added, laughed openly at the weakness of the new African squadron and declared that they never met anything but British cruisers, which could be escaped merely by displaying American colors.[25]

As early as 1841, the American consul at Rio de Janeiro, George W. Slacum, had alerted his government to the growing American participation in the Brazilian slave trade. He cited the case of the brig *Sophia*, which, in the usual pattern, sailed to Africa as an American ship and was transferred to Portuguese control at the moment when some 500 slaves were taken aboard. The American captain then became a passenger, but six American seamen were simply abandoned on the African coast, and five of them failed to survive the ordeal. The *Sophia* returned successfully to Brazil, where, after the landing of the Africans, it was promptly burned, being a telltale liability worth only a small fraction of its recent cargo.[26]

Slacum's warnings were repeated by other consuls and by one American minister after another in the 1840s. None was more eloquent than Henry A. Wise, the staunchly proslavery Virginian who succeeded Proffitt in 1844.

Although he had no instructions on the subject, Wise, according to his biographer, spent at least two-thirds of his time and ultimately ruined his mission trying to suppress American involvement in the Brazilian slave trade.[27] He wrote long dispatches to the secretary of state detailing the offenses committed under cover of the American flag and pleading for corrective action from both Congress and the executive branch. Vigorously pursuing his own investigations, he caused several ships and a number of American citizens to be sent home for trial. His officious conduct antagonized the Brazilian government, as well as the American business community in Rio, neither of which had clean hands where the slave trade was concerned. Wise reserved his strongest denunciations for the capitalists rather than the laborers of the traffic. He protested "the crying injustice of punishing the poor ignorant officers and crews of merchant ships for high misdemeanors and felonies, when the ship-owners in the United States, and their *American consignees, factors, and agents abroad*, are left entirely untouched."[28] Equally guilty, he maintained, were the British manufacturers and merchants who supplied most of the goods used in the slave trade.[29]

Wise's successor, David Tod of Ohio, was likewise appalled at the volume of slave importations into Brazil and the extent to which the traffic depended upon the use of American ships and the American flag. His stream of reports and recommendations went unanswered for three years before a secretary of state took any notice of the subject in official correspondence.[30] Tod and Wise, together with more than one consul, emphasized the need to strike at the whole economic apparatus of the slave trade and not merely at the slavers themselves. They repeatedly urged legislation abolishing or severely limiting the issuance of sea letters, temporary registers for American merchant vessels whose ownership was to be transferred abroad.[31] More drastically, they also proposed that trade in American ships between Brazil and Africa be totally prohibited, since virtually all of it was directly or indirectly a part of the slave trade.[32] At home, their words fell on deaf ears. No president or cabinet member showed any signs of being infected with their zeal. Zachary Taylor's first annual message in 1849 did include a halfhearted recommendation concerning sea letters, but it made no impression on Congress.[33]

Americans of the 1840s, preoccupied with other matters, such as continental expansion and the ulcerating problem of domestic slavery, gave no more than passing thought to the African slave trade, a remote and exotically repulsive criminal enterprise that they nevertheless patronized daily with their consumption of sugar and coffee.[34] Even the most grisly accounts of slave-ship atrocities aroused only limited interest and little sense of national responsibility. Barely noticed and soon forgotten, for instance, were events aboard the *Kentucky* and the *Senator*, American brigs that cleared Rio for Africa in the mid-1840s and returned to Brazil loaded with slaves. The blacks on the *Kentucky* rose in revolt soon after departure and were quickly subdued with gunfire. After summary trials, forty-seven of the mutineers were hanged at the yardarm, shot, and cast overboard. In about a dozen instances, a man's leg was first chopped off to save the irons and separate him from his unconvicted companion. The one woman executed was still alive when thrown into the water and could be seen struggling briefly before she sank beneath the waves.[35] As for the *Senator*, after having been stopped and then released by a United States cruiser, it loaded more than 900 Africans, crammed together so tightly that perhaps as many as 74 died the first night from suffocation and dehydration. Only about 600 were still alive when the vessel reached Brazil. For a time thereafter, the American mate of the *Senator* remained in Rio de Janeiro, talking openly of his immunity from arrest since the United States had no extradition treaty with Brazil.[36]

Slave traders landed more than 350,000 Africans in Brazil during the 1840s, and according to most contemporary estimates, at least half of those importations were achieved with American help of some kind. Yet the navy's Brazil squadron, established in the 1830s, only belatedly received special instructions on the subject and did not take a ship into custody until 1845. Even then, the initiative came from Henry Wise. The vessel in question was the *Porpoise*, which had served on the African coast as a tender to slavers, most recently to the infamous *Kentucky*. Wise engineered its seizure within the harbor of Rio de Janeiro, causing a furious diplomatic controversy that compromised his further usefulness as minister. In the end, however, Brazilian authorities did allow the *Porpoise* to be returned to the United States for trial.[37] The Brazil squadron made only five more captures during the decade, three of them by a single warship, the brig *Perry*, within a two-month period in 1848–49.[38] For the most part, the squadron remained a minor factor in the suppression of the slave trade.

The end of the slave trade into Brazil came with an abruptness that surprised everyone. Estimated annual importations declined from nearly 60,000 in 1849 to fewer than 5,000 in 1851, and by 1853, known landings had ceased entirely.[39] This remarkable change undoubtedly resulted in part from British naval pressure, which was further increased in 1850 when Palmerston openly endorsed and encouraged the seizure of slavers within Brazil's territorial waters. Primarily, however, suppression was achieved because of a shift in Brazilian policy from connivance to vigorous enforcement—a shift made easier by changing public attitudes and by the fact that the great influx of the late 1840s had largely satisfied the need for additional slave labor.[40] With the biggest market for slaves thus suddenly closed, the only other one of any importance remaining open in the western hemisphere was Cuba. Many seasoned participants in the Brazilian traffic accordingly transferred their activities northward.

THE SLAVE TRADE to Cuba, after having declined in the late 1840s, revived markedly during the 1850s. Importations totaled more than twice those of the preceding decade and reached a crescendo of 25,000 in 1859.[41] Spain, which in 1845 had finally passed its first penal law against slave trading, nevertheless continued to wink at the traffic in deference to the wishes of the Cuban planter class. The work of suppression was also hindered by the cross-purposes of Britain and the United States with respect to the future of Cuba. British policy had long been directed not only toward forcible extinction of the Cuban slave trade but toward encouraging the abolition of slavery itself on the island. In contrast, American policy, heavily influenced by fears about British intentions, looked toward annexation of Cuba and the consequent perpetuation of Cuban slavery, though presumably not of the Cuban slave trade.[42] Still another complication was the rise of a movement among certain proslavery extremists to secure the repeal of federal slave-trade laws or put them at defiance.

The campaign to reopen the African slave trade into the United States was launched in 1853–54 by a few South Carolinian extremists who wanted to dramatize southern distinctiveness and hasten the disruption of the Union. Gathering strength from the apprehension and anger aroused in the slave-holding states by the rise of the Republican party, the movement became a major subject of discussion at the southern commercial conventions held annually in the 1850s. It received the enthusiastic support of *De Bow's Review* and a number of influential southern newspapers, including the *Charleston Mercury*, and the *New Orleans Delta*. South Carolina's governor, James H. Adams, drew national attention to the issue in 1856 when he devoted much of his annual legislative message to calling for repeal of the federal anti-slave-trade laws.[43]

Public reaction to Adams's message indicated that the movement had only minority support even in its areas of strength and was decidedly unpopular throughout much of the South. In Washington, Whig congressman Emerson Etheridge of Tennessee offered a resolution condemning proposals for revival of the slave trade as "shocking to the moral sentiment." Any such action by the United States, it declared, would invite "the reproach and execration of all civilized and Christian people." What happened next is highly revealing. The House, after some heated argument, passed the resolution, 152 to 57, but three-quarters of the southerners present voted against it, chiefly on the grounds that Etheridge's wording was unacceptable and had a partisan purpose. Immediately, Democrat James L. Orr of South Carolina offered another resolution declaring that repeal of the slave-trade laws would be "inexpedient, unwise, and contrary to the settled policy of the United States." This formulation the House approved, 183 to 8, echoing its historic, nearly unanimous vote in 1807 for abolition of the slave trade.[44]

One southern congressman who voted against the Etheridge resolution voiced the sentiment of many others when he said that it would be "offensive" to the South. The offensiveness consisted in the resolution's tone of moral reproach, which, although directed at the slave trade, was too easily deflectable to slavery itself. Middle ground is seldom the most logical ground, and southerners responding to abolitionist attacks had never found it easy to explain how the owning of slaves differed ethically from the importation of slaves. Now, proslavery extremists were posing their own versions of the same question. If slave trading was piracy, were not all slaves plunder? If the institution of slavery was beneficial to the black race as well as the white, why should the first step in its establishment be treated as an offense against humanity?[45] The standard southern answer was one that associated slave trading with the criminal violence of abduction and slave owning with the maintenance of an inherited social order.[46] But the distinction had never been very convincing, and most southerners were understandably reluctant to face the troubling moral dilemma that was embedded in Etheridge's resolution and absent from Orr's.

The largely unfavorable public response to the pro-slave-trade crusade did not dampen the enthusiasm of its spokesmen. They knew that, in the Lower South especially, their theoretical arguments carried much more weight than their calls for action. Jefferson Davis was just one leading southerner who, although outside their circle, agreed with them publicly in rejecting moral condemnation of the slave trade, in questioning the constitutionality of federal slave-trade laws, and in maintaining that control of the traffic should be returned to the states.[47] Repeal of the federal laws might be in itself a hopeless quest, but continued agitation of the issue suited the adventuresome spirit of disunionism, even though many secessionists regarded the movement as hazardous to their cause.[48] For a few extremists, moreover, the slave-trade question offered a fine opportunity to flout federal authority and thus retaliate for northern defiance of the fugitive-slave laws. What ensued was an apparent revival of slave importations into the United States—one that proves on close examination, however, to have been largely rumor rather than fact.

Thirty-three-year-old Charles Augustus Lafayette Lamar of Savannah, a mixture of shrewd businessman and southern romantic, decided to vindicate the morality of slaveholding society while turning a good profit in the process. Federal slave-trade law was a "brand of reprobation" that he had resolved to violate, this Georgia fire-eater informed his kinsman, Secretary of the Treasury Howell Cobb. "I will re-open the trade in slaves to foreign countries," he declared, "let your cruisers catch me if they can."[49] Lamar and a group of financial associates bought a luxury yacht, the *Wanderer*, and sent her off to Africa equipped as a slaver. Extremely fast, the schooner eluded naval patrols and in late November 1858 landed about 400 slaves on one of the Georgia sea islands. From there they were distributed clandestinely to various purchasers on the mainland. The buzz of local talk about the landing led federal officials in Georgia to seize the *Wanderer* and proceed against it under admiralty law. Judge John C. Nicoll, although he happened to be Lamar's father-in-law, upheld the libel and declared the vessel forfeited to the United States. Criminal prosecution of Lamar, the ship's captain, and several members of the crew failed in each instance, however.[50]

There were reports, some possibly true, of other slave landings in the late 1850s, but the *Wanderer* remains the only documented case. The spate of rumors, many of which appear to have been mere hoaxes or expressions of southern bravado, gained credence in an atmosphere of political turmoil and national crisis. During the summer of 1859, for example, a correspondent in the *New York Tribune* quoted Stephen A. Douglas as saying that importation of Africans had been carried on extensively for some time and was currently at its highest level in history, amounting to more than 15,000 a year.[51] This alleged assertion, reported by an anonymous source in a politically hostile newspaper, has been offered by some historians as evidence of the "revival" of the African slave trade on the eve of the Civil War.[52] If Douglas actually made such an extravagant statement, he may simply have been echoing reports published several weeks earlier in the *New York Herald*. They came from an anonymous Washington correspondent who cited an unnamed senator as his source for the well-known secret that some sixty or seventy cargoes of African "savages" had been landed on the southern coast within the past eighteen months and that depots for their reception had been established in over twenty cities and towns.[53] During the fall of 1859, the Buchanan administration sent a secret agent into the Lower South to investigate the rumors. In more than a month of travel and inquiry from North Carolina to Texas, he was unable to find any credible evidence of slave landings aside from that of the *Wanderer*.[54] Modern authorities generally agree that there was no significant influx of Africans into the United States during the 1850s.[55]

State action looking toward a reopening of the African slave trade reached its high point not in South Carolina, but in Louisiana, which had a greater need for additional slave labor. There, in 1858, the legislature very nearly enacted a bill authorizing the importation of 2,500 Africans to be "indentured as apprentices" for terms of "not less than fifteen years."[56] A slave-trade movement also developed in Texas and seemed to be prospering until it met virtual repudiation in the election of 1859, which returned the stalwart Unionist Sam Houston to the governorship.[57] The extent to which the white population of the Lower South really favored resumption of the slave trade is difficult to estimate because of the cross-currents always present. Thus, the ranks of apparent supporters were swelled by persons eager to express defiance of federal authority and vindicate the morality of slavery, while the ranks of opponents were reinforced by persons otherwise friendly to the cause who recognized that it posed a dangerous threat to southern unity. Eventually, to be sure, the seven states of the Lower South, organized in convention as the Confederate States of America, placed a constitutional ban on the importation of slaves. That emphatic action undoubtedly reflected a widespread repugnance for the slave trade, but it was, at the same time, too much influenced by considerations of policy to be viewed as an accurate measure of public sentiment. Most of the convention's members understood that reopening the trade, a policy bound to antagonize Virginia and the border states, as well as Britain and most of Europe, was simply not a viable option for the new nation.[58]

IF THE REPORTED flood of African slaves into the United States during the late 1850s was almost entirely myth, the resurgence of slave trading into Cuba certainly was not. Nor can there be any doubt that much of the Cuban traffic originated in American ports and utilized American ships under protection of the American flag. British enforcement activities, which had been substantially reduced during the Crimean War, returned to a higher level in 1857, just when James Buchanan was entering the presidency and installing that inveterate anglophobe Lewis Cass as his secretary of state. With Palmerston now prime minister, the British navy once again began to display the kind of aggressiveness associated with his name, and the Foreign Office intensified its diplomatic pressure on the United States government. As boardings of American vessels along the African coast became more frequent, the British minister in Washington, Lord Napier, confronted Cass with a detailed summary of American involvement. In a note written December 24, 1857, he named more than twenty ships recently proved or strongly suspected to be slavers. Under cover of the American flag, the slave trade was still thriving, he said, but it was now restricted to the Cuban market and could be wiped out entirely if the United States would only meet its obligations under the treaty of 1842 and join Britain in a vigorous naval effort at suppression.[59]

The reply from Cass some three and a half months later was unresponsive. Together with making the usual complaints about British naval excesses and reiterating the American stand on visit and search, he declared that the "joint blockade" of the African coast had proved ineffective and suggested other remedies that might be employed instead. One was a shift of emphasis across the Atlantic. Instead of trying to prevent the export of slaves from Africa, he advised, let Britain induce Spain to "shut the ports of Cuba to their entrance."[60] As it happened, such a change of strategy had been under discussion in London for some time and was just then being put into effect, though by more militant means than Cass had in mind.[61] The American public soon became aware that British naval forces had imposed a virtual blockade of Cuba, detaining and searching vessels of all nations for evidence of slave trading and often firing shots at those that sought to escape inspection. *The New York Times* of May 27 listed twenty-eight acts of aggression against American ships, including harassment within Cuban ports as well as at sea. Even some domestic coasting vessels were caught in the British net.[62]

Amidst the storm of protest that erupted throughout the country, Buchanan dispatched warships to the Gulf of Mexico with orders to "protect all vessels of the United States on the high seas from search or detention by the vessels of war of any other nation."[63] In Congress, which had just concluded a long and rancorous struggle over the Lecompton constitution for

Kansas, there was a remarkable display of national unity, as Republicans competed with Democrats and northerners with southerners in denunciation of British "outrages." If authorized, said Anson Burlingame of Massachusetts, those offenses were acts of war; if not, they amounted to robbery at sea and should be dealt with accordingly. Stephen A. Douglas of Illinois and Robert Toombs of Georgia urged the seizure of British warships in retaliation.[64] Even Gamaliel Bailey's vehemently antislavery *National Era* rallied to the support of the Buchanan administration, declaring that the United States must "resist to the death the insolent assumption of any foreign power to subject our ships to detention and examination."[65]

Dangerous though it seemed at the time, this now forgotten crisis of 1858 lasted only a few weeks and was already subsiding when Congress adjourned on June 14. Leaders of Britain's new Conservative government headed by Lord Derby, which had supplanted the Palmerston regime in February, were clearly perplexed by a furor not of their making. They hastened to rein in the West Indian fleet and disavow its aggressive conduct, but not without stumbling into another round of argument on the subject of visit and search.

Napier, in his Christmas Eve note, made the mistake of declaring that display of the American flag, although it exempted a slaver from search, did not protect it from visit. The foreign secretary, Lord Malmesbury, later spoke in similar terms, thus apparently reasserting a right that Aberdeen had ostensibly renounced in the early 1840s—that is, the right to board *any* vessel for the limited purpose of verifying its nationality.[66] Cass's reply to Napier restated the American position cogently and firmly, but in terms that reflected the moderating influence of Buchanan, a president determined to conduct his own foreign policy. After insisting once again that there was no right of visit or search in peacetime under international law, Cass acknowledged that a vessel falsely assuming an American character had no claim to American protection. Whoever investigated such a vessel, however, did so upon his own responsibility.

> As the identity of a person must be determined by the officer bearing a process for his arrest, and determined at the risk of such officer, so must the national identity of a vessel be determined, at a like hazard to him who, doubting the flag she displays, searches her to ascertain her true character. There, no doubt, may be circumstances which would go far to modify the complaints a nation would have a right to make for such a violation of its sovereignty. If the boarding officer had

just grounds for suspicion, and deported himself with propriety in the performance of his task, doing no injury, and peaceably retiring when satisfied of his
error, no nation would make such an act the subject of serious reclamation.[67]

As late as June 8, Malmesbury appeared unwilling to give up right of
visit, but then, after having consulted the law officers of the Crown, he suddenly reversed himself and declared: "Her Majesty's government recognize
the principles of international law as laid down by General Cass in his note of
the 10th of April."[68] This statement, together with the curbing of Britain's
Cuban squadron, resolved the crisis in a way that left Americans feeling victorious. At a banquet in London on the Fourth of July, the 150 celebrants all
rose to their feet and cheered lustily when the American minister, George M.
Dallas, announced that the long controversy was "finally ended." The *Times*
of London, addressing an editorial to the American nation a few days later,
grudgingly acknowledged: "You have now, it appears, got finally rid of that
remnant of your tutelage, the right of visit."[69] Buchanan reported in his next
annual message that Britain had abandoned its longstanding claims, leaving
American vessels secure from visit or search in peacetime "under any circumstances whatever."[70] Historians have likewise been disposed to portray
the outcome of the affair as a British capitulation. According to a Cass biographer, for instance, it was "one of the most just and most brilliant triumphs
of which to this day our diplomacy can boast."[71]

Yet, as Aberdeen pointed out in the House of Lords, Malmesbury's acceptance of the Cass formulation was little more than a return to the pre-1858
status quo.[72] If anything, the American government made the more substantial concession by acknowledging not only that visitation might sometimes be
appropriate, at the visitor's risk, but also that the circumstances and the manner of boarding might minimize the justification for damages.[73] Moreover,
Malmesbury clearly indicated that the strict new restraints placed on the
British fleet were conditional, pending further negotiations. "Vexatious and
irritating controversies" would surely recur, he warned, unless the two
nations could agree upon a procedure for verifying the nationality of suspected vessels.[74]

Thus, neither the theoretical issue nor the practical problem was resolved
in 1858.[75] The transatlantic wrangling continued. Forcible boarding of American ships, though substantially reduced, did not cease altogether, and some
British naval officers continued the practice of using threats to induce dis-
avowal of a slaver's American character, thereby making it an eligible prize.[76]

In London, Dallas busied himself presenting numerous complaints and claims to the Foreign Office, while British officials at the same time were pleading for American action to suppress the flagrant use of the American flag in the Cuban traffic.[77]

The return of Palmerston as prime minister in 1859 did not tend to reduce Anglo-American friction, and neither did the fact that the flow of slaves into Cuba rose that same year to its highest level since the 1830s. Cass responded to the continual British pressure with increasing vexation. He declared that American involvement in the slave trade was exaggerated and that the United States government was tired of Britain's moralizing representations on the subject. English benevolence might be more credibly exported, he suggested, if it first dealt successfully with English miseries at home.[78] When the British foreign secretary, Lord John Russell, proposed a conference of interested nations on the slave trade, Cass replied with a refusal to participate. When Russell then proposed a system of joint cruising in Cuban waters, he received a similar answer.[79] Traditional American doctrine, having gained additional strength in the recent crisis, still prevailed. The United States would enforce its own slave-trade laws and would submit to no system of international police abridging freedom of the seas.[80]

The Buchanan government recognized, however, that with such reassertion of independence there must go some acceptance of responsibility. Resolved to vindicate American motives in the face of British criticism, and perhaps also seeking to distance himself from proslavery extremism in domestic politics, the president authorized a naval effort that proved to be the strongest attack on the slave trade ever launched by any administration. In 1859, Secretary of the Navy Isaac Toucey took two steps that some naval officers had been advocating for years. He added four steamers to the African squadron and moved its supply base from the Cape Verde Islands to a point on the African mainland much nearer the center of slave-trade activity. At the same time, naval forces in the Gulf of Mexico were reinforced with four steamers for guarding the approaches to Cuba.[81] These measures had striking results. American warships, which had averaged only one prize per year from 1851 through 1858, seized five slavers in 1859 and fifteen in 1860. Of those twenty captures, twelve were made on the African coast and eight in Cuban waters.[82]

Beginning with the *Echo* (also known as the *Putnam*), nine of the twenty-eight vessels captured between August 1858 and April 1861 had slaves aboard, the total coming to more than 5,500.[83] For the first time, federal officials had to deal with the disposition of rescued Africans in large numbers under the slave-trade act of 1819. That law committed such persons to the care of a United States marshal until the president had arranged for their return to Africa.

The *Echo* was taken into Charleston and there condemned in federal court, although the subsequent criminal trial of its crew ended, as everyone expected, in acquittal. Some 300 Africans, many of them needing medical attention, were turned over to Marshal Daniel H. Hamilton and lodged at Fort Sumter in an atmosphere of considerable local excitement about their presence. The federal establishment was poorly prepared for this responsibility suddenly thrust upon it. Congress had not provided funding for such a contingency, and there were no set procedures or administrative guidelines. Hamilton telegraphed the president himself, for example, to find out whether he was authorized to hire a physician.[84] His own expenditure of several thousands of dollars went unreimbursed for more than a year in spite of an extraordinary amount of correspondence between Charleston and Washington on the subject.[85] The administration, after consulting the example set by Monroe in 1819, hurriedly negotiated an agreement with the American Colonization Society whereby the freed slaves were to be received in Liberia and maintained for one year at a total cost of $45,000 (this money was not available for actual payment until Congress appropriated it the following year).[86] On September 19, after about three weeks in Hamilton's charge, the *Echo* Africans were put aboard the steam warship *Niagara* for the voyage back across the Atlantic. Disease had already taken a heavy toll and continued to do so. The approximately 300 slaves brought into Charleston, themselves the wretched remainder of perhaps 450 originally shipped from Africa, were reduced to 270 at boarding and to 200 at the end of their journey.[87]

In April and May of 1860, 1,432 blacks from three slavers captured near Cuba were landed at Key West, and the marshal for southern Florida had to wrestle with the same problem of caring for them until their return to Africa. This time, Congress was in session and responded to a special message from Buchanan with its first legislation in thirty-seven years significantly touching the slave trade. Introduced by Senator Judah P. Benjamin of Louisiana, the measure authorized a general agreement with the Colonization Society and appropriated $250,000 specifically for the care and repatriation of the Africans then in Florida. It also approved a future policy of carrying liberated slaves directly to Africa, if practicable, before taking the captured slaver and its crew to the United States for trial.[88] The bill passed easily in both houses, but not without vehement opposition from many southerners, who denounced it as extravagant and unconstitutional. Jefferson Davis objected especially to providing maintenance for the returnees after their arrival in Liberia. "That," he said, "is carrying sympathy, humanity, or whatever it may be called, to an extreme. Charity begins at home. I have no right to tax our people in order that we may support and educate the barbarians of Africa."[89] As it happened, the total cost of resettling the Florida Africans in Liberia proved to be somewhat lower than estimated because of the frightful mortality rate. The secretary of the interior later reported that 294 died at Key West and another 245 failed to survive the transatlantic voyage.[90]

Despite the navy's record number of captures in 1860, the volume of slave importations into Cuba declined only slightly that year.[91] Furthermore, in the secession crisis erupting after the election of Abraham Lincoln, it became increasingly obvious that the navy might soon have other things to do besides hunt slavers. Following the attack on Fort Sumter in April 1861, the African squadron was called home, except for one ship that remained an additional six months on the Congo coast. Thus, ironically, the first antislavery administration in American history found it necessary to discontinue the vigorous offensive against the slave trade that had been launched by its generally proslavery predecessor.

Plainly, the work of suppressing the slave trade was once again largely in British hands. Although Lincoln's secretary of state, William H. Seward, had been one of those denouncing British naval conduct during the visit-and-search crisis of 1858, he and the president realized that the new circumstances made it advisable to seek a new understanding with the Palmerston government. The outbreak of the Civil War had in any case reversed the historic roles of the two nations with respect to maritime rights. Now it was Britain that experienced the tribulations of a neutral as the United States exercised a belligerent's right of search in order to enforce the blockade of Confederate ports. Americans therefore had good reason to soft-pedal their traditional concern about freedom of the seas. As early as May of 1861, Seward indicated a readiness to be more flexible on the subject. He told the British minister, Lord Lyons, that the Lincoln administration would have "none of the squeamishness about allowing American vessels to be boarded and searched which had characterized their predecessors." Later in the year, he went further and signed a secret memorandum to that effect.[92]

Russell and other British leaders, though pleased by this historic change of attitude, expressed dissatisfaction with the flimsy informality of the arrangement. Further negotiations were delayed because of the *Trent* affair, which brought the two countries to the brink of war in November and December of 1861. When that crisis had been resolved on British terms, the foreign secretary renewed his pressure for a slave-trade convention embracing mutual right of search. By March, Seward was studying a draft of a treaty presented to him by Lyons and ready for his signature. Fearing, however, that the American public would see it as another capitulation to England, he stipulated that the proposal must "have the air of coming originally from the United States." That, he said, would help assure acceptance by the Senate.[93]

Lyons agreed, and the two men immediately proceeded to act out an elaborate charade. Seward began the formalities on March 22 with a letter to Lyons proposing negotiations on the subject, and a few days later he submitted a draft of a slave-trade convention that was virtually a copy of the one prepared in London. Resembling the Anglo-Spanish treaty of 1835, it included mutual right of search, an equipment clause, and mixed courts of adjudication. The secretary of state introduced one change as a matter of political strategy. He added a clause permitting abrogation after ten years. Lyons obligingly went through the motions of opposing this limitation and then yielding in the face of Seward's insistence. The treaty could thus be laid before the Senate as a document ostensibly made in America and not wholly pleasing to the British government. In executive session on April 24, it was approved without a dissenting vote.[94]

The treaty, Seward wrote on the day after he signed it, would "bring the African slave trade to an end immediately and forever."[95] His optimism, though extravagant, proved to be essentially sound. The traffic was in fact already declining when the Anglo-American treaty finally closed the biggest gap in Britain's program of suppression. No longer would the stars and stripes protect a slaver from the Royal Navy, which at last had the search warrant that it needed. Suddenly, New York ceased to be the financial and staging center for the international slave trade. According to a British report, there were 170 slaving voyages organized out of that city in the years 1860–62 and none thereafter.[96] Not surprisingly, importation of Africans into Cuba fell from approximately 14,000 in 1861 to 10,000 in 1862 and to fewer than 4,000 in 1863. Within another three years, the influx had been shut off entirely.[97] In his annual message to Congress of December 8, 1863, Lincoln announced: "It is believed that, so far as American ports and American citizens are concerned, that inhuman and odious traffic has been brought to an end."[98] Legislation dating back to the presidency of George Washington was for the first time totally effective.

After 1820, Congress for nearly four decades ceased to legislate concerning the slave trade. It made no response, for instance, to President Martin Van Buren's recommendation in 1839 that the statutes governing sale of American vessels abroad be revised to prevent acquisition by foreign slave traders.[99] It took no action to remedy the lack of an equipment clause or to restrict American trade between Brazil and Africa, as ministers Henry A. Wise and David Tod advised. The executive and judicial branches thus carried on the work of enforcement with virtually no legislative guidance or assistance. Indeed, on at least one occasion Congress inadvertently made things easier for slave traders. In 1847, with economy in mind, it approved a modification of admiralty law that allowed the owner of a libeled ship, pending disposal of the case, to retain possession by posting a bond.[100] The result was more than one travesty such as that of the bark *Orion*, captured in 1859 and already headed back to Africa on another slaving venture when the court got around to condemning it.[101] As a matter of cold finance, the potential profit from a single voyage far exceeded the amount of the bond and justified the risk.[102]

The processes of slave-trade law were intricate to such a degree that confusing results often occurred. Enforcement always began with action by an agent of the executive branch, such as a naval commander or a federal district attorney, but it was ultimately a judicial responsibility. The act of 1794 and subsequent legislation vested jurisdiction in the federal district and circuit courts, functioning both as courts of admiralty (without juries) and as courts of criminal justice (with trial by jury). Seizure of a slaver could result in two kinds of legal action. One was proceedings *in rem* against the ship and its cargo; the other was indictment and trial of one or more of the malefactors. The outcomes were often incongruent. Thus, Captain Cyrus Libby of the *Porpoise* was acquitted in 1846 by a Maine jury, although the ship itself was later confiscated. Similarly, a federal judge in New York condemned the *Nightingale*, captured in 1861 with 961 Africans aboard, but juries failed to convict the two ship's officers brought to trial.[103]

Slave trading in the early decades of the nineteenth century was an old practice but a new crime, with little grounding in legal precedent. The body of American legislation against the trade, though specific enough in setting penalties, defined offenses in such general language that it left many loopholes for defense attorneys and lodged much discretionary power in the federal judiciary. And since the Supreme Court over the years spoke author-itatively on only a few key questions, the attitudes of individual justices on circuit and of lower-court judges played an important part in shaping national slave-trade policy. Their task was a complicated one, involving the application of federal criminal and admiralty law to cases that often also came within the purview of international maritime law and sometimes raised questions of state-federal relations.

The first major issue to be judicially determined was the question whether slave trading could be punished as an international crime. What proved to be the seminal decision came from an English high court in 1817 when the distinguished jurist Sir William Scott (later Lord Stowell) overruled the capture and confiscation of a French slave ship, the *Louis*. Scott held that there was no maritime right of search in peacetime, except against pirates, and that the slave trade was not piratical or in any other way a breach of interna-tional law. It violated, he said, only the domestic laws of certain nations, each of which had the sole power to enforce its own enactments.[104] Lieutenant Robert F. Stockton's venturous seizure of a French slaver, the *Jeune Eugenie*, brought the same question before an American court in 1822. Justice Joseph Story, sitting as circuit judge for Massachusetts, rejected the *Louis* doctrine in a lofty invocation of natural law. The slave trade, he declared, was "repugnant to the general principles of justice and humanity" and therefore contrary to the law of nations, as well as the law of France. Refusing to restore the vessel to its French owners, he nevertheless stopped short of the confiscation that his argument seemed to justify. Instead, under pressure from the State Depart-ment, he ordered that it be delivered over to the French consul.[105]

Story's compliant disposal of the *Jeune Eugenie* obviated appellate review of the bold opinion with which he had prefaced it. Already, however, another case raising the same fundamental questions was before the federal judiciary. In 1820, the *Antelope*, a Spanish slaver that had fallen prey to a Latin Amer-ican privateer captained by a citizen of the United States, was taken into custody near the coast of Florida with 281 Africans aboard.[106] The federal dis-trict court in Georgia and then the federal circuit court both ruled that the ship and a proportion of the slaves must be restored to the Spanish claimants. In each instance, the judge reasoned his way to an emphatic denial that the slave trade violated international law.[107] The case did not reach the Supreme Court until 1825, shortly after senatorial amendment had wrecked the Anglo-American convention designed by John Quincy Adams—a convention that equated the slave trade with piracy and would have established a mutual right of search. Chief Justice John Marshall, speaking for an obviously divided court, paid his respects to the moralistic views of Story but aligned American law with the hardheaded realism of the *Louis* decision. The slave trade, he said, was contrary to the law of nature but consistent with the law of nations. Therefore, it did not "in itself" constitute piracy and could be made piratical only by statute, which had no force beyond the authority of the legislature enacting it. The lower-court ruling that American seizure of the *Antelope* had been illegal was accordingly allowed to stand.[108]

Marshall thus smothered the idea of achieving by judicial fiat the criminalization of the slave trade in international law. There remained only the hope inscribed in the abortive Convention of 1824 that all the other "maritime and civilized powers" might be persuaded to follow individually the example of Britain and the United States in declaring the trade to be piracy, thereby making it so in international law.[109] Progress toward that goal proved to be slow, however. Brazil, for example, did not pass such legislation until 1850, and Spain was still refusing to do so in the 1860s.[110] Consequently, one finds a federal judge instructing a Pennsylvania jury in 1855 that the slave trade, however horrible it might be, did not constitute piracy—not in the sense of making the trader legally an enemy of the human race who could be brought to trial before any court in any country.[111] The American definition of slave trading as piracy therefore had little or no effect on the law of nations. It served primarily to justify the domestic policy of prescribing the death penalty as punishment.

The most famous of all American slave-trade cases likewise involved Spain and the shadowy reaches of international law. In the summer of 1839, the schooner *Amistad* left Havana for another part of Cuba carrying fifty-three recently imported Africans. En route, the blacks revolted and seized control of the ship, killing the captain and one or more members of the crew. They resolved to set course for a return to Africa, but their two owners, whom they had spared, tricked them into heading toward the coast of the United States. After nearly two months at sea, the *Amistad* wandered into Long Island Sound, where it was seized by a revenue cutter and taken into the port of New London, Connecticut. Amidst much local excitement that soon spread across the country, the Africans were lodged in jail, charged with piracy and murder. Abolitionists rallied to their defense, while the Spanish minister in Washington demanded the return of the ship to its owners and the surrender of the blacks to his government.[112]

The Van Buren administration, which at this very time was protesting

Britain's high-handed tactics of search and seizure, emphatically supported the Spanish claim. In addition to treaty obligations and considerations of international law, the president, facing a difficult campaign for reelection in 1840, could not afford to antagonize the South by lending any semblance of approval to a slave rebellion. Secretary of State John Forsyth and Attorney General Felix Grundy, both southerners, were confident that the whole affair could be handled expeditiously through diplomatic channels, but they reckoned without the independence of the federal judiciary.

The Supreme Court justice on circuit in Connecticut was Smith Thompson, an old enemy of Van Buren in New York politics. He settled one important question when he advised a federal grand jury that the *Amistad* Africans, having staged their mutiny on the high seas, were not indictable under American law.[113] Soon thereafter, in admiralty proceedings before the district court, Judge Andrew T. Judson ruled that the schooner and its contents were Spanish property which must be turned over to the Spanish government—except for the Africans. They had been imported illegally into Cuba, he said, and were therefore not property but free persons under Spanish law. He ordered that they be delivered to the president for transportation back to Africa.[114]

Administration leaders were unwilling to acquiesce in this abolitionist victory, however. So the United States government, acting on behalf of Spain, appealed Judson's decision to the circuit court (consisting of Thompson and Judson) and then to the Supreme Court presided over by Roger B. Taney. The case became all the more a national spectacle when John Quincy Adams agreed to serve as a defense counsel and, in an eight-hour argument extending over two days, vehemently chastised the Van Buren administration for its intervention on the side of slavery.[115] The verdict of the Court, with only one justice dissenting, was delivered by Justice Story on March 9, 1841, nearly two decades after his ambivalent handling of the *Jeune Eugenie* case. This time, he spoke in restrained language calculated to avoid stirring up sectional animosities, but his decision confirmed those of the lower courts in finding the Africans to be neither slaves nor pirates but free persons who had been kidnapped from their homeland and held illegally on the *Amistad*.[116] Later that same year, as a consequence, the thirty-five blacks surviving out of the original fifty-three boarded ship in New York harbor for their return to Africa.[117]

After the judicial disposition of the *Amistad* affair in 1841, it continued for many years to be an irritant in American diplomacy and domestic politics. The Spanish government repeatedly demanded an indemnity, and one administration after another acknowledged the justice of its claim. James

Buchanan, both as secretary of state under Polk and during his own presidency, was especially energetic in seeking the necessary appropriation. Congressional debate on the issue ran along sectional lines, partly because reimbursement was viewed as a vindication of slaveholders' rights and partly because the claim came to be regarded as an impediment to American acquisition of Cuba. As late as 1860, a treaty with Spain was defeated in the Senate because it included indemnification for the *Amistad*. Spanish officials finally gave up the struggle after the Lincoln administration repudiated the policy of its predecessors and brushed aside the *Amistad* claim as having no "obligation in law or conscience."[118]

The *Amistad* decision dramatized the principle of checks and balances in the federal government by imposing judicial restraint on the president's authority to conduct foreign relations. Frustrating to executive policy, it was also embarrassing in the context of international law because Story's opinion went behind the ship's documents to enforce Spanish law against Spanish subjects. That was precisely what the British navy had been doing and the American government had been protesting in the controversy over visit and search. More important, perhaps, the decision disturbed many southerners, who read in it judicial endorsement of a slave's right to rebel against his master. Actually, however, Story had implicitly confirmed that right only in the special circumstance of a person's being held as a slave in violation of positive law, and such was not the condition of American slaves. In spite of all the notoriety and emotionalism surrounding it, the *Amistad* case proved to be something less than a legal landmark. It settled no major issue and contributed little to the development of American slave-trade law.

ENFORCEMENT OF SLAVE-TRADE legislation depended in no small part on the latitude with which it was judicially construed and on the standards of proof employed. Both varied, of course, from court to court and according to the nature of the cause. In admiralty cases, where confiscation of a ship and its cargo was commonly the matter at issue, federal judges generally followed the less stringent rules of civil procedure, discountenancing, for example, the efforts of slave-trade lawyers to exploit legal loopholes and rely on legal niceties. Thus, Justice Thompson, speaking for the Supreme Court in 1824, upheld confiscation of two vessels by the district court in South Carolina, declaring that in admiralty proceedings, a libel did not require "all the formality and technical precision of an indictment at common law."[119] There were exceptions, of course, such as a circuit court decision of John Marshall in

1819, which reversed a judgment of forfeiture by virtue of an exceedingly strict reading of the act in question.[120]

The federal judiciary for the most part proved no more willing than Justice Story to accept the argument that only vessels captured with slaves aboard were liable to confiscation. Despite the lack of a detailed equipment clause in any of the acts of Congress, American courts tended to follow the British example of viewing strong circumstantial evidence as conclusive in the absence of satisfactory refutation. Thus the burden of proof in libel proceedings often came to rest on the owner of the captured ship or whoever claimed it as his property. As early as 1820, Justice Henry B. Livingston made the emphatic pronouncement that "restitution ought never to be made, but in cases which are purged of every intentional violation, by proofs the most clear, the most explicit and unequivocal."[121] Twenty years later, Justice Thompson on circuit in New York, reviewing the case of the schooner *Catharine*, declared: "If the outward voyage of this vessel to the coast of Africa was unconnected with the subsequent employment of the vessel in the transportation of slaves, it certainly requires explanation why she was so peculiarly fitted, in every respect, for the transportation of slaves." Unpersuaded by the explanation offered, he reversed the district court's decision and ordered confiscation of the ship.[122]

A few judges, to be sure, interpreted federal law so strictly as to provide a protective screen for some of its violators. Conspicuous in this respect was Samuel R. Betts of New York, a judicial appointee of John Quincy Adams whose concern for property rights outweighed his pallid interest in suppressing the African slave trade. Among other things, Judge Betts was disposed to regard a vessel's cargo, however well adapted to the slave trade, as not in itself incriminating; and, contrary to several earlier court decisions, including Story's in the case of the *Alexander*, he took the view that a ship did not become engaged in the transportation of slaves until it actually received slaves aboard.[123] His general outlook was well revealed in the case of the *Mary Ann*, a schooner taken over by its crew on the coast of Africa when they became convinced that their captain intended to use it as a slaver. Dismissing the libel, he denounced the action of the crew as "a naked aggression upon the rights of the owner" and denied their claim for wages.[124] Along with Justice Samuel Nelson, who served with him on the circuit court from 1845 onward and tended to share his views, Betts undoubtedly lent some measure of encouragement to slave traders operating out of the port of New York.[125]

Betts's predilections were to some extent curbed by the Supreme Court, which in 1840, for example, explicitly rejected his narrow definition of employment in the transportation of slaves.[126] Consequently, even he appears to have condemned about as many vessels as he released. In the country as a whole during the years 1837 to 1861, over 60 percent of the *in rem* cases carried to a court decision ended in forfeiture.[127] That was well below the British percentage of confiscations, but the circumstances were different. Slavers captured by the Royal Navy were non-British vessels subject to British authority under international arrangements extracted by the British government with heavy-handed diplomacy. Their cases were adjudicated far from England in a short-shrift manner by mixed commissions and British vice admiralty courts that specialized in slave-trade enforcement. Presumption of guilt was so strong that few ships escaped condemnation or destruction—only 42 out of 646 in the period 1821 to 1843.[128] Slavers captured by the U.S. Navy were U.S. ships, often claimed by influential owners having the advantage of expert legal counsel. Their cases were adjudicated at home in various United States district courts by general-purpose judges accustomed to applying common law rules of evidence. The complexity of ownership transfers and lease contracts, together with the tendency of American involvement to be concentrated in the outbound voyages preceding the actual embarkation of slaves, sometimes made confiscation difficult to justify. In these circumstances, a higher average of releases was no doubt inevitable.

In the international effort to suppress the slave trade, confiscation of the offending vessel became the principal sanction and proved over the years to be a far from effective one. The critical factor, as in the case of bonding a captured ship, was the ratio of estimated risk to expected profit. A shipload of Africans was likely to be worth ten or fifteen times the value of the vessel itself. One successful Atlantic crossing could recoup the losses from several captures, and the odds much of the time favored success. Criminal sanction would have been a stronger deterrent if it had been more extensively employed, but the British, as chief enforcers, had no authority to punish foreign nationals with imprisonment or death. They confiscated and destroyed slave ships by the hundreds, but the crews, though sometimes turned over to their own national authorities, usually went free to sail again on subsequent slaving voyages. It was the United States, more than any other nation, that struggled with the problem of using criminal sanction against the slave trade. The frantic efforts of many slaver crews to avoid being arrested as Americans suggest that the penal laws enacted by Congress did have some restraining effect, but the attention of historians has usually been centered on the small number of offenders who actually suffered punishment.

Criminal procedure against alleged slave traders was subject to all the constitutional restraints and common law rules associated with Anglo-American justice, including presumption of innocence, the right to trial by jury, and the requirement of proof beyond reasonable doubt.[129] Particularly important, given the far-flung nature of the slave trade, was the fact that depositions sufficient to justify confiscation of a vessel in a court of admiralty would not serve in a criminal trial, where the accused person had a constitutional right to be confronted with the witnesses against him. Therefore, district attorneys usually had a difficult task assembling the evidence needed for conviction, especially in the face of well-organized resistance from an illicit but entrenched economic interest. Their key witnesses were often out of reach, while the defendant could usually count on exculpatory testimony cut to order. "That perjury will be committed by witnesses of the defence is certain," said one prosecutor. "Pre-arrangements are made for perjury in all slave voyages."[130] Proof of American ownership or American citizenship was almost routinely a stumbling block. Thus, Justice Robert C. Grier on circuit in Pennsylvania refused to accept a ship's registry or "common reputation" as sufficient evidence of ownership. He accordingly instructed the jury in favor of the defendant. The jurymen somewhat rebelliously returned a verdict of "Not guilty under the charge of the court; but guilty in point of fact." Grier made them change it to a simple "Not guilty."[131]

Frequently, however, the jurors proved stubbornly unwilling to convict. This was conspicuously true of several southern juries in the late antebellum period. Sixteen crew members of the notorious *Echo* stood trial in Charleston after Justice James M. Wayne had extracted indictments from a reluctant grand jury. With defense counsel ringing the changes of proslavery argument, they were all found not guilty.[132] Soon thereafter, a Florida jury acquitted the *Echo*'s owner-captain, having been directed to do so on technical grounds.[133] Some thirteen men connected with the equally notorious *Wanderer* were indicted in Georgia, but fewer than half of the cases actually came to trial and no one was convicted.[134] The captain of the *Wanderer*, a South Carolinian, sought refuge in Charleston and was there protected from prosecution by the federal district judge.[135] Attempts to punish persons who knowingly purchased *Wanderer* slaves likewise failed.[136] It appears that after the year 1846, not a single person was convicted on slave-trade charges in a southern federal court.

The great majority of prosecutions were initiated in northern states, most of them in New York. There, about one-sixth of the persons indicted from 1837 to 1861 were ultimately convicted. More than twice as many were acquitted, and the rest likewise gained their freedom, whether via *nolle prosequi*, because of divided juries, by forfeiting bail, or in a few instances, by simply escaping from custody. During that period, according to the records compiled by historian Warren S. Howard, twenty men received prison sentences averaging two years in length, but they served only about one year, on average, because of ten presidential pardons.[137] Fifteen of the convictions were under the law of 1800 and five under the law of 1818, which provided maximum penalties of two years and seven years, respectively. Three men indicted under the Piracy Act of 1820 were allowed to plead guilty to the act of 1800. One was not so lucky.

Captain Nathaniel Gordon, thirty-three-year-old member of a Maine seafaring family, had become involved in slave-trading at a young age, perhaps as early as 1848.[138] His ship, the *Erie*, was seized off the Congo Coast in August 1860 with 897 slaves aboard, and ten months later he went on trial in the circuit court for the southern district of New York, charged with the capital crime of piracy. The jury could not agree on a verdict, primarily because Gordon's two mates swore to his innocence, but the district attorney, a newly installed Republican, determinedly sought more witnesses and instituted a second trial in November 1861. Four members of the *Erie*'s crew were now on hand to testify against their captain. Along with other arguments, defense counsel maintained that the ship, at the time of its capture, was owned and commanded by Spaniards; that Gordon was just a passenger when the slaves were taken aboard; that the crime had been committed in Portuguese rather than international waters; and, most desperately, that Gordon was perhaps not an American citizen because he might have been born abroad during one of his parents' voyages. The court brushed aside all technical objections, and the jury pondered for only twenty minutes before returning a verdict of guilty. Gordon was sentenced to death.[139] The Supreme Court refused to intervene, and so did President Lincoln, except for granting a short reprieve.[140] Gordon, after attempting to poison himself in his cell, died on the gallows on February 21, 1862.[141]

The punishment seemed all the more extreme because of its uniqueness. No other American suffered death as a slave trader or even served a long prison term for the crime. The two mates on the *Erie*, though scarcely less culpable than their captain, were allowed to plead guilty under the act of

1800 and escaped with sentences of eight and nine months.[142] Gordon's conviction has with some justice been labeled a "fluke" that resulted from "the chance conjunction of all the circumstances necessary to hang a pirate." Certainly the Piracy Act of 1820, because of its very harshness, proved almost impossible to enforce in American courts. Yet it is less than accurate to characterize the law as a "dead letter" for forty-two years preceding the execution of Gordon.[143] There is no telling how many Americans were dissuaded from entering the slave trade by the very existence of the law. We do know that the fear of hanging sometimes led culprits to conceal or forswear all connection with the United States and surrender to the British navy as persons subject to its police authority.[144] It was because of the same fear, moreover, that prior to the late 1850s, Americans involved in the slave trade generally avoided association with the actual shipping of slaves. Thus, for most of its life, the Piracy Act seems to have had a deterrent effect that greatly reduced the occasions for its punitive use. Indictments under it were, in any case, very few before 1858.[145]

Most of the American slavers seized with Africans aboard and therefore qualifying as pirates under the act of 1820 were taken during the brief period from April 1860 to April 1861, a time of national crisis culminating in the outbreak of civil war.[146] They were eight ships in all, carrying a total of more than five thousand slaves. Federal courts of admiralty confiscated seven of them: three in New York, one in Virginia, and three in Florida.[147] Criminal prosecution proved much less effective, however, particularly in the South. A Florida grand jury refused to indict one captain; a trial jury acquitted another; and apparently no action at all was taken against the third. Indictment of the slaver captain in Virginia seems likewise to have led nowhere. In New York, where two captains, seven mates, and an owner were indicted, prosecutors did manage to secure five convictions, only one of which, however, was on a capital charge. Their efforts were frustrated in two instances by divided juries and in two others by escapes from custody.[148] Considering the political turbulence of the time and the increased difficulty of assembling the witnesses needed to provide proof beyond reasonable doubt, and considering also the widespread reluctance to impose the death penalty for carrying slaves from Africa to Cuba, it is scarcely surprising that federal attorneys failed to do better.[149] The conviction rate had always been low and for a variety of reasons, not the least of which was the consistent adherence of federal courts to Anglo-American legal rules and principles guarding the rights of accused persons.

AT THE BEGINNING of the nineteenth century, the American nation was importing more slaves than ever before and supplying a good many of the ships and men engaged in the Atlantic slave trade.[150] The famous act of March 2, 1807, for which the ground had been prepared twenty years earlier by the framers of the Constitution, spelled termination of the American role as a market for African slaves. It is true that after the War of 1812, conditions in the Gulf and Caribbean region growing out of the Spanish American revolutions stimulated a burst of slave smuggling into Georgia and Louisiana, but the volume never approached that of the preceding decade, and from about 1820 onward, importation of Africans into the United States was negligible if not nonexistent. The myth to the contrary remains surprisingly durable, owing largely to the influence of W. E. B. Du Bois, who concluded that the act of 1807 "came very near being a dead letter."[151] Repeatedly confusing importation of slaves with the continued flourishing of the international slave trade to Cuba and Brazil, he declared that the influx "noticeably increased about 1835, and reached large proportions by 1860," so large, in fact, as to constitute a virtual "reopening of the slave-trade." The Du Bois estimate of illicit importations totaling at least a quarter of a million over the period 1807–62 would mean the equivalent of more than six hundred *Wanderers*, each landing its cargo of some four hundred Africans on an American shore and doing so with such incredible secrecy that only one of them became the object of public attention.[152]

The act of 1807 was in fact a success, emphatically so if one compares it with analogous efforts in the twentieth century, such as the exclusion of illegal immigrants. Enforcement and the threat of enforcement played a part, but the primary reason for the effectiveness of the legislation was voluntary compliance. Having passed Congress with little opposition, it evoked no popular protest or open talk of defiance. Americans seem to have been near consensus in their readiness to close the gates against further importation of slaves. Although motivated, many of them, by a humanitarian repugnance for the trade, they were plainly most concerned about the racial future of the nation. With Haiti very much in mind, they feared that the African element in the population already exceeded the bounds of safety. Jefferson, in recommending passage of the law, had appropriately justified it as required by "the morality, the reputation, and the best interests of our country."[153] The two groups most adverse to the ban on importations were, in a sense, neutralized by the alternatives available. Because of the natural increase in the American slave population (something that was unique in the western hemisphere), the labor needed by planters in newly settled areas could be supplied largely from slave surpluses in the older South. As for the slave traders themselves, those determined not to abandon their calling could join in the expanding international traffic and do so at a lower risk than if they were to try smuggling Africans into the United States.

It was American participation in the transatlantic slave trade, not importation of Africans into the United States, that persisted until the Civil War in defiance of federal law. Such participation, though substantial at the beginning of the century, had become relatively insignificant by the 1820s, consisting largely of American service on foreign slavers. According to an official British survey, less than one percent of the vessels then engaged in the slave trade were of United States registry.[154] But a great change began to take place in the late 1830s, largely as a result of more vigorous British suppression policies. The increased pressure on Spanish, Portuguese, and Brazilian slave-trading interests led them to seek allies beyond the reach of British authority and spelled tempting opportunity (at a time of financial depression in the United States) for Americans willing to take part, one way or another, in the illegal enterprise. Thereafter, for almost a quarter of a century, American involvement in the transatlantic slave trade lent credence to the image of a republic governed by its slaveholding class.

Besides the seafaring men who actually served on slaving vessels, the taint of American complicity extended to shipowners, commercial agents, and other mercantile elements operating in seaports from New England to Louisiana, as well as in Cuba and Brazil. By the 1850s, New York in particular had become notorious as the place where more slave-trade voyages were being organized, financed, and fitted out than anywhere else in the world. The taint extended also to the United States government, both for failing to exercise adequate control over its own citizens and for allowing foreign slavers to shield themselves behind American registry and the American flag. According to many a contemporary critic and more than one historian, federal officials were chronically negligent in their execution of the slave-trade laws, owing in large part to a systemic proslavery bias.

It is scarcely surprising that Palmerston and other English leaders, for example, should have regarded the seemingly perverse conduct of the United States with respect to the slave trade as a manifestation of southern ascendancy in national affairs. Of course, abolitionists on both sides of the Atlantic shared this conviction, well expressed by the American Anti-Slavery Society when it declared: "That so little should be done by the United States Government to execute its own . . . laws against the foreign Slave-trade, is the most natural consequence conceivable of its complicity with Slaveholding and Slavery-extension, and its servility to the Slave-Power."[155]

Such views were not entirely erroneous. The South did have its own peculiar emotional stake in all the controversy, domestic and foreign, associated with the African slave trade, and the resulting patterns of southern concern were bound to impinge in some ways on government policy. As the vote on the Etheridge resolution graphically revealed, antebellum southerners found it increasingly difficult to reconcile condemnation of the slave trade with a defense of slavery itself. There was a disturbing logic in the argument of George Fitzhugh, among others, that condemnation of the traffic and the very existence of the African squadron cast moral reproach on the slaveholding system.[156] Throughout the antebellum period, the South's hypersensitivity to anything touching slavery plainly affected the administration of federal slave-trade laws, just as it undoubtedly discouraged congressional action needed to improve the effectiveness of those laws. Most important of all, perhaps, was the way in which the mounting southern fear of British antislavery designs served to intensify traditional Anglophobia in the United States and thus impede American cooperation with the international effort against the slave trade.[157]

Yet the relation between southern imperatives and national policy was in this instance more tenuous, as well as more complex and discrepant, than has commonly been supposed. Indeed, the African slave trade is something of an anomaly in American history, for it does not fit well into the familiar pattern of sectional conflict over slavery. Throughout that conflict, a majority of southerners, for reasons ranging from moral repugnance to the most selfish economic considerations, remained opposed to any further introduction of African slaves into the United States. Even the proimportation movement of the late 1850s was for many of its supporters primarily an expression of southern defiance, rather than a program of action. And the Confederate Constitution, created in 1861 by men exclusively from the Deep South, went far beyond the United States Constitution in *forbidding* the importation of Africans and *requiring* congressional legislation to enforce the ban.[158]

As for the international slave trade to Cuba and Brazil, a few southerners were involved, but the South as a whole had no strong interest in its continuation. The federal laws prohibiting the traffic passed Congress with little southern opposition, and certain influential southerners, such as Charles F. Mercer and Henry A. Wise, were among the most eloquent advocates of a vigorous enforcement policy. Southern naval commanders did not hunt slavers with any less dedication than that of northern officers. Southern Supreme Court justices Roger B. Taney, John A. Campbell, and James M. Wayne displayed sterner disapproval of the slave trade than their northern colleagues, Robert C. Grier and Samuel C. Nelson; and it was not until the eve of the Civil War that certain federal courts in the South became conspicuously reluctant to enforce the slave-trade laws.[159] In short, there is little evidence confirming the view that southern men in positions of power made it a practice down through the years to undermine the enforcement program.[160]

For all its sectional overtones, then, the African slave trade never became a major sectional issue in nineteenth-century American politics. The subject did not arise in any of the historic confrontations between North and South. Strikingly, for example, the slave-trade law of 1819 passed Congress with strong bisectional support at the very time that the Missouri controversy was erupting in the House of Representatives. Thereafter, except during the crises with Britain over right of search, American policy makers, both northern and southern, generally tended to view the international slave trade as a problem of marginal relevance to the national interest. The inadequacies of the American suppression program did bear some marks of southern influence, though not of deliberate southern intent. They resulted, however, from a complex of factors that also included preoccupation with other matters of higher priority, considerations of economy in government, ingrained suspicion of British motives, and extremely difficult conditions of enforcement.

7

The Fugitive Slave Problem to 1850

On April 19, 1775, the day of the memorable clashes at Lexington and Concord, two British-born indentured servants launched their own personal rebellion in Fairfax County, Virginia. Thomas Spears (carpenter, pock-marked and freckled, with a drawling voice) and William Webster (brickmaker, well-built, with a roundish face and a broad Scots accent) slipped away from their master's plantation under the cover of night and headed down the Potomac in a small boat. George Washington described them carefully in an advertisement that he placed in the *Virginia Gazette* at Williamsburg. He offered twenty dollars apiece for their capture.[1] The men may have been still at large in June, when Washington accepted appointment as commander in chief of the Continental Army and set out for Massachusetts. By autumn, however, both had returned, or been returned, to Mount Vernon.[2]

Runaways were a common feature of late colonial society, and from Virginia northward, especially, they included white persons as well as black. Washington, who had a relatively small number of white servants on his plantation, was more often bothered by the flight or truancy of a slave. On August 2, 1771, for example, he made this entry in his diary: "At home all day a writing letters and advertisements of Harry who run away the 29th."[3] As president a quarter of a century later, he found the problem as troublesome as ever, and fearing public embarrassment, he was no longer willing to advertise in his own name for the return of a fugitive. In 1796, Mrs. Washington was distressed when her personal servant girl ran off from their house in Philadelphia. A year later, the household regime at

Mount Vernon was disrupted by the disappearance of Hercules the cook. Such "elopements," Washington wrote, were likely to become more frequent in Virginia. "I wish from my soul," he added, "that the legislature of this State could see the policy of a gradual abolition of slavery. It would prevent much future mischief."[4]

Colonial laws dealing with runaway servants and slaves dated back to the seventeenth century. Some responsibility for enforcement rested with sheriffs, magistrates, and other public officers, but more often than not, recovery depended largely on the initiative of the owner. Men like Washington, acting for themselves or through intermediaries, usually took their own steps to locate a fugitive and compel his return to servitude. In doing so, they were presumably exercising a common-law right of "recaption," which, as defined by Sir William Blackstone, permitted private action to recover property wrongfully taken, or a wife, child, or servant wrongfully detained, so long as the exertion did not cause "strife and bodily contention, or endanger the peace of society."[5] Except for a clause in the articles of the New England Confederation (which ceased to exist in 1684), there were no formal intercolonial arrangements for rendition of fugitives. In law and custom, however, the right of recaption was generally assumed to be extrajurisdictional. Thus, Thomas Jefferson in 1769 offered a reward for the return of his mulatto slave Sandy: £2 if captured within Albemarle County, £4 if captured elsewhere in Virginia, and £10 if brought back from another colony. Eight years later, Samuel Chase of Maryland sought the help of Caesar Rodney concerning two escaped slaves recently seen in Sussex County, Delaware. "As I am entirely unacquainted with any one in that County," he wrote, "I beg the favor of You to employ some Person to make Search after them. A Reward of £10 is advertised for each."[6]

The Continental Congress, during most of its fifteen-year existence, took action concerning fugitive slaves only with respect to a special problem growing out of the Revolutionary War. That is, in the treaty of peace with Great Britain and in a series of treaties with Indian tribes, it sought to bring about the return of slaves who had fallen into enemy hands, whether as a result of flight or of capture.[7] Meanwhile, the beginnings of abolition in the North were awakening some slaveholders to the need for express confirmation of their assumed right to pursue runaways across state boundaries. Pennsylvania, in legislation inaugurating a program of gradual emancipation, agreeably provided such reassurance. The state's historic law of 1780 stipulated that the right of an out-of-state owner to recover a fugitive remained unimpaired.[8] In

207 — THE FUGITIVE SLAVE PROBLEM TO 1850

Congress five years later, when Rufus King of New York renewed Jefferson's proposal to exclude slavery from the western territories, the resolution that he subsequently reported from committee included a clause concerning fugitive slaves—the first one ever to come before the national legislature.[9] This resolution in modified form, but with the fugitive slave clause intact, was adopted in 1787 as the sixth article of the Northwest Ordinance. The wording of the clause, like its context, is extremely important: "There shall be neither slavery nor involuntary servitude in the said territory otherwise than in the punishment of crimes, whereof the party shall have been duly convicted; provided always that any person escaping into the same, from whom labor or service is lawfully claimed in any one of the original States, such fugitive may be lawfully reclaimed and conveyed to the person claiming his or her labor or service as aforesaid."[10]

Note particularly the words "may be lawfully reclaimed." In the Ordinance of 1787, as in the Pennsylvania act of 1780, the fugitive slave clause was essentially a recognition of the right of recaption. The provision appeared in both documents, moreover, as a concession to slavery within a larger package of freedom. It was a response to a new situation in which certain slaveholding states were now bordered by jurisdictions where slavery had been abolished.

As a practical matter, flight of slaves across state boundaries was still far from being a significant national problem in 1787. The subject did not even arise in the Constitutional Convention until two weeks before adjournment. It might not have arisen at all without the example of the Northwest Ordinance and the stimulus of a companion item in the emerging draft of the Constitution. Congress, sitting in New York, passed the ordinance on July 13, and the men in Philadelphia were soon familiar with its text. Then, on August 28, the delegates arrived at discussion of the clause dealing with interstate fugitives from justice. Any such person must be "delivered up," it declared, "upon demand of the executive power of the State from which he fled."[11] At this opportune moment, Pierce Butler and Charles C. Pinckney of South Carolina moved to expand the clause by requiring that fugitive servants and slaves "be delivered up like criminals." The proposal, if adopted, would have assimilated the recovery of runaway slaves to the formal process of extradition. There were objections, however, from James Wilson of Pennsylvania and Roger Sherman of Connecticut, both primarily worried about the cost of such a procedure for the state governments involved. Sherman saw "no more propriety in the public seizing and surrendering a slave or servant, than a horse."[12]

Butler and Pinckney, perhaps having second thoughts themselves from the slaveholders' point of view, promptly withdrew their proposition. The next day, Butler submitted a new version that retained no hint of extradition but did echo one phrase in the flight-from-justice clause. Approved without dissent and apparently without discussion by delegates weary after three months of labor, this revised proposal went through two further revisions before emerging as the third and final paragraph of Article IV, Section 2, of the Constitution: "No person held to service or labour in one State, under the laws thereof, escaping into another, shall, in consequence of any law or regulation therein, be discharged from such service or labour, but shall be delivered up on claim of the party to whom such service or labour may be due."13

The crucial phrase derived from the flight-from-justice clause is "shall be delivered up," which contrasts sharply with the "may be lawfully reclaimed" of the Northwest Ordinance. Lacking these words, the fugitive slave clause would have been little more than an injunction against state interference with the right of recaption. But the Butler-Pinckney attempt to merge fugitives from service with fugitives from justice, though speedily abandoned, had affected the text of the Constitution. Now, according to the highest law of the land, a slave must be "delivered up" to the party legitimately claiming his service. But delivered up by whom? Presumably, by anyone holding or harboring him, and presumably also, by agents of the state into which he had fled, if that should prove necessary. The effect of the phrase, though far from clear, appeared to be something *more* than, or something *other* than, mere validation of the right of recaption.14

There was a second and more fundamental difference between the two fugitive slave clauses approved during the summer of 1787. In the case of the Northwest Ordinance, which Congress enacted not for the United States as a whole, but for a dependent area under its exclusive control, the clause was neither national in scope nor compulsive in its effect. Merely a grant of privilege to extrajurisdictional slaveholders, it did not intrude on the sovereignty of any existing state. In contrast, the clause written into the Constitution made interstate rendition of slaves part of the national purpose and did so in the language of legal command. Plainly, it imposed a restriction on state authority, though without specifying the means of enforcing that restriction. At the same time, there is nothing in the text or context to indicate that it was also intended as a mandate to the legislative branch of the new government. The wording of the clause, together with its placement in a section on interstate comity (rather than among the enumerated powers of Congress), seems fairly conclusive on that point. [15]

Discussion of the fugitive slave clause in the state ratifying conventions likewise did not reveal any expectation of its being reinforced by federal statute.[16] Furthermore, the First Congress, in three sessions of hard work putting the Constitution into practice, made no move to implement this or any of the other restrictions on state power contained in Article I, Section 10, and Article IV, Section 2. Constitutional restraints tend, after all, to be self-operative. Slaveholders now had a guaranteed right to reclaim fugitives across state lines without any interference stemming from state authority. If that right should be violated, they could no doubt seek remedy in a court of law, state or federal, for the judges of both were bound by oath to treat the Constitution as the supreme law of the land. Up to this point, therefore, the federal government's involvement with the problem of fugitive slaves was limited to the vague imperative in the Constitution and the likelihood that the federal judiciary would eventually play some part in defining its meaning. By the time the Second Congress assembled in October 1791, however, a running quarrel between Virginia and Pennsylvania had set the stage for congressional intervention.

IN SOUTHWESTERN PENNSYLVANIA, a certain slave named John became legally free in 1783 because his owner had failed to register him in compliance with the state's gradual emancipation law. He was nonetheless retained as a slave and hired out in Virginia. With abolitionist help, he escaped in 1788 and returned to Pennsylvania. Soon thereafter, three Virginians acting on behalf of the lessee entered Pennsylvania, seized John, and hustled him back into slavery. From their point of view, they were exercising a right recognized by Pennsylvania law and guaranteed by the Constitution. But recaption wrongfully practiced amounted to kidnapping, and the three men were indicted *in absentia* under a new Pennsylvania statute that specifically protected free blacks from being carried out of the state for the purpose of enslavement.[17]

More than two years passed without further developments. Then, in 1791, Governor Thomas Mifflin of Pennsylvania, acting under pressure from the Pennsylvania Society for Promoting the Abolition of Slavery, wrote to Governor Beverley Randolph of Virginia, requesting extradition of the three kidnappers and restoration of the slave John to freedom. Randolph, on advice from the Virginia attorney general, refused to comply. Mifflin thereupon sought the help of Washington, with whom he had served and quarreled dur-

ing the Revolution. He suggested that the president might ask the federal legislature to provide such regulations as would, in the future, "obviate all doubt
and embarrassment upon a constitutional question so delicate and important." Washington, after obtaining a somewhat muddled opinion from the
United States attorney general, Edmund Randolph, chose to lay the whole
matter before the newly convened Second Congress.[18]

The problem at hand, it must be emphasized, was extradition of fugitives
from justice, not rendition of fugitive slaves. John, at the time of his seizure
by the three Virginians, had been a free man under Pennsylvania law, and
Virginia authorities never denied it, although of course his captors did.[19] The
question formally at issue between the two states was whether those men
should be returned to Pennsylvania for trial. Still, John's interstate flight with
the aid of abolitionists and his interstate recaption by bounty hunters seemed
to be the very stuff of black fugitivism. That made it easy for members of
Congress to conclude that *both* of the fugitive clauses in the Constitution
required legislative elaboration. Furthermore, other rescue incidents along
the Virginia-Pennsylvania border were at that time alerting southerners to
the need for more precise definition of their constitutional right to recover
runaway slaves anywhere in the country.[20]

As soon as the House of Representatives received Washington's communication, Theodore Sedgwick of Massachusetts moved to create a committee
to prepare legislation "making a general provision in cases of persons charged
with felony, treason, or other crimes, who may flee from a State having cog-
nizance thereof." The House promptly appointed such a committee, with
Sedgwick as chairman, but enlarged the instruction to include legislation
respecting fugitive slaves as well. Who proposed this significant change does
not appear in the record. As it happened, the bill that Sedgwick reported in
November 1791 made no progress on the House floor, and thereafter the initiative passed to the Senate. A precedent had been set, however, for linking
the two subjects in a single statute.[21]

The Senate, after appointing one committee without result, appointed
another in November 1792, authorizing it to draft a bill "respecting fugitives
from justice, and persons escaping from the service of their masters." Four
weeks later, William Johnston of North Carolina presented the committee's
handiwork, which, after several days of apparently heated discussion, was
recommitted. Johnston reported back in early January with amendments
amounting virtually to a new bill. During the debate that followed, this draft
too was extensively modified before the Senate finally passed it on January

18. The House then discussed the bill briefly and approved it by a vote of 48 to 7, having made only one minor verbal change that the Senate readily accepted. On February 12, President Washington signed the measure commonly referred to as the "Fugitive Slave Act of 1793," although only half of its text was devoted to that subject.[22]

The double irony in the whole story would be hard to miss. Just as the fugitive slave clause of the Constitution had been inspired by a seemingly minor concession to slavery in a charter of *freedom* (Article VI of the Northwest Ordinance), so the legislation of 1793 originated in efforts to secure the *freedom* of a man wrongfully held as a slave. In both instances, moreover, the problem of fugitive slaves entered the national purview as a mere addendum to the problem of fugitives from justice. But that emphasis changed during the Second Congress, as the fugitive slave portion of the bill became the center of attention and controversy. Consequently, whereas the first Senate committee, like the House committee before it, consisted of two New Englanders and one southerner, the committee elected by the Senate in November 1792 had a southern majority and a southern chairman. The slaveholding interest, having become more keenly aware of what was at stake, closed ranks to a degree that gave it a pronounced advantage in the shaping of the legislation that eventually emerged.

Much of the Senate's difficulty in framing an acceptable fugitive slave law sprang from the fact that the federal government did not itself have the personnel and other means necessary for effective enforcement. Essentially, there were only two solutions available. One was to require that state and local officials do the work of capturing runaway slaves and turning them over to claimants. The other was to confirm the right of recaption and put teeth into it by providing federal penalties for interference with its exercise. Successive changes in the original Senate bill moved it from the first solution toward the second, leaving only judicial officers—federal, state, and local—involved in the rendition process. The requirement of minimal judicial proceedings before removal of an alleged fugitive proved to be the one positive concession to antislavery sentiment in the shaping of the bill. Another proposed modification, amounting to a kind of statute of limitations, would have given more legal protection to blacks who were longtime residents of a state and claimed to be free. This provision had senatorial approval for a time, but it was struck out in the final hours of debate.[23]

The law signed by Washington contained four sections, the first two of which laid down rules for extradition of fugitives from justice by demand of one governor upon another. Section 3 authorized an owner or his agent to seize an interstate "fugitive from labor" and take him before a federal judge or local magistrate, who, if satisfied of the validity of the claim, was to issue a certificate that would be sufficient warrant for removing the fugitive to the state from which he had fled. The fourth section prescribed a fine of $500 for anyone knowingly concealing such a fugitive or obstructing his arrest or rescuing him from custody. Both halves of the statute constituted intervention by Congress in matters that might have been left to the operation of interstate comity; and both virtually requisitioned the participation of state officials in the execution of federal law.[24]

Congress thus implemented the fugitive slave clause of the Constitution by affirming more explicitly the right of recaption across state lines and reinforcing it with a measure of federal sanction. Recovery of fugitives remained essentially a private undertaking, but one now modestly facilitated and marginally restrained by judicial supervision. Certification amounted to the retroactive licensing of any slave hunter who could satisfy a magistrate (by oral testimony or affidavit) that the person in his custody was indeed a runaway. At the same time, the certification process lent some protection to blacks wrongfully seized, but in this respect it was woefully inadequate. Testimony at the summary hearing was ex parte, and the role of the judge or magistrate was limited to a single ministerial function, beyond which he had no authority to intervene.[25] The statute conferred upon an alleged fugitive no right to speak in his own behalf or to be represented by legal counsel or to have his fate decided by a jury. If his status before flight was in question, the issue could be resolved only in the jurisdiction from which he had fled—that is, according to slave-state law, wherein all blacks were regarded as slaves unless they could prove otherwise.

Still, an alleged fugitive seized in a free state and claiming to be a free person was not wholly at the mercy of national law on the subject—not in a federal republic. In a state such as Pennsylvania, where slavery was in the course of extinction and where blacks were legally presumed to be free in the absence of proof to the contrary, the state government had not only a right but an obligation to protect its citizens and other residents against wrongful treatment amounting to abduction. Under the Constitution alone, the fugitive slave problem might have remained, like the fugitive-from-justice problem, largely a matter of interstate comity, but congressional intervention converted it into a matter of federal relationship, with the national government becoming in the end virtually an agent of the slaveholding interest within free-state jurisdictions.[26] Clashes between state and federal authority were an inevitable consequence of the intervention for the simple reason that effective recovery of fugitive slaves was incompatible with effective protection of free blacks against wrongful seizure.

What turned a difficult problem into an explosive national issue was the developing pattern of outlawry on both sides. On the one hand, some southerners continued the practice of interstate recaption without obtaining the certification specified by the federal law. That is, exercising a common-law right presumably guaranteed by the Constitution, they simply seized alleged fugitives and took them back across state lines to the persons claiming them as slaves. Identification was primitive, however, depending largely on descriptions, and not only were honest mistakes sometimes made, but too often, wrongful seizure was a deliberate act of kidnapping for profit. On the other hand, antislavery resistance to the act of 1793 appeared in a variety of forms, including the reluctance of many free-state magistrates to participate in the recovery process and the active promotion of slave escapes by aggressive abolitionists.

THE LAW SIGNED by George Washington in 1793 continued for fifty-seven [1850] years to be the only federal legislation concerning fugitive slaves. During all that time, attempts to revise or supplement the statute were surprisingly few, considering the widespread dissatisfaction with the way it worked in practice. Most notably, Congress remained completely unresponsive to complaints that the law placed free blacks at risk of enslavement and served as cover for a good deal of outright kidnapping. No bill aimed at ameliorating the racial injustice of the measure was ever introduced or reported in either house, whereas southerners seeking tougher enforcement came close to success on two occasions.

In December 1801, Representative Joseph Nicholson of Maryland reported a bill of remarkable breadth and severity. Designed as an amendment to the act of 1793, it imposed a heavy fine on anyone hiring a black person who did not have a certificate of freedom, and, under threat of the same penalty, it required the employer of a black stranger to advertise a description of that person in two newspapers. Here was a measure that plainly "sought to extend the principles and precautions of a slave regime throughout the nation."[27] Northerners united quickly and defeated it on the third reading by a vote of 46 to 43. Their principal objection, as stated in the meager record, was that "they did not wish to compel every free person of color in the Middle and Eastern States to procure and carry about with them such a certificate."[28]

Sixteen years went by before southern members of Congress mounted another serious effort to amend the act. This time it was a Virginian named James Pindall who reported a bill designed to put more teeth in the recovery process by making northern governors and judicial officers virtually the ministerial agents of southern state officials. Somewhat modified under northern attack, but still invasive of state sovereignty and menacing to the liberties of free blacks, the measure passed the House and was approved by the Senate in amended form. The two houses did not resolve their differences before adjournment, however, and it never became law.[29]

Except as an occasional sounding board for discontent with the act of 1793, Congress played no part in the handling of the fugitive slave problem during the first half of the nineteenth century. The executive department was more active, but mainly in peripheral ways. Federal officials enforced the law in the territories and in the District of Columbia; army troops on the frontier were sometimes used to help owners recover runaway slaves; certain treaties with Indian tribes stipulated the return of fugitives; and the State Department made persistent efforts to secure international agreements for the recovery of fugitives from Spanish Florida, Mexico, and Canada. Among the three branches of the national government, only the judiciary was functionally involved in the interstate rendition process before 1850, and even its role might be regarded as secondary if it were not for one Supreme Court decision of crucial importance.

Interstate recovery of fugitive slaves was essentially a private enterprise conducted under the authority of federal law within an often uncongenial jurisdiction. Certain northern legislatures figure prominently in this, the most melodramatic chapter in the history of American slavery, but the story is primarily an episodic one of pursuers and pursued, of confrontations that occasionally turned violent, and of court cases by the hundreds. In the early decades of the nineteenth century, Pennsylvania and New York were the major centers of controversy, both states being then engaged in the gradual emancipation of their own slave populations. Although a few citizens of those states undoubtedly lent assistance now and then to runaway slaves, there was no extensive desire to interfere with the operation of the law or to encourage an influx of fugitives from the Chesapeake region. At the same time, two persistent problems drove state governments toward intervention. One was the question of how to handle an alleged fugitive's claim that he or

she was in fact free. The other was the evidence that free blacks in considerable numbers were being seized and sold into slavery.

Southerners in Congress, by thwarting all efforts to secure federal
antikidnapping legislation, put added pressure on the free states to provide
some kind of protection for their black residents. Pennsylvania had led the
way in 1788 with an amendment to its abolition statute that included a relatively mild penalty for the kidnapping of a black person with the intention of
selling him into slavery.[30] In 1808, the New York legislature became the first
to pass a law specifically labeled "An Act to prevent the kidnapping of free
people of color." It prescribed very severe penalties that were somewhat moderated in later legislation but continued to include the possibility of as much
as fourteen years' imprisonment.[31] An Ohio antikidnapping law enacted in
1819 is of special interest because it forbade the removal of any alleged fugitive from the state without conformance to the procedure set forth in the
federal law of 1793. In effect, this provision abrogated the slaveholder's right
of direct recaption under common law, a right widely believed to have been
recognized in the Constitution.[32]

In March 1820, shortly after a fierce and protracted controversy in Congress had ended with passage of the Missouri Compromise, the Pennsylvania
General Assembly rather belatedly provided the state with an antikidnapping
law of some force. In addition to its severe punitive provisions, the statute forbade justices of the peace and aldermen to play any part in administration of
the federal fugitive slave law, and it required other state judicial officers to
make and file records of all cases in which they issued certificates of removal
by virtue of that law. [33] Clearly, these restrictions, whatever effect they might
have on the kidnapping of free blacks, were bound to make the legitimate
recovery of fugitives more difficult.

Meanwhile, complaints from the state of Maryland about the escape of
slaves across the Mason-Dixon line were becoming more vehement. Pennsylvania responded in 1826 with a law seemingly designed to strike a balance
between the rights of slaveholders and the protection of free blacks. While
retaining the antikidnapping features of the earlier statute, it authorized the
participation of judges, sheriffs, and local magistrates in the recovery process,
but made that process more complex and difficult than what was required by
federal law. In addition, it repealed the section of the abolition act of 1780 that
had recognized a right of do-it-yourself recaption under common law. As in
Ohio, strictly private capture and removal of a fugitive slave now became the
legal equivalent of kidnapping.[34]

Two years later, as part of a general revision of its statutes, New York likewise prohibited private recaption and established a recovery procedure that involved state officials in the apprehension of runaways, as well as in the judicial disposal of their cases. The New York codifiers went further than Pennsylvania in one respect by permitting an arrested fugitive to sue out a writ *de homine replegiando* and thus have his claim to freedom tried before a jury.[35] Indiana in 1816 and 1824 had already made provision for jury trial in disputed fugitive cases, and the *de homine* writ had long been statutorily available to alleged fugitives in Massachusetts.[36]

In this selective summary of state laws passed before 1830, the principal trend is obvious enough. A desire to prevent kidnapping of free blacks, and especially quasi-kidnapping under the color of law, led a number of state governments to supplement the sketchy, one-sided federal statute of 1793 by imposing their own rules on the rendition process. Such legislation made recovery of fugitives generally more difficult, and it often had the effect of suppressing entirely the common-law right of recaption. The interference with slaveholders' rights was at first a more or less unintended consequence of extending protection to free blacks, but increasingly with the growth of antislavery influence, it became a calculated purpose. The turning point, if there was one, may be said to have come during the 1820s in the aftermath of the Missouri crisis and at a time when militant abolitionism was beginning to emerge as a national movement. Of course, attitudes and policies with respect to fugitives varied considerably from Maine to Illinois. Nevertheless, by 1830, with nullification of federal law about to become forever identified with South Carolina, the fugitive slave legislation of some northern states was tending in the same direction.

Competing federal and state legislation was only one of the legal complexities of the fugitive slave problem, which also involved the application of common law and constitutional imperative, as well as the extrajurisdictional reach of slave-state law into free-state communities, the dual status of slaves as persons and property, and a racial order that almost everywhere limited and complicated the freedom of free blacks. Out of hundreds of separate incidents over the years, each laden with personal drama and each in its own way a dark vignette of American slavery, there arose a variety of issues requiring judicial settlement.

As early as 1795, for instance, the supreme court of New Jersey dealt with the key question of where the burden of proof lay in a contest between a claimant and an alleged fugitive.[37] At about the same time, in a case involving the famous frontier politician John Sevier, the supreme court of Pennsylvania indicated that physical force could be used in recaption if necessary, "without recurring to any constituted authority." A Pennsylvania decision in 1816 held that a child born to a slave after she had fled to Philadelphia could not be claimed as a fugitive. Another in 1819 quashed a writ *de homine replegiando* on constitutional grounds, thereby closing a common-law back door to jury trial for fugitives.[38] In New York, where use of the *de homine* writ had been provided for by statute, the state supreme court ruled it unconstitutional just six years later.[39] Meanwhile, various challenges to the constitutionality of the federal law were being turned aside. In 1816, a federal court in Indiana rejected the argument that Congress lacked the power to enact such legislation.[40] The supreme court of Massachusetts in 1823 rejected the contention that it violated the Fourth Amendment's protection against unreasonable searches and seizures.[41] And in the mid-1830s, a federal court in New York rejected the argument that it violated the Seventh Amendment's guarantee of jury trial.[42]

In the Massachusetts decision, Chief Justice Isaac Parker held that the protection of the Bill of Rights did not extend to slaves because they were not "parties to the Constitution." Whatever may be said about its validity, such a pronouncement begged the central question commonly at issue in fugitive slave cases, namely, whether the alleged fugitive *was* in fact a slave. It amounted to juridical acceptance of the southern rule that blacks were slaves unless they could prove themselves free. Parker also declared that the Constitution, in spite of its delicate reference to slaves as persons, actually embodied an agreement to treat them as property.[43] Both doctrines—presumption of slavery and slaves as property—had been implicitly embraced by Congress in the act of 1793, and northern judges were more disposed than northern legislatures to follow its example. The leading northern court decisions of the time consequently tended to counteract legislative trends by reaffirming the right of recaption, overturning provisions for jury trial, and upholding the supremacy of federal law over that of the states.

In these decisions, one commonly finds the mixture of judicial formalism and moral regret expressed by a Pittsburgh recorder when he returned a fugitive to his master in 1835: "Whilst, as a man, all my prejudices are strong against the curse of slavery, and all its concomitant evils, I am bound by my oath of office to support the constitution of the United States and the constitution of Pennsylvania, not to let my feelings as a man interfere with my duties as a judge."[44]

Such decisions also undoubtedly reflected a social conservatism made more resolute by anxiety about the future of the American Union. The ominous Missouri crisis was still a fresh memory when Andrew Jackson entered the White House in 1829, and during the eight years of his presidency, sectional strains were intensified by the Nat Turner rebellion in Virginia, the nullification movement in South Carolina, the emergence of a more radical abolitionism personified by William Lloyd Garrison, the crusade for abolition of slavery in the District of Columbia, the bitter struggle in Congress over antislavery petitions, the emancipation of slaves in the British West Indies, the beginning of the controversy over annexation of Texas, and an outburst of antiabolitionist riots across the North.

It was in that context that Justice Henry Baldwin of the United States Supreme Court, while charging a circuit court jury in 1833, denounced the "false philanthropy which prostrates the law and the Constitution in its zeal against slavery." Baldwin, a native of Connecticut and a graduate of Yale College, told the Pennsylvania jury that the foundations of the national government were laid on the rights of property in slaves. "The whole structure must fall," he warned, "by disturbing the cornerstones." He reinforced his own reasoning with a quotation from William Tilghman, late chief justice of the Pennsylvania supreme court, who in 1819 had declared: "Whatever may be our private opinions on the subject of slavery, it is well known that our southern brethren would not have consented to become parties to a Constitution . . . unless their property in slaves had been secured."[45] This was the "historical-necessity" doctrine, a proslavery constitutional myth originating in northern ambivalence rather than southern conviction. The idea that the fugitive slave clause had been regarded as indispensable in 1787 and was therefore an especially sacrosanct part of the Constitution did not have much basis in fact, but it fortified the self-justification of more than one northern judge caught between the obligations of duty and the appeals of conscience. Conceived at a time when little was yet known about the proceedings of the Constitutional Convention, the idea survived publication of Madison's *Notes of the Debates* and came to be embraced by a majority of the United States Supreme Court. Of course, southern political leaders gladly appropriated it. "Without this provision of the Constitution," said a Virginia senator in 1850, "it is admitted on all hands, the Union could never have been formed."[46] President James Buchanan made the same assertion during the secession crisis of December 1860, declaring it to be "a well-known historical fact."[47] Ten years later, Alexander H. Stephens was still honoring the myth with solemn reiteration.[48]

IN A GOOD many of the significant fugitive slave cases, no one's freedom was actually at stake. Instead, the central figures were persons being prosecuted or sued for aiding the escape of fugitives or for kidnapping free blacks. One such case proved to be especially historic. In 1837 Edward Prigg, acting as the agent of a Maryland claimant, set out to recover Margaret Morgan—not a recent runaway but rather one who for five years had been living in Pennsylvania with her husband and a growing number of children. At first, Prigg tried to act in accordance with the Pennsylvania law of 1826, but after meeting resistance from the local justice of the peace, he and three associates simply carried the woman and her children off to Maryland. There followed an indictment for kidnapping and an unsuccessful effort to secure his extradition. In some respects, the whole affair resembled the dispute between Pennsylvania and Virginia that had led to passage of the federal law of 1793. Now, Pennsylvania and Maryland, after decades of complaining back and forth across the Mason-Dixon line, agreed to an arrangement whereby their conflicting interests in the fugitive slave problem would be submitted to the highest judicial authority. Prigg was extradited, tried, and convicted; the verdict was upheld *pro forma* by the supreme court of Pennsylvania; and the case was then taken on appeal to the United States Supreme Court.[49] *Prigg v. Pennsylvania*, argued and decided during the early months of 1842, might with more accuracy have been titled "Maryland versus Pennsylvania," or even "Slave States versus Free States."

For nearly half a century there had been no congressional legislation respecting fugitive slaves. The subject had never been discussed in a presidential message or dealt with in a decision of the Supreme Court. This long period of detachment was now about to end. *Prigg v. Pennsylvania* amounted to a resumption of the early movement toward nationalization of the fugitive slave problem that had begun in the Constitutional Convention and culminated in the act of 1793. As a case about the federal relationship, it presented the anomaly of southerners arguing for national supremacy and against state power, doing so before a tribunal that in recent years had been shifting emphasis to the latter. As a case predominantly about slavery, its outcome was largely predetermined by the makeup of the Court, which had a southern majority steadfast in its proslavery allegiance and a northern minority firm in

its conviction that moral repugnance to the institution, however commend-
able, must not be allowed to impair the rule of law or the constitutional
cement of Union. The confusion wrought by the multiplicity of opinions has
obscured the extent to which members reached agreement in the Prigg case.

Displaying a fine strategic sense, Chief Justice Roger B. Taney turned the
writing of the official opinion over to Justice Joseph Story, the country's foremost legal scholar, who combined his judicial career with the role of luminary
in the Harvard Law School. On the bench, Story was most notably a devoted
supporter of federal authority in the tradition of John Marshall. His antislavery sentiments, though sometimes given forceful expression (as in the case of
the *Jeune Eugenie*), were generally subordinated to his professionalism and
conservative nationalism.

Story set the tone of his opinion with an endorsement of the historical-
necessity doctrine, placing the fugitive slave clause in a special constitutional
category as a "fundamental article, without the adoption of which the Union
could never have been formed." He then proceeded to interpret the first part
of the clause as a self-executing guarantee of the slaveholder's "positive,
unqualified right" to recapture a fugitive slave by private effort alone in any
state of the Union and to do so without interference or restraint of any kind,
provided that no breach of the peace were committed. Such had been Prigg's
course of action precisely, and Story concluded by overturning his conviction
after ruling that the Pennsylvania law of 1826 was "unconstitutional and
void" because it purported to punish "the very act of seizing and removing a
slave, by his master, which the Constitution of the United States was designed
to justify and uphold."[50]

Story's sweeping confirmation of the right of recaption and his invalida-
tion of the Pennsylvania statute were the essential parts of his opinion, but by
no means the whole of it. To the argument of Pennsylvania counsel that the
framers of the Constitution had left enforcement of the fugitive slave clause
to the states, he responded by interpreting the latter part of the clause as a
conferral of power and responsibility on Congress. Thus he held the federal
law of 1793 to be "clearly constitutional in all its leading provisions."[51] Up to
this point, it should be said, Story had carried most of the justices with him,
but not so when he turned his attention to the state-federal relationship.
There, his opinion proved to be the least authoritative and yet the most
important in its historical consequences.

Having already declared that an owner's constitutional right to recover
his slave was one that no state law could "in any way qualify, regulate, con-

trol, or restrain," Story went further to deny that state governments, even in the absence of federal legislation, had any power to legislate on the subject. The power, he said, was "exclusive in Congress." What, then, of the provision in the federal act of 1793 authorizing local magistrates to administer it? Story hinted that the constitutionality of the provision might be in doubt. He left undecided the question whether magistrates were *bound* to act under the law but had no doubt that they could *choose* to do so, "unless prohibited by state legislation."[52] Thus he plainly implied that state governments had the option of barring state and local officials from participation in the recovery process. On these two points—the exclusivity of federal power and the obligation of state officials—Story had little support from the other justices. Taney, for one, entered a vehement dissent in which he argued that state governments were constitutionally restrained only from actions *interfering* with a slaveholder's right to recover his property. They had the power and even the duty, he maintained, to assist in the *protection* of that right.[53]

Taney, to be sure, agreed with most of what Story had written, and well he might, for it was emphatically proslavery in tone and substance. At a time when the status of slaves under federal law remained a debatable question in Congress, Story labeled them a "species of property" and held that the right to recover a fugitive was "a right of property" that all departments of the national government were constitutionally bound to protect.[54] His ruling on recaption meant that a slaveholder virtually carried the law of his own state with him when he pursued a fugitive into a free state. That included the presumption that blacks were slaves unless they could prove otherwise. In the course of upholding the federal law and striking down the Pennsylvania law, Story completely ignored the central question of how disputed cases were to be decided. He also ignored the problem of how state governments were to protect free blacks from mistaken or felonious seizure without impinging on the slaveholder's "positive, unqualified" right of recovery.

This proslavery decision nevertheless proved to be of dubious proslavery value. It did ostensibly free owners in pursuit of runaway slaves from all restrictive procedures and other obstructions imposed by state law. But at the same time, it cast shadows of doubt across those features of state law that facilitated rendition, such as the use of local police officers to arrest alleged fugitives.[55] Furthermore, the proslavery thrust of the decision soon provoked resistance of several kinds, including a more determined opposition to the fugitive slave law itself.

One line of resistance was to minimize the scope of judicial review and reassert the power of a state government to intervene in the recovery process, at least to the extent of protecting its own free black population. For example, Governor William H. Seward declared in a message to the New York legislature: "The authority of the decision cannot be extended to cases presenting facts materially varying from those which marked the case thus adjudicated. It is, therefore, believed that the privilege of habeas corpus and the right of trial by jury [for alleged fugitives] as yet remain unimpaired in this state."[56] Seward, a Whig, was soon succeeded by a Democratic governor, who promptly called for repeal of the state's current personal liberty law on the ground that it was incompatible with the Prigg decision. Legislative efforts at repeal never succeeded, however. The statute in question, which had been passed in 1840 to replace the act of 1828, remained on the books with its constitutional status uncertain.[57]

A different kind of counterattack, seemingly in accord with Story's Prigg opinion, was to divorce state facilities entirely from the rendition of fugitive slaves. Massachusetts adopted this alternative in 1843, and similar laws were soon passed in four other New England states. Essentially, they prohibited judges and local magistrates from accepting jurisdiction in fugitive cases, and they forbade the arrest or detention of alleged fugitives by any state officers.[58] Slaveholders, as a consequence, were left without any official aid in the recovery of slaves, except for what little could be supplied by a few federal judges and marshals.

Surprisingly, Pennsylvania did not respond to the Prigg decision until 1847, at a time when, with American armies penetrating deep into Mexico, the question of slavery in an expanding nation was intensifying the sectional conflict. The legislature suddenly enacted a broad statute that combined the Massachusetts strategy of disengagement with Seward's strategy of reasserting state power. Thus, while one section of the law prohibited state officials from participation in the rendition process, another provided punishment for any claimant who exercised the right of recaption in a violent manner, and still another defiantly declared that state judges had the authority at all times "to issue the writ of habeas corpus, and to inquire into the causes and legality of the arrest or imprisonment of any human being within this commonwealth." The law provoked outbursts of rage in the South and especially in the neighboring states of Maryland and Virginia.[59]

Such response by northern state governments to the proslavery impact of *Prigg v. Pennsylvania* reflected a widespread mood of resistance that also manifested itself in increasing private aid to runaways and in occasional outbursts of mass protest. The first major public uproar occurred in Boston and led to passage of the aforementioned Massachusetts law installing a policy of noncooperation. In October 1842, James B. Gray of Virginia ventured to seize George Latimer in Boston, the heartland of abolitionism, claiming him as a runaway slave. Legal maneuvers, first before the state's chief justice, Lemuel B. Shaw, and then before Justice Story, ended favorably for Gray, but final action was postponed several weeks to allow time for the obtaining of testimony from Virginia. In the interval, with the alleged fugitive locked up in the city jail at the request of his alleged owner, militant blacks and abolitionist leaders mobilized a passionate, sometimes riotous public outcry. Intimidated by the threat of a forcible rescue, Gray agreed to sell Latimer at a relatively low price.[60]

The Latimer affair and other confrontations had the effect on many northerners of personalizing a social system that was otherwise a remote generality. Pursuit of fugitives into free states converted vague black images into flesh-and-blood individuals seeking freedom. Furthermore, every such incident dramatized the fact that slavery was, in some respects, a national institution. Thus the fugitive slave issue undoubtedly helped broaden the front of the antislavery crusade, and yet, as a classic problem in the conflict of law and conscience, it also tended to be divisive, both for abolitionists of the 1840s and Republicans of the 1850s. Most notably, it was the *Prigg* and Latimer excitement of 1842 that drove Garrisonians to the extreme of cursing the Constitution and demanding dissolution of the Union—a course of action that completed their divergence from the mainstream of the antislavery movement.[61]

In a nation born of revolution, there were heroic precedents for resistance to unjust laws, but when the revolution gave way to a constitutional order established by popular consent, obedience to law became, in the words of the greatest American revolutionist, "sacredly obligatory upon all."[62] The relative strength of these two traditions as they affected the fugitive slave problem was tested in courts and other public forums throughout the North. The argument for compliance as a matter of constitutional obligation and sound public policy had great logical force. No one put it more emphatically than Justice John McLean, a moderately antislavery Ohioan, who declared again and again from the circuit bench that judges must apply the law as it was written, that objectionable laws should be "respected and obeyed" until they were changed in the prescribed manner, and that substitution of the rule of individual conscience for the rule of law would "overturn the basis of society."[63] At the same time, the moral argument for resistance, drawn from both religious and secular sources, had an emotional appeal that extended well beyond the circles of organized abolitionism and was enhanced by the other sectional antagonisms of the decade. But moral argument carried more weight in mass meetings than it did in courtroom proceedings.

Perhaps the most eloquent effort to blend moral principle with legal argument in a formal attack on the Fugitive Slave Act (and on much of the *Prigg* decision as well) was that of Salmon P. Chase in *Jones v. Van Zandt*, a penalty suit brought against an Ohio farmer for aiding a group of slaves who had escaped from Kentucky. Both in the federal circuit court where he first argued the case and before the United States Supreme Court in 1847, Chase appealed to the law of nature as the appropriate basis for interpreting the constitutional relation of the federal government to slavery. As an institution universally acknowledged to be contrary to natural law, slavery had no existence, he declared, beyond the jurisdiction that gave it legal sanction. The government of the United States therefore had "nothing whatever to do, directly, with slavery" because no part of the Constitution recognized a right of property in human beings. Even the clause dealing with fugitives from service spoke only of "persons," and it made no rule concerning black persons held to labor that did not apply equally to white persons held to labor. Consequently, all immunities secured by the Constitution to persons in general belonged as a matter of right to persons who had escaped from service.[64]

Chase then went on to argue that the act of 1793 was unconstitutional, not only because Congress had lacked the authority to pass it, but also because it violated the protection against unreasonable searches and seizures in the Fourth Amendment, the due process clause of the Fifth Amendment, and the right of trial by jury guaranteed in the Seventh Amendment. These and other provisions of the Bill of Rights, he declared, "were mainly designed to establish as written law, certain great principles of natural right and justice." They did not create restrictions on legislative power but rather affirmed restrictions that were imposed by "the very nature of society and of government." No legislature, Chase intoned, could turn wrong into right or darkness into light or human beings into things. And, he added with what can only be called forlorn hope, "No court is bound to enforce unjust law."[65]

With or without such moral pleading, the antislavery attack on the constitutionality of the fugitive slave law made a good deal of sense as exposition of the pristine Constitution written in 1787 and amended in 1791. After six decades of proslavery gloss, however, it was difficult for any tribunal to take Chase's argument seriously. Speaking for a united Supreme Court, Justice

Levi Woodbury (like Story, a New Englander) brushed aside the defense case in a few sentences. Referring to fugitives simply as "property" and to the fugitive slave clause as one of the "sacred compromises" of the Constitution, he declared that the validity of the act of 1793 "must be considered as among the settled adjudications of this court."[66] Thus the slaveholding interest had again won the legal battle at the highest judicial level, knowing full well that in the world of day-to-day reality it was another empty victory.

REPEATED CONFIRMATION of their constitutional right to reclaim fugitive slaves anywhere in the Union made it all the more frustrating for southerners to be continually prevented from doing so on northern ground. Runaways, they complained, were often induced to flee by abolitionist influence and illegally aided in their escapes by a network of conspirators, black and white (the "underground railroad" of history and legend).[67] Then, when a slave owner entered a free state to recover his property in accordance with federal law, he was likely to be impeded by unfriendly state legislation, uncooperative or feckless local officials, and a hostile, sometimes violent populace. If he exercised the right of reception, he ran the risk of arrest for kidnapping or breach of the peace. If he sought damages for the loss of a slave, the litigation was frequently protracted, the jury was seldom sympathetic, and collection could be difficult even if he won.[68]

Southerners, who, like abolitionists, used a great deal of anecdotal evidence to enrich their argument, apparently found it as infuriating to have a fugitive set free by legal artifice as to have one rescued by physical force. They fiercely resented the antislavery strategy of enmeshing claimants in courtroom technicalities and generally making recovery so vexatious and costly as to discourage other slaveholders from pursuing their runaways into free territory. In one instance, a fugitive discovered aboard a ship was released by a New York judge because the captain holding him did not qualify as an "agent" of the owner. Then, after being reapprehended and brought before a court of sessions in strict accordance with a state law, he was again released on the ground that the said law was unconstitutional because it conflicted with the federal exclusivity doctrine set forth by Justice Story in his *Prigg* decision.[69] As another prime example of northern legal chicanery, the story was told of a fugitive set free in New York City because his owner could not furnish satisfactory proof that Maryland was a slave state.[70]

But of course the most spectacular confrontations were the riotous ones. Early in 1847, at about the time that the Supreme Court was deciding the

Van Zandt case, a group of Kentuckians arrived in Marshall, Michigan, and located the six slaves they were pursuing. Enlisting the aid of a deputy sheriff, they tried to take the fugitives before a magistrate but were prevented from doing so by an angry crowd of several hundred people. They eventually gave up and left town under threats of violence, but not before being charged with trespass and paying a fine of $100. The incident prompted the Kentucky legislature to pass a resolution calling on Congress for new fugitive slave legislation that would inflict on violators "the severest penalty ... that the Constitution of the United States will tolerate."[71]

Such requests had come periodically from the border states without achieving any effect, but in the spring of 1848, as Pennsylvania's new personal liberty law set a tone of increased northern militancy and as the sectional struggle over slavery in the Far West approached its dangerous climax, the Senate judiciary committee responded with a bill cut to southern demands. Presented by the committee chairman, Senator Andrew P. Butler of South Carolina, the bill was aimed primarily at lengthening the list of federal officials from whom certificates of removal could be obtained. Most notably, postmasters and collectors of customs were to be included. The Senate took no action on the measure during that session, but James M. Mason of Virginia reintroduced it in early January of 1850. It was committed and quickly reported with some changes, then debated for several days toward the end of the month.[72] Mason, acting under instructions from the Virginia legislature, was now assuming the leadership of a determined southern effort to obtain more effective fugitive slave legislation.[73]

Not really satisfied with the committee's bill, Mason offered an amendment constituting virtually a whole new measure, which, at his request, was ordered printed and laid on the table to await later action. Its most conspicuous feature was a provision for the appointment of an army of "commissioners," each with the authority to hire subordinate officials, issue warrants, hear fugitive cases, and grant certificates of removal.[74] Thus Mason and Butler as representatives of southern leadership had plainly opted for the creation of an elaborate bureaucracy to facilitate the recovery of fugitive slaves. They did so reluctantly, of course, knowing that any such extension of federal power would be not only a violation of southern principles but perhaps also, in the long run, a threat to southern security. Their strategy amounted to an acknowledgment that Story's dictum undermining state responsibility for the return of fugitives, though unacceptable to them as a reading of law, was all too accurate as a reading of circumstances.

Meanwhile, on January 29, Henry Clay presented the set of resolutions with which he launched his effort to resolve the sectional crisis now threatening the life of the nation. Elaborating on his seventh resolution, which called for a more effectual fugitive slave law, he declared in a speech delivered a week later that he was willing to vote for "the most stringent measures" and impose "the heaviest sanctions" to secure the slaveholder's right to recover his property.[75] Thus the Great Compromiser sought no compromise on this issue—no balancing of sectional claims, no concession to northern sensibilities. Instead, a severely proslavery law was to serve as one of the counterweights to legislation desired by the North. This linkage with other sectional problems in a general scheme of compromise had an effect on the fugitive slave controversy that can scarcely be overstated; for the bill passed in 1850 would surely have failed if it had been considered as an independent measure at any other time.

No less crucial was the fact that the compromise was conceived and designed in the Senate, where the members who could reasonably be called antislavery were outnumbered at least two to one and consequently had little influence on the legislation being drafted. An early move by Seward, for example, to guarantee jury trial in disputed fugitive cases was plainly a hopeless gesture not worth the Senate's time. It succeeded only in provoking one southerner to an outburst of contumely.[76] For abolitionists gloomily watching the trend of events in Congress, the heaviest blow fell when Daniel Webster in his famous Seventh of March speech took the southern side on the fugitive slave issue and announced that he would support the Butler-Mason bill as part of a general settlement.[77]

The ensuing excoriation of Webster in abolitionist circles merged with a broader antislavery protest against the whole compromise movement—a protest in which the harshest language was used to characterize the proposed fugitive slave law. The outcry apparently had some effect on Clay and the special Committee of Thirteen that he headed, since the set of compromise measures reported by him on May 8 included a placatory addition to the Butler-Mason bill. It provided assurance (through the requirement of a bond from the claimant) that a person seized as a fugitive who insisted that he was free would have an opportunity to prove his case before a jury in the state to which he was being returned.[78] This was at best a minor concession to antislavery opinion, being essentially an extension of the southern argument that summary process was appropriate in the rendition of a fugitive slave because it did not constitute a final disposition of the fugitive's status. The proposal satisfied few northern critics and at the same time displeased most southerners, who wanted no mention of jury trial in federal legislation on the subject of slavery.

Webster, shaken by the ferocity of abolitionist attacks upon him, likewise beat a retreat from his earlier position. On June 3, he presented a bill providing that if a person seized as a fugitive denied under oath that he owed service to the claimant, the issue must be tried before a local jury. This remarkable change of heart evoked no recorded senatorial comment.[79] Seven weeks later, after Zachary Taylor's death and the elevation of Millard Fillmore to the presidency, Webster resigned his seat in order to become secretary of state. He thus played no further part in the achievement of compromise.

The Senate all this while continued to leave the fugitive slave question in abeyance while working away on other aspects of the sectional crisis. By mid-August, having passed legislation dealing with California, New Mexico, Utah, and Texas, members were ready to resume the consideration of the Butler-Mason bill that they had begun and suspended in January. On Monday, August 19, Mason started things off by offering, as an amendment, a substitute bill that included the main features of the old one, together with a provision, originally suggested by Clay, for indemnification of owners whose recaptured slaves were forcibly rescued from custody. This new bill also incorporated one rather inconsequential recommendation of the Committee of Thirteen, but conspicuously absent was that body's compromise proposal regarding jury trial.[80] Debate extending over five days centered less on the text of Mason's substitute than on a series of proposed revisions and alternative measures. The discussion and voting revealed the weakness of the antislavery opposition, which had only one militant voice in Salmon P. Chase and consisted otherwise of about a dozen northern senators, principally Whigs.[81] At the same time, certain parts of the debate exposed some cracks in southern unity on the subject of federal protection of slavery.

The Senate rejected an effort to revive Webster's bill providing for a jury trial in the state where a fugitive was captured if he should deny under oath that he owed service to the claimant. The vote of 27 to 11 constituted an emphatic validation of the southern argument that such a provision would make the rest of the bill useless and amount to an abdication of federal responsibility for the return of fugitive slaves.[82] But perhaps the most remarkable feature of the debate at this point was the flat denial by two southern senators that kidnapping of free blacks into slavery had ever been practiced. Claiming to have investigated the matter all the way back to the

Such his much deceit now

1790s, Butler declared: "Not a single case has occurred where a person has pursued and taken a fugitive . . . who was not his property, or the property of one for whom he was acting as an agent." Jefferson Davis issued a similar denial.[83]

Other attempts at affording some legal protection to persons seized as fugitives were likewise brushed aside. Among them, an amendment proposed by Webster's successor, Robert C. Winthrop, which would have reduced the one-sidedness of the certification process and rendered it subject in some measure to state court review, attracted only eleven favorable votes.[84] Later in the week, a substitute bill offered by Henry Clay's Kentucky colleague, Joseph R. Underwood, which included the Committee of Thirteen's proposal to guarantee jury trial in the slave state of origin, was defeated, 22 to 14, with southerners almost solidly opposed.[85] Mason spoke vehemently against both proposals and carried his point that the certificate issued by a commissioner must be conclusive in all respects and unencumbered by any conditions. With that legal force, it would constitute a sufficient return to a writ of habeas corpus or any other court process resorted to in behalf of a fugitive.

For southerners, the one divisive feature of Mason's bill proved to be the indemnity clause, especially so after Thomas G. Pratt of Maryland offered an amendment expanding its coverage to include any slave not delivered up in response to a commissioner's warrant. The division in some degree reflected the difference between the border states, where slave escapes added up to significant financial losses, and the lower South, where the problem, though emotionally charged, was more or less academic. But in addition, reimbursement for fugitive slaves out of the national treasury could not easily be accommodated to southern constitutional theory or to southern concern about the impingement of federal power on the slaveholding system. It was, exclaimed a Tennessee senator, a "monstrous" proposition—one that had no basis in the Constitution, would result in many abuses, and might even become a vehicle of compensated manumission. After some heated argument, the Pratt amendment went down to defeat, 27 to 10, with the slave-state vote evenly divided. Then, on the motion of Jefferson Davis, Mason's more limited provision for indemnification was eliminated.[86] That change left a bill that every southern member could support. The last roll-call vote took place on Friday, August 23. Only fifteen of the thirty northern senators were present, and three of them joined twenty-four southerners in ordering engrossment for a third reading. On the following Monday, the bill was passed by a voice vote and sent on to the other chamber.[87]

As it happened, this Thirty-first House of Representatives had fewer experienced members and somewhat less antislavery energy than its recent predecessors. Furthermore, after nine months of fierce legislative debate and public discussion in an atmosphere of national crisis, the pressure for enactment of the compromise fashioned in the Senate was tremendous. When the Mason bill came up for consideration on September 12, a Pennsylvania Democrat named James Thompson took the lead in railroading it through the various stages of passage in a single afternoon. No debate was allowed before the final vote of 109 to 76. Thirty-one northerners joined 78 southerners to form the majority, while another 27 northerners (chiefly Whigs) failed to vote.[88] The measure passed Congress because southerners in both houses supported it unanimously, while only 54 percent of the total northern membership voted against it.[89] Thus the South had once again profited from its greater unity on the subject of slavery, but that customary advantage was decisively reinforced in this instance by a widespread northern recognition of fugitive slave legislation as an indispensable element in any formula for sectional peace.

8

The Fugitive Slave Problem, 1850 to 1864

The bill signed by President Millard Fillmore on September 18, 1850, was designated an amendment supplementary to the act of 1793. Essentially, it expanded federal power over the interstate rendition of fugitive slaves at the expense of state power to intervene in the process. The central figure in the new system was to be the commissioner, an officer appointed by a United States circuit judge and having "concurrent jurisdiction" with federal judges in the administration of the statute.[1] A commissioner could in turn appoint "one or more suitable persons" to execute his warrants, and he or any such subordinate had the authority to summon the aid of bystanders as a *posse comitatus*. In addition, federal marshals and their deputies were drawn explicitly into the work of enforcement and made financially liable for nonexecution of warrants and the escape of fugitives from their custody.

A pursuing slave owner or his agent could himself seize an alleged fugitive or else obtain a warrant for his arrest by a federal officer. In either case, the captive was to be brought before a commissioner or federal judge, who would conduct a summary hearing and, if the claimant's *ex parte* evidence proved satisfactory, issue a certificate of removal. Testimony from the prisoner was expressly barred, and the certificate was declared to be "conclusive," making its holder immune to "molestation" by court processes of any kind. Thus anyone taken into custody as a fugitive slave was cut off from the traditional legal resorts of an accused person.[2] As for extralegal action in his behalf, the new law made it more hazardous by increasing financial penalties and adding the threat of imprisonment.[3] Furthermore, if there was reason to fear an effort at forcible rescue, the claimant could have the fugitive delivered to him in his own state at government expense—the task to be performed by the marshal or other arresting officer and as many specially hired subordinates as the situation seemed to require.[4]

Here, then, was the ultimate legislative elaboration of the vague fifty-two-word sentence that in August 1787 had been added almost as an afterthought to the Constitution of the United States. Framed by southerners for enforcement among northerners, the law of 1850 never could have been passed except as part of a grand design of compromise at a time of national crisis.[5] It was utterly one-sided, lending categorical federal protection to slavery while making no concession to the humanity of African Americans or to the humanitarian sensibilities of many white Americans. Some of its language and substance seemed gratuitously provocative, as though antislavery noses were being rubbed in the legitimacy of the peculiar institution. Notable in this respect were the reference to free-state legal process as "molestation" and the clause making private citizens liable to impressment as slave catchers. No less offensive was the provision setting a commissioner's fee at ten dollars if he issued a certificate of removal and only five dollars if he refused to do so. The explanation that it required more paper work to remand an alleged fugitive than to release him did not silence antislavery charges that the differential amounted to petty bribery.

The unrelieved abrasiveness of the Fugitive Slave Act raises a question about the motives of its framers. If they really wanted the law to work, why not try to make it a little easier for northerners to live with? The fact is that James M. Mason himself had little faith in its success and said so when he assumed the role of principal author. "I fear," he declared, "that the disease is seated too deeply to be reached by ordinary legislation. . . . I fear it will be found that even this law will be of little worth in securing the rights of those for whose benefit it is intended." Andrew Butler and Jefferson Davis, both of whom contributed to the shaping of the measure, expressed the same pessimism.[6] Yet for these men, southern militants who were uncertain whether the future of the South lay inside or outside the Union, the legislation had symbolic and strategic value transcending its doubtful utility. Passage of the act lent weight to the southern definition of what the federal government owed to slavery, while at the same time setting up an acid test of northern fidelity to the Constitution. Enforcement, if effective, would be a significant victory over the abolitionist enemy; if ineffective, as the three men expected, it would arouse southern indignation and hasten the achievement of southern unity.

Despite secessionist movements in several states, acceptance of the Compromise of 1850 eventually prevailed throughout the South, but it was accompanied by many grim warnings that the North must abide by the terms of the settlement. Everyone knew where the greatest danger now lay. "The continued existence of the United States as one nation," declared the *Southern Literary Messenger*," depends upon the full and faithful execution of the Fugitive Slave Bill." The same belief was expressed in that famous credo of conditional Unionism, the "Georgia platform," which also threatened secession if the law should be repealed or "materially" modified by Congress.[7] These caveats were taken seriously in the North, where Daniel Webster probably spoke for a majority of the population when he insisted over and over that the legislation had been "essential to the peace of the country" and must be enforced.[8] Yet the fury of abolitionist protest made it all too plain that the Fugitive Slave Act would be resisted in such ways as to put the peace of the country at further risk. Ralph Waldo Emerson set the tone for thousands when he declared: "As long as men have bowels, they will disobey."[9]

To nobody's surprise, one of the first confrontations took place in Boston, where a newly organized vigilance committee shielded fugitives William and Ellen Craft from arrest and frightened their pursuers out of town. An even earlier display of resistance in Pennsylvania had raised the question of whether federal troops should be used to enforce the law. President Fillmore, in consultation with his cabinet, resolved to do so when necessary and issued directions to that effect. "God knows that I detest slavery," he declared, "but it is an existing evil for which we are not responsible, and we must endure it and give it such protection as is guaranteed by the Constitution, till we can get rid of it without destroying the last hope of free government in the world."[10]

Several months passed before federal authority was put to a significant test. Then, in mid-February 1851, a coffee-house waiter in Boston was arrested as a fugitive on a warrant issued by the local United States commissioner, George T. Curtis. Before the case had been disposed of, a crowd of blacks broke into the courtroom and carried off Shadrach, the prisoner, who was soon put on his way to safety in Canada.[11] This first forcible slave rescue of the 1850s provoked angry outcries throughout the South and caused a flurry of activity in Washington. At the instance of Henry Clay, the Senate passed a resolution asking the president for information about the affair. Fillmore responded immediately with a message in which he requested clarifying legislation that would make it easier for him to use army, navy, and militia forces in the execution of federal law. With the collaboration of his Secretary of State Daniel Webster, he issued a proclamation calling on citizens to "rally to the support of the laws of their country" and ordering prosecution of all persons who had contributed to Shadrach's escape.[12] Webster, who equated such resistance with treason, supervised the preparations for trial of the eight men eventually indicted.[13] Never before had a president and his administration become so directly and wholeheartedly involved in the work of recovering fugitive slaves.

Another test of strength came soon enough in Boston. Thomas Sims, who had escaped from Georgia by stowing away on a ship, was arrested in early April and brought before Commissioner Curtis for a hearing that continued off and on through the following week. This time, the hand of authority held firm against an astonishing series of efforts on the prisoner's behalf. Twice, the state supreme court refused to grant a writ of habeas corpus, as the venerable chief justice, Lemuel Shaw, turned aside arguments against the constitutionality of the 1850 law. Similar applications to a federal district court judge and to a justice of the United States Supreme Court were likewise unsuccessful. A petition to the state legislature also failed. So did a plan to have Sims charged with a crime and sent to prison in Massachusetts. Meanwhile, despite abolitionist mass meetings and a good deal of violent oratory, all rescue schemes came to nothing because Sims was too well guarded by the marshal's staff, Boston police, and armed volunteers. On Friday, April 11, Curtis at last awarded a certificate of removal to the claimant. Early the next morning, a force of some three hundred men in military array escorted the young slave to the ship that would carry him under heavy guard back to Georgia. The total cost of restoring him to his owner was credibly estimated at $20,000.[14]

The rendition of Sims enraged abolitionists and convinced many southerners that public officials in the North were making a serious effort to enforce the Fugitive Slave Law. But other dramatic episodes that same year changed the picture again. In September, at Christiana, Pennsylvania, a party of men from Maryland, together with a deputy federal marshal, tried to take two fugitives into custody and set off a violent encounter in which the slave owner himself was killed and his son grievously wounded. Several weeks later, a well-organized mob invaded the police station in Syracuse, New York, and forcibly liberated a fugitive known as Jerry, who was then hurried off to Canada.[15] What disturbed southerners and northern conservatives all the more was the fact that punishment of resisters and rescuers proved to be almost impossible. Of the seventy-five persons indicted for their roles in the Boston (Shadrach), Christiana, and Syracuse affairs, only one was convicted.[16] Those three events had revealed not only the intensity of opposition to the new law, but also the federal government's limited capacity for enforcement, given its lack of prison facilities, the often mediocre quality of its local officers, and the loose structure of its criminal prosecution system.

Nevertheless, Fillmore in his annual message of December 2, 1851, offered assurance that the number of active resistants was comparatively small and "believed to be daily diminishing." He congratulated Congress and the country on the "general acquiescence" in the compromise measures and the "spirit of conciliation" that they had produced. This rosy outlook was not entirely illusory. Public excitement declined over the next two years, during which time there was only one slave rescue. At their national conventions in June 1852, the Whig and Democratic parties both endorsed the Fugitive Slave Act and deprecated any attempt to renew the sectional controversy. Accordingly, when Senator Charles Sumner introduced a motion for its repeal a few weeks later, he received support from only three of his colleagues.[17]

The law, in fact, was working—after a fashion. From the date of its passage to the end of 1853, about seventy fugitives were returned to their owners by federal tribunals, whereas only about one-fifth of that number were released or rescued from custody.[18] This record amounted, of course, to little more than a token achievement, but it seems to have taken some of the edge off southern discontent while antagonizing only a minority in the free states. At the same time, the fiery rhetoric and occasional violence of the opposition, together with the prominence of blacks in every rescue incident, undoubtedly drove some northerners toward a conservative, law-and-order point of view. Plainly, the fugitive-slave issue, however inflammatory it might be in an episodic way, was not enough by itself to bring on a national crisis. Dedicated abolitionists could nevertheless take comfort in the expectation that something more would soon turn up. The Massachusetts Anti-Slavery Society, in its annual report for 1853, declared: "The lull which now broods over the land cannot prevail long. Under the surface which looks so stagnant and moveless, mighty passions lurk."[19]

FRANKLIN PIERCE TOOK the oath of office on March 4, 1853, by which time *Uncle Tom's Cabin*, the most famous of all responses to the Fugitive Slave Act, had already sold hundreds of thousands of copies. The new president concluded his inaugural address that day with high praise for the Compromise of 1850, and, in an obvious reference to its most controversial feature, declared that the legislation was "strictly constitutional and to be unhesitatingly carried into effect." Pierce and his attorney general, Caleb Cushing, two New Englanders who shared a hatred of abolitionism, were determined to bolster federal enforcement. Cushing did so repeatedly in his official opinions and rulings. To help protect federal marshals from legal harassment, he approved government payment of their attorneys' fees whenever they were sued or prosecuted for actions related to execution of the Fugitive Slave Law. He defined in exceedingly broad terms a marshal's authority to call members of any police force or military organization into a *posse comitatus*. He spelled out the incapacity of any state court to discharge a fugitive on a writ of habeas corpus. And he recognized the right of a slave owner to recover a fugitive, not only within states and federal territories, but also within the unorganized territory of the United States.[20]

That unorganized territory, most of which had been closed to slavery by the Missouri Compromise, was just then becoming the focus of a major political controversy. Earlier efforts to provide territorial government for the region having been frustrated by southern opposition, the Kansas-Nebraska bill that made its way through Congress between January and May 1854 carried a concession to the South in the form of an explicit repeal of the federal ban on slavery in the area north of 36° 30'. The resulting explosion of northern anger, which transformed the national party system and renewed the sectional conflict in all its bitterness, had a telling effect on the fugitive-slave struggle. Antislavery militancy gained new adherents, many of them supporters of the recent compromise who now felt betrayed and wanted to strike back at the South in some way. Enactment of the Kansas-Nebraska bill, said one conservative Whig, would mean "the complete nullification of the Fugitive Slave Law."[21]

On March 10, 1854, one week after the bill passed the Senate, a fugitive named Joshua Glover was overpowered and taken into federal custody near Racine, Wisconsin. Legal ramifications of the capture would extend into the next decade, but the first result was a huge mass meeting that expressed its outrage in a series of resolutions, one of which read: "Inasmuch as the Senate of the United States has repealed all compromises heretofore adopted by the Congress of the United States, we, as citizens of Wisconsin, are justified in declaring and do hereby declare the slave-catching law of 1850 disgraceful and also repealed." The next day, a mob battered down the door of the Milwaukee jail where Glover was being held and set him free. In addition, the claimant and the deputies who seized Glover were arrested by the county sheriff on charges of kidnapping and assault and battery, the warrant having been issued by the mayor of Racine. The federal district judge intervened to order their release. But efforts to punish two ringleaders of the rescue were frustrated, their convictions in federal court being virtually set aside by the state supreme court, which in an earlier proceeding had already declared the Fugitive Slave Act to be unconstitutional. This bold judicial pronouncement echoed popular sentiment already expressed in the resolutions of a two-day state convention that revived the doctrine of state interposition as a shield against undue expansion of federal power. Thus, once again in American history, the local unpopularity of an act of Congress had raised the specter of nullification.[22]

Another sensational confrontation occurred in late May, coinciding with final passage of the Kansas-Nebraska bill. Several Boston policemen, acting as deputies of the federal marshal and carrying a commissioner's warrant, arrested Anthony Burns, who had recently fled from Richmond, Virginia. Ensuing events followed a familiar pattern. There were legal maneuvers on Burns's behalf, and the claimant was harassed with a countersuit for damages. Antislavery forces called a public meeting at Faneuil Hall, where Wendell Phillips, Theodore Parker, and other impassioned orators linked events in Boston with those in Washington. "Nebraska I call knocking a man down," Phillips exclaimed, "and this is spitting in his face after he is down." Before the night was over a bungled attempt to storm the courthouse and liberate Burns had resulted in the fatal shooting of one of the guards. With the emphatic approval of President Pierce, the Marshal then summoned the aid of nearby marines and army troops, including a company of artillery. On June 2, after Commissioner Edward G. Loring had issued a certificate of removal, Burns, like Thomas Sims before him, was marched to the city wharf amidst a military presence that restrained but did not silence the crowd of angry onlookers.[23]

This second display of federal power in Boston was more formidable and costly than the first. Yet enforcement triumphed only in part. Efforts to prosecute the courthouse rioters got nowhere, and the murder of the guard went unpunished. In addition, federal officials involved in the case were made to feel the heat of public outrage. When Asa Butman, the man who arrested Burns, ventured into Worcester seeking another fugitive slave, a mob abused him with insults, threats, expectorations of tobacco juice, and blows to the head, until he was escorted safely out of town.[24] As for Loring, the central figure in the rendition proceedings, abolitionist pressure cost him his law lectureship at Harvard and eventually brought about his removal from the office of probate judge for Suffolk County.[25] Recovery of fugitives in such a hostile environment was proving too expensive for everyone concerned, and slaveholders soon gave up trying. After Burns, no person was remanded to slavery from Massachusetts or any other part of New England.

Elsewhere, the pattern of dutiful enforcement with intervals of violent resistance continued throughout the decade. Early in 1856, for example, seven fugitives taken into custody near Cincinnati were restored to their Kentucky owners at federal expense, but not before a deputy had been wounded by gunfire and one of the captives, Margaret Garner, had begun cutting the throats of her children rather than see them returned to slavery. From the Garner episode until the end of 1860, forty-four persons in Ohio were delivered to claimants and five persons forcibly liberated, one of them in the memorable Oberlin-Wellington rescue of September 1858.[26] But more important than the rescues and other physical acts of defiance was the growing resistance of state and local governments to execution of the Fugitive Slave Law.

The Massachusetts legislature, as one might expect, responded emphatically to the Burns rendition and the repeal of the Missouri Compromise. In 1855, it approved an elaborate "Act to protect the Rights and Liberties of the People" that in several ways encroached on federal authority. Vetoed as unconstitutional by a governor not unsympathetic to its purpose, the measure was promptly enacted with an overriding vote. Between 1854 and 1858, the six New England states, as well as Michigan and Wisconsin, enacted personal liberty laws of one kind or another.[27] Ostensibly aimed at protecting only free blacks, the laws were in fact usually designed to obstruct rendition of any person claimed as a fugitive slave. Such was most plainly the case with provisions guaranteeing access to the writ of habeas corpus and jury trial. This personal liberty legislation of the 1850s flouted federal authority, infuriated southerners, and contributed heavily to the progress of sectional alienation. Confined as it was, however, to states where geography and popular feeling made slave hunting a poor risk anyhow, it probably did not have a significant effect on recovery of fugitive slaves.

State and federal authority came into conflict most abrasively in certain episodes of enforcement like the Margaret Garner case. There, a state probate judge fined the United States marshal and ordered him to jail for contempt of court because he had not responded to a writ of habeas corpus issued on behalf of the fugitives. The marshal was then freed with a writ of habeas corpus by the area's federal district judge, who in doing so rejected the state judge's argument that the Fugitive Slave Act was unconstitutional.[28] Another jurisdictional clash took place in 1857 at Mechanicsburg, Ohio, after the arrest of a fugitive had been prevented by a crowd of armed men. The affair produced the spectacle of a sheriff struck down in a fight with deputy marshals; the marshals jailed on charges of assault and battery but freed by the federal district judge; and then an assortment of state officials facing trial in federal court for obstructing a federal officer in the performance of his duty. Governor Salmon P. Chase stepped in to arrange a compromise that involved reimbursement of the claimant by popular subscription and discontinuance of the prosecutions.[29]

The Oberlin-Wellington rescue of the following year likewise resulted in cross-indictments, namely of thirty-seven persons by a federal grand jury on charges of violating the Fugitive Slave Act and of a deputy marshal and three other persons by a county grand jury on charges of kidnapping. This standoff ended in a compromise whereby all prosecutions were abandoned, but not before two of the rescuers had been convicted and another kind of state-federal confrontation had been narrowly avoided. Writs of habeas corpus brought the two men before the Ohio supreme court, which heard the state's attorney general argue that they should be discharged because the law allegedly violated was unconstitutional. By a bare majority of 3 to 2, the court rejected that heady argument and remanded the prisoners.[30]

The supreme court of Wisconsin, on the other hand, continued to challenge the Fugitive Slave Act. Its repeated interference with federal authority in the aftermath of the Glover rescue brought it eventually into direct confrontation with the United States Supreme Court. The latter took no action until 1859, when, in *Ableman v. Booth*, it unanimously upheld southern rights with respect to fugitive slaves and issued a ringing affirmation of national judicial supremacy. That was not the end of the story, however, for the state supreme court refused to take notice of the accompanying mandate, and the Wisconsin legislature adopted resolutions declaring the decision to be "void and of no force." The controversy dragged on until the firing on Fort Sumter had made it obsolete.[31]

BEFORE SIGNING THE fugitive slave bill in 1850, President Fillmore consulted his attorney general, John J. Crittenden, and received the Kentuckian's official assurance that it was constitutional.[32] Nine years later in *Ableman v. Booth*,

Chief Justice Roger B. Taney had the concurrence of all his colleagues when he made the same pronouncement as an authoritative judicial ruling.[33] But then, no federal jurist or attorney general ever expressed a contrary opinion about either of the fugitive slave acts. Nor did any state supreme court, except that of Wisconsin, ever rule against their validity, whereas such state tribunals upheld the legislation on a dozen or more occasions.[34] The United States Supreme Court, in three decisions on the subject over a seventeen-year period, treated it each time as a matter already settled and not open to reconsideration. At this highest judicial level, the whole body of argument challenging the constitutionality of the legislation was simply disregarded.

The argument nevertheless seems strong enough in substance to have deserved a more respectful hearing. It suffered, of course, from being associated with the excesses of abolitionism, but among its most notable expositors were men of moderate views on slavery, such as Chief Justice Joseph C. Hornblower of New Jersey and Chancellor Reuben H. Walworth of New York. In opinions written at about the same time in the mid-1830s, both jurists maintained that the fugitive-slave clause of the Constitution vested no responsibility or authority in Congress. Instead, it imposed "a restriction and a duty" upon state governments and their citizenry (Walworth). Its fulfillment therefore depended "upon the enlightened patriotism and good faith of the several States" (Hornblower). Even Daniel Webster acknowledged in 1850 that such had been his understanding of the clause until Justice Story ruled otherwise in the *Prigg* case.

Later, Abram D. Smith of the Wisconsin Supreme Court rejected Story's reasoning and followed the Walworth-Hornblower line of exegesis when he declared: "The Constitution expresses a simple inhibition on the one hand, and enjoins a simple duty on the other. The inhibition on the states is, not to discharge the fugitive by any state law or regulation; the duty enjoined upon the state is, to deliver him up on claim, etc. An inhibition upon the states is not a grant of power to the United States. A duty enjoined upon the states cannot be construed into a grant of power to the United States to do the same thing in case the states do not."[35]

This was strict constructionism of the sort employed by opponents of a national bank and federally sponsored internal improvements. It rested on the literal truth that the fugitive-slave clause contained no express grant of power to Congress and, indeed, made no reference to federal enforcement of any kind. Moreover, contextual evidence strongly reinforces the impression that the framers of the Constitution had no congressional implementation in mind. The clause appears not in Article I with the enumerated powers of Congress, but rather in Article IV, which is about states and statehood, and more specifically in the second section of that article, which is about interstate comity, consisting as it does of the privileges-and-immunities clause, the flight-from-justice clause, and the fugitive slave clause. Of the three other sections in the article, two expressly confer power on Congress, and the other vests power in the "United States"—presumably meaning all three branches of the federal government. In contrast, Section 2 contains no grant of power in any of its three subsections. All this suggests that in Article IV, at least, when the framers intended to confer power, they did so explicitly. Congress itself seems to have come to that conclusion with respect to the other two subsections of Section 2, for neither of them was implemented with federal enforcement legislation.[36] Thus Article IV as context lends no credence and much doubt to the view of the fugitive slave clause as an empowerment of Congress.

Yet all such evidence and argument counted for little in American courts. There, whenever the question of constitutionality arose, the principles of broad construction, reinforced by the weight of precedent, nearly always prevailed. As Justice Story phrased it in the *Prigg* case: "No one has ever supposed that Congress could . . . enact laws beyond the powers delegated to it by the Constitution. But it has on various occasions exercised powers which were necessary and proper as means to carry into effect rights expressly given and duties expressly enjoined thereby. The end being required, it has been deemed a just and necessary implication that the means to accomplish it are given also."[37] It was a strange circumstance that this doctrine of implied power should have been employed in the interest of the region traditionally associated with strict construction of the Constitution. The fugitive slave issue had produced mirror images in which slaveholding southerners invoked national authority, while antislavery northerners pressed the doctrine of state's rights to the verge of nullification.[38]

But even if it were accepted that the fugitive slave clause by implication vested power in Congress, there would remain the question of whether the resulting legislation did not violate rights guaranteed elsewhere in the Constitution. The argument to that effect, presented so forcefully by Chase in the Van Zandt case, gained additional strength from the severity of the enactment of 1850. Its prime illustration might well have been the case of Adam Gibson, one of the first persons returned to slavery under the new law. Seized and brought before a United States commissioner in Philadelphia, he was identified, remanded, and hurried off to Maryland, where, however, his supposed owner honestly acknowledged that he was not the man sought.[39]

The United States Supreme Court persistently ignored the violation-of-rights issue and the threat posed to the free black population. Individually, however, most of its northern members paid some attention to the subject on circuit, and so did a number of district judges as well. The diverse backgrounds and circumstances of this corps of federal jurists did not prevent them from closing ranks against the complaint that the fugitive slave legislation of 1793 and 1850 inflicted deprivation of liberty without jury trial or without any of the other protections implied in the phrase "due process of law." Their response in all its verbal variations followed essentially the dual strategy of citing the substantial body of precedent while defining the rendition process in such narrow terms as to shield it from every constitutional objection.

In late antebellum years, the weight of precedent was all the more compelling because any judicial resistance to it was sure to aggravate the increasingly dangerous sectional conflict. Even Justice McLean, whose antislavery credentials were strong enough to make him the runner-up for the Republican presidential nomination in 1856, showed no inclination to disturb the judicial consensus rejecting all arguments based on the Bill of Rights. The fact that the constitutionality of the act of 1793 had never been denied by any federal or high state court on account of its lack of provision for jury trial seemed to him "no unsatisfactory evidence" of the correct construction for both fugitive slave laws. To be sure, he still had some qualms. "If the decision on such an inquiry as this should finally fix the seal of slavery on the fugitive," he acknowledged, "I should hesitate long, notwithstanding the weight of precedent, without the aid of a jury, to pronounce his fate." Then he added: "But the inquiry is preliminary, and not final."[40]

In those last words, as he shifted his attention from precedent to substance, McLean was relying on what had long been the core of rebuttal to the violation-of-rights argument: the rendition of a fugitive slave was not a judicial process but rather a ministerial act analogous to the extradition of a fugitive from justice;[41] the presiding magistrate or commissioner made no final determination of status but instead merely ascertained whether or not the person in custody was the person claimed in accordance with the law; any dispute about the rightfulness of that claim must be resolved in the state from which the person had fled; there his case for freedom, if he had one, would be decided in a trial before a judge and jury. This line of reasoning, which dated back at least to 1819, became common parlance not only in judicial decisions but in editorials and speeches defending the constitutionality of fugitive-slave legislation. It was especially useful to northern conservatives under abolitionist attack for their support of the act of 1850.[42]

Antislavery leaders viewed the whole formulation as a tissue of fallacies and deceit. Horace Mann compared it to the impious blandishments of Satan in the Garden of Eden.[43] As he pointed out, the analogy between extradition and rendition had little basis in reality. An alleged fugitive from justice was delivered into public custody, having been charged with a crime for which he could be punished only if tried and convicted by due process of law. In contrast, an alleged fugitive from service was delivered as property into the private possession of a claimant. Subject immediately to punishment without trial, he had no assurance and little hope of a day in court. Regarded as a contaminating influence, he was likely instead to be whipped for the edification of other slaves and sold off to a distant buyer. Clearly, there was nothing "preliminary" about the process that relegated him to slavery. "The decision of the commissioner is *final*," Mann declared, disputing assertions to the contrary by Commissioner Curtis in the Sims case. "He might as well doom a man to be hurled from the Tarpeian rock and say that the act is not final because he only commits the victim to the laws of gravitation, as he has committed Sims to the laws of Georgia."[44]

McLean himself, after insisting that rendition was not a final determination of status, went on to concede that the power of a master on his home grounds might well defeat a returned fugitive's suit for freedom. "This must be admitted," he said, "but the hardship and injustice supposed arise out of the institution of slavery, over which we have no control."[45] Similarly, the complaint that a free person might be condemned to slavery was sometimes brushed aside with the observation that defects in a law did not make it unconstitutional or that mistakes could occur in the enforcement of any legislation.[46] In this way, the threat to free blacks inherent in the fugitive slave laws was scaled down from a systemic injustice to one of the casual hazards that are a part of life.

The violation-of-rights argument elicited other judicial refutations as well, some of them narrowly technical. Thus, according to McLean, the Seventh Amendment's guarantee of jury trial "in suits at common law" was not applicable because the rendition of a fugitive slave proceeded under statutory law.[47] Somewhat more plausibly, the due process clause of the Fifth Amendment was held to be irrelevant because it applied only to criminal prosecutions. As for the Fourth Amendment's protection against unreasonable searches and seizures, Justice Story silently disposed of that issue in his *Prigg* decision when he interpreted the fugitive slave clause as a self-enacting, unconditional confirmation of the right of recaption. It thereafter seemed obvious that if a claimant had the constitutional right to seize a fugitive without a warrant, Congress had the power to incorporate that right in legislation.[48] Neither Story nor any other federal judge ever came to grips, however, with the fact that the clause antedated the amendments to the Constitution and was presumably limited by each of them.

Instead, the constitutional status of the fugitive slave laws reflected judicial acceptance of the historical necessity doctrine giving the fugitive slave clause a special priority among the various parts of the Constitution. The doctrine was historically erroneous, but by the 1850s it had acquired a certain prescriptive credibility that was all the more impressive in the context of worsening sectional conflict. Justice Robert C. Grier, instructing the jury in one of the trials following the Christiana riot, declared: "It is well known that, without this clause, the assent of the southern states could never have been obtained to this compact of union." Then he went on to warn that if northerners prevented execution of the clause, they would have no just complaint if southerners resorted to secession.[49] With apprehension thus reinforcing historical error in antebellum judicial reasoning, the right to recover a fugitive outranked competing constitutional rights. A pursuing slaveholder took with him the relevant slave law of his own state, including the definition of slaves as property and the presumption of slavery attaching to all people of color. Better than anything else, the history of the fugitive slave clause and its implementation illustrates the evolution from the unglossed Constitution of 1787 to the functionally proslavery Constitution of 1860.

IN 1855, WITH the Burns rendition bitterly in mind, the Massachusetts legislature approved a resolution calling for repeal of the Fugitive Slave Act on the ground that it violated, not the Fourth, Fifth, or Seventh, but the Tenth Amendment, which reserves to the states and the people "all powers not delegated to the United States by the Constitution, nor prohibited by it to the States."[50] There we have a documentary reminder that the fugitive slave controversy was a conflict of jurisdictions as well as personal rights and part of a larger struggle over the place of slavery in the structure of the republic.

For abolitionists, of course, slavery had no rightful place whatever in that structure. The Liberty party platform of 1844 boldly affirmed an intention to promote overthrow of the institution. It also denounced the fugitive slave clause as robbery of a natural right and therefore "absolutely void." Such was the radical temper of the American antislavery movement in its classic middle period. The abolitionists, though highly effective as social agitators, were too few to play much of a role in politics except as a pressure group that occasionally held the balance of power in a local or state election. At its peak in the presidential contest of 1844, the Liberty party drew only 62,300 votes or 2.3 percent of the total cast.[51] Already at work, however, were forces that would produce a political movement of narrower purpose and broader appeal, one that opposed slavery but conceded its legitimacy in part of the nation. The transcontinental expansion of the 1840s revived the struggle over the extension of slavery that had been dormant since the Missouri Compromise. As a consequence, the slave-centered program of abolitionism was increasingly overshadowed by the Free-Soil and Republican program of restrictionism, which had more to do with white rights than with black wrongs. Abraham Lincoln gave expression to the change in racial emphasis when, speaking of the newly created Kansas and Nebraska territories, he declared: "We want them for homes of free white people."[52]

The emergence of an antislavery movement dedicated to free-soilism rather than abolitionism tended to marginalize the fugitive slave issue, which was closely associated in the public mind with abolitionist sympathies and leadership. The Republican platforms of 1856 and 1860, like the Free-Soil platform of 1848, made no mention of the issue.[53] For a new major party striving to unify and enlarge its conglomerate membership, the whole subject was dangerously divisive. Lincoln warned Chase in June 1859: "The introduction of a proposition for repeal of the Fugitive Slave Law into the next Republican national convention will explode the convention and the party."[54] It is a striking fact that during the first five years of the Republican presence in Congress, there was no bill or resolution introduced, no debate attempted, on the subject of fugitive slaves.[55] The silence prevailed, moreover, at a time when both houses were almost continuously preoccupied with the slavery question in other ways.

At the state level, to be sure, Republican legislators were instrumental in the passage of some new personal liberty laws and a number of resolutions urging repeal of the Fugitive Slave Act, but these actions appear to have been taken largely in retaliation for proslavery gains on the territorial front. The Dred Scott decision in 1857 lent stimulus to an even more radical campaign in Massachusetts and New York aimed at outright repudiation of the fugitive slave laws. Legislation that would have freed every slave coming into the state received strong Republican support, though not enough in either instance to secure enactment.[56] In the North as a whole, however, Republican alignment with abolitionists on the fugitive slave issue was by no means as wholehearted and universal as southerners believed it to be.

The intensity of southern feeling on the subject is something of a historical puzzle. For one thing, slave escapes to the North apparently did not increase in the decade preceding the Civil War. However, recent scholarship, founded upon southern sources, sheds new light upon the matter. By focusing on runaways who stayed within the South and thus never challenged the Fugitive Slave Act, John Hope Franklin and Loren Schweninger reveal that slavery was an institution with serious problems on the eve of the Civil War. They estimate that in 1860 alone, 50,000 slaves took unauthorized leaves, the overwhelming majority of them consisting of fugitives who never left their familiar environs. By contrast, the U. S. Census reported only 803 escapes for that year, a statistic that possibly revealed the proslavery interest's desire to keep hidden the extent of the South's failure to maintain effective control in master-slave relationships close to home. In any case, far fewer fugitives escaped to the northern states or Canada than those runaways who never left the South.[57]

The border states, to be sure, sustained the heaviest losses of slaves escaping north of the Ohio River. According to the census reports, 46 percent of the fugitives in 1850 and 43 percent in 1860 were from Delaware, Maryland, Kentucky, and Missouri, although they contained only 12 percent and 11 percent, respectively, of the total slave population. This was an escape rate six times that for the rest of the South.[58] But therein lies another aspect of the puzzle, for the complaints from the border states were much less menacing than those from farther south, where the threat of secession commonly accompanied insistence on the retention and enforcement of the Fugitive Slave Act. One remark of Senator Jeremiah Clemens of Alabama, a Unionist by disposition, may be taken as typical. After acknowledging that his state did not lose "on average, one Negro in five years," he went on to say: "Convince me that this law cannot be executed, and you convince me that this government is and ought to be at end."[59]

Such depth of feeling about a matter ostensibly of little practical consequence can be explained in some part by the southern tendency, especially strong in the Lower South, to associate the fugitive slave issue with the problem of security. Flight, after all, was a form of resistance in a society haunted by the fear of servile rebellion, and northern violence on behalf of runaways further stimulated the apprehension of incendiary forces at work. The public excitement surrounding many escapes and rescues could scarcely fail to have a subversive effect even in remoter slaveholding regions. News of the Shadrach affair as it spread southward was, said Andrew P. Butler, like "a spark over a powder magazine."[60] Concern for security increased as the decade wore on, but, like the financial losses suffered, it was just one factor in the boiling up of southern anger with respect to fugitive slaves. There was also the sense of being cheated of a right accorded by the Constitution and repeatedly confirmed by every branch of the federal government. And with it went the sense of being personally defiled and humiliated by the constant flow of abolitionist invective on the subject. Most offensive of all were the northern personal liberty laws; each of them, being the work of a legislative majority, seemed to constitute a sovereign expression of hostility to the southern people, as well as a deliberate violation of the federal compact. There is no little significance in the fact that the declaration of the causes of secession issued by South Carolina's secession convention on December 24, 1860, devoted more space to the personal liberty laws than to any other single grievance.[61]

Southern complaints, it should be emphasized, were directed against northern states and the Republican party, not against the federal government, which continued to be the stalwart patron and agent of slaveholders in pursuit of runaway slaves. "There has been no time since its establishment," said Senator Robert Toombs of Georgia in January 1860, "when it has been truer to its obligations, more faithful to the Constitution than within the last seven years."[62] President James Buchanan was as determined as his predecessors to enforce the Fugitive Slave Act, and in his annual message of December 3, 1860, he asserted that the law had been "carried into execution in every contested case since the commencement of the present Administration." With the Lower South now moving toward secession as a result of Lincoln's election, the frantic Buchanan urged that northern states promptly repeal their "unconstitutional and obnoxious enactments." Otherwise, he warned, it would be "impossible for any human power to save the Union" and the slaveholding states "would be justified in revolutionary resistance to the Government." Later in the same message, he proposed an "explanatory amendment" to the Constitution, one section of which would have affirmed the validity of the Fugitive Slave Act and nullified every state law impairing its effectiveness.[63]

In the reconvening Thirty-Sixth Congress, Democrats from the Upper South and Lower North responded to the president's appeal with a variety of proposals, such as federal reimbursement for unreturned fugitives and, in a more retaliatory vein, the denial of representation to states that interfered with the recovery process.[64] Clearly, any program for saving the Union by compromise had to deal with the fugitive slave problem as well as the more critical issue of slavery in the territories. Both the House Committee of Thirty-Three and the Senate Committee of Thirteen sought to do so. Even Abraham Lincoln, who was generally opposed to compromise, privately furnished the Senate some conciliatory resolutions on the subject. One of them, however, aptly revealed the intractability of the whole problem. It declared that the fugitive slave clause ought to be enforced by federal law "with efficient provisions for that object" but also "with the usual safeguards to liberty, securing free men against being surrendered as slaves."[65] Decades of experience had shown that these two purposes were incompatible.

There followed three months of congressional effort that ended in failure, producing no salvational compromise and, indeed, very little legislation of a reconciliatory nature.[66] A bill granting fugitive slaves limited access to jury trial passed the House late in the session, but it foundered in the Senate. So did a joint resolution from the House urging repeal of those personal liberty laws that conflicted with the Constitution and federal law.[67] In one state legislature after another, late-hour attempts to repeal or modify such laws were proving unsuccessful.[68] When Congress arrived at its hour of adjournment on March 3, 1861, the fugitive slave issue remained one of the irreducible elements in the crisis of the Union.

ONE MIGHT EXPECT the Fugitive Slave Act to have been an early casualty of the Civil War. Secession, after all, removed most of its southern defenders from Congress and also canceled out the principal reason for what northern support it had received, namely, preservation of the Union. Within twelve months after the opening battle at Bull Run, Congress abolished slavery in the territories and in the District of Columbia and moved a long way toward general emancipation with the Confiscation Act of 1862. Yet the fugitive slave laws remained in place for two more years. Lincoln entered office committed to their enforcement, although he reiterated his preference for a new statute with more "safeguards of liberty." Attorney General Edward Bates clearly enunciated administration policy in the summer of 1861 when he instructed a federal marshal that all laws must be faithfully executed and that any refusal to do so with respect to fugitive slaves would constitute an official misdemeanor.[69] The controlling influence at this time was undoubtedly the need to retain the loyalty of the border states, where the fugitive problem had always been heavily concentrated. But in addition, after the war began, Congress had other, more urgent matters to consider, and there was less pressure for change because the emphasis of abolitionist agitation shifted to demands for universal emancipation. Furthermore, as the months passed, it seemed increasingly likely that the very nature of the conflict would turn the Fugitive Slave Law into a dead letter.

Enforcement by civil authority appears to have been sporadic and relatively inconsequential, reflecting the attitudes of local federal officials more than administration policy.[70] At the time of the Fort Sumter crisis, for example, there was a brief flurry of activity in Chicago when the Democratic marshal still holding office began arresting known fugitives, causing panic in the black community.[71] The greatest amount of excitement occurred right in Washington, where the Virginia-born federal marshal, Lincoln's intimate friend Ward H. Lamon, pursued a program of vigorous enforcement that lent aid to kidnappers as well as legal owners. His deputies even entered army camps to arrest fugitives for return to their owners.[72] Such conduct angered Republican members of Congress and eventually brought Lamon into direct conflict with the military commander of the district, General James S. Wadsworth. At one point in the spring of 1862, soldiers acting under orders from Wadsworth seized the city jail, arrested the jailer, and released all the alleged fugitives confined within its walls. Lamon and his deputies, with the help of local police, promptly recaptured the jail and arrested the two soldiers that had been left to guard it. The confrontation ended peacefully with an exchange of prisoners, but there were additional clashes in the months that followed.[73]

Far more important than civil enforcement was the military response to the flight of slaves from the control of their masters to the protection of Union armies. Northerners were generally disposed to welcome this flurry of self-liberation as a drain on Confederate strength. But some army commanders viewed the growing number of "contrabands" as a nuisance distracting them from their main duties, and some were more sympathetic than others to the rights of loyal slaveholders under the fugitive slave laws.[74] In the absence of a comprehensive military policy, a number of army officers elected to return fugitives to their owners, thus in effect doing the work of federal marshals. When these practices became known in Washington, antislavery leaders were outraged and hastened to press for countermeasures. After several preliminary efforts and the usual legislative delays, Congress in March 1862 approved an addition to the Articles of War prohibiting the return of fugitives by members of the armed forces.[75] By that time, in any case, the contraband problem was being absorbed into the movement toward general emancipation.

Yet the laws of 1793 and 1850 remained on the federal statute books, retaining theoretically all their quondam force. Antislavery efforts to remove these eyesores were blocked by border-state congressmen and northern Democrats with the help of conservative Republicans. Thus, a Senate bill to repeal the act of 1850, having been introduced in December 1861, was bottled up in committee until February 1863 and then reported unfavorably by the chairman, a New Jersey Republican. Similar efforts in the House in June 1862 and December 1863 were tabled by votes of 66 to 51 and 81 to 73, respectively. As late as April 1864, when the Senate took up a bill for repeal of the fugitive slave laws, it accepted an amendment leaving the act of 1793 in force. Eleven Republicans voted for the amendment, apparently agreeing with its author, John Sherman of Ohio, that certain southerners were still entitled to at least minimal protection of a right guaranteed by the Constitution. Radical Republicans would not support such a compromise, however, and the measure made no further headway. Finally, in June 1864, a bill to repeal both fugitive slave laws was passed by the two houses and signed by the president.[76] Said the *New York Tribune*: The blood-red stain that has blotted the statute-book of the Republic for seventy years is wiped out forever."[77] Few Americans took much notice, however, of what amounted to little more than a *pro forma* action. The federal government laid down quietly the burdensome responsibility that it had quietly and unnecessarily accepted in 1793.[78]

War inevitably disrupted the security of the slaveholding system and neutralized the federal contribution to that security. The flight of slaves to the Union army, which began not long after the firing on Fort Sumter, may rightly be regarded as the first phase of a process that culminated in the Emancipation Proclamation and the Thirteenth Amendment. In short, wartime fugitives had a discernibly significant effect on the nature and outcome of the conflict. Much more difficult to assess is the influence of the fugitive slave controversy on the coming of the Civil War.

Fugitive slaves and their pursuers caused friction between northern and southern states from the earliest years of the American government, but the problem did not pose a major threat to the nation until it became linked with the radical abolitionism that emerged in the 1830s. The fugitive slave issue lent emotional force and dramatic episode to the crusade against slavery, and it provided abolitionists their most popular cause—one that sometimes invited bold action as well as fiery words. At the same time, the fugitive issue, together with the territorial issue, so broadened the antislavery movement that it achieved imposing political power in one northern state after another.

Viewed from the South, the fugitive slave controversy was the clearest manifestation of a bond between radical abolitionism and the supposedly more moderate antislavery element that organized eventually as the Republican party. Here southerners found the strongest evidence that the North was becoming abolitionized and that their constitutional rights were under deadly attack as a consequence. Albert Taylor Bledsoe, a professor of mathematics at the University of Virginia, wrote in the mid-1850s: "It may be supposed, perhaps, by those who have reflected little on the subject, that the controversy respecting the Fugitive Slave Law is merely about the value of a few slaves. It is, in our opinion, far otherwise; it is a great constitutional question. . . . It is a question, as it appears to us, whether the Constitution or the abolitionists shall rule the country."[79] This perception of a menace to be faced, of a world to be defended or lost, was at the core of southern motivation in the secession winter of 1860–61.

In the free states, where the issue inspired division rather than consensus, it no doubt had a less critical influence on the shaping of public attitudes. Still, the Fugitive Slave Law of 1850 was the most intrusive action ever taken by the federal government on behalf of slavery, and it did harden many northern hearts against further concessions to the slave power. Viewed from any direction, the fugitive slave problem contributed significantly to the mutual sectional hostility that eventuated in civil war.

9

Slavery in the Federal Territories

Before he departed for France as a minister plenipotentiary in the summer of 1784, Thomas Jefferson served six months in Congress and managed, even during that brief interval, to leave several more indelible marks on American history. In a masterly paper he laid the foundation for the system of decimal coinage that was subsequently adopted by Congress. He coauthored a plan for the disposal of western lands featuring a grid system of survey that Congress soon incorporated in the Land Ordinance of 1785. Most notably, he drafted and secured passage of a plan of government for the West that became known as the Ordinance of 1784.[1] In the process, moreover, he raised for virtually the first time the question of whether slavery should be restricted geographically or allowed to expand with the expanding nation.

Creation of the national territorial system may be said to have begun in earnest on January 2, 1781, when the Virginia legislature passed an act ceding to the United States its vast land claims north of the Ohio River. Certain conditions attached to the cession proved unacceptable to the Confederation Congress, however, and not until March 1, 1784, did a modified offer from Virginia win congressional approval. On that same day, a committee headed by Jefferson, submitted its "plan for the temporary government of the Western territory."[2] The plan called for division of the entire West into as many as sixteen rectilinear states, each to be largely self-governing from the start and to achieve equal status in the Confederation when its population reached that of the least populous of the original thirteen states.

To this liberal design for state making, the committee added five restrictions, including the provision that "after the year 1800 of the Christian era, there shall be neither slavery nor involuntary servitude in any of the said states, otherwise than in punishment of crimes." During consideration of the measure on the floor of Congress, the antislavery provision was deleted because only six of the required seven state votes could be mustered in its favor.[3] Thus the Ordinance of 1784 as enacted on April 23, like the final version of the Declaration of Independence, was stripped of its Jeffersonian stroke against slavery. At the same time, an amendment added before passage declared that until a temporary government was actually organized, Congress might take measures "for the preservation of peace and good order among the settlers." Here, though limited in scope, was the first assertion of congressional power to govern the West directly.[4]

Forty days later, the North Carolina legislature followed Virginia's lead with a similar act of cession. The offer itself proved abortive and was not renewed for five years, but one of the attached conditions (no doubt inspired by Jefferson's recent antislavery proposal in Congress) required that Congress should make no law tending to emancipate slaves in the ceded area.[5]

In 1785, Rufus King of Massachusetts renewed Jefferson's proposal to exclude slavery from the entire transappalachian West, making it effective immediately, however, rather than after 1800. This, the last effort to enact such a comprehensive ban, had the preliminary approval of all northern delegates and a majority of the Maryland delegation as well. But it never came to a final vote, perhaps because its supporters recognized that such an extreme measure had no chance of success.[6] In 1786, a committee headed by Jefferson's friend James Monroe submitted a new plan for government of the West, but one that applied only to the region already ceded by Virginia—that is, to the Northwest. The plan amounted to a partial first draft of the famous ordinance enacted the next year, which established a centralized territorial system that in many ways resembled the old British colonial system, except for the promise of eventual statehood.[7]

The ordinance as originally drafted and in the revised form that came before Congress on July 11, 1787, contained no mention of slavery. But just before its passage two days later, Nathan Dane of Massachusetts moved an addition to the document's five "articles of compact" between the original states and the people and states of the territory. The proposed article began by declaring: "There shall be neither slavery nor involuntary servitude in the said territory otherwise than in the punishment of crimes, whereof the party shall have been duly convicted." To this emphatic ordainment of freedom there was attached, however, a significant concession to slavery in the form of a proviso legalizing recapture of fugitive slaves that escaped into the territory from any of the original states.[8]

Dane's amendment was accepted without demur, and the entire ordinance then won unanimous approval from the five southern and three northern states participating in the vote. Just why southerners in Congress put aside their earlier opposition to antislavery legislation for the West has been the subject of much speculation and dispute. No doubt the fugitive slave provision made the article more palatable for the South, and it must be remembered that in 1787 the people of the slaveholding states did not yet regard themselves as a minority section in mortal danger from antislavery aggression. Prohibiting slavery north of the Ohio, where it might take root but seemed unlikely to flourish, was no great concession and offered little or no threat to the ongoing expansion of slavery farther south. There, southerners could confidently assume that, as North Carolina had already insisted, territorial law must reflect the realities of southwestern settlement.[9]

The Northwest Ordinance was to remain for seventy-five years the premier antislavery document in American history. Later Congresses incorporated its memorable restriction in the organic act for each territory carved out of the Old Northwest and in the organization of other territories as far west as Oregon. With passing years, the ordinance, as viewed in the northern part of the Union, acquired a celebrative, almost mythic status that placed it alongside the Declaration of Independence and the Constitution as "one of the three title-deeds of American constitutional liberty."[10] The antislavery clause is indeed historically important as the initiation of a national policy on the extension of slavery. Yet the operative effect of the clause has often been questioned, and it soon became clear that the policy was just a half policy with an essentially proslavery counterpart.[11]

Some five weeks after Congress, under the authority of the Articles of Confederation, enacted the Northwest Ordinance in New York, the Constitutional Convention in Philadelphia began to consider the same problem of providing a system of government for the West. Two clear-cut proposals of James Madison were revised into one clause streaked with ambiguity. "The Congress," it declared, "shall have Power to dispose of and make all needful Rules and Regulations respecting the Territory or other Property belonging to the United States." All the contemporary evidence indicates that the rulemaking authority was meant to extend to the establishment of territorial government as well as to the disposal of public land, but the obscure phrasing left room for later controversy.[12]

The territory clause was approved by the Convention, probably without dissent,[13] and it appears to have attracted no criticism during the process of ratification. Madison in *Federalist* 43 called it "a power of very great importance" and emphasized its governmental aspect by associating it with the clause providing for the admission of new states. In August of 1789, the first Congress under the Constitution reenacted the Northwest Ordinance with the antislavery provision intact.[14] No member of either house questioned its authority to do so. George Washington, who had presided over the Constitutional Convention, readily signed the measure into law. Later that same year, the same Congress accepted North Carolina's cession of its western land, to which was attached the condition that "no regulation made or to be made shall tend to emancipate slaves." Accordingly, when Southwest Territory was created in 1790, its organic act, though similar in most respects to the Northwest Ordinance, omitted the ban on slavery.[15] In the circumstances, Congress could scarcely have done otherwise. Especially with slaveholding Kentucky nearly ready for statehood, any effort to impose the ban farther south would have been futile.

By 1790, then, Congress had activated a power and inaugurated a policy concerning the expansion of slavery. Without challenge, it had asserted and exercised its constitutional power to prohibit slavery in federal territory, but at the same time, it had renounced any intention of employing that power south of the Ohio River. The result, pregnant with meaning for the future, was a national policy of having two policies, with the Ohio as the dividing line between them. North of the river slavery was forbidden by federal law; south of the river it was silently permitted though not mandated by federal law. The practical effect, soon accentuated by the admission of Kentucky and Tennessee as slaveholding states, was to extend the Mason and Dixon line westward to the Mississippi.

ARTHUR ST. CLAIR, a Scotsman of uncertain parentage who had risen to the rank of major general during the Revolution, was a delegate to Congress from Pennsylvania and that body's president in 1787 when he received and accepted its appointment as the first governor of Northwest Territory. Reappointed by President Washington in 1789, he served until a quarrel with the Jefferson administration led to his removal in 1802. A man little troubled by diffidence in his exercise of authority, St. Clair took it upon himself to assure

French residents of the Illinois country that the antislavery clause of the Northwest Ordinance did not apply to slaves already held in the region at the time of its enactment. He casually informed the president of his ruling in the postscript of a letter on another subject. Washington and his secretary of state, Thomas Jefferson, silently acquiesced in this high-handed action, which had the effect of reducing the clause from an absolute prohibition to a ban merely on the further importation of slaves.[16]

Support for the St. Clair interpretation, which amounted virtually to an amendment, could be drawn from the language of the Virginia cession and the ordinance itself; both contained special references to the rights and liberties of the French inhabitants. Essentially, however, St. Clair's argument was the simple one that legislation ought not to be retroactive and that uncompensated emancipation of slaves already resident in 1787 would be "an act of the Government arbitrarily depriving a part of the people of a part of their property."[17] Here was an early manifestation of the tendency of federal officials to recognize the property-holding aspect of slavery—something not expressly warranted by the Constitution.

St. Clair's dispensation for a few hundred inhabitants did not in itself seriously impair the antislavery character of the Northwest Ordinance, but it led the way to more flagrant intrusions on the integrity of the document. For one thing, children of slave mothers were also held to be unaffected by the ban, so that, according to the federal census of 1820, for instance, over half the slaves still held in Indiana had been born after 1787. More significant were movements to establish virtual slavery in the form of long-term indentures. Nothing of the kind got beyond the talking stage in Ohio, but in 1803 the territorial governor and judges of Indiana Territory arbitrarily installed such a system, and the territorial legislature, when it came into existence, even provided a rudimentary slave code. The officers of Illinois Territory, created in 1809, followed suit by adopting wholesale the laws of Indiana, with the indenture system included.[18]

The system proved to be most tenacious in Illinois with its largely southern population. Although the state constitution of 1818 prohibited slavery, it authorized some continuation of the use of indentures, and strong objection from a number of northern congressmen did not prevent admission to statehood. In 1823–24, a vigorous movement to revise the Illinois constitution in favor of slavery received the support of the legislature but was defeated at the polls. Thus it was the voters of Illinois who ultimately excluded slavery from its boundaries. Not even the antislavery forces in the struggle viewed the

Northwest Ordinance as legally and conclusively binding on the sovereign power of their state. Indeed, the whole episode could be regarded as the climax of the ordinance's transformation "from a constitutional text into a higher law."[19]

The presence of slavery in early Indiana and Illinois affected only a small number of people and may now be viewed as one of those minor eddies that add complexity to the flow of history without changing its direction. For the people affected, however, it was not a statistical trifle but rather the essence of reality. One is forcibly reminded of that fact when he reads the text of an Indiana indenture binding a boy named Jacob to one Eli Hawkins for a term of ninety years, after which (at the age of 106) he was to be "free to all intents and purposes."[20] The various modifications, evasions, and outright violations of the antislavery article of the Northwest Ordinance originated, of course, in the complaints of certain actual settlers, usually of southern background. But they also reflected the proslavery bias of many territorial officials and a general indifference among higher executive officers in the national capital.

In the Southwest, it was different because federal policy allowing slavery to exist suited the wishes of the population. The only resistance to that policy came from outsiders—that is, from a few antislavery spirits in Congress. There was little left of Southwest Territory after the admission of Tennessee as a slaveholding state in 1796. By that time, however, Spain had relinquished its claim to the "Yazoo Strip" extending across what is now southern Alabama and Mississippi. In 1798, Congress accordingly proceeded to organize Mississippi Territory. Again, as in 1790, the legislation was modeled after the Northwest Ordinance, with the antislavery restriction deleted. In the House of Representatives, George Thacher of Massachusetts moved to strike out the deletion and thereby precipitated the first significant congressional debate on the subject of slavery in the territories. Perhaps the most notable feature of the whole discussion was the absence of any argument that Congress lacked the constitutional authority to impose such a restriction. Thacher's motion had no chance of success. Only eleven congressmen joined him in this last effort to circumscribe slavery in transappalachian America. This defeat was followed, to be sure, by a lesser antislavery victory, for an amendment prohibiting the foreign slave trade into the territory did win acceptance, to the displeasure of many inhabitants.[21]

It was in the territorial governments of the Gulf region (as well as in the government of the District of Columbia) that federal authority became most extensively and intimately involved with the slaveholding system. For instance, the first governor and judges of Mississippi Territory (two of them New Englanders and all of them appointed by President John Adams) promulgated a legal code that included a "Law for the regulation of Slaves." Detailed enough to constitute an elementary slave code, the measure extended to such matters as forbidding any slave to carry a weapon of any kind, own a dog or a horse, keep hogs running at large, engage in trade, or hire himself out, even with his owner's consent.[22] The readiness with which federal officials often sacrificed abstract scruples to concrete circumstances is exemplified in the advice that the secretary of state received from a boundary commissioner in the Yazoo Strip shortly before the creation of Mississippi Territory. "Slavery," the man wrote, "though disagreeable to us northern people, it would certainly be expedient to let it continue in this district; . . . otherwise, emigrants possessed of that kind of property would be induced to settle in the Spanish territory."[23]

On the March day in 1801 when Thomas Jefferson walked from his boarding house to the Capitol and took the prescribed oath as third president of the United States, national policy respecting the expansion of slavery had been set for the whole American West as it then existed—set in terms that only partly realized the liberal purpose of the ordinance he had drafted seventeen years earlier. The capstone of the policy fell into place the following year when the administration accepted Georgia's tardy cession of its western land claims, complete with the same kind of antislavery provision that North Carolina had insisted on in 1790.[24] The West, like the East, was to be divided between freedom and slavery. Jefferson as president probably could not have rescinded or significantly modified that arrangement. Soon, however, the nation would acquire an even larger West, and there would be another opportunity for him to pursue his antislavery ideal, if he chose to do so.

WITH THE PURCHASE of Louisiana from Napoleonic France in 1803, the history of slavery in the territories enters the second of its three major phases. One might have expected the author of the Ordinance of 1784 to view the acquisition as a tabula rasa and make some effort to inhibit the spread of the institution into a vast domain still largely free of white settlement, but Jefferson as president never lifted his hand against slavery, except in the matter of terminating the importation of slaves. Events such as the black revolution in Haiti and the Gabriel conspiracy in Virginia had contributed to an erosion of his antislavery convictions that left him passively pessimistic about the racial future of America. Reinforcing these private tendencies of mind were the exigencies of his role as head of a political party that drew the greater part of its electoral strength from the South. It is therefore not at all astonishing that Jefferson's administration should have been functionally proslavery. His attitude became clear soon enough when he sent to Congress, for use in organizing the new territory, a "Description of Louisiana" that included a digest of laws with a rigorous slave code.[25]

It had already become the accepted rule that slavery was legal in any federal territory from which it had not been excluded by federal law. This was presumably all the more true in the case of Louisiana, where the institution had existed under previous regimes and the inhabitants in the treaty of acquisition had been guaranteed the "free enjoyment" of their property. The Jeffersonian leadership in Congress accordingly drafted an organic act that omitted all reference to slavery. Opposition on antislavery grounds came principally from certain northern Federalists motivated, no doubt, by partisan as well as humanitarian considerations. Their leader, Senator James Hillhouse of Connecticut, offered a series of amendments that aroused extensive and often vehement debate. The boldest among them provided that no slave brought into Louisiana after a date to be specified should be required to serve more than one year beyond his twenty-first (or her eighteenth) birthday. The Senate rejected this semiabolitionist proposal by the fairly close vote of 17 to 11. A similar motion subsequently passed the House, only to be turned down again by the Senate. Both houses did approve amendments that banned the foreign slave trade and severely limited the domestic slave trade into the territory. The latter restriction was the strongest ever imposed on any part of the South before the Civil War. Highly unpopular among local residents, it lasted only a year and was probably never enforced.[26]

The bill enacted in 1804 created Orleans Territory, with boundaries approximating those of the later state of Louisiana. Additional legislation in 1805 assimilated the territory to the Northwest Ordinance, attaching the now familiar southern exemption from the antislavery article of that document. Territorial officials promptly interpreted this change as repealing the Hillhouse restriction on domestic slave trading. At the same time, Congress organized the rest of the Louisiana Purchase as Louisiana Territory without any mention of the ordinance or of slavery, thus employing in its purest form the hands-off strategy later called "nonintervention." The effect, especially in view of slavery's previous existence there, was a tacit federal sanction of the institution everywhere west of the Mississippi.[27]

All of this was done without any resistance from those members like

Hillhouse who had stirred up so much controversy a year earlier. Both measures were rushed through passage during the pressure period near the end of the session, but in light of the precedent already set east of the Mississippi, it seems incredible that no one made an attempt to exclude slavery from the northern part of the Louisiana Purchase as an offset to allowing it in the southern part. The oversight may be said to illustrate the random, spasmodic nature of antislavery sentiment in Congress at this time. The result, in any case, was that slavery established itself ever more firmly along the west bank of the Mississippi as far north as St. Louis, so that by 1810 the slave population of Louisiana Territory had reached 3,000. In 1812, along with admitting Orleans Territory to the Union as the state of Louisiana, Congress reorganized Louisiana Territory and changed its name to Missouri Territory. A motion in the House to prohibit the admission of slaves was quickly defeated. The act in its final form made no mention of slavery, thus continuing the policy of silent sanction.[28]

Federal authority in Orleans Territory during the eight years of its existence served largely to satisfy the needs and desires of the dominant planter class. In 1805, for instance, the presidentially appointed legislative council reaffirmed Spanish laws for the punishment of slaves. Two years later, the new territorial legislature, having already enacted a black code, passed a law severely restricting manumission and ending the slave's right to purchase his own freedom. These measures were approved by the presidentially appointed governor, William C. C. Claiborne. Slaveholders also expected the governor to help them recover their runaway slaves, many of whom fled to Spanish settlements in east Texas. Claiborne, using the threat of possible action by an impatient American citizenry, eventually negotiated an agreement with Mexico for mutual cooperation in the return of fugitives.[29]

One of the most pressing concerns of Claiborne and federal military commanders stationed in the Southwest was the fear of slave revolts, whether locally inspired or encouraged by subversive foreign influences. With blacks constituting nearly half the population of the territory, with memories of the Haitian rebellion enhanced by the presence of many refugees from that bloody upheaval, and with the spirit of revolution sweeping across much of Latin America, frequent rumors of slave conspiracies kept Louisianians in a state of apprehension that sometimes became outright panic. Claiborne was particularly busy in 1804 and 1805 responding to reports, strengthening patrols, dispatching troops to troubled communities, and otherwise seeking to increase security while calming the citizenry.

No open revolt materialized until January 1811, just at the time when the United States was in the process of seizing the western part of Spanish West Florida, having claimed it as part of the Louisiana Purchase. Violence broke out on a plantation north of New Orleans and swept several hundred blacks into the largest slave uprising in American history. The rebels began an organized march southward toward the city but were soon overwhelmed by a swiftly mobilized body of militia, naval troops, and regular army soldiers under the command of General Wade Hampton. The engagement turned into a massacre that left sixty-six black bodies for the counting. In addition, twenty-one of the insurrectionists taken alive were executed after speedy trial and conviction. Their heads were then placed on poles in the vicinity of the uprising as a warning to all who might be tempted to follow their example. In the aftermath of the affair, Claiborne busied himself with securing reimbursement for owners whose slaves had been killed and urging measures for the further improvement of public safety, including tighter curbs on the slave traffic. A Virginian of moderate temper and honest intentions, he was a very model of federal authority operating as proslavery authority in southern territories.[30]

The revolt of 1811 intensified racial apprehensions not only in the nascent state of Louisiana but also in neighboring Mississippi Territory. There, even after the declaration of war on Great Britain, Governor David Holmes regarded the large population of slaves as the greatest threat to security that he faced. "Scarcely a day passes," he wrote to General James Wilkinson, "without my receiving some information relative to the designs of those people to insurrect."[31] The war years passed, however, without any outbreak of the kind feared, and in fact, blacks both free and enslaved played a not insignificant role in Andrew Jackson's historic defense of New Orleans. The admission to statehood of Mississippi in 1817 and Alabama two years later closed the territorial history of the Old Southwest, leaving only the Louisiana Purchase, minus the state of Louisiana, as slaveholding federal territory.

For the most part, national discord over slavery was muted during the years of maritime contention and then outright warfare with England. Even after peace returned, the subject did not for a time cause much disturbance in the deliberations of Congress. As late as April 1818, a motion to prohibit the institution in all states thereafter admitted met swift rejection in the House of Representatives. Yet, within a year, the whole atmosphere had changed, as northern members of Congress precipitated the first major sectional confrontation over the westward expansion of slavery. This abrupt change had complex origins, reflecting, for instance, the last-ditch strategies of a dying Federalist party and the rising social influence of evangelical Protestantism. Whatever the background forces at work, northerners seem to have awakened quite suddenly to a realization that under the "Virginia dynasty" of Jefferson, Madison, and Monroe, the national prospect had been weighted heavily in favor of slavery.

THE MISSOURI CRISIS may be viewed as having actually begun in November 1818, with a resolution for the admission of Illinois, and to have ended in March 1821 with final approval of statehood for Missouri. During that period, Congress admitted two other states (Alabama and Maine) but organized just one new territory (Arkansas). The crisis was indeed over the expansion of slavery, but it centered primarily on the process of making new states rather than on the process of creating and governing federal territories. This feature of the struggle put antislavery elements at a serious disadvantage because any effort to introduce a prohibition or restriction at the state-making stage was likely to be, in practical terms, too late, and in constitutional terms, highly questionable.

The first indication of the approaching sectional quarrel came when thirty-three northern House members voted against the admission of Illinois after a New York congressman had denounced its constitution as insufficiently antislavery. Then, in mid-February of 1819, this same congressman, James Tallmadge, Jr., succeeded in adding a provocative amendment to a new bill for the admission of Missouri. It prohibited the further introduction of slavery into Missouri and provided that slave children born after the date of admission should be free at the age of twenty-five.[32] The ten thousand slaves already resident in Missouri would not have been touched by the amendment, which nevertheless constituted a long-term plan of gradual abolition. In order to justify federal supremacy within the boundaries of a sovereign state, Tallmadge appealed to the Constitution's guarantee clause (Article IV, Section 4), wherein the United States guarantees to every state a "republican form of government." This line of reasoning enraged southerners as it implied that all slave states, even those that participated in the framing of the nation's fundamental law, were not truly republican in form.[33] Tallmadge's argument was a direct challenge to the very notion of a slaveholding republic, and southerners at the time appreciated the historic potential of the guarantee clause for enormous trouble.[34]

In the House, northern members, mostly Republicans, voted almost 9 to 1 for the Tallmadge amendment.[35] In the Senate, southerners were confident that they had the votes to kill the measure. Yet even in that chamber, the constitutional assault against the slaveholding republic continued. Senator Rufus King, a surviving framer of the Constitution, attested that the territories clause (Article IV, Section 3) empowered Congress to establish special conditions for admission of new states into the Union. In 1812, he said, Congress had demanded that Louisiana accept both trial by jury and English as the official language. Holding Missouri to special conditions relating to slavery was of no different order.[36] Outside of Congress, John Jay, also a northern Founding Father of renown, offered an ingenious constitutional argument. Focusing on Article I, Section 9, paragraph 1, relating to Congress's power to restrict the importation of slaves after 1808, he claimed that Congress could ban the importation of slaves into the state of Missouri specifically.[37] In the House, John W. Taylor, also of New York, extended this logic to claim congressional power over any and all interstate traffic in slaves.[38] Justice Joseph Story and Senator Benjamin Ruggles of Ohio both added that the commerce power, located in Article I, Section 8, by itself was sufficient to this end.[39]

Seeing their section under attack, surviving southern Founding Fathers could not long remain silent. James Madison and Charles Pinckney stressed that the Constitutional Convention had not authorized any extraordinary congressional control over slavery.[40] Thomas Jefferson, although not a participant in the Convention of 1787, likewise recoiled against all of the northern constitutional innovations spawned by the Missouri crisis. As for the expansion of slavery that he had once opposed, Jefferson adopted the argument that "diffusion" of the institution in the West would not increase the total number of slaves and "would make them individually happier and facilitate their eventual emancipation." New York's John W. Taylor responded to this weak line of southern defense by branding the rationale a "counterfeit" method of seeking "to palliate disease by the applications of nostrums . . . which saves a finger today, but amputates the arm tomorrow."[41] Despite such individual resistance to southern perceptions, the true character of the northern position became obvious when Tallmadge and his allies made no attempt to block the admission of Alabama as a slave state late in 1819. The creation of Arkansas Territory earlier in the year with no restriction placed on slavery had provided an indication that northern animus toward the institution weakened when more southern regions were under discussion.[42] The distinction between Alabama and Missouri made sense from a practical stand-point, given that Alabama was surrounded by slave states and already held a slave population four times greater than that of Missouri; but if a new slave-holding state in the Deep South did not violate the guarantee clause, then how could one from more northern latitudes?

The collapse of northern resistance concerning Alabama served to signal a return to moderation, a precondition for any eventual compromise.[43] A set-tlement was attempted by linking Missouri and Maine's dual admission, which balanced the addition of one slave state with one that was free. The bill had solid southern support and enough northern acquiescence to give it a chance, but in the end this attempt by itself failed to resolve the matter. Even-tually, threats from southern disunionists drove enough wavering northerners toward a final solution. An amendment offered by Representa-tive Jesse B. Thomas of Illinois to divide the rest of the Louisiana Purchase at 36° 30' latitude, with slavery prohibited north of that line, ultimately com-pleted the settlement. In the end, Maine served as a counterweight to Missouri, and the future course of slavery in what was then the American West was determined.[44]

A second Missouri Compromise, this one occurring in 1821 over the issue of whether Missouri had the authority to bar the entry of free blacks into the new state, basically obfuscated the question at hand simply to restore peace.[45] By that point, antislavery fervor in Congress was spent, and the rel-ative calm that earlier had characterized congressional discourse on slavery returned. Nevertheless, the constitutional logic of the antislavery position permanently affected the collective memory, especially that of southerners. Thereafter, southerners periodically questioned whether the Union itself could long endure.[46] Increasingly, they looked at any congressional power over slavery, even in the federal territories where that authority was well founded, with great suspicion.[47] This supersensitivity on the topic of slavery persuaded a number of northerners to shelve their antislavery views. While extreme constitutional arguments continued in abolitionist pamphlets, such expressions largely disappeared from the speeches of northern congressmen. Occasionally, sporadic flare-ups in Congress were forced by antislavery radi-cals exercising the right of petition. But generally, the North seemed satisfied that slavery's trans-Mississippi northward advance had been halted and cared little to revisit the subject.

Concurrently, the nation's fundamental creed underwent a subtle trans-formation. During the Missouri debates, the presumed national purpose of spreading the blessings of liberty had been frequently raised by northerners, engendering a southern response that the founding national vision embedded in the Declaration of Independence was a mere "fanfaronade of metaphysical abstractions."[48] Following the Missouri Compromise, Americans in general, other than those of a firm antislavery persuasion, seemed to subscribe to a new southern understanding that the Declaration of Independence did not in fact proclaim universal human rights, but rather applied to whites alone. Indeed, during the decade following the crisis, the Jacksonian movement celebrated an equality reserved for white men only. Gradually, the slaveholding republic came to acquire a revised national ideology suitable for maintaining sectional peace.[49]

THE REDEVELOPMENT OF a two-party system in the decades that followed the Missouri crisis served to calm political passions on the slavery issue, at least temporarily. By heightening conflict over issues having nothing to do with slavery directly—such as the Bank of the United States, Henry Clay's "American System" of protective tariffs and federally sponsored internal improvements, together with the controversial leadership style of Andrew Jackson—the emergence of the Whig and Democratic parties effectively redirected the course of American politics. The Democratic party's two-thirds rule, adopted in 1832, that nominees for president and vice president have an extraordinary majority support, subtly restricted any new outburst of anti-slavery agitation, as aspiring northern Democratic leaders knew that they needed southern backing to win the ultimate prize. Party restraints also worked upon southern leaders. For example, President Andrew Jackson reluctantly delayed slaveholding Texas, which had declared its independence from Mexico in 1836, from immediately entering the Union, as he could not risk disrupting his intersectional party in a presidential election year. The new Whig party exercised similar restraining influences, at least up until John Tyler became the first vice president to assume the presidency upon the death of a sitting president. Labeled "His Accidency," Tyler soon alienated his own Whig party and for the rest of his term operated independently of any concern to maintain intraparty unity. A proslavery extremist, Tyler actively sought the annexation of Texas irrespective of the consequences.[50] After two decades of relative intersectional calm, the issue of slavery's expansion into the West reawakened.

Stretching from California to Russian Alaska, the Oregon Country concurrently captured the imaginations of northern free-soil expansionists.

Exploiting Oregon's potential to balance Texas, James K. Polk won the Democratic nomination for the presidency in 1844 upon a dual promise to add both areas to the United States. Seizing upon Polk's narrow victory over an anti-expansionist Henry Clay, annexationists declared a public mandate to admit Texas immediately, which was done by a joint resolution of Congress.[51] Supposedly, clear title to the Oregon half of Polk's platform could follow in due course.

Texas, Oregon, and California were all linked in the westward-looking agenda of the Democratic party. As Mexicans viewed Texas as legitimately part of their nation, American annexation of Texas necessarily meant war, or at the very least very serious negotiations with Mexico in order to prevent hostilities.[52] Whether by war or negotiations, Polk was intent upon acquiring at least part of Alta California. He went to the brink with Great Britain over Oregon as well, despite the fact that this European power could not be bullied as a weak Mexico might.[53] In the contest with Great Britain, California was also key, given both the latter's proximity to Oregon and its extremely vulnerable condition. Several weeks before Polk's inauguration, the Mexican residents of California themselves had expelled their Mexican-appointed governor, effectively ending Mexico's control of that province.[54] From then on, California was more independent than not and fair game for any power seeking to control the Pacific coast.[55]

In order to avoid the possibility of a two-front war, Polk divided the Oregon Country with Great Britain in 1846, at the same time, he went to war with Mexico over Texas to defend an extreme proslavery boundary claim.[56] In retaliation for the president's compromise of free soil, northern congressmen, led by Pennsylvania Democrat David Wilmot, vowed to bar slavery from any territory taken from Mexico. For the first time in American history, a serious attempt was made to use the Constitution's territories clause to ban slavery from the West without any conciliatory gesture toward southern interests. Wilmot's proposal, made in the form of an amendment to a military appropriations bill, read: "*Provided*, That, as an express and fundamental condition to the acquisition of any territory from the Republic of Mexico by the United States, by virtue of any treaty which may be negotiated between them, and to the use by the Executive of the moneys herein appropriated, neither slavery nor involuntary servitude shall ever exist in any part of said territory, except for crime, whereof the party shall first be duly convicted."[57] In the Missouri crisis, northern antislavery forces had not held firm on Arkansas and Alabama, a weakness that eventually led to compromise. No such moderation characterized the Wilmot Proviso, which repeatedly passed the House only to fail in a pro-southern Senate. There, John C. Calhoun countered by proclaiming that slavery followed the flag into any and all acquired provinces. As western territories belonged to all of the states collectively, the property rights of citizens of all the states had to be honored—slaveholders not excluded. His so-called Calhoun Resolutions failed to pass either house but succeeded in inspiring increasing southern support.[58]

The inability of the Wilmot Proviso to pass the senate possibly motivated Supreme Court Justice John McLean to suggest that the proviso's principle was inherent in the Constitution itself. A rare antislavery presence on a proslavery Court, McLean argued that under the Constitution, freedom was national, while slavery was only local, which logically suggested that territory acquired by the nation itself was automatically free soil.[59] Other antislavery activists suggested that the Fifth Amendment's guarantee of individual liberty supported McLean's case. By contrast, slavery's defenders claimed that the Fifth Amendment protected slaveholders' property rights from any federal meddling, such as the Wilmot Proviso.[60] In an environment that was rapidly reducing all political questions to matters of constitutional imperative, President Polk himself tentatively favored a more political approach, that of extending the Missouri Compromise line of 36° 30' into any lands taken from Mexico.[61] Yet none of these positions succeeded in winning sufficient congressional backing. Inexorably, the nation moved toward a new sectional crisis over slavery.

Lewis Cass, who was nominated by the Democrats to succeed Polk, held that the Constitution's territories clause, properly interpreted, did not empower Congress to pass either the Wilmot Proviso or extend the line of 36° 30' into the Far West, as that language provided only the authority to make rules and regulations regarding the disposition of public lands.[62] By his lights, allowing the people of each federal territory to decide the issue of slavery for themselves was in the tradition of the nation's founders, who fought Great Britain supposedly to establish the principle of local self-government.[63] According to this logic, nonintervention, as made operational in 1787 south of the Ohio River, was in the tradition of local self-government, whereas Congress's imposed Northwest Ordinance of that same year was not. Stephen A. Douglas, who soon became the leading spokesman for "popular sovereignty," stopped short of claiming that the Constitution gave Congress no authority over the issue. Rather, he urged that Congress *should* be guided by "the great principle" of local self-government.[64]

One practical problem with popular sovereignty concerned exactly when the principle of local self-government should become operational during the territorial process. Historically, nonintervention, or noninterference by the federal government, had led to the effective establishment of slavery. Slavery, with other vices, could only be kept out of a territory by means of governmental proscription, which Cass hinted was still possible under his plan. In advocating local self-determination, Cass's rhetoric seemed to allow that territorial governments themselves might outlaw slavery well before applying for statehood. Indeed, before northern groups he suggested this option. Yet, when speaking before southern audiences, Cass tightly defined popular sovereignty as operating only at the moment when a territory petitioned Congress for entry into the Union as a sovereign state. Up until that time, laissez faire would allow slavery to become firmly established.[65] Of course, by that late date, the issue would have already been determined by drift. For southern voters, popular sovereignty and nonintervention became synonymous. In the North, popular sovereignty meant something else altogether. With this clever stratagem, Cass succeeded in shaping the national discourse, despite the fact of losing the presidential election to his Whig opponent, Zachary Taylor, hero of the Mexican War.

Although nonintervention and drift had heretofore aided slavery's extension, the Mexican Cession provided unique circumstances that possibly favored freedom, as Mexico had banned slavery by positive enactment prior to American acquisition. Until superceded by new congressional statutes, this Mexican law officially continued into the new American era. If federal officials on the scene had an intent to maintain the legal status quo, Congress's failure to resolve the dispute regarding slavery's extension in this instance clearly favored antislavery.[66] However, the California gold rush prevented this scenario. As soldiers in the American occupying force deserted to the gold fields, California rapidly moved toward anarchy. In the wake of this historical event, drift became intolerable. Upon assuming the presidency in March 1849, Zachary Taylor was forced to act.[67]

In April, Taylor dispatched a special agent to California to work with the American military governor in encouraging the burgeoning new population there to petition Congress for immediate statehood. Without knowledge of this presidential intention, California's military authorities had already begun to move in this direction. Three weeks before Taylor's inauguration, citizens met in San Francisco and called for the creation of a provisional civilian government. Well before Taylor's plan was known, the military governor decided to lead this popular groundswell rather than oppose it.[68] When Taylor's agent arrived on June 4, the process for convening a state constitutional convention in Monterey in September was underway. Of course, the presence of a presidential emissary approving of the course already taken helped move matters forward. Taylor's agent, T. Butler King, was a Georgia slave owner. One-third of the delegates sent to the Monterey convention were slave owners, as was President Taylor himself. Yet all involved recognized that California's young population insisted upon free-state status.[69]

President Taylor saw the entire Mexican Cession as unsuited to slavery. Indeed, had the gold rush not roughly intervened, a slaveholding southern president, intent upon carrying out an antislavery policy in the West through a quiet enforcement of Mexican law by American military administrators in territory left unorganized by Congress, might have effectively calmed the volatile sectional confrontation initiated by the Wilmot Proviso. But, of course, this is not what occurred. Rather, in attempting to resolve the issue of California anarchy, a politically inexperienced Taylor succeeded only in generating a strident opposition from his native South. Surrounded by northern antislavery advisors, Taylor naively convinced himself that by jumping over the normal territorial process and instead pushing for new states in both California and New Mexico he could avoid the issue of slavery in the territories.[70]

North Carolina's Thomas L. Clingman expressed rising southern sentiment by noting that under Taylor's leadership California, Oregon, New Mexico, Deseret (Utah), and Minnesota all seemed likely to join the Union as free states, giving the North practical control of the Senate as well as the House. Once thus empowered, Clingman predicted, the North would soon move to destroy slavery in the southern states themselves. He imagined how a Congress with northern majorities in *both* houses might find the constitutional power to destroy slavery everywhere in the nation: "Would not this majority find the power, as easily as they have done in their State Legislatures, where they have complete sway, to nullify the provision of the Constitution for the protection of fugitive slaves? Have not prominent northern politicians . . . already declared that there is nothing in the Constitution of the United States which obstructs or ought to obstruct the abolition of slavery, by Congress, in the States?" He and others threatened that before the South would bow before this specter of northern domination, the Union itself would be torn asunder.[71] The rage, present in the earlier Missouri crisis, emerged fully resurrected by the end of 1849. Constitutionalization of the issue of slavery in the West, and an emotional hardening of positions that accompanied this process, made an easy resolution virtually impossible.[72]

THE MONTEREY CONVENTION finished its work on October 13, 1849, adopting a constitution prohibiting slavery. The voters of California ratified it on November 13. These actions, culminating on December 4 in President Taylor's recommendation that the new state be quickly admitted, precipitated the nation's greatest crisis over slavery in a generation.[73] Refusing to follow Taylor's presidential leadership, Henry Clay offered his own plan for a sweeping compromise, only one part of which involved California's admission as a free state.[74] The facts that Taylor (the titular head of the Whig party) had no political experience and that Clay (the historic leader of the Whig party) had failed five times to win the prize so easily acquired by Taylor, heightened the drama of this personal confrontation.[75]

By encouraging both California and later New Mexico to become free states by their own initiative, Taylor created the appearance of validating the Wilmot Proviso without having Congress actually enact the measure. By contrast, Clay's plan called for California to become a free state but also divided the remainder of the Mexican Cession into two territories—New Mexico and Utah (the northern half of Taylor's "New Mexico")—"without the adoption of any restriction or condition on the subject of slavery." If and when the House passed Clay's plan, it would thereby formally reject the Wilmot Proviso, thus appeasing southern sensibilities. Clay was enough of a politician to know that symbolic acts are often as significant as material concessions. Few southerners had expectations of slavery actually flourishing in these regions; Daniel Webster reminded his own northern constituents of this fact and urged them to detach themselves from what he regarded as Wilmot's needless taunting of the South.[76]

Despite proslavery elements in Clay's package, some southerners were unwilling to surrender all hope of getting any portion of California. Jefferson Davis, for one, thought that southern California, combined with part of western New Mexico, might make a fine slave state.[77] Loyal to the concept of state sovereignty, southerners could not deny the clear preferences of Californians themselves. On the other hand, southern California had been poorly represented at the Monterey convention, due to the fact of its light population relative to that of the gold-mining regions of northern California. Southern expansionists focused upon the injustice of a regionally concentrated group of young gold-seeking adventurers determining the destiny of southern California. Those attuned to southern interests foresaw that some-day California had to divide into several states given its unusual size, which if replicated on the east coast would incorporate Pennsylvania, South Carolina, and everything in between into a single state.[78] One month after Clay offered his compromise plan, a mass meeting held in Los Angeles petitioned Congress to divide California, so as to leave the southern part of the proposed state as an organized territory. The protest was forwarded to Senator Henry S. Foote of Mississippi, who presented it before the United States Senate on May 9, 1850. Given such expressions emanating from California itself, southerners were encouraged to demand their fair share of the Pacific coast.[79] Likewise, President Taylor, deeply offended by Clay's refusal to follow his lead, stood ready to kill his rival's plan. In the early summer of 1850, both the South and those antislavery Whigs supporting Taylor's plan blocked Clay's progress.[80]

Then, Taylor died on July 9, following a very brief illness. Millard Fillmore, the new president, quickly swore allegiance to Clay as party leader. Yet, even with the elimination of presidential opposition, Clay's proposal stalled. Years of identifying the issue of slavery in the territories with constitutional imperatives seemingly prevented any resolution.[81] Thereupon, an exhausted, aged Clay transferred the congressional management of his compromise plan to Stephen A. Douglas, a younger, more energetic man from the other major party.[82] Concluding that true compromisers were in a minority, Douglas adopted a new strategy, alternatively coupling extreme factions with an unwavering procompromise minority to get each facet of the settlement through Congress in a piecemeal manner. In the months of August and September, Douglas trained the Senate and the House to do his bidding. Voting on each specific measure was largely along sectional lines. In the end, President Fillmore signed all parts of the so-called Compromise of 1850. Because of the extraordinary way in which each part of it was maneuvered through Congress, historian David M. Potter aptly termed the Compromise of 1850 as "a truce perhaps, an armistice, certainly a settlement, but not a true compromise."[83]

California thus became a free state. New Mexico and Utah's situation was more ambiguous. The enigma of Cass's popular sovereignty—which confusingly translated into either Calhoun's constitutional position effectively protecting slavery in the territories up until statehood *or* a possible instrument to kill slavery during the territorial stage well before any application for statehood—was built into the very structure of the settlement. Revealing just how far the issue of slavery in the territories had become constitutionalized, the law provided for any decisions made effecting slavery in either Utah or New Mexico during their territorial stages to be appealed to the United States Supreme Court.[84] Ten years after the settlement, no slaves were reported to reside in New Mexico Territory and only twenty-nine slaves were in Utah Territory. In the end, Webster's judgment that climate and geography effectively banned slavery in the area appeared to be validated by census data. Nevertheless, both territorial legislatures provided legal sanction to slavery. Utah's act was passed in 1852 and New Mexico's in 1859.[85] As neither territory ever enacted a law challenging the property rights of slaveholders, no appeals were ever made to the Supreme Court.

Some parts of the Compromise of 1850 had nothing to do directly with the issue of slavery in the territories. Of these, the Fugitive Slave Act of 1850 is the principal example. Arrangement of Texas's boundary with New Mexico, U.S. absorption of the state's debt, and restriction of the slave trade in Washington, D.C., made up the remaining pieces of the settlement. However, the significance of the package rested primarily in the fact that the issue of slavery in the territories, which had first threatened the Union with the entry of Missouri and later with California, had seemingly been permanently laid to rest. Both Douglas and President Fillmore emphasized this point.[86] However, the matter was far from dead. Four years later, Douglas himself reopened it by devising the Kansas-Nebraska Act, a measure that invited American settlement into the undeveloped part of the Louisiana Purchase above 36° 30'. In the process, the Missouri Compromise line barring slavery's northward advance was repealed. Born in northern reaction to Douglas's symbolic reawakening of an old issue, the Republican party thus came into being, devoted to halting the spread of slavery into new territories. In hindsight, Douglas's behavior seems almost inconceivable, given his earlier central role in supposedly settling the problem for all time.

To explain this course of events, the historian must recreate concerns and expectations of the times. First, one must consider the ambitions of Stephen A. Douglas himself. As a Democrat, he knew that he needed strong southern support if he ever hoped to become president of the United States. The role that he played in shaping the Kansas-Nebraska Act clearly enhanced his reputation in the South, where restriction of slavery north of the line of 36° 30' rankled as a continuing symbol of congressional interference with that section's most significant domestic institution. But Douglas's southward-looking political motivations did not primarily determine his course. More important was his desire to develop economic opportunities for his Illinois constituents.

The nation was then experiencing dynamic technological growth. Railroads especially captured the public imagination. Every town, certainly every city, dreamed of becoming a commercial emporium. The westward migration of the American people continued unabated. Railroad construction promised to direct the course of empire. Yet, prior to the Kansas-Nebraska Act, a swath of wilderness ranging northward from 36° 30' to the Canadian border remained closed to American settlement. Over the years, the federal government had made various treaties with Indian tribes promising them permanent guarantees against future encroachment if they would relocate far from areas of white settlement, beyond the western borders of Arkansas, Missouri, and Iowa. "This policy," wrote Douglas in late 1853, "evidently contemplated the creation of a perpetual and savage barrier to the further progress of emigration, settlement and civilization in that direction."[87] This situation had become the practical negative result of the Missouri Compromise of over a generation before, as southerners stood ready to block any attempt to organize the region above 36° 30' into free territories. Every year that the South succeeded in maintaining the status quo, the potential growth of Chicago and St. Louis remained unrealized, leaving commercial interests in both northern and southern Illinois frustrated.[88] The dynamism of the age augured against any such permanent obstruction. Douglas came to see the Kansas-Nebraska Act as the only practical way to bring about both national development and the growth of his state and region. With California rapidly growing in population, the need for a transcontinental railroad was apparent. If northern and central routes remained blocked by the presence of an Indian wilderness, New Orleans would become by default the great city of the Mississippi River basin. Douglas intended that Chicago and St. Louis remain front runners in this contest for urban supremacy.[89]

In 1853, Jefferson Davis became the secretary of war and directed the Army Corps of Engineers to find the most feasible railroad route across the continent. Its subsequent report was predictable: The extreme southern route, which would best serve the interests of both New Orleans and Davis's Mississippi, was the best of all possible routes. It bypassed the rugged Rockies and the almost impassable Sierra Nevada that burdened more northerly routes. It had only one geographic handicap. A strip of land in Mexico, immediately south of western New Mexico Territory's southern boundary on the Gila River, was needed so that the railroad route would never have to leave the United States on its way to San Diego. As Douglas moved to organize the wilderness north of 36° 30', the U.S. ambassador to Mexico was finalizing the terms of the Gadsden Purchase which would put the extreme southern route entirely on American soil.[90]

Typical of American politicians of all seasons, Douglas explained his purposes in idealistic, democratic rhetoric. Jacksonian Democrats, of whom Douglas was a prime example, saw westward expansion as essential for the perpetuation of both individual freedom and republican government. Anticipating Frederick Jackson Turner, Democrats then typically believed that economic opportunity for the masses could only be kept alive by means of a continuously expanding agricultural frontier. The replanting of democratic institutions, characterized by local self-government, became Douglas's "great principle" underlying popular sovereignty. In his own mind, the Kansas-Nebraska Act was synonymous with American freedom, economic opportunity, and local self-determination, upon which the American democratic experiment rested.[91] Most importantly, he believed in his own powers of political persuasion to communicate this vision to the American people.

Douglas's original bill had proposed to organize the entire area north of 36° 30' as "Nebraska Territory." Dividing it subsequently into both Kansas and Nebraska made it more attractive to southerners, who could see in Kansas a possible future slave state, immediately to the west of slaveholding Missouri. Given the fact that Douglas himself had no strong personal moral revulsion concerning slavery, the change was seen by him as one that merely helped move western development forward. Earlier, in shepherding the Compromise of 1850 through Congress, he had helped eliminate the negative symbolic force of the Wilmot Proviso. Surrendering the moral sense of national prohibition that the Missouri-Compromise line of 36° 30' had come to represent was of no different order. For him, such moral condemnation was only abolitionist posturing over an abstraction, lacking in practical definition and deserving little serious consideration.

Douglas saw the Compromise of 1850 as having made the Missouri Compromise's earlier line of prohibition politically irrelevant. He portrayed the modern method of resolving the issue of slavery in the territories as present in the rules organizing Utah and New Mexico territories.[92] Southerners could readily agree with Douglas, as the Illinois senator did not overemphasize the probable outcome of any meaningful popular sovereignty in Kansas Territory. Most westward-moving Americans were northerners, loyal to northern institutions and northern culture, and likely to restrict the introduction of slave agriculture. As a realist, Douglas knew what popular sovereignty, exercised during the territorial stage, was likely to produce in

Kansas.[93] But, as he prided himself a realist, it is interesting that he did not foresee the southern rage that inevitably resulted when these facts ultimately materialized. Focusing upon the immediate challenge of getting his bill enacted over vociferous antislavery opposition, Douglas chose to let the future take care of itself.

In the session of Congress that immediately followed the passage of the Kansas-Nebraska Act, Douglas gave his primary attention to passing a Pacific Railroad bill, but he did not succeed.[94] For that matter, neither did any of the other aspirants in this transcontinental contest. In fact, nothing happened on this score until the Civil War, when southern desertion of Congress finally allowed the selection of a central route across the continent, partially through territory organized by Douglas in 1854.[95]

SEVENTY PERCENT OF northern Democratic congressmen and senators who voted for the Kansas-Nebraska Act lost their seats in the midterm elections of 1854.[96] Despite their harsh rejection at the polls, northern Democrats generally continued to opt for a harmonious relationship with southern Democrats. As for Douglas himself, he realized that the midterm election results virtually killed his own presidential ambitions for 1856.[97] Nevertheless, he continued to nurture hopes of one day heading a national ticket with the help of southern votes. While the Kansas-Nebraska Act hurt the Democrats, the party at least remained afloat as a national political organization.

Whig losses in the midterm elections were more serious. The deaths of Clay and Webster several years before contributed to the party's unraveling. With its traditional leadership disappearing, the party entered a steep descent. More fundamental problems further encouraged the Whig decline. Whigs had never shown the cleverness in managing the constitutionalization of the issue of slavery in the territories, which had characterized the party of Cass and Douglas. During and after the crisis of 1850, many northern Whigs had revealed themselves as essentially antislavery people, while southern Whigs at times occupied more strident proslavery positions than even southern Democrats. By 1852, the national Whig party appeared to have a sectionalized split personality so far as the slavery issue was concerned.[98]

Webster had provided a model of a sectional Whig leader moderating his message to meet the needs of his national party, but few northern Whigs followed his example. Indeed, Senator William H. Seward's remarks during the debates leading to the Compromise of 1850 especially hurt the cause of southern Whiggery. An advisor to President Taylor, New York's Seward had addressed the emotional needs of his section by preaching against the immorality of slavery rather than effectively representing his president's plan to end the immediate sectional crisis.[99] Accordingly, southerners fell away from the Whig party in droves following the Compromise of 1850. The witness of the Louisiana-slaveholding soldier-hero Taylor being manipulated by the likes of "higher law" Seward produced a southern alienation that contributed to a Democratic landslide in the elections of 1852.[100] Rather than hold onto an increasingly marginalized national Whig party, northern Whigs also exited their party in 1854, further relegating the party of Clay and Webster to a political grave. Two new parties—the national American (or Know-Nothing) party and a sectional, northern Republican party—quickly emerged.[101]

It is important not to overemphasize the role that the slavery issue played in the death of the Whig party. Economic and personal issues had called the party into being in the 1830s, yet they were passé by the early 1850s. Clay's themes of protective tariffs, federally sponsored internal improvements, and the Bank of the United States no longer effectively divided the parties. With the passing of Andrew Jackson in 1845, continuing animosity toward "King Andrew" no longer had any relevance. A growing degree of interparty consensus on economic issues heightened intraparty sensitivities over slavery, especially within the Whig party.[102]

Those northern Whigs gravitating toward the Know-Nothings did not jettison their antislavery views; rather they preferred, temporarily at least, to accentuate a presumably greater concern with cultural issues surrounding the changing demographics of European immigration. German Catholics came to the United States during this time, but it was particularly the increasing numbers of impoverished Irish Roman Catholic immigrants that sparked a nativist reaction among northern Know-Nothings, who experienced the shock of this invasion more directly and immediately than southern Know-Nothings. In the North, Roman Catholic prelates made increasing demands that the Protestant practices of Bible reading and hymn singing be removed from schools supported by public taxation. As there was no public school system in the South, a similar clash did not occur there. Nevertheless, a number of southern Whigs chose to experiment with this new national coalition, framed around a shared, intersectional Protestant distrust of Roman Catholicism. Interestingly, while northern Know-Nothings tried to persuade voters that Irish Catholic newcomers tended to support slavery, southern Know-Nothings argued that immigrants in the North were the natural enemies of slavery and that their demographic growth was the greatest long-term threat that the South faced.[103]

Some northern members of this new nativist party worked to mute their antislavery differences with their southern evangelical brethren, but such efforts were generally unsuccessful. These differences gradually undermined a *national* organization devoted to preserving Protestant practices and cultural understandings in American life and government.[104] Republicans, made up mostly of former northern Whigs but containing antislavery Democrats as well, were not similarly restrained, given the lack of any southern branch in their party. This fact gave them a long-term advantage over the Know-Nothing party in the North. Republicans proudly resurrected the Wilmot Proviso, broadening it to apply to all federal territories, not just the Mexican Cession.[105] Free-soil parties had existed in the past, but they had never represented more than a small minority of the American electorate.[106] The Republican party posed a different threat to the South, for as a contender for major-party status in the most populous section of the Union, it had the ability to win the presidency without garnering a single southern vote.

The Republican party represented many shades of antislavery opinion. Some members were motivated by their hatred of the slave-system's injustices done to African Americans, whereas others were motivated by a racist contempt for blacks themselves and wished the nation to be rid of both slavery and blacks altogether.[107] Republicans also trumpeted negative stereotypes of the arrogant and barbarous slaveholder.[108] In general, Republicans were characterized by their cultural distance from both southern slavery and black people, rather than outright compassion for the slave or hatred for either slaveholders or African Americans. They spoke for many northerners who were tired of perpetually genuflecting before southern sensibilities, as they commonly saw all things southern as corrupting republican virtue and holding back national economic progress. By restricting the spread of slavery, they wanted the West to become culturally northern and entrepreneurial in spirit. In Europe, a little-known social revolutionary by the name of Karl Marx suggested that concepts such as "freedom" and "equality" would be especially exalted by the emerging spokesmen of industrial capitalism, as these ideas best justified depersonalized labor relationships essential for rapid economic development. Such words certainly characterized the rhetoric of the new Republican party, yet usually within a context of expanding economic opportunities in western territories kept free of slavery.[109] Republicans typically did not call for the destruction of slavery in the states where it already existed. Rather, they wished to restrict and slowly undermine slavery, without destroying the nation in the pursuit of immediate abolition.

Republicans wanted to end what they regarded as the unnatural hold of the slaveholding interest upon the government of the United States. They recalled the Declaration of Independence as having founded the nation upon an ideology unfriendly to the very concept of slavery. Spokesmen such as William H. Seward recalled that the Constitutional Convention had revealed its hostility to a perpetual slaveholding republic "by authorizing Congress to prohibit the importation of 'persons' who were Slaves after 1808, and to tax it severely in the meantime." The New Yorker emphasized that the framers intended for the Constitution to provide no meaningful federal support to the slaveholding interest, and yet the exact opposite had occurred piecemeal over the intervening decades. Seward recalled all of the innovative constitutional theories hostile to slavery that had first surfaced on a national stage during the Missouri crisis. He identified the ruling Democratic party as the key to the slave-power's hold over the federal government. Going hand-in-hand with the Republican emphasis on keeping slavery out of the western territories, Seward emphasized that the Republican party first needed to break the grip of the Democratic party upon the reins of national power.[110]

The Republican party wanted a nation guided by one cultural standard rather than remain a "house divided against itself." The focus of this orientation initially was the Republican resolve to put slavery on the course of national extinction. Cultural homogeneity was the watchword of the Know-Nothing party as well. While Republicans generally shunned Know-Nothingism as too extreme, northern nativists sensed that (unlike the Democratic party) Republicans would never be actively antinativist as an organization. Flattering new citizens at election time, individual Republican office seekers at times celebrated the increasing cultural diversity that was coming to characterize the North. As a matter of emphasis, antinativism never became a Republican priority, and Republican antinativists such as William H. Seward were a rare commodity. Typically, Republicans were of Protestant backgrounds, distrusted Roman Catholicism, and were prone toward moralistic crusading, a trait most evident in their evangelical antislavery campaign. When the Know-Nothing party finally died after only several years of operation, most northern Know-Nothings found a welcome home in the Republican party.[111]

Republicans and northern Know-Nothings joined in the fight against slavery in the territories, realizing that in Kansas the national destiny was unfolding. Specifically, the struggle over Kansas challenged whether popular sovereignty could ever serve as a practical solution to the issue of slavery in the territories.[112] At first, fraudulent voting on the part of Missourians masquerading as Kansas settlers carried elections for proslavery.[113] Antislavery forces then erected their own illegal territorial legislature to countermand a legal legislature elected by fraud.[114] Springing up at the grassroots of this western struggle, eventual guerrilla warfare in Kansas sent shock waves across the nation.[115] As small-scale violence in Kansas reached a crescendo in 1856, Republicans and Know-Nothings tested their relative strength in the political arena. The year before, the Know-Nothing party carried many state contests, and it then looked as if it would emerge as the premier rival of the Democrats.[116] But this early assessment was premature, for in the presidential contest of 1856 the Know-Nothings effectively disintegrated over a national-convention plank regarding slavery in the territories. In that election, the Republicans emerged as the only real challenger to continuing Democratic control. Pennsylvania's James Buchanan, the Democratic nominee, went on to win that contest, but he and the rest of his party found the outcome uncomfortably close. The loss of several northern states from Buchanan's column—Pennsylvania and Illinois or Indiana, to be specific—would have given the victory to John C. Frémont, the Republican party's first presidential nominee.[117]

For years, there had been talk of the Supreme Court providing a definitive statement on the issue of slavery in the territories. In 1848, a Senate committee headed by John M. Clayton had first proposed the idea of a judicial solution, which was included as a possibility in the New Mexico and Utah provisions of the Compromise of 1850.[118] In a speech delivered in the Senate on May 2, 1856, Louisiana's Judah P. Benjamin suggested that the Court needed to resolve differences between northern and southern Democrats in interpreting the practical operations of popular sovereignty under the Kansas-Nebraska Act. Both Cass and Douglas immediately praised this suggestion.[119] Finally, President Buchanan noted in his inaugural address on March 4, 1857, that soon the Supreme Court would hand down the long-awaited decision resolving the true meaning of popular sovereignty.[120] Yet when the decision came days later it was not primarily addressed to the issue of popular sovereignty but rather to the inability of Congress to ban slavery from the territories. Only indirectly did the Court's decision effect popular

sovereignty. As creatures of Congress, territorial governments certainly c
not exercise powers forbidden to Congress itself. Taney himself gave only a
few lines to this lesser issue.[121]

Three years before, shortly after the repeal of the Missouri Compromise line of 36° 30', President Pierce's attorney general had reported his opinion that Congress had exceeded its constitutional authority in 1820.[122] Indeed, even before that, John C. Calhoun had thoroughly developed the constitutional reasoning that was ultimately employed in the Dred Scott decision. This logic held that the Constitution prevented congressional meddling with southern property rights in the commonly held federal territories. By fully exploiting the concept of state police powers in defining slave property, the Court transformed a state sovereignty protected by the Tenth Amendment into a doctrine of national proslavery power to determine the future course of the western territories.[123]

Effectively, the Court told the rapidly rising Republican party that it should disband, that it could not carry out its principal *raison d'être*. In this case, the weakest branch of the federal government informed Congress, the strongest branch, that it lacked the power to accomplish the will of an emerging sectionalized national majority. The Court instructed the nation that the Constitution was indeed a proslavery compact.[124] The result was a political explosion in the North. The Dred Scott decision, only the second instance in U.S. history of the Court invalidating a federal statute, was built upon both a weak legal argument and a misrepresentation of history.[125] Republican refusal to accept the judgment followed, as party propagandists spread the notion of a conspiratorial "slave-power" that corrupted not only the government of the United States (including the Court), but even the Constitution itself. Republicans were not undone by the decision but instead were handed a new weapon—that being the well-grounded speculation that Chief Justice Roger Taney's court intended eventually to nationalize slavery by legalizing it within the northern states themselves.[126] The constitutionalization of the issue of slavery in the territories had been developing for at least a decade. It is understandable that rational people might have expected this ideological theorizing to continue until slavery became in fact a national institution.

Typical of Republican newspapers, the *Chicago Tribune* warned that slaves might soon be bought and sold on the streets of Chicago.[127] Fear of the decision's gross exultation of the slaveholder's property rights led the *Indianapolis State Journal* to ask: "Can a slaveholder, defying our State Constitution, bring his slaves here in Indiana and hold them?"[128] Such concerns were not outlandish. A review of the course of American history up to that point demonstrated that the federal government had gradually become a tool of the proslavery interest. The Dred Scott decision especially evidenced this, and by 1858 the Buchanan administration itself would be revealed as uncritically proslavery. These facts encouraged speculation that subsequent court actions, enforced by federal officials, might guarantee slaveholders sojourning rights in free states or invalidate northern state laws freeing slaves illegally held there. The Dred Scott decision, having flirted with the concept of substantive due process of law in Taney's own opinion, could readily be expanded to uphold a broadening principle of vested property rights, so far as slavery's existence in the northern states themselves was concerned.[129] President Buchanan himself encouraged northern paranoia by suggesting that the Dred Scott decision informed him that even if Kansas eventually abolished slavery, any slaves already there would remain in perpetual servitude even after Kansas became a free state.[130] Historian Kenneth Stampp has written: "His novel doctrine denied the right of *any* territory where slaveholders had chosen to settle to become entirely a free state regardless of the wishes of the majority."[131]

New York became one of several northern states to address the broadest proslavery implications of the Dred Scott case. Since 1850, all of the northern states had experienced the new Fugitive Slave law's intrusion within their borders. In this light, the Dred Scott decision warned of possible additional federal interference. "The decision," reported a special joint committee of the New York legislature, "will bring slavery within our borders against our will, with all its unhallowed, demoralizing, and blighting influences." As New York allowed African American men to vote under certain property restrictions, the Dred Scott decision's ruling that free blacks were incapable of state citizenship was direct proof of federal interference with state prerogatives. The joint committee's report closed with a reference to the Virginia and Kentucky Resolutions of 1798, suggesting that state nullification remained as the northern states' ultimate constitutional remedy against proslavery federal oppression.[132]

For more cautious Republicans, who were unwilling to advocate open resistance to federal judicial authority, two dissenting justices in the Dred Scott case offered a convenient escape hatch. Justices John McLean and Benjamin R. Curtis held that as soon as Justice Taney and others ruled that Scott could not be a citizen of state or nation the case effectively ended and that all subsequent argument was merely *obiter dicta*. Modern students of the decision do not give much credence to the position that the court did not effectively decide on the issue of slavery in the territories. Nonetheless, some Republicans claimed so at the time for practical political effect. In this way, Republican office seekers could assert that they were still law-abiding while advocating the election of a Congress intent on outlawing slavery in the territories.[133]

As northerners absorbed the meaning of the court decision, more threatening news arrived. The proslavery territorial legislature of Kansas chose to press the issue of immediate statehood. With each passing month, the real but officially unrecognized antislavery majority in the territory grew larger, which convinced the legislature to act while there was still a slim chance for victory. In an act of nonviolent resistance, antislavery settlers boycotted the election for a state constitutional convention, many of them fearing that their participation would only be overcome by proslavery fraud in any case. Robert J. Walker, Buchanan's handpicked territorial governor, valiantly tried to persuade antislavery voters that he was intent upon conducting a fair election, but his efforts were unsuccessful in getting them to vote. As a result, a proslavery constitutional convention was elected. Convening at Lecompton in the fall of 1857, the convention quickly drafted a proslavery state constitution.[134]

In referring the document back to the people of Kansas for ratification, the convention refused to allow a simple "yes" or "no" vote. Instead it came up with a scheme that made a mockery of popular sovereignty itself. Kansas's voters were given a choice of the Lecompton constitution with slavery unrestricted or with slavery restricted to the current slaves then residing in the territory. If the latter option passed, roughly two hundred slaves already in Kansas would remain slaves for life, as would their descendents.[135] Governor Walker renounced this method of referral as a sham and eventually resigned over the issue. Under extreme pressure from the proslavery wing of the Democratic party, Buchanan himself came out in favor of the unseemly process.[136] Lewis Cass, who was then Buchanan's secretary of state and Governor Walker's supervisor within the cabinet, supported Buchanan. Although himself the father of popular sovereignty, Cass was willing to sacrifice his ideological creation in hopes of keeping intersectional peace.[137] Since 1789, the "slaveholding republic" had been nurtured by this brand of "doughface" accommodation.

Kenneth Stampp has described Buchanan's choice as ripe with historical consequences. Unlike some other scholars, Professor Stampp does not regard Buchanan to have been weak willed and easily manipulated by the proslavery interest. Rather, he portrays Buchanan as regarding the whole affair as over a meaningless symbolism created by noisy abolitionist extremists. In Buchanan's eyes, the will of Kansas's antislavery majority could have been quietly implemented once the territory became a slave state. Then, the proslavery articles of the state constitution could have been repealed. Stubbornly, Buchanan chose to stand his ground against all those who could not see the logic of his position.[138] Professor Stampp credits the president's obstinate resolve to his hatred of abolitionism and a personal indifference to the moral issue of slavery. Stampp speculates that had Buchanan heeded the straightforward advice of Governor Walker and come out against the Lecompton fraud, the southern march toward secession could have been diverted. Buchanan was in a position to lead his southern allies toward realistic outcomes. Instead, he allowed southern passions to fester into predictable political defeat, which in turn drove the South closer to secession. Had Buchanan exercised proper leadership, Stampp emphasizes, the Democratic party would have remained intact and the subsequent Civil War might have been at least postponed. Accordingly, Professor Stampp sees Buchanan as bearing major individual responsibility for the rapid descent toward the national political disintegration that followed.[139]

Stephen Douglas, the principal politician then associated with popular sovereignty, refused to support Buchanan, thus triggering the disruption of the Democratic party. Unlike Buchanan, Douglas had little real choice in determining his course. His senate seat was up for election in 1858. If he followed Cass in backing Buchanan, he knew that his career as an elected official would be over, such was the popular animus in Illinois against the Lecompton fraud. Douglas was forced to come out against this sham if he had any hope of appearing as a man of integrity. Given that he knew that Republican opposition against him would be intense in the senatorial race, Douglas chose not only to oppose the Lecompton constitution but fight it with a dramatic flair that would both confuse his opponents and rally his supporters for the coming campaign.[140] In early December, Douglas inaugurated his anti-Lecompton crusade with these words: "If this constitution is to be forced down our throats, in violation of the fundamental principle of free government, under a mode of submission that is a mockery and insult, I will resist to the last. I have no fear of any party associations being severed. . . . I will stand on the great principle of popular sovereignty, which declares the right of all people to be left perfectly free to form and regulate their domestic institutions in their own way. I will follow that principle wherever its logical consequences may take me."[141]

Over the next several months, he forged a temporary practical alliance with Republicans in Congress. Buchanan, armed with the power of federal patronage to reward and punish, opposed them. In the end, neither side achieved outright victory. Instead, Congress passed the so-called English Compromise, which sent the Lecompton constitution back to the voters of Kansas to be voted up or down as a complete package. By the terms of this "compromise," if the voters voted against Lecompton and slavery, they would be forced to wait several years until the territorial population reached something more than 90,000, the number then used to justify one member of the House of Representatives. On August 2, 1858, with antislavery voters participating in the election, the Kansas electorate killed the Lecompton constitution by a majority of 11,300 to 1788.[142]

Horace Greeley, the widely read Republican editor of the *New York Tribune*, praised Douglas's gallant fight against the Lecompton constitution and urged the Illinois branch of the Republican party not to contest his seat in the November election—advice that was firmly rejected.[143] Illinois Republican leader Abraham Lincoln realized that Douglas was planning a trap even before the Little Giant's formal break with Buchanan. He wrote former Democrat Lyman Trumbull, who had become Illinois' first Republican senator in the previous election, that Douglas was scheming "to draw off some Republicans" in the upcoming campaign. He warned Trumbull that true Republicans should not encourage this trend.[144] When Greeley began to praise Douglas publicly, Lincoln privately exploded, accusing the New York editor of "sacraficing [sic] us here in Illinois."[145] Six months later, and a week before his own nomination to run against Douglas, Lincoln calmed down and wrote calculatingly that he would have to be "patient" regarding the unfortunate "inclination of some Republicans to favor Douglas."[146]

Lincoln knew his challenge in this unique historical context. First, he had to demonstrate to the voters that Douglas was not the quasi-Republican that he often appeared to be during the Lecompton fight. Likewise, he had to portray Douglas as intellectually and emotionally incapable of effectively protecting northern interests. Given that Douglas had effectively stolen the political center with his anti-Lecompton heroics, Lincoln knew that uncharacteristically he himself would have to take advanced antislavery positions to create any significant difference for the voters. Lincoln, who had never come close to achieving his unrelenting political ambitions, knew this as his defining moment. Douglas was a national political force. A contender who could match him blow for blow might become a national leader himself. Such was the test facing this prior one-term Whig congressman (1845–47).

LINCOLN SUCCESSFULLY PRESSURED Douglas to a series of joint debates, to occur between August 21 and October 15,[147] during which he intended to demonstrate that Douglas was still an integral part of the slave-power conspiracy, as much as when he led Congress to pass the Kansas-Nebraska Act. He meant to portray Douglas's role as that of a political salesman to the North, peddling the concept that popular sovereignty was the only rational solution to the problem of slavery in the territories. Once northerners accepted that position, Lincoln's conspiratorial theory concluded, they would be well along toward moral indifference, which was a necessary precondition to nationalizing slavery.

Lincoln's purpose was to expose the difference between true Republican ideology and Douglas's values—a difference that the Little Giant had temporarily successfully blurred during the Lecompton fight. In achieving this, Lincoln had to stray considerably from his party's preferred focus on the practical issue of slavery in the territories and instead emphasize abstract moral values. Nonetheless, this was a modification of tactics only. The basic strategy of convincing the public that slavery should be placed on the course of ultimate extinction through its elimination in the federal territories remained constant. Lincoln knew that Douglas did not share this Republican goal, despite appearances in the anti-Lecompton fight.

Lincoln summarized his campaign focus in this way: "The real issue in this controversy—the one pressing upon every mind—is the sentiment on the part of one class that looks upon the institution of slavery as a wrong, and of another class that does not look upon it as a wrong."[148] Throughout the debates, Lincoln repeated this moral theme.[149] He emphasized that the best thinking of the Founding Fathers supported the current Republican position. He insisted that African Americans had to be included in the meaning of "all men" if the Declaration of Independence was to make any sense. He also claimed that the Constitution itself had been framed so as not to allow slavery any privileged constitutional position. The founders, he said, realized that the nation at the outset did not live up to the ideals of the Declaration. In stating that all persons have human rights, they had not intended to describe human relationships as they existed then or at any time in the recorded past. All that they intended, he emphasized, was to point the new nation in a progressive direction: "They meant to set up a standard maxim for a free society which should be familiar to all: constantly looked to, constantly labored for, and though never perfectly attained, constantly approximated and thereby deepening its influence and augmenting the happiness and value of life to all people of all colors, everywhere."[150] The framers, he asserted, had meant to put slavery on the course of ultimate extinction. But instead, during the interim, the federal government itself had become a tool of the slaveholding interest.[151]

Douglas disagreed that the founders had intended to include black people in the phrase "all men are created equal." Here he sided with Chief Justice Taney's opinion in the Dred Scott decision. The framers, Douglas emphasized, did not intend to proscribe slavery in any way; neither had they intended to promote the institution. Earlier, in a speech at Chicago, Douglas had stated: "The framers of our government never contemplated uniformity in its internal concerns. . . . They well understood that the great varieties of soil, of production and of interests, in a republic as large as this, required different local and domestic regulations in each locality. . . . Diversity, dissimilarity, variety in all our liberties, is the great safeguard of our liberties."[152] Subtly, Douglas contrasted his political party's tolerance of diversity with Republican preference for moral uniformity and cultural homogeneity. Douglas prided himself as being a practical man of the world in contrast to rigid idealists such as Lincoln, and so he readily let Lincoln define him as a person not guided by moral considerations. That which Lincoln intended as a criticism, Douglas accepted as an unintended compliment.

Lincoln warned that if the voting public validated Douglas's amoral stance by returning him to the Senate, the proslavery plan to divert the nation from its original purpose would be furthered. In both his "House Divided" speech at the outset of the campaign and also in the debate held at Ottawa, Illinois, Lincoln fantasized about a possible second Dred Scott case in which Taney would rule that even supposedly free states could not keep slavery outside their borders.[153] He tied this nightmarish projection to Douglas's flexible morality and implied that if the voters wanted slavery in the free states themselves, they should vote for Douglas.[154] At Galesburg, Lincoln went so far as to supply Taney's imagined constitutional logic for forcing slavery upon the northern states: The Dred Scott decision had already affirmed that the Constitution recognized "the right of property in a slave," something that Lincoln denied was good constitutional law. Nonetheless, the Court had decided it. This new Court doctrine, when combined with the Fifth Amendment's property-protecting due process clause and the privileges and immunities clause of Article IV, Section 2, could produce a ruling protecting slavery within the northern states as well as in the western territories.[155]

Before racist crowds, especially in southern Illinois, Douglas emphasized that Lincoln's egalitarian logic led straight toward unthinkable racial amalga-mation. Lincoln replied that he did not favor integrating African Americans into American life as social and political equals. In fact, he wished that Ameri-can blacks could be returned to Africa.[156] He advocated no change in northern society, where free blacks were oppressed at every turn.[157] Lincoln had earlier proclaimed that a house divided against itself could not stand. Yet he saw no inconsistency in continuing the northern methods of maintaining a racially di-vided national community. While this political position was opportune if Re-publicans hoped to achieve majority status, here was an obvious ideological weak spot that eventually would stall their party's progressive advance.

In the Freeport debate, Douglas offered that which would come to be called the "Freeport Doctrine." Lincoln had first challenged him by asking how the senator could continue to support both popular sovereignty and Chief Justice Taney's opinion in the Dred Scott decision, as the two were in seeming contradiction.[158] Douglas offered an answer that was not new. He had stated it before. Others, including Jefferson Davis, also suggested it. But in the context of this particular campaign, the answer took on an ominous character for southerners.[159] Practically, Douglas said, slavery could not exist in the territories unless supported by slave codes that could be provided only by territorial legislatures. Hence, in order to keep slavery effectively out of a territory, that territory's legislature did not have to outlaw slavery directly, which in the Dred Scott decision Taney had suggested that it could not do anyway. All that it had to do was not pass any slave codes, the multifaceted, tyrannical police regulations that every slave society needed to keep its human property well behaved and orderly. By inactivity or indefinite pro-crastination, a territorial legislature could effectively outlaw slavery without ever conducting a frontal assault. Unlike Lincoln, Douglas saw no need to oppose Taney's opinion. He could support essentially meaningless judicial abstractions, while continuing to rely on his "great principle"—the meaning-ful democratic processes of popular sovereignty and local self-determination.

Douglas's reputation in the Democratic party was not negatively affected by the Freeport Doctrine. In the North, his supporters were somewhat inspired by the bold proclamation. In the South and among northern Buchanan Democrats, his reputation had already been severely damaged in the congressional debates over the Lecompton constitution. Publicity of the Freeport Doctrine did have an effect, however, as the South began to demand that Congress enact a slave code for all the territories and thereby overcome the limitations of judicial power which Douglas apparently celebrated.[160]

Eventually, Douglas had to deal with the aftermath of his Freeport Doctrine, but more immediately his challenge was to defeat Lincoln. Little was spared by either side in a campaign that at times was waged on a low level, in stark contrast to the classic character of the debates themselves. The Republican press accused Douglas of promoting the interests of the Roman Catholic church, in that his wife was a Catholic and his children were enrolled in Jesuit schools.[161] In the end, this mean-spirited attack did not help. Following the election, state legislators that were pledged to Douglas reelected their champion in the manner then prescribed by the Constitution.[162] Writing to a friend that he would "now sink out of view, and ... be forgotten," Lincoln added, "I believe I have made some marks which will tell for the cause of civil liberty long after I am gone." He was clearly disappointed at the result and thought that his political career might be at an end.[163] In reality, it had only barely begun. His keen mind and ability to reduce abstract principles to easily remembered fundamental maxims impressed newspaper readers of the debates across the North.[164] For example, his explanation of the Declaration of Independence's meaning was timeless in its persuasive simplicity. In the concluding debate at Alton, he had returned to this theme:

> The authors of that notable instrument intended to include all men, but they did not mean to declare all men equal in all respects. They did not mean to say all men were equal in color, size, intellect, moral development or social capacity. They defined with tolerable distinctness in what they did consider all men created equal—equal in certain inalienable rights, among which are life, liberty and the pursuit of happiness. This they said, and this they meant. They did not mean to assert the obvious untruth, that all were then actually enjoying that equality, nor yet, that they were about to confer it immediately upon them. In fact, they had no power to convey such a boon. They meant simply to declare the right so that the enforcement of it might follow as fast as circumstances should permit.[165]

By comparison, both Douglas and Chief Justice Taney publicly exhibited a poor understanding of the Declaration's political philosophy. Indeed, a convenient forgetfulness regarding the nation's original ideals had facilitated the federal government's gradual seduction by the slaveholding interest.[166] Lincoln's forceful protest demonstrated that the best way to end this pattern of drift was to recall and clearly reexpress first principles.

A decade earlier, John C. Calhoun had argued that the South needed to do more than drift so far as the Declaration of Independence was concerned.

Preferring to begin the hard work of converting the South to a theory that could support both hierarchy and oligarchy, Calhoun wanted to reject Jefferson's old ideology outright, for, as he acknowledged publicly, it clearly included African Americans within its scope. The South Carolinian proslavery thinker/politician found this inclusion completely unacceptable and not correctable by bastardizing its original meaning.[167] Few southerners followed his advice, preferring the easier course, advanced by Taney and Douglas, of merely restricting the Declaration for whites only. Lincoln identified and exploited the weakness of this restrictionist approach. A month before the debates, in a speech at Chicago, he said: "Where will it stop? If one man says it does not mean a Negro, why may not another say it does not mean some other man?"[168] Thereby, Lincoln revealed the problem that had earlier concerned Calhoun, who had known that a restricted Declaration logically eventually had to unravel.

By not allowing Douglas to rest upon his anti-Lecompton accomplishments during the campaign, Lincoln pushed the Republican party to a more advanced position than that advocated by those eastern Republicans who had wanted to allow Douglas to run uncontested in 1858. By his hounding of Douglas during the debates, Lincoln also insured that the clever Illinois senator could never repair his relations with the South. At Jonesboro, he asked Douglas if he would vote for a congressional slave code, if such an opportunity arose. Douglas's quick and negative response, fully in harmony with the principle of popular sovereignty, served notice to southerners that he would always be their enemy.[169] Indeed, it was this very issue of a federal slave code for the territories that drove the generations-long sectional conflict toward its ultimate conclusion.

The Dred Scott decision had proclaimed abstract property rights for slaveholders in the territories, but these were empty promises unless supported by local police regulations, commonly known as slave codes. Southerners keenly felt that such regulations were their due, for without them the practical effect of the Dred Scott decision was undone. The Lecompton constitution's failure demonstrated how the earlier southern hope of the Kansas-Nebraska Act to produce one more slave state had been misplaced. Without a federal slave code for the territories, the Dred Scott decision also was worthless. In the midst of all of these dashed southern expectations was the figure of Stephen A. Douglas. On December 9, 1858, the Democratic senatorial caucus, controlled by the proslavery element in the party, announced that Douglas had been removed from his chairmanship of the committee on territories, a position that he had held for eleven years.[170] The following year, President Buchanan called for Congress to protect slaveholders' property in the territories.[171] On February 2, 1860, Jefferson Davis introduced a set of resolutions calling for a federal slave code for the territories.[172] Knowing that his resolutions lacked the votes to be enacted, Davis focused upon getting the Democratic caucus to approve them as a litmus test of doctrinal acceptability.[173] Meanwhile, Douglas tried vainly to explain the multiple nuances of his popular sovereignty doctrine to a national audience in an article in *Harper's Magazine* that appeared in September 1859. The ironic consensus of both Republicans and southern Democrats that congressional action was needed to resolve the issue of slavery in the territories once and for all revealed the weak position of Douglas entering into a presidential campaign.[174]

On the eve of the Civil War, the South demanded national power to settle the issue of slavery in the territories. In 1859, the proslavery U.S. Supreme Court also promoted a nationalist interpretation of the Constitution in the case of *Ableman v. Booth*, which denied a Wisconsin constitutional challenge to the Fugitive Slave Act of 1850. Ironically, the slaveholding interest, which had long kept a potentially dangerous federal government in check by means of a strict states-rights interpretation of the Constitution, came to rely on a nationalist understanding in its hour of greatest challenge.[175] Over the decades, the federal government had effectively become a proslavery instrument by means of multiple little decisions and unconscious drift. But with a northern majoritarian impulse threatening to overwhelm past practices, the South demanded that the federal government enforce what it had come to regard as binding constitutional guarantees. Of course, this declaration of national supremacy was not without an all-important caveat: If the federal government failed to fulfill its constitutional duty, as southerners perceived it, the dismemberment of the Union itself would necessarily follow.

In April 1860, the Democratic National Convention met at Charleston, South Carolina. The meeting lasted for only ten days, breaking up over Douglas's refusal to support a federal slave code for the territories.[176] On June 18, Democrats met again at Baltimore, with the same result. This time, the convention disintegrated after only six days.[177] Following this second debacle, sectional branches of the party met separately in that city. In this way, two separate Democratic platforms and sets of nominees for the presidency and vice presidency were finalized.[178] Going into the presidential election of 1860, Democrats could find no common ground, thereby virtually assuring the election of Abraham Lincoln, who was nominated as the Republican presidential candidate in May. Lincoln's subsequent election set up the secession crisis and the bloody war that followed. This, and the fight over a federal slave code for the territories that preceded it, are familiar ground. Less known is the fact that the struggle over control of the western territories (beyond the southern symbolic demand for a federal slave code) did not end with Kansas's rejection of the Lecompton constitution. On the very eve of civil war, the final episode began. At issue was the future of southern California.

EXCEPT FOR CUBA, which perennially remained high on the southern agenda, California had no effective rival for irritating the issue of slavery's expansion over an extended period.[179] Missouri had become the centerpiece of a great intersectional compromise in 1820, but after that, except to supply "border ruffians" to foul territorial elections in Kansas, Missouri ceased to affect the issue. By contrast, California seemed to be in the mounting sectional controversy from the time of the Mexican War right up to the Civil War itself. Many saw it as the underlying cause spurring Polk's aggressive policy toward Mexico. Then came the California gold rush, which forced the Compromise of 1850, of which California statehood became the central part. In the years that followed, maneuvering over transcontinental railroad routes to California helped spawn the Kansas-Nebraska Act. Even after that, the presence of California in the American Union remained a disruptive influence, as it served as both a recruiting ground and a base camp for proslavery filibuster expeditions into Central America, led by the likes of William Walker and "General" Henry A. Crabb.[180]

Many a southerner grieved that even though Los Angeles and San Diego existed at approximately the same latitudes as the major cities of South Carolina, southern California was part of a free state. A number of transplanted southerners comprised the most influential citizens in both Los Angeles and San Diego. Indeed, months before the completion of the Compromise of 1850, a mass meeting in Los Angeles had petitioned Congress, protesting the pending admission of California as a free state. This petition called for southern California to become a federal territory, which would have left northern California alone to become a new free state.[181]

The idea of having southern California become a federal territory revived immediately following the passage of the Kansas-Nebraska Act. At that time, a New Orleans newspaper speculated: "The Nebraska principle of popular sovereignty and non-intervention smooths the way for the establishment of a slave State in Southern California. For if the people of California choose to divide their domain, and to set up another State with Southern institutions, of course Congress will not presume to interpose any objection."[182] As for the southern Californians themselves, they kept pushing for their section of the state to be converted into a federal territory.[183] Even some northern Californians welcomed the idea of southern California eventually becoming a separate state, for only by the proliferation of western senators and congressmen could western issues rise on the national political agenda.[184]

Early in 1859, a measure to divide California was presented before the California state legislature. San Luis Obispo and all counties southward were to form the new "Territory of Colorado."[185] This event did not go unnoticed in the East. In Lincoln's Illinois, California's movement in such a direction appeared as more evidence of the slave-power conspiracy.[186] Southern California, combined with an area along the Gila River in present-day Arizona, was promoted in *DeBow's Review* as having potential to support cotton agriculture.[187] In 1859, the New Mexico Territorial legislature enacted a slave code, despite the fact that no slaves then lived in the territory. All of this appeared as preparatory for some larger southern vision. Federal patronage from the Buchanan administration, together with threats not to defend the region adequately against Indian attacks unless the slave code were passed, reportedly persuaded the legislature to take this action.[188] Even after the disappointment following the failure of the Lecompton constitution, some southerners continued to hope for slavery's expansion into the West.[189]

Patronage from the Buchanan administration shaped local politics in California as much as in New Mexico. In the Golden State, "Chiv" (Chivalry) Democrats, backed by the promise of federal favors, arranged for Andrés Pico to front the split-the-state movement. Ostensibly, the proposal for southern California to become a federal territory was to provide relief for Latino land owners, whom the state legislature had heavily taxed.[190] The argument was unconvincing. Why should the state legislature act in this manner, when simply lowering property taxes would have been far easier to achieve? In addition, why did the California legislature suddenly take such a keen interest in helping Latinos? Just a few years earlier, the state legislature had passed measures designed to drive them from the gold fields.[191] Rumors circulated that Pico, who had led "Californio" military resistance during the Mexican War, had been promised the new territorial governor's post.[192] These estimates of Pico's motivations were accurate, for when Abraham Lincoln won the presidency in 1860, Pico did an abrupt political about-face, switching to the Republican party in order to feed (in the words of one of his former southern allies) at "the flesh pots of Abraham."[193]

The state legislature passed the bill to split the state with an interesting twist. Reminiscent of the Lecompton constitution, which had been referred to the voters only in a most restricted sense, the split-the-state referendum was only offered to the voters of southern California, where the outcome was predictable.[194] Such an arrangement revealed the slave-power's workings in California, a matter that had concerned Lincoln himself.[195] In the fall of 1859, Mississippi's governor Henry S. Foote, who had been promoting the division of California for almost a decade, announced: "I believe that in less than two years from this time, if we are wise, we will have a slave State in Southern California. The State has been divided within the last six months for that purpose."[196]

Under the Dred Scott decision, slavery could not be politically barred from any federal territory. Yet, by 1859, southerners realized that abstract principle was meaningless without accompanying territorial slave codes. The recent memory of dashed hopes in Kansas cautioned against any southern enthusiasm about the proposed Territory of Colorado, for the superiority of northern numbers could ultimately dictate an antislavery result.[197] Looking toward secession, most southerners held in abeyance the hope of splitting California. If and when a new southern confederacy became established, then the proslavery interest could reasonably demand its due in California. For northerners, the dizzying events of 1859 to 1860 likewise postponed any consideration of the California proposal. Of course, had anything come of Senator John J. Crittenden's peace plan of December 1860 to divide the West between slavery and freedom, the California request of 1859 would have become a necessary part of implementing the so-called Crittenden Compromise.

With the beginning of the war, the South once again considered southern California, as demonstrated by the westward advance of Confederate troops that ended at the Battle of Glorieta Pass in New Mexico Territory on March 28, 1862.[198] Southern defeat at that place concluded this last effort to extend slavery into the western territories.

10

THE REPUBLICAN REVOLUTION

TWO WEEKS BEFORE the inauguration of Abraham Lincoln on March 4, 1861, Jefferson Davis was sworn in as president of a new republic, erected in less than a hundred days and extending from South Carolina to Texas. Nothing in the history of the Civil War is more remarkable than the speed with which secession proceeded and the Confederacy took shape, once the outcome of the presidential election was known. The rush to action reflected a passion also expressed in much southern rhetoric. A New Orleans editor called Lincoln's election a "deliberate, cold-blooded insult and outrage upon the people of the slaveholding states."[1] *The Richmond Enquirer* declared that it amounted to "an act of war."[2] Private feeling was often as intense as public sentiment. The wife of a Georgia planter exclaimed in a letter to her son: "We have no alternative; and necessity demands that we now protect ourselves from entire destruction at the hands of those who have rent and torn and obliterated every national bond of union."[3]

When it came to choosing a specific course of action, southerners were, as usual, unable to agree, but what proved to be decisive in the winter of 1860–61 was the critical number among them who viewed the election of Lincoln as adequate reason for immediate dissolution of the Union. At the heart of the matter was southern perception of the Republican party not as a mere political opposition, but as a hostile, revolutionary force bent on total destruction of the slaveholding system. "Our enemies are about *to take possession of the Government*," wrote a South Carolinian. "We must expect just that sort of leniency which is shown by the conqueror over a subjugated and craven people."[4] Such apprehensions were widespread, and the list of dangers allegedly activated by Lincoln's victory was a long one. The new party in power was expected to repeal the fugitive slave laws, prohibit interstate trade in slaves, reverse the Dred Scott decision through a reorganization of the Supreme Court, and abolish slavery in the territories, in the District of Columbia, and in the forts and arsenals of the United States. More than that, empowered Republicans would break down southern defenses against abolitionist propaganda and subject slaveholding society to a mounting threat of internal disorder.[5] The platform of the Republican party, according to Senator Clement C. Clay of Alabama, was "as strong an incitement and invocation to servile insurrection, to murder, arson, and other crimes, as any to be found in abolition literature."[6] Republicans must be dealt with as enemies, said a North Carolina editor; their policies would "put the torch to our dwellings and the knife to our throats."[7]

Of course southerners exaggerated the radical tendencies of Republicanism, and they probably overestimated its potential menace. The Republican free-soil principle was actually a political and moral compromise with the institution of slavery, and Republican leaders were something less than willful agents of violent social revolution. Yet southerners made no mistake in perceiving the election of Lincoln as a sharp break with the past. To understand its revolutionary implications for southerners, one must take into account not only the malign countenance of Republicanism in the South, but also the character and conduct of the national government from 1789 to 1861.

Although the nation had been termed "a house divided against itself" and "half slave and half free," in one respect, unity had tended to prevail over duality. The policy of the federal government down through the years, despite several conspicuous exceptions, had been predominantly supportive of slavery. Whatever it might be as a federal union of sovereign states, the antebellum United States, as a sovereignty itself, was a slaveholding republic. That was the impression given by the national capital. That was the image presented in diplomacy to the rest of the world. And that had become the law of the land by edict of the Supreme Court. "The right of property in a slave is distinctly and expressly affirmed in the Constitution," Chief Justice Taney had declared in 1857. The federal government therefore had no power over the institution except "the power coupled with the duty of guarding and protecting the owner in his rights."[8]

But with Lincoln's election, all was suddenly changed. The old republic— which had protected the slaveholding interest on the high seas, in relations with foreign governments, in the District of Columbia, in the federal territories, and to some extent even in the free states—was at an end. Many southerners accordingly came to the conclusion that their only recourse was to erect another federal republic, with its constitution more securely bound to slavery but otherwise modeled closely after the republic they had lost.

Brown reflects Garrisonian position

FOR SOUTHERNERS, JOHN BROWN's raid on Harpers Ferry, Virginia, in mid-October 1859 revealed the true intent of the Republican party. Whereas southerners had viewed the new party as a hostile force before Harpers Ferry, after that event this perception became more visceral than thoughtful, thereby preparing the ground for southern secession and eventual civil war. Coming a mere year before the election of the first Republican president, the impact of John Brown's raid upon the collective southern psyche can scarcely be overemphasized.

Before taking this bold action, Brown had earlier gained notoriety at Pottawatomie, Kansas, in 1856. His subsequent planning of an attack on the federal armory at Harpers Ferry, a bold stroke that he hoped would become the long-awaited Armageddon of American slavery, was faulty to say the least, but his resolve was unstoppable. In his seizure of the federal arsenal there, he hoped to supply escaping slaves with arms in mountain hideouts stretching deep into the southern states.[9] Following the taking of the armory itself, slaves from the surrounding countryside were to gravitate to Brown and his men. In execution, the plan fell apart. Brown's band was overwhelmed by U.S. Horse Marines under the command of Army Colonel Robert E. Lee. Brought to trial in Charlestown, (West) Virginia, Brown was tried, convicted, and executed for murder and treason. The entire process took a month and a half.

Had Brown been killed in his final battle, the impact of this event upon the course of history would certainly have been less. As it was, John Brown alive became a force that perhaps only he had foreseen. Allowed to plead for his life, he instead chose to deliver discourses against the sinful nation that allowed slavery's continuance. As he awaited his execution, every word he uttered or wrote found its way into print. The fact that many northerners, Republican leaders included, dismissed his actions as insane or criminal had little impact upon southerners, who were far more impressed by the multiple expressions of northern public mourning at the news of Brown's hanging.[10] For many southerners, this aspect of the affair made secession virtually inevitable as soon as northerners elected a "Black Republican" president, thereby confirming the North's undying hatred for the South.[11]

From the moment of Brown's capture, evidence revealed a wider conspiracy. Franklin Sanborn, Gerrit Smith, Samuel Gridley Howe, Martin Delany, Augustus Wattles, and Frederick Douglass were implicated. Authorities were particularly interested in Douglass, the premier African American abolitionist.[12] Although Douglass had unsuccessfully tried to talk Brown out of his high-risk sortie, he had known about Brown's plans in advance and understandably did nothing to alert authorities. With Brown captured, this most famous former runaway slave fled again to Great Britain, where earlier in his career he had gone to escape the reach of American slave catchers. There, safe from Virginia justice, Douglass distanced himself from Brown, a strategy that helped ease his eventual return to the United States. Douglass emphasized that under the American constitutional system slavery could be destroyed without violent revolution. Simultaneously, Abraham Lincoln adopted a similar theme as Democratic party prints sought to tie Brown's violence to William H. Seward, the front-runner for the Republican presidential nomination in 1860.[13] Seward's radical image had been earned by his penchant to engage in rash rhetorical flourishes, which made him appear more extreme than he really was. As Seward already commanded the radical flank of the Republican forces, Lincoln took more moderate positions. This move especially made good political sense, as Republicans had to attract former Know-Nothings and Millard Fillmore supporters if they hoped to win in 1860.[14] Beginning to believe that he had a chance of capturing the presidential nomination, Lincoln traveled to Seward's New York to make himself better known among both friends and enemies of the powerful Republican senator.

On February 27, at the Cooper Institute in New York City, looking his best in a new suit of clothes, Lincoln emphasized that the Republican party wanted only to continue the conservative course initiated in the Northwest Ordinance, which had first restricted the spread of slavery into the American West. Unable to ignore the event at Harpers Ferry, Lincoln railed against the "slander" of those who sought to confuse John Brown's murderous course with the Republican party's peaceful, gradualist approach to the problem.[15] At the same time, responding to the taunts of British Garrisonians, Frederick Douglass made a major address in Glasgow. In his message that the Constitution could be used to destroy slavery in the states where it already existed, Douglass was more radical than Lincoln. Nonetheless, he gloried in his relatively moderate stance within the abolitionist movement itself. Later that year, he would publish his Glasgow speech in pamphlet form for wider distribution.[16]

Douglass's constitutional argument was not original. Lysander Spooner and William Goodell had framed it years before.[17] Nevertheless, the effect of a former slave conducting a public seminar on the antislavery powers inherent in the American governmental system could not help but inspire hope that meaningful political change was a real possibility. Douglass urged his hearers not to confuse the long proslavery history of the United States government with the Constitution itself. "They are as distinct from each other," he said, "as the chart is from the course which a vessel may be sometimes steering."[18] By their flawed past management of the federal government, Douglass said, the American people had "trampled upon their own constitution, stepped beyond the limits set for themselves, and in their ever-abounding iniquity, established a constitution of action outside of the fundamental law of the land."[19] Here, similar to Lincoln, he called for his countrymen to reject the heritage of bad political habits, a product of generations, and return instead to the intentions of the Founding Fathers.

Douglass prophesied that under an antislavery administration and an antislavery Congress, the Constitution could become something quite different than it had been up to that time. Taking one constitutional provision after another, he showed how specific sections and paragraphs could be given muscular antislavery interpretations, quite unlike the proslavery views too readily conceded by the Garrisonians. Douglass transformed the famous three-fifths clause, which in the hands of Garrisonians became a key piece of evidence tying the Constitution indelibly to slavery, into a veritable engine for liberty "by holding out to every slaveholding State the inducement of an increase of two-fifths of political power by becoming a free State."[20] Likewise, Article IV, Section 4, which Garrisonians portrayed as requiring the federal government to crush slave insurrections, was reworked by Douglass into a potential mechanism to destroy slavery itself. When faced with a slave insurrection, he said, an antislavery president could end the threat most expeditiously by issuing an emancipation proclamation. The constitutional language simply called upon the authority of the United States to protect the states "against domestic violence." It did not prescribe which means to use in carrying out that charge. As the Constitution's Preamble exalted the desirability of domestic tranquility, Douglass found additional constitutional authorization for his ingenious interpretation.[21]

"The slaveholders have ruled the American government for the last fifty years," he told his Glasgow audience. "Let the anti-slavery party rule the nation for the next fifty years." Then he added, almost in passing: "And, by the way, that thing is on the verge of being accomplished." In the new day that he saw coming, the Constitution would be cleansed of its proslavery interpretations and instead become an antislavery foundation of a new kind of republic.[22]

Heretofore, the Constitution's territories clause (Article IV, Section 3, paragraph 2) had channeled the Republican moderate program. In his remarks at Alton during the debates with Stephen Douglas, Lincoln had justified the cautious Republican approach of focusing upon the territories alone by using the analogy of a cancer patient who chooses to contain and restrict the fatal disease, in preference to dying at the hands of a surgeon attempting to cut the malady out, root and branch, all at once.[23] The unspoken implication remained that after the disease came under proper national control, complete removal might ultimately be attempted. On the eve of Lincoln's nomination for the presidency, Frederick Douglass held up for public view the constitutional surgical tools that could be used at the proper moment. To southerners, the diverse antislavery methods advocated by Lincoln, Douglass, and even Brown were all part of one ideological continuum.

Talk of using constitutional language against slavery was not new. In 1808, Congress had used Article I, Section 9, paragraph 1, to prohibit an international commerce in slaves. This action suggested a possible later use of the commerce clause located in Article I, Section 8, to prohibit the movement of slaves across state lines. When this possibility had been raised during the Missouri crisis, southerners had reacted with vehemence, winning a general deference to their opinion for a generation.[24] Indeed, failure with this radical constitutional interpretation had helped disillusion Garrisonians with the entire political process.[25] But on the eve of the election of the first Republican president, activist uses of old antislavery constitutional interpretations became a distinct possibility.

Historian Arthur Bestor has suggested that use of the commerce power to destroy the domestic slave trade was premature in the middle of the nineteenth century, as the concept of federal police powers did not begin to be employed until several generations later.[26] Yet, as Bestor himself concedes, his argument is essentially ahistorical. We do not know what an antislavery federal government might have done to destroy slavery over time—if civil war had not erupted and if general emancipation had not been applied based on presidential war powers. We do know that at the time of Lincoln's election, political abolitionists had not forgotten the constitutional ways to attack the interstate slave trade.[27] Encouraged by the emergence of a new antislavery majority, their threat was real, for after Lincoln's election, John J. Crittenden and other constitutional compromisers demanded Republican renunciation of this potential use of the commerce clause. [28] Lincoln himself indicated that he cared "but little" about preserving this particular constitutional argument, but his overall rejection of the compromise proposals made that caveat immaterial.[29] John C. Breckinridge, the proslavery Democrat who came in second to Lincoln in electoral votes in the presidential race of 1860, saw the unwillingness of other Republican leaders to renounce this particular constitutional argument as greatly contributing to the ultimate success of the southern secession movement.[30]

Throughout the course of the slaveholding republic, southerners had felt generally secure under the Constitution. This ceased with Lincoln's election, and their mounting discomfort led to secession. South Carolina became the first southern state to enact a formal break on December 20, 1860. The state convention taking this action explained itself by highlighting the Lincoln administration's presumed intent "that a war must be waged against slavery until it shall cease throughout all the United States."[31] In the winter of 1860–61, constitutional perceptions became virtual reality. President-elect Lincoln sent a letter to Alexander Hamilton Stephens, a southerner with whom he had served in Congress over a decade before. "Do the people of the South," Lincoln wrote, "really entertain fears that a Republican administration would directly, or indirectly, interfere with their slaves, or with them, about their slaves? If they do, I wish to assure you, as once a friend, and still, I hope, not an enemy, that there is no cause for such fears."[32] Less than two months later, Stephens became vice president of the Confederate States of America. In the highly charged political environment deriving both from John Brown's raid and the revived antislavery constitutional speculation surrounding Lincoln's election, the president-elect's promises simply were not believed.

SOUTHERNERS DID BELIEVE that, once installed, an antislavery government would move in subtle ways to undermine the tight internal unity that characterized their unique social order. Critical inquiry, which flourished in northern culture, was restricted and restrained in the South. Genuine free speech was a value that a slave society could not tolerate and long survive, especially within a western European civilization that was becoming increasingly hostile to slavery.[33]

Southern intolerance to dangerous ideas had become apparent a generation before, in 1835, when abolitionists inundated the South with literature designed to offend southern sensibilities.[34] In the unsteady years following Nat Turner's rebellion, the U.S. Mail temporarily became an unwitting instrument of abolitionist agitation, as antislavery tracts and newspapers began to arrive in southern post offices for local delivery. Southern complaints pushed President Andrew Jackson to call for a federal ban on such mailings.[35] Interestingly, John C. Calhoun opposed this, sensing a dangerous principle lurking within a seemingly proslavery presidential proposal. The South Carolinian did not oppose censorship. He simply wanted it brought about in a manner harmonious with the constitutional theory that he was then developing for the maintenance of a slaveholding republic. He did not want a federally imposed censorship that might indirectly encourage those advocating a federal prohibition of the interstate slave trade. Calhoun wanted nothing that might suggest a federal police power. He preferred to have the federal government solely supplement enforcement of state police powers in the banning of incendiary literature. In this way, the federal government would become only an agent of state sovereignty and not its master.[36] Even more than Calhoun's opposition, First Amendment guarantees against federal censorship torpedoed Jackson's idea, but a proslavery administrative understanding was implemented that ultimately satisfied Calhoun. In 1836, Congress passed a law requiring that mail be delivered to its destination. But, under the direction of Amos Kendall, Jackson's postmaster general, local postmasters interpreted this to mean that when the mail arrived in their offices, the letter of the law had been obeyed. In those states where local feeling ran against delivery of such mail, it never left the post office.[37]

Southerners feared that Lincoln might terminate this understanding and that new Republican postmasters would flood the South with unwanted radical mail.[38] In justifying the practice of not delivering abolitionist literature, Kendall had written that federal postmasters were obligated to do nothing that might undermine the institution of slavery, which he claimed was "recognized and guaranteed by the Constitution itself."[39] But Lincoln did not hold this view. Therefore, how logical was it to presume that Lincoln would continue this practice that was seen as essential for maintaining good order in the southern states? In addition to the issue of the mail itself was the fact that antislavery postmasters and other federal officers might be assigned to the South. The Buchanan administration had demonstrated how federal patronage could build up a strong proslavery interest even in free states such as California. Clearly, a Republican administration could operate similarly to produce an antislavery force even within slave states.[40] Lincoln himself promised that he would not use federal patronage in this way,[41] but intersectional trust was so low that few, if any, southerners believed him. And why should they have? Did not the spoils belong to the victor in American politics at that time?

Stephen Douglas attempted to persuade the South that such fears were unwarranted. Election day found him in New Orleans, where he issued a statement that the election of Lincoln, by itself, did not warrant secession. While acknowledging the South's minority position, he enumerated indisputable facts: The Democratic party controlled both the new House and the Senate. Northern Democrats remained firmly opposed to the Republican agenda. The proslavery Supreme Court was unchanged by the election. "Even in the distribution of his patronage," Douglas wrote on an especially delicate issue, Lincoln "would be dependent upon the Senate for the confirmation of his nominees to office." If events later proved Douglas wrong and somehow Lincoln did real harm despite his isolated position, the Illinois Democrat emphasized that then would be time to consider stern measures. "Such an outrage would not only make the southern people a unit, but would arouse and consolidate all the conservative elements of the North in firm and determined resistance, by overwhelming majorities." He reminded the South that the only way in which Lincoln could possibly gain the upper hand was by means of southern secession itself, which, if successful, would abandon Congress to unelected Republican dominance and thereby encourage the Republican revolution that they feared.[42]

To southerners, Douglas's analysis was superficial. Occasional senatorial rejection of the most extreme Lincoln appointees could not possibly impede the full impact of Republican federal patronage upon the South. Douglas's argument also ignored that much of his own northern constituency was hostile to slavery and simply preferred a popular sovereignty method of restricting the South. Georgia's Howell Cobb, President Buchanan's secretary of the treasury, a secessionist and soon to be president of the Confederate Constitutional Convention, dismissed "over-anxious friends of the Union at the North," such as Douglas, whom he saw as vainly coming up with only weak arguments. Similar to the style of Douglas's New Orleans statement, Cobb identified irrefutable points: "It is true that without a majority in Congress Lincoln will not be able to carry out *at present* all the aggressive measures of his party. But let me ask if that feeble and constantly decreasing majority in Congress against him can arrest that tide of popular sentiment at the North against slavery which, sweeping down all barriers of truth, justice and Constitutional duty, has borne Mr. Lincoln into the Presidential chair?...Can that majority in Congress control the power and patronage of President Lincoln?"[43] Even if Lincoln did hold true to his pledge and did not use federal patronage in the South to build up an antislavery party there, he certainly would feel no such restraint in the northern states, where Republican favors could be expected to woo away Douglas's constituency. A solid North, emerging from this experience, could in time simply overwhelm the South.

President Buchanan took a position in between that of the secessionist Cobb and the unionist Douglas. In his annual message of December 3, he stated that while secession was unconstitutional, the federal government had neither the moral nor the legal authority to crush it.[44] The nation's chief executive offered no resistance to the South's departure from the old Union, which seemingly could no longer adequately serve the needs of that section. Buchanan's confession of national impotence in the face of this historic crisis thus became the last major act of the federal government truly serving the slaveholding interest. Meanwhile, Lincoln was forced to abide the interminable wait until March 4, 1861, when he was scheduled to take the oath of office.

Buchanan's weak stance made it obvious that serious northern concessions in the form of constitutional amendments alone could prevent eventual civil war. Kentucky's John J. Crittenden assumed a central role in trying to negotiate a settlement, and Douglas supported his efforts even though any centralized package would likely violate his "great principle" of local self-determination. Unity among both secessionists and Republicans against their efforts brought war ever closer. [45] By February 4, exactly one month before Lincoln's inauguration, seven southern states from the Deep South, including South Carolina, Mississippi, Florida, Alabama, Georgia, Louisiana, and Texas, had already enacted ordinances of secession. On that day, a southern convention met in Montgomery to create both a new federal government and a new proslavery constitution to guide it.[46] On the same day, a "Peace Convention," representing the remaining states of the old union, including eight slave states, began one last desperate attempt to negotiate constitutional amendments.[47] Also on that day, Thomas L. Clingman of North Carolina delivered an address in the U.S. Senate "on the State of the Union." Above all, he emphasized the specter of Lincoln administering federal patronage. Together, with a "free post-office distribution of abolitionist pamphlets," he predicted that without secession "you would see a powerful division in portions of the

South."[48] Clingman thus offered the proslavery counterpart of Lincoln's "House-Divided" Speech.

That same month, Virginia's secession convention convened and expressions similar to Clingman's predominated. Many there feared that slavery was too weak in the Upper South to survive the influence of Republican federal patronage. Missouri, Kentucky, Delaware, Maryland, and even Virginia itself were all at risk. A southern Republican party, appealing to nonslaveholding whites and fed by federal favors, a federally encouraged freedom of expression, and especially unrestricted delivery of the mails threatened to awaken an internal debate in the Upper South leading toward abolition.[49] A generation before, immediately following Nat Turner's rebellion, the last real debate over slavery had occurred in Virginia. In the convention of 1861, George Randolph reminded his fellow delegates of this history and warned that proslavery ideology was too recent in origin and too little appreciated by the masses to survive a reopening of such an argument.[50] Secessionists feared that in the uncertainty of slave property during a campaign of this nature, slaveholders would remove their human property to the Deep South for protection, an act that would virtually surrender the Upper South to free soil. The secessionist scenario concluded with slavery restricted to the eight cotton states alone. Then, the prediction went, slavery "like a scorpion girdled with fire," would "sting itself to death."[51] The fact that Lincoln vowed that he would not oppose a constitutional amendment permanently guaranteeing federal noninterference with slavery in the states where it already existed did not reduce the anxiety produced by this secessionist nightmare.[52]

Senator Clingman spoke for many of his fellow southerners when he evaluated the intent of the incoming Lincoln administration as being "to foment revolution." He fantasized that if secession did not precede Lincoln's inauguration, the new president would immediately strip southern armories of all weapons to discourage any further thought of proslavery resistance.[53] Step-by-step, abolition would follow, bringing with it "a large free negro population" and the "destruction of society."[54] Several months before, Henry L. Benning of Georgia had elaborated on the racial reasons to support secession. This associate justice of the Georgia Supreme Court projected that if secession did not occur, and the Lincoln administration succeeded in killing slavery in the states where it existed, then a war between the races would inevitably erupt, followed by northern intervention on behalf of the blacks and a forced exile of the whites. Eventually, he predicted, the Yankees themselves would move in and take the land from the blacks, resulting in the ultimate and inevitable extermination of the latter.[55]

Delegates to the Confederate Constitutional Convention held similar attitudes, for they created a new fundamental law designed to ensure that African Americans would always remain slaves. In contrast to the Constitution of 1787, which approximated a neutral position concerning the institution of slavery, the new Confederate constitution was clearly proslavery. Southern myth holds that a love of states rights, not slavery, led to the establishment of the Confederate States of America and the "war between the states" that followed. Actually, the essential causal ingredient was neither a love of states rights nor of slavery. In the end, the southern refusal to submit to Lincoln's election was over race, an interpretation promoted at the time by the secessionists themselves.[56]

Had race not been a factor in American slavery, the Confederate constitution would not have had to treat the peculiar institution with the amount of protective care that it in fact did. First, it specifically called for a federal protection of slavery in the territories, an issue of recent contention under the Constitution of 1787. Under the Confederate constitution, slaveholders would never have to beg either territorial legislatures or Congress to pass slave codes for the territories. It was mandated in the new fundamental law itself.[57] Likewise, this constitutional protection of slavery applied not only to the territories but within the states themselves. Should any Confederate state ever abolish slavery, that act would be essentially null and void, because under the new constitution slavery was guaranteed "in any of the States or Territories."[58] The Confederate constitution guaranteed the slaveholder's "right of transit and sojourn in any State."[59] As a witness of slavery's dominance over the new constitutional order created in Montgomery, the term "negro slavery" was used repeatedly,[60] in stark contrast to the Constitution of 1787 that had embarrassingly used euphemistic language to mask the existence of the tyrannical institution in a land presumably dedicated to liberty.

As historian Arthur Bestor emphasized a generation ago, in the Confederate constitution "slavery was no longer a local institution." Rather it became a national one.[61] Revealing the ridiculous lengths to which the Confederate founding fathers went to protect slavery, the new constitution even guarded against a national antislavery movement arising in the South by prohibiting the Confederate Congress from ever passing legislation "denying or impairing the right of property in negro slaves," assuming that this could be possible in a constitutional order that hedged against even individual states abolishing slavery.[62] Professor Bestor rightly concluded that the new Confederacy was hardly dedicated to states rights. Instead, at least as far as the institution of slavery was concerned, "the Confederacy was a unitary, consolidated, national state, denying to each one of its allegedly sovereign members any sort of local autonomy with respect to this particular one among its domestic institutions."[63]

Considering the new republic being completely dedicated to slavery, Confederate President Jefferson Davis celebrated the new "grand homogeneous Union."[64] Howell Cobb, wrote to James Buchanan, who unwittingly had served as midwife to the new slaveholding republic by his policy of inaction: "I think you will agree with me in pronouncing our [Confederate] constitution a great improvement upon the constitution of the U.S."[65] Confederate Vice President Alexander Hamilton Stephens praised the new fundamental law as forever clarifying "the proper status of the negro in our form of civilization." Referring to the Declaration of Independence of 1776 that had guided the United States from its outset, Stephens commented: "Our new government is founded upon exactly the opposite idea; its foundations are laid, its corner-stone rests upon the great truth, that the negro is not equal to the white man; that slavery—subordination to the superior race—is his natural and normal condition."[66]

The new constitution allowed that federal judicial officers, "acting solely within the limits of any State," could be "impeached by a vote of two-thirds of both branches of the Legislature thereof."[67] This provision, which was never enforced during the brief history of the Confederacy, was more a reflection of past complaints than constituting a "significant embodiment of the theory of states rights," as claimed by one historian.[68] In fact, the provision was created because a federal judge residing in South Carolina four decades before had fought the constitutionality of a state law that required free black seamen to be locked up while on liberty in the state's ports.[69]

The Confederate constitution reconfirmed the United States 1808 prohibition against importing slaves from Africa or foreign countries, albeit exempting the United States itself.[70] Continuing this historic ban served as an inducement to the Upper South to join the Confederacy. States such as Virginia had vehemently opposed any consideration of reopening the importation of Africans. The source of opposition was twofold: (1) given strong racial feelings, many southerners did not want any more blacks living among them; (2) a reopening of the international slave trade threatened to diminish greatly the economic value of slave property already in place.[71]

While technically allowing the importation of slaves from the United States, the new constitution also encouraged the Confederate Congress to "prohibit the introduction of slaves from any State not a member of, or Territory not belonging to, this Confederacy."[72] This provision was designed to pressure the states of the Upper South to join the Confederacy, for if they did not they were forewarned that their surplus slaves might never again be allowed to be sold off to the Deep South. Virginia, Arkansas, Tennessee, and North Carolina subsequently did join the Confederacy but not because of this threat. Lincoln's call for volunteers to suppress the rebellion following the firing on Fort Sumter was a more immediate determining factor.[73]

The new constitution continued the "three-fifths" enumeration of slaves for purposes of representation and direct taxes, with the only protest coming from South Carolina, a state with an African American majority. Some whites there argued that slaves should be counted in full so as to increase that state's representation within the Confederacy.[74] In any case, South Carolina overwhelmingly approved of the document as presented to it, as did all of the other participating states.[75] Overall, the amount of consensus in the Deep South in establishing a new government so quickly was remarkable. The cause of this haste lay in the widely popular secessionist scenario of the fate that would befall the South should it make the fatal mistake of trying to live, even temporarily, under an antislavery federal administration.

Meanwhile, Stephen Douglas internalized what he regarded as a most negative course of events. Southern secession called a rude halt to his lifelong vision of an expanding democratic American empire. Three months after Lincoln's inauguration, the Little Giant was dead, supposedly the victim of a sudden onslaught of acute rheumatism.[76] At the end, unable to move his arms, he transcribed one last letter to a secretary. In it, he blamed the South for the impasse. Southerners, he claimed, would not consent to any compromise, "not even if we would furnish them with a blank sheet of paper and permit them to inscribe their own terms."[77] At Montgomery, southerners had inscribed their own terms for a new slaveholding republic. Nothing offered by Crittenden, Douglas, or the Peace Convention that met in Washington, D.C., in February could compete with that alternative.[78]

LINCOLN'S ASSURANCES failed to divert the Deep South from initiating secession. As military operations got under way with the fall of Fort Sumter, driving still more states to secede, the new president faced another test of his ability to communicate effectively. Specifically, he needed to lead the remaining states, some of which were of split loyalties, not only to crush southern secession but also preserve the best qualities of the old republic while building a new one not dedicated to slavery. Awkward and gangly, with a high voice and a backwoods accent, Lincoln did not fit the beau ideal of a president. Yet, he was president, a fact that he effectively communicated to his initially wayward secretary of state, William H. Seward.[79] Amidst the chaos of organizing his administration for the nation's severest crisis, those closest to him came to respect his unique interpersonal skills and leadership qualities.

His foremost challenge was to articulate a vision for the new antislavery republic being born. He had to do this in such a way that would inspire not only his Republican supporters, but also those who had heretofore opposed him. As Lincoln was versed in the Bible, he was probably familiar with the prediction from the book of Proverbs that a people without a vision perish.[80] In any case, he set to work instructing the northern people about American nationalism's foremost ideals, as he understood them. Others might handle the details of raising, training, provisioning and equipping armies, but he alone could supply a national vision. While waiting for his inauguration, he seemed to pay especial attention to this duty, which could easily get sidetracked after his inauguration on March 4. On February 11, at the time of his departure for Washington, D.C., he began this preinaugural campaign of testing the effect of his vision before audiences in a farewell address to his Springfield neighbors. Without God's direction and assistance, he said, he could not succeed as president.[81] Intellectually attracted to a philosophy that held that "the human mind is impelled to action, or held in rest by some power, over which the mind itself has no control," Lincoln had also been marked by the predestinarian beliefs of his upbringing. [82] Not the kind of politician to indulge mindlessly in religious sentiment, Lincoln injected matters of faith into his public discourse to steel the nation for a cataclysmic struggle that he sensed was coming.[83] He closed his Springfield farewell by commenting that if Providence were behind him, he could not fail. Including both himself and the nation as controlled by mysterious forces, his vision for the nation was constructed upon this publicly proclaimed spiritual foundation.[84] Julia Ward Howe later supplemented Lincoln's own rhetoric with her inspiring lyric to the melody of "John Brown's Body," renamed "The Battle Hymn of the Republic." Men and women, believing that they were holy instruments of "the coming of the Lord," were led to make great sacrifices.

Moving east by rail toward the burdens of office, Lincoln continued to flesh out his national vision. If Divine will was of primary significance, Lincoln saw popular will as a close second. "When the people rise in masses in behalf of the Union and the liberties of their country," Lincoln said at a stop in Indiana, "truly may it be said, 'The gates of hell shall not prevail against them.'"[85] "This is essentially a People's contest," he would say five months later.[86] Lincoln emphasized that ultimately the nation's destiny would be determined by popular resolve, without which the superiority in northern population figures and material wealth could not become significant factors. "I...look to the American people and to that God who has never forsaken them," Lincoln reported to the Ohio state legislature on February 13.[87] Similar to his reliance upon Divine authority, Lincoln's deference to the people was not empty propaganda. A month later, in his Inaugural Address, in recalling the Dred Scott decision that had been delivered by the nation's premier legal experts, he emphasized that the people themselves, not the Supreme Court or any other public officials, are the ultimate constitutional authority in American government. The people, he emphasized, are "their own rulers."[88]

Anarchy.*

Speaking before an audience of German immigrants in Cincinnati, Lincoln inserted the next essential component of this developing creed. Indeed, this last piece became the most important of all the set, for relying merely upon Divine and popular will begged an essential question: What necessarily is the will of a people that is in harmony with God? "I hold that while man exists," Lincoln proclaimed, "it is his duty to improve not only his own condition, but to assist in ameliorating mankind."[89] The people's contest, which he saw developing, was a matter of foundational communal purpose. Ten days later in Philadelphia, he explored this theme more fully. The United States, he said, provides "hope to the world for all future time." A corollary of this axiom was that Americans did not exist for their own individual pursuits of happiness. Individual liberty alone could not provide the necessary binding material for an enduring national existence. At the birthplace of American freedom, he talked about a common purpose of lifting weights "from the shoulders of all men" and providing "that all should have an equal chance."[90]

Lincoln seemed aware of the symbolism accompanying speeches made at certain national places or on specific national dates. In his first July Fourth address as president, he later returned to the theme that he raised at Philadelphia in February. The United States, he said, should not survive merely to provide a political framework to protect individual desire, which, among other things, had fed the selfish purposes of secession. Subtly, Lincoln intended that the new antislavery republic not only fulfill the ideals of the Declaration of Independence, but improve upon them as well. The Declaration had provided a tight focus upon individual rights. Lincoln sought to highlight a more communal purpose for national existence. Collectively, he noted, all Americans were involved in a noble "experiment" to uplift humankind, beginning with the people making up the United States but not ending there. A society wholly dedicated to individualism, Lincoln warned, would eventually fall because of that value's inherent disintegrating principle, upon which "no government can possibly endure." He reached beyond a national purpose limited only to mid-nineteenth-century America. On July 4, 1861, he proclaimed: "This issue embraces more than the fate of these United States. It presents to the whole family of man the question whether a constitutional republic or democracy—a government of the people by the same people—can or cannot maintain its territorial integrity against its own domestic foes."[91]

Lincoln emphasized that at the heart of the crisis facing that generation was the question whether human beings are capable of governing themselves, or whether their selfish nature ultimately requires masters, kings, and dictators to direct their destiny. While not ignoring the importance of individual rights, he called upon something more profound that could inspire many to sacrifice their individual lives so that self-government itself might survive them. Seven months into the war, Lincoln tersely explained his administration's guiding purpose in a note to Sweden's new ambassador: "This country, Sir, maintains, and means to maintain, the rights of human nature and the capacity of man for self government."[92] In scattered fashion, within the first year following his election, Lincoln offered all of the ideas later to appear in finished form in the Gettysburg Address.

Unavoidably, Congress soon joined Lincoln in drafting a national mission statement. In contrast to Lincoln's own soaring views, the Crittenden-Johnson Resolutions of July 1861 were tightly earthbound, stating that the nation was going to war not to liberate slaves but rather to preserve the Union as it had been under the old order.[93] The virtue of this statement was that it encouraged those who had not contributed to Lincoln's election victory to follow his leadership. As he had won only 39 percent of the popular vote, and was commonly cast as a "Black Republican" by his political enemies, it was essential for him to win the support of non-Republicans. During the next year, in the interest of maintaining a semblance of harmony within the North, Lincoln basically deferred to the narrow Crittenden-Johnson statement of war aims.

In recent years, some historians have exaggerated a portrait of an overly conservative Abraham Lincoln, waging war solely to restore a disintegrating empire, ordering generals in the field to halt their unilateral liberation of slaves, and vainly pursuing an antiquated policy of compensated emancipation for owners and colonization for any slaves thus liberated.[94] To a degree, this portrait is a legitimate corrective of Lincoln's long-standing mythological image as the "Great Emancipator" that is even more overblown. In addition, it cannot be denied that much of the interpretation made by Lincoln's critics is founded upon solid evidence.[95] But it is as false to portray Lincoln as one caring nothing about the slavery issue as it is to make him into the premier humanitarian of his age. In fact, Lincoln was a politician first and foremost. He was devoted to certain long-range principles that consistently guided his course, but concurrently he obeyed the necessity of balancing diverse and often conflicting political interests.

It is important to understand what "saving the Union" meant to Lincoln. It did not mean mere preservation of national empire, which might have been the case if, for example, Stephen A. Douglas had been president during the Civil War. For Lincoln, saving the Union was not separate from the eventual elimination of slavery from American life. For him, any Union worth preserving had as a prerequisite that slavery should first be restricted and ultimately be eliminated. Even before the war, secessionists had accurately sensed this about the meaning of this first Republican national administration. And William Lloyd Garrison agreed. A month before the election, Garrison wrote to a friend that Lincoln's victory would signify a sharp shift in national policy, "which, in process of time, must ripen into . . . decisive action."[96] Eventually, all who lived through the conflagration became equally appreciative of this fact.

"Communication and inspiration," James M. McPherson has aptly written, "are two of the most important functions of a president in times of crisis."[97] More than any other person who has ever occupied the presidency, Lincoln had both an ability to define and articulate the meaning of the American national experiment and politically negotiate a deeply divided people toward progressive change. Out of a deep respect for Lincoln's leadership abilities, a distinguished southern historian once speculated that the Union would have lost the war if Jefferson Davis had been president of the United States and Lincoln had led the Confederacy.[98] Of course, such counterfactual musings are ultimately meaningless. Jefferson Davis would never have led the nation in an antislavery direction. Also, Lincoln would never have defended a permanent maintenance of slavery as called for in the Confederate constitution. In the final analysis, neither man can be divorced from the distinct ideological position that each represented.

In recent decades, historians have argued that less adulation should be given to Lincoln's leadership abilities and more to the thousands of anonymous slaves, who by escaping southern captivity during the war, eventually forced Lincoln to support a formal emancipation policy. "Slaves set others in motion. Slaves were the prime movers in the emancipation drama," Ira Berlin has written. "It does no disservice to Lincoln—or to anyone else—to say that his claim to greatness rests upon his willingness to act when the moment was right."[99] A close review of the movement of Lincoln toward an emancipation policy reveals that the antislavery president was often passive, tardy, and at times discouraging of moving in this direction on his own accord. That which pressed him to act ultimately was indeed a de facto emancipation being initiated by the slaves themselves.

It was General Benjamin Butler, not Lincoln, who in May 1861 began the policy of treating runaway slaves as "contraband" of war.[100] In this action, involving both risk-taking African Americans and a politically entrepreneurial general, the president remained essentially passive.[101] Likewise, the important role played by slaves in building Confederate military fortifications, pushed Congress to take a first step beyond the tight focus of the Crittenden-Johnson Resolutions. The result became the Confiscation Act of August 6, 1861, which Republicans supported overwhelmingly and Democrats opposed. The bill, which Lincoln signed reluctantly, emancipated any slaves serving the needs of the Confederate military.[102]

Fear of alienating loyal border-state slaveholders explained Lincoln's cautious attitude, as he believed that the secession of Kentucky might lose the war for the North. Indeed, the president seemed to take the initiative in matters concerning slavery only to protect the institution in the border states, such as when he countermanded General Frémont's military emancipation in Missouri.[103] Lincoln also expressed concern when Republicans began to renounce the Crittenden-Johnson Resolutions, for fear that more radical war aims might lose essential border-state support.[104] At one point, for the same reason, he also chastised his secretary of war for endorsing the idea of arming runaway slaves.[105]

In April 1862, when Congress emancipated slaves in the District of Columbia, the most that Lincoln said in support was that it met his criteria of "expediency." He also praised the bill for including both provisions for compensating owners and colonizing the freedmen.[106] Three weeks earlier, he had written Horace Greeley that he was "a little uneasy" about liberating the District's slaves.[107] Meanwhile, Lincoln continued countermanding generals who issued unauthorized emancipation policies and pleaded with border-state slaveholders to accept a compensated emancipation plan.[108] While modern Lincoln critics have argued that justice would have been "better served by compensating slaves for their long years in bondage," some of these scholars grudgingly acknowledge that his persistence with the compensation idea subtly helped advance the concept of a governmentally administered emancipation.[109]

In the summer of 1862, the political momentum for emancipation began to outstrip Lincoln's political management of the issue. In June, Congress abolished slavery in all U.S. territories without any provision for either compensation or colonization.[110] In July, Congress enacted a Second Confiscation Act, emancipating the slaves of all rebels. Lincoln accepted this only after he had exacted concessions from Congress to provide funds to finance a voluntary colonization of the freedmen involved. He also let it be known that he did not like Congress contradicting his earlier emphasis that the Constitution did not allow congressional interference with slavery within the states.[111]

This step-by-step history of Lincoln's behavior during his first year in office shows him seemingly being led by events. But, from another perspective, it also shows him keeping diverse elements working together as the circumstances emphasized by Professor Berlin made increasing headway. Lincoln negotiated with abolitionist generals who thought that he was going too slowly and with proslavery generals who threatened to resign if abolition ever became an official war aim. Some states were eager to destroy slavery, whereas others pursued a bitter-end policy to preserve slavery. Most importantly, Lincoln sought to keep both abolitionist and proslavery voters backing the war effort. But in the summer of 1862, the president concluded that to maximize his effectiveness in leading this chaotic mix of conflicting interests he had to move closer to the abolitionist position. Two years later, he explained this shift to a Kentucky newspaper editor. He recalled that during his first year, he had kept Kentucky uppermost on his mind. Then, as the pace of events began to indicate that some form of emancipation was coming, he vainly tried to persuade border-state slaveholders to adjust to the emerging reality with the idea of compensated emancipation. Eventually, because of their rejection of this generous solution, he was forced to shift his strategy and move out in front of emancipation's advancing columns.[112]

Congress's Second Confiscation Act was inadequate as a practical mechanism for a general emancipation, as individual legal determinations of whether or not owners were loyal would have to occur in each instance of *de jure* liberation.[113] In any case, the act's real significance was in forcing Lincoln's decision to lead the political emancipation struggle. On July 22, he presented his cabinet members with a draft of a presidential emancipation proclamation. He also discussed with them the enlisting of African Americans in the army. Postmaster General Montgomery Blair predicted a harsh political backlash, which Lincoln was willing to absorb. The president was influenced more by Secretary of State Seward, who warned that both at home and abroad an emancipation proclamation at that moment would probably be interpreted as an act of desperation. Given a string of Union military defeats resulting from General George B. McClellan's ineffectual campaign in Virginia, Great Britain and France might even intervene to stop the mass butchery in America. Fearing that Seward was right, Lincoln decided to keep his new policy under wraps until a victory in the field occurred. Then, he determined, would be the proper moment to act.[114] As ever, the art of political timing dictated Lincoln's course.

While waiting, Lincoln put on his best poker face. No good could come from rumors of a dramatic shift in policy before the proper moment of public announcement. On August 4, he told a group of Indiana visitors that nothing had changed. They asked him to reconsider his opposition to enlisting African Americans in the army, and he dutifully repeated his old saw about how changing that policy might result in the loss of Kentucky.[115] Not only did Lincoln make public statements as conservative as any that he had given; while waiting for a significant military victory he also portrayed himself as more conservative than ever before. On August 14, he met with a faction of African Americans about a federal colonization of their race outside of the United States. He told them that he had determined that colonization in Liberia was impractical, given the costs of transporting America's black population back to Africa, and deemed a mass migration to Central America more feasible.[116] Reports of this meeting drove abolitionists into a collective rage.[117] Perhaps this effect was intended by Lincoln. In the weeks preceding issuance of his emancipation policy, Lincoln deliberately widened the distance between himself and the humanitarian reformers who had long fought for black liberation. Abraham Lincoln was preparing the political ground.

There is a slim possibility that Lincoln was informed in advance that Horace Greeley of the *New York Tribune* was going to blast his policy in his editorial columns.[118] In any case, when the blow came, in two blistering editorials on August 19 and 22, Lincoln took full advantage of the situation. He replied to Greeley in language that modern Lincoln critics are fond of quoting out of context: "My paramount object in this struggle is to save the Union, and is not either to save or destroy slavery. If I could save the Union without freeing any slave, I would do it. . . . What I do about slavery and the colored race, I do because I believe it helps to save this Union."[119] With that, conservatives were assured that Lincoln would never adopt any war aim other than saving the Union. Cleverly concealing his future emancipation policy within a package of unalloyed nationalism, he sought to guarantee its ultimate acceptance by a white racist nation.

What can be made of Lincoln's apparent fixation with the idea of colonization? It was an idea that attracted more than just Lincoln. Harriet Beecher Stowe's *Uncle Tom's Cabin* (1852), a novel that worked to convert the North to antislavery, closed with a white racist fantasy that America's blacks would eventually return to their "homeland" in Africa.[120] The colonization idea certainly revealed a blind spot in the vision of both white America in general and Abraham Lincoln in particular. Yet, given Lincoln's analytical mind, it is hard to believe that he ever thought that such an idea could ever be carried out, given the overwhelming logistical problems involved even in settling former slaves in the nearby Caribbean area. He knew that African Americans overwhelmingly had no desire to leave their true homeland, the place of their birth and collective heritage. Likewise, as he never proposed anything other than voluntary colonization, one can wonder why he expended so much public energy on the subject. The obvious answer lies in remembering that this man was a consummate politician. He knew what corollaries were necessary to prepare his white countrymen to tolerate a policy of emancipation.[121]

The tone of his reply to Greeley also made excellent political propaganda. Certainly, if "Honest Abe" does not deserve the appellation "The Great Emancipator," he should be appreciated as a most skillful dissimulator. Charles Sumner, the abolitionist senator from Massachusetts, practiced a far more open, honest, and transparent form of politics. Throughout the Civil War, he regularly butted heads with the president over the latter's apparent insensitivity and slowness of movement. Yet in 1868, when later reflecting upon the political style that regularly bears the best results, Sumner wrote: "Every man must have certain theories, principles by which governments should be conducted. But where we undertake to apply them to practical problems, there are many difficulties to be overcome, many concessions which must be made in order to accomplish the desired result. The old proverb has it 'the shortest way across is often the longest way round,' and nowhere is this truer than in legislation. It is not every Gordian knot that can be cut: some must be patiently untied."[122] Interestingly, while Lincoln lived, Sumner regularly chastised him for not simply cutting Gordian knots.

In Lincoln's annual address for 1862, made several months after finally revealing his emancipation policy but still on the eve of actually initiating it, the president again returned to the idea of colonization. In his remarks, again one can see him placating white racism, which he knew would show itself more viciously once the walls of slavery were broken. Then, abruptly, he turned from the colonization idea to urge white America to greet black emancipation with as much grace as it could muster. "In times like the present," he reported, "men should utter nothing for which they would not willingly be responsible through time and in eternity." His following commentary revealed that he did not believe that a mass black migration out of the country would ever really occur. Turning toward advocating a more practical racial accommodation at home, he never mentioned colonization publicly again.[123]

Searching for a "prime mover" in the historical drama of emancipation is ultimately a futile enterprise. The prime mover certainly was not Lincoln. But was it the runaway slaves collectively, as Professor Berlin has suggested? Historian Mark Voss-Hubbard has challenged that position by emphasizing that generations of abolitionists "furnished the conceptual legacies necessary for justifying emancipation during and after the war."[124] Does this fact make them the prime movers? In fact, many contributed to general emancipation. Of all the participants, Lincoln regularly played an often distasteful, but nonetheless essential, political role.[125] On September 13, which unknown to him at that time was only a week before his own unveiling of presidential emancipation, Lincoln met with a two-man religious delegation from Chicago. Similar to so many other well-meaning people, they told him that they knew that God wanted immediate emancipation. Frustrated at the long wait for news of a victorious battle, the president shot back that it would help if God revealed himself "directly" "on a point so connected with my duty."[126] The men then tried to persuade him that a presidential emancipation policy would energize the people of the North: "No one," one of them said, "can tell the power of the right word from the right man to develop the latent fire and enthusiasm of the masses." All that Lincoln could reply was, "I know it."[127] In this one brief conversation were all of the elements of the national vision that Lincoln had framed at the outset of his presidency—a people inspired by God to lift burdens from the shoulders of oppressed humanity.

Four days later, near Sharpsburg, Maryland, along a creek called Antietam, God's "terrible swift sword" created the war's bloodiest day. Decimated, Lee's army retreated back into Virginia. McClellan's Army of the Potomac had also been wounded, but seeing the hand of Divine Providence at work, Lincoln politically proclaimed the victory for which he had been waiting for two months. Five days after the battle, he issued the Preliminary Emancipation Proclamation.[128] In the eyes of some, it did not constitute the inspiring declaration of freedom for which they had hoped.[129] Indeed, Lincoln the politician deliberately crafted the statement to be as boring as possible. There would be time enough later for thrilling words, after his new policy was securely established. Frederick Douglass commented at that historic moment that the president's political style had at least one virtue: "Abraham Lincoln ... , in his own peculiar, cautious, forebearing and hesitating way, slow, but we hope sure, has, while the loyal heart was near breaking with despair, proclaimed [emancipation]. . . . The careful, and we think, the slothful deliberation which he has observed in reaching this obvious policy, is a guarantee against retraction."[130] Lincoln had taken the old proverb's "longest way round."

ACCOUNTS OF LINCOLN'S political vacillation on the issue of emancipation often leaves a false impression. James M. McPherson has played a leading role in trying to set the record straight. He rightly claims that for all of the president's temporary and tactical stalling on the matter, Lincoln resolutely and skillfully navigated by a "lodestar that never moved." McPherson emphasizes that before the war, Lincoln was easily characterized as a "one-issue man" tightly focused on restricting the spread of slavery. At the outset of his presidency, Lincoln remained steadily on course, defining a national vision, which on an abstract level included putting slavery on the course of ultimate extinction. Importantly, in 1861 he refused to compromise either on the expansion of slavery or on holding Fort Sumter, when others in his party wavered. In the final analysis, Lincoln preferred war to compromising the slavery issue. McPherson reminds us that "without the war, the door to freedom would have remained closed for an indeterminate length of time."[131] Steadily, over the course of his four years in office, Lincoln fulfilled his vision, transforming noble, abstract principles into an emancipation policy that eventually took root. Working within a context of conflicting passions on fundamental questions, Lincoln needed all of the patience and skill inherent within him to bring about ultimate success.

Ironically, McPherson's portrayal of Lincoln as an active, purposeful leader appears to be undermined by Lincoln's own words. In a letter to Albert G. Hodges of Kentucky, written in 1864, Lincoln stated: "I aver that, to this day, I have done no official act in mere deference to my abstract judgment and feeling on slavery. . . . I claim not to have controlled events, but confess plainly that events have controlled me."[132] Yet when one places this frequently quoted comment in the context of the complete letter, the impression of an essentially passive leader is dispelled. Lincoln concluded the letter with remarks that suggested that God, not he, was in control and that he as president was operating as the Almighty's principal negotiator in the American political arena: "Now, at the end of three years struggle the nation's condition is not what either party, or any man devised or expected. God alone can claim it. Whither it is tending seems plain. If God now wills the removal of a great wrong, and wills also that we of the North as well as you of the South, shall pay fairly for our complicity in that wrong, impartial history will find therein new cause to attest and revere the justice and goodness of God."[133]

Lincoln was not a conventional Christian believer.[134] He belonged to no church. At times, he was regarded by some as a skeptic. Indeed, his unsentimental habit of plumbing issues to bedrock depths did not encourage any simplistic acceptance of biblical teachings. Yet both the personal tragedies of his household and the collective festering wound of civil war, which he knew his own decisions had helped bring about, drove him to discover a mysterious God directing not only bloody events on numerous American battlefields but his own will as well. As such, Lincoln's admission to Hodges of not being in control was essentially a religious confession. The deepening personal conviction that it represented proved to be "the only adequate counterweight for a burden of responsibility too heavy to carry alone."[135]

The America of Lincoln's day was more attuned to the notion of God controlling the nation's destiny than is so today.[136] The philosophies of history that most attracted thinkers throughout all of western civilization at that time agreed that history followed an inevitable progressive course. Many of them held that history was directed by a Divine purpose. In accepting these views, Lincoln was simply accepting the leading philosophical assumptions of his age. Similar to portrayals of Providence appearing in the philosophies of Kant and Hegel, Lincoln's God was not a traditional Christian deity paying scant attention to a material pursuit of happiness. Bearing a close resemblance to the deity of ancient Hebrew belief, Lincoln's image of God was very much focused upon this world. As it took shape during his presidency, Lincoln's belief, while modern in some ways, was not the rather impersonal godhead that was typical of Enlightenment thinkers. Rather, it was a most personal God of Wrath. In his Second Inaugural Address, Lincoln elaborated upon this theme, which had appeared earlier in the Hodges letter:

> The Almighty has His own purposes.... He now wills to remove [slavery], and ... He gives to both North and South, this terrible war, as the woe due to those by whom the offense came.... Fondly do we hope—fervently do we pray—that this mighty scourge of war may speedily pass away. Yet, if God wills that it continue, until all the wealth piled by the bond-man's two hundred and fifty years of unrequited toil shall be sunk, and until every drop of blood drawn with the lash, shall be paid by another drawn with the sword, as was said three thousand years ago, so still it must be said "the judgments of the Lord, are true and righteous altogether."[137]

Lincoln was most proud of this speech and regarded it as possibly his best rhetorical work, outshining even the Gettysburg Address.[138] In the Second Inaugural, he revealed his most deeply held convictions to a national audience in a way that no other president has done throughout all of American history. In this religious belief, Lincoln had found strength to persevere, and at the time of his Second Inaugural when it was apparent that the Union cause would eventually be won, he publicly acknowledged its tenet that the final outcome had been foreordained all along. It must be emphasized that this view had not bred within Lincoln any passivity or Hamlet-like indecisiveness; rather, just the opposite. The Marxist historical philosopher Georgi Plekhanov has written that a belief in the inevitability of ultimate historical results, instead of encouraging noncommitment in the face of events presumably beyond human control, steels the will and encourages historical actors to "display the most indomitable energy ... [and] perform the most astonishing feats." This, wrote Plekhanov, was the shared psychology of Muhammad and Oliver Cromwell, as well as Martin Luther, when he proclaimed, "Here I stand, I can do no other."[139] Lincoln exhibited a similar resolve throughout the Civil War.

While Lincoln often described God's purposes as mysterious, he appears to have had little doubt that he as president discerned the mind and will of the Almighty. In his 1863 Proclamation of Thanksgiving, which officially inaugurated the national holiday, Lincoln interpreted the war as "the most high God ... dealing with us in anger for our sins." While slavery was nowhere specifically mentioned in the proclamation, there can be little doubt how Lincoln himself regarded what he termed "our national perverseness and disobedience."[140] Years before, he had initially gained fame preaching to political rallies that the nation's founders had intended to put slavery on the course of ultimate extinction. In the midst of the Civil War, he emphasized that God as well intended that result. In a letter to Eliza P. Gurney, written immediately after his darkest days of doubt during the entire war, Lincoln emphasized that God intended "some great good to follow this mighty convulsion, which no mortal could make, and no mortal could stay."[141] Likewise, in his Second Inaugural, he revealed his own belief that God intended to keep the nation at war until emancipation was a guaranteed result, something that was not completed even at that late date.[142] Days later, in writing to Thurlow Weed, Lincoln commented: "Men are not flattered by being shown that there has been a difference of purpose between the Almighty and them. To deny it, however, in this case, is to deny that there is a God governing the world."[143]

Lincoln reportedly once said that his mind was like a piece of steel, "very hard to scratch anything on it and almost impossible after you get it there to rub it out."[144] Once that he determined that he knew the truth about anything, he typically repeated it over and over again in speeches and letters until it achieved its highest statement in some piece of polished rhetoric. This habit of mind bred within him an ultimate certainty that God had forced the nation to go through an unavoidable bloodbath for the sole purpose of redeeming the Union from its generations-long experiment as a slaveholding republic. For Lincoln, American history up to that point had mocked the nation's Providential role as a beacon for liberty and material progress available to all. While he often played the role of a humble public servant, who never let his private antislavery views affect public policy, he occasionally revealed that the truth was otherwise. In his own mind, he was God's holy instrument carrying out a Divine mandate of liberty and justice for all. On March 4, 1865, in his Second Inaugural, he shared this view with his countrymen. A month later, this interpretation was exalted by his own martyred death on Good Friday. In crafting the inexorable logic of his Second Inaugural, Lincoln ironically played a part in the subsequent development of his own mythological persona that almost immediately proved irresistible.[145] Lincoln's transfiguration into an American statesman of Christ-like proportions was also encouraged by a whole genre of contemporary popular literature, epitomized in Julia Ward Howe's widely popular poem, "The Battle Hymn of the Republic."[146]

It is not clear exactly when Lincoln determined that the war would continue until slavery was completely destroyed. Immediately before the war, he had done no more than hold firm against any compromise that might allow its extension into the territories. During the first year of the war, Lincoln apparently had hoped that the conflict might end without the social revolution that immediate emancipation was likely to bring in its wake. Even following the Battle of Antietam, at the time of issuing the Preliminary Emancipation Proclamation, Lincoln appreciated the tentativeness of his new policy. Exercising untested presidential war powers,[147] Lincoln threatened states and districts in active rebellion that unless they ceased all resistance before the beginning of the new year, slaves residing therein would be regarded by the national authority as free. In the preliminary proclamation, Lincoln also promised to begin the constitutional amending processes to end slavery throughout the nation at large, a reform that he eventually revealed two and a half months later in his Annual Message.[148] The first and the last of three constitutional amendments that he then proposed called for a gradual emancipation that would compensate former owners and colonize liberated slaves outside the nation. These indications of presidential purpose apparently were primarily intended only to demonstrate that Lincoln was not going to employ merely a temporary wartime policy that could be reversed once the war was over. Indeed, the second proposed amendment addressed this issue directly. "All slaves who shall have enjoyed actual freedom by the chances of war," the proposal read, "shall be forever free."[149]

On January 1, 1863, Lincoln delivered the real Emancipation Proclamation, declaring free "all persons held as slaves" within the Confederacy. The military was ordered to "recognize and maintain the freedom of said persons" as the Confederacy gradually fell before the progress of Union arms.[150] In this decree, the death knell of the slaveholding republic was broadcast throughout the land. "Thus ended one of the strangest paradoxes in human history," Dwight L. Dummond noted one hundred years later at a ceremony commemorating the event. "The President of the United States pronounced the death sentence upon slavery in a country which had been dedicated to freedom eighty-seven years before."[151]

The proclamation also called for the active recruitment of African Americans into the armed services.[152] The employment of black soldiers had actually been inaugurated by Congress as early as July 17, 1862, but Lincoln had delayed implementation. In the late summer and fall of 1862, the president made a first step by authorizing the organization of several black regiments in South Carolina's captured sea islands.[153] Following the Emancipation Proclamation, black recruitment for military service was vastly expanded, with much publicity given to the organization of Robert Gould Shaw's Fifty-fourth Massachusetts Volunteers.[154] In the months that followed, Lincoln placed a great emphasis upon African American recruitment, which he viewed as significant not only for its potential to fill the army's insatiable manpower needs but also as a means whereby his emancipation policy could gain a greater acceptance among whites.[155] The president wrote eloquently of "black men . . . with clenched teeth, and steady eye, and well poised bayonet" fighting to preserve a Union dedicated to the principle that all men are created equal.[156] Nonetheless, Lincoln condoned a policy of racial discrimination within the military. Blacks were required to be led by whites. African American troops were not paid at the same rates as white soldiers. Lincoln the politician knew that real equality had to come piecemeal if at all. He was fond of using the comparison of an egg not being a chicken but on the way to becoming one. He used this same metaphor differently in describing his freeing of some blacks, while leaving others within loyal districts temporarily enslaved. "Broken eggs cannot be mended," he wrote concerning his emancipation policy.[157] He knew that some Democrats viewed even his incomplete emancipation program as grounds for impeachment.[158] Accordingly, he moved cautiously to bring northern Democrats gradually to accept the inevitability of emancipation and its consequences. Some of his contemporaries and many modern observers have found Lincoln's penchant to adopt half measures most frustrating. In this case, he approved and encouraged black enlistment while allowing racial discrimination within the ranks. In Lincoln's mind, he wanted whites to accept black enlistment before pressing for equal treatment. In the words of LaWanda Cox, this was simply "his way of placing first things first."[159]

Simultaneous with pursuing an emancipation program, Lincoln began to think about returning captured Confederate states to their normal place in the Union. In 1862, he began trying to convince whites in portions of such areas to begin the process of forming loyal state governments.[160] In the following year, these initial efforts evolved and by the end of the year Lincoln revealed his presidential Reconstruction policy. Utilizing his constitutional pardoning power, he decreed that whenever 10 percent of the white voters in any Confederate state swore to be loyal in the future, they could create a loyal state government. He suggested a specific loyalty oath that included acceptance of his emancipation policy, but tactfully added that he was open to discuss possible alternate oaths.[161] Essentially, he was trying to engage those who had opposed his presidency by force of arms to begin a conversation with him that would lead to their renunciation of the Confederacy. While firmly wedded to his emancipation policy, he nonetheless knew that chickens must be hatched from delicately formed eggs. Balancing one desire to further black freedom with another to wean southern whites from secessionism, he merely suggested to Michael Hahn, the governor of the presidentially reconstructed state of Louisiana, that some blacks be allowed to vote under the new order.[162] Lincoln believed that a gradual local white acceptance of black civil rights, beginning with a small minority operating under his Ten Percent Plan, would be more effective than having both emancipation and black suffrage forced upon a defeated enemy. As long as the war raged, his approach had to appear somewhat reasonable to southern whites, whom he wanted to convince to quit the fight.[163] Accordingly, he pursued a policy designed to maximize what he regarded as latent white unionist sentiment in the South rather than fulfilling African American desires for immediate and full equality.

At the outset, Charles Sumner and other Radicals in Congress accepted Lincoln's Ten Percent Plan, as they liked its apparent prerequisite that emancipation be supported as part of the pledge of future loyalty.[164] But soon they were complaining about General Nathaniel Banks's policy of working with conservative Unionists in Louisiana rather than with local Radicals who were calling for black suffrage as part of any meaningful Reconstruction.[165] Ultimately, Lincoln clarified his conservative Louisiana policy with language that had come to characterize his approach to virtually all problems: "Concede that the new government of Louisiana is only to what it should be as the egg is to the fowl, we shall sooner have the fowl by hatching the egg than by smashing it."[166]

Republicans in Congress feared that if opportunities for reform were not grasped boldly, they might be lost forever. Land reform was one of their major concerns, which they knew that a conservative regime in Louisiana would never allow. Banks and Lincoln, at least for the time being, seemed willing to settle for African American labor contracts, which left freedmen landless and stuck in a "halfway house between slavery and freedom."[167] In early July 1864, Congress enacted the Wade-Davis bill, in a bold move to direct Reconstruction policy. The measure did not require black voting but insured that the entire Reconstruction process would be put on hold until 50 percent of a state's white voters pledged their future loyalty. In fact, this was not likely to occur until the war was over and the Confederacy was no more. However, as soon as that condition was met, and as soon as 10 percent of white voters could swear to past as well as future loyalty, then the latter cohort would be allowed to create a loyal state government, one more likely to be dominated by persons willing to enact radical reforms than the president's model, which was actively welcoming the inclusion of former rebels.[168] Lincoln pocket vetoed the measure on the grounds that he had had no time to study the issue closely and that he was as yet unprepared to commit to a fixed Reconstruction policy.[169] In point of fact, the president never did commit himself to any Reconstruction concept not closely tied to his short-term goal of persuading rebels to quit the fight.

Radicals in Congress temporarily exploded in anger over the president's refusal to accept congressional direction, but soon the politics of the presidential reelection campaign dampened their rage. While Lincoln had radical challengers to his office, none could muster sufficient support to prevent the president's renomination. With the alternatives of Lincoln or the Democratic candidate, Radicals swung into line behind their president, especially as the people at large were expressing dissatisfaction with high casualty rates and few victories to show for the profligate expenditure of Union lives and treasure.

By late August, a dejected Lincoln was convinced that George McClellan, his likely Democratic challenger, would be elected in November.[170] Believing that the Union cause, which included emancipation, was supported by Providence, Lincoln nonetheless was tempted to consider a ploy whereby he would portray himself to wavering voters as willing to abandon emancipation in exchange for a simple restoration of the Union. The plan was this: Lincoln would propose to Jefferson Davis a restoration of the Union without emancipation being a prerequisite, the assumption being that Davis would immediately reject the offer, as it called for an abandonment of southern independence. The idea was proposed as political propaganda to sway Democrats friendly to the war effort to back Lincoln rather than the Democratic candidate, who would be running on a peace platform calling for a negotiated settlement that would likely result in the survival of the Confederacy.[171] In the end, Lincoln rejected the idea, probably because it would have involved the appearance of betraying African Americans on a massive scale, which certainly would have impacted negatively upon both black enlistments and fighting spirit. Putting the plan into operation would also have probably led to a complete break between Lincoln and the Radicals, who were already in a sour mood over the demise of the Wade-Davis bill. Meanwhile, McClellan's backers exulted that Lincoln's political life was almost over and that "Old Abra'm" was "gliding over the dam."[172]

In tight moments before, Lincoln had left important decisions to Providence. Gideon Welles, Lincoln's secretary of the navy, wrote in his diary that following the Battle of Antietam, Lincoln had confessed to the entire cabinet that before the battle he had "made a vow, a covenant, that if God gave us the victory in the approaching battle, he would consider it an indication of Divine will, and that it was his duty to move forward in the cause of emancipation." Welles added that in the past the president "had in this way submitted the disposal of matters when the way was not clear to his mind what he should do."[173] Apparently, before the Battle of Gettysburg, a little over nine months later, Lincoln again left the war in God's hands, vowing to be emancipation's faithful instrument if a victory was granted.[174] As his letter to Albert G. Hodges amply revealed, Lincoln saw God pushing the war for a Divine purpose of emancipation.[175] Accordingly, Lincoln left the outcome of the presidential election, which all knew would determine the outcome of the war itself, in God's hands. In this moment of ultimate testing, he refused to compromise his emancipation policy for temporary political advantage. Deliverance quickly came in William T. Sherman's capture of Atlanta and in Phil Sheridan's successes in the Shenandoah Valley. With victories in the field, Lincoln's confidence returned, together with an even deeper certainty that he was God's holy instrument to complete a Providential design of African American emancipation, a conviction that was underwritten by a landslide victory at the polls in November.

Sherman's unobstructed march from Atlanta to the sea in late November put the Confederacy on notice that Lee's army was eventually to be crushed in a vice between Sherman's force moving northward from Savannah and Grant's Army of the Potomac holding Lee in place for a final engagement in Virginia. With the advantage of time completely on Lincoln's side, he lobbied House Democrats to join Republicans in completing the congressional role in the ratification of the Thirteenth Amendment, which called for the end of slavery nationwide. On January 31, 1865, with the help of presidential favors and promises of patronage, Lincoln's effort succeeded, and the antislavery amendment was sent on to the states for final approval.[176] Days later, Lincoln and Secretary of State Seward met with Confederate delegates to discuss conditions for peace. Attempting to engage these representatives in a discussion about the possibilities for a Confederate surrender, Lincoln made appearances of being willing to talk about a restoration of the Union without emancipation as a necessary prerequisite. Lincoln biographer David Donald concludes that this only revealed Lincoln playing a politics of misinformation with the enemy in preliminary discussions and not indicating any presidential change of policy. Even this ploy, however, did not succeed in getting these high-ranking officials to consider the possibility of renouncing southern independence.[177]

After nearly four years of war, Lincoln was desperate to break the Confederate will to resist by almost any means necessary. A week after his failed negotiations with Confederate leaders, Lincoln proposed to his cabinet that possibly an offer of compensated emancipation might end the southern resolve to continue the fighting.[178] He also schemed to manipulate the Confederate Virginia legislature to surrender independently, but that too came to naught.[179] On the eve of Lee's surrender at Appomattox, Lincoln was concerned lest the war conclude formally only to devolve rapidly into an ugly unending guerrilla struggle combining rebel obstinacy with simple banditry.[180] Accordingly, in the weeks leading to his Second Inaugural Address, which would define the nation as in the grasp of Divine purposes, Lincoln talked of the heightened need for "Christian Charity."[181] In this time of war's end, the clearest implication that Lincoln made about the shape of his future Reconstruction policy was that his administration would not engage in a peace of vengeance and retribution.[182]

During the last months of his life, Abraham Lincoln seemed overeager to win over his defeated foe by means of generous treatment. Nevertheless, he never forgot that justice for the freedmen was equally a necessary part of "charity for all." His overtures to the Confederates had never seriously considered abandoning African Americans on an altar of sectional reunification. At the time of his assassination on April 14, 1865, the requisite number of states had not yet ratified the Thirteenth Amendment, an event that would not occur until eight months later. In early 1865, emancipation as part of the Constitution was a probability but not yet a certainty. Given this ambiguity, Lincoln emphasized that he personally would never abandon the cause of emancipation. He conceded that the Thirteenth Amendment might yet be defeated. He acknowledged that even his wartime emancipation policy might someday be overturned. But he stated in unambiguous language that he personally would never collaborate with any such ignominious conclusion to the Civil War and would resign his office if necessary: "If the people should, by whatever mode or means, make it an Executive duty to re-enslave such persons," he told the nation in his last Annual Message of December 1864, "another, and not I, must be their instrument to perform it."[183]

While Lincoln often waxed eloquently about the sovereign will of the majority and a government of, by, and for the people, ultimately, in his own mind, he was not the people's agent. Instead, he was a determined but presumably humble instrument of a Divine will driving the United States to fulfill its original promise of being a harbinger of universal human rights. Lincoln's portrait painter, who observed the president frequently in 1864, later wrote of a visiting clergyman who told Lincoln that he hoped that God was on the Union side. Lincoln reportedly replied: "I know that the Lord is *always* on the side of *right*. But," he added, "it is my constant anxiety and prayer that I and this *nation* should be on the Lord's *side*."[184] This is what Lincoln possibly intended when he spontaneously injected into his delivery of the Gettysburg Address that the nation's "new birth of freedom" would necessarily have to be "under God."[185] Conformity to Divine purposes was Lincoln's lodestar. This understanding provided greater power to his own purposes than would have been possible without it, revealing a style of leadership that inspired millions and eventually led to his canonization in a national civil religion tightly connected to an emancipation struggle that continues to this day.[186]

SOME MAY DISAGREE with Dwight L. Dumond's estimate that the slaveholding republic ended with Lincoln's Emancipation Proclamation of January 1, 1863.[187] Even at the end of Lincoln's life a little over two years later, it was not yet a certainty that slavery would be permanently outlawed in the United States. Ratification of the Thirteenth Amendment at the end of 1865 might be a more appropriate ending date of the slaveholding republic. But who can legitimately claim that full emancipation occurred even then? Indeed, for some African Americans trapped in the ruts of intergenerational poverty, real emancipation has yet to occur, despite over a century of changing both the Constitution and federal and state statutes.

In writing about Reconstruction, many scholars have sought to find some central clue why that effort fell short of full emancipation. Some have focused upon the lack of any meaningful land reform in the southern states. Others have found in the flawed leadership of Andrew Johnson the key to lost opportunity. Still others fault the failure of most Republicans to persist in the quest of radical change. A few have blamed Republican leaders for pushing too quickly for radical change and, as a consequence, producing a popular reaction that stopped all progress. Yet, for all of these modern desires for a different outcome, there is another theme in the historical literature on Reconstruction that suggests that any effort to bring about a quick and significant improvement for the mass of freedmen was doomed from the outset, due to a deep and abiding white racial consciousness combined with a strong American preference for localized governmental decision making.

Disillusionment followed the first Reconstruction. By the end of the century, most white Americans concluded that the North had been right in insisting upon the death of formal slavery, but that subsequently the South was correct in refusing to accept African American equal citizenship.[188] An enduring racial prejudice ensured that the caste spirit of the slaveholding republic lived on into the new age. Yet the strength of the national vision that Lincoln had both articulated and partially implemented also remained intact, eventually to be employed again by reformers such as Martin Luther King, Jr. In the twentieth century, the modern civil rights movement marked a second American Reconstruction, but again partial successes bred a renewed disillusionment.

At the end of the Civil War, government leaders recognized an immediate need to secure the freedmen's new free status, but did not foresee that making African Americans special wards of the nation would be anything but a short-term commitment. One day before Lincoln's second inauguration, the Freedmen's Bureau was established for one year's duration.[189] The new agency, born of wartime experiments conducted under both the War and Treasury Departments, met the immediate needs of dislocated persons, both black and white. In addition to providing food, the Freedmen's Bureau set up schools and also promised land reform, but in the end this last-mentioned hope did not materialize, for land confiscated from rebels could only be withheld during the lifetime of the former owner. This meant that "loyal" heirs would eventually get it back.[190] Because of this fundamental weakness in the Confiscation Acts enacted during the war, creating any meaningful black ownership of farms was an unlikely prospect. Over time, Freedmen's Bureau agents concentrated more on working out labor contracts between freedmen and former slave owners than upon land reform.[191] As President Johnson's pardons relieved former rebels of even the temporary effects of the Confiscation Acts, all hope for land reform died. Congressional refusal to bring about any other result guaranteed inaction, despite the cry of Thaddeus Stevens for "40 acres and a mule."[192]

At first perceived as one who would be harsher on wealthy rebels than

Lincoln had been, Andrew Johnson indiscriminately granted presidential pardons, working toward a restoration of the South's old economic order.[193] Leading former Confederates quickly returned to their old roles in the South and assumed control over the presidentially reconstructed governments being erected by Johnson. Elected to state legislatures, they enacted Black Codes, modeled on the defunct Slave Codes that had long served to control the South's African American population. These laws amounted to gun-control laws for blacks only, alcohol prohibition for blacks only, and vagrancy laws for blacks only. African Americans were forbidden either to insult whites or to marry them. They were excluded from testifying in court or from bringing suits. Demeaning and severe punishments were reserved for them regarding crimes that were treated far more leniently when whites were the perpetrators. Overall, the Black Codes were designed to insure that black workers remained a powerless source of reliable plantation labor.[194] Observing the rapid restoration of their former enemies to economic and political supremacy, Republicans saw the need for corrective action.

Unreconstructed former rebels were elected to Congress but were not seated. Indeed, earlier Congresses had refused to let representatives of Lincoln's few reconstructed state governments take their chairs.[195] The reason for this was clear. With the end of slavery, freedmen suddenly counted fully for purposes of representation, whereas under slavery their numbers had been factored at three-fifths of their full strength. With this change, the defeated southern states increased in political power while they denied any political voice to the source of that increased representation.[196] Republicans, who had saved the Union, risked losing political control of it to a Democratic coalition in which those who had attempted to destroy the nation would have a leading voice. As southern state governments revealed their postwar attitudes in the Black Codes, Republicans resolved that they had to act to make meaningful both the saving of the Union and the destruction of slavery for which so many had died.

Coming back into session after an eight-month absence, the Republican Congress enacted both an extension of the Freedmen's Bureau's life and the nation's first civil rights bill, which was designed to nullify the state-based Black Codes.[197] The civil rights bill involved a new experience for the federal government—that of protecting individual civil liberties against the actions of state governments.[198] The Civil Rights Act of 1866 was based on the Thirteenth Amendment, which had become officially part of the Constitution at the end of 1865, yet some doubted that this was proper. The bill reversed the

Dred Scott decision, declaring that the freedmen were citizens and entitled to such rights as suing and testifying in court as well as exercising the property rights associated with citizenship. It demanded an end to racially discriminatory state laws, such as the Black Codes. To some, this inappropriately went beyond the narrow boundaries of the Thirteenth Amendment, which they claimed had been designed only to destroy the formal institution of slavery.[199]

When the Thirteenth Amendment was being drafted in 1864, Charles Sumner had advocated that its wording clearly authorize an assault on the effects of slavery that were sure to linger after the declaration of formal emancipation. Sumner's version would have read: "Everywhere within the limits of the United States, and of each State or Territory thereof, all persons are equal before the law, so that no person can hold another as a slave."[200] This language suggested that any status below a full equality before the law constituted a form of partial slavery. In the end, Congress approved a more ambiguous instrument. The Thirteenth Amendment as passed focused only on obliterating slavery, saying nothing about equality before the law, but allowing Congress to enforce the ban against slavery by means of "appropriate legislation." The new Freedmen's Bureau Act and the Civil Rights Act of 1866, both passed over President Johnson's veto, became law, but the lingering doubts surrounding the ability of one or both of them to survive a constitutional challenge motivated Congress to draft a new constitutional amendment that would clearly cover such legislation.[201] This effort, which eventually became the Fourteenth Amendment, was to have far-reaching consequences.

On its face, the new amendment, which was proposed in 1866 and became part of the Constitution two years later, provided the federal government with an unambiguous power to protect individuals' civil rights from inappropriate state authority.[202] But eventually this new language would be used by Reconstruction's enemies to find much subsequent congressional Reconstruction legislation unconstitutional. Under the Fourteenth Amendment's authority, Congress would later pass acts forbidding private individuals from engaging in racially discriminatory behavior. The federal courts later struck these down as beyond the limits of the Fourteenth Amendment. Additionally, as soon as the Fourteenth Amendment was added to the Constitution, the most restrictive interpretation of the Thirteenth Amendment possible was informally validated.[203]

One cannot deny that the Fourteenth Amendment is a most powerful constitutional instrument. Indeed, it has worked a constitutional revolution in this century. It has been used to void multiple expressions of state police power attempting to curb sexual and reproductive behaviors. The application of the first nine amendments to the states through an expansive interpretation of the due process clause of the Fourteenth Amendment covers a gamut of additional issues in law enforcement procedures, church and state concerns, and state regulation of speech and public assembly, among other matters. It has made the Bill of Rights a living reality for the people as never before. However, as a weapon against the residual habits of a slaveholding culture, it is not as unlimited as the latent power of the Thirteenth Amendment that was effectively erased by the adoption of the Fourteenth Amendment.[204]

Reconstruction Republicans used the Thirteenth and Fourteenth Amendments to undo wrongs initiated at state and local levels. As such, they were primarily reactive tools. Leaders such as Frederick Douglass called for black manhood suffrage, a reform that could prevent the enactment of discriminatory state laws in the first place.[205] With the Black Codes under seige by Freedmen's Bureau agents, the bulk of Reconstruction Republicans became convinced that African American voting power was needed to preserve the principles for which the war had been fought. This realization was slow in coming. Lincoln had toyed with the idea of black veterans and educated blacks enjoying the suffrage, but he had never insisted on it. In the language of the Fourteenth Amendment's second section, the South had been warned that, if African American men were not allowed to vote, southern political representation in the House of Representatives and electoral power in presidential contests would be trimmed—a threat that has never been enforced.[206] The first definite move to insist upon African American voting occurred in the First Reconstruction Act of March 2, 1867, in which Congress formally took the direction of Reconstruction away from the president.[207]

Throughout American history, a heritage of local control over most matters has bred a deep suspicion of federal power. In the slaveholding republic, southerners viewed any hint of federal interference with their peculiar institution with a most watchful eye. At the same time, northerners opposed federal intrusions to protect slavery, such as those authorized by the Fugitive Slave Act of 1850. This preference for local decision making had not wholly been formed by concerns surrounding slavery, but it was not separate from slavery's political influence either. In any case, most northern Republicans wanted this tradition of local control to survive the centralizing forces spawned by the Civil War. African American voting held the promise that this might be achieved while at the same time safeguarding the civil liberties of the freedmen. If the bulk of southern blacks and at least a minority of southern whites formed political coalitions that resulted in state governments pledged to equality under the law, then the federal government's involvement as a guarantor of black civil rights could be minimized.[208] Even Robert J. Kaczorowski, who has emphasized that the new constitutional amendments provided for the creation of a unitary national government and the virtual obliteration of state sovereignty, admits that during Reconstruction, the federal government had neither the tradition, the resources, nor the will to take on the new function of serving as the national guarantor of civil rights.[209] For this reason, Radicals hoped that black voting might enable social justice to be accomplished at the local level.

Following a brief period of Congressional Reconstruction, during which ten southern state conventions were created to draft new state constitutions providing for African American voting on an equal par with whites, Congress approved of the new constitutions and then seated the representatives elected to Congress from these states. By 1870, the process was complete and direct federal control of Reconstruction was ostensibly over. After that time, Congress expected the southern states to manage their own affairs, hopefully with only minimal federal interference. At the outset, every reconstructed state except for Virginia elected a Republican government backed by a coalition of African Americans and whites.[210] In 1870, the Fifteenth Amendment was added to the Constitution, insuring that the suffrage that had been granted African Americans during the state-reforming processes of Congressional Reconstruction would never be denied on racial grounds. However, obvious loopholes in the amendment did provide for a later disfranchisement upon nonracial grounds, such as illiteracy, a fact that urged these new southern state governments to adopt new public education systems as a high priority.[211] These new educational systems took over where the Freedmen's Bureau schools left off, as that agency went out of existence at about the same moment.[212]

Unfortunately, the experiment in a locally based Reconstruction did not go well. First, southerners priding themselves as "unreconstructed rebels" formed the secretive and infamous Ku Klux Klan that intimidated Republican voters and disrupted the new public schools with acts of terrorism.[213] Within the Republican interracial coalitions, additional trouble festered. African Americans complained that they typically provided the voting strength of the party but received only a minority of the nominations for office. Over time, as black politicians became more assertive for what they regarded as their fair share of the offices, southern whites participating in the coalition fell away, being unwilling to continue bearing the wrath of their fellow whites under the new circumstances.[214] Political corruption, often surrounding the new expensive public school systems, also worked to give these struggling Republican coalitions a bad reputation not only in the South but in northern Republican circles as well. The new Republican-run federal Bureau of Education systematically reported news regarding these southern school systems that revealed that often school administrators could not account for funds put in their trust, that illiterate teachers were valued more for their skill in getting out the black vote than as teachers, and that more southern school systems collapsed from internal malfeasance than through Klan violence.[215]

Congress stepped in to battle Klan terrorism, passing three Enforcement Acts in 1870–71.[216] These efforts superficially succeeded, breaking up the Klan as a formal organization. However, the "unreconstructed-rebel" spirit lived on, appearing in new white-supremacist organizations that were not specifically outlawed by congressional statute. With white southern hostility unabated, a split in northern Republican ranks indicated future trouble. In 1872, those Republicans who could not justify the mounting evidence of southern Republican corruption, nor tolerate that associated with the national administration of President Ulysses S. Grant, openly disapproved of federal intervention in southern local affairs. These complainers joined the Liberal Republican movement. While failing to topple Grant, the Liberal Republicans did reveal a crack in the armor of Reconstruction Republicans that Democrats eagerly exploited.[217]

In 1873, the onslaught of the nation's worst depression up to that time worked to deprive the federal government of needed revenue just at the time that it was expanding its operations to enforce national civil-rights legislation in the southern states.[218] Running out of funds, the Reconstruction Republicans backed off of both federal expansion into the judicial affairs of the South and plans to institute federal aid to southern public education.[219] Charles Sumner, however, refused to retreat. He insisted that Reconstruction not end until federally mandated racial integration made full equality before the law a reality. Public accommodations reserved solely for whites, together with racially segregated public schools, represented to the Republican senator the lingering effects of slavery. On his deathbed in 1874, he pleaded with old friends to see this culminating reform through to completion. For years, Sumner had been trying to persuade his colleagues to enact his Supplementary Civil Rights Bill to fulfill these purposes, but they had sensed political

danger and denied him the votes needed for passage. An outpouring of sentiment immediately following his death succeeded where he had failed in life.
On May 23, 1874, the Republican Senate passed the bill and sent it to the
Republican House, which refused to enact the measure as every Republican
House seat was at risk in the upcoming congressional elections, then just a
few months away. Only one-third of the Senate seats were on the line,
accounting for the greater courage in that body. Democrats were overjoyed at
this Republican identification with "racial amalgamation" and looked forward to victory in the fall.[220]

Historians disagree about the impact that this political association of racial
integration with the Republican party had in determining the Democratic
party landslide.[221] In any case, the Republican loss of the House in the fall
elections determined the end of Reconstruction. At the midnight hour of the
lame-duck Reconstruction Congress, just before it passed from existence, it enacted the Civil Rights Act of 1875, which was Sumner's Supplementary Civil
Rights Act with the requirement for racially integrated schools removed to
make it less offensive to whites.[222] From then on, because of a divided Congress, the Republicans could pass no new civil rights legislation. However, the
Senate and the president were still in Republican hands. With white terrorism
rampant in Louisiana threatening to topple the Republican state government
there, President Grant initiated his last bold Reconstruction stand immediately
before the enactment of the new Civil Rights Act. Grant ordered the U.S.
Army to act as a federal police force in Louisiana to restore public order and
preserve, at least temporarily, one southern Republican state government.[223]

One by one, throughout the mid-1870s, southern Republican governments were defeated at the polls. Several factors were involved. One was the
demoralizing guerrilla warfare of white supremacists who moderated their
tactics to fit each situation; sometimes outright violence on a mass scale was
used, as in the Colfax Massacre in Louisiana in 1873, when a white posse
killed approximately 100 African Americans, mutilating their bodies afterward to terrorize blacks in the vicinity.[224] Mississippi whites refined the arts
of intimidation, which they touted as the "Mississippi Plan," which, together
with applications of outright violence, succeeded in "redeeming" that state to
white supremacy and Democratic party rule in 1875.[225] However, "redemption" succeeded for more reasons than white threats and guerrilla attacks. The
southern-white minority that had voted Republican left the party not only
because of the increasing African American insistence on more offices, but
also because of the indelible Republican identification with integrated public

education following the Senate's passage of the Sumner bill in 1874. In eastern Tennessee, where Unionist sentiment ran strong throughout the Civil War and where white Republicans abounded during the early days of Reconstruction, the "mixed-schools" proposal created a white exodus from the Republican party that could not be reversed.[226] By 1876, only three Republican state governments remained in the South, and everyone sensed that they could not long be maintained.

Rutherford B. Hayes has received much blame for abandoning southern blacks in the so-called Compromise of 1877 that followed the contested election results in the presidential election of 1876. But far more than one man's opinion determined this result. In the presidential campaign of 1876, even a blatant anti-Catholic Republican strategy designed to appeal to the strong prejudices of the national Protestant majority proved unable to counterbalance the public's disinclination to continue the cause of black liberation.[227] By 1877, Reconstruction was all but dead. Democrats still controlled the house and in addition claimed to deserve the presidency. Hayes did well to insist upon promises from "redemption" leaders such as South Carolina's Wade Hampton that state public education programs for blacks would be maintained. Thereupon, Hayes ordered the U.S. Army to cease protecting the few remaining Republican regimes, which in any case could not even collect local taxes to survive in any self-sustaining way.[228] The true determining agents in this tragedy were the northern voters themselves. They simply tired of the commitment to bring about a meaningful emancipation, and by 1877 they refused to sustain any government dedicated to that end.

Many historians sympathetically explain the northern attitude that eventually led to Reconstruction's end. "The amount of intervention that was needed to sustain [the collapsing Reconstruction governments] did appear to be boundless," Michael Perman has written. "Nothing ever was enough; more action, it seemed, was always needed."[229] Unwilling to create a permanent national police force and court system capable of handling the problem, Reconstruction Republicans had put their faith in state governments elected by means of African American voting strength. And that foundation was not sufficient to last. Both Professors Perman and Richard H. Abbott emphasize the difficulties involved in maintaining a biracial party in the South at that time.[230] Jeffrey Rogers Hummel emphasizes that weak African American community organization and economic dependence on whites undermined any sustained Reconstruction effort based in the southern states themselves.[231] Similarly, James M. McPherson notes the justifiable distrust of the kind of military intervention that President Grant attempted in Louisiana in 1875.[232] Carl Schurz, who had started the postwar experiment as a Radical, became a Liberal Republican by 1872, and openly expressed his fear of the kind of autocratic centralism under the name of "Reconstruction" that he had known in the Germany of his youth.[233]

During the existence of the slaveholding republic, a proslavery gloss had reconstituted the original Constitution into William Lloyd Garrison's "covenant with death." In the North's retreat from Reconstruction, a similar process began to interpret the Reconstruction amendments so that they significantly minimized Lincoln's foretold "new birth of freedom." The United States Supreme Court, which in the Dred Scott decision two decades before had failed to finalize the constitutionalization of the slaveholding republic, succeeded in a "constitutional counterrevolution" dismantling Reconstruction.[234] While some scholars, led by Michael Les Benedict, have claimed that the Court decisions involved were true to the intent of the Reconstruction amendments' framers, most have agreed with Robert J. Kaczorowski that the Supreme Court opportunistically exploited white racism and the popular disillusionment with Reconstruction to restrict the meaning of the amendments in ways not intended by the framers.[235] Specifically, the Court ruled that the Fourteenth Amendment could not be used to justify federal legislation aimed at private acts of racial discrimination and that the Thirteenth Amendment was scarcely more than an historical artifact tied to the death of formal slavery in 1865.[236] The Court emphasized the loopholes in the Fifteenth Amendment and defined the accompanying clauses of each of the three Reconstruction amendments authorizing Congress to pass "appropriate legislation" as restrictive rather than opportunities for expanded meanings.[237] By the end of the century, the Fourteenth Amendment had been transformed by judicial interpretation into more of a protector of the property rights of railroad corporations than the civil rights of African Americans.[238]

In the *Civil Rights Cases* (1883) decision, which voided the Civil Rights Act of 1875, the Court spelled out the distinct limits of the antislavery republic. Justice Joseph P. Bradley's majority opinion stated it was foolish for African Americans to expect federal legislation "abolishing all badges and incidents of slavery in the United States." The Reconstruction Amendments as interpreted in 1883 gave Congress only the authority to "vindicate those fundamental rights which appertain to the essence of citizenship, and the enjoyment or deprivation of which constitutes the essential distinction between freedom and slavery."[239] Ten years before, in a case ostensibly having nothing to do with African Americans, the Court had severely limited the rights of national citizenship, thereby potentially minimizing "the essential distinction between freedom and slavery" for a hated minority whose civil liberties were left unprotected by state and local decisions.[240] Private acts of racial discrimination, stated Bradley's opinion in 1883, had "nothing to do with slavery or involuntary servitude."[241] Only under the aegis of state police powers, he suggested, could such acts be punished, but that was up to each state to decide and not a matter of concern for the federal government. Bradley continued: "When a man has emerged from slavery, . . . there must be some stage in the progress of his elevation when he takes the rank of a mere citizen, and ceases to be the special favorite of the laws."[242]

The antislavery republic had eliminated private ownership in human beings. Slaves could no longer be found in the nation's capital. American foreign relations were no longer strained to protect that particular past economic interest. Interstate relations were no longer kept in tension by quarreling over fugitive slaves. And the worry of slavery expanding into new federal territories had become only a fading memory. The Republican Revolution had succeeded in eliminating all of these past concerns. But after an experiment with reconstructing America's racial relationships, it was decided, first by the voters and later by their leaders, that it would be foolish to advance the condition of the freedmen beyond what the absolute minimum definitions of freedom required.

11

CONCLUSION

SHORTLY AFTER THE Supreme Court handed down the *Civil Rights Cases* in 1883, a mass meeting was called for Lincoln Hall in the nation's capital. Two prominent Republican orators—one black and one white—were the featured speakers. Frederick Douglass—the runaway slave who had become an avid student of the Constitution in the course of his career as an abolitionist—spoke first. Robert G. Ingersoll—highly valued as a Republican orator despite his outspoken atheist views—closed the program. In some ways, the event was a political rally, similar to others that had characterized both the long battle against slavery and the heady early days of Reconstruction. But this day was different, for everyone present in the hall named for the nation's "Great Emancipator" knew that it marked the end of an era—and not a satisfying conclusion at that. It was a wake without any happy accompanying festivities.

Douglass sensed that new life would not quickly follow that being mourned. Resigned that a renewal of racial progress would occur only long after his lifetime, he urged his hearers to not react out of understandable anger. He specifically cautioned against violence. "Patient reform is better than violent revolution," Douglass said, sounding very much as he had in Glasgow when he had distanced himself from John Brown in the winter of 1859–60.[1] But in that prior event, he had been optimistic and looking forward to the election of an antislavery president. Progress had then been anticipated. Working within the constitutional system then promised that slavery itself might be destroyed. By contrast, in 1883, Douglass saw no grounds for immediate optimism, but still cautioned against any action that might produce an even greater defeat than the one represented in the Court's decision. Ingersoll too urged his hearers to remain law-abiding and work for peaceful change.[2] The fact that both men stressed this point indicated a fear that some might respond to the Court's action in unpredictable ways.

Charles Fairman has analyzed intersectional white newspaper support of the decision and has found that it was overwhelming. Some of the editorial commentary from Republican papers expressed in words the tremendous obstacle that Douglass sensed confronted his race at the close of the nation's first civil rights struggle. The *New York Tribune* suggested that the voided Civil Rights Act of 1875 that had required equal access to public accommodations such as railroad cars, theaters, hotels, and amusement parks had only served "to irritate public feeling." The *Portland Oregonian* offered that nothing was really lost as "social rights" can never be legislated—an opinion seconded by the *Milwaukee Sentinel*. The *Chicago Tribune* advised that "time and better education," not civil rights legislation, was the most effective way to fight racial prejudice, which it naively predicted would be eliminated in a generation.[3] Perhaps worst of all, the recorded private thoughts of Justice Joseph Bradley, who delivered the Court's majority opinion in the case, indicated that he viewed legislation requiring racial integration, such as that required in the Civil Rights Act of 1875, as a form of "slavery."[4]

The Court's decision was no Dred Scott decision that could rally Republicans in popular opposition. To the contrary, a white Republican Supreme Court had relieved an interracial party of responsibility for civil rights legislation that lacked the support of an intersectional majority. "This decision takes from seven millions of people the shield of the Constitution," said Ingersoll, speaking for the minority of white Republicans angered by the Court's action. "It leaves the best of the colored race at the mercy of the meanest white."[5] Both Douglass and Ingersoll grieved that most whites refused to admit that there was an injustice involved. Douglass articulated that the decision was in favor of "slavery, caste and oppression."[6] He confessed to feeling as he had when the Court in 1857 had handed down the Dred Scott decision, making this comparison in order to emphasize the continuing "conflict between the spirit of liberty and the spirit of slavery."[7] The slaveholding republic, he conceded, was gone. But "the spirit or power of slavery" lived on.[8]

In slavery times, Douglass emphasized, the Court had strongly supported slavery, manipulating the Constitution in order to protect the institution in ways never intended by the Founding Fathers. Yet following the formal death of slavery, the Court was only lukewarm for liberty. He looked forward to a time when "a Supreme Court of the United States . . . shall be as true to the claims of humanity, as the Supreme Court formerly was to the demands of slavery."[9] He recalled how the Court had upheld the Fugitive Slave Act of 1850, which was blatantly unconstitutional given its casual disregard of the Bill of Rights. In that case, the Court had concocted an original intent of the Constitution's fugitive slave clause, without any evidence to support its claim. Yet, in the *Civil Rights Cases*, the Court clearly ignored the well-documented intent of the authors of the Thirteenth and Fourteenth Amendments. In a case involving freedom, the Court's decision absolved the states from dedicating themselves to a national standard, whereas in a case involving fugitive slaves the outcome had been otherwise.[10]

The United States did not deserve to be called a nation, charged Douglass, for under the state-centered interpretation of the Court the federal government was incapable of protecting "the rights of its own citizens upon its own soil."[11] Why had this decision been made? The answer to him was clear. White Americans did not identify with the daily oppression experienced by black people in a land dominated by white people. When white men observed a hotel clerk refusing lodging to black female travelers, they did not see such treatment as equivalent to their own wives and daughters being abused in a similar manner. Big trouble loomed, he warned, if common decency continued to be so casually discarded. Sounding as Lincoln had in his Second Inaugural, Douglass suggested: "No man can put a chain about the ankle of his fellow man, without at last finding the other end of it fastened about his own neck. . . . The evil day may be long delayed, but so sure as there is a moral government of the universe, so sure will the harvest of evil come."[12]

In his time at the lectern, Ingersoll emphasized that the Court's decision invited whites to inflict "involuntary servitude" upon blacks. This, he said, had been outlawed by the Thirteenth Amendment, which partially supported the Civil Rights Act of 1875. "A man is in a state of involuntary servitude," he noted, "when he is forced to do, or prevented from doing, a thing, not by the law of the State, but by the simple will of another."[13] By this interpretation, every refusal of service by a person involved in running a public accommodation constituted an act of "involuntary servitude." His argument necessarily ignored the reality that the enactment of the Fourteenth Amendment had encouraged a far more restricted meaning for the Thirteenth Amendment than he presented. In any case, the audience left Lincoln Hall at the conclusion of the meeting with no assurances of any coherent plan to reverse the Court's ruling.

IRONICALLY, THE *Civil Rights Cases* produced one apparent benefit by assuring white southern politicians that they had nothing to fear from Republican Henry Blair's plan to enact federal aid for the improvement of impoverished southern public-school systems, black as well as white. By weakening the federal government's ability to direct and oversee issues of racial equity, the Court's decision persuaded many state-centered southern Democrats that no good reason existed for them to oppose the Blair bill. Indeed, after the decision, some of Blair's closest allies came from the ranks of southern Democrats. Nevertheless, the leadership of the Democratic party in the house remained firmly in opposition and managed to kill Blair's proposals throughout the 1880s.[14]

Finally, in 1888, the Republican party acquired majorities in both houses of Congress and won the presidency as well. The divided government, which had ushered in the end of Reconstruction, gave way to Republican control. Yet, nothing was done to ameliorate the wretched condition of most African Americans, suffering in an environment of quasi slavery. In 1890, when the Blair bill failed to pass, it was clear that the failure was due to northern Republican apathy.[15] Former president Rutherford B. Hayes, who had presided over the formal end of Reconstruction but had thereafter committed himself to the cause of African American education in the southern states, was crushed by his party's behavior. Calling others devoted to the cause to meet with him at Lake Mohonk in Ulster County, New York, Hayes tried to set a tone that would inspire at least this minority to work for social change despite the Republican Congress's clear lack of interest. Hayes emphasized white America's obligation to the freedmen: "We are responsible for their presence and condition on this continent. Having deprived them of their labor, liberty, and manhood, and grown rich and strong while doing it, we have no excuse for neglecting them. . . . In truth, their welfare and ours, if not one and the same, are inseparable. These millions who have been so cruelly degraded must be lifted up, or we ourselves will be dragged down."[16] Hayes's appeal was too late. That same year, in addition to killing the Blair bill, the Republican Congress failed to pass Henry Cabot Lodge's proposal to force the South to conduct honest elections. Mississippians interpreted these two actions as Republican encouragement to treat the "Negro question" any way they saw fit. Beginning in a convention writing a new state constitution, they

fashioned a program both to disfranchise African Americans and to re
even the scanty educational opportunities then available to blacks.[17] Over
the next several years, the rest of the South moved in the same direction.[18]

In 1890, and for many years thereafter, whites concentrated on deepening the degradation of African Americans rather than engaging in any
program of assistance. At the outset of the twentieth century, lynching blacks
at times seemed to become a blood sport in parts of the nation.[19] Whites
often justified exceptional cruelty toward blacks with pseudoscientific proofs
that African Americans were permanently "unassimilable."[20] In the first generation experiencing it, formal emancipation did not produce a meaningful
freedom for most former slaves. One hundred years later, much has changed;
but in spite of significant progress, race relations remain in a state of unease
and mutual distrust, punctuated by occasional outbursts of mass violence and
daily incidents of ugly individual confrontation. To this day, aspects of the
slaveholding republic's legacy remain, both in whites unable to fathom the
depth of African American grievances and in blacks deeply alienated by a
long history of oppression. The bitter harvest, referred to both in Abraham
Lincoln's Second Inaugural Address of 1865 and in Frederick Douglass's well-
reasoned forecast of 1883, unhappily promises to continue well into the
future.

NOTES

CHAPTER 1

1. *HR*, 19 Cong., 1 sess., No. 58 and No. 146 (Serial 141); 20 Cong., 1 sess., No. 27 (Serial 176).

2. *RD*, 20 Cong., 1 sess., 899–901.

3. Ibid., 905.

4. Ibid., 1475–76. For condemnation of slavery by southern participants in the debate, see 907, 974, 991, 1093.

5. Ibid., 907.

6. Ibid., 1062–63.

7. Ibid., 1050–51.

8. Ibid., 910, 920–21.

9. Ibid., 920–21.

10. Ibid., 974–75; William W. Freehling, *Prelude to Civil War: The Nullification Controversy in South Carolina, 1816–1836* (New York: Harper & Row, 1966), 134–35.

11. *RD*, 20 Cong., 1 sess., 1058.

12. Ibid., 913.

13. Ibid., 919.

14. Ibid., 1108.

15. Ibid., 1017, 1020.

16. Ibid., 1479.

17. Ibid., 904–5, 984–85, 1082; Hunter Miller, *Treaties and Other International Acts of the United States of America*, vol. II (Washington, D.C.: Government Printing Office, 1931), 99–100, 575.

18. *RD*, 20 Cong., 1 sess., 974, 1017–18. The act referred to was that of July 22, 1813, but Congress had actually imposed a direct tax on slaves as early as 1798. *SAL*, I: 598; ibid., III:26.

19. *RD*, 20 Cong., 1 sess., 1016–17. Section 34 of the act of September 24, 1789, declared: "The laws of the several states, except where the constitution, treaties or statutes of the United States shall otherwise require or provide, shall be regarded as rules of decision in trials at common law in the courts of the United States in cases where they apply." *SAL*, I: 92.

20. See, for example, *RD*, 20 Cong., 1 sess., 912, 919.

21. Ibid., 1110–11.

22. Ibid., 1114–15.

23. Ibid., 1011.

24. Freehling, *Prelude to Civil War*, 135–36.

25. *RD*, 20 Cong., 1 sess. 1122. The amendment, first offered and then withdrawn by Livingston, was subsequently renewed by another Louisiana congressman, Henry H. Gurley. Ibid., 900, 989, 1048.

26. Ibid., 1459–62.

27. Ibid., 1486.

28. *SAL*, VI:411.

29. *HR*, 30 Cong., 1 sess., No. 187 (Serial 524), 1–3; Virginia Bergman Peters, *The*

Florida Wars (Hamden, Conn.: Archon Books, 1979), 105–7; John K. Mahon, *History of the Second Seminole War, 1835–1842* (Gainesville: University of Florida Press, 1967), 104–6; Frank Laumer, *Massacre!* (Gainesville: University of Florida Press, 1968); Kenneth W. Porter, "Three Fighters for Freedom," *JNH* 28 (1943): 65–72.

30. *HR*, 30 Cong., 1 sess., No. 187 (Serial 524). The quoted words are from pp. 4 and 24.

31. *CG*, 30 Cong., 2 sess., 173, 249.

32. Ibid., 177, 187.

33. Ibid., 39, 84.

34. Charles M. Wiltse, *John C. Calhoun, Sectionalist, 1840–1850* (Indianapolis: Bobbs-Merrill Co., 1951), 378–85.

35. *CG*, 30 Cong., 2 sess., 216.

36. Ibid., 303.

37. *SR*, 30 Cong., 2 sess., No. 282 (Serial 535).

38. William M. Wiecek, *The Sources of Antislavery Constitutionalism in America, 1760–1848* (Ithaca, N.Y.: Cornell University Press, 1977), 15–16.

39. *RD*, 20 Cong., 1 sess., 975.

40. Ibid., 921.

41. See, for example, Robert J. Turnbull, *The Crisis, or Essays on the Usurpations of the Federal Government* (Charleston, S.C.: A. E. Miller, printer, 1827), 131; Thomas Cooper to James Hammond, January 8, 1836, James Hammond Papers, Manuscript Division, Library of Congress.

42. *CG*, 30 Cong., 2 sess., 247.

43. *AC*, 6 Cong., 1 sess., 231; *Dred Scott v. John F. A. Sandford*, 19 Howard 451–52.

44. *RD*, 20 Cong., 1 sess., 1060.

45. For example, John M. Berrien to Charles J. Jenkins, December 10, 1849, John M. Berrien Papers, Southern Historical Collection, University of North Carolina, Chapel Hill. See also J. H. Thornwell, *State of the Country* (Columbia, S.C.: Southern Guardian Press, 1861), 13–14.

46. *CG*, 28 Cong., 2 sess., 88. See the comment by Hannibal Hamlin of Maine, ibid., App., 376.

47. Robert Toombs, "Slavery: Its Constitutional Status, and Its Influence on Society and the Colored Race," *De Bow's Review* 20 (1856): 581.

48. The amendment approved by Congress in 1861 and subsequently ratified by three states read as follows: "No amendment shall be made to the Constitution which will authorize or give to Congress the power to abolish or interfere, within any State, with the domestic institutions thereof, including that of persons held to labor or service by the laws of said State." Herman V. Ames, *The Proposed Amendments to the Constitution of the United States During the First Century of Its History*, vol. II of *Annual Report of the American Historical Association for the Year 1896* (Washington, D.C.: Government Printing Office, 1897), 196.

49. *Charleston Courier*, January 7, 1850. J. Thomas Scharf, *History of Maryland from the Earliest Period to the Present Day*, 3 vols. (1879; Hatboro, Penn.: Tradition Press, 1967), facsimile, III: 240. Similarly, Senator Henry S. Foote of Mississippi declared in 1849 that the "sacred provisions" of the Constitution guaranteed "per-

petual protection to slavery against all foes, either foreign or domestic." *CG*, 31 Cong., 1 sess., 54.

50. *Boston Liberator*, February 3, 1843.

51. Marshall's speech, presented in Hawaii on May 6, 1987, to a seminar of the San Francisco Patent and Trademark Law Association, was widely reported in the press. The complete text is in *Howard Law Journal* 30 (1987): 915–20.

52. William M. Wiecek, "'The Blessings of Liberty': Slavery in the American Constitutional Order," in *Slavery and Its Consequences: The Constitution, Equality, and Race*, ed. Robert A. Goldwin and Art Kaufman (Washington, D.C.: American Enterprise Institute, 1988), 32.

53. Avern Cohn's letter of October 24, published in the *New York Times*, November 11, 1986, p. 24.

54. J. Clay Smith, Jr., "Toward a Pure Legal Existence: Blacks and the Constitution," *Howard Law Journal* 30 (1987): 925; Clarence R. Lawrence III: "Promises to Keep: We Are the Constitution's Framers," ibid., 942.

55. Manning Marable, "The Racial Contours of the Constitution," *Howard Law Journal* 30 (1987): 953.

56. Thurgood Marshall, "The Constitution: A Living Document," *Howard Law Journal* 30 (1987): 918; Vincent Harding, *There Is a River: The Black Struggle for Freedom in America* (New York: Harcourt Brace Jovanovich, 1981), 46; Donald L. Robinson, *Slavery in the Structure of American Politics, 1765–1820* (New York: Harcourt Brace Jovanovich, 1971), 247; John Hope Franklin, *From Slavery to Freedom*, 5th ed. (New York: Alfred A. Knopf, 1980), 96.

57. Wendell Phillips, *The Constitution a Pro-Slavery Document, or Selections from the Madison Papers, etc.* (New York: American Anti-Slavery Society, 1844), 4–5.

58. Herbert Aptheker, ed., *A Documentary History of the Negro People in the United States*, 3 vols. (New York: Citadel Press, 1964), I: 318.

CHAPTER 2

1. Fred Shelley, ed., "Ebenezer Hazard's Travels through Maryland in 1777," *Maryland Historical Magazine* 44 (1951): 50.

2. *JCC*, I:77.

3. *JCC*, IV:258.

4. W. E. Burghardt Du Bois, *The Suppression of the African Slave Trade to the United States of America, 1638–1870* (New York: Longmans Green & Co., 1896), 46–47. According to John Drayton, *Memoirs of the American Revolution . . .*, 2 vols. (Charleston, S.C.: A. E. Miller, printer, 1821), I:181, the association was "punctually complied with" in South Carolina. He adds on p. 182 that "a cargo of near three hundred slaves, was sent out of the Colony by the consignee; as being interdicted by the second article of the association."

5. Julian P. Boyd, et al., eds., *The Papers of Thomas Jefferson*, 27 vols. to date (Princeton, N.J.: Princeton University Press, 1950–97), I: 317–18.

6. Ibid., 314–15. Jefferson's explanation of the deletion was written no later than 1783 and most probably in the late summer or autumn of 1776. See ibid., 304, 308.

7. For example, Merrill D. Peterson, *Thomas Jefferson and the New Nation: A Biography* (New York: Oxford University Press, 1970), 91–92.

8. See, for example, the statements of Chief Justice Roger B. Taney in *Dred Scott v. John F. A. Sandford*, 19 Howard 409–10 (1857); and of Stephen A. Douglas, during his debates with Abraham Lincoln, in *CWAL*, III:113, 177–78, 216, 296.

9. *JCC*, XXV: 660; XXVI: 13–14. The members of the committee making the recommendation were David Howell of Rhode Island, Arthur Lee of Virginia, and Samuel Osgood of Massachusetts.

10. Du Bois, *Suppression*, 50–51; *AC*, 1 Cong., 2 sess., 1183.

11. Du Bois, *Suppression*, 51–52, 224–29; Elizabeth Donnan, "The New England Slave Trade After the Revolution," *New England Quarterly* 3 (1930): 252–54.

12. Paul H. Smith, ed., *Letters of Delegates to Congress, 1774–1789*, 17 vols. to date (Washington, D.C.: Library of Congress, 1976–91), VII:308–9.

13. Smith, ed., *Letters of Delegates*, V:11.

14. Benjamin Quarles, *The Negro in the American Revolution* (Chapel Hill: University of North Carolina Press, 1961), 10–11, 15; Pete Maslowski, "National Policy Toward the Use of Black Troops in the Revolution," *South Carolina Historical Magazine* 73 (1972): 2–3.

15. "Diary of Richard Smith in the Continental Congress, 1775–1776," *AHR* 1 (1895–96): 292; *JCC*, III:265, 266; Maslowski, "Use of Black Troops," 3–4.

16. See the general order of December 30, and Washington to John Hancock (president of Congress), December 31, 1775, in W. W. Abbot et al., eds., *The Papers of George Washington*, Revolutionary War Ser., 7 vols. to date (Charlottesville: University Press of Virginia, 1985–97), II: 620–23; Maslowski, "Use of Black Troops," 4–5.

17. *JCC*, IV:60.

18. Quarles, *Negro in the American Revolution*, 16–18, 51–60; Lorenzo L. Greene, "Some Observations on the Black Regiment of Rhode Island in the American Revolution," *JNH* 37 (1952): 142–56.

19. Smith, ed., *Letters of Delegates*, X:602–4.

20. *JCC*, XIII:385–88; Maslowski, "Use of Black Troops," 6–11; Gregory D. Massey, "The Limits of Antislavery Thought in the Revolutionary Lower South: John Laurens and Henry Laurens," *JSH* 63 (1997): 509–25.

21. Maryland was the only southern state to authorize the enlistment of slaves. In Virginia and elsewhere, slaves were sometimes surreptitiously enrolled as substitutes for their masters, and the use of slaves as military laborers was common throughout the South. Quarles, *Negro in the American Revolution*, 56–58, 98–105, 183; L. P. Jackson, "Virginia Negro Soldiers and Seamen in the American Revolution," *JNH* 27 (1942): 251, 253–55.

22. Christopher Gadsden to Samuel Adams, July 6, 1779, in Richard Walsh, ed., *The Writings of Christopher Gadsden, 1746–1805* (Columbia: University of South Carolina Press, 1966), 166; Maslowski, "Use of Black Troops," 12.

23. Washington to Henry Laurens, March 20, 1779, in John C. Fitzpatrick, ed., *The Writings of George Washington from the Original Manuscript Sources, 1745–1799*, 39 vols. (Washington, D.C.: Government Printing Office, 1931–44), XIV:267; Walter H. Mazyck, *George Washington and the Negro* (Washington, D.C.: Associated Publishers, 1932), 70–72.

24. Quarles, *Negro in the American Revolution*, 64–67.

25. *JCC*, V:425.

26. Charles Francis Adams, ed., *The Works of John Adams, Second President of the United States*, 10 vols. (Boston: Charles C. Little and James Brown, 1850), II:365.

27. *JCC*, I:25; Smith, ed., *Letters of Delegates*, I:168; Jack N. Rakove, *The Beginnings of National Politics: An Interpretive History of the Continental Congress* (New York: Alfred A. Knopf, 1979), 140–41.

28. Since the number of inhabitants could not be immediately ascertained, Congress assigned temporary quotas that were roughly proportionate to population. *JCC*, II:221–22.

29. *JCC*, V:548, 550.

30. *JCC*, VI:1079–80, 1098–1100, 1104; Donald L. Robinson, *Slavery in the Structure of American Politics, 1765–1820* (New York: Harcourt Brace Jovanovich, 1971), 146–49.

31. *JCC*, VI:1080, 1100–1101.

32. Ibid., 1102.

33. *JCC*, IX:800–802; Merrill Jensen, *The Articles of Confederation: An Interpretation of the Social-Constitutional History of the American Revolution, 1774–1781* (Madison: University of Wisconsin Press, 1940, 1959), 148–49. The vote was 5 to 4, with New Jersey joining Maryland, Virginia, North Carolina, and South Carolina to form the majority. The Pennsylvania and New York delegations were divided.

34. *MPP*, I:15. Congress followed the rule during the years before the Articles were ratified. On September 16, 1776, for instance, it authorized an army of eighty-eight battalions, with Massachusetts and Virginia each to supply fifteen, *JCC*, V:762. For a summary, see Mark Mayo Boatner, *Encyclopedia of the American Revolution*, vol. III (New York: David McKay, 1966), 262–63.

35. *JCC*:XI:638, 639, 650–51, 652; Jensen, *Articles of Confederation*, 193–94; Robinson, *Slavery in American Politics*, 152–53.

36. Letter of Maryland delegates to the Maryland Assembly, June 22, 1778, in Smith, ed., *Letters of Delegates*, X:175–76.

37. Edmund C. Burnett, ed., *Letters of Members of the Continental Congress*, 8 vols. (Washington, D.C.: Carnegie Institution, 1921–34), VII:98.

38. *JCC*, XXIV:173–74.

39. Madison's "Notes on Debates," in *The Papers of James Madison*, ed. William T. Hutchinson, et al., 17 vols. to date (Chicago: University of Chicago Press; Charlottesville: University Press of Virginia, 1962–91), VI:402.

40. Ibid., 406–8; *JCC*, XXIV:214–16.

41. *JCC*, XXIV:223–24, 260–61.

42. Hutchinson et al., eds., *Papers of Madison*, VI:425.

43. Madison to Edmund Randolph, April 8, 1783, ibid., 440.

44. *JCC*, XXIV:280–82; XXX:102–7.

45. *JCC*, XXVI:322; XXXI:703.

46. *JCC*, XXIV:249; Adams, ed., *Works of John Adams*, III:336.

47. *JCC*, XXIV:363–64; ibid., XXV:825; ibid., XXVII:368; ibid., XXVIII:46, 123; ibid., XXXII:378.

48. See, for example, Elbridge Gerry to John Adams, February 24, 1785, in Burnett, ed., *Letters of Continental Congress*, VIII:39.

49. JCC, XXXI:863–66, 872. The report even included a little lesson on racial prejudice. Suppose, Jay wrote, that France, in a war with Algiers, should encourage those Americans captured and held as slaves by the Algerians to run away and seek protection within French lines. "What would Congress, and indeed the world, think and say of France, if, on making peace with Algiers, she should give up those American Slaves to their former Algerine Masters? Is there any other difference between the two cases than this, Viz. that the American Slaves at Algiers are white people, whereas the African Slaves at New York were *black* people?"

50. Boyd et al., eds., *Papers of Jefferson*, VI:603–4. The other two members of the committee were Jeremiah Townley Chase of Maryland and David Howell of Rhode Island.

51. Ibid., 611–12; JCC, XXVI:247, 275–79. The use of the phrase "free inhabitants" might be read as implying the continued existence of slavery in the West.

52. Boyd et al., eds., *Papers of Jefferson*, X:58.

53. Don E. Fehrenbacher, *The Dred Scott Case: Its Significance in American Law and Politics* (New York: Oxford University Press, 1978), 78–79.

54. JCC, XXXVIII:164–65, 239.

55. Ibid., 164. The vote was on the motion to commit King's original proposal. Two Marylanders and one Virginian supported the motion; eight southerners opposed it. The vote by states was 8 to 3 in favor of commitment.

56. JCC, XXX:251–55; Jack Ericson Eblen, *The First and Second United States Empires: Governors and Territorial Government, 1784–1912* (Pittsburgh: University of Pittsburgh Press, 1968), 28–36.

57. One man who called upon Congress to take action against slavery was David Cooper, a Quaker, in his pamphlet, *A Serious Address to the Rulers of America* (Trenton, N.J.: Isaac Collins, 1783), 15. "It hath been a matter of wonder to many," he declared, "that that body, who have been so much employed in the study and defence of the *rights* of *humanity*, should suffer so many years to elapse without any effectual movement in this business."

58. Mary Stoughton Locke, *Anti-Slavery in America, from the Introduction of African Slaves to the Prohibition of the Slave Trade, 1619–1808* ([1901]; reprint, Gloucester, Mass.: Peter Smith, 1965), 98, 136–37.

59. During the Convention, James Madison said that there were five southern states, divided from the other eight by "the institution of slavery and its consequences." He thus classified Delaware as northern. Max Farrand, ed., *The Records of the Federal Convention*, rev. ed., 4 vols. (New Haven, Conn.: Yale University Press, 1937, 1966), II:10 (July 14).

60. Farrand, ed., *Records*, I:20 (May 29).

61. Ibid., 242–45 (June 15).

62. Farrand, ed., *Records*, II:15–16 (July 16).

63. Ibid., I:193, 201–2 (June 11).

64. Ibid., 243 (June 15).

65. Ibid., 35–36 (May 30), 486–87 (June 30). Madison renewed the suggestion on July 9, ibid., 562.

66. Ibid., 460, 468 (June 29); 509, 510 (July 2); 524 (July 5); 548–51 (July 7).

67. Ibid., 557–60 (July 9).

68. Ibid., 575, 580–81 (July 11).

69. Ibid., 581–82, 583, 588 (July 11); 593 (July 12).

70. On the issue of slavery as a "tool of political opposition" in the Convention, see Howard Albert Ohline, "Politics and Slavery: The Issue of Slavery in National Politics, 1787–1815" (Ph.D. diss., University of Missouri, Columbia, 1969), 54–55.

71. Farrand, ed., Records, I:587 (July 11).

72. Ibid., 577, 586–88 (July 11). According to Daniel Carroll as quoted by Madison, the negative vote of Maryland was motivated by a desire for a change of phrasing that would make the three-fifths clause more acceptable to people in New England and the middle states.

73. Ibid., 591, 597 (July 12).

74. Farrand, ed., Records, I:603, 606 (July 13); Ibid., II:13–15 (July 16). The great compromise was approved by a vote of 5 to 4, with Massachusetts divided and Pennsylvania, Virginia, South Carolina, and Georgia opposed. Essentially, the division reflected the disagreement between larger and smaller states over the retention of state equality in one branch of the legislature.

75. Farrand, ed., Records, II:16 (July 16).

76. Ibid., I:591–93, 595 (July 12). Morris's motion linking representation with direct taxation was approved unanimously. The motion did not signify that Morris had changed his mind about the three-fifths ratio. He continued to oppose it.

77. Farrand, ed., Records, II:221 (August 8).

78. Ibid., III:255 (King, speaking in the Massachusetts ratifying convention, January 17, 1788).

79. Ibid., II:181, 183 (August 6). In addition to Rutledge, the members of the Committee of Detail were Edmund Randolph of Virginia, Nathaniel Gorham of Massachusetts, Oliver Ellsworth of Connecticut, and James Wilson of Pennsylvania.

80. Ibid., 220–23 (August 8).

81. Ibid., 308 (August 16).

82. Ibid., 354–55 (August 21).

83. Ibid., 354, 364 (August 21); 370 (August 22).

84. Ibid., 364–65, 369–75, 378 (August 21, 22).

85. Ibid., 396 (August 24).

86. Ibid., 412, 414–16 (August 25).

87. See, for example, Christopher Collier and James Lincoln Collier, Decision in Philadelphia: The Constitutional Convention of 1787 (New York: Random House, 1986), 145.

88. Farrand, ed., Records, II:417, 449–53 (August 25, 29). The attempt to restore and broaden the two-thirds requirement was made by Charles Pinckney, but he was outvoted in the South Carolina delegation. The evidence does suggest that there was some kind of understanding between Connecticut and South Carolina delegates.

89. Ibid., 443, 453–54 (August 28, 29).

90. JCC, XXXII:343.

91. Staughton Lynd, "The Compromise of 1787," *Political Science Quarterly* 81 (1966): 225–50, argues that the Constitutional Convention joined with the members of Congress (then meeting in New York) to fashion a sectional compromise on slavery "essentially similar to those of 1820 and 1850." The main features of this "Compromise of 1787" were the three-fifths clause of the Constitution, the antislavery clause of the Northwest Ordinance, and the fugitive-slave clauses in both documents. It is difficult to believe, however, that such an agreement could have been achieved without leaving more documentary traces. Lynd's best piece of evidence is a recollection by Madison, as reported by his one-time secretary in the 1850s. Significantly, it speaks only of the two fugitive-slave clauses and says nothing about the three-fifths compromise. Other historians have accepted the Lynd thesis, for example, Collier and Collier, *Decision in Philadelphia*, 160–65. For a critique, see James H. Hutson, "Riddles of the Federal Constitutional Convention," *William and Mary Quarterly*, 3d ser., 44 (1987): 416–18.

92. Farrand, ed., *Records*, II:559, 629.

93. Jonathan Elliot, ed., *The Debates in the Several State Conventions on the Adoption of the Federal Constitution*, 2d ed., 5 vols. (Philadelphia: J. B. Lippincott, 1891), III:454.

94. Ibid., 269–70, 452–53.

95. Ibid., 455–56, 589–91.

96. Ibid., 453, 599. See Ohline, "Politics and Slavery," 110–14.

97. Elliot, ed., *Debates*, IV:285–86.

98. Ohline, "Politics and Slavery," 77–78, 93–94, 96.

99. Elliot, ed., *Debates*, II:452, 484.

100. *CWAL*, III:11–12, 18, 114–15, 117–18, 178, 219, 274, 276, 306–8, 311–16, 322–23.

101. Walter M. Merrill, ed., *The Letters of William Lloyd Garrison*, 6 vols. (Cambridge, Mass.: Harvard University Press, Belknap Press, 1971–81), I:249; *Boston Liberator*, February 3, 1843.

102. Robert M. Cover, *Justice Accused: Antislavery and the Judicial Process* (New Haven, Conn.: Yale University Press, 1975), 154–58; William M. Wiecek, *The Sources of Antislavery Constitutionalism in America, 1760–1848* (Ithaca, N.Y.: Cornell University Press, 1977), 249–75; Don E. Fehrenbacher, "Slavery, the Framers, and the Living Constitution," in *Slavery and Its Consequences: The Constitution, Equality, and Race*, ed. Robert A. Goldwin and Art Kaufman (Washington, D.C.: American Enterprise Institute, 1988), 23; William M. Wiecek, "'The Blessings of Liberty': Slavery in the American Constitutional Order," in ibid., 36.

103. Smith to John Greenleaf Whittier, July 18, 1844, published in the *Boston Liberator*, August 31, 1844.

104. Ohline, "Politics and Slavery," 5–12, 19–21. For an example of post–Civil War Garrisonianism, see Henry Wilson, *History of the Rise and Fall of the Slave Power in America*, 3 vols. (Boston: J. R. Osgood, 1872–77), I:74.

105. See, for example, Robinson, *Slavery in American Politics*, 166–67; Merton L. Dillon, *The Abolitionists: The Growth of a Dissenting Minority* (DeKalb: Northern Illinois University Press, 1974), 17; Staughton Lynd, *Class Conflict, Slavery, and the United States Constitution* (Indianapolis, Ind.: Bobbs-Merrill Co., 1967), 183;

Raymond T. Diamond, "No Call to Glory: Thurgood Marshall's Thesis on the Intent of a Pro-Slavery Constitution," *Vanderbilt Law Review* 42 (1989): 93–131; and various essays in the *Howard Law Journal* 30, no. 4 (1987).

106. Vincent Harding, *"There Is a River": The Black Struggle for Freedom in America* (New York: Harcourt Brace Jovanovich, 1981), 46. See also Robinson, *Slavery in American Politics*, 247; John Hope Franklin, *From Slavery to Freedom*, 5th ed. (New York: Alfred A. Knopf, 1980), 96; Collier and Collier, *Decision in Phildelphia*, 177; Paul Finkelman, "Slavery and the Constitutional Convention: Making a Covenant with Death," in *Beyond Confederation: Origins of the Constitution and American National Identity*, ed. Richard Beeman, Stephen Botein, and Edward C. Carter II (Chapel Hill: University of North Carolina Press, 1987), 225.

107. Finkelman, "Slavery and the Constitutional Convention," 193; Wiecek, "Blessings of Liberty," 32. See also William M. Wiecek, "The Witch at the Christening: Slavery and the Constitution's Origins," in *The Framing and Ratificatification of the Constitution*, ed. Leonard W. Levy and Dennis J. Mahoney (New York: Macmillan Publishing Co., 1987), 178–84.

108. Wendell Phillips, *The Constitution a Pro-Slavery Document, or Selections from the Madison Papers, etc.* (New York: American Anti-Slavery Society, 1844), 4, 6.

109. Wendell Phillips, *Review of Lysander Spooner's Essay on the Unconstitutionality of Slavery* (Boston: Andrews & Prentiss, 1847), 33. The clause is in Article I, Section 2.

110. For a forceful presentation of this point of view in 1844, see the report of Thomas W. Gilmer, a Virginia congressman, in *HR*, 28 Cong., 1 sess., No. 404 (Serial 446), 39–40.

111. Philip S. Foner, ed., *Life and Writings of Frederick Douglass*, 4 vols. (New York: International Publishers, 1950), II:472.

112. Article I, Section 9.

113. See Article V: "Provided that no amendment which may be made prior to the year one thousand eight hundred and eight shall in any manner affect the first and fourth clauses in the ninth section of the first Article."

114. The slave-trade clause, said Madison during the ratification debate in Virginia, "was a restraint on the exercise of a power expressly delegated to Congress; namely, that of regulating commerce with foreign nations." Elliot, *Debates*, III:455.

115. Merrill Jensen et al., eds., *The Documentary History of the Ratification of the Constitution*, 18 vols. to date (Madison: State Historical Society of Wisconsin, 1976–95), II:417.

116. Benjamin Rush to John Coakley Lettsom, September 28, 1787, in John P. Kaminski, et al., eds., *Commentaries on the Constitution, Public and Private*, vol. I, 262–63. This is the thirteenth volume of Merrill Jensen, et al., eds., *The Documentary History of the Ratification of the Constitution*, 18 vols. (Madison: State Historical Society of Wisconsin, 1976–1997).

117. *AC*, 9 Cong., 2 sess., 486–87.

118. Antislavery advocates later argued that the word "migration" constituted an explicit acknowledgment of congressional power over the interstate movement of slaves, but southerners replied that the word referred to immigration of free persons. Historians have continued the debate. See, for example, Walter Berns, "The Consti-

tution and the Migration of Slaves," *Yale Law Journal* 78 (1968): 198–228; David Brion Davis, *The Problem of Slavery in the Age of Revolution, 1770–1823* (Ithaca, N.Y.: Cornell University Press, 1975), 125–30. It should be noted, however, that the southern argument, if accepted, would not demonstrate the absence of congressional power over the interstate slave trade but only the absence of a specific recognition of that power in Article I, Section 9.

119. *SAL*, I:347; ibid., II:70–71.

120. The other two clauses in Section 2 are the privileges-and-immunities clause and the flight-from-justice clause. Neither was implemented with federal enforcement legislation, although Congress in 1793 did designate the state governors as the officers responsible for the return of fugitives from justice.

121. Farrand, ed., *Records*, II:601, 628 (September 12, 15).

122. Article I, Section 8; and Article IV, Section 4.

123. Richard B. Morris in *The Forging of the Union, 1781–1789* (New York: Harper & Row, 1987), 264–65. According to Morris, the Shays uprising "touched off a wave of backcountry resistance to debt recovery and tax collection" from New England to South Carolina, and that in turn "conveyed a sense of urgency to the nationalists, who now recognized that in addition to setting up a more efficient government with powers over taxation and commerce, there was a need for a central government that could maintain civil order in the states." See also Forrest McDonald, *Novus Ordo Seclorum: The Intellectual Origins of the Constitution* (Lawrence: University Press of Kansas, 1985), 177–78.

124. Phillips, *Constitution a Pro-Slavery Compact*, 4.

125. Wiecek, *Antislavery Constitutionalism*, 63, referring to Article I, Section 9: "No Tax or Duty shall be laid on Articles exported from any State"; and Article I, Section 10: "No State shall, without the Consent of the Congress, lay any Imposts or Duties on Imports or Exports, except what may be absolutely necessary for executing its inspection Laws." The same two clauses are labeled "indirect protections of slavery" by Paul Finkelman, "Slavery and the Constitutional Convention: Making a Covenant with Death," in Beeman, Botein, and Carter, eds., *Beyond Confederation*, 191.

126. Farrand, ed., *Records*, II:305–8, 355, 359–64 (August 16, 21). The vote was 7 to 4, with Connecticut and Massachusetts joining the five southern states in support of the restriction on federal power.

127. Ibid., 436, 442 (August 28).

128. Finkelman, "Slavery and the Constitutional Convention," 191 n, acknowledges that no southern state would have levied an export tax on the products of slave labor. Nevertheless, he declares, "a free state like New York, Massachusetts, or Pennsylvania might conceivably have taxed products produced in other states but exported through the harbors of New York, Boston, or Philadelphia." The alleged proslavery element in the clause thus becomes exceedingly tenuous, which may explain, as Finkelman does not, why it received little support from southern delegates.

129. Ibid., 190–92.

130. *Boston Liberator*, August 31, 1844.

CHAPTER 3

1. *Washington Union*, April 20, 1848; *Washington National Intelligencer*, April 19, 1848; *New York Herald*, April 19, 1848, [Richard Hildreth], *Personal Memoir of Daniel Drayton, for Four Years and Four Months a Prisoner (for Charity's sake) in Washington Jail, Including a Narrative of the Voyage and Capture of the Schooner Pearl*, 2d ed. (Boston: B. Marsh, 1854), 26–33; Samuel Gridley Howe, *Slavery at Washington: Narrative of the Heroic Adventures of Drayton, an American Trader, in "The Pearl". . .* (London: Ward & Co., [1848]), 5–8. The Drayton and Howe accounts are reproduced in *Slave Rebels, Abolitionists, and Southern Courts*, ed. Paul Finkelman, 2 vols. (New York: Garland Publishing Co., 1988), II:445–592. For evidence that Hildreth ghostwrote the *Memoir*, see Donald E. Emerson, *Richard Hildreth*, in *Johns Hopkins University Studies in Historical and Political Science*, ser. 64 no. 2 (Baltimore: Johns Hopkins University Press, 1946), 45. The most extensive secondary treatment is Stanley C. Harrold, Jr., "The *Pearl* Affair: The Washington Riot of 1848," *Columbia Historical Society Records* 50 (1980): 140–60. It was reported that one of the missing slaves belonged to Dolley Madison. *Boston Liberator*, April 21, 1848.

2. According to some accounts, there were 77 fugitives. The *Washington National Intelligencer* of April 19, for instance, reported 38 men, 26 women, and 13 children in the group.

3. *Washington National Intelligencer*, April 19, 1948; *Memoir of Daniel Drayton*, 33–40, 53; Harrold, "*Pearl* Affair," 142–44. The drayman was identified as Judson Diggs by Harriet Beecher Stowe in *A Key to Uncle Tom's Cabin* (Boston: J. P. Jewett, 1853), 157–59. Chester English, cook and deckhand, was also indicted, but the charges against him were dismissed.

4. *Washinton National Intelligencer*, April 20, 21, 22; *New York Herald*, April 19, 20, 21; *Charleston Courier*, April 28, *Boston Liberator*, April 21, May 5, 1848; Stanley Harrold, *Gamaliel Bailey and Antislavery Union* (Kent, Ohio: Kent State University Press, 1986), 125–27; Harrold, "*Pearl* Affair," 145–58.

5. *CG*, 30 Cong., 1 sess., 649–73. The resolution that provoked the debate was introduced by John G. Palfrey of Massachusetts. It was tabled by a vote of 130 to 42. James Brewer Stewart, *Joshua R. Giddings and the Tactics of Radical Politics* (Cleveland: Case Western Reserve University Press, 1970), 152, says that Giddings had "full knowledge" of the Drayton plot beforehand.

6. *CG*, 30 Cong., 1 sess., App., 500–510. See also Richard H. Sewell, *John P. Hale and the Politics of Abolition* (Cambridge, Mass.: Harvard University Press, 1965), 115–18. John Davis of Massachusetts made a mild speech defending the reasonableness of Hale's bill.

7. *New York Herald*, April 23, 1848. The *Herald* correspondent reported that "one likely fellow was exchanged for a Durham bull."

8. *CG*, 30 Cong., 1 sess., 671; Joshua R. Giddings, *Speeches in Congress* (Boston: J. P. Jewett and Co., 1853), 233, 242. The latter is a written-out, extended version of the hour-long speech that Giddings delivered in Congress on April 25, 1848.

9. *Memoir of Daniel Drayton*, 65–69; "Sketch of the Opening Argument in the Case of the United States *vs.* Daniel Drayton," in *Slavery: Letters and Speeches*, Horace Mann (Boston: B. B. Mussey, 1853), 90–94; *Drayton v. U.S.*, 7 Federal Cases

1063–68 (1849). The figure 74 resulted from the fact that two of the 76 slaves were from Virginia and therefore not covered by the laws of the District of Columbia.

10. *Memoir of Daniel Drayton*, 100–102; Charles Sumner, *Charles Sumner: His Complete Works*, 20 vols. (1900; reprint, New York: Negro Universities Press, 1969), III:222. Sumner prepared a legal opinion upholding the power of the president to pardon Drayton and Sayres so as to relieve them from imprisonment, without necessarily releasing them from the obligation to pay their fines, one-half of which were by law apportioned to the slave owners.

11. *Memoir of Daniel Drayton*, 112–20; Fillmore to John J. Crittenden, April 17, 1852, in Frank H. Severance, *Millard Fillmore Papers*, ed. vols. X and XI of *Publications of the Buffalo Historical Society*, 2 vols. (Buffalo, N.Y.: Buffalo Historical Society, 1907), I:362–63; Fillmore to Dorothea Dix, August 13, 1852, in Charles M. Snyder, ed., *The Lady and the President: The Letters of Dorothea Dix and Millard Fillmore* ([Lexington]: University of Kentucky Press, 1975), 136.

12. *CG*, 30 Cong., 2 sess., App., 320, 322.

13. *RD*, 24 Cong., 2 sess., 713; *CG*, 25 Cong., 2 sess., App., 56.

14. According to the Census of 1850, the city of Washington (comprising only a part of the District of Columbia) had 2,113 slaves and a total population of 40,001; the District of Columbia had 3,687 slaves and a total population of 51,687.

15. *JCC*, XXV:707–14; ibid., XXVII:699–701; ibid., XXIX:735; Joseph L. Davis, *Sectionalism in American Politics, 1774–1787* (Madison: University of Wisconsin Press, 1977), 59–75; Lawrence Delbert Cress, "Whither Columbia? Congressional Residence and the Politics of the New Nation, 1776 to 1787," *William and Mary Quarterly*, 3d ser., 32 (1975): 581–600; Kenneth R. Bowling, *The Creation of Washington, D.C.: The Idea and Location of the American Capital* (Fairfax, Va.: George Mason University Press, 1990), 30–70.

16. James Madison to Edmund Pendleton, September 14, 1789, in William T. Hutchinson et al., eds., *The Papers of James Madison*, 17 vols. to date (Chicago: University of Chicago Press; Charlottesville, Va.: University of Virginia Press, 1962–91), XII:402–3. For a good brief summary of the contest in the first session of the First Congress, see ibid., 59–62. The most extensive treatment is in Kenneth Russell Bowling, "Politics in the First Congress, 1789–1791" (Ph.D. diss., University of Wisconsin, 1968), 154–70.

17. *AC*, 1 Cong, 1 sess., 836–37. For the calendar of actions in the House and Senate on the "Seat of Government" bill (HR-25), see Linda Grand De Pauw, ed., *Documentary History of the First Federal Congress*, vol. VI, *Legislative Histories* (Baltimore: Johns Hopkins University Press, 1986), 1850–55.

18. *AC*, 1 Cong, 1 sess., 837–74.

19. Ibid., 881; De Pauw, ed., *Legislative Histories*, 1863. Two Maryland votes against the Lee amendment constituted the only break in the sectional alignment. For the series of resolutions and various proposed amendments with which legislation on this subject began, see De Pauw, ed., *First Federal Congress*, vol. III, *House of Representatives Journal* (Baltimore: Johns Hopkins University Press 1977), 184–94.

20. De Pauw, ed., *House Journal*, 191, 221–22; *AC*, 910–11. The vote on the bill was 31 to 17.

21. Morris's excuse for turning against the Susquehannah was a proviso added to the House bill requiring the states of Pennsylvania and Maryland to legislate for

removal of obstructions in the river. In Morris's view, any such improvement of navigation on the Susquehannah would tend to draw commerce away from the Delaware and thus from Pennsylvania. See Edgar S. Maclay, ed., *Journal of William Maclay* (New York: D. Appleton & Co., 1890), 156, 159; Bowling, "Politics in the First Congress," 167–68.

22. De Pauw, ed., *First Federal Congress*, vol. I, *Senate Legislative Journal* (Baltimore: Johns Hopkins University Press, 1972), 187; *AC*, 1 Cong., 1 sess., 85. The vote was 10 to 8.

23. De Pauw, ed., *Senate Legislative Journal*, 187–89; *AC*, 1 Cong., 1 sess., 85–86; Maclay, ed., *Journal of William Maclay*, 162–65.

24. Maclay, ed., *Journal of William Maclay*, 159, 161, 162.

25. *AC*, 1 Cong., 1 sess., 92, 923, 926; De Pauw, ed., *Senate Legislative Journal*, 201, 203; Bowling, "Politics in the First Congress," 170; Maclay, ed., *Journal of William Maclay*, 168–69. The New York senators, Rufus King and Philip John Schuyler, were concerned primarily with keeping the temporary seat of government in New York City for as long as possible.

26. *AC*, 1 Cong., 2 sess., 939, 1078–80.

27. In a letter to Henry Lee, October 4, 1789, Madison spoke of the "improbability or remoteness of the success of the Potomac," and he remained pessimistic almost until the day of decision. Hutchinson et. al., ed., *Papers of Madison*, XII:425–26.

28. Vermont's ratification in 1790 balanced North Carolina in the Senate but added only one northerner to the House.

29. On Washington's role, see Bowling, "Politics in the First Congress," 194–95; Maclay, ed., *Journal of William Maclay*, 312. For Jefferson's early interest, see Julian P. Boyd, et al., eds., *The Papers of Thomas Jefferson*, 27 vols. to date (Princeton, N.J.: Princeton University Press, 1950–97), VI:364–68.

30. Maclay, ed., *Journal of William Maclay*, 190.

31. Madison to Edmund Pendleton, June 22, 1790, Hutchinson et al., eds., *Papers of Madison*, XIII:252.

32. Boyd et al., eds., *Papers of Jefferson*, XVII:205–07.

33. See Jacob E. Cooke, "The Compromise of 1790," *William and Mary Quarterly*, 3d ser., 27 (1970): 523–45; Kenneth R. Bowling, "Dinner at Jefferson's: A Note on Jacob E. Cooke's 'The Compromise of 1790'," *William and Mary Quarterly*, 3d ser., ibid. 28 (1971): 628–40, with "Rebuttal" by Cooke, 640–48. See also Bowling's article, "The Bank Bill, the Capital City, and President Washington," *Capitol Studies* 1 (1972): 69 n. 1, where he quotes the following contemporary statement by a congressman: "The assumption . . . was effected by a Bargain, three o[r] four members agreeing to vote for the measure provided the permanent seat of the Government was established on the Potomac." Cooke maintains that the Hamilton-Jefferson-Madison agreement did not significantly affect passage of either measure. Bowling insists that it was of critical importance in both instances. He acknowledges that the agreement changed no votes on the residency bill, but argues (unconvincingly in my opinion) that Hamilton assured its passage by persuading the Massachusetts delegation not to "interfere" with the Philadelphia-Potomac arrangement, except by voting against it.

34. De Pauw, ed., *Senate Legislative Journal*, 375, 390–91, 396–97; *HJ*, III: 505–6; *AC*, 1 Cong., 2 sess., 995, 1000, 1002. For the text of the "Residence Act" (S-12), and

the calendar of Senate and House actions leading to its passage, see De Pauw, ed., *Legislative Histories*, 1767–74.

35. Madison to Pendleton, June 22, 1790, Hutchinson, et al., eds., *Papers of Madison*, XIII:252.

36. Bowling, "Bank Bill," 60–63, 67–70.

37. Ibid., 64–66; *MPP*, I:100–101 (January 24, 1791), 106 (October 25, 1791). On Jefferson's assistance, see Boyd et al., eds., *Papers of Jefferson*, XVII:452–71.

38. The beginnings of Washington are detailed in Wilhelmus Bogart Bryan, *A History of the National Capital*, 2 vols. (New York: Macmillan Publishing Co. 1914–16), I:105–356. A briefer account is in Constance McLaughlin Green, *Washington: Village and Capital, 1800–1878* (Princeton, N.J.: Princeton University Press, 1962), 12–22.

39. *AC*, 1 Cong., 2 sess., 1662–63. The congressman was Aedanus Burke.

40. Washington to Tobias Lear, April 12, 1791, in John C. Fitzpatrick, ed., *The Writings of George Washington from the Original Manuscript Sources*, 39 vols. (Washington, D.C.: Government Printing Office, 1931–44), XXXVII:573; Stephen Decatur, Jr., *The Private Affairs of George Washington, from the Records and Accounts of Tobias Lear, Esquire, His Secretary* (Boston: Houghton Mifflin & Co., 1933), 239; Douglas Southall Freeman, *George Washington: A Biography*, 7 vols. (New York: Charles Scribner's Sons, 1948–57), VI:226, 308–9, 384.

41. *Butler v. Hopper*, 4 Federal Cases 904 (1806).

42. Washington to David Stuart, March 28, 1790, in Fitzpatrick, ed., *Papers of Washington*, XXXI:30.

43. Maclay, ed., *Journal of William Maclay*, 217.

44. Bowling, "Politics in the First Congress," 174.

45. *SAL*, I:130.

46. *SAL*, II:103–04.

47. Green, *Washington, 1800–1878*, 21.

48. See, for example, the argument of John Nicholas of Virginia, *AC*, 6 Cong., 2 sess., 867–68.

49. Bryan, *National Capital*, I:387–99, 441–43, 447.

50. Ibid., 400–401, 445–47; ibid., II:103–8, 115–16, 193–98; F. Regis Noel, *The Court-House of the District of Columbia* (Washington, D.C.: Law Reporter Printing Co., 1939), 47–61. The mayor of Washington was elected by the council from 1812 to to 1820 and by popular vote thereafter. Congress established a criminal court for the District of Columbia in 1838, *SAL*, V:306.

51. Worthington G. Snethen, *The Black Code of the District of Columbia* (New York: William Harned, 1848), 15.

52. *SAL*, III:323; Alfred Garrett Harris, "Slavery and Emancipation in the District of Columbia, 1801–1862" (Ph.D. diss., Ohio State University, 1946), 45.

53. *HR*, 21 Cong., 1 sess. No. 269 (Serial 200), 1–7.

54. *RD*, 21 Cong., 1 sess., 753–55, 822–27, 1121; 21 Cong., 2 sess., 260; *SAL*, IV:448–50; Harris, "Slavery and Emancipation," 46–47. The act also provided heavy penalties for the abduction of free blacks—up to twelve years in prison and a $5,000 fine.

55. Snethen, *Black Code*, 21–22, 36, 42, 43, 44, 53.

56. *SAL*, X:642–43; ibid., XI:794–95; *Washington National Intelligencer*, February 16, 1858; Harris, "Slavery and Emancipation," 47–48; Bryan, *National Capital*, II:439.

57. William Frank Zornow, "The Judicial Modifications of the Maryland Black Code in the District of Columbia," *Maryland Historical Magazine* 44 (1949): 25–27.

58. Ibid., 24. In 1813, under a Maryland law of 1751, a slave was sentenced to death and executed for the attempted rape of a white woman. *U.S. v. Patrick*, 27 Federal Cases 460 (2 Cranch C.C. 66).

59. *U.S. v. Wright*, 28 Federal Cases 790 (1803).

60. *Minchin v. Docker*, 17 Federal Cases 437 (1806).

61. *U.S. v. King*, 26 Federal Cases 786 (1807).

62. *U.S. v. Brockett*, 24 Federal Cases 1241 (1823).

63. *Crawford v. Slye*, 6 Federal Cases 778 (1834).

64. *U.S. v. Lloyd*, 26 Federal Cases 987 (1834).

65. *U.S. v. Frye*, 25 Federal Cases 1222 (1835).

66. *U.S. v. Henning*, 26 Federal Cases 265, 267 (1835, 1836).

67. *U.S. v. Bowen*, 24 Federal Cases 1207 (1835).

68. *Hickerson v. U.S.*, 30 Federal Cases 1087 (1856).

69. *SAL*, III:588.

70. Snethen, *Black Code*, 42.

71. Ibid., 40, 41, 45, 46.

72. Ibid., 29–30.

73. Ibid., 12–13, 31–32; *HR*, 19 Cong., 2 sess., No. 43 (Serial 159); *RD*, 19 Cong., 2 sess., 555–56, 559–60; William Jay, *View of the Action of the Federal Government in Behalf of Slavery* (New York: American Anti-Slavery Society, 1839), 53. According to the report of a House committee in 1829, of the 179 blacks committed to the Washington jail as suspected runaways during the preceding three years, 147 were claimed as slaves, 26 proved to be free and were discharged, and 6 were unclaimed and sold for maintenance and fees. *HR*, 20 Cong., 2 sess., No. 60 (Serial 190).

74. *HR*, 28 Cong., 1 sess, No. 29 (Serial 445).

75. *HR*, 20 Cong., 2 sess., No. 60 (Serial 190), 7.

76. *CG*, 37 Cong., 2 sess., 26, 88; *Washington National Republican*, March 31, 1862.

77. Basil Hall, *Travels in North America in the Years 1827 and 1828*, 3d ed., 3 vols. (Edinburgh: Robert Cadell, 1830), III:34–41, recorded his attendance at such a marshal's sale.

78. *SAL*, II:116, 193–95, 757; Snethen, *Black Code*, 34.

79. Bryan, *National Capital*, II:134–35; Charles Francis Adams, ed., *Memoirs of John Quincy Adams, Comprising Portions of His Diary from 1795 to 1848*, 12 vols. (Philadelphia: J. B. Lippincott & Co., 1874–77), IX:417–18; Leonard Falkner, *The President Who Wouldn't Retire* (New York: Coward-McCann, 1967),181–85. The *Washington National Intelligencer* of October 23, 1837, contains an advertisement for the sale of Dorcas Allen and her two surviving children after a jury had acquitted her on grounds of insanity.

80. *AC*, 8 Cong., 2 sess., 995–96. Six Federalists and 25 Republicans voted for the

resolution. Of the 30 favorable northern votes, 20 came from the three middle Atlantic states and 10 from the five New England states. John Archer of Maryland was the only southerner to support the resolution.

81. Washington *National Intelligencer*, January 22, 1802, quoted in Constance McLaughlin Green, *The Secret City: A History of Race Relations in the Nation's Capital* (Princeton, N.J.: Princeton University Press, 1967), 20; *RD*, 20 Cong., 2 sess., 177.

82. Ralph L. Ketcham, "The Dictates of Conscience: Edward Coles and Slavery," *Virginia Quarterly Review* 32 (1960): 52.

83. Snethen, *Black Code*, 22–24. Harris, "Slavery and Emancipation," 51–55, 312–13; William T. Laprade, "The Domestic Slave Trade in the District of Columbia," *JNH* 11 (1926): 28–31. Harris puts the number annually gathered in Washington and shipped south at 1,000 to 1,500 in the period 1828–36. This estimate is probably too low. One firm alone, Franklin and Armfield of Alexandria, sent about 1,000 to 1,200 south every year during that period. Wendell Holmes Stephenson, *Isaac Franklin, Slave Trader and Planter of the Old South* ([1938]; reprint, Gloucester, Mass.: Peter Smith, 1968), 34.

84. *AC*, 14 Cong., 1 sess., 1115–17; Bryan, *National Capital*, II:135.

85. *AC*, 16 Cong., 1 sess. Alexander Smyth of Virginia likewise affirmed the power of Congress to abolish slavery in the District of Columbia, but he indicated that it could not be done without the "just compensation" required by the Fifth Amendment. Ibid., 998–99, 1003.

86. Glover Moore, *The Missouri Controversy, 1819–1821* (Lexington: University of Kentucky Press, 1953), 295, 348–49.

87. Robert Y. Hayne, *RD*, 19 Cong., 1 sess., 166; [Robert J. Turnbull], *The Crisis: or, Essays on the Usurpations of the Federal Government* (Charleston: A. E. Miller, printer, 1827), 132. William M. Wiecek, *The Sources of Antislavery Constitutionalism in America, 1760–1848* (Ithaca, N.Y.: Cornell University Press, 1977), 131.

88. *The Genius of Universal Emancipation*, October 1823, p. 49; ibid., January 1824, pp. 98–99; ibid., March 1824, p. 130; ibid., April 1824, p. 146; ibid., May 3, 1824, p. 181.

89. Ibid., March 4, 1826, p. 213; ibid., June 10, 1826, pp. 322–23; *HJ*, 19 Cong., 1 sess. (Serial 130), 559; Mary Tremain, *Slavery in the District of Columbia: The Policy of Congress and the Struggle for Abolition* (New York: G. P. Putnam's Sons, 1892), 60–61. The resolution declared that the District of Columbia "ought to exhibit to the Nation and the World, the purest specimen of government, vindicating the superior excellence of free institutions."

90. *AC*, 19 Cong., 2 sess., 1099–1101.

91. *The Genius of Universal Emancipation*, February 2, 1828, p. 28; ibid., February 9, 1828, p. 38; ibid., April 26, 1828, p. 94; *HD*, 20 Cong.,1 sess., No. 215 (Serial 173).

92. *RD*, 20 Cong., 2 sess., 180.

93. Ibid., 167–68, 175–87.

94. *HJ*, 20 Cong., 2 sess. (Serial 183), 137–39. The preamble was defeated, 141 to 37; the resolutions were approved, 120 to 59 and 114 to 66. McDuffie voted against both resolutions; so did a future president, James K. Polk of Tennessee; so did Edward Bates of Missouri, later attorney general in the Lincoln administration.

95. Tremain, *Slavery in the District of Columbia*, 67; *RD*, 20 Cong., 1 sess., 1122.

The members were John C. Weems and George C. Washington of Maryland, Mark Alexander and Robert Allen of Virginia, George Kremer of Pennsylvania, Ralph I. Ingersoll of Connecticut, and John Varnum of Massachusetts. Only Ingersoll voted against the D'Auterive claim.

96. *HR*, 20 Cong., 2 sess., No. 60 (Serial 190), 1–4.

97. Ibid., 4–6. Between 1820 and 1830, the white population of the district increased 22 percent and the free black population, 52 percent.

98. Ibid., 4; *HJ*, 20 Cong., 2 sess. (Serial 183), 216–17, 405; 21 Cong., 1 sess. (Serial 194), 549; Tremain, *Slavery in the District of Columbia*, 69. The text of the bill is in the *Washington National Intelligencer*, February 7, 1829, and April 22, 1830.

99. *The Genius of Universal Emancipation*, February 2, 1828, p. 31.

100. *Washington National Intelligencer*, August 20, 1830.

101. Samuel Flagg Bemis, *John Quincy Adams and the Union* (New York: Alfred A. Knopf, 1956), 329.

102. *RD*, 22 Cong., 1 sess., 1425–26.

103. Adams, ed., *Memoirs of John Quincy Adams*, VIII:454–55.

104. *RD*, 21 Cong., 2 sess., 1442.

105. *RD*, 22 Cong., 2 sess., 1585; 23 Cong., 2 sess., 253.

106. *HJ*, 23 Cong., 2 sess. (Serial 270), 387–89.

107. See the graph of mob incidents in Leonard L. Richards, *"Gentlemen of Property and Standing": Anti-Abolition Mobs in Jacksonian America* (New York: Oxford University Press, 1970), 15.

108. W. Sherman Savage, *The Controversy over the Distribution of Abolition Literature, 1830–1860* (Washington, D.C.: Association for the Study of Negro Life and History, 1938), 13–15.

109. *Washington National Intelligencer*, August 12–15, 1835; Bryan, *National Capital*, II:144–45; Neil S. Kramer, "The Trial of Reuben Crandall," *Records of the Columbia Historical Society* 50 (1975–76): 123–25. According to the *Intelligencer*, the disorder in Washington was partly inspired by a riot over bank policy that took place a few days earlier in Baltimore. See David Grimsted, "Rioting in Its Jacksonian Setting," *AHR* 77 (1972): 374–78.

110. *Washington National Intelligencer*, August 15, 1835.

111. *U.S. v. Crandall*, 25 Federal Cases 684 (1836); Kramer, "Trial of Reuben Crandall," 129–39. There are two pamphlet accounts of Crandall's trial, both reproduced in Finkelman, ed., *Slave Rebels*, 317–428. Key strongly resented abolitionist attacks upon the African colonization movement, in which he had played a leading role. Also, the vigorous prosecution of Crandall by an appointee of Andrew Jackson may have been politically motivated, serving as a response to the widespread southern suspicion that Martin Van Buren, the Jacksonian heir apparent, was not sufficiently hostile to abolitionism.

112. *Boston Liberator*, March 16, 1838. Some of the literature was indeed incendiary. For instance, one sentence read into the court record spoke of the day when the slave would strike back against the slaveholder: "His torch will be at the threshhold, and his knife at the throat of the planter. Horrible and indiscriminate will be the vengeance." The charge of "publishing" such material rested, however, on the lend-

ing of one pamphlet and on the fact that several others carried the words "read and circulate" in Crandall's handwriting.

113.   *HJ*, 24 Cong., 1 sess. (Serial 285), 47–67; *CG*, 24 Cong., 1 sess., 24–25.

114.   *CG*, 24 Cong., 1 sess., 27, 77–78, 225; Charles M. Wiltse, *John C. Calhoun: Nullifier, 1829–1839* (Indianapolis: Bobbs-Merrill Co., 1949), 178–79.

115.   *CG*, 24 Cong., 1 sess., 27, 39–40, 221. The Senate did not settle the question of reception until March 9, 1836, when it voted against Calhoun, 36 to 10.

116.   Ibid., 39, 50, 75, 103.

117.   Ibid., 133.

118.   Ibid., 155.

119.   Ibid., 156; Drew Gilpin Faust, *James Henry Hammond and the Old South: A Design for Mastery* (Baton Rouge: Louisiana State University Press, 1982), 178–79; Charles M. Wiltse, *John C. Calhoun: Sectionalist, 1840–1850* (Indianapolis, Ind.: Bobbs-Merrill Co., 1951), 284–85.

120.   *CG*, 24 Cong., 1 sess., 156–57, 161.

121.   Martin Van Buren, *Opinions of Martin Van Buren, Vice President of the United States, upon the Powers and Duties of Congress, in Reference to the Abolition of Slavery Either in the Slave-Holding states or in the District of Columbia . . .* (Washington, D.C.: Blair & Rives, 1836).

122.   *CG*, 24 Cong., 1 sess., 383; *HR*, 24 Cong., 1 sess., No. 691 (Serial 295).

123.   *CG*, 24 Cong., 1 sess., 405–6.

124.   The attitude of the House was demonstrated when it inadvertently referred one petition to the committee for the District and then, after considerable debate, reconsidered and tabled it. *HJ*, 24 Cong., 1 sess. (Serial 285), 74, 84–87; *CG*, 24 Cong., 1 sess., 27, 35, 40, 45, 50.

125.   Robert P. Ludlum, "The Antislavery 'Gag Rule': History and Argument," *JNH* 26 (1941): 208–14.

126.   Ibid., 214–15; *CG*, 26 Cong., 1 sess., 150–51. This ultimate gag was imposed by the relatively close vote of 114 to 108.

127.   *CG*, 28 Cong., 2 sess., 7, 18; Adams, *Memoirs of John Quincy Adams*, XII:115–16, 120. Henry H. Simms, *Emotion at High Tide: Abolition as a Controversial Factor, 1830–1845* (Baltimore: Moore & Co., 1960), 166–68.

128.   *CWAL*, IV:152.

129.   *CG*, 25 Cong., 3 sess., 177; App., 355–56. Calhoun said that an attack on slavery in the District was as much an attack on slavery in the states "as firing a train to blow up a magazine would be an attack on the magazine itself." *CG*, 25 Cong., 2 sess., App., 56.

130.   *CG*, 24 Cong., 1 sess., App., 108, 134. Among southerners issuing the warning was William Drayton of South Carolina, who had opposed the nullification movement. In *The South Vindicated from the Treason and Fanaticism of the Northern Abolitionists* (n.p.: H. Manly, 1836; reprint, New York: Negro Universities Press, 1969), 225, he wrote: "It cannot be denied, and need not be concealed, that the abolition of slavery in the District of Columbia by Congress, would be the signal for an immediate dissolution of the Union."

131.   For an example of this argument and for Slade's counterargument, see *CG*, 24 Cong., 1 sess., App., 53, 84–85. Henry Clay, presenting an anti-interference petition

in the Senate on February 7, 1839, claimed that it represented "the almost unanimous sentiment" of District residents, CG, 25 Cong., 3 sess., App., 355.

132. CG, 25 Cong., 2 sess., 36; CWAL, I:75n.

133. CG, 30 Cong., 2 sess., 212.

134. CWAL, III:41–42, 96. As late as March 24, 1862, Lincoln wrote to Horace Greeley that he wanted a bill for abolition in the District to include three features: "gradual—compensation—and vote of the people." Ibid., V:169.

135. HR, 24 Cong., 1 sess., No. 691 (Serial 295), 11–12.

136. Van Buren, Opinions of Martin Van Buren, 6. Van Buren also asserted that if the framers had foreseen so much agitation of the question, they would have made the right to hold slaves in the District an exception to the unrestricted governing power vested in Congress.

137. John T. Scharf, History of Maryland from the Earliest Period to the Present Day, 3 vols. (1879; reprint, Hartboro, Pa: Tradition Press, 1967), II:569. Scharf's presentation of this subject illustrates how well the proslavery myth survived the institution of slavery itself. "As slavery," he wrote, "was a species of property and existed in the District of Columbia before the Act of cession, it was regarded as included in the compact . . . and therefore not to be annulled without the consent of all the parties." A good abolitionist rebuttal to the argument of an implied compact is in S. B. Treadwell, American Liberties and American Slavery (Boston: Weeks, Jordan, & Co., 1838), 89–91.

138. CG, 24 Cong., 1 sess., 125. Pamphleteer Francis E. Brewster, in Slavery and the Constitution (Philadelphia: n.p., 1850), likewise maintained that the District was ceded only as a site for government buildings. "It was not expected," he wrote, "that any authority should be held over it, except which is incident to these objects."

139. CG, 31 Cong., 1 sess., App., 1641. Like many proslavery arguments, this one had its antislavery counterpart. Thus, Horace Mann, in denying that Congress had any constitutional power to establish or support slavery in the District, went on to declare that if it could do so, it could legalize the institution in the forts, arsenals, and customs houses of the free states. CG, 30 Cong., 2 sess., 325.

140. Thus, Henry Wise declared: "Slavery is interwoven with our very political existence, is guaranteed by our Constitution." But at the same time he said: "The nation has nothing to do with slave property." CG, 23 Cong., 2 sess., 253. See also, for example, the resolution of Joseph R. Ingersoll and the remarks of William C. Preston, James Garland, and Richard French. CG, 24 Cong., 1 sess., 45; ibid., App., 53; CG, 28 Cong., 1 sess., 64; RD, 24 Cong., 1 sess., 81.

141. Charleston Courier, January 14, 1836. See also, for example, the statements of Calhoun and William C. Rives in RD, 24 Cong., 2 sess., 711, 721. In a Senate committee report prepared but not filed, the future president, John Tyler, declared: "Slavery existed within the territorial limits of the District before the cession, and was recognized and guaranteed by the constitution. Under what pretense, then, can property vested in a slave be dispossessed, any more than in any other subject?" Niles Weekly Register, September 17, 1836, pp. 44–45.

142. For examples of this argument, see the speeches of William C. Preston, Benjamin W. Leigh, and Francis W. Pickens in CG, 24 Cong., 1 sess., 82, 119, 125.

143. Ibid., 82.

144. The Fifth Amendment also declared: "nor shall private property be taken for

public use without just compensation." This, said John Robertson of Virginia, lent no legitimacy to compensated emancipation because emancipation would not involve public use. Ibid., 399.

145. Ibid., 25 Cong., 2 sess., App., 56–57.

146. Ibid., 64.

147. *SAL*, IX:35–37.

148. *CG*, 30 Cong., 1 sess., 852; ibid., App., 958. For similar arguments by Horace Mann and William H. Seward, see *CG*, 30 Cong., 2 sess., 324–25; ibid., 31 Cong., 1 sess., 1648.

149. *CG*, 30 Cong., 1 sess., 870, 872.

150. *CG*, 30 Cong., 1 sess., 60, 179, 268, 786, 788.

151. *CG*, 30 Cong., 2 sess., 83–84.

152. Ibid., 216; Wiltse, *Calhoun: Sectionalist*, 377–88.

153. *CG*, 30 Cong., 2 sess., 212; Donald W. Riddle, *Congressman Abraham Lincoln* (Urbana: University of Illinois Press, 1957), 169–75.

154. *CG*, 30 Cong., 2 sess., 216.

155. Ibid., 415–16. The House on February 20, 1849, tabled a similar bill introduced in the first session by William W. Wick of Indiana. Ibid., 569.

156. Richard Malcolm Johnston and William Hand Browne, eds., *Life of Alexander H. Stephens*, rev. ed. (Philadelphia: J. B. Lippincott & Co., 1883), 238.

157. *CG*, 31 Cong., 1 sess., 247–48; Holman Hamilton, *Prologue to Conflict: The Crisis and Compromise of 1850* (Lexington: University of Kentucky Press, 1964), 53–59.

158. *CG*, 31 Cong., 1 sess., 944–48.

159. David Outlaw to his wife, July 29, 1850, David Outlaw Papers, Southern Historical Collection, University of North Carolina, Chapel Hill; *New York Evening Post*, quoted in *Boston Liberator*, August 16, 1850.

160. *Washington National Intelligencer*, August 10, November 15, 1850; *Washington News*, August 10, 17, 1850; *Washington Republic*, August 10, 12, 1850; *The Case of William Chaplin* . . . (Boston: Chaplin Committee, 1851), 22–50, reprinted in Finkelman, ed., *Slave Rebels*; Ralph Volney Harlow, *Gerrit Smith, Philanthropist and Reformer* (New York: Henry Holt & Co., 1939), 290–95. Accounts of the affair vary in their details. According to abolitionist reports, for instance, Chaplin himself was unarmed and unaware that the slaves carried guns. See *Boston Liberator*, September 13, 1850.

161. *National Era*, August 15, 1850; *Boston Liberator*, August 16, 23, 1850.

162. David Outlaw to his wife, July 29, 1858, Outlaw Papers.

163. *CG*, 31 Cong., 1 sess., 1743–44, 1750; ibid., App., 1630–37; *SJ*, 31 Cong., 1 sess. (Serial 548), 589, 597–99.

164. *CG*, 31 Cong., 1 sess., App., 1630–33.

165. Ibid., 1637–42.

166. Ibid., 1642–49. Seward's bill called for a referendum within six months of passage. If the District electorate approved the measure, it was to go into effect immediately.

167. Ibid., 1642–64; *SJ*, 31 Cong., 1 sess. (Serial 548), 626.

168. *CG*, 31 Cong., 1 sess., App., 1665–74.

169. *CG*, 31 Cong., 1 sess., 1830, 1837.

170. Six were Whigs and four were Democrats. The three best-known names among them were Clay, Benton, and Sam Houston. See the tabulations in Hamilton, *Prologue to Conflict*, 191–92, 195–200.

171. *CG*, 31 Cong., 1 sess., App., 1644, 1645.

172. Pursuant to a court order in December, 1858, for example, two women and several children were advertised for sale at public auction. *Washington National Era*, December 23, 1858.

173. *AC*, 14 Cong., 1 sess., 1117.

CHAPTER 4

1. Joel Barlow, *An Oration Delivered at the North Church in Hartford, at the Meeting of the Connecticut Society of the Cincinnati: July 4, 1787* (Hartford: Hudson & Goodwin, 1787), 20.

2. George Bancroft, *Literary and Historical Miscellanies* (New York: Harper & Brothers, 1855), 516.

3. [Thomas Paine], *Common Sense* (Philadelphia: n.p., 1776), 58.

4. Horst Dippel, *Germany and the American Revolution, 1770–1800*, trans. Bernhard A. Uhlendorf (Chapel Hill, N.C.: n.p., 1977), 149, 151.

5. Philip S. Foner, *The Democratic-Republican Societies, 1790–1800: A Documentary Sourcebook of Constitutions, Declarations, Addresses, Resolutions, and Toasts* (Westport, Conn.: Greenwood Press, 1976), 353.

6. *CG*, 32 Cong., 1 sess., 104–6.

7. Ibid., 165. The congressman was Meredith P. Gentry.

8. *New York Herald*, March 12, 24, 1848.

9. *CG*, 28 Cong., 2 sess., App., 73. The congressman was Samuel C. Sample. Luther Severance of Maine declared his opposition to extending "the black flag of slavery" and then added, "Let us rather extend the 'area of freedom' by our wisdom, our moderation . . . our bright and shining example as a pattern republic." Ibid., 376. Albert K. Weinberg, *Manifest Destiny: A Study of Nationalist Expansionism in American History* (Baltimore: Johns Hopkins University Press, 1935), 100–129.

10. Lord Aberdeen to Richard Pakenham, December 26, 1843, in *Diplomatic Correspondence of the United States: Inter-American Affairs, 1831–1860*, ed. William R. Manning, 12 vols. (Washington, D.C.: Carnegie Endowment for International Peace, 1932–39), VII:18–22; John C. Calhoun to Pakenham, April 18, 1844, ibid., 252–53.

11. John C. Fitzpatrick, ed., *The Writings of George Washington from the Original Manuscript Sources, 1745–1799*, 39 vols. (Washington, D.C.: Government Printing Office, 1931–44), XXVI:274–75, 364–65. For the losses of slaves by Virginians generally, see Robert McColley, *Slavery and Jeffersonian Virginia*, 2d ed. (Urbana: University of Illinois Press, 1973), 82–84.

12. Hunter Miller, ed., *Treaties and Other International Acts of the United States of America, 1776–1863*, 8 vols. (Washington, D.C.: GPO, 1931–1948), II:99–100, 155. On the whole subject of American slaves carried away by the British in two wars, see

Arnett G. Lindsay, "Diplomatic Relations Between the United States and Great Britain Bearing on the Return of Negro Slaves, 1783–1828," *JNH* 5 (1920): 391–419.

13. Fitzpatrick, ed., *Writings of Washington*, XXVI:402–09; Benjamin Quarles, *The Negro in the American Revolution* (Chapel Hill: University of North Carolina Press 1961), 158–81. The number 4,000 is an estimate. Jefferson later stated the total to be "3,000 negroes, of whom our commissioners had inspection, and a very large number more, in public and private vessels, of whom they were not permitted to have inspection." Julian P. Boyd et al., eds., *The Papers of Thomas Jefferson*, 24 vols. to date (Princeton, N.J.: Princeton University Press, 1950–90), XXIII:568.

14. Charles R. Ritcheson, *Aftermath of Revolution: British Policy Toward the United States, 1783–1795* (Dallas: Southern Methodist University Press, 1969), 70–75, 100, 236; Donald L. Robinson, *Slavery in the Structure of American Politics, 1765–1820* (New York: Harcourt Brace Jovanovich 1971), 348–49; Howard Albert Ohline, "Politics and Slavery: The Issue of Slavery in National Politics, 1787–1815" (Ph.D. diss., University of Missouri, Columbia, 1969), 265–67; Jefferson to George Hammond, December 15, 1791; May 29, 1792, Boyd et al., eds., *Papers of Jefferson*, XXII:410; XXIII:568–73. During the debate on Jay's Treaty in 1796, John Nicholas of Virginia said that the issue of the carried-away slaves was important primarily because "it justified the United States from the charge of breaking the Treaty of Peace." *AC*, 4 Cong., 1 sess., 1005.

15. Frederic Austin Ogg, "Jay's Treaty and the Slavery Interests of the United States," *Annual Report of the American Historical Association for the Year 1901* (Washington, D.C.: Government Printing Office, 1902), I:275–86; Robinson, *Slavery in American Politics*, 349–53; Jay to Secretary of State Edmund Randolph, September 13, 1794, February 6, 1795, *ASP, Foreign Relations*, I:485, 518.

16. *AC*, 4 Cong., 1 sess., 860–65; Robinson, *Slavery in American Politics*, 354–55. The Senate at the same time voted overwhelmingly in favor of a resolution calling for further negotiations with Britain on the slavery issue, but added a proviso that those negotiations should be "distinct from, and subsequent to" negotiations respecting trade with the British West Indies. Southern opposition to the proviso prevented final approval of the resolution.

17. *AC*, 4 Cong., 1 sess., 977–78, 1070, 1291; Robinson, *Slavery in American Politics*, 357–61; Ogg, "Jay's Treaty," 290–94. For many pertinent excerpts from the debate in the House, see William Renwick Riddell, "Jay's Treaty and the Negro," *JNH* 13 (1928): 189–91.

18. Responding to a senatorial resolution of inquiry sponsored by Robert M. T. Hunter of Virginia in 1850, Secretary of State John M. Clayton reported that there were no records in the State Department of any correspondence with Britain on the subject after 1794. *CG*, 31 Cong., 1 sess., 469–70; *SD*, 31 Cong., 1 sess., No. 46 (Serial 558).

19. *ASP, Indian Affairs*, I:26, 546; *HD*, 20 Cong., 2 sess., No. 91 (Serial 186); Charles J. Kappler, ed., *Indian Affairs: Laws and Treaties*, vol. II, *Treaties* (Washington, D.C.: Government Printing Office, 1904), 26, 46, 196; Daniel F. Littlefield, Jr., *Africans and Creeks, From the Colonial Period to the Civil War* (Westport, Conn.: Greenwood Press, 1979), 32–36, 96–98.

20. Miller, *Treaties*, II:574–75.

21. *ASP, Foreign Relations*, IV:106–26; John Bassett Moore, *History and Digest of the International Arbitrations to Which the United States Has Been a Party*, 6 vols.

(Washington, D.C.: Government Printing Office, 1898), I:350–57. In addition to the slaves aboard ship, the British naval commander in the Chesapeake refused to return the slaves on certain islands occupied by British forces. He argued, for instance, that since "none of the slaves now in Tangier were captured there," they did not come within the stipulations of the treaty.

22. John Quincy Adams to Lord Castlereagh, August 9, 1815, *ASP Foreign Relations*, IV:115–16.

23. Adams to James Monroe, August 22, 1815, ibid., 116–17. Samuel Flagg Bemis, *John Quincy Adams and the Foundations of American Foreign Policy* (New York: Alfred A. Knopf, 1949), 231–32.

24. *ASP, Foreign Relations*, IV:363–4, 376, 381, 385–86, 391, 393, 397, 407.

25. Charles Francis Adams, ed., *Memoirs of John Quincy Adams, Comprising Portions of His Diary from 1795 to 1848*, 12 vols. (Philadelphia: J. B. Lippincott & Co., 1874–77), V:160.

26. *ASP, Foreign Relations*, V:220. Adams, in his memoirs, sardonically remarked: "The decision is in our favor, but is expressed in language needing explanation more than the paragraph of the article which was in question." Adams, *Memoirs of John Quincy Adams*, VI:45.

27. *ASP, Foreign Relations*, V:214–17.

28. Moore, *International Arbitrations*, I:366–67. Among other things, Cheves had been speaker of the House of Representatives and president of the Bank of the United States. Hay, who had prosecuted Aaron Burr for treason in 1807, lived in the White House during Monroe's presidency.

29. Report of Henry Clay, March 7, 1826, *ASP, Foreign Relations*, V:800–801, also in *Niles Weekly Register*, March 18, 1826, pp. 45–46.

30. Ibid.; Moore, *International Arbitrations*, I:370–77.

31. *ASP, Foreign Relations*, VI:339–55, 637–38 (text of the convention), 745–53; Moore, *International Arbitrations*, I:377–82.

32. *SAL*, IV:219–21.

33. *ASP, Foreign Relations*, VI:856.

34. Moore, *International Arbitrations*, I:384–85. Henry Clay estimated that only about 500 out of 2,400 deported Chesapeake slaves could be brought within the terms of the treaty. *ASP, Foreign Relations*, VI:342.

35. *ASP, Foreign Relations*, VI:883–86. Cheves's work on the commission is summarized in Archie Vernon Huff, Jr., *Langdon Cheves of South Carolina* (Columbia: University of South Carolina Press, 1977), 136–41.

36. In this appearance before the commission, Wirt was not speaking for the federal government but rather engaging in private practice. The official duties of an attorney general were then relatively light and occupied only part of his professional time.

37. *ASP, Foreign Relations*, VI:855–57; *RD*, 20 Cong., 1 sess., 408–10; *HR*, 20 Cong., 1 sess., No. 208 (Serial 178).

38. *ASP, Foreign Relations*, VI:882–92; *RD*, 20 Cong., 1 sess., 406–11, 786–87, 1811–14, 1830–35, 2314–17, 2575–76; Moore, *International Arbitrations*, I:385–90; *MPP*, II:419–20 (December 2, 1828).

39. From 1823 to 1827, Congress appropriated a total of $56,887 for half the cost of

the mixed commission and the full cost of the awards commission (Moore, *International Arbitrations*, I:367n.) This constituted only part of the direct and indirect financial cost to the federal government.

40. The question did arise twenty years later during one last regurgitation of the problem of the carried-away slaves. On May 13, 1848, the House took up consideration of a private bill for the relief of "legal representatives of Benjamin Hodges, deceased." Hodges, it seems, had lost a slave to the British in 1814 but had failed to get his name on the official list of claimants. The proposal to rectify the omission by paying $280 to the Hodges estate provoked several hours of heated discussion in which members argued the status of slavery under federal law, just as they would soon do again in the debate on the Pacheco claim. The bill was passed by the House, 125 to 28 (Abraham Lincoln voting with the majority), but it did not get past the introductory stage in the Senate. *CG*, 30 Cong., 1 sess., 764, 1028; ibid., App., 540–44; *HJ*, 30 Cong., 1 sess. (Serial 513), 225, 824–25; *SJ*, 30 Cong., 1 sess. (Serial 502), 521, 782.

41. *JCC*, XXXIV:430–31, 458–60; Harold C. Syrett and Jacob E. Cooke, eds., *The Papers of Alexander Hamilton*, 26 vols. (New York: Columbia University Press, 1961–79), V:205–6; Boyd et al., eds., *Papers of Jefferson*, XVII:472–73.

42. Howard Albert Ohline, "Politics and Slavery: The Issue of Slavery in National Politics, 1787–1815" (Ph.D. diss., University of Missouri, Columbia, 1870), 187–91; Boyd et al., eds., *Papers of Jefferson*, XIX:430–33, 518–20.

43. Jefferson to the governor of Georgia (Edward Telfair), July 3, 1792; May 22, 1793; Jefferson to Randolph, October 28, 1792; Randolph to Jefferson, December 3, 1792, Thomas Jefferson Papers, Library of Congress microfilm; Ohline, "Politics and Slavery," 191–95.

44. Jackson to Edmund P. Gaines, April 8, 1816, John Spencer Bassett, ed., *Correspondence of Andrew Jackson*, 6 vols. (Washington, D.C.: Carnegie Institution of Washington, 1926–35), II:238–39; James W. Silver, *Edmund Pendleton Gaines, Frontier General* (Baton Rouge: Louisiana State University Press, 1949), 59–63.

45. An account of the destruction of the fort written by the American naval officer in command is Jairus Loomis to Daniel T. Patterson, August 13, 1816, in *ASP, Foreign Relations*, IV:559–60. An extensive secondary account is in James Parton, *Life of Andrew Jackson*, 3 vols. (New York: Mason Brothers, 1860), II:397–407. See also Kenneth Wiggins Porter, "Negroes and the Seminole War, 1817–1818," *JNH* 36 (1951): 259–65; Rembert W. Patrick, *Aristocrat in Uniform: General Duncan L. Clinch* (Gainesville: University of Florida Press, 1963), 27–33. Clinch, then a colonel, was the army officer commanding the attack.

46. Daniel T. Patterson to Benjamin W. Crowninshield, August 15, 1816, *ASP, Foreign Relations*, IV:561.

47. *SAL*, VI (Private Laws, 1789–1845):778. Joshua R. Giddings, *The Exiles of Florida: Or, the Crimes Committed by Our Government against the Maroons, Who Fled from South Carolina and Other Slave States, Seeking Protection under Spanish Laws*, facsimile reproduction, 1858 (Gainesville: University of Florida Press, 1964), 43–44.

48. *ASP, Military Affairs*, I:687; Edwin C. McReynolds, *The Seminoles* (Norman: University of Oklahoma Press, 1957), 80–81; Giddings, *Exiles of Florida*, 47–48; Porter, "Seminole War, 1817–1818," 268–69.

49. *MPP*, II:31 (March 25, 1818).

50. Porter, "Seminole War, 1817–1818," 270–80; J. Leitch Wright, Jr., *Creeks and Seminoles: The Destruction and Regeneration of the Muscogulge People* (Lincoln: University of Nebraska Press, 1986), 202–8; Robert V. Remini, *Andrew Jackson and the Course of American Empire* (New York: Harper & Row, 1977), 351–65.

51. Kappler, ed., *Indian Affairs*, II:203–4; McReynolds, *Seminoles*, 98–99.

52. Kenneth Wiggins Porter, "Negroes and the Seminole War, 1835–1842," *JSH* 30 (1964): 427.

53. *ASP, Foreign Relations*, VI:580–81, 612, 950; William R. Manning, *Early Diplomatic Relations Between the United States and Mexico* (Baltimore: Johns Hopkins University Press, 1916), 229–31, 240–42. The article as approved by the Senate read as follows: "It is likewise agreed that, in the event of any slaves escaping from their owners residing in the States or Territories of one of the contracting parties, and passing over into the States or Territories of the other, it shall be lawful for the owner or owners of such slaves, or their lawful agents, to require the assistance of the authorities of the country where they may be found for their arrest, detention, and custody, and for that purpose the proprietors, or their agents, shall address themselves to the nearest magistrate or competent officer. On such demand being made, it shall be the duty of the magistrate or competent officer to cause the said slaves to be arrested and detained; and if it shall appear that such slaves be actually the property of the claimant, the magistrate or competent officer shall surrender them to the proprietors, or their agents, to be conveyed back to the country from whence they had escaped, the claimants paying the expenses incurred by the arrest, detention, and custody of such slaves, and none another." Here, quite clearly, was an international version of a fugitive-slave law.

54. Manning, *United States and Mexico*, 242–43; *Journal of the Executive Proceedings of the Senate*, III:606–7 (May 1, 1828).

55. Manning, *United States and Mexico*, 243–46.

56. Ibid., 250–51.

57. *Austin Texas State Times*, June 2, 1855, quoted in Ronnie C. Tyler, "The Callahan Expedition of 1855, Indians or Negroes?" *Southwestern Historical Quarterly* 70 (1966–67): 574–75.

58. Tyler, "Callahan Expedition," 575; J. Fred Rippy, "Border Troubles along the Rio Grande, 1848–1860," *Southwestern Historical Quarterly* 23 (1919–20): 99–104; Paul Neff Garber, *The Gadsden Treaty* (Philadelphia: Press of the University of Pennsylvania, 1923), 159–60; Randolph B. Campbell, *An Empire for Slavery: The Peculiar Institution in Texas, 1821–1865* (Baton Rouge: Louisiana State University Press, 1989), 62–64; Forsyth to Secretary of State William L. Marcy, February 2, 1857, in Manning, ed., *Diplomatic Correspondence: Inter-American*, IX:890 (this John Forsyth was the son of the John Forsyth who served as secretary of state under Jackson and Van Buren).

59. Robin W. Winks, *The Blacks in Canada: A History* (New Haven, Conn.: Yale University Press, 1971), 240.

60. William R. Manning, ed., *Diplomatic Correspondence of the United States: Canadian Relations, 1784–1860*, 3 vols. (Washington, D.C.: Carnegie Endowment for International Peace, 1940–43), I:294.

61. Ibid., 909–10.

62. William Renwick Riddell, "The Fugitive Slave in Upper Canada," *JNH* 5

(1920): 343–44. In *Somerset v. Stewart* (1772), Lord Mansfield had ruled that English law provided no sanction for holding a slave against his will. See William M. Wiecek, "*Somerset*: Lord Mansfield and the Legitimacy of Slavery in the Anglo-American World," *University of Chicago Law Review* 42 (1974): 86–146.

63. Manning, ed., *Diplomatic Correspondence: Canadian*, II:100–101, 132–33, 135.

64. Ibid., 634.

65. Ibid., 181.

66. Ibid., 771–72.

67. Roman J. Zorn, "An Arkansas Fugitive Slave Incident and Its International Repercussions," *Arkansas Historical Quarterly* 16 (1957): 139–49; Zorn, "Criminal Extradition Menaces the Canadian Haven for Fugitive Slaves, 1841–61," *Canadian Historical Review* 38 (1957): 284–91; Riddell, "Fugitive Slave in Upper Canada," 342–54.

68. Zorn, "Criminal Extradition," 292–94; Robert C. Reinders, "The John Anderson Case, 1860–1861: A Study in Anglo-Canadian Imperial Relations," *Canadian Historical Review* 56 (1975): 393–415. The fullest account is Patrick Brode, *The Odyssey of John Anderson* (Toronto: University of Toronto Press, 1989).

69. *SD*, 24 Cong., 2 sess., No. 174 (Serial 298); Joe Bassette Wilkins, Jr., "Window on Freedom: The South's Response to the Emancipation of the Slaves in the British West Indies, 1833–1861," (Ph.D. diss., University of South Carolina, 1977), 173–74; Beverly Miller, "Forcible Liberation of American Slaves in British Colonial Ports, 1830–1855" (M.A. thesis, University of Chicago, 1952), 12–16; Barbara Layenette Green, "Slaves, Ships, and Citizenship: Congressional Response to the Coastwise Slave Trade and Status of Slaves on the High Seas, 1830–1842" (M.A. thesis, North Texas State University, 1975), 12–16.

70. Livingston to the chargé d'affaires, Aaron Vail, February 26, 1833, in *SD*, 24 Cong., 1 sess., No. 174 (Serial 298), 4.

71. *SD*, 24 Cong., 1 sess., No. 174 (Serial 298), 6, 35; Miller, "Forcible Liberation," 17–22.

72. Forsyth to Stevenson, May 19, 1836, Andrew Stevenson Papers, Manuscript Division, Library of Congress. On Stevenson generally, see Francis Fry Wayland, *Andrew Stevenson, Democrat and Diplomat, 1785–1857* (Philadelphia: University of Pennsylvania Press, 1949).

73. Stevenson to Forsyth, July 14, August 6, 1836; Stevenson to Palmerston, July 29, 1836, Stevenson Papers. Most of the official correspondence on the subject is printed in *SD*, 24 Cong., 2 sess., No. 174 (Serial 298), and 25 Cong., 3 sess., No. 216 (Serial 340).

74. Palmerston to Stevenson, January 7, 1837, Stevenson Papers.

75. Stevenson to Palmerston, May 12, 1837, Stevenson Papers.

76. Stevenson to Palmerston, December 23; Stevenson to Forsyth, December 27, 1837, Stevenson Papers.

77. *RD*, 24 Cong., 2 sess., 725.

78. *CG*, 26 Cong., 1 sess., 233, 328–29; App., 266–70; Henry Clay questioned the wisdom of the resolutions but voted for them.

79. *SD*, 34 Cong., 1 sess., No. 103 (Serial 824), 238. The vessel was sometimes mistakenly called the "*Formosa*." See *CG*, 27 Cong., 2 sess., 47; Howard Jones, *To the*

Webster-Ashburton Treaty: A Study in Anglo-American Relations, 1783–1843 (Chapel Hill: University of North Carolina Press, 1977), 80–81.

80. Forsyth to Stevenson, March 12, June 6; Stevenson to Palmerston, April 17, July 10; Palmerston to Stevenson, September 10; Stevenson to Forsyth, October 30, November 5, 1838, Stevenson Papers.

81. Stevenson to Palmerston, February 8, October 30, December 4, 1838; January 26, May 6, 1839; Palmerston to Stevenson, September 13, 1838; May 2, 1839, October 2, 1839; Stevenson to Forsyth, May 8, August 6, December 20, 1839, Stevenson Papers.

82. *HD*, 27 Cong., 2 sess., No. 242 (Serial 405).

83. *CG*, 27 Cong., 3 sess., 276–77.

84. Wayland, *Stevenson*, 183–89; Samuel Eliot Morison, *"Old Bruin": Commodore Matthew C. Perry, 1794–1858* (Boston: Little, Brown & Co., 1967), 137–38. Perry was one of two American visitors in London with whom Stevenson consulted about challenging O'Connell. The other was James Hamilton, the nullification governor of South Carolina. It was Hamilton whose letters home publicized the affair in America.

85. *SD*, 27 Cong., 2 sess., No. 51 (Serial 396); Edward D. Jervey and C. Harold Huber, "The Creole Affair," *JNH* 65 (1980): 196–211. Two of the nineteen mutineers died while in custody, one from natural causes and the other from wounds received during the mutiny.

86. This is a fact not generally recognized. Herbert Aptheker, *American Slave Revolts* (New York: Columbia University Press, 1943), makes no mention of the *Creole* affair. Neither does Eugene D. Genovese in *From Rebellion to Revolution: Afro-American Slave Revolts in the Making of the Modern World* (Baton Rouge: Louisiana State University Press, 1979).

87. *CG*, 27 Cong., 2 sess., 47.

88. Wilbur Devereux Jones, "The Influence of Slavery on the Webster-Ashburton Negotiations," *JSH* 22 (1956): 49.

89. Webster to Everett, January 29, 1842, *SD*, 27 Cong., 2 sess., No. 137 (Serial 397); H. Jones, *Webster-Ashburton Treaty*, 83–84.

90. W. D. Jones, "Influence of Slavery," 50–51.

91. H. Jones, *Webster-Ashburton Treaty*, 148–49; Charles M. Wiltse, *John C. Calhoun: Sectionalist, 1840–1850* (Indianapolis, Ind.: Bobbs-Merrill Co., 1951), 72–73.

92. *SD*, 34 Cong., 1 sess., No. 103 (Serial 824), 16, 18, 455–59. The commissioners first offered the appointment to Martin Van Buren, who declined.

93. Ibid., 31, 38, 52, 57, 187–245. The cases are summarized with excerpts from the arguments and decisions in John Bassett Moore, *A Digest of International Law*, 8 vols. (Washington, D.C.: Government Printing Office, 1906), II:350–61; and in Moore, *International Arbitrations*, I:391–425.

94. *SD*, 34 Cong., 1 sess., No. 103 (Serial 824), 237, 245.

95. Ibid., 52, 57.

96. *CG*, 27 Cong., 2 sess., 342.

97. Ibid., 343, 345–46, 349; James Brewer Stewart, *Joshua R. Giddings and the Tactics of Radical Politics* (Cleveland: Case Western Reserve University Press, 1970), 73–76.

98. See Webster to Ashburton, August 1, 1842, *SD*, 27 Cong., 3 sess, No. 1 (Serial 413), 116–22.

99. Thomas O. Ott, *The Haitian Revolution, 1789–1804* (Knoxville: University of Tennessee Press, 1973). On the refugees, who were predominantly white but included some persons of color and even some slaves, see Alfred N. Hunt, *Haiti's Influence on Antebellum America: Slumbering Volcano in the Caribbean* (Baton Rouge: Louisiana State University Press, 1988), 37–83; John E. Bauer, "International Repercussions of the Haitian Revolution," *Americas* 26 (1969–70): 395–403.

100. Taney to J. Mason Campbell, October 19, 1860, Benjamin C. Howard Papers, Maryland Historical Society. Reports of the Haitian revolution appear to have powerfully affected the attitudes of slaves as well as of white southerners. See, for example, James Sidbury, "Saint Domingue in Virginia: Ideology, Local Meanings, and Resistance to Slavery, 1790–1800," *JSH* 63 (1997): 531–52.

101. Rayford W. Logan, *The Diplomatic Relations of the United States with Haiti, 1776–1891* (Chapel Hill: University of North Carolina Press, 1941), 34–36. For a more extensive treatment, see Timothy M. Matthewson, "Slavery and Diplomacy: The United States and Saint Domingue, 1791–1793" (Ph.D. diss., University of California, Santa Barbara, 1976); also, see his "George Washington's Policy Toward the Haitian Revolution," *Diplomatic History* 3 (1979): 321–36.

102. Logan, *Diplomatic Relations with Haiti*, 98–111; 119–21; Alexander DeConde, *The Quasi-War: The Politics and Diplomacy of the Undeclared War with France, 1797–1801* (New York: Charles Scribner's Sons, 1966), 134–36, 322–23.

103. *AC*, 9 Cong., 1 sess., 138, 515–16; App., 1228–29; *AC*, 9 Cong., 2 sess., 77, 373, 608; App., 1262; Robinson, *Slavery in American Politics*, 370–75.

104. *AC*, 9 Cong., 1 sess., 34, 118, 512–3, 515; Logan, *Diplomatic Relations with Haiti*, 153, 177–79. The southern response to the Haitian revolution is well treated in Hunt, *Haiti's Influence*, 107–46.

105. Monroe's report of the uprising is in Stanislaus Murray Hamilton, *The Writings of James Monroe*, 7 vols. (New York: G. P. Putnam's Sons, 1898–1903), III:234–43. See also Harry Ammon, *James Monroe: The Quest for National Identity* (New York: McGraw-Hill, 1971), 186–89; Aptheker, *American Slave Revolts*, 219–26; Gerald W. Mullin, *Flight and Rebellion: Slave Resistance in Eighteenth-Century Virginia* (New York: Oxford University Press, 1972), 140–53; and especially, Douglas R. Egerton, *Gabriel's Rebellion: The Virginia Slave Conspiracies of 1800 and 1802* (Chapel Hill: University of North Carolina Press, 1993), 50–115, 186–87. For Aptheker, thirty-five is a conservative estimate of the number executed. Ulrich⋅ Bonnell Phillips, *American Negro Slavery: A Survey of the Supply, Employment and Control of Negro Labor as Determined by the Plantation Régime* (New York: D. Appleton & Co., 1918), 475, fixed the number at twenty-five, and Egerton agrees with him.

106. *ASP, Miscellaneous*, I:464. Jefferson had already suggested to Monroe that deportation of rebellious slaves was the "proper measure on this and all similar occasions." Paul Leicester Ford, ed., *The Writings of Thomas Jefferson*, 10 vols. (Washington, D.C.: G. P. Putnam's Sons, 1892–99), VII:457–58.

107. *ASP, Miscellaneous*, I:464–66.

108. Charles R. King, ed., *The Life and Correspondence of Rufus King, Comprising His Letters, Private and Official, His Public Documents and Speeches*, 6 vols. (New York: G. P. Putnam's Sons, 1894–1900), IV:171–75, 197; Jefferson to Governor John

Page, December 27, 1804, *ASP, Miscellaneous*, I:467. After the purchase of Louisiana, the Virginia legislature passed a resolution proposing that a portion of that territory "be appropriated to the residence of such people of color as have been or shall be emancipated in Virginia, or may hereafter become dangerous to the public safety." *ASP, Miscellaneous*, I:466. On the search for a place of asylum generally, see Egerton, *Gabriel's Rebellion*, 151–62.

109. *AC*, 11 Cong., 1 sess., 443–46.

110. *HD*, 27 Cong., 3 sess., No. 36 (Serial 420); John M. Clayton to Benjamin M. Green, June 13, 1849, in Manning, ed., *Diplomatic Correspondence: Inter-American*, VI:8–9; Charles Callan Tansill, *The United States and Santo Domingo, 1798–1873: A Chapter in Caribbean Diplomacy* (Baltimore: Johns Hopkins University Press, 1938), 113–15.

111. Logan, *Diplomatic Relations with Haiti*, 194–95.

112. Ibid., 197–98.

113. *MPP*, II:204–5 (February 25, 1823).

114. *Niles Weekly Register*, September 27, 1823, p. 53.

115. *MPP*, II:205 (February 25, 1823).

116. Adams, ed., *Memoirs of John Quincy Adams*, VI:530.

117. Ibid., VII:440–41; *HD*, 27 Cong., 3 sess., No. 36 (Serial 420), 114–16. The first agent, Septimus Tyler, was transported to Haiti on an American warship in 1817.

118. For the agenda, see Jose Maria Salazar to Clay, November 2, 1825, in *RD*, 19 Cong., 1 sess., App., 45.

119. *RD*, 19 Cong., 1 sess., 166, 2150.

120. Ibid., 290–91, 330.

121. Logan, *Diplomatic Relations with Haiti*, 231–32.

122. Ibid., 235.

123. [Mary S. Legaré, ed.], *Writings of Hugh Swinton Legaré*, 2 vols. (Charleston, S.C.: Burges & James, 1846), 322, 327.

124. Adams, ed., *Memoirs of John Quincy Adams*, XI:333; Logan, *Diplomatic Relations with Haiti*, 235.

125. Calhoun to Buchanan, August 30, 1845, in John Bassett Moore, ed., *The Works of James Buchanan*, 12 vols. (Philadelphia: J. B. Lippincott & Co., 1911), VI:230; Tyler to Calhoun, October 7, 1845, in *Calhoun Correspondence, American Historical Association Annual Report for the Year 1899*, vol. II (Washington, D.C.: Government Printing Office, 1900), 1058–59; Logan, *Diplomatic Relations with Haiti*, 238–39, 244–49, 281–92; Ludwell Lee Montague, *Haiti and the United States, 1714–1938* (Durham, N.C.: Duke University Press, 1940), 56–58, 60, 94–96.

126. Fillmore to his secretary of state, Daniel Webster, July 16, 1852, in Frank H. Severance, ed., *Millard Fillmore Papers*, vols. X and XI of *Publications of the Buffalo Historical Society* (Buffalo, N.Y.: Buffalo Historical Society, 1907), X:372–73.

127. For example, see the petition of Boston merchants, June 17, 1852, summarized in Logan, *Diplomatic Relations with Haiti*, 277–78, and the editorial in the *Washington National Era*, December 23, 1852.

128. Montague, *Haiti and the United States*, 65.

129. On the remarkable scope of the slave-power argument, see David Brion Davis, *The Slave Power Conspiracy and the Paranoid Style* (Baton Rouge: Louisiana State University Press, 1969), 62–86.

130. In his diary entry for February 22, 1819, the day on which the treaty was signed, Adams listed his various worries and reservations about the treaty. The fact that it added new slave territory to the United States was not one of them. Adams, ed., *Memoirs of John Quincy Adams*, IV:275–76.

131. Ibid., V:54. The Senate approved the treaty unanimously in 1819 and reaffirmed its approval in 1821 by a vote of 40 to 4, with all the opposition coming from Kentucky and Tennessee. *Journal of the Executive Proceedings of the Senate*, III:177–78, 242–44.

132. Monroe to Thomas Jefferson, May (no specific day indicated) 1820, and to Andrew Jackson, May 23, 1820, in Hamilton, *Writings of James Monroe*, VI:119–23, 127–28.

133. *ASP: Foreign Relations*, VI:580.

134. Manning, ed., *United States and Mexico*, 286–348; John Spencer Bassett, "Martin Van Buren"; Francis Rawle, "Edward Livingston"; Eugene Irving McCormac, "Louis McLane"; Eugene Irving McCormac, "John Forsyth," all in Samuel Flagg Bemis, ed., *The American Secretaries of State and Their Diplomacy*, 10 vols. (New York: Alfred A. Knopf, 1928), IV:194–97, 245–47, 290, 292–93, 317–18; Robert V. Remini, *Andrew Jackson and the Course of American Freedom, 1822–1832* (New York: Harper & Row, 1981), 218–20; Remini, *Andrew Jackson and the Course of American Democracy, 1833–1845* (New York: Harper & Row, 1984), 352–56. The only northerner among five secretaries of state between 1825 and 1836 was Martin Van Buren, who served approximately two years. The three ministers to Mexico during this period were all southerners.

135. Remini, *Jackson and American Democracy*, 362–64, 367–68; James C. Curtis, *The Fox at Bay: Martin Van Buren and the Presidency, 1837–1841* (Lexington: University Press of Kentucky, 1970), 152–55, 169; Richard Williams Smith, "The Career of Martin Van Buren in Connection with the Slavery Controversy Through the Election of 1840" (Ph.D. diss., Ohio State University, 1959), 288–89.

136. Notably, Benjamin Lundy and John Quincy Adams. See Henry H. Simms, *Emotion at High Tide: Abolition as a Controversial Factor, 1830–1845* (Richmond, Va.: William Byrd Press, 1960), 180–81; Samuel Flagg Bemis, *John Quincy Adams and the Union* (New York: Alfred A. Knopf, 1956), 355–57.

137. Memucan Hunt to John Forsyth, August 4, and Forsyth to Hunt, August 25, 1837, *HD*, 25 Cong., 1 sess. No. 40 (Serial 311), 2–13; *CG*, 25 Cong., 2 sess., 450, 453, 454–55, 498, 501. In the Senate, all the support for the resolution came from southerners. Seven southerners joined 17 northerners in tabling it, 24 to 14.

138. On Tyler and Texas generally, see Frederick Merk, *Slavery and the Annexation of Texas* (New York: Alfred A. Knopf, 1972); Norma Lois Peterson, *The Presidencies of William Henry Harrison and John Tyler* (Lawrence: University Press of Kansas, 1989), 176–259.

139. The fullest treatment of this subject is Joe Bassette Wilkins, Jr., "Window on Freedom: The South's Response to the Emancipation of Slaves in the British West Indies, 1833–1861" (Ph.D. diss., University of South Carolina, 1977).

140. Lord Aberdeen to Richard Pakenham, December 26, 1843, Robert L. Meriwether, W. Edwin Hemphill, and Clyde N. Wilson, eds., *The Papers of John C. Calhoun*, 18 vols. to date (Columbia: University of South Carolina Press, 1959–88), XVIII:53.

141. Green to Tyler, July 3, 1843, in Merk, *Slavery and Texas*, 221–24.

142. Jackson to Francis Preston Blair, May 7, 1844, Papers of Andrew Jackson, Microfilm Supplement, 1986.

143. Upshur to Calhoun, August 14; Calhoun to Upshur, August 27, 1843, Meriwether et al., eds., *Papers of Calhoun*, XVII:355, 381–83. See also Calhoun to Duff Green, April 2, 1842, ibid., XVI:209; Upshur to Edward Everett, September 28, 1843, Manning, ed., *Diplomatic Correspondence: Inter-American*, VII:11–14; Calhoun to William R. King, August 12, 1844, Merk, *Slavery and Texas*, 281–88.

144. The danger is given considerable credence in Justin H. Smith, *The Annexation of Texas* (New York: Baker & Taylor Co., 1911), 84–94; it is minimized in David M. Pletcher, *The Diplomacy of Annexation: Texas, Oregon, and the Mexican War* (Columbia: University of Missouri Press, 1973), 120–27. See also Ephraim Douglass Adams, *British Interests and Activities in Texas, 1838–1846* (Baltimore: Johns Hopkins University Press, 1910), 137–47; William J. Cooper, Jr., *The South and the Politics of Slavery, 1828–1856* (Baton Rouge: Louisiana State University Press, 1978), 192–93; Wiltse, *Calhoun: Sectionalist*, 153–55; Thomas R. Hietala, *Manifest Design: Anxious Aggrandizement in Late Jacksonian America* (Ithaca, N.Y.: Cornell University Press, 1985), 16–26.

145. See especially Tyler's message to Congress, April 22, 1844, *MPP*, IV:309–10. See also Merk, *Slavery and Texas*, 77–78, 201; Hietala, *Manifest Design*, 24.

146. Hietala, *Manifest Design*, 25; Davis, *Slave Power Conspiracy*, 46. "The New York *Herald* and other prints charge the whole of the abolition movement here to the machinations of England," wrote John Greenleaf Whittier in 1842. Annie Heloise Abel and Frank J. Klingberg, *A Sidelight on Anglo-American Relations* (Lancaster, Pa.: Lancaster Press, 1927), 92.

147. See, for example, Calhoun to Gilmer, December 25, 1843, Meriwether et al., eds., *Papers of Calhoun*, XVII:641.

148. Walker's letter is conveniently reproduced in Frederick Merk, *Fruits of Propaganda in the Tyler Administration* (Cambridge, Mass.: Harvard University Press, 1971). See especially p. 235.

149. Smith, *Annexation of Texas*, 122–23, 147–69; Merk, *Slavery and Texas*, 23–25, 33–43; Pletcher, *Diplomacy of Annexation*, 127–35; Claude H. Hall, *Abel Parker Upshur, Conservative Virginian, 1790–1844* (Madison: State Historical Society of Wisconsin, 1963), 199–212.

150. For the controversy over whether Tyler really wanted to appoint Calhoun or was maneuvered into doing so by Henry Wise, see Robert Seager II, *And Tyler too: A Biography of John and Julia Gardiner Tyler* (New York: McGraw-Hill, 1963), 216–17; Craig M. Simpson, *A Good Southerner: The Life of Henry A. Wise of Virginia* (Chapel Hill: University of North Carolina Press, 1985), 57–58; Wiltse, *Calhoun: Sectionalist*, 161–63; John Niven, *John C. Calhoun and the Price of Union: A Biography* (Baton Rouge: Louisiana State University Press, 1988), 273 n; Merk, *Slavery and Texas*, 54.

151. Wiltse, *Calhoun: Sectionalist*, 163–67; *MPP*, IV:307–13 (April 22, 1844).

152. *SJ*, VI:268–69, 272, 283, 284–85. The motion to print was made by an apparently unabashed Tappan. The Senate printing is *SD*, 28 Cong., 1 sess., No. 341 (Serial 435).

153. Upshur to Edward Everett, September 28, 1843 (2 dispatches), in Manning, ed., *Diplomatic Correspondence: Inter-American*, VII:6–17.

154. Meriwether et al., eds., *Papers of Calhoun*, XVIII:273–78. In a subsequent note to Pakenham, Calhoun solemnly denied that this letter was intended as a defense of slavery. (Ibid., 349).

155. For summaries of the debate, see Cooper, *South and Slavery*, 375–76; Peterson, *Harrison and Tyler*, 216–18.

156. Upshur to William S. Murphy, U.S. chargé d'affaires in Texas, January 16, 1844, *SD*, 28 Cong., 1 sess., No. 341 (Serial 435), 47.

157. For the platform and record of the balloting, see Charles Sellers, "Election of 1844," in *History of American Presidential Elections, 1789–1968*, ed., Arthur M. Schlesinger, Jr., Fred L. Israel, and William P. Hansen, 4 vols. (New York: Chelsea House, McGraw-Hill Book Co., 1971), II:799–801, 829–52.

158. *SJ*, VI:312. Thomas Hart Benton of Missouri was the only southern Democrat to vote against the treaty. John Henderson of Mississippi was the only Whig of either section to vote for the treaty.

159. *MPP*, IV:323–27 (June 10, 1844).

160. Ibid., 344 (December 3, 1844).

161. *CG*, 28 Cong., 2 sess., 194, 362, 372. For a summary of the debates in the House and Senate, see Smith, *Annexation of Texas*, 339 n–41 n. The division in the House on January 25 was both sectional and partisan, but more emphatically the latter. Democrats were 80 percent for annexation, Whigs were 90 percent against; southerners were 79 percent for, northerners were 60 percent against. All northern Whigs and southern Democrats voted with their sections; 69 percent of southern Whigs and 65 percent of northern Democrats voted against their sections.

162. Adams, ed., *Memoirs of John Quincy Adams*, XII:173.

163. The Senate amendment offered the president the alternative of reopening negotiations with Texas. It was at Calhoun's urging that Tyler immediately implemented the House version of the resolution, rather than leaving the decision to Polk. See Wiltse, *Calhoun: Sectionalist*, 214; Merk, *Slavery and Texas*, 160–61; Peterson, *Harrison and Tyler*, 257–58.

164. Tyler to the editor of the *Richmond Enquirer*, published June 5, 1847; Tyler to Alexander Gardiner, June 17, 1847, in Lyon G. Tyler, *The Letters and Times of the Tylers*, 3 vols. (Richmond, Va.: Whittet & Shepperson, 1884–96), II:426.

165. *CG*, 28 Cong., 2 sess., 200.

166. Upshur, the lesser known of the two, was if anything the more apprehensive about external threats to slavery. As secretary of the navy in 1841, at a time when the Texas question was relatively dormant, he presented a report calling for enlargement of the navy on the grounds that a wartime enemy (meaning Britain) might try to "subvert our social systems" (meaning incite southern slaves to revolt). *HD*, 27 Cong., 2 sess., No. 2 (Serial 401).

167. Meriwether et al., eds., *Papers of Calhoun*, XVII:383.

168. Richard Kerwin MacMaster, "The United States, Great Britain and the Suppression of the Cuban Slave Trade, 1835–1860" (Ph.D. diss., Georgetown University, 1968), 257–63.

169. [James Hamilton], *Speech of Mr. Hamilton, of South Carolina, on the Panama Mission, Delivered in the House of Representatives, April 6, 1826* (Washington, D.C.: Office of the United States Telegraph, 1826), 24.

170. M. W. Cluskey, ed., *Speeches, Messages, and Other Writings of the Hon. Albert G. Brown*, 2d ed. (Philadelphia: J. B. Smith & Co., 1859), 595.

171. Jefferson to Monroe, October 24, 1823, in Merrill Peterson, ed., *Jefferson: Writings*, 1482–83; Philip S. Foner, *A History of Cuba and Its Relations with the United States*, 2 vols. (New York: International Publishers, 1962–63), I:124–27.

172. Adams to Hugh Nelson, newly appointed minister to Spain, April 28, 1823, in Worthington Chauncey Ford, ed., *The Writings of John Quincy Adams*, 7 vols. (New York: Macmillan Publishing Co., 1913–17), VII:372–73.

173. Manning, ed., *Diplomatic Correspondence: Inter-American*, XI:6–7, 53, 70.

174. Clay to Alexander Everett, April 27, and to Henry Middleton, May 10, 1825, in James F. Hopkins, et al., eds., *The Papers of Henry Clay*, 9 vols. to date (Lexington: University Press of Kentucky, 1959–88), IV:297, 361; Foner, *History of Cuba*, I:150–61; John J. Johnson, *A Hemisphere Apart: The Foundations of United States Policy Toward Latin America* (Baltimore: Johns Hopkins University Press, 1990), 143–47, 161. Secretary of State Martin Van Buren asserted in 1829 that the Mexican-Colombian attack on Cuba had been "arrested chiefly by the timely interposition" of the United States government. Van Buren to Cornelius P. Van Ness, minister to Spain, in William R. Manning, ed., *Diplomatic Correspondence of the United States Concerning the Independence of the Latin-American Nations*, 3 vols. (New York: Oxford University Press, 1925), I:305.

175. Daniel Webster to Robert B. Campbell, January 14, 1843, in Manning, ed., *Diplomatic Correspondence: Inter-American*, XI:27.

176. Foner, *History of Cuba*, I:212–17; II:9–19; MacMaster, "United States, Great Britain, and Cuban Slave Trade," 266–74.

177. Lopez fled to the United States in 1848 when his revolutionary intentions were discovered. He failed in three filibustering expeditions to Cuba and in the end was executed. Foner, *History of Cuba*, II:24–26, 41–60.

178. James Buchanan to Romulus M. Saunders, June 17, 1848; Saunders to Buchanan, July 29, December 14, 1848, Manning, ed., *Diplomatic Correspondence: Inter-American*, XI:54–64, 446, 458; Paul H. Bergeron, *The Presidency of James K. Polk* (Lawrence: University Press of Kansas, 1987), 108–10.

179. Foner, *History of Cuba*, II:66–85; MacMaster, "United States, Great Britain, and Cuban Slave Trade," 359–85; Stanley Urban, "The Africanization of Cuba Scare, 1853–55," *Hispanic American Historical Review* 37 (1957): 29–40; Basil Rauch, *American Interest in Cuba: 1848–1855* (New York: Columbia University Press, 1948), 264–75; Robert E. May, *The Southern Dream of a Caribbean Empire, 1854–1861* (Baton Rouge: Louisiana State University Press, 1973), 46–58; Robert E. May, *John A. Quitman, Old South Crusader* (Baton Rouge: Louisiana State University Press, 1985), 270–82. In a generally exculpatory examination of alleged presidential complicity in filibustering ventures of the 1840s and 1850s, May acknowl-

edges that Pierce "may have hinted during his first year in office that he would support filibuster projects." See his essay, "The Slave Power Conspiracy Revisited: United States Presidents and Filibustering, 1848–1861," in *Union and Emancipation: Essays on Politics and Race in the Civil War Era*, ed. David W. Blight and Brooks D. Simpson (Kent, Ohio: Kent State University Press, 1997), 26.

180.   Marcy to Soulé, April 3, 1854, Manning, ed., *Diplomatic Correspondence: Inter-American*, XI:175–78; Ivor Debenham Spencer, *The Victor and the Spoils: A Life of William L. Marcy* (Providence, R.I.: Brown University Press, 1959), 320–22. For a detailed study of Soulé 's diplomacy, see Amos Aschbach Ettinger, *The Mission to Spain of Pierre Soulé, 1853–1855: A Study in the Cuban Diplomacy of the United States* (New Haven, Conn.: Yale University Press, 1932).

181.   The exact words were: "After we shall have offered Spain a price for Cuba, far beyond its present value, and this shall have been refused, it will then be time to consider the question, does Cuba in the possession of Spain seriously endanger our internal peace and the existence of our cherished Union. Should this question be answered in the affirmative, then, by every law human and Divine, we shall be justified in wresting it from Spain." It has been argued that this phrasing made the threat of seizure conditional rather than direct and, indeed, little more than a "guarded hint" to Spain. See Roy F. Nichols, *Franklin Pierce, Young Hickory of the Granite Hills*, 2nd ed. (Philadelphia: University of Pennsylvania Press, 1958), 596; Philip Shriver Klein, *President James Buchanan: A Biography* (University Park: Pennsylvania State University Press, 1962), 240. But such an interpretation ignores the fact that the authors of the manifesto had answered their own question with the assertion that any delay in the acquisition of Cuba would be "exceedingly dangerous to the United States" and that the island had already become "an unceasing danger, and a permanent cause of anxiety and alarm."

182.   The text of the manifesto, dated October 18, 1854, is in Manning, ed., *Diplomatic Correspondence: Inter-American*, VII:579–85. Its other two authors were Buchanan, minister to Great Britain, and John Y. Mason, minister to France. See also Soulé to Marcy, October 20, 1854, in ibid., XI:825–26; Ettinger, *Mission of Soulé*, 339–412, 490–94.

183.   Washington (D.C.), *National Era* March 29, 1855.

184.   Spencer, *Victor and Spoils*, 340–41; May, *Quitman*, 283–95; Rauch, *American Interest in Cuba*, 295–300; Foner, *History of Cuba*, II:104–05. Marcy's response to the manifesto rejected its more aggressive implications and so displeased Soulé that he resigned. Soulé 's successor, August C. Dodge raised the question of purchase again in August 1855 and was told that "all the treasure of the earth" could not buy Cuba. Dodge also asked for and received assurance that Spain would make no change in the institution of slavery on the island. See Manning, *Diplomatic Correspondence: Inter-American*, XI:886–91.

185.   "It is the capital object on which the President has fastened his hopes for popularity now and fame hereafter." So reported Lord Napier, the British minister in Washington, on May 26, 1857. Napier surprisingly suggested that Britain acquiesce in American annexation of Cuba. He listed eight reasons for such a reversal of British policy, one of which was that it would allay anglophobic feeling in the United States. Lord Palmerston, the prime minister, commented sardonically that Napier should remember that he had not yet become a naturalized citizen of the United States. "As to propitiating the Yankees by countenancing their schemes of annexation," Palmerston added, "it would be like propitiating an animal of prey by giving

him one of one's travelling companions." Gavin B. Henderson, ed., "Southern Designs on Cuba, 1854–57, and Some European Opinions," *JSH* 5 (1939): 383–85.

186. *MPP*, V:510–11 (December 6, 1858).

187. *CG*, 35 Cong., 2 sess., App., 90–95; May, *Southern Dream*, 169–72.

188. *CG*, 35 Cong., 2 sess., 1363, 1385.

189. *CG*, 36 Cong., 1 sess., 199, 2456; *MPP*, V:561 (December 19, 1859) V:642 (December 3, 1860); May, *Southern Dream*, 185–86.

190. August C. Dodge to Lewis Cass, January 5, 1859, in Manning, ed., *Diplomatic Correspondence: Inter-American*, XI:963–64. See also William Preston to Cass, March 9, 1859, ibid., 965–67.

191. *CG*, 35 Cong., 2 sess., 1363. The attitude of the militants was well expressed by Congressman Reuben Davis of Mississippi, who introduced a resolution calling upon the president to seize Cuba and hold it until Spain paid certain debts and removed certain causes of complaint. Plainly, his expectation was that American possession would be permanent. He acknowledged that such action might lead to war. Ibid., 196, 703–6.

192. May, *Southern Dream*, 186.

193. Dunbar Rowland, ed., *Jefferson Davis, Constitutionalist: His Letters, Papers and Speeches*, 10 vols. (Jackson: Mississippi Department of Archives and History, 1923), IV:79–85.

194. Edwin Hodder, *The Life and Work of the Seventh Earl of Shaftesbury, K.G.*, 3 vols. (London: Cassell & Co., 1893), II:397.

195. Henry Barrett Learned, "William Learned Marcy," and Lewis Einstein, "Lewis Cass," in Bemis, ed., *Secretaries of State*, VI:234, 236, 308, 362; Lord Clarendon to Lord Napier, November 20, 1857, in Manning, ed., *Diplomatic Correspondence: Inter-American*, VII:732 n; Moore, ed., *Works of Buchanan*, X:127.

CHAPTER 5

1. *AC*, 6 Cong., 1 sess., 686–90, 699.

2. Jay Coughtry, *The Notorious Triangle: Rhode Island and the African Slave Trade, 1700–1807* (Philadelphia: Temple University Press, 1981), 25.

3. During the years 1804–7 when South Carolina permitted importation of slaves, although the American share of the maritime slave trade was then at its peak, foreign ships still brought more slaves to Charleston than did American ships. *AC*, 16 Cong., 2 sess., 77; James A. Rawley, *The Transatlantic Slave Trade: A History* (New York: W. W. Norton & Co., 1981), 328, 415. According to Coughtry, *Notorious Triangle*, 170, 176, only about one-third of the Rhode Island slavers operating from 1700 to 1807 delivered their human cargoes to the North American continent. But Roger Anstey has estimated that about 60 percent of the slaves carried away from Africa in American ships between 1791 and 1810 were landed in the United States. See "The Volume of the North American Slave-Carrying Trade from Africa, 1761–1810," *Revue Française d'Histoire d'Outre-Mer* 40 (1973): 64.

4. *AC*, 1 Cong., 2 sess., 1473–74. The authority was presumably claimed by virtue of the clause empowering Congress to "regulate commerce with foreign nations," but in later argument it was also justified as an exercise of congressional power to

define and punish "offenses against the law of nations." See, for example, *AC.*, 9 Cong., 2 sess., 271.

5. *AC*, 9 Cong., 2 sess., 486–87. The act entitled "An act to prohibit the importation of slaves into any port or place within the jurisdiction of the United States, from and after the first day of January, in the year of our Lord 1808" was enacted on March 2, 1807. See *SAL*, II:426–29.

6. The February 23 vote of 283 to 16 in the House of Commons was on the second reading of the bill. The American act of March 3, 1807, did not become effective until January 1, 1808, the earliest date possible under the Constitution, whereas the British act of March 25 became effective on May 1, 1807. Roger Anstey, *The Atlantic Slave Trade and British Abolition, 1760–1810* (Atlantic Highlands, N.J.: Humanities Press, 1975), 397–98.

7. William Jay, *View of the Action of the Federal Government in Behalf of Slavery*, 2d. ed. (New York: American Anti-Slavery Society, 1839), 106; W. E. B[urghardt] Du Bois, "The Enforcement of the Slave-Trade Laws," *American Historical Association Annual Report for 1891* (Washington, D.C.: Government Printing Office, 1892), 173; W. E. Burghardt Du Bois, *The Suppression of the African Slave-Trade to the United States of America, 1638–1870* (New York: Longmans, Green & Co., 1896), 109, 115, 116, 127, 129, 160. Christopher Lloyd, *The Navy and the Slave Trade: The Suppression of the African Slave Trade in the Nineteenth Century* (London: Longman's, Green, 1949), 167–68; Warren S. Howard, *American Slavers and the Federal Law, 1837–1862* (Berkeley: University of California Press, 1963), 206.

8. *AC*, 1 Cong., 1 sess., 336.

9. Ibid., 336–42, 903; Donald L. Robinson, *Slavery in the Structure of American Politics, 1765–1820* (New York: Harcourt Brace Jovanovich, 1971), 299–301.

10. *AC*, 1 Cong., 2 sess., 1182–91; Thomas E. Drake, *Quakers and Slavery in America* (New Haven, Conn.: Yale University Press, 1950), 102–4.

11. *AC*, 1 Cong., 2 sess., 1197–98.

12. Ibid., 1198–1205; *HJ*, 1 Cong., 2 sess., 34–35.

13. *AC*, 1 Cong., 2 sess., 1413–17, 1450–74; Madison to Benjamin Rush, March 20, 1790, in William T. Hutchinson et al., eds., *The Papers of James Madison*, 17 vols. to date (Chicago: University of Chicago Press; Charlottesville: University Press of Virginia, 1962–91), XIII:109. The most notable proslavery speech during the debate was made by William Loughton Smith of South Carolina, but James Jackson was more abusive of Quakers. On the two men, see George C. Rogers, Jr., *Evolution of a Federalist: William Loughton Smith of Charleston, 1758–1812* (Columbia: University of South Carolina Press, 1962); and William Omer Foster, Sr., *James Jackson: Duelist and Militant Statesman, 1757–1806* (Athens: University of Georgia Press, 1960). Jackson's speech was satirized by the eighty-four-year-old Benjamin Franklin in a public letter published just a few weeks before his death. See J. A. Leo Lemay, ed., *Franklin: Writings* (New York: Library of America, 1987), 1157–60.

14. *HJ*, 1 Cong., 2 sess., 62–64; Du Bois, *Suppression*, 78–79. The principal substantive change made by the committee of the whole was a more categorical denial of federal power over slavery in the states. The select committee's report seemed to imply that some such power might exist after 1807. For a detailed examination of the report and the debate upon it, see Howard Albert Ohline, "Politics and Slavery: The Issue of Slavery in National Politics, 1787–1815" (Ph.D. diss., University of Missouri, Columbia, 1969), 137–57.

15. *HJ*, 1 Cong., 2 sess., 61–64; *AC*, 1 Cong., 2 sess., 1472–74.

16. Ohline, "Politics and Slavery," 134–37.

17. Ibid., 211–13.

18. Anstey, "Slave-Carrying Trade," 64–65; David Eltis, *Economic Growth and the Ending of the Transatlantic Slave Trade* (New York: Oxford University Press, 1987), 247.

19. Ohline, "Politics and Slavery," 213–19.

20. Du Bois, *Suppression*, 80–81, and other historians following his lead have attributed congressional action in 1794 almost entirely to the Haiti uprising and the fear of similar revolts that it engendered on the American mainland. This judgment is effectively challenged by Ohline in "Politics and Slavery," 243–44. As he says, it is difficult to see how stopping the slave trade to foreign ports could have been expected to reduce the danger of slave rebellion in the United States.

21. *AC*, 3 Cong., 1 sess., 72, 483; *SAL*, I:347–49.

22. *ASP, Miscellaneous*, II:76.

23. Robinson, *Slavery in American Politics*, 312, says that the law "had virtually no effect." John R. Spears, *The American Slave-Trade: An Account of Its Origin, Growth, and Suppression* (New York: Charles Scribner's Sons, 1900), 116, declares that it "never injured the slavers to the extent of a dollar."

24. Coughtry, *Notorious Triangle*, 213–16; James B. Hedges, *The Browns of Providence Plantations: Colonial Years* (Cambridge, Mass.: Harvard University Press, 1952), 83. Brown's prosecution was instigated by the local abolition society, which had been organized a few years earlier by his brother Moses Brown, a Quaker.

25. *SAL*, II:70–71; Coughtry, *Notorious Triangle*, 216–17, 221–22; Judd Scott Harmon, "Suppress and Protect: The United States Navy, the African Slave Trade, and Maritime Commerce, 1794–1862" (Ph.D. diss., College of William and Mary, 1977), 61–62, 238; Ohline, "Politics and Slavery," 245–55. The act of 1800 made it unlawful for any citizen or other resident of the United States to serve on board a vessel or to have any right of property in a vessel transporting slaves from one foreign place to another. To the fine of $2,000 prescribed in the law of 1794, it added imprisonment for a maximum of two years.

26. Coughtry, *Notorious Triangle*, 28, 212; Anstey, "Slave-Carrying Trade," 65; Eltis, *Economic Growth*, 248; Seymour Drescher, *Econocide: British Slavery in the Era of Abolition* (Pittsburgh, Pa.: University of Pittsburgh Press), 31.

27. Coughtry, *Notorious Triangle*, 38, 226–29. The Jefferson appointee was Charles Collins, who held the office for twenty years. Collins had himself captained several slave-trade voyages. He was connected by marriage to Rhode Island's foremost slave-trading family, the D'Wolfs. See also Peter J. Coleman, *The Transformation of Rhode Island, 1790–1860* (Providence, R.I.: Brown University Press, 1963), 51–57.

28. Coughtry, *Notorious Triangle*, 174, 176. American importations of slaves into Havana during the early 1790s were roughly equal to the British and Spanish shares and constituted about one-fourth of the total. See Herbert S. Klein, "North American Competition and the Characteristics of the African Slave Trade to Cuba, 1790–1794," *William and Mary Quarterly*, 3 ser., 28 (1971): 92.

29. Drescher, *Econocide*, 31.

30. Quoted in Daniel P. Mannix and Malcolm Cowley, *Black Cargoes: A History of the Atlantic Slave Trade, 1518–1865* (New York: Viking Press, 1962), 188.

31. *SAL*, II:205–6. The law was drafted particularly in response to a memorial from inhabitants of Wilmington, N.C., where some emancipated slaves from the French island of Guadeloupe had been landed. At the insistence of certain northerners, the original draft was amended to except natives, citizens, and registered seamen of the United States. The vote for passage in the House was 48 to 15, with no southerners in opposition. In the Senate, the bill was passed without a recorded vote. Signed February 28 by Jefferson, the law took effect on April 1, 1803. *AC*, 7 Cong., 2 sess., 207, 385–86, 534; *HJ*, 7 Cong., 2 sess., 264–65; *SJ*, 7 Cong., 2 sess., 111; Ohline, "Politics and Slavery," 341–47.

32. Ohline, "Politics and Slavery," 348–51. The collector was James Simons, a Charleston merchant and political ally of United States Senator Jacob Read.

33. Elizabeth Donnan, *Documents Illustrative of the History of the Slave Trade to America*, 4 vols. (Washington, D.C.: Carnegie Institution, 1930–35), IV:500–502; *AC*, 8 Cong., 1 sess., 992. Ulrich Bonnell Phillips, *American Negro Slavery: A Survey of the Supply, Employment and Control of Negro Labor as Determined by the Plantation Regime* (New York: D. Appleton & Co., 1918), 136–37; Patrick S. Brady, "The Slave Trade and Sectionalism in South Carolina, 1787–1808," *JSH* 38 (1972): 601–20; Ohline, "Politics and Slavery," 352–53. In a speech justifying the repeal, Congressman Thomas Lowndes said that South Carolina's prohibitory laws had proved totally unenforcible and that for several years Africans had been imported "in numbers little short. . . of what they would have been had the trade been a legal one." *AC*, 8 Cong., 1 sess., 992.

34. Often cited are the figures provided from customhouse records by Senator William Smith of South Carolina in 1820, namely, 202 ships landed 39,075 slaves in Charleston during the years 1804–7. Newspaper advertisements indicate, however, that this summary understates the total number of arrivals. *AC*, 16 Cong., 2 sess., 77; Elizabeth Donnan, "The New England Slave Trade," *New England Quarterly* 3 (1930): 275–76; Donnan, *Slave Trade*, IV:504–6, 508–10, 513–16, 521–25.

35. Donnan, *Slave Trade*, IV:519–20. By 1807, there was more support in lowcountry than in up-country South Carolina for continuation of foreign slave importations, apparently because of mercantile investment in the revived trade. See Brady, "Slave Trade and Sectionalism," 613–14.

36. Herman V. Ames, *The Proposed Amendments to the Constitution of the United States During the First Century of Its History, Annual Report of the American Historical Association for the Year 1896*, Vol. II (Washington, D.C.: Government Printing Office, 1897), 208–9, 326, 327, 328.

37. *AC*, 8 Cong., 1 sess., 820.

38. Ibid., 992–1036. Sectional alignments are revealed in roll-call votes on two motions to postpone further consideration until the next session of Congress. The motions were defeated, 62 to 54 and 62 to 55. Ibid., 1020, 1035–36.

39. Ibid., 1020, 1036; *HJ*, 8 Cong., 1 sess., 434–35; Ohline, "Politics and Slavery," 402–3.

40. *AC*, 8 Cong., 2 sess., 313; 9 Cong., 1 sess., 272–73, 274, 323, 346–52, 358–75, 397, 434–40, 442–44; *HJ*, 9 Cong., 1 sess., 197–99, 200–201, 229–30, 252–53, 288–90, 299, 362; Du Bois, *Suppression*, 91–92.

41. In December 1805, for example, David R. Williams moved postponement of the ten-dollar tax proposal, saying that the South Carolina legislature was considering and would probably pass a measure to reinstall prohibition. *AC*, 9 Cong., 1 sess., 274.

42. Phillips, *Slavery*, 138.

43. *AC*, 9 Cong., 1 sess., 20–21, 437–39; Everett Somerville Brown, ed., *William Plumer's Memorandum of Proceedings in the United States Senate, 1803–1807* (New York: Macmillan Publishing Co., 1923), 353–54; Ohline, "Politics and Slavery," 410. Senator John Quincy Adams maintained that the Bradley proposal was constitutionally impermissible.

44. *MPP*, I:408 (December 2, 1806); *AC*, 9 Cong., 2 sess., 16–17, 19, 151.

45. *AC*, 9 Cong., 2 sess., 172.

46. Ibid., 113, 151, 167–68, 170. The congressional history of the slave-trade act of 1807 is treated extensively in Du Bois, *Suppression*, 95–108; Robinson, *Slavery in American Politics*, 324–37; Ohline, "Politics and Slavery," 412–27; Mary Staughton Locke, *Anti-Slavery in America from the Introduction of African Slaves to the Prohibition of the Slave Trade, 1619–1808* (Boston: Ginn & Co., 1901), 149–54.

47. *AC*, 9 Cong., 2 sess., 168–170, 173–75, 265–66.

48. Du Bois, *Suppression*, 96 n–97 n, lists twelve different propositions for the disposal of imported Africans.

49. *AC*, 9 Cong., 2 sess., 181–84, 264–67.

50. Ibid., 189–90, 200, 231–44. The vote replacing the death penalty with a term of imprisonment was 63 to 53, with southerners 34 to 16 in favor of the substitution and northerners 37 to 29 against it. In later proceedings, the House restored the death penalty, then removed it again. Ibid., 477, 483–84.

51. Ibid., 270–73. *HJ*, 9 Cong., 2 sess., 124–26. Northerners voted 61 to 6 for recommitment and southerners 40 to 15 against it.

52. *AC*, 9 Cong., 2 sess., 19, 33, 36, 45, 47; *SJ*, 9 Cong., 2 sess., 23–24, 30, 68–69, 100, 103. In his diary for January 15, Senator John Quincy Adams wrote that the slave-trade bill was discussed at length in the committee of the whole. "I took, and intend to take, no part in debates on this subject," he added. On January 26, he noted: "The debate on the bill to prohibit the importation of slaves was resumed, but seemed to have lost all its interest. The amendments which had been so warmly agitated were this day rejected, after very little said." His entry for the next day says only: "The Slave Prohibition bill passed without a division." Charles Francis Adams, ed., *Memoirs of John Quincy Adams, Comprising Portions of His Diary from 1795 to 1848*, 12 vols. (Philadelphia: J. B. Lippincott & Co., 1874–77), I:444.

53. *AC*, 9 Cong., 2 sess., 427, 477–87.

54. Ibid., 68, 69, 527–28; *SJ*, 9 Cong., 2 sess., 156, 158.

55. *AC*, 9 Cong., 2 sess., 71, 79, 87–88, 626–27; *SJ*, 9 Cong., 2 sess., 164, 191, 192–93.

56. Coughtry, *Notorious Triangle*, 281–85.

57. Rawley, *Transatlantic Slave Trade*, 415.

58. Donnan, *Slave Trade*, IV:526–27.

59. Michael E. Stevens, "'To get as many Slaves as you can': An 1807 Slaving Voyage," *South Carolina Historical Magazine* 87 (1986): 187–92.

60. *SAL*, II:426–30.

61. Donnan, "New England Slave Trade," 277; Coughtry, *Notorious Triangle*, 233.

62. Compare Du Bois, *Suppression*, 109–19, with Ohline, "Politics and Slavery,"

435-38, and see Philip D. Curtin, *The Atlantic Slave Trade: A Census* (Madison: University of Wisconsin Press, 1969), 73-75.

63. John Watkins to John Graham, September 6, 1805, in Clarence Edwin Carter, ed., *The Territorial Papers of the United States*, vol. IX, *The Territory of Orleans, 1803-1812* (Washington D.C.: Government Printing Office, 1934), 503; John E. Fisher, "Slavery and the Slave Trade in the Louisiana Purchase, 1803-1812," *Essays in History* (University of Virginia), 13 (1967-68): 42-58.

64. Joe G. Taylor, "The Foreign Slave Trade in Louisiana After 1808," *Louisiana History* 1 (1960): 38-39; Raymond W. Thorpe, *Bowie Knife* ([Albuquerque]: University of New Mexico Press, 1948), 122-23. According to the later account of John J. Bowie, the brothers made it a practice to turn their slaves over to a customs officer as soon as they entered Louisiana. They then repurchased them at the federal marshal's sale, receiving back half the price as informers (as provided for in the supplementary slave-trade act of April 20, 1818). These transactions made the slaves lawful merchandise in any slaveholding state.

65. Du Bois, *Suppression*, 112-14; Harmon, "Suppress and Protect," 118-23. For a congressional report explaining and justifying the seizure of Amelia Island, see *ASP, Foreign Affairs*, IV:132-34; for a customs official's description of the operations from Galveston Island, see ibid., 134-35.

66. As one indication, Howard, *American Slavers*, 302-3, points to the fact that the federal census of 1870 records only 1,984 natives of Africa in a black population of nearly five million. This figure suggests, he says, that there was no large-scale importation of slaves after 1820.

67. Du Bois relied heavily on episodic evidence and unsubstantiated assertions, some from dubious sources such as Richard Drake, *Revelations of a Slave Smuggler* (New York: R.M. DeWitt, 1860), now generally considered to be spurious. See especially *Suppression*, 117-18, 124-25, 165-66. Acknowledging that there appeared to be "little positive evidence of a large illicit importation into the country for a decade after 1825," Du Bois nevertheless concluded that such absence of evidence of smuggling constituted "presumptive evidence" of official collusion in the continuation of the trade at the rate of "many hundreds per year." Ibid., 128.

68. Curtin, *Atlantic Slave Trade*, 74-75; Eltis, *Economic Growth*, 249; Howard, *American Slavers*, 255-57. The belief that slaves in large numbers were imported from Cuba after 1807 is challenged in Kenneth F. Kiple, "The Case Against a Nineteenth-Century Cuba-Florida Slave Trade," *Florida Historical Quarterly* 49 (1970-71): 346-55. See also David Eltis, "The Nineteenth-Century Transatlantic Slave Trade: An Annual Time Series of Imports into the Americas Broken Down by Region," *Hispanic American Historical Review* 67 (1987): 135 n. Mannix and Cowley, *Black Cargoes*, presented the old, exaggerated picture of illegal importations after 1807. For example, they cited one contemporary report in 1817 that 20,000 slaves per year were being smuggled from Florida into Georgia (p. 203). Yet, during the entire decade from 1810 to 1820, the slave population of Georgia grew from 113,000 to only 150,000, and a large part of the increment must be attributed to natural increase and to imports from the upper South.

69. Richard Sutch, "The Breeding of Slaves for Sale and the Westward Expansion of Slavery, 1850-1860," in *Race and Slavery in the Western Hemisphere: Quantitative Studies*, ed. Stanley L. Engerman and Eugene D. Genovese (Princeton, N.J.: Princeton University Press, 1975), 179-80.

70. Eltis, *Economic Growth*, 249.

71. Dwight F. Henderson, "Federal Justice in Louisiana: The First Quarter Century," in *Essays on Southern History Written in Honor of Barnes F. Lathrop*, ed. Gary W. Gallagher (Austin: University of Texas Press, 1980), 44–45; *AC*, 11 Cong., 1 sess., 34, 36, 41, 42–43, 48–49, 462–65; *SAL*, II:549–50. Most of the French refugees were persons who had fled from Haiti to Cuba in the 1790s. The Napoleonic conquest of Spain in 1808 made them undesirable residents in the eyes of Spanish officials governing Cuba. Only one member of Congress, John Ross of Pennsylvania, raised any objection to the legislation.

72. *MPP* , I:485–86 (December 5, 1810), 577 (December 3, 1816).

73. Measures were introduced in both houses, but it was the Senate bill, amended by the House, that became law on April 20, 1818. *AC*, 15 Cong., 1 sess., 266, 267, 307, 358, 378, 379, 650, 1662, 1715, 1718, 1720, 1744.

74. *SAL*, III:450–53. Fines of $20,000, $5,000, and $1,000 to $10,000 in the act of 1807 were changed to a uniform $1,000 to $5,000. The prison term of 5 to 10 years was reduced to 3 to 7 years.

75. Under the act of 1807, the penalty for buying or selling contraband slaves was $800 per slave. Under the act of 1818, the penalty for importing, holding, or selling contraband slaves was a fine of $1,000 to 10,000 and imprisonment for 3 to 7 years. For holding, buying, or selling, there was also a forfeiture of $1,000 per slave.

76. Du Bois, *Suppression*, 118–20, which is inaccurate and distorted in its treatment of the act of 1818, gives the false impression that the system of rewarding informers was introduced at this point. Actually, the principle was an integral part of preceding federal slave-trade legislation in the acts of 1794, 1800, 1803, and 1807.

77. See, for example, the petitions to the Senate on the subject in *AC*, 15 Cong., 2 sess., 77, 88, 90, 97, 113, 162, 167, 173, 176, 189.

78. Ibid., 279–80, 1430–31.

79. Ibid., 279–80, 540, 1433–34, 1435–36; *SAL*, III:532–34. This measure was not intended to "revise" the supposedly ineffectual act of 1818, as Du Bois asserts in *Suppression*, 120. Instead, it was designed to reinforce all previous slave-trade legislation.

80. *AC*, 16 Cong., 1 sess., 576–77, 603–4, 638, 641, 689, 693–94, 2053, 2207–11 (Mercer's report), 2231, 2236; *SAL*, III:600–601, 721. Unlike Pindall's amendment rejected by the Senate in the preceding Congress, the 1820 law did not impose the death penalty for knowingly *purchasing* contraband slaves. That offense continued to be punishable only by fines and forfeitures.

81. Leonard D. White, *The Jeffersonians: A Study in Administrative History, 1801–1829* (New York: Macmillan Publishing Co., 1951), 340. Federal marshals and district attorneys did not come under the direction of the attorney general until the act of August 2, 1861. *SAL*, XII:285.

82. *ASP, Foreign Relations*, IV:134–37; *U.S. v. Vickery*, 28 Federal Cases 374 (1803).

83. *ASP Miscellaneous*, II:957–75; 134; Du Bois, *Suppression*, 115.

84. *Historical Statistics of the United States, Colonial Times to 1957* (Washington, D.C.: Government Printing Office, 1960), 719, 737.

85. "We know that most piracies, recently committed, have been by vessels

engaged in this traffic," wrote the commander of the *Grampus*. See *ASP, Naval Affairs*, III:865–71; Harmon, "Suppress and Protect," 125–30.

86. P. J. Staudenraus, *The African Colonization Movement, 1816–1865* (New York: Columbia University Press, 1961), 51; Lloyd, *Navy and the Slave Trade*, 15–16.

87. Adams, ed., *Memoirs of John Quincy Adams*, IV:292–94; Chase C. Mooney, *William H. Crawford, 1772–1834* (Lexington: University Press of Kentucky, 1974), 188–91; Staudenraus, *Colonization Movement*, 51–56; Katherine Harris, "The United States, Liberia, and Their Foreign Relations to 1847" (Ph.D. diss., Cornell University, 1982), 88–92,

88. *MPP*, II:63–65 (December 17, 1819); Harry Ammon, *James Monroe: The Quest for National Identity* (New York: McGraw-Hill, 1971), 522–23.

89. Staudenraus, *Colonization Movement*, 57. Approximately two-thirds of the black passengers on the *Elizabeth* were women and children. The *Cyane*, which had been captured from the British during the War of 1812, was referred to in some naval reports as a "corvette," the French term for a ship-rigged vessel that was smaller than a frigate. The more common designation in the United States was "sloop-of-war" or sometimes "ship-sloop." A good discussion of American naval vessels of the early nineteenth century is in Harmon, "Suppress and Protect," 35–45.

90. Staudenraus, *Colonization Movement*, 58–65; Harris, "United States, Liberia," 96–102; Samuel Eliot Morison, *"Old Bruin": Commodore Matthew C. Perry, 1794–1858* (Boston: Little, Brown & Co., 1967), 63–65. Ayres, who was acting as dual agent of the government and the Colonization Society, gave Stockton primary credit for securing the cession of land. At one tense moment in the negotiations, Stockton pointed his pistol at the head of King Peter, the principal ruler, while assuring him that the Americans came as benefactors, not as enemies.

91. Earl E. McNeilly, "The United States Navy and the Suppression of the West African Slave Trade, 1819–1862" (Ph.D. diss., Case Western Reserve University, 1973) 46–47; Morison, *"Old Bruin,"* 65–66.

92. McNeilly, "Navy and the Slave Trade," 47–48.

93. Morison, *"Old Bruin,"* 73–75. The *Shark* was Perry's first independent command. He had served as first officer on the *Cyane* in 1820. For French predominance in the slave trade at this time, see the report of Sir George Collier, commodore of the British West African Squadron, September 16, 1820, in C. W. Newbury, *British Policy Towards West Africa: Select Documents, 1786–1874* (Oxford: Clarendon Press, 1965), 140–42.

94. McNeilly, "Navy and the Slave Trade," 50–51; According to John Quincy Adams, the French minister threatened war over the *Jeune Eugenie* and two other seizures of French ships. Adams, ed., *Memoirs of John Quincy Adams*, V:416.

95. *HR*, 17 Cong., 1 sess., No. 92 (Serial 71), 2, 15–16; *ASP, Naval Affairs*, I:1099. A report of the British African Institution in 1825 listed over 200 vessels engaged in, or strongly suspected of engaging in, the slave trade. Nearly all of them were Portuguese, Spanish, or French. Only one was American. See *HR*, 21 Cong., 1 sess., No. 348 (Serial 201), 276–78.

96. *MPP*, II:109 (December 3, 1821), 309–10 (December 6, 1825). Adams declared: "The African slave trade has long been excluded from the use of our flag, and if some few citizens of our country have continued to set the laws of the Union as well as those of nature and humanity at defiance by persevering in that abominable traffic,

it has been only by sheltering themselves under the banners of other nations less earnest for the total extinction of the trade than ours."

97. Harmon, "Suppress and Protect," 104–6, 239, 254–56; McNeilly, "Navy and the Slave Trade," 59–61, 87–88. The frigate *Java*, for example, made a six-day call at Monrovia in February 1831, and this was the first naval visit in more than two years. The sloop-of-war *Vandalia* was on the African coast from July to October in 1842 but seems to have done little except ride at anchor in various harbors. According to its log, only one suspected vessel was boarded during that time.

98. After Adams in 1825, the next mention of the problem was by Van Buren in 1839. *MPP*, III:538 (December 2, 1839).

99. The importation of slaves into Brazil remained legal under Brazilian law until 1830, but most non-Brazilian participants in the importation were violating the laws of their own countries.

100. D[avid] Eltis, "The Direction and Fluctuation of the Transatlantic Slave Trade, 1821–1843: A Revision of the 1845 Parliamentary Paper," in *The Uncommon Market: Essays in the Economic History of the Atlantic Slave Trade*, ed. Henry A. Gemery and Jan S. Hogendorn (New York: Academic Press, 1979), 284, 291.

101. Howard, *American Slavers*, 30–32, 241–54.

102. A Danish royal decree in 1792 had prohibited the slave trade, effective in 1802. American abolition had been accomplished piecemeal in acts of Congress passed between 1794 and 1807. Britain abolished the trade in 1807; Sweden, in 1813; the Netherlands, in 1814. Napoleon, upon his return from Elba in 1815, issued an abolition decree that was subsequently confirmed by the restored French monarchy but not implemented in legislation until 1818. Spain and Portugal, though more resistant, had by 1815 agreed, in treaties with Britain, to the principle of abolition in the near future and to certain limitations on their continued sanction of the trade. By virtue of another treaty with Britain signed in 1817, the Spanish slave trade was abolished, effective immediately north of the equator and in 1820 south of that line. Portugal, by treaty in 1817, retained its right to trade in slaves south of the equator and only vaguely reiterated its promise of total abolition at some future time. Not until 1836 was that promise completely fulfilled.

103. In an 1817 decision regarding a captured French slave ship, the *Louis*, the British High Court of Admiralty confirmed that there was no right in peacetime to interfere with the maritime commerce of another nation except such as might be arranged by convention. John Dodson, *Reports of Cases Argued and Determined in the High Court of Admiralty*, 2 vols. (London: A. Strahan, 1815–28) II:210–64.

104. Lewis Hertslet, comp., *A Complete Collection of the Treaties and Conventions, and Reciprocal Regulations, at Present Subsisting Between Great Britain and Foreign Powers . . .* , later volumes supertitled *Hertslet's Commercial Treaties* (31 vols.; London: Harry Butterworth, 1840–1924), I:381–407 (Netherlands), II:73–121 (Portugal), II:273–309 (Spain); Charles K. Webster, *The Foreign Policy of Castlereagh, 1815–1822* (London: G. Bell & Son), 1947), 454–66; Leslie Bethell, *The Abolition of the Brazilian Slave Trade: Britain, Brazil and the Slave Trade Question, 1807–1869* (Cambridge: Cambridge University Press, 1970), 15–25; Suzanne Miers, *Britain and the Ending of the Slave Trade* (New York: Africana Publishing Co., 1975), 10–15.

105. *ASP, Foreign Affairs*, V:69–76; Adams, ed., *Memoirs of John Quincy Adams*, IV:150–52; V:181–84, 189–90, 320–21; Richard Rush, *A Residence at the Court of London* (London: Richard Bentley, 1833), 169–70, 255–58; Hugh G. Soulsby, *The*

Right of Search and the Slave Trade in Anglo-American Relations, 1814–1862 (Baltimore: Johns Hopkins University Press, 1933), 14–17, 20–22.

106. Rush, writing to Castlereagh, December 21, 1818 (*ASP, Foreign Affairs,* V:74–75), pointed out that the mixed commissions might violate the clauses of the Constitution vesting all federal judicial power in a supreme court and such inferior courts as Congress might establish, while providing that the judges of those courts should hold their offices during good behavior and be subject to impeachment.

107. *ASP, Foreign Affairs,* V:73.

108. Soulsby, *Right of Search,* 18.

109. *HD,* 21 Cong., 1 sess., No. 348 (Serial 201), 131.

110. *AC,* 14 Cong., 2 sess., 939–41; ibid., 15 Cong., 1 sess., 71–78, 94–108. The Senate approved a resolution instructing committee inquiry into the expediency of taking measures in concert with other nations to suppress the slave trade. The critical vote showed northerners 12 to 4 in favor and southerners 12 to 5 against.

111. *AC,* 16 Cong., 1 sess., 698–99; 2236–37. Final action in the Senate was prevented by a vote of 13 to 12.

112. *AC,* 16 Cong., 2 sess., 1064–71; *ASP, Foreign Relations,* V:92–93, 140–41.

113. For cabinet discussion of the case of the *Jeune Eugenie* as it related to the right of search, see Adams, ed., *Memoirs of John Quincy Adams,* V:387–91.

114. Ibid., VI:37.

115. *AC,* 17 Cong., 2 sess., 1147–55; Samuel Flagg Bemis, *John Quincy Adams and the Foundations of American Foreign Policy* (New York: Alfred A. Knopf, 1949), 415–27. An amendment explicitly endorsing a limited right of search was not accepted, but everyone understood that negotiation would surely lead in that direction. For discussion, see the House committee report of February 16, 1825, in *ASP, Foreign Relations,* V:631–32.

116. Bemis, *Adams and Foreign Policy,* 427–28.

117. *ASP, Foreign Affairs,* V:316–22, 332–39, 341–43.

118. *MPP,* II:243–47 (May 21, 1824).

119. Adams, ed., *Memoirs of John Quincy Adams,* VI:328.

120. Responding to abolitionist pressure, the British ministry in 1823 inaugurated a policy of pressuring colonial governments to make various ameliorative changes in the slaveholding system. The action inspired alarm not only among the West Indian planters directly affected, but also in the American South. Frank Joseph Klingberg, *The Antislavery Movement in England, A Study in English Humanitarianism* (New Haven: Yale University Press, 1926), 336–50; Betty Fladeland, *Men and Brothers: Anglo-American Antislavery Cooperation* (Urbana: University of Illinois Press, 1972), 173–76. The most comprehensive study of southern reaction is Joe Bassette Wilkins, Jr., "Window on Freedom: The South's Response to the Emancipation of the Slaves in the British West Indies, 1833–1861" (Ph.D. diss., University of South Carolina, 1977).

121. *Senate Executive Journal,* III:374, 383–84, 385–87; Bemis, *Adams and Foreign Policy,* 434–35.

122. *ASP, Foreign Relations,* V:362–67; 733–35; Soulsby, *Right of Search,* 37.

123. Charles Vaughan to Palmerston, December 12, 1833; Palmerston to Vaughan, July 7, 1834; Forsyth to Vaughan, October 4, 1834, in the Foreign Office, *British and*

Foreign State Papers, 1834–35, XXIII:135–37, 140–42, 145–47; Soulsby, *Right of Search*, 45.

124. Curtin, *Atlantic Slave Trade*, 234, 248; Eltis, *Economic Growth*, 249.

125. *Hertslet's Commercial Treaties*, IV:109–47; Miers, *Ending of the Slave Trade*, 15–16. On French suppression policies generally, see Serge Daget, "France, Suppression of the Illegal Trade, and England, 1817–1850," in *The Abolition of the Atlantic Slave Trade: Origins and Effects in Europe, Africa, and the Americas*, ed. David Eltis and James Walvin (Madison: University of Wisconsin Press, 1981), 193–217.

126. *Hertslet's Commercial Treaties*, VI:625–59; Leslie Bethell, *The Abolition of the Brazilian Slave Trade: Britain, Brazil and the Slave Trade Question, 1807–1869* (Cambridge: Cambridge University Press, 1970), 154–66, 187–88.

127. *HD*, 26 Cong., 2 sess., No. 115 (Serial 386), 46–50. For other examples, see ibid., 92–166. In this instance, the complex precautions all came to naught. A British warship captured the schooner and took it to Sierra Leone, where it was condemned and broken up, the slaves being set free. But according to Eltis, *Economic Growth*, 97–99, the odds against capture averaged about 4 to 1. This made the financial risk statistically worthwhile. Palmerston's detailed description of how the American flag was fraudulently used is summarized in Stevenson to Forsyth, February 29, 1840, Andrew Stevenson Papers, Manuscript Room, Library of Congress.

128. "It does not appear that the American flag began to be extensively employed for the protection of the slave-trade until between two and three years ago." So wrote the British minister to the United States, Henry Fox, to Secretary of State John Forsyth in October 1839. "But from that time to this," he continued, "the abuse has continued to increase in a regular and terrible proportion." *HD*, 26 Cong., 2 sess., No. 115 (Serial 386), 105.

129. Howard, *American Slavers*, 37–38; McNeilly, "Navy and the Slave Trade," 98–100.

130. *HD*, 26 Cong., 2 sess., No. 115 (Serial 386), 4–92; 27 Cong., 1 sess., No. 34 (Serial 392), 3–11; 27 Cong., 2 sess., No. 22 (Serial 401), 25–41. The Anglo-American discussion of right of visit is well covered in Soulsby, *Right of Search*, 58–69. For other summaries of Stevenson's exchanges with Palmerston on the slave trade, see Francis Fry Wayland, *Andrew Stevenson, Democrat and Diplomat, 1785–1857* (Philadelphia: University of Pennsylvania Press, 1949), 121–30; Richard Kerwin MacMaster, "The United States, Great Britain, and the Suppression of the Cuban Slave Trade, 1835–1860" (Ph.D. diss., Georgetown University, 1968), 163–70.

131. Warnings of British designs on Cuba came from the American minister to Spain, John H. Eaton (who may have gotten the idea from his wife Peggy), and from the American consul in Havana, Nicholas P. Trist. MacMaster, "Cuban Slave Trade," 46–50, 52–53.

132. Henry Fox to Forsyth, October 30, 1839, and Forsyth's delayed reply, February 12, 1840, *HD*, 26 Cong., 2 sess., No. 115 (Serial 386), 120–21, 163–66, 167, 168. The first section of the act of 1794 began as follows: "That no citizen or citizens of the United States, or foreigner, or any other person coming into, or residing within the same, shall, for himself or any other person whatsoever, either as master, factor or owner, build, fit, equip, load or otherwise prepare any ship or vessel, within any port or place of the said United States . . . for the purpose of carrying on any trade or traffic in slaves, to any foreign country." *SAL*, I:347–49.

133. Trist to Forsyth, January 12, 1839, Despatches from United States Consuls in

Havana, record group T-20, microfilm roll 9, National Archives; Trist to the British commissioners, Kennedy and Dalrymple, July 2, 1839, *SD*, 26 Cong., 2 sess., No. 125 (Serial 377), 135. Trist acknowledged that a feeling of "defiance" toward Britain had affected his attitude toward the slave trade.

134. *HD*, 26 Cong., 2 sess., No. 115 (Serial 386), 116–18 and 122–66 passim.

135. *New York Herald*, June 15, 1839; Adams, ed., *Diary of John Quincy Adams*, X:255. Trist was also under attack for alleged mistreatment of American seamen in Havana.

136. *A Letter to Wm. E. Channing, D.D. in Reply to One Addressed to Him by R. R. Madden, on the Abuse of the Flag of the United States in the Island of Cuba, for Promoting the Slave Trade* (Boston: William D. Ticknor, 1840). On Trist in Cuba generally, see MacMaster, "Cuban Slave Trade," 31–36, 41–43, 55–92.

137. *HD*, 26 Cong., 2 sess., No. 115 (Serial 386), 169, 468–95, 505–766; MacMaster, "Cuban Slave Trade," 80–91.

138. *MPP*, III:538 (December 2, 1839); *HD*, 26 Cong., 2 sess., No. 115 (Serial 386), 40.

139. *SD*, 29 Cong., 1 sess., No. 377 (477), 121–22; McNeilly, "Navy and the Slave Trade," 100–103.

140. McNeilly, "Navy and the Slave Trade," 104.

141. The text of the treaty, signed at London, December 20, 1841, is in the Foreign Office, *British and Foreign State Papers*, 1841–42, XXX:269–98.

142. (London) *Times*, January 5, 1842.

143. Reading the *Times* (London) on the treaty, President John Tyler thought that it "looked confoundedly as if the ratification by the five powers was afterward to be proclaimed as equivalent to the establishment of a new rule of international law." George Ticknor Curtis, *Life of Daniel Webster*, 5th ed., 2 vols. (New York: D. Appleton & Company, 1889), II:183. In the case of *The Antelope*, 10 Wheaton 66 (1825), Chief Justice John Marshall had ruled that the slave trade was not piracy in international law.

144. Cass's pamphlet and his letter to Guizot of February 13, 1842, are reprinted in William T. Young, *Sketch of the Life and Public Services of General Lewis Cass, with the Pamphlet on the Right of Search and Some of His Speeches on the Great Political Questions of the Day* (Philadelphia: E. H. Butler, 1853), 136–70. The letter to Guizot may also be read, together with Cass's explanatory dispatch to Webster of February 15, in Kenneth E. Shewmaker et al., eds., *The Papers of Daniel Webster: Diplomatic Papers, 1841–1843*, 2 vols. (Hanover, N.H.: University Press of New England, 1983–88), I:502–13.

145. Webster to Cass, April 5, 1842, in Shewmaker et al., eds., *Webster: Diplomatic Papers*, I:529–32. Webster and Tyler were embarrassed by Cass's action and suspected him of furthering his presidential ambitions, but the sentiments expressed in the letter to Guizot were in accord with administration policy as stated in the president's first annual message of December 7, 1841. *MPP*, IV:77–78 (December 7, 1841).

146. Young, *Lewis Cass*, 142.

147. Trist to Forsyth, January 12, 1839, Despatches from United States Consuls in Havana, record group T-20, microfilm roll 9.

148. Bell to Secretary of the Navy James K. Paulding, July 28, 1840. This letter was soon available for public reading in *HD*, 26 Cong., 2 sess., No. 115 (Serial 386),

57–59. Palmerston quickly denied Bell's charge that British naval officers, for reasons of prize money, were interested only in capturing ships with Africans aboard. Since 1835, he said, British warships had seized 20 Spanish and Brazilian ships with slaves actually aboard and 103 ships merely equipped for slave trading. Palmerston to Stevenson, December 8, 1840, *HD*, 26 Cong., 2 sess., No. 115 (Serial 386), 89.

149. Wilkins, "Window on Freedom," 44–50, 64–69.

150. St. George L. Sioussat, "Duff Green's 'England and the United States': With an Introductory Study of American Opposition to the Quintuple Treaty of 1841," *Proceedings of the American Antiquarian Society*, new ser., XL (1930): 230–32, 266.

151. Calhoun to Upshur, August 27, 1843, Robert L. Meriwether et al., eds., *The Papers of John C. Calhoun*, 18 vols. (Columbia: University of South Carolina Press, 1959–1998), XVII:381. See also Calhoun's letter of instructions to William R. King, U.S. minister to France, August 12, 1844, Richard K. Crallé, ed., *The Works of John C. Calhoun*, 6 vols. (New York: D. Appleton & Co., 1851–56), V:383–88.

152. Eric Williams, *Capitalism and Slavery* (Chapel Hill: University of North Carolina Press, 1944). See also Barbara L. Solow and Stanley L. Engerman, eds., *British Capitalism and Caribbean Slavery: The Legacy of Eric Williams* (Cambridge: Cambridge University Press, 1987).

153. Sioussat, "Duff Green's 'England and the United States,'" 267–70; unsigned review, "Thornton on Slavery," *Southern Literary Messenger* 8 (1842): 235–36; Harry Bluff [Matthew Fontaine Maury], "On the Right of Search," in ibid., 300–301.

154. The slave trade is referred to as "one of the minor problems of the conference" in Wilbur Devereux Jones, "The Influence of Slavery on the Webster-Ashburton Negotiations," *JSH* 22 (1956): 48. Howard Jones, *To the Webster-Ashburton Treaty: A Study in Anglo-American Relations, 1783–1843* (Chapel Hill: University of North Carolina Press, 1977), 78, describes the Anglo-American argument over the slave trade as "low-key" and never a "major controversy."

155. Everett to Webster, January 21, 1842; March 31, 1843, in Shewmaker et al., eds., *Webster: Diplomatic Papers*, I:492, 792; Soulsby, *Right of Search*, 83–86.

156. Shewmaker et al., eds., *Webster: Diplomatic Papers*, I:547–48, 550–56; Ephraim Douglass Adams, "Lord Ashburton and the Treaty of Washington," *AHR* 17 (1911–12): 774.

157. The text of the treaty is printed in Jones, *Webster-Ashburton Treaty*, 181–87.

158. Ashburton to Aberdeen, April 25, 1842, quoted in Soulsby, *Right of Search*, 82.

159. Shewmaker et al., eds., *Webster: Diplomatic Papers*, I:710–13, 716–21, 724–75. Buchanan and Benton both maintained that the U.S. naval commitment in the treaty was the price paid for exemption from British search and seizure. *CG*, 27 Cong., 3 sess., App., 9, 404.

160. *MPP*, IV:196 (December 6, 1842).

161. Aberdeen to Fox (to be read to Webster), January 18, 1843, in the Foreign Office, *British and Foreign State Papers, 1843–44*, XXXI:443–44; *Times* (London), December 31, 1842. In the House of Commons on February 2, Peel declared, "In signing that treaty we consider that we have abandoned no right of visitation." He pointed out, as Aberdeen had done before him, that American warships themselves frequently practiced visitation of suspicious vessels, particularly in the Gulf of Mexico. *Hansard's Parliamentary Debates*, 3d ser., LXVI (1843):88–91; Soulsby, *Right of Search*, 90–91.

162. *MPP*, IV:231 (February 27, 1843).

163. Aberdeen to Everett, December 20, 1841; Everett to Webster, March 23, 1842, *SD*, 29 Cong., 1 sess., No. 377 (Serial 477), 87. The *Tigris* was boarded and searched on the African coast by a British naval officer and sent to the United States for adjudication. The federal district court in Boston dismissed the libel, which was instituted in behalf of the British officer, rather than by the United States government. *The Tigris*, 23 Federal Cases 1220 (1841); MacMaster, "Cuban Slave Trade," 166–67.

164. Stevenson to Palmerston, November 13, 1840, Stevenson Papers; Everett to Aberdeen, November 12, 1842; Everett to Webster, November 18, 1842; Fox to Webster, February 2, 1843; and other correspondence, *SD*, 29 Cong., 1 sess., No. 377 (Serial 477), 11, 35–37, 52–54, 107–12, 117–27; Shewmaker et al., eds., *Webster: Diplomatic Papers*, II:122–23, 134–36.

165. Everett to Aberdeen, March 29, May 20, 1842; November 13, 1843; Aberdeen to Everett, November 23, 1842; August 28, 1843, in the Foreign Office, *British and Foreign State Papers, 1842–43*, XXXI:699–70, 712, 724; (1843–44), XXXII:490, 499–500; John Bassett Moore, *History and Digest of the International Arbitrations to Which the United States Has Been a Party*, 6 vols. (Washington, D.C.: Government Printing Office, 1898), I:417, 418.

166. *SD*, 29 Cong., 1 sess., No. 377 (Serial 477), 87–88; 31 Cong., 1 sess., No. 66 (Serial 562), 30–31. The same instructions were attached to a new Anglo-French treaty signed in 1845 (*Hertslet's Commercial Treaties*, VII:345–46), which substituted joint cruising for the mutual right of search incorporated in the treaty of 1831. This amounted to French acceptance of the British distinction between right of search and a limited right of visit.

167. Levin M. Powell to Francis H. Gregory, April 1850, *SD*, 31 Cong., 1 sess., No. 66 (Serial 562), 5–6; Andrew H. Foote, *Africa and the American Flag* (New York: D. Appleton & Co., 1854), 263.

168. Soulsby, *Right of Search*, 118. On pp. 104–5, Soulsby says that after 1842, "the only subsequent case of visitation prior to 1857 was that of the 'Roderick Dhu,' an American vessel detained on the African coast in January 1843."

169. *SD*, 29 Cong., 1 sess., No. 377 (Serial 477), 7–8; Foote, *Africa*, 263 n.

170. *SD*, 31 Cong., 1 sess., No. 66 (Serial 562), 28–31.

CHAPTER 6

1. Samuel Eliot Morison, *"Old Bruin": Commodore Matthew C. Perry, 1794–1858* (Boston: Little, Brown & Co., 1967), 163–68. Perry was no favorite of the Tyler administration. Only the year before, his brother-in-law, Alexander Slidell Mackenzie, commanding a naval training cruise, had forestalled a mutiny by executing the three ringleaders, one of whom happened to be the scapegrace son of Tyler's secretary of war. Two of Perry's sons were officers on the cruise. Ibid., 144–62.

2. Upshur to Perry, March 30, 1843, *HD*, 35 Cong., 2 sess., No. 104 (Serial 1008), 3–7. Upshur's instructions drew heavily upon earlier ones, and those issued to later commanders were similar. Ibid., 7–21; Earl E. McNeilly, "The United States Navy and the Suppression of the West African Slave Trade, 1819–1862" (Ph.D. diss., Case Western Reserve University, 1973), 100–101. Tyler at the time refused to provide the House with a copy of the instructions to Perry, declaring that it would be "incompatible with the public interests" to do so. *MPP*, IV:320 (May 18, 1844).

3. *HD*, 31 Cong., 1 sess., No. 73 (Serial 578), 3; Warren S. Howard, *American Slavers and the Federal Law, 1837–1862* (Berkeley: University of California Press, 1963), 239–40. Compare W. E. Burghardt Du Bois, *The Suppression of the African Slave-Trade to the United States of America, 1638–1870* (New York: Longmans, Green & Co., 1896), 186; and Hugh G. Soulsby, *The Right of Search and the Slave Trade in Anglo-American Relations, 1814–1862* (Baltimore: Johns Hopkins University Press, 1933), 87, 130; with Judd Scott Harmon, "Suppress and Protect: The United States Navy, the African Slave Trade, and Maritime Commerce, 1794–1862" (Ph.D. Diss., College of William and Mary, 1977), 35, 42–46.

4. *SD*, 28 Cong., 2 sess., No. 150 (Serial 458), 110–12. McNeilly, "Navy and the Slave Trade, 133–44; Harmon, "Suppress and Protect," 177–78; Morison, "*Old Bruin,*" 168–78. It is perhaps significant that Morison, in his chapter on Perry's command of the African squadron, says not a word about specific operations against the slave trade.

5. McNeilly, "Navy and the Slave Trade," 145–46; Howard, *American Slavers,* 214–15, 239.

6. *HD*, 31 Cong., 1 sess., No. 73 (Serial 578), 2. Actually, by the time of Secretary William B. Preston's report, the African squadron had seized eleven ships as slavers. Preston was apparently not counting those vessels that had already escaped condemnation in the courts, but if so, the records indicate that the correct figure was six, rather than seven; for he listed the *Patuxent,* the case against which was dismissed. *HD,* 36 Cong., 2 sess., No. 7 (Serial 1095), 628. Two more seizures later in the year brought the cumulative total for the period 1843–50 to thirteen, of which eight were condemned. See the tabulation in Howard, *American Slavers,* 214–16.

7. Christopher Lloyd, *The Navy and the Slave Trade: The Suppression of the African Slave Trade in the Nineteenth Century* (London: Longmans, Green & Co., 1947), 275–76.

8. McNeilly, "Navy and the Slave Trade," 174–81; George M. Brooke, Jr., "The Role of the United States Navy in the Suppression of the African Slave Trade," *American Neptune* 21 (1961): 35–36; Alan R. Booth, "The United States African Squadron, 1843–1861," in *Papers in African History,* Jeffrey Butler, ed., vol. I (Boston: Boston University Press, 1964), 100–105. The Paine-Bell report had recommended inclusion of one steamer in the African squadron at a time when steam power was just coming into naval use. In 1852, the navy had fourteen steamers in commission, none of them assigned to Africa. The squadron's supply base was Porto Praia in the Cape Verde Islands, and remained there even after the bulk of slave-trading activity had shifted southward to the Congo region. One squadron commander, Francis H. Gregory, complained that ships stationed south of the equator lost two-thirds of their time going back and forth to Porto Praia for supplies. *SD,* 31 Cong., 1 sess., No. 66 (Serial 562), 1–2; *SD,* 36 Cong., 2 sess., No. 4 (Serial 1082), 18.

9. Harmon, "Suppress and Protect," 234; McNeilly, "Navy and the Slave Trade," 176.

10. Harmon, "Suppress and Protect," 205–9.

11. Andrew Stevenson to John Forsyth, February 29, 1840, Andrew Stevenson Papers, Manuscript Division, Library of Congress. As late as 1860, the British foreign secretary harbored the misapprehension that an American cruiser could not touch a slaver unless it actually had slaves aboard. Lord John Russell to Lord Lyons, February 6, 1860, *HD,* 36 Cong., 2 sess., No. 7 (Serial 1095), 389–90.

12. George W. Slacum to Upshur, October 6, 1843, *HD*, 29 Cong., 1 sess., No. 43 (Serial 482), 21–22.

13. Du Bois, *Suppression*, 160: "According to orders of cruisers, only slavers with slaves actually on board could be seized"; William Law Mathieson, *Great Britain and the Slave Trade, 1839–1865* (London: Longmans, Green & Co., 1929), 157: "American cruisers . . . could not capture their own slavers unless the negroes were on board"; Daniel P. Mannix and Malcolm Cowley, *Black Cargoes: A History of the Atlantic Slave Trade, 1518–1865* (New York: Viking Press, 1962), 222: "Slaves had to be found on board; the mere fact that she was fitted out as a slaver was not enough under American law"; Howard Jones, *To the Webster-Ashburton Treaty: A Study in Anglo-American Relations, 1783–1843* (Chapel Hill: University of North Carolina Press, 1977), 72: "If an American cruiser halted a slave ship on its outward voyage it likewise would go free; there were no slaves on board"; David R. Murray, *Odious Commerce: Britain, Spain, and the Abolition of the Cuban Slave Trade* (Cambridge: Cambridge University Press, 1980), 265: "Legally, they were powerless to capture slave ships with equipment for the slave trade but no slaves on board."

14. James K. Paulding to Paine, December 30, 1839, quoted in McNeilly, "Navy and the Slave Trade," 100–101.

15. *The Alexander*, 1 Federal Cases 362 (1823); *U.S. v. Isaac Morris*, 14 Peters 464 (1840). Even before the *Alexander* decision, a federal judge had rejected the argument that only a vessel with slaves aboard was in violation of the act of 1820. See *U.S. v. Andrews*, 24 Federal Cases 815 (1820).

16. Howard, *American Slavers*, 102–6; Isaac Toucey to James Buchanan, *HD*, 35 Cong., 2 sess., No. 104 (Serial 1008), 1–2. The two vessels seized were the *Malaga*, by Lieutenant John E. Bispham of the U.S.S. *Boxer*, and the *Casket*, by Lewis E. Simonds of the U.S.S. *Marion*. The decision on the *Malaga* suit is reported in 16 Federal Cases 535 (1849). Sir Charles Hotham, recent commander of the British African squadron, declared before a parliamentary committee in 1849 that although half the slave ships arriving from Brazil were flying the American flag, U.S. warships did not interfere because of the fear that they would be "convicted in costs." *Report from the Select Committee of the House of Lords Appointed to Consider the Best Means Which Britain Can Adopt for the Final Extinction of the African Slave Trade, Reports from Committees*, 1849 Session, 144–45.

17. *New York Tribune*, August 16, 1860; Howard, *American Slavers*, 108. The ship in question was the *Thomas Achorn*, seized by Lieutenant William E. LeRoy of the U.S. steamer *Mystic*. If a court dismissed a libel but issued a certificate of probable cause, the arresting officer was protected from suit for damages.

18. *CG*, 36 Cong., 1 sess., 2207–11; *SJ*, 36 Cong., 1 sess. (Serial 1022), 394, 485, 835; Howard, *American Slavers*, 108.

19. Howard, *American Slavers*, 132–33.

20. Harmon, "Suppress and Protect," 212–14, 241–42. Harmon's study embraced commanders of the African squadron from 1843 to 1861, the Brazil squadron from 1843 to 1851, and four steamer commanders assigned to the Cuban coast in the late 1850s.

21. David Eltis, *Economic Growth and the Ending of the Transatlantic Slave Trade* (New York: Oxford University Press, 1987), 245, estimates 181,600 slaves imported in 1831–40, and 50,800 in 1841–50. See also Lloyd, *Navy and the Slave Trade*, 116; Murray, *Odious Commerce*, 244.

22. Leslie Bethell, *The Abolition of the Brazilian Slave Trade: Britain, Brazil, and the Slave Trade Question, 1807–1869* (Cambridge: Cambridge University Press, 1970), 155–64, 187, 255–66. The so-called Palmerston Act of 1839 authorized the seizure of Portuguese ships (and ships of no nationality) carrying slaves or equipped for slave trading, whether north or south of the equator, and their adjudication before British vice admiralty courts. The law, as it applied to Portugal, was replaced by the treaty of 1842, which contained an equipment clause and in general resembled the Anglo-Spanish treaty of 1835. The Aberdeen Act of 1845 followed the same course with respect to Brazil at a time when treaty provisions for mutual right of search were about to lapse. Unlike Portugal, however, Brazil steadfastly refused to accept British terms for a new slave-trade treaty, and the law consequently remained in effect until 1869, long after it had ceased to have any practical meaning. On the shift in the 1840s from trial before mixed commissions to trial in British admiralty courts, and the reasons for it, see Leslie Bethell, "The Mixed Commissions for the Suppression of the Transatlantic Slave Trade in the Nineteenth Century," *Journal of African History* 7 (1966): 90–91.

23. Eltis, *Economic Growth*, 244; Bethell, *Brazilian Slave Trade*, 388–95.

24. Proffitt to Upshur, February 27, 1844, quoted in Lawrence F. Hill, *Diplomatic Relations Between the United States and Brazil* (Durham, N.C.: Duke University Press, 1932), 121. Proffitt was exaggerating when he said "almost entirely," but by the later 1840s there was wide agreement that a majority of the ships engaged in the slave trade to Brazil were American built and made use of the American flag. See, for example, the statements of the British naval officer, Arthur Cumming, *SD*, 31 Cong., 1 sess., No. 66 (Serial 562), 8; and American minister David Tod, *SD*, 31 Cong., 2 sess., No. 6 (Serial 588), 25.

25. Hill, *United States and Brazil*, 122. It should be remembered that the squadron, under Perry's command, was at this time cruising only north of the equator, whereas the Brazil trade was concentrated south of that line.

26. George W. Slacum to Daniel Webster, September 4, 13, 1841, *SD*, 28 Cong., 1 sess., No. 217 (Serial 434), 10–11, 14–15.

27. Craig M. Simpson, *A Good Southerner: The Life of Henry A. Wise of Virginia* (Chapel Hill: University of North Carolina Press, 1985), 61–69.

28. Henry A. Wise to John C. Calhoun, December 14, 1844, *HD*, 28 Cong., 2 sess., No. 148 (Serial 466), 55. For other Wise dispatches, see *HD*, 30 Cong., 2 sess., No. 61 (Serial 543), 70–223; *SD*, 30 Cong., 1 sess., No. 28 (Serial 506), 1–135.

29. Wise to Hamilton C. Hamilton, the British minister to Brazil, December 1, 1844, *HD*, 28 Cong., 2 sess., No. 148 (Serial 466), 56–63. In this letter, Wise used the device of quoting gossip among resentful Brazilians and Portuguese to bring a variety of charges against British business interests and the British navy for complicity in the slave trade. Tyler repeated the accusations in one of his last messages to Congress, declaring that British policy seemed "calculated rather to perpetuate than to suppress the trade by enlisting very large interests in its favor." There was naturally an angry reaction in England. Aberdeen's belated response demonstrated that Wise and Tyler had some of the facts wrong, but in Parliament, the prime minister himself acknowledged Britain's economic ties with the slave trade. *MPP*, IV:362–64 (February 20, 1845); Aberdeen to Hamilton, December 4, 1845; *SD*, 30 Cong., 1 sess., No. 28 (Serial 506), 3–65; ibid., Wise to Hamilton, July 31, 1846, *Hansard's Parliamentary Debates*, 3d ser., vol. LXXVIII (1845): 1154.

30. Tod to John M. Clayton, June 20, 1850, *SD*, 31 Cong., 2 sess., No. 6 (Serial 588), 42–43.

31. With Wise's support, Consul Gorham Parks at first refused to grant sea letters, except for a return to the United States, but he was instructed from Washington that he had no choice in the matter. After that, Parks reported, he issued sea letters for a total of seventeen ships. Fifteen of them proceeded to Africa, undoubtedly involved in the slave trade. Parks to Tod, January 29, 1850, ibid., 35. For a discussion of sea letters and how they had the effect of releasing owners from bond, see Andrew K. Blythe to Lewis Cass, April 24, 1857, in *HD*, 36 Cong., 2 sess., No. 7 (Serial 1095), 63–65. Howard, *American Slavers*, 275, says that sea letters were "apparently introduced by departmental initiative in the early 'forties,' " but the act of March 2, 1803, made reference to them. *SAL*, II:209.

32. Tod's successor, Robert C. Schenck, made the same recommendations. *HD*, 28 Cong., 2 sess., No. 148 (Serial 466), 39–40; *SD*, 31 Cong., 2 sess., No. 6 (Serial 588), 3, 10, 27; *SD*, 33 Cong., 1 sess., No. 47 (Serial 698), 5–6.

33. *MPP*, V:15 (December 4, 1849).

34. In 1848, for example, the United States imported approximately 400 million pounds of coffee and sugar, a major part of it produced with slave labor. In dollar value, this amounted to about half of American food imports and about 11 percent of all imports.

35. *SD*, 30 Cong., 1 sess., No. 28 (Serial 506), 71–77; *HD*, 30 Cong., 2 sess., No. 61 (Serial 543), 70–149 passim; [Society of Friends], *An Exposition of the African Slave Trade, From the Year 1840, to 1850, Inclusive* (Philadelphia: J. Rakestraw, 1851), 63–65. A detailed eyewitness account of what happened on the *Kentucky* was provided by one of its crew, an Englishman named William Page. His testimony seems not to have been printed in any congressional document, but it may be read in British Parliamentary Papers, House of Commons, Class A,: *Correspondence with the British Commissioners Relating to the Slave Trade, 1845*, L (London: William Clowes and Sons, 1846), 514–19. According to Page, six women and about twenty men received the lesser punishment of beatings so severe that all the women died.

36. *HD*, 30 Cong., 2 sess., No. 61 (Serial 543), 5, 8–14; *SD*, 31 Cong., 2 sess., No. 6 (Serial 588), 2–7; Howard, *American Slavers*, 104. The number of slave deaths aboard the *Senator* varies with the witnesses all the way from 246 to 373. Efforts of the American consul in Rio to secure the arrest of the mate by Brazilian authorities were unsuccessful.

37. *HD*, 30 Cong., 2 sess., No. 61 (Serial 543), 70–159, 181; Harmon, "Suppress and Protect," 160–61. The *Porpoise* was condemned in 1845. Wise failed in his efforts to secure extradition of the captains and mates of the *Kentucky* and *Porpoise*, but Captain Cyrus Libby of the *Porpoise* returned home voluntarily and was tried and acquitted in Maine. Wise was reprimanded for his excessive zeal. See Buchanan to Wise, September 27, 1845, in John Bassett Moore, ed., *The Works of James Buchanan*, 12 vols. (Philadelphia: J. B. Lippincott & Co., 1908–11), VI:267–71.

38. Howard, *American Slavers*, 214–216. A second ship sent home for trial in 1845 was the *Albert*, likewise seized on the initiative of a consul, Alexander H. Tyler at Bahia. *HD*, 30 Cong., 2 sess., No. 61 (Serial 543), 181–209.

39. Eltis, *Economic Growth*, 244; Bethell, *Brazilian Slave Trade*, 388–90.

40. Bethell, *Brazilian Slave Trade*, 324–63; Lloyd, *Navy and the Slave Trade*, 139–48.

41. Eltis, *Economic Growth*, 245. Ironically, British free-trade policies introduced in the 1840s greatly increased British importation of Cuban sugar and thus indirectly stimulated the Cuban slave trade. See Murray, *Odious Commerce*, 208, 242–243; Howard Temperley, *British Antislavery, 1833–1870* (London: Longman, 1972), 163–65.

42. With American annexation of Cuba, according to James Buchanan, "the last relic of the African slave trade would instantly disappear." *MPP*, V:510 (December 6, 1858).

43. *Charleston Courier*, December 16, 1857, contains the pertinent part of Adams's message. See also Ronald T. Takaki, *A Pro-Slavery Crusade: The Agitation to Reopen the African Slave Trade* (New York: Free Press, 1971), 1–6, 9–22; Harvey Wish, "The Revival of the African Slave Trade in the United States, 1856–1860," *MVHR* 27 (1940–41): 570–72. The central figure in the movement was Leonidas W. Spratt, editor of the Charleston *Standard* and a member of the state legislature.

44. *CG*, 34 Cong., 3 sess., 123–26; Takaki, *Pro-Slavery Crusade*, 7–8. *Richmond Enquirer*, December 23, 1856, declared that the Etheridge resolution "insulted the memory of our forefathers with the gratuitous accusation of inhumanity" and that it was designed to divide Democrats while linking southern Know-Nothings with northern Republicans.

45. Takaki, *Pro-Slavery Crusade*, 68–69; William Sumner Jenkins, *Pro-Slavery Thought in the Old South* (Chapel Hill: University of North Carolina Press, 1935), 97. Moral comparison of the domestic slave trade and the foreign slave trade had long been an especially effective abolitionist tactic. See, for example, *The Genius of Universal Emancipation* [newspaper], June 1825, p. 129; *Norwich (Conn.) Republican*, clipped in the *Boston Liberator*, May 14, 1836, p. 80; *South Side Democrat*, clipped in the *Washington National Era*, October 7, 1858.

46. See, for example, the remarks of Calhoun in *RD*, 24 Cong., 1 sess., 209; and Reverdy Johnson in the *Richmond Enquirer*, December 26, 1856. No southerner believed that traffic in slaves was immoral, wrote a South Carolina clergyman. But the African trade, he added, was not a traffic in slaves. It was a system of "kidnapping and man-stealing." James Henry Thornwell, *State of the Country* (Columbia, S.C.: Southern Guardian Steam Power Press, 1861), 9.

47. Dunbar Rowland, ed., *Jefferson Davis, Constitutionalist: His Letters, Papers and Speeches*, 10 vols. (Jackson: Mississippi Department of Archives and History, 1923), VI:65–71; Clement Eaton, *Jefferson Davis* (New York: Free Press, 1977), 95. Upon returning home to Mississippi in the spring of 1859, Davis found "a rapidly increasing feeling in favor of opening the African Slave Trade." Davis to Clement C. Clay, May 17, 1859, in Lynda Lasswell Crist, Mary Seaton Dix, et al., eds., *The Papers of Jefferson Davis*, 9 vols. to date (Baton Rouge: Louisiana State University Press, 1971–97), VI:251.

48. Takaki, *Pro-Slavery Crusade*, 104–5. Robert Barnwell Rhett, editor of the *Charleston Mercury*, supported the pro-slave-trade movement in 1854 but had changed his mind by 1857. For the southern argument on reopening the slave trade, see also Jenkins, *Proslavery Thought*, 95–103; John McCardell, *The Idea of a Southern Nation: Southern Nationalists and Southern Nationalism, 1830–1860* (New York: W. W. Norton & Co., 1979), 133–40.

49. *The Reply of C. A. L. Lamar, of Savannah, Georgia, to the Letter of Hon. Howell Cobb, Secretary of the Treasury of the United States, Refusing a Clearance to the*

Ship Richard Cobden (Charleston, S.C.: Walker, Evans & Co., 1858), 10. Lamar was the son of Gazaway Bugg Lamar, one of the South's wealthiest businessmen.

50. Tom Henderson Wells, *The Slave Ship Wanderer* (Athens: University of Georgia Press, 1967), 7–62; Takaki, *Pro-Slavery Crusade,* 201–12. When the *Wanderer* was auctioned in Savannah by the U.S. marshal, Lamar repurchased it for $4,000 and promptly knocked down the one man who had dared to bid against him. The ship was condemned a second time as a slaver in June 1860. See the case of *The Wanderer,* 29 Federal Cases 150; *HD,* 36 Cong., 2 sess., No. 7 (Serial 1095), 630, 631.

51. *New York Tribune,* August 23, 1859. The obvious purpose of the communication was to aggravate Douglas's quarrel with southern Democrats. The correspondent, who signed himself "A Native Southerner," reported that Douglas spoke "sneeringly" of the South, "as though he had it in his breeches pocket."

52. For example, Du Bois, *Suppression,* 181–82; Wish, "Revival of the African Slave Trade," 582.

53. *New York Herald,* July 12, August 6, 1859. That the unnamed senator was Douglas seems unlikely because he was mentioned by name in the same article.

54. The report of the agent, Benjamin F. Slocumb, appears in Robert Ralph Davis, Jr., ed., "Buchanan Espionage: A Report on Illegal Slave Trading in the South in 1859," *JSH* 37 (1971): 272–78.

55. See, for example, Eltis, *Economic Growth,* 249; Howard, *American Slavers,* 154, 301–2; Wells, *Wanderer,* 86–87.

56. Takaki, *Pro-Slavery Crusade,* 170–74; James Paisley Hendrix, Jr., "The Efforts to Reopen the African Slave Trade in Louisiana," *Louisiana History* 10 (spring 1969): 97–123. The measure passed the House and narrowly failed in the Senate. It was renewed in 1859 but received less support. For the fate of an apprentice scheme in Mississippi, see Takaki, *Pro-Slavery Crusade,* 178.

57. Takaki, *Pro-Slavery Crusade,* 180–84; Earl W. Fornell, "Agitation in Texas for Reopening the Slave Trade," *Southwestern Historical Quarterly* 60 (1956): 245–59; W. J. Carnathan, "The Proposal to Reopen the African Slave Trade in the South, 1854–1860," *South Atlantic Quarterly* 25 (1926): 427–28. Houston defeated the incumbent Democrat, Hardin R. Runnels, who favored reopening the slave trade, although his party had refused to take such a position.

58. Takaki, *Pro-Slavery Crusade,* 231–38. For a cogent discussion of southern attitudes toward reopening the slave trade, see David M. Potter, *The Impending Crisis, 1848–1861,* completed and edited by Don E. Fehrenbacher (New York: Harper & Row, 1976), 398–401.

59. Napier to Cass, December 24, 1857, *SD,* 35 Cong., 1 sess., No. 49 (Serial 929), 16.

60. Cass to Napier, April 10, 1858, ibid., 42–55.

61. For discussion of transferring the primary naval effort to Cuban waters, see the *Post* (London) article of January 9, 1857, reprinted in *New York Times,* January 26, 1857; also *London Times,* May 21, 25, 1857: "If, then, England wishes to make a great effort to put down the trade in its last stronghold, *it will do well to turn its attention to the Cuban coast itself.*"

62. For specific incidents, see *SD,* 35 Cong., 1 sess., No. 59 (Serial 930), 6–7, 16–19; ibid., No. 61 (Serial 930), 21–36. The *Mobile,* for example, was on its way from Alabama to New York when fired at and boarded. The boarding officer reportedly said that he had orders to detain "every vessel going up and down the Gulf."

63. *MPP*, V:507 (December 6, 1858).

64. *CG*, 35 Cong., 1 sess., 2494–98. See also the resolution and speech of Reuben Davis (Mississippi) in the House, *CG*, 35 Cong., 1 sess., App., 494–99.

65. *Washington National Era*, May 27, June 3, 1858.

66. Malmesbury to Napier, June 4, 1858, *HD*, 36 Cong., 2 sess., No. 7 (Serial 1095), 94–95.

67. *SD*, 35 Cong., 1 sess., No. 49 (Serial 929), 49.

68. Dallas to Cass, June 8; Malmesbury to Napier, June 11, 1858, *HD*, 35 Cong., 2 sess., No. 2 (Serial 997), 34–39.

69. *Times* (London) July 6, 7, 1858.

70. *MPP*, V:507 (December 6, 1858).

71. Andrew C. McLaughlin, *Lewis Cass* (Boston: Houghton, Mifflin & Co., 1891), 330. See also Soulsby, *Right of Search*, 163–64; Eltis, *Economic Growth*, 218; Lewis Einstein, "Lewis Cass," in *American Secretaries of State and Their Diplomacy*, Samuel Flagg Bemis, ed., 10 vols. (New York: Alfred A. Knopf, 1927–29), VI:321–23; Frank B. Woodford, *Lewis Cass: The Last Jeffersonian* (New Brunswick: Rutgers University Press, 1950), 319–20; Mathieson, *Slave Trade*, 155–57.

72. *Hansard's Debates*, 3d ser., vol. CLI (1858):2085–88.

73. Cass also acknowledged that the refusal of a merchant vessel to show its colors (a fairly common stratagem) would justify boarding.

74. *HD*, 35 Cong., 2 sess., No. 2 (Serial 997), 35–36, 39. Malmesbury said in Parliament that the standard orders to the British fleet, which had been in effect for many years and which permitted boarding to verify nationality, were not altered but were suspended, pending further negotiations. *Hansard's Debates*, 3d ser., vol. CLI (1858): 2089–90. Since those negotiations made little progress, the suspension presumably did not last beyond the life of the Derby ministry, which ended in June 1859.

75. The flurry of British naval aggressiveness in the spring of 1858 was never satisfactorily explained by British authorities. A spokesman for the Foreign Office asserted in the House of Commons (*Hansard's Debates*, 3d ser. vol. CLI [1858]:48) that the blockade of Cuba had been "instituted on the suggestion of the American Government," but Cass's letter of April 10 was received much too late to have provided the original impetus, which came in fact from the Palmerston ministry before its fall in February. Palmerston himself said in June that the shift of emphasis to Cuban waters had been adopted "in deference to the frequently expressed wishes of Parliament and of numerous deputations which waited upon the late Government." Ibid., 52–53. The excessiveness of the blockade could not easily be accounted for, however. It was ascribed by various British leaders to misplaced zeal, inexperienced officers, and American exaggeration. They might well have added hunger for prize money, which was an ever present spur to intemperate action. Mathieson, *Slave Trade*, 158, makes the preposterous statement that the crisis was "no more than what in the jargon of our own day would be called a 'newspaper stunt,' got up by the slave traders and their friends." The problem of responsibility is more sensibly discussed in Richard W. Van Alstyne, "British-American Diplomatic Relations" (Ph.D. diss., Stanford University, 1928), 236–37.

76. The *Jehossee* and the *George William Jones* were boarded in early 1860, for example. *HD*, 36 Cong., 2 sess., No. 7 (Serial 1095), 417, 430–34, 588–93. The threat to turn a slaver and its crew over to an American warship or send it into an Ameri-

can port apparently persuaded more than a few captains to throw flag and papers overboard. Examples are the *Louis McLane* (captured in October 1857), the *Caroline* and the *Cortez* (captured in April, 1858), and the *Rufus Soulé* (captured and burned in October 1858). Ibid., 137–43, 193, 330–32, 400–414, 561–71; *HD*, 35 Cong., 1 sess., No. 49 (Serial 929), 69–73; ibid., No. 132 (Serial 959), 4–19.

77. See, for example, Dallas to Malmesbury, July 7, August 24, September 11, 1858; January 31, 1859; Lord Lyons to Cass, May 23, 1859, *HD*, 36 Cong., 2 sess., No. 7 (Serial 1095), 132–34, 193, 240–43, 303–4, 337–38.

78. Soulsby, *Right of Search*, 150–55.

79. Russell to Lyons, February 6, 1860; Cass to Lyons, April 3, 1860, *HD*, 36 Cong., 2 sess., No. 7 (Serial 1095), 390, 414–16; Van Alstyne, "British-American Relations," 245–46.

80. In his annual message of December 8, 1858, Buchanan declared: "The occasional abuse of the flag of any nation is an evil far less to be deprecated than would be the establishment of any regulations which might be incompatible with the freedom of the seas." *MPP*, V:508 (December 6, 1858).

81. Report of the Secretary of the Navy, December 2, 1859, *SD*, 36 Cong., 1 sess., No. 1 (Serial 1025), 1138–39.

82. See the tables compiled from government records in Harmon, "Suppress and Protect," 241–43, and Howard, *American Slavers*, 216–22. They are identical, except that Howard also lists ships arrested in American ports, totaling twenty-five from 1851 through 1858 and fourteen from 1859 through 1860.

83. In addition to these nine heavily laden slavers (*Echo, Wildfire, William, Bogota, Erie, Storm King, Cora, Bonito,* and *Nightingale*), a tenth, the *W.R. Kibby,* had three African boys aboard when captured.

84. Hamilton to Buchanan, August 31, 1858, Records of the Department of the Interior, record group M160, microfilm roll 3, National Archives.

85. Many details of Hamilton's troubled quest for reimbursement are in his numerous letters to South Carolina congressman William Porcher Miles, including those of March 15, 30, December 30, 1859; January 11, February 2, 27, March 15, 19, 1860, in the William Porcher Miles Papers, Southern Historical Collection, University of North Carolina, Chapel Hill.

86. *MPP*, V:527–29 (December 6, 1858); *SAL*, XI:404 (March 3, 1859). The special appropriation was $75,000, larger than any to that date except for the $100,000 appropriated in the slave-trade act of 1819.

87. Howard, *American Slavers*, 223, 238; Takaki, *Pro-Slavery Crusade*, 214.

88. *SAL*, XII:40–41.

89. *CG*, 36 Cong., 1 sess., 2303–09, 2638–42. The quoted words of Davis are on p. 2304. The votes for passage were 41 to 14 in the Senate and 122 to 56 in the House. Nearly all of the 70 negative votes came from southerners.

90. Jacob Thompson to Lewis Cass, Department of the Interior Records, record group M160, microfilm roll 1; F. J. Moreno to Thompson, May 10, 24, 28, June 10, 25, July 26, 1860, ibid., Roll 6. The total cost of about $212,000 included $35,000 in bounties ($25 per slave) paid to officers and crews of the capturing vessels, as provided for in the act of March 3, 1819.

91. Eltis, *Economic Growth*, 245, estimates slave imports into Cuba at 25,000 for 1859 and 21,000 for 1860.

92. A. Taylor Milne, "The Lyons-Seward Treaty of 1862," *AHR* 38 (1932–33): 512.

93. Ibid., 512–13, 519–20.

94. Ibid., 522–23; in the Foreign Office, *British and Foreign State Papers, 1862–63,* LIII:1425–30; *SD,* 37 Cong., 2 sess., No. 57 (Serial 1122), 2–15; *Journal of the Executive Proceedings of the Senate of the United States of America from December 2, 1861 to July 17, 1862, Inclusive* (Washington: Government Printing Office, 1887), XII:254, 256. On the treaty generally, see also Conway W. Henderson, "The Anglo-American Treaty of 1862," *CWH* 15 (1969): 308–19.

95. Seward to Charles Francis Adams, April 8, 1862, *Papers Relating to Foreign Affairs* (Washington, D.C.: Government Printing Office, 1862), 65. This series subsequently came to be titled *Foreign Relations of the United States.*

96. Murray, *Odious Commerce,* 305–6.

97. Eltis, *Economic Growth,* 245.

98. *CWAL,* VII:36.

99. *MPP,* III:538 (December 2, 1839).

100. *SAL,* IX:181. The stated purpose of the law was to reduce government expense in admiralty proceedings. It made no distinction between ordinary maritime libels and those associated with the slave trade.

101. *The Orion,* 18 Federal Cases 817 (1859); Howard, *American Slavers,* 170–76, 306–7. Howard lists six other ships that went off on slaving voyages while under bond. For a list of alleged slavers bonded in New York, 1852–62, see *SD,* 37 Cong., 2 sess., No. 53 (Serial 1122), 2–3.

102. The *Orion* was, in fact, captured by H.M.S *Pluto* with slaves aboard and without colors or papers. Condemned in a British vice admiralty court, it was broken up. Howard, *American Slavers,* 175.

103. *U.S. v. Libby,* 26 Federal Cases 928 (1846); *The Porpoise,* 19 Federal Cases, 1064 (1855); *U.S. v. Westervelt,* 28 Federal Cases, 529 (1861); Howard, *American Slavers,* 203–4. Libby, it should be noted, was indicted not for the *Porpoise's* services to the notorious *Kentucky,* but on a rather dubious capital charge (under the Piracy Act of 1820) for bringing a single African aboard his own ship with the intent to enslave him.

104. John Dodson, *Reports of Cases Argued and Determined in the High Court of Admiralty,* 2 vols. (London: A. Strahan, 1815–28), II:210–64. The case is summarized by John Marshall in *The Antelope,* 10 Wheaton 66 (1825), 118.

105. *U.S. v. La Jeune Eugenie,* 26 Federal Cases 832, 846, 851 (1822). Story's decision, together with the argument for the French claimants, is conveniently available as a reprinted pamphlet in Paul Finkelman, ed., *The African Slave Trade and American Courts: The Pamphlet Literature,* 2 vols. (New York: Garland Publishing, 1988), I:31–144. On Story and the slave trade, see R. Kent Newmyer, *Supreme Court Justice Joseph Story: Statesman of the Old Republic* (Chapel Hill: University of North Carolina Press, 1985), 347–50.

106. John T. Noonan, Jr., *The Antelope: The Ordeal of the Recaptured Africans in the Administrations of James Monroe and John Quincy Adams* (Berkeley: University of California Press, 1977), 26–31. Noonan's monograph is definitive, but see also John Quincy Adams's summary of the *Antelope* case in his argument before the Supreme Court as counsel for the *Amistad* Africans, reprinted in Finkleman, ed., *African Slave Trade,* I:334–74.

107. Noonan, *Antelope*, 53–65.

108. Ibid., 93–112; *The Antelope*, 10 Wheaton 66. The case of the *Antelope*, which returned twice to the Supreme Court (11 Wheaton 413 [1826]; 12 Wheaton 546 [1827]), was complicated by the fact that more than half of the blacks found on board had been removed from other slavers, one of them American and several Portuguese. In the end, 37 Africans were consigned to slavery as property of the Spanish claimants, and in 1827, about 120 were transported to Liberia as liberated persons. The rest of the 281 had died or disappeared. Noonan, *Antelope*, 127–28, 134–35, 140.

109. *ASP, Foreign Affairs*, V:321.

110. Murray, *Odious Commerce*, 182–83, 254–56, 310, 313, 319–20. The Anglo-Brazilian treaty of 1826 declared the slave trade to be piracy, but its legal effect remained a matter of controversy between the two countries and even among British officials. Bethell, *Brazilian Slave Trade*, 65–66, 89–95, 255–66, 325–26.

111. Judge John K. Kane in *U.S. v. Darnaud*, 25 Federal Cases 754, 760–61 (1855).

112. Howard Jones, *Mutiny on the Amistad: The Saga of a Slave Revolt and Its Impact on American Abolition, Law, and Diplomacy* (New York: Oxford University Press, 1987), 3–6, 22–29. Other secondary accounts are Christopher Martin [Edwin Palmer Hoyt], *The Amistad Affair* (London: Abelard-Schuman, 1970); Mary Cable, *Black Odyssey: The Case of the Slave Ship Amistad* (New York: Viking Press, 1971).

113. *Trial of the Prisoners of the Amistad on the Writ of Habeas Corpus, Before the Circuit Court of the United States, for the District of Connecticut, at Hartford* (New York, 1839), 9–10, 21–22, reprinted in Finkelman, ed., *African Slave Trade*, I:153–54, 165–66.

114. *Gedney v. L'Amistad*, 10 Federal Cases 141, 145, 146–47, 151 (1840); Jones, *Mutiny on the Amistad*, 96–99, 119–135. Judson's ruling was a pleasant surprise to abolitionists, for in 1833 he had been one of the leaders of community opposition to Prudence Crandall and her school for African American girls in the Connecticut village of Canterbury.

115. Finkelman, ed., *African Slave Trade*, I:241–408, contains not only Adams's argument but also the shorter and probably more effective one of his cocounsel, Roger S. Baldwin, later a Connecticut governor and United States senator. For an account of Adams's role in the case, see Samuel Flagg Bemis, *John Quincy Adams and the Union* (New York: Alfred A. Knopf, 1956), 384–411.

116. *U.S. v. the Amistad*, 15 Peters 518 (1841); Jones, *Mutiny on the Amistad*, 188–93. Only three of the five southern justices, including Taney, participated in the decision. The lone dissenter was Henry Baldwin of Pennsylvania.

117. Jones, *Mutiny on the Amistad*, 203–5. Story's decision overruled the order of the district court that the *Amistad* blacks be returned to Africa under presidential auspices. Instead, they were simply pronounced free, and their return home had to be financed by private means.

118. Martin, *Amistad Affair*, 215–25; Jones, *Mutiny on the Amistad*, 205–18; R. Earl McClendon, "The *Amistad* Claims: Inconsistencies of Policies," *Political Science Quarterly* 48 (1933): 392–412. The indemnity demanded by Spain was largely for the Africans but also for the *Amistad* itself, which, although confirmed as Spanish property by the district court, had been sold for salvage and other charges.

119. *The Emily and the Caroline*, 9 Wheaton 381, 385 (1824).

120. *The Caroline*, 5 Federal Cases 90 (1819). This was a different ship from the *Caroline* in the note above.

121. *The Josefa Segunda*, 5 Wheaton 338, 357 (1820).

122. *U.S. v. The Catharine*, 25 Federal Cases 332, 341 (1840). See also *The Plattsburgh*, 10 Wheaton 132 (1825), in which Story ruled that equipment for the slave trade, as soon as it was begun, made a ship liable to confiscation; *The Porpoise*, 19 Federal Cases 1064 (1855); *The Orion*, 18 Federal Cases 817 (1859); *The Slavers. (Kate)*, 2 Wallace 350 (1864).

123. Howard, *American Slavers*, 158–69. See Betts's pretrial statement in *U.S. v. Isaac Morris* (concerning the schooner *Butterfly*), as reported in the *New York Herald*, November 2, 1839, and the report of the trial, ibid., December 2, 1839; also *U.S. v. Isaac Morris*, 14 Peters 464, 466 (1840).

124. *The Mary Ann*, 16 Federal Cases 949 (1848); Howard, *American Slavers*, 188–89. The captain of the *Mary Ann* was a convicted slave trader who had just been released from prison after receiving a presidential pardon.

125. Horace Greeley's *New York Tribune*, July 10, 1857, criticized the "severe spirit of strict construction" displayed by Betts and Nelson. "These two learned judges," it charged, "strain every nerve . . . in efforts substantially to nullify the acts for the suppression of the slave trade."

126. *U.S. v. Isaac Morris*, 14 Peters 464, 476 (1840). The decision of the court, written by Chief Justice Roger B. Taney, virtually compelled a reluctant Betts to condemn Morris's vessel, the *Butterfly*, in admiralty proceedings. The Betts decision is printed in the Foreign Office, *British and Foreign State Papers, 1840–41*, XXIX:649–55.

127. Of 41 cases decided in the southern district of New York from 1837 to 1861 (as listed in Howard, *American Slavers*, 213–23), 22 ended in confiscation. Although several of these decisions are known to have been made by other judges, most of them were presumably rendered by Betts. In the nation as a whole, including New York, there were 57 confiscations and 34 dismissals. In southern courts there were 26 confiscations out of 38 decisions; in the North, 31 out of 53.

128. Eltis, "The Transatlantic Slave Trade, 1821–1843" (Ph.D. diss., University of Rochester, 1978), 210–11.

129. As already noted, the slave-trade law of 1818 did shift the burden of proof to persons charged with bringing foreign blacks into the United States or "purchasing, holding, selling, or otherwise disposing" of them. *SAL*, III:452.

130. *U.S. v. Darnaud*, 25 Federal Cases 754, 758 (1855).

131. *U.S. v. Brune*, 24 Federal Cases 1280 (1852). The act of 1820 provided for punishment of any person serving on an American slave ship or any American citizen serving on a foreign slave ship. Therefore, either American ownership of the vessel or the American citizenship of the defendant had to be proved. For an example of the citizenship problem, see the Darnaud case cited above.

132. *Report of the Trials in the Echo Cases, in Federal Court, Charleston, S.C., April, 1859* (Columbia, S.C.: R. W. Gibbes, 1859), reprinted in Finkelman, ed., *African Slave Trade*, II:55–167; Howard, *American Slavers*, 144. In the two trials of ten men and six men, the juries deliberated one hour and one-half hour, respectively, to reach their verdicts. Five persons on the first jury, having already voted for ten acquittals, were recruited for service on the second jury. Charlestonians nevertheless congratu-

lated themselves on the fairness and decorum with which the trials were conducted. *Charleston Courier*, April 20, 22, 1859.

133. *New Orleans Picayune*, May 28, 29, 1859, partially quoted in Howard, *American Slavers*, 300.

134. Wells, *Wanderer*, 54–59; Howard, *American Slavers*, 230, 231.

135. Wells, *Wanderer*, 38–39, 49–50, 59–62. Efforts by Attorney General Jeremiah S. Black to have William C. Corrie transferred to Savannah for trial were frustrated by Judge A. G. Magrath with the mysterious acquiescence of his colleague on the circuit court, Justice Wayne, who in recent grand-jury charges had expressed strong support for enforcement of the slave-trade laws. McGrath issued a strict-constructionist opinion in which he denied that the Piracy Act of 1820 had anything to do with slave trading. *U.S. v. Corrie*, 25 Federal Cases 658 (1860).

136. See *U.S. v. Gould*, 25 Federal Cases 1375 (1860).

137. Howard, *American Slavers*, 190–91, 224–35, 308–9. Presidential clemency had become common for all kinds of offenses. As early as 1820, John Quincy Adams grumbled privately about the pressures for pardoning convicted murderers: "The moment a man is sentenced to die . . . religion, humanity, family influence, female weakness, personal importunity, pious fraud, and counterfeit benevolence all join in a holy league to swindle a pardon from the Executive. The murderer is pumped and purged into a saint, or certified into an idiot. Fathers and mothers, brothers and sisters, travel hundreds of miles to work by personal solicitation upon the kindly feelings of the President. First they extort a reprieve, then they worry out indulgences, and finally screw out a pardon." Charles Francis Adams, ed., *Memoirs of John Quincy Adams, Comprising Portions of this Diary from 1795 to 1848*, 12 vols. (Philadelphia; J.B. Lippincott & Co., 1874–77), V:168. Even Abraham Lincoln pardoned one convicted slave trader because of ill health after he had served only seven months of a five-year sentence. Howard, *American Slavers*, 189, 233–34. Indeed, it appears from the records that all together, Lincoln received petitions for clemency from seven persons convicted under the slave-trade laws and that he pardoned four of them. J. T. Dorris, "President Lincoln's Clemency," *Illinois State Historical Society Journal* 20 (1927–28): 547–68.

138. *New York Times*, February 22, 1862; Howard, *American Slavers*, 88–90.

139. *New York Times*, June 21, 22, 1861; *U.S. v. Gordon*, 25 Federal Cases 1364 (1861); Howard, *American Slavers*, 199–202; The first jury was said to have been divided 7 to 5 in favor of conviction.

140. *Ex Parte Gordon*, 1 Black 503 (1861); CWAL, V:128.

141. *New York Times*, February 21, 22; *New York Herald*, February 22; *New York Tribune*, February 22, 1862. Criminal trial under any of the slave-trade acts originated in a federal circuit court, consisting of a district judge and the Supreme Court justice assigned to that circuit, or either of them sitting alone. In response to Gordon's applications for writs of prohibition and certiorari, Chief Justice Taney declared that the Supreme Court had no appellate power in a federal criminal case except if the judges of the circuit court should certify that they had opposing opinions on a question raised during the trial. In this instance, there was no such disagreement between Judge William D. Shipman and Justice Samuel Nelson. Lincoln granted Gordon a two-week reprieve but rejected pleas from "a large number of respectable citizens" that he commute the sentence to imprisonment for life. See, for example, Rhoda E. White to Lincoln, February 17, 1862, Robert Todd Lincoln Collection,

Manuscript Division, Library of Congress, reporting that Gordon's wife and aged mother were in Washington with a petition signed by 11,000 New Yorkers urging commutation. Gordon, in the throes of strychnine poisoning, was so plied with whiskey to ease the pain that he went to his death only vaguely aware of what was happening to him.

142. Howard, *American Slavers*, 202–3, 232. Gordon, it appears, was the only person executed for slave trading by *any* European or American nation. See Eltis, *Economic Growth*, 90.

143. Howard, *American Slavers*, 196, 202.

144. Surrender to British authority was a way for an American captain to escape criminal sanction entirely. In 1857, for example, the master of the *Louis McLane* threw his papers overboard and then signed the following statement, presumably drafted by his captors: "Having forfeited the right to the protection of any flag, and the schooner under my command (whose name I refuse to divulge) being equipped for the slave trade, and when boarded by your boat quite ready for the embarkation of six hundred slaves, I deliver her up as a lawful prize, and request you will land me, without my crew, as near the Congo as convenient to you." Enclosed with Napier to Cass, April 16, 1858, *HD*, 36 Cong., 2 sess., No. 7 (Serial 1095), 81–82.

145. One man before Gordon was convicted under the Piracy Act, having commanded a vessel that was burned on the coast of Cuba in 1854 after landing more than 500 slaves. Justice Nelson declared a mistrial, however, acknowledging an error in his charge to the jury. The captain, James Smith, whose citizenship was in some doubt anyhow, subsequently pleaded guilty to violating the Act of 1800. His punishment was two years in prison and a fine of $1,000 that President Buchanan later kindly remitted. *U.S. v. Smith*, 27 Federal Cases 1131 (1855); Howard, *American Slavers*, 192–96.

146. The two principal exceptions were the *Pons*, captured in 1845, and the *Echo* (*Putnam*), captured in 1858.

147. The *Erie*, the *Cora*, and the *Nightingale* were condemned in New York; the *Storm King*, in Virginia; the *Wildfire*, the *William*, and the *Bogota*, in Florida. The disposition of the *Bonito* in New York is unknown. Howard, *American Slavers*, 220–23.

148. Ibid., 202–4, 232–34. The first mate of the *Cora* escaped from custody soon after the vessel arrived in port, and the captain, whose identification was in any case a matter of controversy, eventually did the same. Ibid., 232; *New York Times*, December 11, 12, 18, 1860; ibid., January 12, 1861; *New York Tribune*, December 12, 18, 1860; ibid., January 12, 1861. Three mates of the *Nightingale* were indicted on piracy charges. After the trials of two of them had resulted in deadlocked juries, all three were released on bail and their cases abandoned. Howard, *American Slavers*, 203–4, 234. See the *New York Times*, November 15, 1861, for a report of one of these trials, with editorial comment blaming New York civic leaders, including the clergy, for the city's involvement in the slave trade. Some crew members were also indicted, but it was virtually impossible to secure conviction of ordinary seamen, who could claim ignorance or lack of intent and whose citizenship was often difficult to verify. Nearly all the slave traders tried and convicted in the United States were captains, mates, owners, or supercargoes.

149. In the fall of 1860, the federal district attorney in New York City, J. J. Roosevelt, angered antislavery elements with a pronouncement that public opinion

would no longer support the execution of slave traders and that the president would not permit a death sentence to be carried out. *New York Times,* December 12, 27, 1860; ibid., February 21, 1862.

150. Scholarly estimates of Africans brought into the United States and of slaves transported from Africa to the western hemisphere in American vessels run as high as 235,000 and 201,000, respectively, for the period 1790 to 1810. See Roger Anstey, "The Volume of the North American Slave-Carrying Trade from Africa, 1761–1810," *Revue Francaise d'Histoire d'Outre Mer* 62 (1973): 63, 65. It should be noted, however, that the estimate of 235,000 importations is a questionable statistical inference drawn from the census record of decennial increases in the American slave population by Robert William Fogel and Stanley L. Engerman. Their total for 1800–1810 alone, as reported to Anstey, was 156,000, twice that of any other decade in American history, with more than two-thirds of the importations being presumably illegal. There is no direct evidence to confirm such a huge influx of contrabands, which would have overshadowed the notorious legalized flow into South Carolina, from 1804 to 1807. See Fogel and Engerman, *Time on the Cross: The Economics of American Negro Slavery,* 2 vols. (Boston: Little, Brown & Co., 1974), I:24–25; ibid., II (*Evidence and Methods*):30–31. A graph (ibid., I:25) shows only 110,000 importations for 1800–1810, but a similar graph in Robert William Fogel, *Without Consent or Contract: The Rise and Fall of American Slavery* (New York: W. W. Norton & Co., 1989), 33, fixes the total at 145,000. Anstey used the Fogel-Engerman figure of 235,000 for 1790–1810 in calculating that approximately 201,000 slaves were exported from Africa to the western hemisphere in American ships during that period. His estimate, too, is therefore probably an inflated one. Eltis, in *Economic Growth,* 247, likewise used the Fogel-Engerman estimates of 79,000 for 1790–1800 and 156,000 for 1800–1810.

151. Du Bois, *Suppression,* 109. The Du Bois influence can be seen, for example, in John Hope Franklin, *From Slavery to Freedom: A History of Negro Americans,* 6th ed. (New York: Alfred A. Knopf, 1988), 86, 111. "The law," Franklin declares, "went unenforced." So much so that in the 1850s "a repeal was unnecessary to reopen the trade."

152. Du Bois, *Suppression,* 155, 178; W. E. B. Du Bois, "The Enforcement of the Slave-Trade Laws," *American Historical Association Annual Report for 1891* (Washington, D.C.: Government Printing Office, 1892), 173. The tendency of some historians to confuse slave importations with participation in the international slave trade is well illustrated in Carl B. Swisher, *The Taney Period, 1836–64* (New York: Macmillan Publishing Co., 1974), 691–92, where it is declared: "The traffic was variously between Africa at one end and Brazil or Cuba or some part of the United States at the other, with the United States usually the intended final destination."

153. *MPP,* I:408 (December 2, 1806).

154. Philip D. Curtin, *The Atlantic Slave Trade: A Census* (Madison: University of Wisconsin Press, 1969), 248.

155. *Annual Reports of the American Anti-Slavery Society, by the Executive Committee, for the Years Ending May 1, 1857, and May 1, 1858* (New York: American Anti-Slavery Society, 1859), 57.

156. [George Fitzhugh], "The Conservative Principle, or Social Evils and Their Remedies, Part II: Slave Trade," *De Bow's Review* 22 (1857): 461.

157. On southern Anglophobia, see Kenneth S. Greenberg, *Masters and Statesmen:*

The Political Culture of American Slavery (Baltimore: Johns Hopkins University Press, 1985), 106–23.

158. Charles Robert Lee, Jr., *The Confederate Constitutions* (Chapel Hill: University of North Carolina Press, 1963), 162, 181. The Confederate Congress complied with the constitutional requirement on February 9, 1861, when it enacted legislation continuing in force "all laws of the United States . . . not inconsistent with the Constitution of the Confederate States." William M. Robinson, Jr., *Justice in Grey: A History of the Judicial System of the Confederate States of America* (Cambridge, Mass.: Harvard University Press, 1941), 23.

159. Both Campbell and Wayne delivered charges to southern grand juries strongly supportive of the slave-trade laws. Henry G. Connor, *John Archibald Campbell* (Boston: Houghton Mifflin & Co., 1920), 102–3; *Charge of Mr. Justice Wayne . . . to the Grand Jury of the Sixth Circuit Court of the United States, for the Southern District of Georgia* (Savannah, Ga., 1859), reprinted in Finkelman, ed., *African Slave Trade*, II:1–29. See also Campbell's judgment in *U.S. v. Hahn*, 26 Federal Cases 227 (1860). Taney's judicial conduct with respect to the slave trade was exemplary from an antislavery point of view. See especially *Strohm v. U.S.*, 23 Federal Cases, 240 (1840); and *U.S. v. Morris*, 14 Peters 464 (1840). Howard, *American Slavers*, 39, credits Taney with frightening Baltimoreans out of the business of building ships specifically for sale to slave traders. This, he asserts, was "the federal government's only real success against the slave trade."

160. Du Bois, *Suppression*, 188, speaking of southern leaders in 1861, says that they had been "attacking the slave-trade laws for a decade, and their execution for a quarter-century."

CHAPTER 7

1. John C. Fitzpatrick, ed., *The Writings of George Washington from the Original Manuscript Sources, 1745–1799*, 39 vols. (Washington, D.C.: Government Printing Office, 1931–44), III:289.

2. See the letters of Lund Washington, October 15, December 3, 1775, in Philander D. Chase, ed., *The Papers of George Washington: Revolutionary War Series*, vol. II (Charlottesville: University Press of Virginia, 1987), 174, 175 n, 480.

3. Donald Jackson and Dorothy Twohig, eds., *The Diaries of George Washington*, 6 vols. (Charlottesville: University Press of Virginia, 1976–79), III:45.

4. Fitzpatrick, ed., *Writings of Washington*, XXXV:154, 171, 201–2, 297–98; ibid., XXXVI:2, 70, 123–24, 148; ibid., XXXVII:578.

5. Sir William Blackstone, *Commentaries on the Laws of England*, 4 vols. (Oxford: Clarendon Press, 1765–69), III:4–5; Thomas D. Morris, *Free Men All: The Personal Liberty Laws of the North, 1780–1861* (Baltimore: Johns Hopkins University Press, 1974), 3–4. In 1847, Salmon P. Chase argued persuasively that recaption as Blackstone defined it referred to recovery of a servant wrongfully detained by another person, not to recapture of a runaway servant against his will. See S. P. Chase, *An Argument for the Defendant Submitted to the Supreme Court of the United States, at the December Term, 1846, in the Case of Wharton Jones vs. John Van Zandt* (Cincinnati: R. P. Donogh & Co., 1847), 89–91, as reprinted in Paul Finkelman, ed., *Fugitive Slaves and American Courts: The Pamphlet Literature*, 4 vols. (New York: Garland Publishing, 1988), I:429–31.

6. Lathan A. Windley, "Runaway Slave Advertisements of George Washington and Thomas Jefferson," *JNH* 63 (1978): 373–74; Paul H. Smith, ed., *Letters of Delegates to Congress, 1774–1789*, vol. VII (Washington, D.C.: Library of Congress, 1981), 376 n. Washington, advertising the escape of four slaves in 1761, offered a higher reward if any were captured outside the colony.

7. Summaries of the provisions in Indian treaties for recovery of slaves are in Marion Gleason McDougall, *Fugitive Slaves (1619–1865)* (Boston: Ginn & Co., 1891), 12–13, 104–5.

8. Specifically, the law provided that "such owner, master or mistress, shall have like right and aid to demand, claim and take away his slave or servant as he might have had in case this act had not been made." *Statutes at Large of Pennsylvania from 1682 to 1801*, 16 vols. (Harrisburg: C.M. Busch, State Printer 1896–1904), X:71–72.

9. *JCC*, XXVIII:164, 239.

10. *JCC*, XXXII:343.

11. Article IV of the Articles of Confederation contained such a provision. It was incorporated with only verbal changes in the Constitution.

12. Max Farrand, ed., *The Records of the Federal Convention*, rev. ed., 4 vols. (New Haven, Conn.: Yale University Press, 1937, 1986), II:443.

13. Ibid., 446, 453–54, 601–2, 662.

14. The flight-from-justice clause, by requiring that a fugitive be delivered up "on demand of the executive authority of the state from which he fled," clearly signified delivery by agency of the recipient state; for to whom else could a state executive direct his demand except to the executive of another state? There was no such clarifying specification in the fugitive-slave clause.

15. See Chapter 2 for further elaboration.

16. See, for example, the remarks of James Madison and Patrick Henry in the Virginia convention, Jonathan Elliott, *The Debates in the Several State Conventions on the Adoption of the Federal Constitution . . .* rev. ed., 5 vols., (Philadelphia: J. B. Lippincott Co., 1891), III:453, 456.

17. Paul Finkelman, "The Kidnapping of John Davis and the Adoption of the Fugitive Slave Law of 1793," *JSH* 56 (1990): 400–402; William R. Leslie, "A Study in the Origins of Interstate Rendition: The Big Beaver Creek Murders," *AHR* 55 (1951–52): 66–67.

18. *ASP: Miscellaneous*, I:38–43. Mifflin, of Quaker parentage, had served as quarter-master general of the Continental Army but was part of the notorious Conway Cabal that aimed at removal of Washington from command.

19. Some Virginians did vehemently insist that John was a slave "seduced from his rightful owner." See William P. Palmer and Sherwin McRae, eds., *Calendar of Virginia State Papers and Other Manuscripts . . .* , vol. V (Richmond: n.p., 1885), 396–97, 402.

20. Ibid., 402–3.

21. *AC*, 2 Cong., 1 sess., 147, 148, 179; *HJ*, 2 Cong., 1 sess., 15, 17, 30; Finkelman, "Kidnapping of John Davis," 407–10. Finkelman's article is the most thorough examination of the drafting of fugitive-slave legislation in 1791–93.

22. *AC*, 2 Cong., 2 sess., 616; *SJ*, 2 Cong., 1 sess., 170; ibid., 2 sess., 16, 24, 25, 28,

29, 33–34, 35, 47, 48, 53, 57; *HJ*, 2 Cong., 2 sess., 105; Finkelman, "Kidnapping of John Davis," 412–18.

23. Finkelman, "Kidnapping of John Davis," 414, 417.

24. *SAL*, I:302–5.

25. See the charge to the jury by Justice Bushrod Washington in *Worthington v. Preston*, 30 Federal Cases 645 (1824).

26. The act of 1793 imposed upon state executives the duty of arresting and delivering up fugitives from justice, but extradition continued to depend on comity and was sometimes refused. The Supreme Court held in *Kentucky v. Dennison*, 24 Howard 66 (1860), that the judiciary could not compel a governor's compliance.

27. Donald L. Robinson, *Slavery in the Structure of American Politics, 1765–1820* (New York: Harcourt Brace Jovanovich, 1971), 290–91; Howard Albert Ohline, "Politics and Slavery: The Issue of Slavery in National Politics, 1787–1815" (Ph.D. diss., University of Missouri, 1969), 328–31.

28. *AC*, 7 Cong., 1 sess., 423, 425.

29. *AC*, 15 Cong., 1 sess., 226, 231–39, 242–55, 446–47, 513, 825–31, 837–40, 1339, 1393. For a full discussion of the Pindall bill, see Morris, *Free Men All*, 35–41.

30. *Statutes at Large of Pennsylvania from 1682 to 1801*, XIII:56; Morris, *Free Men All*, 26. Kidnapping occurred often enough to cause public concern, but because of its nature, no numerical estimate is possible. On the subject generally, see Carol Wilson, *Freedom at Risk: The Kidnapping of Free Blacks in America, 1780–1865* (Lexington: University Press of Kentucky, 1994).

31. *New York Session Laws*, 31st sess. (Albany: John Barber, 1808), 108–9; *Revised Laws of the State of New York*, 36th sess. (Albany: H. C. Southwick & Co., 1813), II:209–10; *New York Session Laws*, 40th sess. (New York: William Gould and David Banks and Stephen Gould, 1818), 143; Morris, *Free Men All*, 28.

32. *Ohio Session Laws* (1818–19) 17th sess. (Chillicothe; State Printer, 1819), 56–8. An earlier Ohio law had set a recovery procedure that by implication outlawed recaption. *Ohio Session Laws* (1804–5) 3d sess. (Chillicothe: N. Willis, 1805; reprinted Norwalk, Ohio: The Laning Company, 1901), 358–59; Morris, *Free Men All*, 28–29.

33. *Pennsylvania Session Laws* (1819–20) 44th sess. (Harrisburg: C. Gleim, 1820) 104–06.

34. *Pennsylvania Session Laws* (1825–26) 50th session (Harrisburg: Cameron B. Krause, 1826), 150–55; Morris, *Free Men All*, 46–53, gives an excellent account of the passage of this law, which began as a proslavery bill drafted by commissioners from Maryland. Morris sees the law as a compromise between "the demands of the fugitive slave clause and the responsibility to protect the personal liberty of free blacks." For the view that the law was intended to make the recovery of fugitives "virtually impossible," see William R. Leslie, "The Fugitive Slave Act of 1826," *JSH* 18 (1952): 444–45. Leslie pointed in particular to a provision excluding the oath of an owner as evidence that the alleged fugitive was his property. The law recapitulated the act of 1820 by allowing judges and recorders, but not the more numerous justices of the peace and aldermen, to follow the simpler procedures of the federal law of 1793.

35. *The Revised Statutes of the State of New York*, 3 vols. (Albany: Packard and Van Benthuysen, 1829), II:464–65. Morris, *Free Men All*, 53–57. For alleged fugitives, the ancient and cumbersome writ *de homine replegiando* (replevin of a person)

had one traditional advantage over the writ of *habeas corpus* in that it led to a jury trial rather than just to a hearing before a judge.

36. John Codman Hurd, *The Law of Freedom and Bondage in the United States*, 2 vols. (Boston: Little, Brown & Co., 1858–62), II:30, 127–28, 129. The Indiana laws, since they also permitted recovery under the federal statute of 1793, did not make jury trial obligatory. See William R. Leslie, "The Constitutional Significance of Indiana's Statute of 1824 on Fugitives from Labor," *JSH* 13 (1947): 338–53. In the 1830s, Massachusetts briefly abolished and then restored the writ *de homine replegiando*. In other states the writ was sometimes resorted to under common law, but the tendency as time passed was rather to associate the more easily managed writ of *habeas corpus* with jury trial for fugitives. See Morris, *Free Men All*, 11–12, 64, 76–79, 83, 169–70, 177.

37. *State v. Heddon*, 1 Coxe 328 (New Jersey, 1795); Kempes Y. Schnell, "Court Cases Involving Slavery: A Study of the Application of Anti-Slavery Thought to Judicial Argument" (Ph.D. diss., University of Michigan, 1955), 164–66.

38. *Respublica v. Richards*, 1 Yeates 480, 482 (Pennsylvania, 1795); *Commonwealth v. Holloway*, 2 Sergeant and Rawle 305 (Pennsylvania, 1817); *Wright v. Deacon*, 5 Sergeant and Rawle 62 (1819).

39. *Jack v. Martin*, 12 Wendell 311, 324 (New York Supreme Court, 1834); Morris, *Free Men All*, 65–69.

40. *In re Susan*, 23 Federal Cases 444 (1818).

41. *Commonwealth v. Griffith*, 2 Pickering 11, 14–15 (Massachusetts, 1823).

42. *In re Martin*, 16 Federal Cases 881, 883 (New York, [undated but either 1834 or 1835]).

43. *Commonwealth v. Griffith*, 2 Pickering 18.

44. *Report of the Case of Charles Brown, a Fugitive Slave Owing Labour and Service to Wm. C. Drury of Washington County, Maryland; Decided by the Recorder of Pittsburgh, February 7th, 1835* (Pittsburgh, 1835), 55; reproduced in Finkelman, ed., *Fugitive Slaves*. For similar pronouncements, see Robert M. Cover, *Justice Accused: Antislavery and the Judicial Process* (New Haven, Conn.: Yale University Press, 1975), 119–21.

45. *Johnson v. Tompkins et al.*, 13 Federal Cases 840, 852 (1833); *Wright v. Deacon*, 5 Sergeant and Rawle 63 (Pennsylvania, 1819).

46. Speech of Robert M. T. Hunter, *CG*, 31 Cong., 1 sess., App., 377. See ibid., 528, for the assertion of another Virginian, Thomas H. Bayly, that the fugitive-slave clause "had been made an indispensable condition by the southern States of their sanction of the Constitution." For endorsement of the historical-necessity doctrine by Massachusetts chief justice Lemuel Shaw, see Leonard W. Levy, "Sims' Case: The Fugitive Slave Law in Boston in 1851," *JNH* 35 (1950): 57. For discussion of the case, see the speech of Charles Sumner in the Senate on August 26, 1852, *CG*, 32 Cong., 1 sess., App., 1106–7; also, Hurd, *Law of Freedom and Bondage*, II:439n; Donald M. Roper, "In Quest of Judicial Objectivity: The Marshall Court and the Legitimation of Slavery," *Stanford Law Review* 21 (1969): 538.

47. *MPP*, V:630 (December 3, 1860).

48. Alexander H. Stephens, *A Constitutional View of the Late War Between the States*, 2 vols. (Philadelphia: National Publishing Co., 1868–70), II:26. An interesting extension of the myth may be found in *U.S. v. Copeland*, 25 Federal Cases 646

(1862), wherein the presiding judge rejected the argument that the Fugitive Slave Act did not apply to the District of Columbia. "Maryland and Virginia," he declared, "would not have consented to the Union if this District was to be a refuge for their fugitives." Of course at the time when the Constitution was written and ratified, no one knew where the federal district would be located.

49. Carl B. Swisher, *The Taney Period, 1836–1864*, vol. V of *The Oliver Wendell Holmes Devise History of the Supreme Court of the United States* (New York: Macmillan Publishing Co., 1974), 537–38; Paul Finkelman, "*Prigg v. Pennsylvania* and Northern State Courts: Anti-Slavery Use of a Pro-Slavery Decision," *CWH* 25 (1979): 6–8.

50. *Prigg v. Pennsylvania*, 16 Peters 539, 611, 613, 625–26 (1842). On the right of recaption, as Story traced it to Blackstone's exposition of English common law, see note 5 above. On the Prigg case generally, see Joseph C. Burke, "What Did the Prigg Decision Really Decide?" *Pennsylvania Magazine of History and Biography* 93 (1969): 73–85; Finkelman, "*Prigg v. Pennsylvania*," 5–35; Barbara Holden-Smith, "Lords of Lash, Loom, and Law: Justice Story, Slavery, and *Prigg v. Pennsylvania*," *Cornell Law Review* 78 (1992–93): 1086–1151; Swisher, *Taney Period*, 535–47; Morris, *Free Men All*, 94–104; Don E. Fehrenbacher, *The Dred Scott Case: Its Significance in American Law and Politics* (New York: Oxford University Press, 1978), 43–45; Harold M. Hyman and William M. Wiecek, *Equal Justice Under Law: Constitutional Development, 1835–1875* (New York: Harper & Row, 1982), 107–9; R. Kent Newmyer, *Supreme Court Justice Joseph Story: Statesman of the Old Republic* (Chapel Hill: University of North Carolina Press, 1985), 370–75; David P. Currie, *The Constitution in the Supreme Court: The First Hundred Years, 1789–1888* (Chicago: University of Chicago Press, 1985), 241–45.

51. *Prigg v. Pennsylvania*, 16 Peters 618–22 (1842).

52. Ibid., 612, 622–25. Story, after denying that the states had any concurrent power over the interstate rendition of fugitive slaves, proceeded to confuse matters by acknowledging that a state might, as a matter of protecting public safety, employ its general police power to arrest runaways and remove them from its borders. Such regulations, if they did not interfere with the "just rights of the owner to reclaim his slave," would be constitutional. Thus Story seemed to leave room for state legislation strictly supportive of recovery. On this point, see Finkelman, "*Prigg v. Pennsylvania*," *CWH* 25 (1979): 9–10, 19–20.

53. *Prigg v. Pennsylvania*, 626–33.

54. Nine years earlier, in his *Commentaries on the Constitution of the United States*, 3 vols. (Boston: Hilliard, Gray & Co., 1833), II:110 (section 637), Story had declared that a slave was "in every practical sense property."

55. The very Pennsylvania statute struck down by the Court included an arrest procedure involving local magistrates, sheriffs, and constables. In contrast, the federal law made no provision for arrest but only for a summary process of certification after the fugitive had been privately seized by the owner or his agent.

56. Seward's message of August 16, 1842, in *Niles' National Register* 63: 28 (September 10, 1842).

57. Morris, *Free Men All*, 119–23.

58. *Acts and Resolves Passed by the Legislature of Massachusetts in the Year 1843* (Boston: Dutton and Wentworth, Printers to the State, 1843), 33; Morris, *Free Men All*, 112–15. The laws passed by Vermont (1843), Connecticut (1844), New Hamp-

shire (1846), and Rhode Island (1848) are cited in Finkelman, "*Prigg v. Pennsylvania*," 21 n. Their provisions are summarized in Joseph L. Nogee, "The Prigg Case and Fugitive Slavery, 1842–1850," *JNH* 39 (1954): 200–202.

59. *Pennsylvania Session Laws*, 71st sess. (Harrisburg: J.M.C. Lescure, 1847), 206–8; Morris, *Free Men All*, 117–19. The statute also legalized testimony by a slave "against any person whatsoever" (presumably including claimants under the fugitive-slave law), and it canceled the longstanding right of sojourners to keep slaves with them in the state for up to six months. On July 15, 1847, Charles J. Faulkner of Berkeley County, Virginia (later a member of Congress and minister to France), wrote to John C. Calhoun that the statute was "the most deliberate and perfidious violation of all the guaranties of the Constitution which the fanaticism and wickedness of the abolitionists have resorted to, and the most serious and dangerous attack yet made on the institution of slavery." Slaves, he said, had begun to flee Maryland and Virginia "in gangs of tens and twenties." Chauncey S. Boucher and Robert P. Brooks, eds., "Correspondence Addressed to John C. Calhoun, 1837–1849," *American Historical Association Annual Report*, 1929 (Washington, D.C.: American Historical Association, 1930), 385–87.

60. Morris, *Free Men All*, 109–11; Leonard W. Levy, *The Law of the Commonwealth and Chief Justice Shaw* (Cambridge, Mass.: Harvard University Press, 1957), 78–84. Latimer's case was complicated by his claim that he had been freed by the will of a former owner and by the fact that Gray also accused him of theft and sought his extradition as a fugitive from justice.

61. Walter M. Merrill, *Against Wind and Tide: A Biography of William Lloyd Garrison* (Cambridge, Mass.: Harvard University Press, 1963), 204–5; Irving H. Bartlett, *Wendell Phillips, Brahmin Radical* (Boston: Beacon Press, 1961), 117–19. In an address issued two years later, the executive committee of Garrison's American Anti-Slavery Society declared: "As soon as that appalling decision of the Supreme Court was enunciated, in the name of the Constitution, the people of the North should have risen *en masse*, if for no other cause, and declared the Union at an end." Wendell Phillips, *The Constitution a Pro-Slavery Compact, or Selections from the Madison Papers, etc.* (New York: American Anti-Slavery Society, 1844), 106–7.

62. George Washington's "Farewell Address," MPP, I:224 (September 17, 1796).

63. *Jones v. Van Zandt*, 13 Federal Cases 1047 at 1048–49 (1843); *Norris v. Newton*, 18 Federal Cases 322 at 326–327 (1850). See also Cover, *Justice Accused*, 260–61, and the cases quoted therein. Twenty-nine-year-old Abraham Lincoln expressed the same sentiment publicly in 1838. "Let every man remember," he declared, "that to violate the law, is to trample on the blood of his father . . . although bad laws, if they exist, should be repealed as soon as possible; still while they continue in force, for the sake of example, they should be religiously observed." *CWAL*, I:112.

64. Chase, *Argument in the Case of Jones vs. Van Zandt*, 82–83,85–87. For the case in the circuit court, see *Jones v. Van Zandt*, 13 Federal Cases 1040, with later litigation at 1047–58. See also Swisher, *Taney Period*, 548–53; John Niven, *Salmon P. Chase: A Biography* (New York: Oxford University Press, 1995), 76–83.

65. Chase, *Argument in the Case of Jones vs. Van Zandt*, 88–104. William H. Seward associated himself with Chase as counsel for Van Zandt before the Supreme Court and likewise argued that the act was unconstitutional. See his argument as reprinted in Finkelman, ed., *Fugitive Slaves*, I:473–86.

66. *Jones v. Van Zandt*, 5 Howard 215, 228–230.

67. On southern complaints about the underground railroad, see Larry Gara, *The Liberty Line: The Legend of the Underground Railroad* (Lexington: University of Kentucky Press, 1961), 152–60.

68. An eloquent statement of southern grievances on the subject is the resolution of the Virginia legislature adopted February 7, 1849, *Virginia Session Laws* (1849–1850), 73rd and 74th years of the Commonwealth (Richmond: William F. Ritchie, 1850), 240–54. For an account of eight years of litigation that ended with the slave owner collecting only part of the damages originally awarded (*Norris v. Newton*), see Paul Finkelman, "'The Law, and Not Conscience, Constitutes the Rule of Action': The South Bend Fugitive Slave Case and the Value of Justice Delayed," in *The Constitution, Law, and American Life: Critical Aspects of the Nineteenth Century Experience*, ed., Donald G. Nieman (Athens: University of Georgia Press, 1992), 23–51. Another account of this complex case is Patrick J. Furlong, "The South Bend Fugitive Slave Case," in *We the People: Indiana and the United States Constitution* (Indianapolis: Indiana Historical Society, 1987), 7–24. In a resolution asking for federal legislation in 1844, the Maryland legislature pointed out that damage suits on the part of slave owners were often impractical because slave rescues were carried out by persons owning no property. *HD*, 28 Cong., 1 sess., No. 228 (Serial 443).

69. Finkelman, "*Prigg v. Pennsylvania*," 30–31.

70. *CG*, 31 Cong., 1 sess., 235.

71. *SR*, 30 Cong., 1 sess., No. 143 (Serial 512), 1–5.

72. *CG*, 31 Cong., 1 sess., 99, 103, 171, 220, 228, 233–37. A copy of the bill as reported in 1850 with amendments is in ibid., App., 79; and also in *SR*, 31 Cong., 1 sess., No. 12 (Serial 565), 14–16.

73. *Virginia Session Laws* (1849–50), 254. The legislative history of the Fugitive Slave Law is well covered in Morris, *Free Men All*, 131–45; and in Ralph A. Keller, "Extraterritoriality and the Fugitive Slave Debate," *Illinois Historical Journal* 78 (1985): 113–28.

74. *CG*, 31 Cong., 1 sess., 270–71.

75. Ibid., 244–47; ibid., App., 123, 124.

76. *CG*, 31 Cong., 1 sess., 236–37. The irate senator was Henry S. Foote of Mississippi, who declared that Seward's effort to plunder southern rights should be looked upon "with pointed disapprobation, with hot contempt, with unmitigated loathing, and abhorrence unutterable."

77. Ibid., 481. Webster subsequently insisted that the *Congressional Globe*, by printing a single word out of place, had misrepresented him as giving unqualified support to the Mason bill when in fact he was determined to have it amended. For details, see M[oses] Stuart, *Conscience and the Constitution, with Remarks on the Recent Speech of the Hon. Daniel Webster in the Senate of the United States on the Subject of Slavery* (Boston: Crocker & Brewster, 1850), 67–68.

78. *CG*, 31 Cong., 1 sess., 947–48.

79. Ibid., 1111. Webster declared that he had drafted the bill back in February, after consultation with a "high judicial authority" and other eminent members of the legal profession. The evidence does not support this assertion, however. See, for example, his letter of May 15, 1850, to certain citizens of Newburyport in Charles M. Wiltse and Michael J. Birkner, eds., *The Papers of Daniel Webster: Correspon-*

dence, vol. VII (Hanover, N.H.: University Press of New England, 1986), 88–89, 91. See also Morris, *Free Men All*, 135, 138.

80. *CG*, 31 Cong., 1 sess., 946; ibid., App., 1582.

81. Besides Chase, a Free-Soiler, the opposition's chief spokesmen and strategists were all Whigs. Several northern Democrats voted with them but took little or no part in the debate. John P. Hale, the other Free-Soiler in the Senate, and William H. Seward, the most prominent antislavery Whig, were both absent throughout the week. So, for that matter, were the two major architects of the Compromise of 1850, Henry Clay and Stephen A. Douglas.

82. *CG*, 31 Cong. 1 sess., App., 1583–89. The author of this amendment was William L. Dayton, who in 1856 became the Republican party's first nominee for vice president.

83. Ibid., 1585, 1588. There are, of course, no reliable statistics on the number of free blacks abducted into slavery, but a vast amount of anecdotal evidence and the antikidnapping legislation of southern as well as northern states testify to the absurdity of the Butler-Davis assertion. See Ira Berlin, *Slaves Without Masters: The Free Negro in the Antebellum South* (New York: Random House, 1974), 99–101, 160–61; Gary B. Nash and Jean R. Soderlund, *Freedom by Degrees: Emancipation in Pennsylvania and Its Aftermath* (New York: Oxford University Press, 1991), 196–201; . Carol Wilson, *Freedom at Risk: The Kidnapping of Free Blacks in America, 1780–1865* (Lexington: University Press of Kentucky, 1994), 9–66.

84. *CG*, 31 Cong., 1 sess., App., 1589–90.

85. Ibid., 1609–13, 1625. The only slave-state support for the Underwood substitute came from the two Delaware senators. However, certain sections of the substitute were approved by Mason and, on his motion, incorporated in his bill.

86. Ibid., 1591, 1594–98, 1600–1609; *SJ*, 31 Cong., 1 sess., 573 (Serial 548). The *Globe*'s report of the roll-call vote on the Pratt amendment is slightly inaccurate.

87. *CG.*, 31 Cong., 1 sess., App., 1630, 1660.

88. *CG*, 31 Cong., 1 sess., 1806–7.

89. More specifically, 87 percent of the southern membership voted, and 100 percent of those voting favored the bill; whereas 74 percent of the northern membership voted, and 79 percent of those voting opposed the bill.

CHAPTER 8

1. Although the number of such commissioners was increased after passage of the Fugitive Slave Act in 1850, the office itself dated back to 1812. Edward G. Loring, who ordered the rendition of Anthony Burns in 1854, had held the office of commissioner of the United States Circuit Court since 1840.

2. The writ of habeas corpus was technically still available but rendered useless by the mandated conclusiveness of the certificate of removal. See Winthrop's amendment and the discussion following, *CG*, 31 Cong., 1 sess., App., 1589. Legal representation for alleged fugitives, which the law neither required nor forbade, was often volunteered by local antislavery lawyers.

3. The maximum criminal penalties were a $1,000 fine and six months in prison, to which could be added civil damages of $1,000 for every fugitive lost to his owner.

4. *SAL*, IX:462–65. The statute in its final form was the work of several hands.

Sections 1–3, having to do with the appointment of commissioners, were incorporated, with Mason's approval, from the rejected Underwood bill. Sections 4–9 were Mason's bill, first introduced in January and amended during the August debate, at which time he attributed the original text to an unnamed northerner. (*CG*, 31 Cong., 1 sess., App., 1613). The tenth and last section, drawn from the bill submitted in May by the Committee of Thirteen, offered a claimant the option of presenting the facts of the case to a judge in his own state and receiving a transcript that would serve as evidence before a federal judge or commissioner in any other state.

5. Thomas Hart Benton wrote several years later: "The wonder is how such an act came to pass. . . . Under other circumstances—in any season of quiet and tranquillity—the vote of Congress would have been almost general against the complex, cumbersome, expensive, annoying, and ineffective bill." Thomas Hart Benton, *Thirty Years View*, 2 vols. (New York: D. Appleton & Co., 1865), II:780.

6. *CG*, 31 Cong., 1 sess., 233 (Mason); ibid., App., 79 (Butler), 1588 (Davis). See also ibid., App., 1622, where David L. Yulee of Florida declares: "I have considered that the measure is phantasmagorian. No law which can be made here can have much effect." In 1851, after the first slave rescue in Boston, Butler pronounced the law impossible to execute, adding that one "might as well expect to keep a maniac quiet by singing a lullaby." Ibid., 2 sess., App., 298–99.

7. Unsigned editorial, "The Fugitive Slave Bill," *Southern Literary Messenger*, 16 (November 1850), 697; Henry Steele Commager, *Documents of American History*, 7th ed., 2 vols. (New York: Appleton-Century-Crofts, 1962), I:324. The Georgia platform, a series of resolutions passed by a state convention in December 1850, "epitomized the attitude of the great majority of southerners in 1850." David M. Potter, *The Impending Crisis, 1848–1861*, completed and edited by Don E. Fehrenbacher (New York: Harper & Row, 1976), 128.

8. Charles M. Wiltse and Michael J. Birkner, eds., *The Papers of Daniel Webster: Correspondence*, vol. VII (Hanover, N.H.: University Press of New England, 1986), 174 n, 182–83, 250, 318; Irving H. Bartlett, *Daniel Webster* (New York, W. W. Norton & Co., 1978), 263–65.

9. Len Gougeon and Joel Myerson, eds., *Emerson's Antislavery Writings* (New Haven, Conn.: Yale University Press, 1995), 60.

10. Fillmore to Webster, October 23, 28, 1850, in Wiltse and Birkner, eds., *Papers of Webster: Correspondence*, VII:163–64, 172. The story of the Crafts is summarized in John E. Talmadge, "George Tests the Fugitive Slave Law," *Georgia Historical Quarterly* 49 (1965): 57–64; and in Robert J. Rayback, *Millard Fillmore: Biography of a President* (Buffalo: Buffalo Historical Society, 1959), 271–73.

11. *Boston Liberator*, February 21, April 11, 1851; Stanley W. Campbell, *The Slave Catchers: Enforcement of the Fugitive Slave Law, 1850–1860* (Chapel Hill: University of North Carolina Press, 1968), 148–51; Jane H. Pease and William H. Pease, *They Who Would Be Free: Blacks' Search for Freedom, 1830–1861* (New York: Atheneum, 1974), 219–21.

12. *CG*, 31 Cong., 2 sess., 580, 596–600; *MPP*, V:101–6 (February 19, 1851), 109–10 (March 4, 1851). The reception of Fillmore's message set off a two-day debate in the Senate (*CG*, 31 Cong., 2 sess., App., 292–326), during which Clay insisted that the law was being well enforced everywhere except in Boston, while Mason, for one, emphatically disagreed.

13. Wiltse and Birkner, eds., *Papers of Webster: Correspondence*, VII:221–27,

229–30. Of the Shadrach rescue specifically Webster said in a public letter: "This is levying war against the United States, and is nothing less than treason." George Ticknor Curtis, *Life of Daniel Webster*, 4th ed., 2 vols. (New York: D. Appleton & Co., 1872), II:90. For other examples of Webster's repeated use of the word "treason," see his speeches at Buffalo and Syracuse in May 1851, respectively, in Daniel Webster, *The Writings and Speeches of Daniel Webster*, 18 vols. (Boston: Little, Brown & Co., 1903), XIII:419; and Charles M. Wiltse and Alan R. Berolzheimer, eds., *The Papers of Daniel Webster: Speeches and Formal Writings*, vol. II (Hanover, N.H.: University Press of New England, 1988), 595.

14. This paragraph is largely based on Leonard W. Levy's excellent article, "Sims' Case: The Fugitive Slave Law in Boston in 1851," *JNH* 35 (1950): 39–74. Justice Levi Woodbury, on circuit duty, actually granted a writ of habeas corpus but then, in the subsequent hearing, remanded Sims to the custody of the federal marshal.

15. Campbell, *Slave Catchers*, 151–57; Pease and Pease, *They Who Would Be Free*, 223–27. For a full account of the Christiana affair, see Thomas P. Slaughter, *Bloody Dawn: The Christiana Riot and Racial Violence in the Antebellum North* (New York: Oxford University Press, 1991). For an account of the Jerry rescue by an abolitionist participant, see Samuel J. May, *Some Recollections of Our Antislavery Conflict* (Boston: Fields, Osgood & Co., 1869), 373–84.

16. In each instance, some of the most indictable culprits (principally blacks) fled to Canada or otherwise escaped arrest. At Christiana, a foolish decision (undoubtedly reflecting Webster's influence) to charge the offenders with treason made the prosecution's task especially difficult. The one man convicted in Syracuse was Enoch Reed, an African American tried under the act of 1793.

17. *MPP*, V:136–38 (December 2, 1851); Arthur M. Schlesinger, Jr., ed., *History of American Presidential Elections, 1789–1968*, 9 vols. (New York: Chelsea House Publishers, 1985), II:952, 957. *CG*, 32 Cong., 1 sess., 1950; ibid., App., 1125; David Donald, *Charles Sumner and the Coming of the Civil War* (New York: Alfred A. Knopf, 1961), 224–37.

18. Campbell, *Slave Catchers*, 199–201.

19. *Twenty-First Annual Report Presented to the Massachusetts Anti-Slavery Society by Its Board of Managers, January 26, 1853* (Boston: Massachusetts Anti-Slavery Society, 1853), 76.

20. *MPP*, V:202 (March 4, 1853); Cushing to Pierce, November 14, 1853, and February 18, May 27, September 11, 1854, in C. C. Andrews, ed., *Official Opinions of the Attorneys General of the United States*, vol. VI (Washington, D.C.: Government Printing Office, 1856), 221–23, 306–7, 466–74, 713–14; Claude M. Fuess, *The Life of Caleb Cushing*, 2 vols. (New York: Harcourt, Brace & Co., 1923), II:144–45.

21. Amos A. Lawrence to William Appleton, March 6, 1854, quoted in Jane H. Pease and William H. Pease, *The Fugitive Slave Law and Anthony Burns: A Problem in Law Enforcement* (Philadelphia: J. B. Lippincott & Co., 1975), 28.

22. Vroman Mason, "The Fugitive Slave Law in Wisconsin, with Reference to Nullification Sentiment," *Proceedings of the State Historical Society of Wisconsin . . . 1895*, (Madison: State Historical Society of Wisconsin, 1895) 122–44; Carl B. Swisher, *The Taney Period, 1836–1864* (New York: Macmillan Publishing Co., 1974), 653–60. It is a curious coincidence that the claimant, Benammi S. Garland of Missouri, had for many years been the agent of John F. A. Sanford in respect to Dred Scott.

23. The fullest account is in David Russell Maginnes, "The Point of Honor: The

Rendition of the Fugitive Slave Anthony Burns, Boston, 1854" (Ph.D. diss., Columbia University, 1973) 80–204. See also Campbell, *Slave Catchers*, 124–30; Pease and Pease, *Fugitive Slave Law and Anthony Burns*, 28–33, 38–48. Efforts to free Burns by purchase at the time of his arrest did not succeed, but in 1855 he was bought with money raised largely by the black community of Boston.

24. Tilden G. Edelstein, *Strange Enthusiasm: A Life of Thomas Wentworth Higginson* (New Haven, Conn.: Yale University Press, 1968), 167–70. Higginson, the man who led the abortive attempt to rescue Burns, nevertheless acted as Butman's protector in the Worcester riot.

25. Robert M. Cover, *Justice Accused: Antislavery and the Judicial Process* (New Haven, Conn.: Yale University Press, 1975), 179–82; Irving H. Bartlett, *Wendell Phillips, Brahmin Radical* (Boston: Beacon Press, 1961), 186–87. Phillips led the crusade to punish Loring. Many documents of the Loring removal are conveniently assembled in Paul Finkelman, ed., *Fugitive Slaves and American Courts: The Pamphlet Literature*, 4 vols. (New York: Garland Publishing Co., 1988), III:1–330.

26. Julian Yanuck, "The Garner Fugitive Slave Case," *MVHR* 40 (1953–54): 47–66; Campbell, *Slave Catchers*, 203–6. For the Oberlin-Wellington rescue, see Nat Brandt, *The Town That Started the Civil War* (Syracuse, N.Y.: Syracuse University Press, 1990).

27. For analysis of these laws, see Thomas D. Morris, *Free Men All: The Personal Liberty Laws of the North, 1780–1861* (Baltimore: Johns Hopkins University Press, 1974), 195–98; Campbell, *Slave Catchers*, 171–84; Norman L. Rosenberg, "Personal Liberty Laws and Sectional Crisis, 1850–1861," *CWH* 17 (1971): 30–44. Ohio's name is sometimes added to this list, but the mild legislation enacted by the state in 1857 was substantially repealed within a year.

28. *Ex parte Robinson*, 20 Federal Cases, 965 (1856); Yanuck, "Garner Case," 64.

29. Campbell, *Slave Catchers*, 161–64; and for a longer account, presenting many of the documents, see Benjamin F. Prince, "The Rescue Case of 1857," *Ohio Archaeological and Historical Society Publications* 16 (1907): 292–309. This was the Mechanicsburg or Addison White rescue.

30. *Ex parte Bushnell, Ex parte Langston*, 9 Ohio State Reports 78 (1859); Campbell, *Slave Catchers*, 164–67; Brandt, *Town That Started Civil War*, 115–237. Bushnell, a white man, and Langston, a black, served out sentences of sixty and twenty days, respectively.

31. Swisher, *Taney Period*, 653–72. Sherman M. Booth, the central figure in the affair, was a Milwaukee editor who played a leading role in the rescue of Joshua Glover. Arrested and released by order of the state supreme court, he was re-arrested, tried in federal court, and convicted, only to be released again by the state supreme court. After both cases had been reviewed and federal authority upheld in *Ableman v. Booth*, 21 Howard 506 (1859), Booth was imprisoned once more, then rescued and recaptured, and finally pardoned in 1861 by President James Buchanan. The course of the Wisconsin supreme court in these complex proceedings was crisply summarized by Chief Justice Taney in *Ableman v. Booth*, 507–14. See also Mason, "Fugitive Slave Law," 117–44; A. J. Beitzinger, "Federal Law Enforcement and the Booth Cases," *Marquette Law Review* 41 (1957): 7–32.

32. Crittenden to Fillmore, September 18, 1850, in Benjamin F. Hall, comp., *Official Opinions of the Attorneys General of the United States*, vol. V (Washington, D.C.: Government Printing Office, 1852), 254–59, esp. 257.

33. *Ableman v. Booth*, 21 Howard 526 (1859). Taney used only a single sentence to make the ruling on constitutionality.

34. In *Ex parte Bushnell*, 187–88 (1859), Chief Justice Joseph R. Swan listed fourteen cases in which state supreme courts had upheld the constitutionality of the fugitive slave legislation. Swan added that he had been "unable to find a single decision of any Supreme Court of any state in the Union, denying to Congress the power to legislate upon this subject." Swan insisted that only one member of the Wisconsin supreme court had issued such a denial, but a majority of two did so in *In re Booth*, 3 Wisconsin 1 (1854), and again in *In re Booth and Rycraft*, 3 Wisconsin 157 (1854). The dissenting opinion of Milton Sutcliffe in *Ex parte Bushnell*, 229–315, is perhaps the most extensive statement by a state supreme court justice holding the act of 1850 to be unconstitutional. A pamphlet version is reprinted in Finkelman, ed., *Fugitive Slaves*, IV:23–119.

35. Hornblower in *State v. The Sheriff of Burlington*, unreported (1836), but the pamphlet text of his opinion is reproduced in Finkelman, ed., *Fugitive Slaves*, I:99–103; Chancellor Reuben H. Walworth of New York in *Jack v. Martin*, 14 Wendell 524–30 (New York, Court of Errors, 1835); Smith in *In Re Booth*, 3 Wisconsin 127.

36. Congress in the act of 1793 merely designated state governors as the officers responsible for the return of fugitives from justice.

37. 16 Peters 619. Here, Story was of course following John Marshall's classic statement of the doctrine of implied powers in *McCulloch v. Maryland*. So was Justice John McLean eleven years later in *Miller v. McQuerry*, 17 Federal Cases 338: "If the Constitution guarantees a right to the master of a slave, and that he shall be delivered up, the power is given to effectuate that right." For the same argument from Henry Clay, see his speech in the Senate, February 18, 1851, *CG*, 32 Cong., 1 sess., App., 321.

38. There were some southerners, to be sure, who regarded the Fugitive Slave Act of 1850 as a dangerous sacrifice of strict-constructionist principles. See, for example, the *Charleston Mercury* editorial, reprinted in the *Washington National Era*, October 11, 1855. See also Larry Gara, "The Fugitive Slave Law: A Double Paradox," *CWH* 10 (1964): 233.

39. *Boston Liberator* (with reports from several other newspapers), January 3, 1851.

40. *Miller v. McQuerry*, 17 Federal Cases 340 (1853). At the same time that McLean upheld the constitutionality of federal fugitive slave legislation and insisted that it must be enforced, his statutory construction (and that of several other federal judges) sometimes limited its punitive effect. He held, for example, that advising, feeding, and clothing a fugitive did not constitute the harboring or concealing that would be in violation of the law. *Jones v. Van Zandt*, 13 Federal Cases 1048 (1843); Jordan Marshall Smith, "The Federal Courts and the Black Man in America, 1800–1883: A Study of Judicial Policy Making" (Ph.D. diss., University of North Carolina, 1977), 193–203.

41. Classification of rendition as an administrative rather than a judicial process served also to answer antislavery attacks on the office of commissioner in which it was contended that Congress had no power to vest judicial authority in persons not appointed in the constitutionally prescribed way. Yet Attorney General John J. Crittenden had declared in an official opinion written September 18, 1850, that the

issuance of a certificate by a commissioner was "the act and judgment of a judicial tribunal having competent jurisdiction." See John Codman Hurd, *The Law of Freedom and Bondage in the United States*, 2 vols. (Boston: Little, Brown & Co., 1858–62), II:653–97, 719; and Hall, comp., *Opinions of Attorneys General* , V:257.

42. See *Wright v. Deacon*, 5 Sergeant and Rawle 62, 63 (Pennsylvania, 1819). In a case on circuit in the 1830s, Justice Smith Thompson declared that the rendition process was "only a preliminary examination to authorize the claimant to take back the fugitive to the State from which he fled; and the question whether he is a slave or not is open to inquiry there." *In re Martin*, 16 Federal Cases 881, 883. For the assertion of James M. Mason, principal author of the act of 1850, that rendition affected only "custody" and not "title," see *CG*, 31 Cong., 1 sess., App., 1590. Justice Samuel Nelson in a charge to a federal grand jury in 1851 said of the rendition proceeding: "It settles conclusively no right of the claimant to the service of the fugitive, except for the purpose of removal to the state from which he or she fled." 30 Federal Cases 1011. This same line of reasoning was followed by the historian Allen Johnson in his influential article, "The Constitutionality of the Fugitive Slave Acts," *Yale Law Journal* 31 (1921–22): 174–79.

43. Horace Mann, *Slavery: Letters and Speeches* (Boston: B. B. Mussey & Co., 1851), 499.

44. Ibid., 495.

45. *Miller v. McQuerry*, 17 Federal Cases 340.

46. See, for instance, the opinion written in November 1850 by Benjamin R. Curtis as counsel for the United States marshal, quoted in Hurd, *Law of Freedom and Bondage*, II:723 n.

47. *Miller v. McQuerry*, 17 Federal Cases 340. The generally accepted interpretation, as set forth by Justice Story in *Parsons v. Bedford*, 3 Peters 433, 445–46 (1830), was that the amendment embraced all suits except those in equity and admiralty. McLean had dissented in that case and was apparently resolved to ignore Story's ruling.

48. 16 Peters 540–41; Hurd, *Law of Freedom and Bondage*, II:740–41.

49. *United States v. Hanway*, 26 Federal Cases 105, 123 (1851).

50. *HD*, 34 Cong., 1 sess., No. 81 (Serial 867).

51. Of course the Liberty party represented something less than the full strength of abolitionism because it was opposed by the Garrisonian wing of the movement.

52. *CWAL*, II:268.

53. In 1852, the platform of the Free Democratic party, a thinner, more radical continuation of the Free Soil movement, did denounce the Fugitive Slave Act of 1850 and demand its repeal.

54. *CWAL*, III:386.

55. According to the *Congressional Globe*, no legislation on the subject was proposed in the Thirty-Fourth Congress or the Thirty-Fifth, and none in the Thirty-Sixth until March 26, 1860, when Harrison G. Blake of Ohio offered a bill for repeal that was referred to the judiciary committee but never reported. *CG*, 36 Cong., 1 sess., 1356.

56. Morris, *Free Men All*, 188–93; Rosenberg, "Personal Liberty Laws," 38–39.

57. John Hope Franklin and Loren Schweninger, *Runaway Slaves: Rebels on the Plantation, 1790–1860* (New York: Oxford University Press, 1999), 48, 116, 122, 239, 241–42, 279, 282, 291; John Hope Franklin and Alfred A. Moss, Jr., *From Slavery to*

Freedom: A History of African Americans, 7th ed. (New York: Alfred A. Knopf, 1994), 187–88; Allan Nevins, *The Emergence of Lincoln,* 2 vols. (New York: Charles Scribner's Sons, 1950), II:489; J. C. Furnas, *Goodbye to Uncle Tom* (New York: William Sloane Associates, 1956), 239–40; Larry Gara, *The Liberty Line: The Legend of the Underground Railroad* (Lexington: University of Kentucky Press, 1961), 153, 162, 189.

58. The seven coastal states from South Carolina around to Texas reported 312 fugitives in 1850, but it is doubtful that many of them reached a free state. Of 694 fugitives recorded in William Still's *Underground Railroad Records,* only 35 came from the cotton South (Furnas, *Goodbye to Uncle Tom,* 242). A study of North Carolina fugitives leaving the state down to 1840 indicates that fewer than half of them went to the North. Freddie L. Parker, *Running for Freedom: Slave Runaways in North Carolina, 1775–1840* (New York: Garland Publishing, 1993), 395.

59. *CG,* 31 Cong., 2 sess., App., 304. Similarly, Senator Walker Brooke declared during another debate: "We do not regard this law as having any merits, so far as we in Mississippi are concerned, but its repeal would be an act of bad faith . . . and we contend that a Union preserved under such circumstances would be worse than no Union at all." *CG,* 32 Cong., 1 sess., 1951.When some 2,500 citizens of Massachusetts responded to the Burns affair by petitioning Congress for repeal of the law, Senator James C. Jones of Tennessee exclaimed that the memorial was "surcharged with treason and with blood," and that repeal would mean secession. *CG,* 33 Cong., 1 sess., 1514.

60. *CG,* 31 Cong., 2 sess., App., 299. For the most extensive assessment of southern anxiety about slave rebellion, see Steven A. Channing, *Crisis of Fear: Secession in South Carolina* (New York: Simon & Schuster, 1970).

61. Edward McPherson, *The Political History of the United States of America During the Great Rebellion* (Washington, D.C.: Philp & Solomons, 1864), 15–19. Drafted by Christopher G. Memminger, later secretary of the treasury in the Confederate government, the declaration was criticized by several delegates for its emphasis on the fugitive-slave problem.

62. *CG,* 36 Cong., 1 sess., App., 88.

63. *MPP,* V:630, 638 (December 3, 1860).

64. *CG,* 36 Cong., 2 sess., 77, 78. Morris, *Free Men All,* 203–8, presents an excellent summary of congressional activity with respect to fugitive slaves in the secession winter of 1860–61.

65. *CWAL,* IV:156–57. See also David M. Potter, *Lincoln and His Party in the Secession Crisis* (New Haven, Conn.: Yale University Press, 1942), 167–69. Another resolution declared that all state legislation in conflict with such federal law ought to be repealed.

66. The principal actions were Senate and House approval of a constitutional amendment in effect guaranteeing the perpetuity of slavery and passage of bills organizing three new territories with slavery not expressly forbidden therein. See Potter, *Lincoln and His Party,* 277–78, 301.

67. *CG,* 36 Cong., 2 sess., 1262, 1266, 1328, 1350; Morris, *Free Men All,* 204, 207. The bill provided that a fugitive claiming to be free should have a jury trial in a federal district court of the state from which he had allegedly fled.

68. Morris, *Free Men All,* 208–18.

69. *CWAL*, IV:263–64; Campbell, *Slave Catchers*, 192.

70. Federal courts had almost nothing to do with the subject throughout the war. The prime exception is *U.S. v. Copeland*, 25 Federal Cases 646 (1862), in which the circuit court of the District of Columbia held that the fugitive slave laws applied to the District.

71. *Chicago Tribune*, April 9, 10, 11, 1861.

72. *New York Tribune*, April 3, 1862.

73. *Washington National Republican*, May 24, 1862; Henry Greenleaf Pearson, *James S. Wadsworth of Geneseo* (New York: Charles Scribners' Sons, 1913), 138–40. Lamon's account of the affair is in his *Recollections of Abraham Lincoln, 1847–1865*, ed. Dorothy Lamon Teillard, 2d ed. (Washington, D.C.: The Editor, 1911), 254–57. At a conference with Lincoln on June 11, Lamon and Wadsworth agreed to peace terms proposed by Orville H. Browning. For details see Theodore Calvin Pease and James G. Randall, eds., *The Diary of Orville Hickman Browning*, 2 vols. (Springfield: Illinois State Historical Library, 1925–33), I:549–50. On July 1, Lincoln told Browning that administration policy was to return no Negroes to slavery, but induce none to escape. Ibid., 555

74. "Contraband" was a term used in the international law of warfare to designate certain goods of a neutral nation (such as munitions) that could not without risk of confiscation be supplied to a belligerent nation. General Benjamin F. Butler, stationed at Fortress Monroe in the spring of 1861, first applied the word to fugitive slaves entering army lines. His argument that slaves put to military use by the enemy became seizable as contrabands of war was endorsed by Secretary of War Simon Cameron and incorporated in the Confiscation Act of August 6, 1861. See Louis S. Gerteis, *From Contraband to Freedman: Federal Policy Toward Southern Blacks, 1861–1865* (Westport, Conn.: Greenwood Press, 1973), 11–16.

75. The text of the article and material related to its passage is in McPherson, *Political History of the Rebellion*, 237–38. See also Henry Wilson, *History of the Rise and Fall of the Slave Power in America*, 3 vols. (Boston: James R. Osgood & Co., 1875–77), III:294–97.

76. McPherson, *Political History of the Rebellion*, 235–37, conveniently presents the data on which this paragraph is based. For a guide to congressional consideration of the issue during this session, see Marion Gleason McDougall, *Fugitive Slaves, 1619–1865* (Boston: Ginn & Co., 1891), 123. See also Allan G. Bogue, *The Earnest Men: Republicans of the Civil War Senate* (Ithaca, N.Y.: Cornell University Press, 1981), 188–94.

77. *New York Tribune*, June 24, 1864.

78. Even William Lloyd Garrison's newspaper had little to say on the subject, except that it chastised Democrats for voting against repeal. *Boston Liberator*, June 17, July 1, 1864.

79. Albert Taylor Bledsoe, *An Essay on Liberty and Slavery* (Philadelphia: J. B. Lippincott & Co., 1856), 379. Bledsoe, a West Point graduate, practiced law for ten years in Springfield, Illinois, and was associated with Abraham Lincoln in local Whig politics. He served for a time in the Confederate government, and after the war, as founder and editor of the *Southern Review*, he was one of the fiercest defenders of the Lost Cause.

CHAPTER 9

1. Merrill D. Peterson, *Thomas Jefferson and the New Nation* (New York: Oxford University Press, 1970), 276–78. For the question of whether the plan of government truly became an "ordinance," see Richard P. McCormick, "The 'Ordinance' of 1784?" *William and Mary Quarterly*, 3d ser., 50 (1993): 112–22; but cf. Francis S. Philbrick, ed., *The Laws of Illinois Territory, 1809–1818* (Springfield: Illinois State Historical Library, 1950), cclxii–cclxiii.

2. Julian P. Boyd et al., eds., *The Papers of Thomas Jefferson*, 26 vols. to date (Princeton, N.J.: Princeton University Press, 1950–95), VI:581–607. See also Peter S. Onuf's excellent book, *Statehood and Union: A History of the Northwest Ordinance* (Bloomington: Indiana University Press, 1987), 46–49, where the document in the revised form approved by Congress is reprinted. A year earlier, as Onuf (p. 110) points out, Timothy Pickering had sought to exclude slavery from a proposed military colony in the Ohio country.

3. *JCC*, XXVI:247; Donald L. Robinson, *Slavery in the Structure of American Politics, 1765–1820* (New York: Harcourt Brace Jovanovich, 1970), 379–80. A motion to strike the antislavery provision having been made, the rules of Congress required the approval of at least seven states to retain it. The vote by states was 6 to 3 in favor of retention, with North Carolina divided and New Jersey not counted because it had only one delegate present. The vote by delegates was 16 to 7 in favor. Jefferson was outvoted in his own Virginia delegation. See his letter to Madison, April 25, 1784, and his later comment on the closeness of the vote in Boyd et al., eds., *Papers of Jefferson*, VII:118; ibid., X:58.

4. Boyd et al., eds., *Papers of Jefferson*, VI:612, 613, 615; Jack Ericson Eblen, *The First and Second United States Empires: Governors and Territorial Government, 1784–1912* (Pittsburgh: University of Pittsburgh Press, 1968), 23–24. The amendment was offered by Elbridge Gerry of Massachusetts but apparently written by Jefferson. On the connections between the ordinances of 1784 and 1787, see Robert F. Berkhofer, Jr., "Jefferson, the Ordinance of 1784, and the Origins of the American Territorial System," *William and Mary Quarterly*, 3d ser., 29 (1972): 231–62.

5. Walter Clark, ed., *The State Records of North Carolina*, 26 vols. (n.p.: Goldsboro, N.C., 1886–1905), XXIV:561–63.

6. *JCC*, XXVIII:164–65, 239. The favorable vote on the King proposal was for commitment. The committee, headed by King, restored the Jefferson date and added a fugitive-slave clause. Its report was not acted upon. For a discussion, see Charles R. King, ed., *The Life and Correspondence of Rufus King*, 6 vols. (New York: G. P. Putnam's Sons, 1894–1900), I:41n–42 n.

7. *JCC*, XXX:402–6; Monroe to Jefferson, May 11, 1786, in Boyd et al., eds., *Papers of Jefferson*, IX:510–11. See also *JCC*, XXXI:669–73, for the revised version of Monroe's plan presented by another committee in September 1786.

8. *JCC*, XXXII:313–20, 334–43.

9. For general discussion of this question, see Robinson, *Slavery in American Politics*, 381–86; Don E. Fehrenbacher, *The Dred Scott Case: Its Significance in American Law and Politics* (New York: Oxford University Press, 1978), 80–81. An economic motive was attributed to southerners by William Grayson, a congressman from Virginia. "The clause respecting slavery," he wrote, "was agreed to by the

southern members for the purpose of preventing tobacco and indigo from being made on the N.W. side of the Ohio, as well as for several other political reasons." Grayson to James Madison, August 8, 1787, Edmund C. Burnett, ed., *Letters of Members of the Continental Congress*, 8 vols. (Washington, D.C.: Carnegie Institution, 1921–34), VIII:632. The much discussed role of Manasseh Cutler and other New England land speculators forming the Ohio Company is well summarized in Paul Finkelman, "Slavery and the Northwest Ordinance: A Study in Ambiguity," *Journal of the Early Republic* 6 (1986): 351–53.

10. The words are those of Senator George Frisbie Hoar of Massachusetts in 1887, as quoted in Onuf, *Statehood and Union*, 133.

11. Stephen A. Douglas, in defending the Kansas-Nebraska Act and the principle of popular sovereignty in 1854, argued that neither the ordinance nor any other congressional intervention had ever prevented slavery from going into a western territory. Abraham Lincoln replied that the facts proved otherwise, pointing especially to the difference between Illinois and Missouri. "They lie side by side, the Mississippi River only dividing them," he said, "while their early settlements were within the same latitude. Between 1810 and 1820 the number of slaves in Missouri *increased* 7,211; while in Illinois, in the same ten years, they *decreased* 51. . . . During this time, the ordinance forbid slavery to go into Illinois, and *nothing* forbid it to go into Missouri. It *did* go into Missouri and did *not* go into Illinois. That is the fact." *CWAL*, II:276–77. Finkelman's "Slavery and the Northwest Ordinance" is the most extensive effort by a modern scholar to minimize the efficacy of the ordinance. For a partial dissent, see David Brion Davis, "The Significance of Excluding Slavery from the Old Northwest in 1787," *Indiana Magazine of History* 84 (1988): 75–89.

12. Max Farrand, ed., *The Records of the Federal Convention of 1787*, rev. ed., 4 vols. (New Haven, Conn.: Yale University Press, 1937), II:321, 324, 458–59, 466, 578, 602, 662; Fehrenbacher, *Dred Scott Case*, 82–84.

13. There is some confusion in the record about Maryland's vote.

14. *AC*, 1 Cong., 1 sess., 56, 660.

15. *AC*, 1 Cong., 2 sess., 942, 948, 951–52, 963–64, 1477–78, 1549, 1556, 2208–12, 2226–27. The North Carolina act of cession (December 22, 1789) and deed of cession (February 25, 1790), together with the congressional act of acceptance (April 2, 1790) and the act organizing the "Territory South of the River Ohio" are reproduced in *TP*, IV:3–19.

16. St. Clair to Washington, May 1, 1790, in *TP*, II:248; Finkelman, "Slavery and the Northwest Ordinance," 365–67. For a persuasive critique of the argument that the ordinance was prospective only, see Philbrick, ed., *Laws of Illinois Territory* ccxxxiii-ccxlix.

17. William Henry Smith, ed., *The St. Clair Papers: The Life and Public Services of Arthur St. Clair*, 2 vols. (Cincinnati: R. Clarke, 1882; reprint, New York: Da Capo Press, 1971), II:31. The Virginia deed of cession required that the French inhabitants should "have their possessions and titles confirmed to them and be protected in the enforcement of their rights and liberties." The ordinance permitted retention of the "laws and customs now in force among them relative to the descent of property." It is by no means clear that either clause conferred upon this one group the special privilege of remaining slaveholders in a region where slavery had been abolished. The ordinance also seemed to acknowledge a continuing presence of servitude when it referred in one passage to "free inhabitants" and in another to "free male inhabi-

tants," but this ambiguity reflected nothing more than the fact that the antislavery provision was added at almost the last moment, without any accompanying revision of other parts of the document.

18. Smith, ed., *St. Clair Papers*, II:331; Francis S. Philbrick, ed., *The Laws of Indiana Territory, 1801–09* (Springfield: Illinois State Historical Library, 1930), 42–43, 136–39, 203–4, 463–67, 523–26; J. P. Dunn, *Indiana: A Redemption from Slavery* (Boston: Houghton, Mifflin & Co., 1888), 314–16, 329–34; Philbrick, ed., *Laws of Illinois Territory*, 5. For a proposal that the first Ohio constitution allow a limited form of slavery, see Alfred Mathews, *Ohio and Her Western Reserve* (New York: D. Appleton & Co., 1902), 253–55. The Indiana governor was the future president, William Henry Harrison; the Illinois governor was Ninian Edwards, whose son would become Abraham Lincoln's brother-in-law.

19. Emile Joseph Verlie, ed., *Illinois Constitutions* (Springfield: Illinois State Historical Library, 1919), 38–39; *AC*, 15 Cong., 1 sess., 306–10; Dwight Harris, *History of Negro Slavery in Illinois and of the Slavery Agitation in That State* (Chicago: A. C. McClurg & Co., 1906), 27–49; Onuf, *Statehood and Union*, 123–30. As late as 1840, the federal census reported 331 slaves in Illinois. The indenture system lasted nominally until its omission from the new state constitution of 1848.

20. Emma Lou Thornbrough, *The Negro in Indiana: A Study of a Minority* ([Indianapolis]: Indiana Historical Bureau, 1957), 8–11.

21. *AC*, 5 Cong., 2 sess., 515, 1306–12, 1314, 1318; Robinson, *Slavery in American Politics*, 387–92; Fehrenbacher, *Dred Scott Case*, 87–89, 622; *TP*, V:67, 85.

22. *Sargent's Code: A Collection of the Original Laws of the Mississippi Territory Enacted 1799–1800 by Governor Winthrop Sargent and the Territorial Judges* (Jackson, Miss.: Historical Records Survey, 1939), 44–48; see also 113–14. Sargent, a native of Gloucester, Massachusetts, who had served for a decade as the secretary of Northwest Territory, married into a prominent Mississippi family and spent the last years of his life as a planter near Natchez.

23. Andrew Ellicott to Timothy Pickering, September 24, 1797, in Carter, ed., *TP*, V:5.

24. Of the three members of Jefferson's cabinet who negotiated the agreement with Georgia, two were northerners and all three had antislavery credentials. They were James Madison, Albert Gallatin, and Levi Lincoln.

25. *AC*, 8 Cong., 1 sess., 1498–1578. Among the many writings on Jefferson and slavery, see especially David Brion Davis, *The Problem of Slavery in the Age of Revolution, 1770–1823* (Ithaca, N.Y.: Cornell University Press, 1975), 164–84; John C. Miller, *The Wolf by the Ears: Thomas Jefferson and Slavery* (New York: Free Press, 1977); Winthrop D. Jordan, *White Over Black: American Attitudes Toward the Negro, 1550–1812* (Chapel Hill: University of North Carolina Press, 1968), 429–81.

26. *AC*, 8 Cong., 1 sess., 240–42, 244; Everett S. Brown, ed., "The Senate Debate on the Breckinridge Bill for the Government of Louisiana, 1804," *AHR* 22 (1916–17): 340–64; Robinson, *Slavery in American Politics*, 396–400; Fehrenbacher, *Dred Scott Case*, 91–96; *TP*, IX:261, 265.

27. *AC*, 8 Cong., 2 sess., 47, 48, 54, 59–61, 68, 69, 1201, 1209–11, 1213, 1215; *TP*, IX:405–7, 547–48; ibid., XIII:87–89, 92–95.

28. *TP*, XIV:552–59; *AC*, 12 Cong., 1 sess., 242–43, 244, 1248, 1279, 1434.

29. *TP*, VII:385 n; Joseph T. Hatfield, *William Claiborne, Jeffersonian Centurion in the American Southwest* (Lafayette: University of Southwestern Louisiana Press,

1976), 180–83. On the background of French and Spanish slave law in Louisiana, see Thomas N. Ingersoll, "Slave Codes and Judicial Practice in New Orleans, 1718–1807," *Law and History Review* 13 (1995): 23–62.

30. Dunbar Rowland, ed., *Official Letter Books of W. C. C. Claiborne, 1801–1816*, 6 vols. (Jackson: Mississippi State Department of Archives and History, 1917), III:5–7; ibid., V:93–97, 99–100, 101, 110, 121–24 (address to territorial legislature), 130–31; Hatfield, *William Claiborn*, 183–87; James H. Dormon, "The Persistent Specter: Slave Rebellion in Territorial Louisiana," *Louisiana History* 18 (1977): 389–404. Claiborne reported that the number of insurgents was variously estimated from 180 to 500. In 1812, Claiborne became the first governor of the state of Louisiana. He died in 1817 at the age of forty-two, soon after having been elected to the United States Senate.

31. *AC*, 12 Cong., 1 sess., 242–43, 244, 1248, 1279, 1434.

32. Glover Moore, *The Missouri Controversy, 1819–1821* (Lexington: University of Kentucky Press, 1953), 34, 35, 52–53; the objectionable part of the Illinois constitution was its continuation of the indenture system, though future indentures were limited to one year. Verlie, ed., *Illinois Constitutions*, 38–39.

33. For the most complete exposition of the guarantee clause argument during this episode, see Timothy Fuller of Massachusetts in *AC*, 15 Cong., 2 sess., 1180–81. Despite flawed logic, Fuller, unlike some other northerners, emphasized that the original slave states, unlike Missouri, would never be affected by the guarantee clause. See William M. Wiecek, *The Guarantee Clause of the U.S. Constitution* (Ithaca, N.Y.: Cornell University Press, 1972), 143–44.

34. *AC*, 16 Cong., 1 sess., 323, 338–39; Robinson, *Slavery in American Politics*, 412; Fehrenbacher, *Dred Scott Case*, 112. Indeed, four decades later, after the eventual destruction of slavery by federal authority, the guarantee clause would be called upon again, this time to cleanse southern state governments of the institution's lingering effects. See Wiecek, *Guarantee Clause*, 166–243.

35. Don E. Fehrenbacher, *Sectional Crisis and Southern Constitutionalism* (Baton Rouge: Louisiana State University Press, 1995), 129.

36. Charles R. King, ed., *The Life and Correspondence of Rufus King*, 6 vols. (New York: G. P Putnam's Sons, 1894–1900), VI:690–703.

37. Henry P. Johnston, ed., *The Correspondence and Public Papers of John Jay*, 4 vols. (New York: G.P. Putnam's Sons, 1890–93), IV:430–31.

38. *AC*, 16 Cong., 1 sess., 959.

39. Ibid., 281; Joseph Story, *Slavery and the Slave Trade. From Judge Story's Charge to the Grand Jury of the U.S. Circuit Court in Portsmouth, N.H. May Term, 1820* (Boston: n.p., 1820), 2–4.

40. For Madison's opinion, see *Letters and Other Writings of James Madison*, 4 vols. (Philadelphia: J. B. Lippincott & Co., 1865), III:167–69; For Pinckney's statement, see AC, 16 Cong., 1 sess., 1316.

41. Paul Leicester Ford, ed., *The Writings of Thomas Jefferson*, 10 vols. (New York: G. P. Putnam's Sons, 1892–99), X:157–58; David N. Mayer, *The Constitutional Thought of Thomas Jefferson* (Charlottesville: University Press of Virginia, 1994), 288–89; *AC*, 15 Cong., 2 sess., 1175.

42. William R. Johnson, "Prelude to the Missouri Compromise: A New York Con-

gressman's Effort to Exclude Slavery from Arkansas Territory," *New York Historical Society Quarterly* 48 (1964): 42–44; Robinson, *Slavery in American Politics*, 413.

43. *AC*, 16 Cong., 1 sess., 11, 20, 710.

44. The most delicate element of the compromise (that concerning the removal of any congressional restriction on the future of slavery in Missouri) passed by a 90 to 87 margin. A unanimous southern vote in favor, together with fourteen northern votes, created the slim majority. See *AC*, 16 Cong., 1 sess., 1576–86; Robinson, *Slavery in American Politics*, 418–20; Moore, *Missouri Controversy*, 105.

45. Peter B. Knupfer, *The Union As It Is: Constitutional Unionism and Sectional Compromise, 1787–1861* (Chapel Hill: University of North Carolina Press, 1991), 99–101; William M. Wiecek, *The Sources of Antislavery Constitutionalism in America, 1760–1848* (Ithaca, N.Y.: Cornell University Press, 1977),123–24; Fehrenbacher, *Dred Scott Case*, 68.

46. In 1850, Virginia Senator Robert M. T. Hunter recalled Rufus King's speeches as a declaration of the war upon slavery that was waged, despite some momentary lulls, ever thereafter. See *CG*, 31 Cong., 1 sess., App., 375–76. In writing his opinion in the Dred Scott case, Justice John A. Campbell recalled the "subversive" influence of the Tallmadge amendment. See *Dred Scott v. John F.A. Sandford*, 19 Howard 393 (1857), 508–9.

47. Wiecek, *Guarantee Clause*, 146.

48. David W. Blight, "Perceptions of Southern Intransigence and the Rise of Radical Antislavery Thought, 1816–1830," *Journal of the Early Republic* 3 (1983): 139–63; Robinson, *Slavery in American Politics*, 409.

49. For northern discourse in Congress on the Declaration of Independence during the Missouri crisis, see Horace Greeley, ed., *A History of the Struggle for Slavery Extension or Restriction in the United States, from the Declaration of Independence to the Present Day* . . . (New York: Dix, Edwards & Co., 1856), 10; Wiecek, *Sources of Antislavery Constitutionalism*, 120–21, 264–65; John Ashworth, *Slavery, Capitalism, and Politics in the Antebellum Republic*, vol. 1, *Commerce and Compromise* (Cambridge: Cambridge University Press, 1995), 63–64; William Sumner Jenkins, *Pro-slavery Thought in the Old South* (1935, reprint, Gloucester, Mass.: Peter Smith, 1960), 59–60; Moore, *Missouri Controversy*, 307–9; Charles M. Wiltse, *John C. Calhoun: Sectionalist, 1840–1850* (1951; reprint, New York: Russell & Russell, 1968), 334–36. For the original intent of the Declaration, see Allen Jayne, *Jefferson's Declaration of Independence: Origins, Philosophy and Theology* (Lexington: University of Kentucky Press, 1998), 124–25.

50. Robert V. Remini, *Andrew Jackson and the Course of American Democracy, 1833–1845* (New York: Harper & Row, 1984), 360; James C. N. Paul, *Rift in the Democracy* (1951; reprint, New York: A. S. Barnes & Co., 1961), 20–32; Michael F. Holt, *The Political Crisis of the 1850s* (New York: W.W. Norton & Co., 1978), 19–20, 24, 31, 40–44; Richard H. Brown, "The Missouri Crisis, Slavery, and the Politics of Jacksonianism," *South Atlantic Quarterly* 65 (1966): 69–70. The workings of the Democratic party's two-thirds rule to punish antislavery radicalism was most clearly demonstrated in the party's convention of 1848. See Bryon E. Shafer, *Bifurcated Politics: Evolution and Reform in the National Party Convention* (Cambridge: Harvard University Press, 1988), 12–13.

51. *CG*, 28 Cong., 2 sess., 129, 154, 193, 244, 359–62; Frederick Merk, *Manifest Destiny and Mission in American History: A Reinterpretation* (New York: Alfred A.

Knopf, 1963), 43–45; Norman A. Graebner, *Empire on the Pacific: A Study in American Continental Expansion* (1955; reprint, Santa Barbara: ABC-Clio, 1983), 108.

52.   Wilson Shannon to James Buchanan, April 6, 1845, in William Manning, ed., *Diplomatic Correspondence of the United States: Inter-American Affairs, 1831–1860*, 12 vols. (Washington, D.C., 1932–39), VIII:709–11.

53.   *MPP*, IV:392–98 (December 2, 1845), 449–50 (June 10, 1846), 452 (June 16, 1846); David M. Pletcher, *The Diplomacy of Annexation: Texas, Oregon, and the Mexican War* (Columbia: University of Missouri Press, 1973), 236–38.

54.   Shannon to Buchanan, April 6, 1845, Manning, ed., *Diplomatic Correspondence: Inter-American*, Thomas O. Larkin to James Buchanan, July 10, 1845, in *The Larkin Papers*, George P. Hammond, ed., 10 vols. (Berkeley: University of California Press, 1951–68), III:265–68; Andrew F. Rolle, *California: A History*, 2d ed. (New York: Thomas Y. Crowell Co., 1969), 166–68; Thomas R. Hietala, *Manifest Design, Anxious Aggrandizement in Late Jacksonian America* (Ithaca, N.Y.: Cornell University Press, 1985), 70–71.

55.   James Buchanan to Thomas O. Larkin, October 17, 1845, in John Bassett Moore, ed., *The Works of James Buchanan*, 12 vols. (1908–11; reprint, New York: Antiquarian Press Ltd., 1960), VI:275–78; diary entry dated October 24, 1845, in *The Diary of James K. Polk During His Presidency, 1845 to 1849*, ed. Milo Quaife, 4 vols. (Chicago: A. C. McClurg, 1910), I:71–72.

56.   Frederick Merk, *The Oregon Question: Essays in Anglo-American Diplomacy and Politics* (Cambridge, Mass.: Harvard University Press, Belknap Press, 1967), 409–13; Julius W. Pratt, "James K. Polk and John Bull," *Canadian Historical Review* 24 (1943): 343–49.

57.   *CG*, 29 Cong., 1 sess., 1217; Chaplain W. Morrison, *Democratic Politics and Sectionalism: The Wilmot Proviso Controversy* (Chapel Hill: University of North Carolina Press, 1967), 16–20, 34, 37, 180–81 n; Richard R. Stenberg, "Motivation of the Wilmot Proviso," *MVHR* 18 (1932): 535–41.

58.   *CG*, 29 Cong., 2 sess., 424–25, 555; Richard K. Crallé, ed., *The Works of John C. Calhoun*, 6 vols. (New York: D. Appleton & Co., 1854–57), VI:303; William J. Cooper, Jr., *The South and the Politics of Slavery, 1828–1861* (Baton Rouge: Louisiana State University Press, 1978), 253.

59.   *Washington National Intelligencer*, December 22, 1847; Francis P. Weisenburger, *The Life of John McLean* (1937; reprint, New York: Da Capo Press, 1971), 118.

60.   Salmon P. Chase to James G. Birney, April 2, 1844, in Dwight L. Dumond, ed., *Letters of James Gillespie Birney, 1831–1857*, 2 vols. (New York: D. Appleton-Century Co., 1938), II:805–6; William Goodell, *Views of American Constitutional Law, In Its Bearing upon American Slavery* (Utica: Lawson & Chaplin, 1845), 57–63; Fehrenbacher, *Dred Scott Case*, 122–23. During the next two decades, the antislavery Fifth Amendment argument was publicized in the platforms of the Liberty party (1844), the Free-Soil party (1848), and the Republican party (1856 and 1860). See Kirk H. Porter and Donald Bruce Johnson, comps., *National Party Platforms, 1840–1964* (Urbana: University of Illinois, 1966), 5, 13, 27, 32. The proslavery Fifth Amendment argument was ultimately incorporated into the Dred Scott decision. See *Dred Scott v. John F. A. Sandford*, 19 Howard 450.

61.   Entry for January 16, 1847, in Quaife, ed., *Diary of James K. Polk*, II:331; David M. Potter, *The Impending Crisis, 1848–1861*, completed and edited by Don E.

Fehrenbacher (New York: Harper & Row, 1976), 56; Eugene I. McCormac, *James K. Polk: A Political Biography* (Berkeley: University of California Press, 1922), 619–21.

62. For Cass's enunciation of popular sovereignty in the "Nicholson Letter," see *Washington Union*, December 30, 1847; *CG*, 34 Cong. 3 sess., 85–86; Allen Johnson, "Genesis of Popular Sovereignty," *Iowa Journal of History and Politics* 3 (1905): 3–19.

63. Milo Milton Quaife, *The Doctrine of Non-Intervention with Slavery in the Territories* (Chicago: M. C. Chamberlain, 1910), 45–55.

64. *CG*, 31 Cong., 1 sess., 343, 398, 454, 528; ibid., App., 72–73, 151–52; Stephen A. Douglas, "The Dividing Line Between Federal and Local Authority: Popular Sovereignty in the Territories," *Harper's Magazine* 19 (1859): 519–37.

65. Don E. Fehrenbacher, *The South and Three Sectional Crises* (Baton Rouge: Louisiana State University Press, 1980), 39.

66. In early 1849, the senate passed a civil appropriations bill, which, if approved in the House, would have abrogated Mexican antislavery law in the Mexican Cession. All sides were aware of the significance of this factor. See *CG*, 30 Cong., 2 sess., 190–92, 573, 607–8, 666–698; ibid., App., 253–55; Holman Hamilton, *Zachary Taylor: Soldier in the White House* (Indianapolis: Bobbs-Merrill Co., 1957), 153.

67. Hamilton, *Soldier in the White House*, 177–78.

68. Cardinal Goodwin, *The Establishment of State Government in California, 1846–1850* (New York: Macmillan Publishing Co., 1914), 66–70.

69. William H. Ellison, *A Self-Governing Dominion: California, 1849–1860* (Berkeley: University of California Press, 1950), 30.

70. First Annual Message of President Taylor, December 4, 1849, in *The State of the Union Messages of the Presidents, 1790–1966*, ed. Fred L. Israel, 3 vols. (New York: Chelsea House Publishers, 1967), I:783; Hamilton, *Soldier in the White House*, 256–66.

71. *CG*, 31 Cong., 1 sess., 200–209, and ibid., App., 74–78; Hamilton, *Soldier in the White House*, 262–63, 270.

72. Avery O. Craven, *The Growth of Southern Nationalism, 1848–1861* (Baton Rouge: Louisiana State University Press, 1953), 59–65; Allan Nevins, *Ordeal of the Union*, 2 vols. (New York: Charles Scribner's Sons, 1947), I:240–52; Wiltse, *Calhoun: Sectionalist*, 394–410; *SD*, 30 Cong., 2 sess., Nos. 41, 51, 58 (Serial 533); *HD*, 30 Cong., 2 sess., No. 54 (Serial 544); *SD*, 31 Cong., 1 sess., No. 24 (Serial 563).

73. *MPP*, V:18–19 (December 4, 1849); ibid., 27–29 (January 23, 1850); John Ross Browne, *Report of the Debates in the Convention of California on the Formation of the State Constitution, in September and October, 1849* (Washington, D.C.: J. T. Towers, printer, 1850), 474–77; App., IV.

74. *CG*, 31 Cong., 1 sess., 244–52.

75. Ibid., App., 1091–93; Hamilton, *Soldier in the White House*, 333; Glyndon G. Van Deusen, *The Life of Henry Clay* (Boston: Little, Brown & Co., 1937), 408.

76. *CG*, 31 Cong., 1 sess., App., 269–76; Robert V. Remini, *Henry Clay: Statesman for the Union* (New York: W. W. Norton & Co., 1991), 736.

77. Jefferson Davis referred to the Taylor plan as "the plan of concealing the Wilmot Proviso under a so-called state constitution." See Jefferson Davis to W. R. Cannon, January 8, 1850, Civil War Collection, Huntington Library, San Marino, Calif.; *CG*, 31 Cong., 1 sess, App., 154.

78. James Buchanan to Mr. King, May 13, 1850, in *Works of James Buchanan,* ed. Moore, VIII:384–85; Buchanan to Mr. Foote, May 31, 1850, ibid., 387.

79. *CG,* 31 Cong., 1 sess., 967; Lewis Publishing Co., *An Illustrated History of Los Angeles County, California* (Chicago: Lewis Publishing Co., 1889), 94.

80. *CG,* 31 Cong., 1 sess., App., 612–16, 1091–93; Hamilton, *Soldier in the White House,* 334–35.

81. *CG,* 31 Cong., 1 sess., 1491; ibid., App., 1470–88; George Rawling Poage, *Henry Clay and the Whig Party* (Chapel Hill: University of North Carolina Press, 1936), 254–57; Holman Hamilton, *Prologue to Conflict: The Crisis and Compromise of 1850* (Lexington: University of Kentucky Press, 1964), 109–17.

82. Calvin Colton, *The Last Seven Years of the Life of Henry Clay* (New York: A. S. Barnes & Co., 1856), 756–57.

83. *SAL,* IX:446–58, 462–65, 467–68; Potter, *Impending Crisis,* 113; also see Don E. Fehrenbacher, "The New Political History and the Coming of the Civil War," *Pacific Historical Review* 54 (1985): 131–32.

84. *SAL,* IX:450, 455–56; for a southern interpretation of the meaning of popular sovereignty in the Utah and New Mexico bills, see Ulrich B. Phillips, ed., "The Correspondence of Robert Toombs, Alexander H. Stephens, and Howell Cobb," *Annual Report of the American Historical Association, 1911,* Vol. II (Washington, D.C.: n.p., 1913), 283.

85. U.S. Census Office, *Population of the United States in 1860; Compiled from the Original Returns of the Eighth Census* (Washington, D.C.: Government Printing Office, 1864), 572, 574–75; Newell G. Bringhurst, "The Mormons and Slavery—A Closer Look," *Pacific Historical Review* 50 (1981): 329, 333, 335; Loomis Morton Ganaway, *New Mexico and the Sectional Controversy, 1846–1861* (Albuquerque: University of New Mexico Press, 1944), 60–76.

86. "To the Editor of the Washington Union," March 19, 1852, in *The Letters of Stephen A. Douglas,* ed. Robert W. Johannsen (Urbana: University of Illinois Press, 1961), 243; *CG,* 32 Cong., 1 sess., 976–83; ibid., App., 65–68; *MPP,* V:93 (December 2, 1850).

87. Stephen A. Douglas to J. H. Crane, D. M. Johnson, and L. J. Eastin, December 17, 1853, Johannsen, ed., *Letters of Douglas,* 269; James C. Malin, "The Motives of Stephen A. Douglas in the Organization of Nebraska Territory: A Letter Dated December 17, 1853," *Kansas Historical Quarterly* 19 (1951): 351–52.

88. James C. Malin, *The Nebraska Question, 1852–1854* (Lawrence, Kan.: n.p. 1953), 18–19, 81–82, 443–48; Robert W. Johannsen, *Stephen A. Douglas* (New York: Oxford University Press, 1973), 397–98.

89. *CG,* 32 Cong., 2 sess., 469–75, 542–44, 556–65; Robert R. Russel, *Improvement of Communication with the Pacific Coast as an Issue in American Politics, 1783–1864* (Cedar Rapids, Iowa: Torch Press, 1948), 156–59.

90. To deemphasize his own sectional identification with a central route, Douglas advocated that three transcontinental railroads be built—this, to satisfy backers of northern, central, and southern routes. Clearly, the nation could only afford one road initially. See *CG,* 33 Cong., 2 sess., 210; Frank Hodder, "The Railroad Background of the Kansas-Nebraska Act," *MVHR* 12 (1925): 15–17; Paul Neff Garber, *The Gadsden Treaty* (Philadelphia: Press of the University of Pennsylvania, 1923), 81–82, 112–13.

91. *CG,* 33 Cong. 1 sess., 275–80; Stephen Douglas to Howell Cobb, April 2, 1854,

Johannsen, ed., *Letters of Douglas*, 300; Michael A. Morrison, *Slavery and the American West: The Eclipse of Manifest Destiny and the Coming of the Civil War* (Chapel Hill: University of North Carolina Press, 1997), 16, 99, 122, 142, 147, 152; Holt, *Political Crisis of the 1850s*, 144–48; Bruce Collins, "The Ideology of the Ante-Bellum Northern Democrats," *Journal of American Studies* 11 (1977): 103–21.

92. *SR*, 33 Cong., 1 sess., No. 15, 1–4; Robert W. Johannsen, "Stephen A. Douglas, Popular Sovereignty and the Territories," *Historian* 22 (1960): 385. For the Kansas-Nebraska Act, see *SAL:X:277–90*.

93. Collins, "Ideology of Northern Democrats," 106.

94. *CG*, 33 Cong., 2 sess., 210, 224, 251, 281–82, 285–91, 316–19, 329–38, 805–14; Robert W. Johannsen, *The Frontier, The Union, and Stephen A. Douglas* (Urbana: University of Illinois Press, 1989), 92–93.

95. *SAL*, XII:489–98.

96. Jon Fackler, "An End to Compromise: The Kansas-Nebraska Bill of 1854" (Ph.D. diss., Pennsylvania State University, 1969) 321–22.

97. Johannsen, *Douglas*, 477–78.

98. Morrison, *Slavery and the American West*, 138–40.

99. *CG*, 31 Cong., 1 sess., App., 265; Hamilton, *Soldier in the White House*, 321–22.

100. William, J. Cooper, Jr., *The South and the Politics of Slavery, 1828–1856* (Baton Rouge: Louisiana State University Press, 1978), 284–85, 340–44, 355; Arthur C. Cole, *The Whig Party in the South* (Washington, D.C.: American Historical Association, 1913), 183.

101. William E. Gienapp, *The Origins of the Republican Party, 1852–1856* (New York: Oxford University Press, 1987), 89–100.

102. Holt, *Political Crisis of the 1850s*, 33–34, 109–10.

103. Tyler Anbinder, *Nativism and Slavery: The Northern Know Nothings and the Politics of the 1850s* (New York: Oxford University Press, 1992), xiii, 10–11, 24, 104, 106, 115, 135–37; W. Darrell Overdyke, *The Know-Nothing Party in the South* (Baton Rouge: Louisiana State University Press, 1950), 198–200; Stephen E. Maizlish, "The Meaning of Nativism and the Crisis of the Union: The Know-Nothing Movement in the Antebellum North," in *Essays on American Antebellum Politics, 1840–1860*, ed. Stephen E. Maizlish and John J. Kushma (College Station: University of Texas at Arlington; Texas A & M University Press, 1982), 166–98.

104. Anbinder, *Nativism and Slavery*, 168, 171–73, 185, 193.

105. Gienapp, *Origins of the Republican Party*, 335; for the Republican platform of 1856, see Donald Bruce Johnson, *National Party Platforms*, 2 vols (1956; reprint, Urbana: University of Illinois Press, 1978), I:27–28.

106. In 1844, Liberty party presidential nominee James G. Birney received 2.3 percent of the popular vote. In 1848, Free-Soil party presidential nominee Martin Van Buren received 10.1 percent of the popular vote. In 1852, Free-Soil party presidential nominee John P. Hale received 5.0 percent of the popular vote. See George Brown Tindall and David E. Shi, *America: A Narrative History*, 5th ed. (New York: W. W. Norton & Co., 1999), [App.] A38–A39.

107. James D. Bilotta, *Race and the Rise of the Republican Party* (New York: P. Lang, 1992), 365–96; Eric Foner, *Free Soil, Free Labor, Free Men: The Ideology of the Republican Party Before the Civil War* (1970; reprint, New York: Oxford University Press, 1995), 262; Eugene H. Berwanger, *The Frontier Against Slavery: Western*

Anti-Negro Prejudice and the Slavery Extension Controversy (Urbana: University of Illinois Press, 1967), 128–37; V. Jacque Voegeli, *Free But Not Equal: The Midwest and the Negro During the Civil War* (Chicago: University of Chicago Press, 1967), 1–9.

108. *Chicago Tribune*, January 31, 1856; Jeter Allen Isely, *Horace Greeley and the Republican Party, 1853–1861* (Princeton, N.J.: Princeton University Press, 1947), 147–50.

109. Karl Marx, "The Materialist Conception of History," in *Theories of History*, ed. Patrick Gardiner (New York: Free Press, 1959), 130; Foner, *Free Soil, Free Labor, Free Men*, 56–57.

110. William H. Seward, *The Slaveholding Class Dominant in the Republic: Speech of William H. Seward, At the Mass Republican Convention, Held at Detroit, October 2d, 1856* (n.p.: n.p., 1856), 2–10.

111. Over the last two decades, a debate over the nature of the Republican party in the middle of the nineteenth century has at times been heated. The "new political history" has cast a spotlight on the ethnocultural biases prominent in the party at that time, whereas traditionalists have continued to emphasize the dynamics of the party's struggle against slavery. Unfortunately, each position has often been reduced by its opponents into a caricature that fails to convey the essential character of the new party. It is important to emphasize that the Republicans of the 1850s were neither *modern* civil rights advocates nor *modern* religious bigots. But, in a strange way, they were the forebears of each of these two modern positions which have little in common with each other. The Republicans of the 1850s were unique to their time and place and can best be appreciated in their own historical context. For representations of each side of this debate, together with several attempts at synthesizing both views, see Richard H. Sewell, *Ballots for Freedom: Antislavery Politics in the United States, 1837–1860* (New York: Oxford University Press, 1976), 265–77, 266 n; Paul Kleppner, *The Third Electoral System, 1853–1892: Parties, Voters, and Political Cultures* (Chapel Hill: University of North Carolina Press, 1979), 48, 51, 68–69; Gienapp, *Origins of the Republican Party*, 61–64, 365–67, 418–21; Joel H. Silbey, *The American Political Nation, 1838–1893* (Stanford: Stanford University Press, 1991), 171–75; Anbinder, *Nativism and Slavery*, xiii, 10–11, 24, 266–67; also see Ward M. McAfee, *Religion, Race, and Reconstruction: The Public School in the Politics of the 1870s* (Albany: State University of New York Press), 3–5, 215–16; and especially Fehrenbacher, "The New Political History and the Coming of the Civil War," 134–42.

112. CG, 34 Cong., 1 sess., App., 57–63, 89–109, 115–18, 129–34; Charles Sumner, *The Crime Against Kansas* (1856; reprint, New York: Arno Press, 1969); Samuel Augustus Johnson, "The Emigrant Aid Company in the Kansas Conflict," *Kansas Historical Quarterly* 6 (1937): 21–33.

113. Johannsen, *Douglas*, 472–74.

114. Ibid., 474–75.

115. Fanny Hunter, *Western Border Life; or, What Fanny Hunter Saw and Heard in Kanzas [sic] and Missouri* (New York: Derby and Jackson, 1856), 347–51, 357–67.

116. Anbinder, *Nativism and Slavery*, 194, 198, 207, 209, 243–45.

117. Andrew Rolle, *John Charles Frémont: Character As Destiny* (Norman: University of Oklahoma Press, 1991), 174.

118. John M. Clayton, *Speech of John M. Clayton of Delaware in Defense of the Bill to Organize Territorial Governments in Oregon, California and New Mexico, Popularly Known As the Territorial or Compromise Bill. Delivered in the Senate of the United States, August 3, 1848* (Washington, D.C.: n.p., 1848), 7–10; Knupfer, *The Union As It Is,* 173–74.

119. *CG,* 34 Cong., 1 sess., 1093, 1097, 1100.

120. *MPP,* V:431 (March 4, 1857).

121. Fehrenbacher, *Dred Scott Case,* 314.

122. Ibid., 361, 666 n.

123. Harold M. Hyman and William M. Wiecek, *Equal Justice Under Law: Constitutional Development, 1835–1875* (New York: Harper & Row, 1982), 174, 178, 183; Arthur Bestor, "The American Civil War as a Constitutional Crisis," *American Historical Review* 69 (1964): 350; Jesse T. Carpenter, *The South as a Conscious Minority, 1789–1861: A Study in Political Thought* (1930; reprint, Gloucester, Mass.: Peter Smith, 1963), 150–55; for a proslavery argument explaining why the precedent of the Northwest Ordinance had no antislavery import, see Robert Toombs, "Slavery: Its Constitutional Status," *DeBow's Review* 20 (1856): 588–90.

124. Alfred L. Brophy, "Let Us Go Back And Stand Upon The Constitution: Federal-State Relations in *Scott v. Sandford,*" *Columbia Law Review* 90 (1990): 221.

125. Fehrenbacher, *Dred Scott Case,* 384.

126. Ibid., 423.

127. *Chicago Tribune,* March 12, 14, 16, 1857.

128. Quoted in *Indianapolis State Sentinel,* March 25, 1857.

129. See commentary on *Lemmon v. The People,* 20 N.Y. 562 (1860), in William M. Wiecek, "*Somerset*: Lord Mansfield and the Legitimacy of Slavery in the Anglo-American World," *University of Chicago Law Review* 42 (1974): 136–40; Fehrenbacher, *Dred Scott Case,* 453, 475; Brophy, "Federal-State Relations in Scott," 211–16, 221–23; Hyman and Wiecek, *Equal Justice Under Law,* 194; *CG,* 35 Cong., 1 sess., 385, 665; ibid., 2 sess., 1249–51.

130. *MPP,* V:454 (December 8, 1857).

131. Kenneth M. Stampp, *America in 1857: A Nation on the Brink* (New York: Oxford University Press, 1990), 300.

132. New York (State) Legislature, *Assembly Documents,* 80th sess., no. 201 (Albany: C. Van Benthuysen, Printer to the Legislature, 1857), 1–6; *New York Herald,* April 12, 1857; Fehrenbacher, *Dred Scott Case,* 433.

133. Fehrenbacher, *Dred Scott Case,* 331–34, 336, 438–39; also see Daniel W. Gooch, *The Supreme Court and Dred Scott. Speech of Hon. Daniel W. Gooch, of Massachusetts, Delivered in the U.S. House of Representatives, May 3, 1860* (n.p.: n.p., 1860), 1.

134. James A. Rawley, *Race and Politics: "Bleeding Kansas" and the Coming of the Civil War* (Philadelphia: J. B. Lippincott & Co., 1969), 202–56; *Transactions of the Kansas State Historical Society* 5 (1889–96): 264–561—in this source especially see a letter from Walker to Cass, dated November 3, 1857, on pp. 402–3; Willard Carl Klunder, "Lewis Cass and Slavery Expansion: The Father of Popular Sovereignty and Ideological Infanticide," *CWH* 32 (1986): 313.

135. *MPP,* V:453 (December 8, 1857).

136. Philip Shriver Klein, *President James Buchanan: A Biography* (University

Park: Pennsylvania State University, 1962) 308; Allan Nevins, *Emergence of Lincoln*, 2 vols. (New York: Charles Scribner's Sons, 1950), I:239–47.

137. Klunder, "Lewis Cass and Slavery Expansion," 314–16.

138. Stampp, *America in 1857*, 300; James Buchanan, *Mr. Buchanan's Administration on the Eve of the Rebellion* (New York: D. Appleton & Co., 1866), 44.

139. Stampp, *America in 1857*, 282, 330–31; also see Robert W. Johannsen, "A Nation on the Brink," *Reviews in American History* 19 (1991): 499–504.

140. Johannsen, *Douglas*, 586–92.

141. *CG*, 35 Cong., 1 sess., 18.

142. *SAL*, XI:269–72; Damon Wells, *Stephen Douglas: The Last Years, 1857–1861* (Austin: University of Texas Press, 1971), 46–51; F. G. Adams, ed., "Governor Denver's Administration," in *Transactions of the Kansas State Historical Society* 5 (1889–96): 540.

143. Potter, *Impending Crisis*, 331; Johannsen, *Douglas*, 593, 632–35, 640, 650; Isely, *Horace Greeley and the Republican Party*, 244–47.

144. Abraham Lincoln to Lyman Trumbull, November 30, 1857, HM Manuscripts, Huntington Library, San Marino, Calif.

145. Abraham Lincoln to Lyman Trumbull, December 28, 1857, HM Manuscripts.

146. Abraham Lincoln to Ward Hill Lamon, June 11, 1858, Lamon Collection, Huntington Library; David Herbert Donald, *Lincoln* (New York: Simon & Schuster, 1995), 205.

147. Abraham Lincoln to Stephen Douglas, July 24 and July 29, 1858, in *Abraham Lincoln, Speeches and Writings, 1832–1858: Speeches, Letters, and Miscellaneous Writings, The Lincoln-Douglas Debates*, comp. by Don E. Fehrenbacher (New York: Library of America, 1989), 479, 481–82; Stephen A. Douglas to Abraham Lincoln, July 24 and July 30, 1858, in ed., Johannsen, *Letters of Douglas*, 423–25; Wells, *Douglas: The Last Years*, 83–86.

148. *CWAL*, III:312.

149. Ibid., 181; Fehrenbacher, comp., *Lincoln, Speeches and Writings*, 581.

150. *CWAL*, III:301. Also see David Zerefsky, *Lincoln, Douglas, and Slavery: In the Crucible of Public Debate* (Chicago: University of Chicago Press, 1990), 149–54; Merrill D. Peterson, *The Jeffersonian Image in the American Mind* (New York: Oxford University Press, 1960), 162–63, 205, 221–22; Harry V. Jaffa, *Crisis of the House Divided: An Interpretation of the Lincoln-Douglas Debates* (Seattle: University of Washington Press, 1959), 369; Paul M. Angle, ed., *Created Equal? The Complete Lincoln-Douglas Debates of 1858* (Chicago: University of Chicago Press, 1958), 100–101.

151. *CWAL*, II:491, 494, 514–15; ibid., III:306–8.

152. Angle, *Created Equal?*, 18–20; also see Robert W. Johannsen, *Lincoln, the South, and Slavery: The Political Dimension* (Baton Rouge: Louisiana State University Press, 1991), 81.

153. CWAL, II:467; ibid., III:18, 27.

154. Ibid., II:514.

155. Ibid., III:230–31, 251; Fehrenbacher, *Dred Scott Case*, 492; Hyman and Wiecek, *Equal Justice Under Law*, 194.

156. *CWAL*, II:255; ibid., III:296–97, 298–99.

157. Abraham Lincoln to James N. Brown, October 18, 1858, in Fehrenbacher, comp., *Lincoln, Speeches and Writings*, 822; *CWAL*, III:312; Leon Litwack, *North of Slavery, The Negro in the Free States, 1790–1860* (Chicago: University of Chicago Press, 1961).

158. *CWAL*, III:43, 51.

159. Fehrenbacher, *Dred Scott Case*, 498–501.

160. Wells, *Douglas: The Last Years*, 122, 124; Potter, *The Impending Crisis*, 403.

161. Johannsen, *Douglas*, 675–76; Lincoln himself reflected the cultural identifica-tion of his party with anti-Irish feeling when he expressed fear that an influx of rough Irish railway workers (which he sardonically referred to as "Celtic gentle-men") might tip the election to Douglas. See Abraham Lincoln to Norman B. Judd, October 20, 1858, in Fehrenbacher, comp., *Lincoln, Speeches and Writings*, 824.

162. Don E. Fehrenbacher, *Prelude to Greatness: Lincoln in the 1850s* (Stanford: Stanford University Press, 1962), 118–20.

163. Abraham Lincoln to Anson G. Henry, November 19, 1858, in Fehrenbacher, comp., *Lincoln, Speeches and Writings*, 831; Donald, *Lincoln* (New York: Simon & Schuster, 1995), 228.

164. Johannsen, *Lincoln, the South, and Slavery*, 65.

165. *CWAL*, III:301; also see ibid. II:545–47; Jayne, *Jefferson's Declaration of Inde-pendence*, 124–25.

166. Larry E. Tise identifies several early proslavery modifications of the Declara-tion's ideology. See his *Proslavery: A History of the Defense of Slavery in America, 1701–1840* (Athens: University of Georgia Press, 1987), 39, 248, 342.

167. For Calhoun's outright rejection of both Lockean theory and Jefferson's Decla-ration of Independence, see his Speech on the Oregon Bill, June 27, 1848, reprinted in *Union and Liberty: The Political Philosophy of John C. Calhoun by John C. Cal-houn*, ed. Ross M. Lence (Indianapolis: Liberty Fund, 1992), 565–70; also see Merrill D. Peterson, *The Great Triumvirate: Webster, Clay, and Calhoun* (New York: Oxford University Press, 1987), 410.

168. *CWAL*, II:500.

169. *CWAL*, III:132, 141–42, 269–70. After the Freeport and Jonesboro debates, Lin-coln thought that Douglas could never again restore good relations with southern Democrats, but he was not entirely sure. See Abraham Lincoln to Lyman Trumbull, December 11, 1858, HM Manuscripts.

170. *New York Times*, December 9, 10, 14, 1858; Johannsen, *Douglas*, 685–87.

171. *MPP*, V:554 (December 19, 1859).

172. *CG*, 36 Cong., 1 sess., 658–59.

173. Ibid., 2155–56.

174. Robert W. Johannsen, "Stephen A. Douglas, 'Harper's Magazine,' and Popular Sovereignty," *MVHR* 45 (1959): 606–31; Harry V. Jaffa and Robert Johannsen, eds., *In the Name of the People: Speeches and Writings of Lincoln and Douglas in the Ohio Campaign of 1859* (Columbus: Ohio Historical Society, 1959), 58–125, 173–99. This latter source contains both Douglas's *Harper's* essay and a rejoinder by Buchanan's attorney general.

175. Arthur Bestor, "State Sovereignty and Slavery: A Reinterpretation of Proslav-ery Constitutional Doctrine, 1846–1860," *Journal of the Illinois State Historical*

Society 54 (1961): 136–42; for the opposite (but corresponding) development in the North at the same time, see Richard Paul Grau, "The Slavery Issue and the Compact Theory in the North During the 1850s: The Emergence of States-Rights Nationalism" (Ph.D. diss., Georgetown University, 1973) 11–52, 525–633.

176. Murat Halstead, *Caucuses of 1860: A History of the National Political Conventions of the Current Campaign: Being a Complete Record of the Business of all the Conventions* (Columbus, Ohio: Follett, Foster & Co., 1860), 1–2, 92–97; Roy F. Nichols, *The Disruption of American Democracy* (1948; reprint, New York: Collier Books, 1962), 288–322; Robert W. Johannsen, "Douglas at Charleston," in *Politics and the Crisis of 1860*, ed. Norman A. Graebner (Urbana: University of Illinois Press, 1961), 61–90.

177. National Democratic Executive Committee, *Proceedings of the Conventions at Charleston and Baltimore. Published by Order of the National Democratic Convention* (Washington, D.C.: Maryland Institute, 1860), 238–41; Halstead, *Caucuses of 1860*, 159–60, 202.

178. Halstead, *Caucuses of 1860*, 202–30.

179. *MPP*, V:561 (December 19, 1859); Robert E. May, *The Southern Dream of a Caribbean Empire, 1854–1861* (Baton Rouge: Louisiana State University Press, 1973), 16–19, 22–76, 163–89.

180. Moore, ed., *Works of James Buchanan*, X:357–58, 362; William Frank Stewart, *Last of the Filibusters; or, Recollections of the Siege of Rivas* (Sacramento: Henry Shipley & Co., 1857), 7–85.

181. *CG*, 31 Cong., 1 sess., 967.

182. *New Orleans Creole* clipping enclosed in letter from Samuel Hopkins Willey to Benjamin Davis Wilson and Margaret S. Hereford Wilson, December 30, 1854, Benjamin Davis Wilson Papers, Huntington Library, San Marino, Calif.

183. Ward M. McAfee, "California's House Divided," *CWH* 33 (1987): 115–30.

184. Ibid., 128.

185. *Journal of the Senate of the State of California at the Eleventh Session of the Legislature* (Sacramento: State Printer, 1860), 126.

186. Editorial, Dixon (Ill.) *Republican and Telegraph* reprinted in Los Angeles, *Southern Vineyard* , June 17, 1859; also see (Los Angeles), *El Clamor Público*, August 13, 1859.

187. N.a., "Slavery in New Mexico," *DeBow's Review* 26 (January-June 1859): 601; n.a., "The Cotton Fields of Arizona Territory," *DeBow's Review* 24 (January-June 1858): 320–21.

188. Loomis Morton Ganaway, *New Mexico and the Sectional Controversy, 1846–1861* (Albuquerque: University of New Mexico Press, 1944), 60–76.

189. Los Angeles *Star*, May 28, 1859.

190. William Henry Ellison, "The Movement for State Division in California, 1849–1860," *Southwestern Historical Quarterly* 17 (1914): 111–19, 122–24.

191. Richard H. Peterson, "Anti-Mexican Nativism in California, 1848–1853: A Study of Cultural Conflict," *Southern California Quarterly* 62 (1980): 310–13; William Robert Kenny, "Mexican-American Conflict on the Mining Frontier, 1848–1852," *Journal of the West* 6 (1967): 589–91.

192. John G. Downey to Pablo de la Guerra, October 8, 1860, John G. Downey Papers, Huntington Library, San Marino, Calif.; *Sacramento Daily Union*, February 5, 1859.

193. John S. Griffin to Cave Johnson Couts, November 1, 1864, Couts Papers, Huntington Library, San Marino, Calif.; *CWAL*, IV:519.

194. *Statutes of California, 10th Session* (Sacramento: State Printer, 1859), 310–11; also see "Communication of Governor Latham, January 12, 1860," *Journal of the Senate (California), 11th Session* (Sacramento: State Printer, 1860), 129.

195. *CWAL*, II:300–301.

196. Henry S. Foote, "Speech of the Hon. H. S. Foote, of Mississippi," *DeBow's Review* 27 (July-December 1859): 219.

197. Philip A. Roach to Jefferson Davis, June 27, 1859, reprinted in *Jefferson Davis, Constitutionalist, His Letters, Papers and Speeches*, ed. Dunbar Rowland, 10 vols. (Jackson: Mississippi Department of Archives and History, 1923), IV:59–61.

198. L. Boyd Finch, *Confederate Pathway to the Pacific: Major Sherod Hunter and Arizona Territory, CSA* (Tucson: Arizona Historical Society, 1996), 155–56; Robert Lee Kerby, *The Confederate Invasion of New Mexico, 1861–1862* (Los Angeles: Westernlore Press, 1958), 97–105.

CHAPTER 10

1. Avery O. Craven, *The Growth of Southern Nationalism, 1848–1861* (Baton Rouge: Louisiana State University Press, 1953), 358.

2. Ibid.

3. Robert Manson Myers, ed., *The Children of Pride: A True Story of Georgia and the Civil War* (New Haven, Conn.: Yale University Press, 1972), 641.

4. [John Townsend], *The Doom of Slavery in the Union: Its Safety Out of It* (Charleston, S.C.: Evans & Cogswell, printers, 1860), 4.

5. See, for example, *Kentucky Statesman*, January 6, 1860, and *Richmond Examiner*, November 9, 1860, in Dwight Lowell Dumond, ed., *Southern Editorials on Secession* (New York: Century Co., 1931), 4, 223.

6. *CG*, 36 Cong., 2 sess., 486.

7. Joseph Carlyle Sitterson, *The Secession Movement in North Carolina* (Chapel Hill: University of North Carolina Press, 1939), 135.

8. *Dred Scott v. Sandford*, 19 Howard 393 (1857), 451–52.

9. Frederick Douglass, *"John Brown": An Address, by Frederick Douglass, and Delivered at Harper's Ferry, May 30, 1881, on the Occasion of the Fourteenth Anniversary of the Storer College* (1881; reprint, Institute, W. Va.: West Virginia State College, 1953), 19–20; Otto J. Scott, *The Secret Six: John Brown and the Abolitionist Movement* (New York: Times Books, 1979), 257–58; F. B. Sanborn, ed., *John Brown: Liberator of Kansas and Martyr of Virginia* (Cedar Rapids, Iowa: Torch Press, 1910), 538–40.

10. Stephen B. Oates, *To Purge This Land With Blood: A Biography of John Brown*, 2d ed. (Amherst: University of Massachusetts Press, 1984), 310–12. For northern sermons portraying Brown as an avenging saint and Christian martyr, see

Rev. W. W. Patton, *The Execution of John Brown; A Discourse Delivered at Chicago, December 4th, 1859, in the First Congregational Church* (Chicago: Church, Goodman & Cushing, 1859), 3–14; Nathaniel Hall, *The Iniquity: A Sermon Preached in the First Church, Dorchester, on Sunday, December 11, 1859* (Boston: John Wilson & Son, 1859), 5–19; Charles Gordon Ames, *The Death of John Brown: A Discourse at the Free Congregational Church, Bloomington, Ill., December 4, 1859* (1859; reprint, n.p.: n.p., October 1909), 3–38.

11. David M. Potter, *The Impending Crisis, 1848–1861*, completed and edited by Don E. Fehrenbacher (New York: Harper & Row, 1976), 378–79.

12. Oates, *To Purge This Land*, 312–15.

13. New York Democratic Vigilant Association, *Rise and Progress of the Bloody Outbreak at Harper's Ferry* (New York: John F. Trow, printer, 1860), 16–18.

14. David Herbert Donald, *Lincoln* (New York: Simon & Schuster, 1995), 240, 255.

15. *CWAL*, III:522–50.

16. Frederick Douglass, *The Constitution of the United States: Is It Pro-Slavery or Anti-Slavery? By Frederick Douglass. A Speech Delivered in Glasgow, March 26, 1860, in Reply to an Attack Made Upon His View by Mr. George Thompson* (Halifax: T. & W. Birtwhistle, printers, 1860).

17. William Goodell, *The Constitutional Duty of the Federal Government to Abolish American Slavery: An Exposé of the Position of the American Abolition Society* (New York: American Abolition Society, 1856); Lysander Spooner, *The Unconstitutionality of Slavery* (Boston: B. Marsh, 1845).

18. John W. Blassingame et al., eds., *The Frederick Douglass Papers, Series One: Speeches, Debates, and Interviews*, 5 vols. (New Haven, Conn.: Yale University Press, 1979–92), III:345.

19. Ibid., 349.

20. Ibid., 352.

21. Ibid., 354–55, 361.

22. Ibid., 365.

23. *CWAL*, III:313; for Lincoln's repeated use of this analogy, see ibid., V:327.

24. David L. Lightner, "The Door to the Slave Bastille: The Abolitionist Assault Upon the Interstate Slave Trade, 1833–1839," *CWH* 34 (1988): 236, 241, 247–48.

25. Ibid., 249.

26. Arthur Bestor, "The American Civil War as a Constitutional Crisis," *AHR* 69 (1964): 340–43.

27. John Jay, *The Rise and Fall of the Pro-Slavery Democracy, and the Rise and Duties of the Republican Party. An Address to the Citizens of Westchester County, New York . . . , November 5, 1860* (New York: R. Lockwood & Co., 1861), 41.

28. *CG*, 36 Cong., 2 sess., 82–83, 112–16.

29. *CWAL*, IV:183.

30. *CG*, 36 Cong., 2 sess., 1468.

31. Convention of the People of South Carolina, *Declaration of the Immediate Causes which Induce and Justify the Secession of South Carolina from the Federal Union; And the Ordinance of Secession* (Charleston, S.C.: Evans & Cogswell, 1860), 10.

32. Abraham Lincoln to Alexander Hamilton Stephens, December 22, 1860, in Don E. Fehrenbacher, comp., *Abraham Lincoln, Speeches and Writings, 1859–1865:*

Speeches, Letters, and Miscellaneous Writings, Presidential Messages and Proclamations (New York: Library of America, 1989), 194.

33. Clement Eaton, *Freedom of Thought in the Old South* (Durham, N. C.: Duke University Press, 1940), 99–117, 149–50.

34. William Sherman Savage, "Abolitionist Literature in the Mails, *1835–1836*," *JNH* 13 (1928): 150–56.

35. *MPP*, III:175, 176 (December 7, 1835); Amos Kendall to Andrew Jackson, August 7, 1835; Andrew Jackson to Amos Kendall, August 9, 1835, ibid., in *Correspondence of Andrew Jackson*, ed. John Spencer Bassett, 6 vols. (Washington, D.C.: Carnegie Institution of Washington, 1926–33), V:359–61.

36. Richard K. Crallé, ed., *Reports and Public Letters of John C. Calhoun*, 6 vols. (New York: D. Appleton & Co., 1851–56), V:200–202; Harold W. Thatcher, "Calhoun and Federal Reinforcement of State Laws," *American Political Science Review* 36 (1942): 773–80.

37. *CG*, 24 Cong., 1 sess., App., 6–10; *SAL*, V:87; Thomas Hart Benton, *Thirty Years' View; or, A History of the American Government from 1820 to 1850*, 2 vols. (New York: D. Appleton & Co., 1897), I:580–82; William Sherman Savage, *The Controversy Over the Distribution of Abolition Literature, 1830–1860* (Washington, D.C.: Association for the Study of Negro Life and History, 1938), 81.

38. Clement L. Eaton, "Censorship of the Southern Mails," *AHR* 48 (1943): 280.

39. Quoted in Edward McPherson, *The Political History of the United States of America, During the Great Rebellion . . .*, 4th ed. (Washington, D.C.: James J. Chapman, 1882), 189.

40. *Richmond Enquirer*, July 10, 1860, in *Southern Editorials on Secession*, Dwight Lowell Dumond, ed. (New York: Century, 1931), 141.

41. Abraham Lincoln to John A. Gilmer, December 15, 1860, *CWAL*, IV:152.

42. Stephen A. Douglas to Ninety-Six New Orleans Citizens, November 13, 1860, Robert W. Johannsen, ed., *The Letters of Stephen A. Douglas* (Urbana: University of Illinois Press, 1961), 499–503.

43. Howell Cobb to the People of Georgia, December 6, 1860, *Annual Report of the American Historical Association, for the Year 1911*, Vol. II (Washington, D.C.: n.p., 1913), 513–14. For a study of how Lincoln actually used federal patronage in the slave states left under his control, see Harry J. Carman and Reinhard H. Luthin, *Lincoln and the Patronage* (New York: Columbia University Press, 1943), 186–227.

44. *MPP*, V. 630–38 (December 3, 1860).

45. Johannsen, ed., *Douglas*, 814–19, 825.

46. Confederate States of America, *Provisional and Permanent Constitutions of the Confederate States* (Richmond: Tyler, Wise, Allegre & Smith, printers, 1861).

47. L. E. Chittenden, *A Report of the Debates and Proceedings in the Secret Sessions of the Conference Convention, for Proposing Amendments to the Constitution of the United States, Held in Washington, D.C., in February, A.D., 1861* (New York: D. Appleton & Co., 1864), 9.

48. Thomas L. Clingman, "Speech on the State of the Union. Delivered in the Senate of the United States, February 4, 1861," *Southern Pamphlets on Secession, November 1860–April 1861*, ed. Jon L. Wakelyn (Chapel Hill: University of North Carolina Press, 1996), 289.

49. George H. Reese, ed., *Proceedings of the Virginia State Convention of 1861*, 4 vols. (Richmond: Virginia State Library, 1965), I:250–71.

50. Ibid., 757–58.

51. Ibid., II:82.

52. *CWAL*, IV:270; *CG*, 36 Cong., 2 sess., 1340; *SAL*, XII:251.

53. Clingman, "Speech," 289–90.

54. Ibid., 287.

55. William W. Freehling and Craig M. Simpson, eds., *Secession Debated: Georgia's Showdown in 1860* (New York: Oxford University Press, 1992), 119–20.

56. Upon occasion, southern historians have been quite straightforward in recognizing that something other than states rights has historically been the central theme of southern political history. See Ulrich B. Phillips, "The Central Theme of Southern History," *AHR* 34 (1928): 30–43.

57. See Article IV, Section 3, clause 3. James D. Richardson, comp., *A Compilation of the Messages and Papers of the Confederacy, Including the Diplomatic Correspondence, 1861–1865*, 2 vols. (Nashville: United States Publishing Co., 1905), I:51.

58. Ibid.

59. See Article IV, Section 2, paragraph 1, ibid., 50.

60. A. L. Hull, "The Making of the Confederate Constitution," *Publications of the Southern History Association* 9 (1905): 291.

61. Arthur Bestor, "State Sovereignty and Slavery: A Reinterpretation of Proslavery Constitutional Doctrine, 1846–1860," *Journal of the Illinois State Historical Society* 54 (1961): 178.

62. Article I, Section 9, paragraph 4. Richardson, comp., *Compilation of the Messages and Papers of the Confederacy*, I:43.

63. Bestor, "State Sovereignty and Slavery," 178.

64. Linda Lasswell Crist et al., eds., *The Papers of Jefferson Davis*, 9 vols. to date (Baton Rouge: Louisiana University Press, 1971–97), VII:44.

65. Howell Cobb to James Buchanan, March 26, 1861, *Annual Report of the American Historical Association, 1911*, II:555.

66. Alexander Hamilton Stephens, "Corner-Stone Speech," March 21, 1861, reprinted in Henry Cleveland, *Alexander H. Stephens, in Public and Private: With Letters and Speeches* (Philadelphia: National Publishing Co., 1866), 721.

67. Article I, Section 2, paragraph 5. Richardson, comp., *Compilation of the Messages and Papers of the Confederacy*, I:38.

68. Charles Robert Lee, Jr., *The Confederate Constitutions* (Chapel Hill: University of North Carolina Press, 1963), 92.

69. John Lofton, *Denmark Vesey's Revolt: The Slave Plot that Lit a Fuse to Ft. Sumter* (Kent, Ohio: Kent State University Press, 1964), 201–10; *HR*, 27 Cong., 3 sess., No. 80, 21–23; *Elkison v. Deliesseline*, 8 Federal Cases 493 (1823), 496.

70. Article I, Section 9, paragraph 1. Richardson, comp., *Compilation of the Messages and Papers of the Confederacy*, I:43.

71. Donald E. Reynolds, *Editors Make War: Southern Newspapers in the Secession Crisis* (Nashville: Vanderbilt University Press, 1970), 91.

72. Article I, Section 9, paragraph 2. Richardson, comp., *Compilation of the Messages and Papers of the Confederacy*, I:43.

73. William C. Davis, *"A Government of Our Own": The Making of the Confederacy* (New York: Free Press, 1994), 334; Daniel W. Crofts, *Reluctant Confederates: Upper South Unionists in the Secession Crisis* (Chapel Hill: University of North Carolina Press, 1989), 314–15, 329, 332–52; Robert P. Sutton, *Revolution to Secession: Constitution Making in the Old Dominion* (Charlottesville: University Press of Virginia, 1989), 143.

74. Lee, *Confederate Constitutions*, 136.

75. Ibid.

76. Johannsen, *Douglas*, 870, 872.

77. Stephen A. Douglas to Virgil Hickox, May 10, 1861, Johannsen, ed., *Letters of Douglas*, 512.

78. The February "Peace Convention" closed with no agreement on constitutional amendments that would have had slaves recognized as property, something that the Constitution of 1787 had not explicitly done. See Chittenden, *Debates and Proceedings*, 596. For a modern account that holds Lincoln primarily responsible for the failure to reach a compromise, see Crofts, *Reluctant Confederates*, 353–60.

79. Abraham Lincoln to William H. Seward, April 1, 1861, Fehrenbacher, comp., *Lincoln, Speeches and Writings*, 227–28; Phillip Shaw Paludan, *The Presidency of Abraham Lincoln* (Lawrence: University Press of Kansas, 1994), 60–63.

80. Proverbs, 29:18.

81. "Farewell Address at Springfield, Illinois," February 11, 1861, Fehrenbacher, comp., *Lincoln, Speeches and Writings*, 199.

82. Douglas C. McMurtrie, ed., *Lincoln's Religion, The Text of Addresses Delivered by William H. Herndon and Rev. James A. Reed…* (Chicago: Black Cat Press, 1936), 80–83; Abraham Lincoln, *The Philosophy of Abraham Lincoln In His Own Words*, comp. William E. Baringer (Indian Hills, Colo.: Falcon's Wing Press, 1959), 121; Charles B. Strozier, "Abraham Lincoln and the Apocalyptic at Mid Century," in *Abraham Lincoln: Contemporary. An American Legacy*, ed. Frank J. Williams and William D. Pederson (Campbell, Calif.: Savas Woodbury Publishers, 1995), 193–202; Donald, *Lincoln*, 14–15, 48–49.

83. Phillip Shaw Paludan, *"A People's Contest": The Union and Civil War, 1861–1865* (New York: Harper & Row, 1988), 339–74, esp. 371–72. Lincoln's articulation of a communal national purpose under Divine guidance succeeded in winning him the overwhelming support of the nation's Protestant churches by the time of his reelection campaign in 1864. See Donald, *Lincoln*, 542.

84. *CWAL*, VIII:332–33.

85. "Reply to Oliver P. Morton at Indianapolis, Indiana," February 11, 1861, Fehrenbacher, comp., *Lincoln, Speeches and Writings*, 199–200.

86. *CWAL*, IV:438.

87. "Address to the Ohio Legislature, Columbus, Ohio," February 13, 1861, Fehrenbacher, comp., *Lincoln, Speeches and Writings*, 205.

88. *CWAL*, IV:268.

89. "Speech to Germans at Cincinnati, Ohio," February 12, 1861, Fehrenbacher, comp. *Lincoln, Speeches and Writings*, 203.

90. "Speech at Independence Hall, Philadelphia, Pennsylvania," February 22, 1861, Ibid., comp. Fehrenbacher, 213.

91. *CWAL*, IV:426. Lincoln's rhetoric, while making repeated reference to the Declaration of Independence, was far less devoted to individualism than that document. For example, the Declaration itself makes frequent use of the word "rights," a term not to be found in the Gettysburg Address. Lincoln preferred to talk of enlarging liberty for masses of people rather than for individuals.

92. Ibid., V:17–18.

93. *CG*, 37 Cong., 1 sess., 243.

94. Lerone Bennett, Jr., "Lincoln, a White Supremacist," in *The Leadership of Abraham Lincoln*, ed. Don E. Fehrenbacher (New York: John Wiley & Sons, 1970), 129–40; Nathan Irvin Huggins, *Slave and Citizen: The Life of Frederick Douglass* (Boston: Little, Brown & Co., 1980), 77–86. For a discussion of this tendency within modern popular portrayals of Lincoln, see Stephen B. Oates, *Abraham Lincoln: The Man Behind the Myths* (New York: Harper & Row, 1984), 25–30.

95. For example, see *CWAL*, IV:506–7, 517–18, 531–32; ibid., V:29–31, 144–46, 169, 192, 222–23, 317–19, 324.

96. William Lloyd Garrison to a "friend," October 11, 1860, in William E. Cain, ed. *William Lloyd Garrison and the Fight Against Slavery: Selections from The Liberator* (Boston: St. Martin's Press, Bedford Books 1995), 161.

97. James M. McPherson, *Abraham Lincoln and the Second American Revolution* (New York: Oxford University Press, 1991), 112.

98. David M. Potter, "If the Union and the Confederacy Had Exchanged Presidents," in *The Leadership of Abraham Lincoln*, ed. Fehrenbacher, 63; Waldo W. Braden, *Abraham Lincoln, Public Speaker* (Baton Rouge: Louisiana State University Press, 1988).

99. Ira Berlin, "The Slaves Were The Primary Force Behind Their Emancipation," in *The Civil War: Opposing Viewpoints*, ed. William Dudley (San Diego: Greenhaven Press, 1995), 280, 283. Also see Leon F. Litwack, *Been In The Storm So Long: The Aftermath of Slavery* (New York: Vantage Books, 1980), 118, 177, 180, 181, 182, 186, 187.

100. Benjamin Butler to Simon Cameron, July 30, 1861, in Frank Moore, ed., *The Rebellion Record: A Diary of American Events, With Documents...*, 11 vols. (New York: G. P. Putnam's Sons, 1861–63; D. Van Nostrand, 1864–68), II:437–38; Benjamin F. Butler to Winfield Scott, May 24, 1861; in *Private and Official Correspondence of Gen. Benjamin F. Butler, During the Period of the Civil War*, ed. Jessie Ames Marshall, 5 vols. (Norwood, Mass.: Plimpton Press, 1917), I:102–8. John B. Cary to Benjamin F. Butler, March 9, 1891, ibid.

101. Donald, *Lincoln*, 343.

102. *CG*, 37 Cong., 1 sess., 219, 434; ed., Moore, *Rebellion Record*, II:475–76; *SAL*, XII:319; Donald, *Lincoln*, 314.

103. Abraham Lincoln to John C. Frémont, September 2 and 11, 1861; *Lincoln, Speeches and Writings*, Fehrenbacher, comp. 266–70; Abraham Lincoln to David Hunter, September 9, 1861, ibid., Abraham Lincoln to Orville H. Browning, September 22, 1861, ibid.

104. *CWAL*, V:49.

105. Paludan, *Presidency of Lincoln*, 103.

106. *CWAL*, V:192; *CG*, 37 Cong., 2 sess., 347–48; Edward McPherson, *The Political History of the United States of America During the Great Rebellion . . .* (Washington, D.C.: James J. Chapman, 1882), 211–12; Michael J. Kurtz, "Emancipation in the Federal City," *CWH* 24 (1978): 250–67.

107. *CWAL*, V:169.

108. Ibid., 22–23, 317–19.

109. Ira Berlin et al., *Slaves No More: Three Essays on Emancipation and the Civil War* (Cambridge: Cambridge University Press, 1992), 29–30.

110. *SAL*, XII:432; E. McPherson, *Political History of the Rebellion*, 254–55.

111. E. McPherson, *Political History of the Rebellion*, 197–98; Don E. Fehrenbacher and Virginia Fehrenbacher, eds., *Recollected Words of Abraham Lincoln* (Stanford, Calif.: Stanford University Press, 1996), 64–65.

112. Abraham Lincoln to Albert G. Hodges, April 4, 1864, *Lincoln, Speeches and Writings*. Fehrenbacher, comp., 585–86.

113. *SAL*, XII:589–92; Harold M. Hyman and William M. Wiecek, *Equal Justice Under Law: Constitutional Development, 1835–1875* (New York: Harper & Row, 1982), 252.

114. Entry for July 22, 1862, in ed., David Donald *Inside Lincoln's Cabinet, The Civil War Diaries of Salmon P. Chase* (New York: Longmans, Green & Co., 1954), 97–100; John T. Morse, Jr., introduction to *Diary of Gideon Welles*, 3 vols. (Boston: Houghton Mifflin & Co., 1911), I:70–71; William Ernest Smith, *The Francis Preston Blair Family in Politics*, 2 vols. (New York: Macmillan Publishing Co., 1933), II:203.

115. *New York Tribune*, August 5, 1862.

116. *CWAL*, V:370–75; George B. Vashon to Abraham Lincoln, September 1862, C. Peter Ripley et al., eds. *The Black Abolitionist Papers*, 5 vols. (Chapel Hill: University of North Carolina Press, 1985–92) V:152–55.

117. *Boston Liberator*, August 22, 1862. William Lloyd Garrison's editorial described Lincoln's comments to the African American delegation as "puerile, absurd, illogical, impertinent, untimely." Also see Frederick Douglass to Gerrit Smith, September 8, 1862, *The Life and Writings of Frederick Douglass*, ed. Philip S. Foner, 4 vols. (New York: International Publishers, 1950–55), III:260–70. "The Spirit of Colonization," September 1862, ibid. "The President and His Speeches," September 1862 ibid. Tellingly, Douglass commented at this time: "The President of the United States seems to possess *an ever increasing passion* for making himself appear silly and ridiculous, if nothing worse." Ibid., 266.

118. James R. Gilmore, *Personal Recollections of Abraham Lincoln and the Civil War* (Boston: L. C. Page & Co., 1898), 81–83; Harlan Hoyt Horner, *Lincoln and Greeley* (n.p.: University of Illinois Press, 1953), 246–48, 263. There is reason to doubt the claim made by Gilmore that Lincoln knew of Greeley's plans in advance. See Fehrenbacher and Fehrenbacher, eds., *Recollected Words*, 526 n.

119. Abraham Lincoln to Horace Greeley, August 22, 1862, Fehrenbacher, comp., *Lincoln, Speeches and Writings*, 357–58.

120. Harriet Beecher Stowe, *Uncle Tom's Cabin, or, Life Among the Lowly* (1881; reprint, New York: Collier Books, 1962), 494–97.

121. Don E. Fehrenbacher, "Only His Stepchildren: Lincoln and the Negro," *CWH* 20 (1974): 306.

122. Charles Sumner to John Wolcott Phelps, April 18, 1868, in Beverly Wilson

Palmer, ed., *The Selected Letters of Charles Sumner*, 2 vols. (Boston: Northeastern University Press, 1990), II:424.

123. *CWAL*, V:534–36; Fehrenbacher, "Only His Stepchildren," 308.

124. Mark Voss-Hubbard, "The Political Culture of Emancipation: Morality, Politics, and the State in Garrisonian Abolitionism, 1854–1863," *Journal of American Studies* 29 (1995): 160.

125. Jeffrey Rogers Hummel, in his *Emancipating Slaves, Enslaving Free Men: A History of the American Civil War* (Peru, Ill.: Open Court Publishing Co., 1996), 352–53, 355, claims that Lincoln's role in destroying slavery was not essential. He writes that slavery was inevitably doomed, even had Lincoln "permitted the small Gulf Coast Confederacy to depart in peace." Professor Hummel imagines that slaves escaping to what was left of the United States would have eventually undermined the entire slave system. This thesis harmonizes with Professor Berlin's self-emancipation theme, but does this counterfactual musing have merit? We do know [to borrow Professor Hummel's words] that "State violence directed from the top down" actually destroyed slavery in the United States. We also know that despite this bloody, organized, national sacrifice, an ideology of white supremacy and enslavement of "inferior" peoples almost succeeded on a global scale under the leadership of Adolf Hitler eight decades later. Reason suggests that slavery's chances to survive and flourish into the twentieth century and beyond could only have been enhanced if Lincoln had not resisted southern secession with military force. For counterfactional imaginings diametrically opposed to those of Professor Hummel, see Robert W. Fogel, *Without Consent or Contract: The Rise and Fall of American Slavery* (New York: W. W. Norton & Co., 1989), 411–17.

126. "Reply to Chicago Emancipation Memorial, Washington, D.C.," Fehrenbacher, comp., *Lincoln, Speeches and Writings*, 361, 740 n.

127. Ibid., 366–67.

128. Moore, ed., *Rebellion Record*, V:479–80.

129. William Lloyd Garrison to Fanny Garrison, September 25, 1862, Walter M. Merrill, et al., eds., *The Letters of William Lloyd Garrison*, 6 vols. (Cambridge, Mass.: Harvard University Press, Belknap Press, 1971–81), V:114–15. One modern version of the standard complaint against the Emancipation Proclamation can be found in Richard Hofstadter, *American Political Tradition* (1948; reprint, New York: Vintage Books, 1960), 132.

130. Frederick Douglass, "Emancipation Proclaimed," September 1862, in Foner, ed., *Life and Writings of Douglass*, III:273–77.

131. J. McPherson, *Lincoln and the Second American Revolution*, 114, 125; James M. McPherson, "Lincoln Freed the Slaves," in *The Civil War: Opposing Viewpoints*, ed. William Dudley (San Diego, Calif.: Greenhaven Press, 1995), 267, 269–70.

132. Abraham Lincoln to Albert G. Hodges, April 4, 1864, in *Lincoln, Speeches and Writings*, Fehrenbacher, comp., 585–86.

133. Ibid., 186.

134. Fehrenbacher and Fehrenbacher, eds., *Recollected Words*, 110–11, 191, 245, 372–74, 436–37.

135. Don E. Fehrenbacher, "The Weight of Responsibility," in *Lincoln in Text and Context*, Don E. Fehrenbacher (Stanford, Calif.: Stanford University Press, 1987), 161; also see Richard N. Current, "The Instrument of God," *The Lincoln Nobody*

Knows (New York: McGraw-Hill Book Co., 1958), 51–75; Ronald C. White, Jr., "Lincoln's Sermon on the Mount: The Second Inaugural," in *Religion and the American Civil War*, ed. Randall M. Miller et al. (New York: Oxford University Press, 1998), 208–25.

136. Charles Reagan Wilson, "Religion and the American Civil War in Comparative Perspective," in *Religion and the Civil War*, ed. Miller et al., 396, 402.

137. "Second Inaugural Address," March 4, 1865, Fehrenbacher, comp., *Lincoln, Speeches and Writings*, 687.

138. Abraham Lincoln to Thurlow Weed, March 15, 1865, Ibid., 689; James M. McPherson, *Abraham Lincoln and the Second American Revolution*, 111–12.

139. George Plekhanov, *The Role of the Individual in History* (New York: International Publishers, 1940), 12.

140. "Proclamation of Thanksgiving, By the President of the United States," Fehrenbacher, comp., *Lincoln, Speeches and Writings*, 520–21.

141. Abraham Lincoln to Eliza P. Gurney, September 4, 1864, ibid., 627.

142. "Second Inaugural Address," ibid., 686–87.

143. Abraham Lincoln to Thurlow Weed, March 15, 1865, ibid., 689.

144. Fehrenbacher and Fehrenbacher, eds., *Recollected Words*, 413.

145. For examples of later popular literature portraying Lincoln in an almost mythological way, see John Wesley Hill, *Abraham Lincoln: Man of God* (New York: G. P. Putnam's Sons, 1920); Ralph G. Lindstrom, *Lincoln Finds God* (New York: Longmans, Green & Co., 1958).

146. Elizabeth Fox-Genovese, "Days of Judgment, Days of Wrath: The Civil War and the Religious Imagination of Women Writers," Miller et al., eds., *Religion and the Civil War*, 236.

147. Joel Parker, "Constitutional Law," *North American Review* 94 (1862): 449–54; William Lloyd Garrison, *The Abolition of Slavery: The Right of the Government Under the War Power* (Boston: R. F. Wallcut, 1862), 6–12; Grosvenor Porter Lowrey, *The Commander-In-Chief; A Defense Upon Legal Grounds of The Proclamation of Emancipation . . .* (New York: G. P. Putnam, 1863), 7–34.

148. *CWAL*, V:433–34.

149. Ibid., 530.

150. Ibid., VI:28–30.

151. Dwight Lowell Dumond, *The Emancipation Proclamation: Freedom in the Fullness of Time* (Ann Arbor: University of Michigan Press, 1963), 1.

152. *CWAL*, VI:28–30.

153. James M. McPherson, *The Struggle for Equality: Abolitionists and the Negro in the Civil War and Reconstruction* (Princeton, N.J.: Princeton University Press, 1964), 196–98.

154. Ibid., 202–3; *CG*, 37 Cong., 3 sess., App., 72–86, 103–6.

155. Herman Belz, *Emancipation and Equal Rights: Politics and Constitutionalism in the Civil War Era* (New York: W. W. Norton & Co., 1967), 53; La Wanda Cox, *Lincoln and Black Freedom: A Study in Presidential Leadership* (Columbia, S. C.: University of South Carolina Press, 1981) 23.

156. Abraham Lincoln to James C. Conkling, August 26, 1863, in Fehrenbacher, comp., *Lincoln, Speeches and Writings*, 499.

157. Abraham Lincoln to John A. McClernand, January 8, 1863, ibid., 428.

158. *CG*, 37 Cong., 3 sess., 15, 92.

159. Cox, *Lincoln and Black Freedom*, 35.

160. *CWAL*, V:303, 445, 462–63, 504–5; *HR*, 37 Cong., 3 sess., No. 22, No. 23., No. 46; *CG*, 37 Cong., 3 sess., 832–33.

161. "Proclamation of Amnesty and Reconstruction, By the President of the United States of America," December 8, 1863, Fehrenbacher, comp., *Lincoln, Speeches and Writings*, 555–58; Abraham Lincoln to Nathaniel P. Banks, January 31, 1864, ibid., 570–71.

162. Abraham Lincoln to Michael Hahn, March 13, 1864, ibid., 579.

163. Hyman and Wiecek, *Equal Justice Under Law*, 270; Eric Foner, *Reconstruction: America's Unfinished Revolution, 1863–1877* (New York: Harper & Row, 1988), 36; William B. Hesseltine, *Lincoln's Plan of Reconstruction* (Tuscaloosa, Ala.: Confederate Publishing Co., 1960), 19–21.

164. Peyton McCrary, "The Party of Revolution: Republican Ideas About Politics and Social Change, 1862–1867," *CWH* 30 (1984): 341–42.

165. Ibid., 342; Wendell Phillips to Edward Gilbert, May 27, 1864, E. McPherson, *Political History of the Rebellion*, 412.

166. "Speech on Reconstruction, Washington, D.C.," April 11, 1865, Fehrenbacher, comp., *Lincoln, Speeches and Writings*, 700.

167. McCrary, "The Party of Revolution," 339. LaWanda Cox emphasizes that Lincoln's intent in Louisiana and elsewhere was that the freedmen ultimately be provided with real opportunities to become landowners. In her estimation, Andrew Johnson almost single-handedly prevented the implementation of a modest land reform program after the war. See Cox, *Lincoln and Black Freedom*, 178–79, 190 n-191 n. For a racist argument against land reform that helped shape the political landscape of the time, see Samuel F.B. Morse et al., *Emancipation and Its Results* (New York: Society for the Diffusion of Political Knowledge, 1863), 15, 18–19, 23–24, 30–32.

168. E. McPherson, *Political History of the Rebellion*, 317–18; *CG*, 38 Cong., 1 sess., 2107–8, 3518; Herman Belz, *Reconstructing the Union: Theory and Policy During the Civil War* (Ithaca, N.Y.: American Historical Association, 1969), 210; Belz, *Emancipation and Equal Rights*, 91–93.

169. "Proclamation Concerning Reconstruction, By the President of the United States," in Fehrenbacher, comp., *Lincoln, Speeches and Writings*, Fehrenbacher, comp., 605.

170. "Memorandum on Probable Failure of Re-election," August 23, 1864, ibid., 624.

171. Abraham Lincoln to Charles D. Robinson, August 17, 1864, ibid. Abraham Lincoln to Henry J. Raymond, August 24, 1864, ibid., 620–22, 625, 754 n; Donald, *Lincoln*, 526–29, 553; Paludan, *Presidency of Lincoln*, 284; Cox, *Lincoln and Black Freedom*, 17.

172. "We're Bound to Beat Old Abe," *Little Mac: Campaign Songster* (New York: E. P. Patten, 1864), 11.

173. Welles, *Diary*, I:142–43.

174. William J. Wolf, *The Almost Chosen People: A Study of the Wartime Religion of Abraham Lincoln* (Garden City, N.Y.: Doubleday & Co., 1959), 124–26; Fehrenbacher and Fehrenbacher, eds., *Recollected Words*, 387–88.

175. Lincoln to Hodges, April 4, 1864, Fehrenbacher, comp., *Lincoln, Speeches and Writings*, 586.

176. Oates, *Lincoln: Man Behind the Myths*, 116–17.

177. Donald, *Lincoln*, 552, 559–60.

178. Ibid., 560–61.

179. Ibid., 589–90.

180. Abraham Lincoln to Thomas C. Fletcher, February 20, 1865, Fehrenbacher, comp., *Lincoln, Speeches and Writings*, 684.

181. Ibid.

182. "Second Inaugural Address," in Fehrenbacher, comp., *Lincoln, Speeches and Writings*, 687.

183. "Annual Message to Congress," December 6, 1864, ibid., 661.

184. Francis B. Carpenter, *Six Months at the White House With Abraham Lincoln: The Story of a Picture* (New York: Hurd & Houghton, 1866), 282; emphases are Carpenter's.

185. The qualification "under God" was not in Lincoln's written text at Gettysburg but the two words were apparently spontaneously added in the act of delivery, as newspaper accounts reported the president as having said them. See *CWAL*, VII:19, 19 n-20 n, 21 n, 23. Garry Wills in his *Lincoln at Gettysburg: The Words That Remade America* (New York: Simon & Schuster, 1992), 194, speculates that it would have been "uncharacteristic" of Lincoln to alter the text in the act of delivery "in front of a huge audience." Nonetheless, Wills notes that the newspaper accounts placed the words "under God" awkwardly in the text, which is suggestive of a literal reporting of a spontaneous presidential inclusion. Ibid., 198. In the final text, used for historical publication, the words "under God" were included in such a way to satisfy critics of presidential syntax. Wills also notes that Lincoln himself later endorsed inclusion of the two words into the speech. Ibid., 202–3, 263.

186. Richard N. Current, "Lincoln, the Civil War, and the American Mission," in *The Public and the Private Lincoln: Contemporary Perspectives*, ed. Cullom Davis et al. (Carbondale: Southern Illinois University Press, 1979), 145–46; Phillip Shaw Paludan, *"A People's Contest": The Union and the Civil War, 1861–1865* (New York: Harper & Row, 1988), 372–74; Fehrenbacher, "The Death of Lincoln," *Lincoln in Text and Context*, 175–77. In our own time, Martin Luther King, Jr., has acquired a similar status in this ongoing national civil religion.

187. Dumond, *Emancipation Proclamation*, 1.

188. Thomas J. Pressly, *Americans Interpret Their Civil War* (1954; reprint, New York: Collier Books, 1962), 167–70.

189. *SAL*, XIII:507–09.

190. Louis S. Gerteis, *From Contraband to Freedman: Federal Policy Toward Blacks, 1861–1865* (Westport, Conn.: Greenwood Press, 1973), 187.

191. O. O. Howard, *Autobiography of Oliver Otis Howard, Major General, United States Army . . .*, 2 vols. (New York: Baker & Taylor Co., 1908), II:212–14, 250, 312–13, 423; Sidney Andrews, "Three Months Among the Reconstructionists," *Atlantic Monthly* 16 (February 1866): 243; Donald G. Nieman, introduction to *To Set the Law in Motion: The Freedmen's Bureau and the Legal Rights of Blacks, 1865–1868* (Millwood, N.Y.: Kraus, 1979); Sara Rapport, "The Freedmen's Bureau as a Legal Agent for Black Men and Women in Georgia," in *The Freedmen's Bureau*

and Black Freedom, ed. Donald G. Nieman (New York: Garland Publishing Co., 1994), 267–72.

192. Gerteis, *From Contraband to Freedman*, 187–88; Michael Perman, *Emancipation and Reconstruction, 1862–1879* (Arlington Heights, Ill.: Harlan Davidson, 1987), 36, 41–42; Foner, *Reconstruction: Unfinished Revolution*, 159–61, 235; Eric Foner, "Thaddeus Stevens, Confiscation, and Reconstruction," in *The Hofstadter Aegis, A Memorial*, ed. Stanley Elkins and Eric McKitrick (New York: Alfred A. Knopf, 1974), 160, 179, 182.

193. *MPP*, VI:310–14 (May 29, 1865); Cox, *Lincoln and Black Freedom*, 178–79, 190 n-191 n; Foner, *Reconstruction: Unfinished Revolution*, 183, 191.

194. Hyman and Wiecek, *Equal Justice Under Law*, 319, 321; Foner, *Reconstruction: Unfinished Revolution*, 199–200.

195. Belz, *Emancipation and Equal Rights*, 99–100.

196. C. Vann Woodward, "Seeds of Failure in Radical Race Policy," in *American Counterpoint* (Boston: Little, Brown & Co., 1971), 171.

197. *SAL*, XIV:27–30, 173–77.

198. Harold M. Hyman, "Reconstruction and Political-Constitutional Institutions: The Popular Expression," in *New Frontiers of the American Reconstruction* (Urbana: University of Illinois Press, 1966), 11.

199. Belz, *Emancipation and Equal Rights*, 111–12, 117; Hyman and Wiecek, *Equal Justice Under Law*, 405–6.

200. E. McPherson, *Political History of the Rebellion*, 255.

201. *CG*, 39 Cong., 1 sess., App., 158.

202. Robert J. Kaczorowski, "To Begin the Nation Anew: Congress, Citizenship, and Civil Rights after the Civil War," *AHR* 92 (1987): 54.

203. Harold M. Hyman and William M. Wiecek argue that the Thirteenth Amendment should not be given "a tightly limited meaning" because when it was enacted most of its framers regarded it as having the potential to apply the Bill of Rights to the states. While Hyman and Wiecek report the fact that the Fourteenth Amendment was created in deference to a minority of Republicans who saw the Thirteenth Amendment as an inadequate foundation for the Civil Rights Act of 1866, they ignore the inevitable consequence of this concession. The Thirteenth Amendment might have become a truly expansive constitutional instrument had the Fourteenth Amendment never been adopted. But, as it would be illogical to regard the Fourteenth Amendment as redundant, the adoption of the new amendment necessarily imparted "a tightly limited meaning" to its predecessor. See Hyman and Wiecek, *Equal Justice Under Law*, 389, 391, 405–6, 413.

204. In modern times, the Fourteenth Amendment's equal protection clause is a bulwark for opponents of affirmative action programs, which could easily be justified by an expanded interpretation of the Thirteenth Amendment were such logic now feasible. Ironically, affirmative action's principal modern constitutional foundation is state police power, which historically was used to suppress African American liberty. See ibid.; *Regents of the University of California v. Bakke*, 438 U.S. 265 (1978); Michael Lynch, "Racial Preferences Are Dead: Anti-Quota Activist Ward Connerly on the End of Affirmative Action, *Reason* 29 (February 1998): 32–38; William J. Bennett, et al., "Is Affirmative Action on the Way Out? Should It Be?" *Commentary* 105 (March 1998): 18–57.

205. Foner, ed., *Life and Writings of Douglass*, IV:158.

206. Hyman and Wiecek, *Equal Justice Under Law*, 408.

207. *SAL*, XIV:428–30.

208. Belz, *Emancipation and Equal Rights*, 103; Michael Les Benedict, "Preserving the Constitution: The Conservative Basis of Radical Reconstruction," *JAH* 61 (1974): 68–71, 76–77, 81, 84, 89–90.

209. Kaczorowski, "To Begin the Nation Anew," 58. Also see Robert J. Kaczorowski, *The Politics of Judicial Interpretation: The Federal Courts, Department of Justice and Civil Rights, 1866–1876* (New York: Oceana Publications, 1985), 3.

210. Michael Perman, *The Road to Redemption: Southern Politics, 1869–1879* (Chapel Hill: University of North Carolina Press, 1984), 4–5, 9, 11, 19, 23, 25, 162.

211. *CG*, 41 Cong., 2 sess., App., 45; Edgar W. Knight, "Reconstruction and Education in Virginia," *South Atlantic Quarterly* 15 (January/April 1916): 29–35; Henry Wilson, "New Departure of the Republican Party," *Atlantic Monthly* 27 (January 1871): 114–20.

212. Ronald E. Butchart, *Northern Schools, Southern Blacks, and Reconstruction, Freedmen's Education, 1862–1875* (Westport, Conn.: Greenwood, 1980), 20, 97–114; Paul A. Cimbala, "Making Good Yankees: The Freedmen's Bureau and Education in Reconstruction Georgia, 1865–1870," Nieman, ed., *The Freedmen's Bureau and Black Freedom*, 57–66.

213. George C. Rable, *But There Was No Peace: The Role of Violence in the Politics of Reconstruction* (Athens: University of Georgia Press, 1984), 97–98; Allen W. Trelease, *White Terror: The Ku Klux Conspiracy and Southern Reconstruction* (New York: Harper & Row, 1971), 36, 117, 287–301.

214. Perman, *The Road to Redemption: Southern Politics*, 139.

215. Ward M. McAfee, *Religion, Race, and Reconstruction: The Public School in the Politics of the 1870s* (Albany: State University of New York Press, 1998), 90–103.

216. *SAL*, XVI:140–46, 433–40; *CG*, 42 Cong., 1 sess., App., 335–36; Belz, *Emancipation and Equal Rights*, 127–28; Kaczorowski, "To Begin the Nation Anew," 61; Everette Swinney, "Enforcing the Fifteenth Amendment, 1870–1877," *JSH* 28 (1962): 202–18.

217. Everette Swinney, *Suppressing the Ku Klux Klan: The Enforcement of the Reconstruction Amendments, 1870–1877* (New York: Garland Publishing Co., 1987), 318; William Gillette, *Retreat From Reconstruction, 1869–1879* (Baton Rouge: Louisiana State University Press, 1979), 60–72.

218. *CG*, 43 Cong., 1 sess., 612–13; James Garfield, *Revenues and Expenditures, Speech of Hon. James A Garfield, of Ohio, in the House of Representatives, Thursday, March 5, 1874* (Washington, D.C.: J. H. Cunningham, 1874), 5, 7.

219. Kaczorowski, *The Politics of Judicial Interpretation*, 110–13; McAfee, *Religion, Race, and Reconstruction*, 122–23.

220. *Cincinnati Daily Enquirer*, May 24, 1874, 2:1; *Wilmington, N.C., Daily Journal*, May 28, 1874, 2:3; *Louisville, Ky., Courier Journal*, May 25, 1874, 2:4.

221. Gillette, *Retreat From Reconstruction*, 198–99, 218, 220, 223, 238–58; Foner, *Reconstruction: Unfinished Revolutions*, 512, 524; Mark Wahlgren Summers, *The Era of Good Stealings* (New York: Oxford University Press, 1993), 255.

222. *SAL*, XVIII:335–37.

223. William S. McFeely, *Grant: A Biography* (New York: W. W. Norton & Co., 1981), 416–18.

224. Hummel, *Emancipating Slaves, Enslaving Free Men*, 318; Hyman and Wiecek, *Equal Justice Under Law*, 488; *U.S. v. Cruikshank*, 92 U.S. 542 (1876).

225. William C. Harris, "Mississippi: Republican Factionalism and Mismanagement," *Reconstruction and Redemption in the South*, ed. Otto H. Olsen (Baton Rouge: Louisiana State University Press, 1980), 93–108.

226. Minutes of the Fentress County [Tennessee] Democratic and Conservative Meeting, Jamestown, Tenn., September 7, 1874, Special Collections, Hoskins Library, University of Tennessee, Knoxville; *Harper's Weekly* 18 (September 26, 1874): 790; *Wilmington, N.C., Daily Journal*, August 8, 1874, 1:2.

227. Vincent P. De Santis, "Rutherford B. Hayes and the Removal of the Troops and the End of Reconstruction," *Region, Race and Reconstruction: Essays in Honor of C. Vann Woodward*, ed. J. Morgan Kousser and James M. McPherson (New York: Oxford University Press, 1982), 417–46; McAfee, *Religion, Race, and Reconstruction*, 175–220; Tyler Anbinder, "Ulysses S. Grant, Nativist," *CWH* 43 (1997): 135–39; Ward M. McAfee, "Reconstruction Revisited: The Republican Public Education Crusade of the 1870s," *CWH* 42 (1996): 145–49.

228. McAfee, "Reconstruction Revisited," 149–51.

229. Michael Perman, *Emancipation and Reconstruction, 1862–1879* (Arlington Heights, Ill.: Harlan Davidson, 1987), 128.

230. Perman, *The Road to Redemption: Southern Politics*, 135–39; Richard H. Abbott, *The Republican Party and the South, 1855–1877, The First Southern Strategy* (Chapel Hill: University of North Carolina Press, 1986), 229.

231. Hummel, *Emancipating Slaves, Enslaving Free Men*, 318–19.

232. J. McPherson, *Lincoln and the Second American Revolution*, 150–52.

233. Frederick Bancroft, ed., *Speeches, Correspondence and Political Papers of Carl Schurz*, 6 vols. (New York: G. P. Putnam's Sons, 1913), III:121, 125, 130–31, 141, 144, 151–52.

234. J. McPherson, *Lincoln and the Second American Revolution*, 147.

235. Michael Les Benedict, "Preserving Federalism: Reconstruction and the Waite Court," *Supreme Court Review* (1978), 39–41, 46–48, 50–52, 56, 61–63, 77–78; Phillip S. Paludan, *A Covenant With Death: The Constitution, Law, and Equality in the Civil War Era* (Urbana: University of Illinois Press, 1975), 55; Kaczorowski, "To Begin the Nation Anew," 45–47, 45 n-47 n, 49, 60, 64–68; Hyman and Wiecek, *Equal Justice Under Law*, 500.

236. *U.S. v. Cruikshank*, 92 U.S. 542 (1876), 542–60; *U.S. v. Harris*, 106 U.S. 924 (1883), 629–33, 639–44; *Civil Rights Cases*, 109 U.S. 3 (1883), 5–12, 22, 25; Laurent B. Frantz, "Congressional Power to Enforce the Fourteenth Amendment Against Private Acts," *Yale Law Journal* 73 (1964): 1366–67; Hyman and Wiecek, *Equal Justice Under Law*, 505–7.

237. *U.S. v. Reese*, 92 U.S. 214 (1876), 214–17; Swinney, "Enforcing the Fifteenth Amendment," 208.

238. *Plessy v. Ferguson*, 163 U.S. 537 (1896); *Smyth v. Ames*, 169 U.S. 466 (1898); Rayford W. Logan, *The Betrayal of the Negro: From Rutherford B. Hayes to Woodrow Wilson* (London: Collier Books, 1965), 105–24; Charles McCurdey,

"Justice Field and the Jurisprudence of Government-Business Relations," *JAH* 61 (1975): 1003–4.

239. *Civil Rights Cases*, 109 U.S. 20, 22.

240. *Slaughterhouse Cases*, 16 Wallace 36 (1873); Stanley I. Kutler, *Judicial Power and Reconstruction Politics* (Chicago: University of Chicago Press, 1968), 166; Robert J. Kaczorowski, "Revolutionary Constitutionalism in the Era of the Civil War and Reconstruction," *New York University Law Review* 61 (1986): 937–39; Kaczorowski, *The Politics of Judicial Interpretation*, 151–53.

241. *Civil Rights Cases*, 109 U.S. 24.

242. Ibid., 25.

CHAPTER 11

1. Washington, D.C., Citizens, *Proceedings of the Civil Rights Mass Meeting Held at Lincoln Hall, October 22, 1883, Speeches of Hon. Frederick Douglass and Robert G. Ingersoll* (Washington, D.C.: C. P. Farrell, 1883), 5.

2. Ibid., 18.

3. Charles Fairman, *Reconstruction and Reunion: 1864–88*, 2 vols. (New York: Macmillan Publishing Co., 1971–87), II:568–82.

4. Ibid., 288–89, 564.

5. Washington, D.C., Citizens, *Civil Rights Mass Meeting, October 22, 1883*, 17.

6. Ibid., 4.

7. Ibid., 5.

8. Ibid., 11.

9. Ibid.

10. Ibid., 9–11.

11. Ibid., 7.

12. Ibid., 8.

13. Ibid., 21–23.

14. Gordon Canfield Lee, *The Struggle for Federal Aid, First Phase: A History of the Attempts to Obtain Federal Aid for the Common Schools, 1870–1890* (New York: Bureau of Publications, Teachers College, Columbia University, 1949), 140–47, 155–58.

15. Henry W. Blair, "National Aid to Education," *Proceedings of the Department of Superintendence of the National Educational Association at its Meeting in Washington, March 6–8, 1889* (Washington, D.C.: Government Printing Office, 1889), 297–99; John S. Barbour, *Aid to Common Schools, Speech of Hon. John S. Barbour, of Virginia, in the Senate of the United States, Wednesday, March 5, 1890* (Washington, D.C.: Government Printing Office, 1890), 6, 8, 10, 13; Isabel C. Barrows, ed., *First Mohonk Conference on the Negro Question, Held at Lake Mohonk, Ulster County, New York, June 4, 5, 6, 1890* (Boston: George H. Ellis, printer, 1890), 11–12.

16. Barrows, ed., *First Mohonk Conference*, 9.

17. *Atlanta Constitution*, May 6, 1890, 9:1; ibid., July 18, 1890, 4:1; ibid., July 27, 1890, 14:3; ibid., August 16. 1890, 4:3; *Chicago Daily Tribune*, September 20, 1890, 4:3; Mississippi Constitutional Convention, *Journal of the Proceedings of the*

Constitutional Convention, State of Mississippi: Begun at the City of Jackson on August 12, 1890 (Jackson, Miss.: E. L. Martin, printer, 1890), 11, 83–88, 618–20.

18. Robert A. Margo, *Race and Schooling in the South, 1880–1950: An Economic History* (Chicago: University of Chicago Press, 1990), 21–22; J. Morgan Kousser, *The Shaping of Southern Politics: Suffrage Restriction and the Establishment of the One-Party South, 1880–1910* (New Haven, Conn.: Yale University Press, 1974), 139–81 (Kousser emphasizes that southern states inaugurated sophisticated disfranchisement mechanisms even prior to Mississippi's blatant action in 1890; he also emphasizes that their intent was to disfranchise Populist whites as well as Republican blacks; see pp. 39–44); John Hope Franklin, "Legal Disfranchisement of the Negro," *Journal of Negro Education* 26 (1957): 241–48.

19. John Hope Franklin, *From Slavery to Freedom: A History of Negro Americans*, 3d ed. (New York: Alfred A. Knopf, 1967), 342, 439–44.

20. John Roach Straton, "Will Education Solve the Race Problem?" *North American Review* 170 (1900): 789–97, 800.

INDEX